TERRIFIC PACIFIC COOKBOOK

BY ANYA VON BREMZEN
AND JOHN WELCHMAN
ILLUSTRATIONS BY CHARLENE RENDEIRO

WORKMAN PUBLISHING · NEW YORK

"The Well-Rounded Coconut," page 350, appeared in a slightly different version in *Gourmet*, November, 1994.

Library of Congress Cataloging-in-Publication Data
von Bremzen, Anya.
Terrific Pacific cookbook/by Anya von Bremzen and John Welchman.
p. cm.
Includes index.
ISBN 1-56305-868-5—ISBN 1-56305-172-9 (pbk)
1. Cookery, Southeast Asian. 2. Cookery, Australian. 3. Cookery—Pacific Area--Social life and customs. I. Welchman, John. II. Title.
TX724.5.A1V66 1995
641.591823--dc20
95-2381 CIP

Cover design by Lisa Hollander
Book design by Lisa Hollander with Lori S. Malkin
Cover and book illustrations by Charlene Rendeiro
Back cover photograph by John Welchman

Workman Publishing Company, Inc.
708 Broadway
New York, NY 10003

First printing September 1995
10 9 8 7 6 5 4 3 2

TO OUR PARENTS

ACKNOWLEDGMENTS

When John had an offer to relocate to Australia in 1990 we were thrilled but also a little hesitant. How would we manage for several years at the other end of the world? But we were both already in love with the allure—and especially the food—of the Pacific; this book is our heartfelt testimony to a perfect marriage of destiny and decision.

First thanks go to our friends and colleagues Down Under who inspired and nurtured us. Julie and Philip Meyer, in whose house this project began, are both artists and travelers, who taught us to love and respect their continent as they do. The ebullient Ronnie di Stasio made our spirits soar, and our stomachs glow with his extraordinary food, wine, and bonhomie. Gabrielle Pizzi, Charles Green and Lindell Brown, Ian Friend and Robyn Daw, and Anna and Morry Schwartz in Melbourne, and Jani Laurence and Brian Zuleika in Sydney, all sustained us with friendship far from home. Geoff Slattery, Terry Durrack, and Mietta O'Donnell kindly welcomed us to the Melbourne food scene, and David Turner contributed great recipes.

Talented Sydney chefs Chris Manfield, Tetsuya Wakuda, David Thompson, and Philip Searle opened our eyes to the marvelous possibilities of fusion cooking at its very best. Their recipes and ideas helped form the backbone of this book; their passionate commitments to culinary integrity and experiment are world class. In Sydney, we also thank Helen Greenwood, Girard Madani, Dietmar Sawyere, Matthew Moran, and Charmaine Solomon; and Carolyn Lockhart, Meg Thomason, and Carol Selvarajah of *Gourmet Traveller*.

In Thailand, thanks to the chefs and managers of Bangkok's Lemongrass, Seven Seas, Celadon, and Spice Market restaurants, and Takrai restaurant in Chiang Mai, for sharing their recipes and ideas. Prameran Krongkaew gave generously of her knowledge of Thai cuisine. In Bangkok, Danny McCafferty at the beautiful Dusit Thani hotel provided a home away from home, and Jacques Lafargue arranged wonderful afternoons with the cooks in the kitchens of the excellent Benjarong and Thien Doung restaurants. The folks at the Thai Cooking School at the Oriental Hotel shared recipes and information. Their classes are a must for anyone interested in Thai cuisine. Thanks also to the Tourism Authority of Thailand for coordinating meetings and travel plans.

In Singapore, hats

off to Juliet David, a food personality extraordinaire, who spun us around (and out of) town with great energy, enthusiasm, and knowledge. At the fabled Raffles Hotel, we thank Puri and Baliram Sangkaran for the tiffin treats. We joined Geraldene LoweIsmail for one of her fascinating walking tours through the city; and spent a perfect evening with Mr. and Mrs. Guih, an enchanting Baba-Nonya couple, who educated us about Peranakan history and traditions. We also thank the Goodwood Park Hotel, Li Bai restaurant at the Sheraton Towers, Tradewinds Restaurant at the Hilton Hotel, Omni Marco Polo Hotel, and Ho Juan Inn at the Tea Chapter for their help with recipes and information. The Singapore Tourist Promotion Board was a model of courtesy and efficiency, helping us to get the very best from this fragrant island.

In Malaysia, we thank Christobelle Savage (aka Auntie Belle) whose promise to cook us a Devil Curry "like you never thought" was our first introduction to the seductive cuisine of this wonderful land. Thanks also to her family in the Portuguese settlement in Melaka. In Penang, the Khor family and the Dragon King restaurant shared some of the great wealth of Nonya cooking and lore. Chef Hassan Kasim and Yap Yoon Lian in Kuala Lumpur, chef Gerhard Albrecht of Kuching Hilton, and the Tourist Development Corporation of Malaysia were most helpful during our stay.

In New Zealand, thanks to Jan Bilton for being such a generous and insightful guide to the Auckland food scene, and for introducing us to the culinary joys of the kiwi. Thanks also to Elizabeth Pedersen of the New Zealand Herald for her wonderful cake recipes.

In San Francisco, a big thanks to Agnes Ng and Dawn Jackson; their assistance was invaluable. Clifford Chow, Andy Wai, and the staff at the Harbor Village, my adopted Chinese family, initiated me into the secret world of Chinese dining. Irene Trias, Bruce Hill, Ken Oringer, Joseph and Cecilia Chung, Chris Yeo, and Bruce Cost shared recipes, ideas, and more. Thanks to Gerry di Vecchio at *Sunset* magazine for her kindness and sharing information.

Hotel dining in the 90s is a far cry from the tired selection of look-alike international dishes of the recent past. The better hotel chains in the Pacific have developed some of the outstanding and reputed restaurants in the region. Their regular local food promotions, chef's exchanges, culinary shows, and book publishing efforts have made a great contribution to the preservation and reinvention of the food cultures of Southeast Asia. We are especially grateful to the Hyatt International Hotels for introducing us to the new Pacific flavors and their first-class chefs at the Park Hyatt in Sydney, the Hyatt Regency in Singapore, and the Park Hyatt in Canberra. We also thank the Regent Hotels whose chefs and staff helped us so much in our travels to Sydney, Auckland, Kuala Lumpur, and Bangkok. While researching this book we often found ourselves in the unenviable position of shuttling between Melbourne, Moscow (for another project), Kuala Lumpur, New York, and California. We thank Qantas, Singapore Airlines, Malaysian Airlines, and Japan Airlines for their assistance.

On home ground in San Diego, thanks to Steve Fagin for his inimitable fellowship at a hundred tables, Diane and Jerry Rothenberg, lovers of good food and always kind hosts, and to all our friends at the University of California. We tested many of the recipes that follow in Nora and Frederick Sargent's wonderful house overlooking the Pacific in La Jolla, and thank them for their support. Also thanks to Japengo and Azzura Point restaurants for their recipes.

In New York, our friends Orshi Drozdik, Mark Cohen and Ivone Margulies, Dr. Yvonne Shafir, Sonya Gropman, and Berta Jottar ate with us, listened to our stories, looked at our photographs and indulged us beyond deserving—we love you all! Our agent Alice Martell was, as always, unflappable, inexhaustible, and full of savoir faire. Thank you to Zanne Zakroff, Kemp Minifie, and Gail Zweigenthal of *Gourmet* magazine for sharing our enthusiasm for Pacific flavors and for making us look forward to every issue of *Gourmet*. Sylvia Carter of *Newsday* has been generous and supportive throughout, and is always a source of inspiration.

At Workman, we thank Suzanne Rafer, our editor and friend, for her enthusiasm and unswerving attention to detail. Also thanks to Lisa Hollander, for her dashing design and Lori S. Malkin for carrying it through so

attractively; and Andrea Glickson for her tireless publicity efforts. Thanks, too, to Margery Tippie, for making us feel so secure about the manuscript. And, of course, to Peter Workman who shared our belief that Pacific flavors will seduce the world.

Finally, we want to thank our parents, Larisa Frumkin and Sergei Bremzen, and Barbara and John Welchman Sr. They have always been wonderfully supportive of our comings and goings. When all is said and done, they put us on the road, and it is to them that this book is dedicated.

CONTENTS

FINGER FOODS

2

Inspired by the street snacks of Southeast Asia, these small bites pack big flavors. Offerings include Imperial Rolls, Thai-Style Pizza, Tuna Tartare and Wasabi Mayonnaise, Colonial High Tea Curry Puffs, and the world-famous Singapore Sling.

ESSAY
Gurney Drive: Fast-Food Paradise

37

PACIFIC RIM STARTERS

40

Spice-infused first courses like Shrimp and Shiitake Ravioli with Lemongrass-Lime Oil, Gingered Salmon Parcels in Saffron Broth, and White-Cooked Chicken with Black Bean Sambal quicken the palate and set the stage for the meal to . . come.

ESSAY
The Spice Trade

56

SOUP

60

Sensual mulligatawny, aromatic Vietnamese *pho*, and fiery Thai *tom*—at once comforting and exotic, soups made in the Asian tradition nurture the body while evoking adventures in far off lands.

ESSAY
True Thai Tastes

87

SALADS

94

In the kitchens of the Pacific Rim, a handful of fresh herbs, a bit of fish or meat, and a touch of fire ring out in vibrant orchestrations like Tuna *Poke* Salad with Nashi Pear, Vietnamese Lemon Beef Salad, Green Papaya Slaw, and more.

ESSAY
Sydney and Melbourne

116

FISH AND SEAFOOD

122

Asian cooks have dozens of ways to bring out the best in seafood: The mild sweetness of sea bass is accentuated with steaming and a shot of black vinegar, while bold crabs are wok-seared and smothered in sweet and sour chile sauce.

P O U L T R Y   A N D   G A M E
1 6 4

The whole world adores a plump chicken, and nowhere is this bird (and feathered friends) treated with more respect than in Asia. Try Cold Poached Chicken with Asparagus and Honey-Miso Dressing, Aromatic Steamed Chicken Pudding, and Pan-Fried Quail in a Rich Curry Sauce.

B E E F   A N D   V E A L
2 0 4

Although beef and veal are relative strangers at the Asian table, they get along famously with the fiery chiles, sweet glazes, and ethereal aromatics of the Pacific— Seared Steak with Black Bean Sherry Sauce, Red-Braised Beef with Shiitake Mushrooms, and Veal Chops with Macadamia Nut Crust.

L A M B   A N D   P O R K
2 2 8

Pork and lamb stand up to the heady perfumes of star anise, dried tangerine peel, and sherry in dishes like Red-Braised Lamb Shanks and Spare Ribs with Mango Barbecue Sauce. But in a lighter dish, such as Stir-Fried Pork Ribbons, these meats won't overpower delicate aromatics like lemongrass and kaffir lime.

C U R R I E S
2 5 8

There are as many curries as there are cooks, but each one starts the same way: Pounded aromatics are slowly cooked in oil, then augmented with freshly ground spices. Not until the entire house is redolent with curry paste do any more ingredients join in. Some tempting curries are Lamb Korma, Eggplant and Raisin Tamarind Curry, and Fragrant Ceylonese Fish Curry.

V E G E T A B L E S
2 8 6

Radiant Chinese greens, tender asparagus, luscious eggplant, earthy mushrooms,

pungent turnips—vegetables are flash-fried and spiked with soy and garlic or slowly simmered in a complex curry. From the great vegetarian traditions of China, India—and California.

Rice is revered throughout Asia, but in China, noodles are also a national treasure. And, yes, it *is* bad manners not to slurp loudly as you enjoy Broad Rice Noodles with Chinese Sausage and Shrimp. Also: Salmon *Biriyani* from San Francisco and Steamed Sticky Rice with Swordfish and Shiitakes.

The lush textures, bright flavors, and vivid colors of native Pacific fruits turn ordinary cakes, creams, puddings, and pastries into tantalizing tropical jewels—like Seduction Pineapple Upside-Down Cake, Mango Gratin with Champagne Sabayon, and Banana and Kiwi Spring Rolls.

Basic steamed rice, chicken stock, toasted nuts, and homemade spice mixes, sweet soy sauce, and hot chile sauce.

INTRODUCTION:
THE FRAGRANT FLAVORS OF
THE PACIFIC RIM

Call their union what you will—Pacific Rim, fusion, or East-meets-West—Oriental and Occidental flavors have finally embraced each other with open arms. The great culinary traditions of Europe and Asia, long distant and remote, each exotic to the other, have blended, fused, and overlapped—sometimes with seismic effects. The heartland of this new cuisine is a great loop of countries strung like a necklace around the edges of the seemingly endless Pacific Ocean.

The Pacific Rim is an infinitely complex culinary mosaic: Thai, Malay, Japanese, Indian, regional Chinese, Vietnamese, Polynesian, colonial Western, and contemporary European influences mingle to produce the most varied, exciting, and sophisticated culinary landscape in the world. It is a universe of cuisine bursting with vibrant tastes: the warming tingle of spices; the exquisite perfume of lemongrass, coconut, ginger, and herbs; the heat of chiles and the tang of lime; the crunch of peanuts; and the irresistible tastes of tropical fruit. Once considered mysterious and foreign, these flavors are quickly becoming a staple part of the American food experience. The fragrant breezes of Pacific cooking are about to waft into the American home kitchen.

But this vivid gastronomic exchange is not all one-way. While Western cooks are experimenting with Oriental flavors, their Asian counterparts are likewise discovering Western tastes and techniques. While we tuck into noodles and curry, in Asia they are going out for pasta and enchiladas. Food is on the wing as well as on the table. Pacific Rim cuisine is not a figment of the culinary imagination—a gourmet fantasy that will soon give way to the next new fad—but a contemporary global phenomenon rooted in the history, geography, economics, and social reality of everyday fin-de-siècle life. It is the flavor base for tomorrow, an exciting new vocabulary of tastes and techniques for the next millennium. Much more than a collection of ethnic recipes, the *Terrific Pacific Cookbook* offers you a vivid, and we hope, well-rounded, sketch of this crucial new culinary style.

A cuisine of the present and for the future, yes. But the fusion palate was not born of the whims of gastronomic fashion or the advent of global communications technology—East and West didn't meet for the first time in the kitchen of a pastel-hued California café or on the enormous tables of a new Hong Kong hotel. For centuries, spice merchants plied the oldest trade routes on the globe. They hauled new flavors on camel-back over the Central Asian deserts, until Portuguese, Dutch, and British ships opened up the sea routes that founded their empires in the fifteenth and sixteenth centuries. The colonial history of

Southeast Asia includes an intriguing, colorful patchwork of tastes and traditions, and is the most enduring source of culinary union and improvisation. The robust stews enjoyed by Portuguese seamen can still be found in the old spice port of Melaka; French baguettes are the base for a typical Vietnamese sandwich; Dutch cakes form the centerpiece of the traditional Indonesian Christmas table; British high tea and Sunday roasts are revered rituals in Malaysia and Singapore. And in the "melting pot" cuisine of Australia, the overlays and combinations have become as subtle and exact as the finest marquetry.

The idea for *Terrific Pacific* was born out of a two-year sojourn in Australia in the early '90s. Half-expecting to subsist on meals of overcooked roast, three vegetables, and canned lager, John and I were stunned to discover that these clichés were a decade out of date and we had entered the incredible kingdom of food Down Under. A Pacific country with strong European traditions, naturally situated on the crossroads between East and West, Australia was emerging as the most convincing point of connection between Oriental and Occidental products and cuisines. We were en-

chanted by the imaginative creations of Australian chefs, who presented us with a Five-Spice Duck Pie with Ginger Glaze, Miso-Flavored Oyster Gratin, and New Zealand Scampi with Green Tea Sauce.

Australasian food is the Pacific equivalent of border cuisine, like Tex-Mex in the American Southwest. It is multicultural eating at its best. I was astonished by the ease, casualness, and skill with which even Australian home cooks juggle Asian and European ingredients and techniques.

Soon I became so beguiled by the flavors of the Pacific Rim, that I craved them as the basis of my own cooking. This was the way I wanted to cook for myself and for friends. Here, I thought, was a vision of what the American food scene would be in several years. Today in the United States, I can buy fresh galangal, banana leaves, and flowering chives; canned coconut milk has its own place on supermarket shelves; Thai curry pastes and Chinese noodles turn up prettily packaged in gourmet shops and more recently in supermarkets; and Pacific recipes appear next to Mediterranean ones in newspapers and food magazines. I think I was right.

With Australia as our base, John and I traveled high and low in search of terrific Pacific flavors. We journeyed to Thailand, New Zealand, Indonesia, Malaysia, Japan, and Singapore before completing our tour with a long stay in California. We learned kitchen secrets and culinary lore from roadside hawker stalls, market vendors, food writers, grandmothers, magazine editors, and five-star chefs. With help we transcribed recipes from Thai and Hokkien and interpreted chefs' scribbles in Tamil, Vietnamese, and Bahasa Malay. We sampled the staggering variety of street food on the enchanted island of Penang; we shared the excitement of fusing new flavors with the talented young chefs of Sydney and Melbourne; we shopped for the freshest produce at Asian wet markets. We scoured for local legends about spices and tropical fruit; we ate some of the best Pacific seafood at water's-edge seafood paradises—often nothing more than roofs on teetering stilts. We visited vast *dim sum* palaces, cozy noodle shops, chic tea houses, and popular banana leaf restaurants. We chatted with globe-trotting hotel chefs (Berlin one year, Bangkok the next); we studied the history of colonial fare at fabled old hotels; and we cooked with fishermen in the Portuguese settlement near Melaka. Back home on the Pacific Rim side of the United States, we watched as the kitchens of a famous Cantonese restaurant in San Francisco turned out a banquet for five hundred, and toured ethnic grocery stores and restaurants wherever we traveled.

In assembling recipes for this collection, my aim was to bring the drama, excitement, and sheer excellence of Pacific Rim food to the American table—but to do it in a way that would be fun, casual, and gentle on the home cook. It was daunting to reduce the mountain of recipes and information I collected into the relative molehill of a single book—I still have material for a dozen sequels. After all, we were dealing with three continentsful of culinary traditions. For *Terrific Pacific*, I have selected the recipes I thought would be best understood by, and most accessible to, American cooks. This is an introduction to the vibrant flavors of various Pacific Rim countries and a sampling of the best of fusion cuisine; it is not an ethnic cookbook or a *Larousse Gastronomique* of Asian flavors. There are recipes here for those already familiar with the Asian palate as well as for those who have not yet set eyes on galangal or tamarind. Some are truly authentic Asian recipes, others are casual creations by Australian and Californian chefs, which can be thrown together in minutes.

A word of caution: The marriage of Eastern and Western flavors is not always a perfect union. I am not an advocate of randomly mixing disparate flavors in the name of culinary experimentation. Too often, much of what passes for East-West food in this country ends up doing a disservice to both traditions. As this project progressed, my admiration for the depth and complexity of Asian cuisines grew. Not even the most dazzling creations of the finest fusion chefs can compare with the conceptual brilliance of Thai, the complexity of Chinese, the inherent elegance of Vietnamese, or the creative borrowings of Malaysian cuisines. It is for this reason that much of the book is devoted to authentic Southeast Asian recipes. Much as I admire the overlay of flavors—ancient and modern—in the Pacific world, I am a passionate advocate of respect for the integrity of great traditions. When fusing styles, it is important to depart from a solid base, either Eastern or Western. Once you've mastered the authentic preparation, whether it's a pasta or curry, it is much easier to begin your experiments—perhaps adding a subtle hint of coconut milk and ginger to a silky French sauce, or giving a French or Italian twist to an ethnic Asian dish. I hope this book will show you the way.

Terrific Pacific fusions often come with a touch, sometimes definite, sometimes feather-light: An authentic Thai curry is served with Western-style roast turkey; a velvety American pumpkin soup is enhanced by Asian spices and coconut milk; a ginger-laced Japanese vinaigrettte dresses a potato salad; tangy Indian pakora batter coats chunks of salmon.

The foods and traditions in this book are diverse and complex, but if I had to point to the key continuities in their ingredients and cooking techniques it would be the profusion of spices and aromatics, an emphasis on grilling and stir-frying, and a love of salads, curries, and noodles. Many recipes begin with a fragrant pounded paste of fresh garlic, ginger, chiles, and lemongrass. And a range of dry spices infuse almost every dish from appetizers to desserts. The flavors are light, tangy, sweet, and utterly refreshing.

"Isn't it easier and cheaper to go around the corner to a neighborhood Thai or Vietnamese, than to attempt these exotic cuisines at home?" you might ask. Our answer might surprise you. For while there are wonderful, tongue-tingling exceptions, the vast majority of ethnic Southeast Asian restaurants serve up the equivalent of the overcooked chow mein or spaghetti and meatballs that passed for Chinese and Italian food before we became familiar with the *real thing.* Yet, with just a base stock of ingredients and good recipes to follow, you can end up with food infinitely fresher, tastier, and healthier than anything that you will encounter in even the better restaurants. Once you become more familiar with basic Pacific ingredients and techniques, tossing an Asian-inspired meal together is as simple as whipping up a pasta sauce or mixing a guacamole. I hope the recipes and stories in this book will open the door to a new world of food! The millennia of refinement and sheer culinary craft invented in Southeast Asia is finally seducing the world.

—Anya von Bremzen

TERRIFIC PACIFIC RECIPES

Spiced Nuts

Shrimp Chips with
Coconut-Peanut Dip

Seven Seas Roast Chile Dip with
Grilled Pork Strips

Thai Crabmeat Dip in Endive Spears

Colonial High Tea Curry Puffs

Thai-Style Pizzas with Two Toppings

Curried Potato Fritters with
Herbed Yogurt Dip

Crispy Stuffed Mushrooms

Seafood-Filled Rice Paper Rolls with
Two Dipping Sauces

Tuna Tartare with Wasabi
Mayonnaise on Fried Wonton Skins

Marinated Shrimps with
Mango in Lettuce Parcels

Sushi Rice Sandwiches

Imperial Rolls

Popiah

Salmon and Spinach Pakoras

Crispy Crescents Filled with
Herbed Shrimp and Pork

Grilled Chicken Slices with
Tamarind Dip

Thai Chicken with
Toasted Coconut in Lettuce Parcels

Spice-Crusted Chicken Liver Nibbles

Five-Spice Beef Brochettes

Mixed Satays with Spicy Peanut Sauce

Cucumber Boats with Lemon Beef
Salad

Lamb Toasts with a Tropical Sambal
and Avocado Cilantro Cream

Horses Galloping on Star Fruit

Griddle Bread with Curried Lamb

For parties, drinks, and pre-dinner snacking, nothing beats the Southeast Asian hors d'oeuvre. Just think of the choices: skewers of lightly smoky satay dipped in a spicy peanut sauce; juicy strips of chicken with a beguiling tart and sweet tamarind dip; plump shrimp, sweet with coconut and tart with lime juice, wrapped in a cooling lettuce leaf; crispy, spicy, thumb-size spring rolls or their uncooked counterparts, paper-thin rounds of rice paper, seductively wrapped around seafood, sprigs of aromatic herbs, and delicate rice vermicelli. To make the food even more entertaining, I often like to follow the Asian "wrap it yourself" tradition and present a rainbow of little dishes accompanied by leafy salad greens, rice paper, or delicate spring roll skins, as well as a variety of dipping sauces.

As ideally suited to Western entertaining as these foods are, the paradox is that they function very differently in their traditional contexts. Take Thailand, for example. A complete Thai meal, consisting of several types of dishes all served with rice and all arriving at the same time, would inevitably include a dip (usually based on pounded chiles) accompanied by slices of meat, fried fish, cooked and raw vegetables, or omelet strips. Hence, the delightful dips in this chapter are pure Thai in spirit but Western in presentation.

The Chinese *dim sum* ritual is another alluring, small-bite tradition that offers great finger food ideas. In China, these tempting morsels are steamed, boiled, or fried, and passed around in carts to throngs of hungry breakfasters. This wonderful family concept inspired many Southeast Asian countries to adopt the endlessly imaginative repertoire of dumplings, fritters, spring rolls, and meatballs—only now they are filled and wrapped with local ingredients according to regional preferences.

But this chapter takes its real inspiration from the traditional street foods sold by vendors throughout Asia. Easily handled and conveniently picked up, these toothsome little snacks, which fortify workers throughout the continent, are often eaten on the run. Transplanted to a western-style party, they do not lose their allure, but become even more seductive.

SPICED NUTS

Hot, sweet, and spicy, these nuts are an ideal nibble before a meal. Macadamias, cashews, and almonds, indigenous to the Pacific region, make the best combination, but you can use the nuts of your choice. The nuts will keep in an airtight container for up to a week.

2 tablespoons canola oil
½ teaspoon best-quality curry powder
1 teaspoon pure chile powder
1 teaspoon paprika
1 teaspoon ground cumin
1 teaspoon ground coriander
¼ teaspoon ground cayenne pepper
2 cups mixed raw nuts (such as macadamia, peanuts, cashews, and almonds)
4 teaspoons sugar
2 teaspoons salt, or more to taste

1. Preheat the oven to 300°F.

2. Heat the oil in a small skillet over medium heat. Add the curry and chile powders, paprika, cumin, coriander, and cayenne and stir until fragrant, about 1 minute.

3. Place the nuts in a mixing bowl. Add the spiced oil, sugar, and salt and toss thoroughly. Spread the nuts on a baking sheet. Bake, shaking occasionally, until the nuts are fragrant and golden, about 20 minutes. Serve warm, or cool and store in an airtight container.

MAKES 2 CUPS

SHRIMP CHIPS
with Coconut-Peanut Dip

Munched throughout Southeast Asia, these shrimp crackers are served as pre-dinner bites or used for scooping up dips or salads. They are entertaining to cook, as you watch a piece of hard plastic-looking stuff, which looks anything but edible, puff and wiggle itself into a gloriously fat chip. To make a show of it, invite guests to make their own batch. The coconut dip can be beefed up with cooked ground chicken or pork, or crabmeat.

*1 package (8 ounces) shrimp chips
    (prawn crackers)
Peanut oil, for deep-frying
Quick Coconut-Peanut Dip
    (recipe follows)*

Pour oil to a depth of 1¹/₂ inches in a large skillet and heat it over medium-high heat to

350°F. Fry the chips, in batches, until they puff up, about 15 seconds. Immediately transfer them with a slotted spoon to a plate lined with paper towels. Make as many as you wish. Cool before serving with the peanut dip. The shrimp chips will keep for several days in an airtight container.

Quick Coconut-Peanut Dip

*1 tablespoon peanut oil
3 tablespoons finely chopped onion
2 cloves garlic, crushed through a press
1 small fresh hot chile, green or red, stemmed,
    seeded, and minced
¹/₄ teaspoon best-quality curry powder
¹/₄ teaspoon ground turmeric
1 teaspoon paprika
1 tablespoon smooth unsalted, unsweetened
    peanut butter
³/₄ cup canned unsweetened coconut
    milk, well stirred
1¹/₂ teaspoons soy sauce
1 teaspoon fresh lemon
    juice
Salt, to taste*

Heat the oil in a small saucepan over medium-low heat. Add the onion, garlic, and chile and cook until the onion is translucent, about 3 minutes. Add the curry powder, turmeric, and paprika and stir for 1 minute. Stir in the peanut butter and coconut milk, bring to a simmer, and simmer, stirring for 5 minutes. Remove from the heat and add the soy sauce, lemon juice, and salt. Cool to room temperature before serving.

SERVES 4 TO 6

SEVEN SEAS ROAST CHILE DIP

with Grilled Pork Strips

Seven Seas, in the trendy Sukhumvit area, is one of the most exciting restaurants in Bangkok. Run by seven young partners (hence the name), most of them artists and designers, it doubles as an art gallery.

This sophisticated dip of roasted chiles and eggplant is one of endless variations on *nam prik*, a blistering concoction of pounded chiles, garlic, and fish sauce. This version uses the juice and leaves of fragrant kaffir limes. While the frozen leaves are certainly available at Thai groceries, supplies of the lime itself are more intermittent. Sometimes the limes are available whole, other times their shredded rind is sold in plastic packages. If you can't find kaffir lime, use the zest and juice of a common lime, though the unmistakable delicate perfume will unfortunately be lost. And use the larger green chiles, which are only medium-hot. Do not use jalapeños or serranos.

Traditionally, Thai dips such as this one are served with slices of meat, fried fish,

omelet strips, or cooked vegetables. Although I suggest grilled pork strips, it also tastes great with slices of grilled chicken breast, crudités, or just crackers.

12 large fresh medium-hot green chiles (4 to
   5 inches long), such as Anaheims
2 Chinese or Japanese eggplants (about
   12 ounces total), stemmed
Vegetable oil, for the skillet
½ cup very finely chopped red onion
3 small firm, ripe plum tomatoes, finely
   chopped
2 cloves garlic, crushed through a press
1½ tablespoons fresh kaffir or other lime
   juice, or more to taste
2 teaspoons grated kaffir or other lime zest
2 tablespoons Asian fish sauce, such as
   nam pla
1½ teaspoons sugar
2 tablespoons chopped scallions
3 tablespoons chopped fresh cilantro leaves
Salt, to taste
3 center-cut boneless pork chops (about
   1 pound)
1 tablespoon soy sauce

1. Preheat the broiler.

2. Broil the chiles, turning occasionally, until soft and lightly charred all over, about 7 minutes. Leave the broiler on. Place the chiles in a paper bag, wrap in a towel, and let stand for at least 10 minutes. Stem, peel, seed, and coarsely chop the chiles. Do not remove the seeds.

3. Lightly oil a cast-iron skillet and heat over medium heat. Add the eggplant and pan-roast, turning several times, until soft and charred on all sides, about 12 minutes. Cut in half lengthwise and scoop out the pulp.

4. Process the chiles and eggplant in a food processor until minced but not puréed. Transfer to a bowl and add the onion, tomatoes, garlic, lime juice, fish sauce, sugar, scallions, cilantro, and salt and stir well.

5. Brush the pork chops with soy sauce and rub with salt. Grill on both sides until cooked through, about 12 minutes. Cool. Slice crosswise into medium-thick slices.

6. Place a bowl filled with the dip in the middle of a plate and arrange the pork slices around it.

SERVES 6

THAI CRABMEAT DIP
in Endive Spears

Slightly bitter endive spears provide a nice foil for the sweetness of crabmeat bathed in coconut milk and perfumed with lemongrass. However, cucumber or lettuce cups, or wedges of red bell pepper make a fine substitute.

1 serrano chile, stemmed, seeded, and
*   chopped*
1 clove garlic, minced
1 tablespoon very finely sliced fresh
*   lemongrass (3 inches of the lower stalk,*
*   tough outer leaves discarded)*
2 teaspoons grated lemon zest
2 teaspoons Asian fish sauce, such as
*   nam pla*
2 tablespoons fresh lime juice
Salt, to taste
2 cups lump crabmeat, preferably Alaskan,
*   picked over*
3 tablespoons slivered fresh basil leaves
2 tablespoons torn fresh cilantro leaves
4 tablespoons canned unsweetened coconut
*   milk, well stirred*
3 medium heads Belgian endive

1. In a large bowl combine the chile, garlic, lemongrass, lemon zest, fish sauce, lime juice, and salt. Add the crabmeat, basil, cilantro, and coconut milk and toss gently to combine.

2. Separate the endive into spears. Fill with the crab mixture and serve.

SERVES 6

SINGAPORE SLING BASH

. . . .

SPICED NUTS

SEVEN SEAS ROAST CHILE DIP
with Grilled Pork Strips

VEGETABLE MEDLEY
with Indonesian Peanut Dip

THAI CRABMEAT DIP
in Endive Spears

IMPERIAL ROLLS

GRILLED CHICKEN SLICES
with Tamarind Dip

SINGAPORE SLINGS

COLONIAL HIGH TEA CURRY PUFFS

In Malaysia, the culinary traditions inherited from years of British colonial rule are still very much alive today.

These curry puffs—a Southeast Asian spin on Indian *samosas*—are a mandatory offering at a Malaysian high tea, a ceremony that displays the tantalizing array of local foods in a European context.

The curry puff recipe presented here is essentially a lazy version, made with a filling of delicious curried potatoes and peas that is wrapped in puff pastry (which the Malaysians love). The curry puffs are quite large, so I would figure on one per person, if served with other appetizers. You can easily double the recipe for a large buffet.

2 tablespoons unsalted butter

1 tablespoon vegetable oil

¾ cup chopped onion

2 teaspoons grated fresh ginger

2 teaspoons minced garlic

1 teaspoon cumin seeds

¾ teaspoon best-quality curry powder

½ teaspoon ground coriander

½ teaspoon ground cayenne pepper

½ teaspoon garam masala

2¼ cups diced cooked potatoes

⅓ cup fresh or frozen green peas, thawed
    if frozen

¼ cup Chicken Stock (page 384), canned
    broth, or water

2 tablespoons fresh lemon juice

Salt and freshly ground black pepper, to taste

1½ sheets frozen puff pastry, thawed

1 egg yolk, mixed with 1 teaspoon milk

1. Heat the butter and oil in a large skillet over medium heat. Add the onion and cook until wilted, about 5 minutes. Add the ginger and garlic and cook, stirring, for another 3 minutes. Stir in the cumin seeds, curry powder, coriander, cayenne, and garam masala and stir for 1 minute. Add the potatoes, peas, and stock, stirring well to coat with the spice mixture, and cook until the mixture is fairly dry, about 5 minutes. Add the lemon juice and season with salt and pepper. Transfer to a bowl and cool completely.

2. Preheat the oven to 375°F.

3. On a lightly floured board, roll the puff pastry ¹⁄₁₆ inch thick. With a large cookie cutter or the rim of a small bowl, cut out 4½-inch circles. When cutting out circles, make them as close together as possible so you don't waste pastry.

4. Place a heaping tablespoon of the filling on the lower half of each circle, spreading it out a little. Fold the other half of the circle over the filling to form a half-moon. Pinch the edges tightly and crimp decoratively. You should have 11 to 12 curry puffs.

5. Arrange the curry puffs on a large baking sheet, brush with the egg wash, and bake until golden, about 17 minutes. Serve warm.

MAKES 11 TO 12 CURRY PUFFS

THAI-STYLE PIZZAS
with Two Toppings

In Bangkok, wood oven-baked pizza is second in popularity only to nachos. So in the best Thai spirit, here are dainty cocktail party–size pizzas with two piquant Thai-inspired toppings, one of lightly marinated shrimp, red peppers, and oyster mushrooms, another of *larb*, a tangy mixture of minced spiced pork and aromatic herbs.

The dough and each topping recipe will make eighteen 4-inch pizzas. Each topping recipe is easily halved, and the dough recipe easily doubled, so you can adjust the pizza types to suit your taste.

CRUST
1 package active dry yeast
½ teaspoon sugar
1⅓ cups lukewarm water
1½ tablespoons vegetable oil
1 teaspoon salt
3¾ to 4 cups all-purpose flour
Cornmeal, for sprinkling the pan

1 recipe Shrimp Topping or Larb Topping
(recipes follow)

1. In a large bowl, combine the yeast, sugar, and water and let stand until foamy, about 5 minutes. Stir in the oil and the salt.

2. Gradually add 3¾ cups flour, mixing well with a wooden spoon after each addition. Transfer the dough to your work surface and knead until it is smooth and elastic, about 8 minutes, adding more flour if it is too sticky.

3. Shape the dough into a ball and place in a large oiled bowl. Turn to coat with the oil, cover with plastic wrap, and let rise in a warm, draft-free place until doubled in bulk, about 1 hour. Punch the dough down.

4. Preheat the oven to 500°F for 30 minutes. Lightly oil 3 medium-size baking sheets and sprinkle them with cornmeal.

5. Divide the dough into thirds, then divide each third into 6 balls. Let stand, covered, for 5 minutes. On a floured surface with a floured rolling pin, roll out each dough ball to a round 4 inches in diameter.

6. Place 6 rounds of dough on each baking sheet and arrange the topping on the pizzas as directed in the following recipes. Bake 2 sheets at a time on the bottom rack placed at the lowest level of the oven until the crust is browned, 10 to 12 minutes. Repeat with the remaining pizzas.

MAKES EIGHTEEN 4-INCH PIZZAS

Shrimp Topping

27 large shrimp (about 1¼ pounds), peeled, deveined, and halved lengthwise
3 tablespoons olive oil
2 tablespoons fresh lime juice
1 teaspoon minced fresh ginger
½ cup finely chopped onion
4 cloves garlic, minced
3½ cups firm, ripe tomatoes, peeled, seeded, and chopped
2 teaspoons sambal oelek (page 388) or Chinese chile paste with garlic
5 tablespoons chopped fresh cilantro leaves
1 small red onion, halved and thinly sliced lengthwise
1 large red bell pepper, stemmed, seeded, and julienned
10 oyster mushrooms, cut into strips
Salt and freshly ground black pepper, to taste

1. In a large bowl, toss the shrimp with 1 tablespoon of the olive oil, 1 tablespoon of the lime juice, and the ginger and marinate for 1 hour.

2. Meanwhile, heat the remaining 2 tablespoons oil in a large skillet over medium heat. Add the onion and garlic and cook, stirring, for 3 minutes. Add the tomatoes and cook, stirring, until the tomatoes are softened and reduced somewhat, about 10 minutes. Remove from heat and stir in the remaining 1 tablespoon lime juice, the *sambal oelek,* and cilantro and season with salt and pepper. Cool to room temperature.

3. Spoon some of the tomato mixture on the prepared pizza rounds, top each with 3 shrimp halves, cut side down, and then with some red onion, red pepper, and oyster mushrooms. Bake as directed in the crust recipe.

MAKES ENOUGH TOPPING FOR EIGHTEEN 4-INCH PIZZAS

PACIFIC TASTES DRINKS PARTY

. . . .

THAI-STYLE PIZZAS
with Two Toppings

LAMB TOASTS
with a Tropical Sambal and
Avocado Cilantro Cream

SUSHI RICE SANDWICHES

CURRIED POTATO FRITTERS
with Herbed Yogurt Dip

MARINATED SHRIMP
WITH MANGO
in Lettuce Parcels

Larb
Topping
for Pizza

1 tablespoon peanut oil

1 pound lean ground pork

3 tablespoons fresh lime juice

*1½ tablespoons Asian fish sauce, such as
    nam pla*

½ teaspoon sugar

*2 small fresh hot chiles, green or red,
    stemmed, seeded, and chopped*

¼ teaspoon dried red pepper flakes

*1 small red bell pepper, stemmed, seeded,
    and finely diced*

1 tablespoon grated fresh ginger

½ cup finely chopped red onion

*3 large firm, ripe tomatoes, peeled, seeded,
    and chopped*

*Salt and freshly ground black pepper,
    to taste*

*3 tablespoons chopped fresh mint leaves,
    plus additional for garnish*

*3 tablespoons chopped fresh cilantro leaves,
    plus additional for garnish*

*¼ cup chopped roasted peanuts,
    for garnish*

1. Heat the oil in a large skillet over medium-high heat. Add the pork and cook, stirring and breaking up the lumps with a fork, until the pork is no longer pink, about 5 minutes. With a slotted spoon, shaking off the excess liquid, transfer the pork to a large bowl. Add the remaining ingredients, except the garnish, to the pork, and mix well.

2. Spread the prepared pizza rounds evenly with the topping and bake as directed in the crust recipe. Before serving, garnish the pizzas with extra chopped mint and cilantro, and the peanuts.

MAKES ENOUGH TOPPING FOR EIGHTEEN 4-INCH PIZZAS

THE SPICE OF LIFE

For the many ethnic Indians of Southeast Asia, spices are the key to life. Cardamom is used as a slimming agent. Fenugreek reduces fever and intestinal inflammations. Cumin is prescribed in Hindu medicine for all sort of diseases, including jaundice and piles, and its seeds are mixed to a paste and applied to the body to relieve arthritic pains. Aniseed, when crushed with some clove oil and then rubbed into forehead and temples, is said to cure nervous headaches. Tamarind is an aphrodisiac, a breath freshener, a teeth whitener, and a meat tenderizer. When mixed with water and rock sugar, it is also held to relieve cuts and sores; rock sugar alone ensures a sweet married life.

Nutmeg cures heart conditions when mixed with boiling water and sugar. Taken morning and evening, a glass of ginger water will keep illness at bay. Coriander is used to relieve constipation and insomnia and as an aid during childbirth. Cinnamon relieves the common cold. Chiles cure paralysis.

Turmeric is good for the complexion, and is rubbed on newborn babies. Women mix it with water for use as a moisturizer. The Malays mix it with fried salty fish and serve the dish to women in childbirth.

CURRIED POTATO FRITTERS
with Herbed Yogurt Dip

Small potato fritters, laced with southern Indian spices, make terrific finger food. And when shaped into generous (3-inch) patties or croquettes, they make a fine side dish or vegetarian entrée.

3 tablespoons unsalted butter
¾ cup finely chopped onion
¾ teaspoon ground turmeric
¾ teaspoon ground coriander
½ teaspoon best-quality curry powder
¼ teaspoon pure chile powder, or more
    to taste
1½ teaspoons cumin seeds
3 large baking potatoes (about 1½ pounds),
    cooked and peeled
⅓ cup dessicated (dried) coconut, soaked in
    warm water for 15 minutes and drained
1 to 2 serrano chiles, stemmed, seeded, and
    chopped
¼ cup chopped fresh cilantro leaves
2 large eggs, lightly beaten
⅔ cup fine dry bread crumbs
Salt, to taste
Herbed Yogurt Dip (recipe follows)
Canola or peanut oil, for deep frying the
    fritters

1. Melt the butter in a medium-size skillet over medium heat. Cook the onion until translucent, about 7 minutes. Add the turmeric, coriander, curry powder, chile powder, and cumin and stir over low heat for 1 minute. Remove from the heat.

2. In a large bowl, mash the potatoes coarsely. Add the seasoned onion, coconut, chiles, and cilantro. Stir in the eggs and ¼ cup of the bread crumbs. Mix well and season with salt to taste.

3. Spread the remaining bread crumbs on a cutting board. Shape the potato mixture into 2-inch patties and roll in the crumbs.

4. Pour oil to a depth of 1 inch in a deep fryer or a large skillet and heat to 360°F over medium-high heat. Working in batches, fry the fritters on both sides until deep golden, 3 to 4 minutes. Drain on paper towels. Let cool slightly and serve with Herbed Yogurt Dip.

SERVES 6 TO 8

Herbed Yogurt Dip

¼ cup heavy (or whipping) cream
1 cup low-fat plain yogurt
4 tablespoons chopped fresh mint leaves
3 tablespoons chopped fresh cilantro leaves
1 small serrano chile, stemmed, seeded, and
*   minced*
1 clove garlic, chopped
2 teaspoons fresh lemon juice, or to taste
Pinch of sugar, or to taste
Salt, to taste

Place all the ingredients in a food processor and process just until the solids are finely minced. Do not overprocess. Let stand at room temperature for at least 30 minutes before serving for the flavors to develop.

MAKES ABOUT 1¼ CUPS

CRISPY STUFFED MUSHROOMS

A dim sum-inspired dish, these mushroom caps are filled with spicy minced pork, then fried in a light batter. You can stuff the mushrooms ahead of time, but serve them as soon as you fry them for the juiciest of fillings, encased in the crispiest of shells.

FILLING
12 ounces ground pork
2 teaspoons grated fresh ginger
2 cloves garlic, crushed through
*   a press*
1 tablespoon rice wine or dry sherry
4 teaspoons soy sauce
3 tablespoons chopped fresh
*   cilantro leaves*
½ teaspoon dried red pepper flakes
1½ teaspoons cornstarch
1 large egg white
Salt, to taste

1 pound (at least 30) medium button
*   mushrooms, preferably uniform size,*
*   wiped clean*
¼ cup all-purpose flour
¼ cup cornstarch
1 teaspoon baking powder
5 tablespoons ice water
¼ cup cold milk
Oil, for deep frying

Soy-Scallion Dipping Sauce (recipe follows)

1. Combine all of the filling ingredients in a medium-size bowl and stir well in one direction. Cover the bowl and refrigerate for 2 to 4 hours.

2. Use your fingers to remove the entire stem from each mushroom. With a small sharp knife, gently remove the rim around the edge of the caps. Stuff the mushrooms with the pork mixture, making a nice rounded top.

3. Sift the flour, cornstarch, and baking powder into a bowl. Whisk in the water and the milk until smooth. Let stand for 10 minutes.

4. Pour oil to a depth of 2 inches into a deep fryer or wok and heat over medium-high heat to 350°F.

5. Using a fork, dip one mushroom at a time in the batter until evenly coated. Gently shake off the excess batter. Drop the mushrooms, 6 to 8 at a time, into the hot oil, filled side down, and fry until deep golden and crisp, 6 to 7 minutes, returning the oil to 350°F before each new batch. Remove with a slotted spoon to paper towels to drain. Serve at once with Soy-Scallion Dipping Sauce.

MAKES ABOUT 30 MUSHROOMS, ENOUGH TO SERVE 8 TO 10 AS AN APPETIZER

ORIENTAL APPETIZER BUFFET

. . . .

CRISPY STUFFED MUSHROOMS

THAI CRABMEAT DIP
in Endive Spears

THAI SEAFOOD AND RICE NOODLE SALAD

SPICE-CRUSTED CHICKEN LIVER NIBBLES

MIXED SATAYS
with Spicy Roast Peanut Sauce

Soy-Scallion Dipping Sauce

½ cup good-quality dark soy sauce
1 clove garlic, minced
¾ teaspoon minced fresh ginger
3 tablespoons Chicken Stock (page 384) or
*   canned broth*
2 teaspoons rice vinegar
1 teaspoon sugar
1¼ teaspoons Oriental sesame oil
3 tablespoons thinly sliced scallions

Whisk all the ingredients together in a small bowl. Let stand at room temperature for 15 minutes before serving.

MAKES ABOUT ⅔ CUP

SEAFOOD-FILLED RICE PAPER ROLLS
with Two Dipping Sauces

To me, these enticing rice paper parcels filled with seafood, rice vermicelli, and an assortment of fresh herbs exemplify the alluringly light, crisp, clean flavors of Vietnam. They make perfect finger food: exotic, fun to eat, low in calories, easily prepared ahead of time, and utterly delicious.

This recipe makes quite plump, bountiful rolls, replete with two kinds of seafood, herbs, and an assortment of crisp shredded vegetables. For an easier, lighter version, use only the shrimp, and substitute halved small green or red lettuce leaves for the shredded lettuce and cucumber, placing them on the rolls with the herbs. Serve the rolls with the two sauces and a mound of lettuce leaves. Then show your guests how to wrap a roll in a lettuce leaf and dip in either or both of the sauces.

3 ounces rice vermicelli
¾ cup shredded iceberg lettuce
¾ cup bean sprouts
1 medium cucumber, peeled, seeded,
*   and julienned*
1¼ cups lump crabmeat, picked over
12 large cooked shrimp, peeled, deveined,
*   and cut in half lengthwise*
12 round 8½-inch rice-paper wrappers
12 large sprigs fresh mint
12 large sprigs fresh cilantro
Green-leaf lettuce leaves, for wrapping
*   the rolls*
Hoisin Dipping Sauce (recipe follows)
Vietnamese Tangy Lime Dipping Sauce
*   (recipe follows)*

1. Soak the rice vermicelli in cold water for 20 minutes. Meanwhile, bring a large saucepan of salted water to a boil. Drain the vermicelli and gently separate it with your fingers. Drop the vermicelli into the boiling water and cook for 30 seconds. Drain, then rinse under cold running water and drain again until dry. Cut into 2-inch lengths. Place in a bowl and reserve.

2. Combine the lettuce, bean sprouts, and cucumber in a large bowl and toss with your fingers until well combined.

3. Place the crabmeat and shrimp in two separate bowls.

4. Working with 4 rounds of rice-paper wrappers at a time, lay them on your work surface. With a pastry brush, brush both sides of each wrapper generously with lukewarm water. Let stand until the wrappers are soft

and pliable, 1½ to 2 minutes. If parts of the wrappers still look dry, lightly brush with some more water.

5. Have bowls of the filling ingredients at the ready in your work area. Place a sprig of mint and a sprig of cilantro in a line across the lower third of a wrapper. Top with some rice vermicelli, shaping it into a compact log. Place about 1½ tablespoons of the lettuce mixture on top, shaping it into a compact log. Top with some crabmeat, and place 2 shrimp halves lengthwise along the roll. Fold the bottom flap of the wrapper up and over the filling, then roll it up gently but tightly, folding the sides in as you go. The rice paper will seal by sticking to itself. Repeat with the remaining wrappers and filling ingredients.

6. You can either serve the rolls whole or cut in half crosswise. To serve, arrange the rolls on a large platter and serve a pile of lettuce leaves and the two sauces separately. To eat, wrap each roll in a lettuce leaf and dip in one of the sauces.

MAKES 12 ROLLS TO SERVE 6

Hoisin
Dipping Sauce

The Vietnamese sometimes serve bottled hoisin sauce with rice-paper rolls. I find the taste to be too dense and thick, so I lighten it up with a little lemon juice and sugar, a touch of sesame oil, and a sprinkling of peanuts.

¾ cup hoisin sauce
1 tablespoon fresh lemon juice
½ teaspoon sugar
1½ teaspoons Oriental sesame oil
1½ tablespoons finely chopped roasted peanuts

EDIBLE RICE PAPER

Very thin parchment-like rice paper is the least fussy of all "wrappers." All it needs is to be moistened with water, allowed to sit for a couple of minutes, and it's ready to roll. Dried rice-paper rounds can be purchased in Asian grocery stores, where they may also be called spring roll skins, galettes de riz, or banh trang. They will keep almost indefinitely in a cupboard, so do not take up valuable freezer or refrigerator space. Rice paper does, however, tend to get crumbly and tear easily when old, so, when buying it, look for packages containing paper without any signs of cracks or crumbling edges. Making a perfectly compact, tight roll without tearing the paper takes some practice, so count on making and eating several trial rolls until you get it right.

Once you have mastered the simple art of wrapping food in rice paper, the combinations of filling are endless. Traditional fillings always include aromatic herbs such as mint, cilantro, and Asian or purple basil, and refreshing cucumber and rice noodles. Additional fillings are limited only by your imagination. Try poached chicken breast meat, cooked ground pork spiced with ginger and garlic, poached fish, or very thinly sliced grilled beef, pork, or smoked salmon. You can create your own combinations using your favorite aromatic herbs (chives are especially nice), salad greens, arugula or radicchio, asparagus, mushrooms, crisp julienned radish or jicama, or carrot or fennel neatly cut into matchsticks.

At a convivial gathering of friends, or to break the ice at an informal dinner party, place bowls of assorted fillings on the table and let your guests make up their own rolls. The results are guaranteed to be as revealing as they are entertaining.

Combine the hoisin sauce, lemon juice, sugar, and sesame oil in a small bowl and stir well. Sprinkle with chopped peanuts and serve.

MAKES ABOUT ¾ CUP

Vietnamese Tangy Lime Dipping Sauce

Nouc cham, the versatile Vietnamese dipping sauce, is an excellent accompaniment to a number of dishes in this book, including Imperial Rolls, Crispy Crescents filled with Herbed Shrimp and Pork, and Thai Drumsticks for a Crowd. Check the Index for page numbers.

FAST FOOD

The stands of hawker trolleys and kiosks that line the thronging streets of Southeast Asian cities are home to one of the great culinary pleasures on Earth—stall cuisine. And nowhere is the tradition so vibrant and successful as in Malaysia and Singapore.

Stall cuisine thrives on a wonderfully improvised mix-and-match. It's not unusual to find an Indian vendor (usually Tamil), for example, selling Hokkien rice noodles, but with a dash of lamb curry added to create south Indian style stir-fried noodles. Nearby, a Malay hawker may sell curry puffs, adapted from colonial British cooking. And while there is a good deal of rivalry between the different groups, it is common for diners to browse at a range of ethnically different stalls.

Once good stalls are discovered, the news spreads lightning-fast. I know a stall in Kuala Lumpur where lines for the famous Malay breakfast of nasi lemak (coconut rice with curries and condiments) stretch around the block. Stalls are so precious that they are passed down like family jewels. Consistently well patronized ones are worth their weight in gold. Successful proprietors own a house, drive flashy cars, and perhaps send their children overseas to college.

DELICIOUS RESEARCH

John and I made the rounds of hawker stalls in Penang, Kuala Lumpur, and Singapore until our legs gave way and our stomachs said "no more." One night we went quite late to the Chinatown night market in Kuala Lumpur. The food stalls were set out on the cross streets, while the main drag was given over to the evening trade in clothes and bric-a-brac.

We settled upon Chinese fondue and tucked into do-it-yourself skewers of mushrooms, peppers, and cubes of beef, squid, and cuttlefish, which we boiled at the table in a cauldron of bubbling broth and ate dipped in either the curry or chile sauces provided. Opposite was a kiosk dispensing sugarcane juice from four ornate samovars. The liquid was poured into little plastic sacks—the kind in which you take home goldfish from the fair—and hung on a row of hooks, ready to go. Next door, another drinks kiosk didn't have its American marketing quite right. Its sign read "honey, sea, and coconut juice."

The best hawkers have the wit and wisdom of a London cab driver, the speed and patience of a Japanese assembly worker, and the cooking skills of a grand master. They boast long and loud about the VIPs who have visited their stalls, or give you an opinionated rundown on current affairs, or anoint your purchase with a few well-chosen words of advice. Gossip and news come together in a spectacle of passions. Millionaires happily rub elbows with trishaw drivers, just to get a plateful of the best fried noodles in town. Hawker stalls are just about the best dinner show around.

5 tablespoons fresh lime juice
6 tablespoons Asian fish sauce, such as
    nam pla
1 small fresh hot chile, green or red,
    stemmed, partially seeded, and minced
1 teaspoon distilled white vinegar
3½ tablespoons sugar, or more to taste
3½ tablespoons hot water
2 tablespoons chopped fresh cilantro leaves

In a small bowl, combine all the ingredients and stir well until the sugar is dissolved. Let stand at room temperature for at least 30 minutes before serving.

MAKES ABOUT ¾ CUP SAUCE

T U N A   T A R T A R E   W I T H   W A S A B I   M A Y O N N A I S E

on Fried Wonton Skins

This hors d'oeuvre is my easy rendition of the trendy *ahi napolenos* (raw tuna stacked on fried wonton skins), which seems to have replaced the eighties "tuna carpaccio" on fusion restaurant menus from coast to coast. Despite the fancy-sounding title, it is a cinch to put together. Here, a minimum amount of effort and a minor splurge on a half-pound of top-quality (impeccably fresh sashimi-quality) tuna will invariably produce dazzling results.

Peanut oil, for deep frying the skins
12 round or square wonton skins,
    thawed if frozen
8 ounces very fresh ahi or other
    sashimi-quality tuna, cut into
    ¼-inch dice
½ teaspoon coarse (kosher) salt
2 teaspoons finely grated fresh ginger
1 tablespoon plus 1 teaspoon
    tamari soy sauce
1 teaspoon Oriental sesame oil
2 tablespoons seasoned rice vinegar
1 teaspoon distilled white vinegar
2 tablespoons thinly sliced scallion
    greens
1 Kirby cucumber, seeded and sliced
    into long, paper-thin strips with
    a vegetable peeler
1 tablespoon Japanese pink pickled ginger,
    thinly julienned
2 tablespoons Wasabi Mayonnaise (page 52),
    or as needed

1. Pour oil to a depth of 2 inches into a large, deep skillet and heat it over medium-high heat to 350°F. Deep-fry as many wonton wrappers as will fit comfortably until puffed and golden, about 30 seconds. Drain well on a double layer of paper towels. Repeat with the remaining wrappers.

2. Place the tuna in a bowl and rub with salt and ginger. Add the tamari, sesame oil, and 1½ teaspoons of the rice vinegar. Stir in the scallions. (You can make the tuna ahead of time, but don't add the scallions until right before serving.)

3. Use your hands to squeeze the excess juice out of the cucumber strips and place in a small bowl with the pickled ginger. Add the remaining rice vinegar and the white vinegar and let stand for 10 minutes.

4. Place about 1 tablespoon of the tuna on a wonton skin, spreading it all over the surface. Drizzle a little of the Wasabi Mayonnaise decoratively on the tuna or pipe it out in lattice fashion. Arrange a small heap of the cucumber-ginger mixture on top. Repeat with the rest of the ingredients, then arrange on a decorative serving platter and serve at once.

MAKES 12 HORS D'OEUVRES

MARINATED SHRIMP WITH MANGO

in Lettuce Parcels

Set in a glass pavilion overlooking exquisite water gardens, the restaurant Celadon at the Sukothai Hotel in Bangkok offers the most daring and authentic Thai cuisine in the city, reflecting all of the country's four culinary regions. The German-born executive chef, Sven Krauss, is an exception to the jaded Bangkok expatriate chefs in that he pursues a passionate interest in traditional regional Thai cooking. In his quest for authentic flavors, he often takes a long rice barge "up-country" for tastings at the homes of friends and relatives of his staff.

It was at the Celadon that I tasted a delectable appetizer of enormous prawns from the Gulf of Thailand, lightly cooked in coconut milk, marinated in a lively mixture of lime juice, garlic, red shallots, green chiles, and fish sauce, and presented on lettuce leaves. Wonderful as it was, to me the tart marinade required a note of sweetness, so I have added a touch of finely diced

mango. The shrimp also taste delicious without the lettuce wrappers, served as an appetizer salad.

> 2 cups canned unsweetened coconut milk, well stirred
> 24 extra-large shrimp, peeled and deveined
> 7 tablespoons fresh lime juice
> 1½ tablespoons Asian fish sauce, such as nam pla
> 1½ teaspoons sugar
> 2 small fresh hot chiles, green or red, stemmed, seeded, and finely chopped
> 4½ tablespoons finely chopped red shallots or red onion
> ¼ cup finely diced firm ripe mango
> 2 tablespoons diced red bell pepper
> 24 small Boston lettuce leaves, rinsed and patted dry

1. Bring the coconut milk to a simmer in a medium-size saucepan, over medium-low heat. Add the shrimp and poach until they just turn pink, about 2½ minutes. (Cover the pan with a splatter screen if the milk splatters.) Do not overcook. Remove with a slotted spoon to a bowl.

2. Toss together 3 tablespoons of the poaching liquid, the lime juice, fish sauce, sugar, chiles, shallots, mango, and bell pepper in a medium-size bowl. Toss the shrimp with this mixture, cover with plastic wrap, and chill for 2 to 6 hours.

3. To serve, place a shrimp on a lettuce leaf, spoon some shallot and mango mixture over it, and roll it up.

MAKES 24 SHRIMP PARCELS

19

LEMONGRASS TEA

*D*elicious tea can be brewed from fresh or dried lemongrass stalks. It's better made from whole stalks, but you can still have a nice cup of tea made from the upper part of the stalk. Rinse the trimmed tops and allow them to air-dry until completely dry. Store in an airtight container on the lowest shelf of the refrigerator or in the freezer until you make the tea.

You will need 4 whole stalks of fresh lemongrass or 8 dried upper stalks per cup of boiling water. Crush and break the lemongrass into pieces to extract as much flavor as possible. Place in a teapot with a couple of lightly smashed thick slices of fresh ginger and add boiling water. Cover the pot and allow to steep for 20 minutes, then strain. Lemongrass tea is also tasty iced, with some sugar and a dash of fresh lemon or orange juice.

SUSHI RICE SANDWICHES

*H*ere is a very Pacific *amuse-gueule*, just right for a chic cocktail party. Sweet marinated cucumber, sushi rice, and smoked salmon are layered, then cut into squares. The rice needs time to compress, so make it several hours ahead or the day before serving. You can marinate the cucumbers up to 2 days before serving.

Serve these with soy sauce and wasabi (Japanese horseradish) or with Wasabi Mayonnaise (see Index).

SUSHI RICE
1¼ *cups short-grain rice*
1¾ *cups water*
2 *tablespoons rice vinegar*
1½ *teaspoons sugar*
Salt, to taste

¼ *cup rice vinegar*
2 *teaspoons soy sauce*
2 *tablespoons sugar*
1 *teaspoon finely julienned fresh ginger*
½ *teaspoon salt*
2 *firm, small hothouse cucumbers,*
    peeled and thinly sliced
7 to 8 *ounces thinly sliced smoked salmon*
Snipped fresh chives, for garnish

1. Make the sushi rice: Rinse the rice thoroughly in several changes of cold water. Place in a sieve and drain well.

2. Combine the rice and water in a medium-size saucepan and bring to a boil over medium heat. Partially cover and cook for 10 minutes. Then reduce the heat to low, cover completely, and simmer for 5 minutes. Remove from the heat and let stand, without removing the lid, for 20 minutes.

3. Combine the vinegar and sugar in a small nonreactive saucepan and heat, stirring, until the sugar is dissolved. Cool. Stir carefully but thoroughly into the rice. Season with salt. Place the rice in a bowl and keep covered with a damp cloth until ready to use.

4. Combine the vinegar, soy sauce, sugar, ginger, and salt in a small saucepan and heat until the sugar dissolves. Remove from the heat and allow to cool. Place the cucumbers in a small bowl and pour the mixture over them. Refrigerate, covered, for at least 2 hours or as long as overnight. Drain well.

5. Line a 9-inch square baking pan with plastic wrap, leaving enough wrap hanging over the edges so that you'll be able to completely cover the top with it. Spread half the rice on the plastic wrap, smoothing it out to all corners of the pan with the back of a large wet spoon. Spread the salmon slices evenly over the rice, then place the cucumbers on the salmon, slightly overlapping the slices. Top with the remaining rice, again smoothing it out with the back of a wet spoon.

6. Fold the plastic wrap over so that it completely covers the surface of the rice and top with a cutting board or a platter that fits just inside the pan. Place a heavy weight, such as a heavy iron skillet or cans of food on top and refrigerate for at least 4 hours or overnight.

7. Remove the weight and cutting board or platter. Lift the sides of the plastic wrap and carefully turn the square out onto a cutting board. Remove the plastic wrap. With a sharp knife, cut into 1½-inch squares, wetting the knife before each slice. Arrange the squares on a platter and garnish with chives.

SERVES 6

IMPERIAL ROLLS

For a Westerner, these classic rolls, wrapped in delicate rice paper and filled with seafood, vegetables, and rice vermicelli, are usually the first introduction to Vietnamese cuisine. While the rolls are terrific on their own, it is the presentation—the hot, crispy, and slightly sweet rolls, wrapped

in the cooling lettuce leaf and dipped in the sour-salty-sweet sauce—that makes the dish so distinct and exciting. Select rice paper rounds that look strong and intact, discarding the cracked brittle ones. You will need about 24 for this recipe.

4 ounces rice vermicelli
8 large dried shiitake mushrooms
8 ounces lean pork, finely diced or coarsely ground in a food processor
6 ounces shrimp, peeled, deveined, and minced in a food processor
1½ tablespoons minced garlic
¼ cup chopped scallions
1 cup grated carrot
1 cup shredded napa or regular cabbage
2½ tablespoons chopped fresh cilantro leaves
2 large eggs
3 tablespoons Asian fish sauce, such as nam pla
5 teaspoons plus 1 tablespoon sugar
Salt, to taste
About 1 cup flat beer, at room temperature
1 package 8½-inch round rice-paper wrappers
Peanut oil, for deep frying

GARNISHES
Double recipe of Vietnamese Tangy Lime Dipping Sauce (page 15)
1 cup grated carrot
Fresh cilantro sprigs
Fresh mint sprigs
2 heads butter lettuce, leaves separated, rinsed, and patted dry

1. Soak the rice vermicelli in warm water for 20 minutes. Drain until completely dry. Cut the vermicelli into 1½-inch lengths. You should have about 1 cup. (Draining will take at least 2 hours; so if you can, prepare the vermicelli the day before.)

2. Soak the shiitake mushrooms in cold water for 1 hour. Drain the mushrooms, remove and discard the tough stems, and finely chop the caps.

3. In a large bowl, combine the pork, shrimp, vermicelli, mushrooms, garlic, scallions, carrot, cabbage, and cilantro. Add the eggs, fish sauce, and the 5 teaspoons sugar. Season with salt and mix well.

4. In a bowl, combine the beer and remaining sugar and stir well. Working with 4 rounds of rice-paper wrappers at a time, lay them on your work surface. With a pastry brush, brush both sides of each wrapper evenly with beer. Let stand for about 1½ minutes until the wrappers are soft. If the wrappers look dry, brush them lightly with more beer, but don't make them too wet, otherwise they will tear.

5. Lay a softened wrapper on your work surface and fold up the lower third. Place about 1½ tablespoons of the filling along the folded portion of the wrapper, about ¾ inch from the bottom, shaping it into a 4½-inch log. Fold the bottom and sides of the wrapper in over the filling and roll up carefully but tightly, starting with the filled portion. If the rolls are too loose, they will burst during cooking. Repeat with the remaining wrappers and filling.

6. Pour oil to a depth of 2 inches into a wok or a large deep skillet and heat to 360°F over medium-high heat. Fry the rolls in batches, without crowding, until golden brown on all sides, 10 to 12 minutes. Make sure the oil returns to 360°F before each new batch, but do not let it get too hot. Transfer the finished rolls to a platter lined with paper towels. If you are not serving the rolls immediately, keep the fried ones warm in a 200°F oven.

7. To serve, place the Vietnamese Tangy Lime Dipping Sauce in a bowl and add the carrot. Place the cilantro and mint sprigs and lettuce leaves on decorative platters. (It may be easier to do this before you fry the rolls.) Cut each fried roll in half crosswise.

8. To eat, place a lettuce leaf on a plate and top with a cilantro and mint sprig. Place one of the half-rolls on the lettuce and roll up. Dip into the sauce and eat.

MAKES 24 ROLLS

P O P I A H

Like Mexican tortilla-wrapped snacks, the Straits Chinese *popiah* are filling finger foods, and you won't need more than salad and dessert to complete a meal. The recipe here is for an authentic version, but you can stretch the concept of multi-fillings as far as you like. After you have tried the classic recipe, experiment with seafood, thin slices of grilled meat or chicken, purchased barbecued duck and salad greens. And if you don't want to make the wrappers yourself, use purchased *popiah, lumpia,* or spring roll wrappers, which can be obtained in Asian grocery stores. (I recommend Menlo brand.) Store-bought wrappers should be steamed over boiling water for 10 minutes before using.

FRESH EGG ROLL WRAPPERS

1⅔ cups all-purpose flour

¾ cup cornstarch

3 large eggs, beaten

3 cups water

1 tablespoon peanut oil, plus additional for
    frying the wrappers

FILLING

3½ tablespoons peanut or canola oil

12 ounces boneless loin pork chops, cut into
    very thin strips

4 cloves garlic, pounded or processed to a
    paste

1 cup canned bamboo shoots, drained and
    shredded

1 cup shredded daikon radish

3 cups shredded jicama

1½ cups water

2 teaspoons sugar

1½ tablespoons preserved soybeans
    (optional)

1½ tablespoons fresh lemon juice

2 tablespoons sliced scallions

GARNISHES

12 to 15 cloves garlic (optional)

4 ounces fresh hot red chiles, stemmed and
    seeded, to taste; or sambal oelek (page 388);
    or Thai siracha chile sauce

1½ cups bean sprouts, rinsed and patted dry

1 large head romaine lettuce, leaves
    separated, rinsed, and patted dry

1 large cucumber, grated (with skin)

1½ cups lump crabmeat, picked over and
    flaked

12 ounces cooked small shrimp

4 Chinese sausages, steamed for 10 minutes
    and thinly sliced

1 recipe Omelet Strips (page 106)

1 cup fresh cilantro leaves

½ cup roasted peanuts, crushed

¾ cup hoisin sauce, or ketjap manis

Lime wedges

1. Make the wrappers: Sift the flour and cornstarch together into a large bowl. Make a well in the middle and gradually beat in the eggs, water, and 1 tablespoon oil until you have a smooth, thin batter. Alternatively, you can mix all the ingredients in a food processor. Cover with plastic wrap and let rest for 30 minutes.

2. Heat an 8-inch crepe pan or a nonstick skillet over medium heat. Pour some oil into a small bowl. Stick a fork into a 2-inch-thick slice of potato or daikon. Dip it into the oil and use it to brush the bottom of the pan with oil. When the oil is very hot, tilt the pan at an angle and quickly pour in a small ladleful of the batter, starting on the raised side of the pan. Very quickly rotate the pan until the batter covers it in a very thin layer. (It will take you several attempts to know exactly how much batter to use and how much to tilt and rotate the pan. Be patient.) Fry on one side until opaque and slightly bubbly, about 45 seconds. Turn and fry on the other side for 15 seconds more. Slide the wrapper onto a plate. Repeat with the rest of the batter, oiling the pan before each wrapper and stacking the wrappers on the plate. You should have about 20 wrappers. Cover the wrappers with aluminum foil until ready to use. They can be made a day ahead of time and kept refrigerated.

3. Make the filling: Heat 1½ tablespoons of the oil in a large skillet over medium heat. Add the pork and cook, stirring occasionally, until opaque. Remove from the skillet and reserve. Pour off any accumulated juices from the skillet.

4. Add the remaining 2 tablespoons oil to the skillet and heat over medium heat. Add the garlic and cook for 30 seconds. Add the bamboo shoots, daikon, and jicama and cook, stirring, for 5 minutes. Return the pork to the skillet, add the water, sugar, and soybeans and cook, stirring from time

MELINA'S POPIAH PARTY

While chatting with Juliet David, a food writer and consultant who is considered the first lady of the Singapore food world, I expressed an interest in tasting an authentic version of popiah, the renowned Straits Chinese delicacy. "La, nothing can be easier," exclaimed Juliet, as she reached for her cellular phone. Surrounded by phones and beepers, Juliet is one of those ebullient people who never stand still. She seems to have more audiences than the Thai royal family, and is probably invited to more dinners and receptions than Princess Di. "La, I will introduce you to Melina Teo, one of the best cooks and certainly the most accomplished popiah maker in town." One phone call later, John and I were invited for a demonstration and assemble-it-yourself popiah party.

On the day of the party, we arrived at the elegant home of Dr. and Mrs. Teo to find that the ever-efficient Juliet had even arranged a photo shoot of Melina's famous popiah, so that we would have a visual record to take with us.

The beautifully prepared popiah ingredients were all attractively laid out on the dining table. The meal consisted of a mound of ethereal paper-thin homemade egg crepe wrappers surrounded by a dizzying array of savory fillings, garnishes, and sauces. It was clear that we needed a lesson in how to properly construct a popiah and Melina and some of her guests were happy to give us novices their expert advice. We each lined a wrapper with a lettuce leaf, then spread some spicy garlic sauce on top, and added a hearty mixture of braised pork, jicama, and daikon. We topped that with some crabmeat, shrimp, Chinese sausages, omelet strips, crushed peanuts, and sprigs of fresh herbs. A squeeze of lime juice completed this intriguing bouquet of flavors, and the popiahs were rolled up like a spring roll and consumed with great gusto. As was the next one and the one after that. The popiahs were irresistible and the photographs, while memorable, are no match for my taste memory of Melina's fabulous popiah.

to time, until the filling is soft and all the water has been absorbed, about 20 minutes. Stir in the lemon juice and scallions, transfer to a bowl, and cool to warm or room temperature. The filling can be served either cold or warm.

5. Prepare the garnishes: Using a mortar and pestle or a small food processor, pound or process the garlic to a paste, if using. Clean the mortar or processor and pound or process the chiles to a paste.

6. Blanch the bean sprouts in boiling water for 15 seconds. Refresh under cold running water.

7. To serve the *popiah*, arrange the wrappers on a platter and place a bowl with the filling next to it. Place the lettuce leaves, pounded garlic, pounded chiles or chile sauce, bean sprouts, cucumber, crabmeat, shrimp, sausages, omelet strips, cilantro, peanuts, hoisin sauce, and lime wedges in separate bowls and on platters and arrange on the table around the wrappers.

8. To eat, place a wrapper on a plate and

top with a lettuce leaf. Spread the leaf with a little garlic, chile, and hoisin sauce. On the bottom portion of the leaf, place some filling, a couple of shrimp, some crabmeat, omelet strips, sausage, cucumber, bean sprouts, cilantro, and peanuts. Squeeze some lime juice on top. Roll up the wrapper, egg roll fashion, and eat.

SERVES 8 TO 10

SALMON AND SPINACH PAKORAS

akoras are crisp Indian fritters, coated with a delicious batter of spicy chick-pea flour *(besan)*. Although *pakoras* are most commonly made with various vegetables, here is a fresh and pretty California version using salmon and spinach leaves. *Besan* can be found at all Indian markets, and once you have mastered the simple art of making *pakoras,* try it with vegetables, such as small mushrooms, pieces of bell pepper, red onion, or cooked cauliflower. Serve these with a spicy sauce, such as Herbed Yogurt Dip, Tamarind Dip, Mint Relish, or Spicy Tomato Chutney (see Index).

1½ cups chick-pea flour (besan)
1 teaspoon baking powder
1 teaspoon paprika
½ teaspoon ground turmeric
Salt
1¼ cups warm water
2 cloves garlic, crushed through a press
Peanut oil, for deep frying
12 ounces skinless salmon fillet, cut into
2 x 1-inch rectangles
12 large spinach leaves, rinsed and
patted dry

1. Combine the chick-pea flour, baking powder, paprika, turmeric, and 1 teaspoon salt in a large bowl. Gradually add the water, stirring until you have a smooth batter. Stir in the garlic.

2. Pour oil to a depth of 2 inches in a wok and heat it over medium-high heat to 375°F.

3. Rub the salmon lightly with salt and place 4 pieces in the batter, mixing gently with a fork. Using tongs, remove the salmon pieces from the batter and slide them into the hot oil. Fry, turning once, until the salmon is golden and cooked through, about 4 minutes. Reduce the heat if the salmon begins to brown too fast. With a slotted spoon remove the *pakoras* to drain on paper towels. Repeat with the rest of the salmon, bringing the oil back to 375°F before each batch.

4. If there is too much debris in the oil, heat fresh oil to 375°F. Place half of the spinach leaves in the remaining batter and turn to coat. Remove with tongs, gently shaking off the excess batter. Fry until puffed and golden, about 2 minutes, and remove to drain on paper towels. Repeat with the rest of the spinach.

5. To serve, arrange the salmon and spinach on a serving platter and serve with one or two of the suggested dipping sauces.

SERVES 6

CRISPY CRESCENTS

Filled with Herbed Shrimp and Pork

These light, deep-fried dumplings explode in your mouth with a juicy sweet-and-sour herbed Thai filling. After the filling is made—which can be done ahead of time—these crescents can be put together in minutes. Once filled, they can be frozen and then deep fried in a flash, "in the event of the slightest guest," as my Russian grandmother used to put it. The crescents can be served with a number of dipping sauces. Try Soy-Scallion Dipping Sauce, Vietnamese Tangy Lime Dipping Sauce, or Tamarind Dip (see Index).

5 dried shiitake mushrooms

About 1½ tablespoons canola or peanut oil, plus more for deep frying the crescents

¼ cup chopped shallots

1 large clove garlic, crushed through a press

¼ pound lean ground pork

8 medium shrimp, peeled, deveined, and finely chopped

3 tablespoons grated carrot

5 teaspoons Asian fish sauce, such as nam pla

1 tablespoon fresh lime juice

1 teaspoon sugar

1½ tablespoons chopped scallions

1½ tablespoons chopped fresh basil or mint leaves

Salt, to taste

24 to 26 round wonton skins, thawed if frozen

1 large egg white, beaten

1. Soak the mushrooms in lukewarm water to cover for 1 hour. Drain, then pat dry with paper towels. Discard the stems and finely chop the caps.

2. Heat 1½ tablespoons of the oil in a wok over medium-high heat until almost smoking. Swirl the wok to coat with the oil. Add the shallots and garlic and cook, stirring, until translucent, about 2 minutes. Add the pork and cook, breaking up the lumps with a fork, until the pork is thoroughly cooked and all the liquid it released has evaporated.

3. Add a little more oil, if necessary, and add the shrimp, carrot, and mushrooms. Cook, stirring, for 2 minutes. Raise the heat to high and add the fish sauce, lime juice, and sugar. Cook, stirring, until the mixture is dry, about 1 minute. Stir in the scallions, basil, and salt, if needed. Let the mixture cool before proceeding to the next step.

4. Working with 6 at a time, place the wonton skins on your work surface, keeping the other ones covered with a dampened towel. Brush the edges of the skins with egg white. Place a heaping teaspoon of the filling on a skin, slightly off center. Fold the upper edge down over the filling to form a crescent and press together to secure. Repeat to make the rest of the crescents.

5. Pour oil to a depth of 1½ inches into a deep fryer and heat over medium-high heat to 350°F. Fry as many crescents as will comfortably fit until golden and crisp, about 1½ minutes. Transfer with a slotted spoon to dry paper towels. Serve at once with one of the suggested dipping sauces.

MAKES 24 TO 26 CRESCENTS

GRILLED CHICKEN SLICES

with Tamarind Dip

Slices of spiced grilled chicken make attractive and easy party food when presented on a platter around a delicious dip. As the sweet-and-sour tamarind dip here is a takeoff on an Indian tamarind chutney, the chicken is likewise coated with a tandoori-style yogurt marinade.

The dip is wonderful and versatile and makes a great gift, though if you are giving it away, don't add the cilantro, since it discolors.

4 large skinless, boneless chicken breast
    halves (about 2 pounds total)
Salt and freshly ground black pepper, to taste
½ cup low-fat plain yogurt
3 cloves garlic, crushed through a press
1 tablespoon grated fresh ginger
½ teaspoon ground cayenne pepper
1 teaspoon paprika
½ teaspoon ground turmeric
1½ tablespoons fresh lemon juice
Tamarind Dip (recipe follows)

1. Rub the chicken with salt and pepper and place in a shallow bowl. Whisk together the yogurt, garlic, ginger, cayenne, paprika, turmeric, and lemon juice. Pour over the chicken and turn to coat. Cover and refrigerate for at least 2 hours.

2. Prepare coals for grilling or preheat the broiler. Bring the chicken to room temperature.

3. Grill or broil the chicken until golden and cooked through but still juicy, about 4 minutes per side. Cover loosely with foil and let stand until cool enough to handle.

4. To serve, cut the chicken on the diagonal into medium-thick slices. Place the bowl of Tamarind Dip in the middle of a large platter and arrange the chicken slices around it.

SERVES 6 AS AN APPETIZER

Tamarind Dip

1½ tablespoons tamarind pulp, preferably
    from Thailand
½ cup plus ⅓ cup Chicken Stock (page 384)
    or canned broth, boiling hot
1 tablespoon soy sauce
2 tablespoons dry sherry
4 teaspoons honey, or more to taste
1½ tablespoons ketchup
1½ teaspoons cornstarch, diluted in
    2 teaspoons cold water
1 teaspoon minced garlic
¼ teaspoon dried red pepper flakes, or more
    to taste
3 tablespoons chopped fresh cilantro leaves

1. Soak the tamarind pulp in ½ cup boiling stock off the heat for 15 minutes. Stir and mash it with a fork to help it dissolve. Strain through a fine strainer into a bowl, pressing on the solids with the back of a wooden spoon to extract all the liquid.

2. Combine the tamarind liquid, the remaining ⅓ cup stock, soy sauce, sherry, honey, and ketchup in a nonreactive saucepan and bring to a simmer over medium-low heat. Slowly drizzle in the cornstarch mixture and heat, stirring, until the sauce thickens, about 2 minutes. Off the heat, stir in the garlic and pepper flakes. Let the sauce stand for 15 minutes, then strain into a serving bowl and add the cilantro.

MAKES ABOUT 1¼ CUPS

SINGAPORE SLING

*T*he notorious Singapore Sling was created by bartender Ngiam Tong Boom at Raffles Hotel in 1915. Here it is, straight from the Raffles bar.

1 cup gin
½ cup Cherry Heering
¼ cup fresh lime juice
4 cups unsweetened pineapple juice
⅓ cup Grenadine
Dash of Benedictine D.O.M.
Dash of Triple Sec
Few drops of Angostura bitters
3 slices orange, halved, for garnish

Stir all the ingredients together in a large pitcher filled with ice cubes. Strain or pour into tall glasses over ice. Garnish each glass with half of a fresh orange slice.
Makes 6 drinks

THAI CHICKEN WITH TOASTED COCONUT

in Lettuce Parcels

*T*he recipe below is a cosmopolitan version of *larb*, a ground meat dish, flavored with lime juice and fish sauce, that originates in the highlands of northern Thailand. Here, the tart and sweet chicken mince is enlivened by ginger and cilantro, sprinkled with toasted coconut and peanuts, and tucked into a lettuce parcel. The inspiration for this dish comes from a lovely Bangkok restaurant called Lemongrass. Narin, the chef/co-owner and antique dealer, constantly experiments with authentic up-country recipes, modernizing and adjusting them to the taste of his predominantly expatriate (though not tourist) clientele. This dish, he claims, is one of his more successful inventions. The more "authentic" version, he notes, would use minced pigeon meat.

Because this is such a perfect cocktail or buffet party dish, this recipe feeds twelve, but it is easily halved or quartered. The chicken can be made ahead of time, but the cilantro should be added right before serving.

The pile of lettuce and bowls of condiments next to the chicken may produce a bit of confusion, so if you don't feel like doing all the explaining, place a little sample parcel on a plate next to the dish.

2 tablespoons peanut oil, or more as needed
2½ pounds ground chicken
1½ cups chopped red onion
¼ cup grated fresh ginger
4 to 6 small fresh hot red chiles, stemmed, seeded, and chopped
1½ cups torn fresh cilantro leaves
¾ cup fresh lime juice
6 tablespoons Asian fish sauce, such as nam pla
2 tablespoons sugar
3 tablespoons hot water
Salt, to taste
1 cup toasted shredded coconut, fresh or dessicated (dried)
⅔ cup chopped roasted peanuts
2 heads romaine lettuce, separated into leaves, rinsed and patted dry, large leaves halved crosswise

1. Heat the oil in a wok or a large skillet over medium-high heat until almost smoking. In batches, cook the chicken until browned, breaking it up thoroughly with a fork, about 7 minutes. If the chicken throws off too much liquid, tilt the skillet and spoon it out. If the chicken begins to stick to the bottom, add a little more oil. Make sure the chicken is not lumpy and you have a fine mince. Transfer to a bowl and cool. Add the onion, ginger, chiles, and cilantro and toss well.

2. In a small bowl, combine the lime juice, fish sauce, sugar, and water and stir well to dissolve the sugar. Toss the chicken with the dressing. Season with salt, if necessary. Place the chicken on a large platter and sprinkle with some coconut and peanuts. (This should be done right before serving.) Place the rest of the coconut and peanuts in bowls next to the chicken.

3. To eat, place some chicken on a lettuce leaf, sprinkle with coconut and peanuts, and wrap.

SERVES 12 AS AN APPETIZER OR PART OF A BUFFET

S P I C E - C R U S T E D
C H I C K E N   L I V E R
N I B B L E S

The intriguing Chinese-inspired blend of spices in this recipe, with its zing of dried tangerine peel, provides a perfect counterpoint to the rich, buttery flavor of the chicken livers. These can be served as cocktail nibbles, with Tamarind Dip (see Index), or as a light first course on a bed of wild greens, sparingly drizzled with a balsamic vinaigrette.

Be sure the livers are bone dry before you roll them in flour and fry them, otherwise you and the kitchen will get splattered with hot oil. Double or triple the Spice Mixture recipe and keep in an airtight container to use as a deliciously unusual spice rub.

1/4 cup all-purpose flour
Chinese Spice Mixture (recipe follows)
1/4 cup canola or safflower oil
1 pound chicken livers, trimmed, rinsed, and
*   patted thoroughly dry*

1. On a plate, combine the flour with the Spice Mixture.

2. Heat the oil in a large skillet, over medium-high heat. Roll the chicken livers in the flour mixture, then cook, without crowding them in the skillet, until crispy on the outside and still pink inside, about 3 minutes per side. Drain on paper towels and serve at once, either as finger food with Tamarind Dip, or atop a bed of greens.

SERVES 6 TO 8 AS AN APPETIZER, 4 AS A FIRST COURSE

Chinese Spice
Mixture

1 teaspoon fennel seeds
2 teaspoons black peppercorns
3 star anise points
1 1/2 teaspoons coriander seeds
1 piece (1 inch) dried tangerine peel, broken
*   into pieces*
1/4 to 1/2 teaspoon ground cayenne pepper
1/8 teaspoon ground cinnamon
Salt, to taste

In a spice or coffee grinder, combine the fennel seeds, peppercorns, star anise, coriander, and tangerine peel. Grind into a not-too-fine powder. Transfer to a small bowl and add cayenne, cinnamon, and salt to taste.

MAKES ABOUT 2 TABLESPOONS

FIVE-SPICE BEEF BROCHETTES

Lamb or pork cubes would also take well to the whiff of sweet spices in the marinade and the rich soy and black vinegar glaze. Prepare the skewers of beef ahead of time, so all that remains is to pop them on a grill or under a broiler. If you want to make a meal of it, cut the meat into larger cubes and use large skewers.

½ teaspoon five-spice powder

1½ teaspoons freshly ground black pepper

1 teaspoon ground coriander

½ teaspoon dried red pepper flakes, or more to taste

1 pound beef sirloin, cut into ½ inch cubes

2 tablespoons soy sauce

1½ tablespoons Chinese rice wine or dry sherry

2 tablespoons Chinese black vinegar or balsamic vinegar

2 cloves garlic, crushed through a press

1½ cups pearl onions (small white boiling onions)

2 large red bell peppers, stemmed, seeded, and cut into 1½-inch pieces

8 ounces small button mushroom caps

1. Stir the five-spice powder, black pepper, coriander, and pepper flakes in a small bowl to mix well. Rub into the meat, then place the meat in a large bowl. Add the soy sauce, rice wine, vinegar, and garlic and toss to coat well. Marinate the meat in the refrigerator for 2 to 6 hours.

2. Prepare coals for grilling or preheat the broiler. Soak 14 medium-size bamboo skewers in water for 1 hour.

3. Blanch the onions in boiling water for 1½ minutes. Plunge into cold water, drain, and remove the skins. Pat dry with paper towels.

4. Remove the meat from the bowl, reserving any marinade. Thread 3 cubes of meat on each skewer, alternating each cube with pieces of pepper, mushrooms, and onions. Place the skewers on a grilling rack or broiling tray and brush with the marinade. Grill 3 inches away from the heat until medium-rare, about 3 to 4 minutes per side. Serve at once.

MAKES 14 BROCHETTES

MIXED SATAYS
with Spicy Peanut Sauce

From Indonesia to Malaysia to Thailand, bamboo skewers supporting tasty charcoaled morsels of meat with a sweet and spicy peanut sauce are as ubiquitous a street snack as hot dogs at a baseball stadium. Needless to say, there are countless variations of the recipe. I found my favorite at the street stalls of Malaysia, where the peanut sauce is intricately spiced, sour from the tamarind and sweet with palm sugar.

I suggest using both lamb and chicken in this recipe. If you wish, double the amount of one or the other, or try beef sirloin. The traditional presentation features sweet-and-sour cucumber salad, which in Malaysia also includes fresh pineapple. Ideally, satays should be served straight from the grill or broiler, so to make life easier, thread the meat on skewers ahead of time and grill as the guests arrive. The sauce can be prepared up to a day ahead, and the salad several hours ahead.

MARINADE

¼ cup chopped onion

1 tablespoon chopped garlic

1½ tablespoons chopped fresh ginger

2 tablespoons chopped cilantro roots and/or stems

1 teaspoon ground turmeric

½ teaspoon best-quality curry powder

½ teaspoon ground cayenne pepper

¾ cup canned unsweetened coconut milk, well stirred

2 tablespoons soy sauce

2 tablespoons rice vinegar

1½ tablespoons (packed) light brown sugar

Salt, to taste

8 ounces skinless, boneless chicken breast, cut into 12 strips 3 inches long and ¾ inch wide

1 pound boneless lamb or pork (1 inch thick), cut into ¾-inch cubes

Red kale leaves or shredded red cabbage, for garnish

Spicy Peanut Sauce (recipe follows)

Cucumber and Pineapple Salad (recipe follows)

1. Place all the marinade ingredients in a food processor and process to a paste. Divide the marinade between 2 bowls. Add the chicken to one bowl and the meat to another. Toss both with the marinade. Cover with plastic wrap and refrigerate for at least 6 hours or overnight, turning occasionally.

2. Soak 24 bamboo skewers in water for 1 hour. Prepare coals for grilling or preheat the broiler.

3. Thread 1 strip of chicken on each of 12 skewers. Thread 4 pieces of meat on each remaining skewer.

4. Grill or broil the chicken until cooked through and slightly charred, about 3 minutes on each side. Keep warm. Grill the meat, 2 minutes on each side for lamb, or 3 minutes on each side for pork.

5. Line a platter with red kale or shredded red cabbage. Place the bowl of Spicy Peanut Sauce in the middle, and arrange skewers of chicken and meat around it. Serve the Cucumber and Pineapple Salad alongside.

MAKES 24 SATAYS, TO SERVE 6 TO 8

Spicy Peanut Sauce

Y ou can make the sauce up to several days ahead. As it is extraordinarily delicious and freezes well, you might want to make a double batch. The sauce will thicken and mellow on standing, so stir in some more coconut milk or water when you reheat it, and liven up the flavor with some additional vinegar, paprika, and cayenne. If you freeze the sauce, defrost and heat to warm before serving. If tamarind is not easy to find, substitute fresh lemon or lime juice to taste.

1½ tablespoons tamarind pulp, preferably
    from Thailand
⅓ cup boiling water
2 small fresh hot chiles, green or red,
    stemmed, seeded, and chopped
1 tablespoon chopped fresh ginger
4 cloves garlic, chopped
1 tablespoon chopped fresh lemongrass
    (3 inches of the lower stalk, tough outer
    leaves discarded)
1½ tablespoons peanut oil
½ cup chopped onion
1 teaspoon ground turmeric
1 teaspoon ground cumin
1 teaspoon ground coriander
½ teaspoon freshly ground black pepper
1 teaspoon paprika, plus more to taste
⅛ teaspoon ground cayenne pepper, or to taste
1¼ cups canned unsweetened coconut milk,
    well stirred
¾ cup water
⅔ cup finely ground unsalted roasted
    peanuts
¼ cup coarsely ground unsalted roasted
    peanuts
1 tablespoon soy sauce
1½ teaspoons (packed) light brown sugar
Dash of rice vinegar, or to taste

1. Soak the tamarind pulp in the boiling water off the heat for 15 minutes. Stir and mash it with a fork to help it dissolve. Strain through a fine strainer into a bowl, pressing on the solids with the back of a wooden spoon to extract all the liquid. Set the tamarind liquid aside.

2. Using a mortar and pestle or a small food processor, crush the chiles, ginger, garlic, and lemongrass to a paste. If using a food processor, add a little coconut milk to assist the process.

3. Heat the oil in a wok or heavy medium-size saucepan over medium heat and cook the onion until softened, 5 minutes. Add the chile paste, turmeric, cumin, coriander, black pepper, paprika, and cayenne. Reduce the heat to low and cook the mixture, stirring frequently, until it no longer tastes raw, about 5 minutes. Add a little coconut milk, 1 tablespoon at a time, if the mixture begins to stick. Stir in the remaining coconut milk and water and cook over medium heat until slightly reduced. Reduce the heat to low, stir in the fine and coarse peanuts and the reserved tamarind liquid, and cook, stirring, until the sauce thickens, about 5 minutes. Add the soy sauce and sugar and simmer for 1 minute. Adjust the seasoning, adding salt, and more paprika and cayenne, if desired, and stir in the vinegar.

MAKES ABOUT 2 CUPS

Cucumber and Pineapple Salad

This is a lovely, refreshing relish-type salad to be served alongside spicy grills or rich curries.

*1 cup diced, seeded, peeled firm
    cucumber*
1 cup diced fresh pineapple
½ cup diced red onion
2 tablespoons rice vinegar
1 tablespoon sugar
1½ teaspoons hot water
*1 hot red chile, fresh or dried,
    stemmed, seeded, and
    minced*
*2 tablespoons chopped fresh cilantro
    leaves*

Combine the cucumber, pineapple, and onion in a medium-size bowl. In another bowl, whisk together the vinegar, sugar, hot water, and chile until the sugar is dissolved. Toss the cucumber mixture with the dressing and let stand for 30 minutes at room temperature before serving. Stir in the cilantro.

SERVES 8 AS AN ACCOMPANIMENT

CUCUMBER BOATS
with Lemon Beef Salad

Although this dish sounds like the ultimate '80s American cocktail fare, the idea of presenting food in carved, hollowed-out vegetables is quintessentially Thai. Whenever I have leftover grilled beef or roast lamb, the next day I mix it into a refreshingly tart and spicy Thai salad and stuff it into crisp, cooling cucumber shells. Make sure to select firm, fresh cucumbers for a nice crunch.

*1 cup thinly sliced grilled rare beef or
    roast lamb*
4 lemon slices, chopped with skin on
¼ cup very thinly sliced red onion
¼ cup julienned red bell pepper
*3 tablespoons slivered fresh basil or
    mint leaves*
3 tablespoons torn fresh cilantro leaves
2 tablespoons fresh lemon juice
1 tablespoon rice vinegar
*2 tablespoons Asian fish sauce, such as
    nam pla*
1 tablespoon sugar
*2 small fresh hot chiles, green or red,
    stemmed, seeded, and minced*
*6 medium firm Kirby cucumbers,
    peeled*
Fresh mint sprigs, for garnish

1. Cut the beef or lamb slices into bite-size pieces. In a large bowl, toss the meat with the lemon, onion, bell pepper, basil, and cilantro.

2. In a bowl, whisk together the lemon juice, vinegar, fish sauce, sugar, and chiles and stir to dissolve the sugar. Toss the beef with the dressing and let stand for 15 minutes.

3. Cut the cucumbers in half lengthwise and then crosswise. Scoop out the pulp, leaving a ¼-inch thick shell. Slice off enough to flatten the bottom of each cucumber boat so that it will stand still on a serving platter. Place the cucumber boats on a serving platter and fill with the beef salad. Serve garnished with mint sprigs.

SERVES 6 TO 8

LAMB TOASTS

with a Tropical Sambal and Avocado Cilantro Cream

I enjoyed this appetizer at a cocktail party in New Zealand, and think it a great way to use leftover leg of lamb. You can also use smoked venison, very thinly sliced cold pork loin, or roast beef.

TROPICAL SAMBAL
½ cup finely diced papaya
2 firm, ripe kiwis, peeled and diced
¼ cup finely chopped red onion
1½ tablespoons chopped fresh cilantro
*   leaves*
1 serrano chile, stemmed, seeded, and
*   chopped*
2 tablespoons fresh lime juice
¼ teaspoon Tabasco, or more to taste
Salt, to taste

AVOCADO CILANTRO CREAM
½ cup crème fraîche, or sour cream
3 tablespoons heavy (or whipping) cream
1 small ripe avocado, peeled, pitted, and
*   chopped*
3 tablespoons chopped fresh cilantro leaves
1 clove garlic, crushed through a press
3 tablespoons fresh lime juice
Salt and freshly ground black pepper,
*   to taste*

¼ cup light olive oil (do not use virgin or
*   extra-virgin), or more as needed*
24 slices French bread
6 to 8 ounces thinly sliced cooked leg
*   of lamb*

1. Make the *sambal*: Combine all the ingredients in a large bowl and let marinate at room temperature for 30 minutes to 2 hours.

2. Make the avocado cream: Combine all the ingredients in a food processor and process until smooth. Transfer to a pastry bag fitted with a decorative tip.

3. Heat the oil in a large skillet over medium heat and fry the bread in batches until light golden on both sides. Add more oil if necessary. Drain on paper towels.

4. Pipe the avocado cream decoratively in a circle on each piece of toast. Place a slice of lamb on each toast and spoon some *sambal* on top.

MAKES 24 APPETIZERS

HORSES GALLOPING ON STAR FRUIT

The name of this Thai dish is *ma hor*, which literally means "galloping horses." Traditionally, the horsemen (minced sweet and spicy ground pork) usually gallop on slightly underripe pineapple slices, showing off the Thai skill of mixing and matching textures and flavors. I, however, see this savory snack as a golden opportunity to do something creative with star fruit, which is showing up in local supermarkets more frequently nowadays. If, however, star fruit disappear from sight just when you need them most, you can happily revert to pineapple wedges.

4 teaspoons peanut or vegetable oil
4 shallots, finely chopped
2 teaspoons minced garlic
1 teaspoon minced cilantro roots and/or stems
½ pound ground pork
1½ tablespoons palm sugar or (packed) light brown sugar
1½ tablespoons Asian fish sauce, such as nam pla
2 tablespoons water
1 tablespoon soy sauce
¼ cup roasted unsalted peanuts, coarsely crushed
Salt and freshly ground black pepper, to taste
4 to 5 star fruit, cut into ¼-inch-thick slices (you can substitute slightly underripe pineapple wedges)
Thinly sliced fresh hot red chiles, for garnish
Fresh cilantro and mint leaves, for garnish

1. Heat the oil in a medium-size skillet over medium heat. Add the shallots, garlic, and cilantro and cook, stirring, for 1 minute. Add the pork, sugar, fish sauce, water, soy sauce, and peanuts and cook, stirring, until the pork is cooked through and the liquid it throws off has evaporated, 6 to 7 minutes. Remove from the skillet and cool to room temperature. Season with salt and pepper.

2. Place a heaping teaspoon of the pork mixture on each slice of star fruit, patting it into a compact shape with your fingers. Garnish with chiles, cilantro, and mint.

SERVES 6 TO 8

GRIDDLE BREADS
with Curried Lamb

Murtabak are filled griddle breads devised by the Indians who migrated to Malaysia. And, as is often the case with Southeast Asian migrant food, they are found only in Malaysia and not in India. Malaysians usually enjoy them at street stalls as a before-work breakfast, accompanied by a glass of strong, cardamom-scented tea with condensed milk. As a more filling option, they are eaten dipped in a rich coconut curry. In a Western context I like to serve *murtabak* cut into bites and accompanied with a yogurt dip. Like all filled breads,

SINGING FOR SUPPER

In Malaysia, young unmarried women were strictly forbidden to sing in the kitchen while cooking. If they did, they would end up marrying old men.

these take a bit of work, but 12 large ones, cut into quarters, will feed a crowd. The breads can easily be made a day ahead and crisped in a 400°F oven before serving.

2 tablespoons vegetable oil
1½ cups finely chopped onion
1½ pounds ground lamb
⅓ cup dark raisins
1 tablespoon chopped garlic
2 teaspoons grated fresh ginger
1 teaspoon minced seeded fresh hot green
    chile
1½ teaspoons best-quality curry powder
½ teaspoon pure chile powder, or more to
    taste
1 teaspoon ground coriander
1 teaspoon ground cumin
4 large eggs, lightly beaten
Salt and freshly ground black pepper, to taste
1 tablespoon fresh lemon juice
Pinch of sugar, or more to taste
¼ cup chopped fresh cilantro leaves
¼ cup chopped fresh mint leaves
Griddle Bread Dough (recipe follows)
3 tablespoons vegetable oil, or more as
    needed, for frying the breads
Herbed Yogurt Dip (page 12)

1. Heat the oil in a large skillet over medium-low heat. Add the onion and cook until softened, about 7 minutes. Raise the heat to medium-high, add the lamb and raisins, and cook, breaking the lamb up with a fork until it is no longer pink, about 5 minutes. If the lamb throws off too much liquid, tilt the skillet and spoon it out. Add the garlic, ginger, green chile, curry powder, chile powder, coriander, and cumin and cook, stirring, for 3 minutes.

2. Add the eggs and cook, stirring well, until the eggs are cooked through, about 3 minutes. Season to taste with salt and pepper. Add the lemon juice, sugar, cilantro, and mint. Transfer to a bowl and let cool. (The filling can be prepared up to a day ahead.)

3. Spread about 3 tablespoons of the filling in the middle of a square of griddle bread dough, leaving a 2-inch border. Fold the top and bottom edges over the filling to meet in the center, then fold in the sides. Flatten each packet with your hands, pushing the filling into the corners, until you have a thin 5-inch square. Repeat the procedure with the remaining balls of dough and filling.

4. Preheat a large griddle or cast-iron skillet over medium-high heat and brush with some oil. Add a *murtabak* and fry until crisp and golden, about 1½ minutes on each side, keeping the uncooked breads covered with plastic wrap. Repeat with the rest of the breads, transferring the cooked ones to a large platter.

5. Cut each bread into 4 squares and serve hot or warm, with Herbed Yogurt Dip.

**MAKES 12 BREADS
TO SERVE 8 TO 10**

Griddle Bread Dough

2¼ cups all-purpose flour, plus about
   ¼ cup, as needed
½ cup whole-wheat flour
¾ teaspoon salt
2 large eggs
¾ cup low-fat plain yogurt
2 tablespoons butter, melted
Vegetable oil

1. Sift the flours and salt into a large bowl. Make a well in the center and pour in the eggs, yogurt, and melted butter. Mix in the flour with your hands until you get a rather soft dough. Transfer the dough to a floured board and knead, adding more flour as necessary, until the dough is smooth and elastic, and no longer sticky, about 10 minutes. Shape the dough into a ball, coat with oil, cover with plastic wrap and let stand to "relax" for 1 hour. (The dough can be made a day ahead, covered with plastic wrap, and refrigerated.)

2. Divide the dough into 12 parts and shape each one into a ball. Brush each ball generously with oil and let stand, covered, for 15 minutes.

3. On a floured surface, with a floured rolling pin, roll out one ball as thin as you can manage, to form a square. With your hands, stretch the dough carefully in all directions, especially around the edges, until it is paper thin. You should have about an 8-inch square. Fill as directed in the recipe above.

MAKES 12 BREADS

GURNEY DRIVE:
FAST-FOOD PARADISE

For lovers of street food, Gurney Drive in Georgetown on the island of Penang in northern Malaysia, is the Holy Grail. At seven in the evening, as the tropical heat subsided, we hired a trishaw (a man-powered bicycle-*cum*-taxicab) to make the two-mile pilgrimage from the center of the island to this fabled gastronomic suburb by the sea. We were pedaled with immense dignity by an old man with wire-thin legs.

"I won't wait for you. You'll make too much snail-pace after too much dinner," he joked with us.

As we plodded along Julan Sultan, which the locals call Millionaire's Row because of the lavishly scaled palaces and mansions that line it, he waved his hand at the Christmas tree glory of the Hotel Metropol, emblazoned with neon signs advertising "laser-lit karioke" and trussed up in dazzling fairy lights. Dusk had fallen, Penang had come to life and a colorful evening was just beginning.

Gurney Drive is a seaside culinary nirvana: a huge esplanade of kiosks and booths, tables and chairs, and a tropical art-deco-style main building holding the largest of kitchens and undercover seating. Even from a distance, the excitement begins to build, but still nothing can prepare you for the real thing. The heady aromas tease at a hundred yards. By fifty, you break into a run. Once inside the food compound, you are immersed in a riot of action and bombarded from all sides by tastes and smells. You slowly emerge from a blissed-out

stupefaction with the realization that what makes everything here possible is sheer freshness and exquisite expertise.

There are hawker stalls for every ingredient, every preparation, and every shade and nuance of the region's cuisines.

Each of these tiny, hyperactive booths is owned and run by people who are quite simply the best at what they do. The booths are passed down from generation to generation. Family secrets and mystery ingredients are jealously guarded. If a stall with a reputation should come up for sale, the utensils, the secrets, and sometimes even the cook will go with it. And the business can command an enormous price. Gurney Drive is the stock exchange of Southeast Asian food. It is fast, competitive, and filled with virtuoso technicians.

SO MANY CHOICES

The art of self-indulgence on the Drive isn't hard to master. You sit down at one of the tables, order a cooling tropical juice—maybe one made with tangy lime or soothing sugarcane or refreshing star fruit. Leaving your drink in charge of the table, you make your first tour of inspection, browsing and grazing from the cornucopia of pick-and-choose foods. Each time something tempting takes your fancy, you order a portion and yell out your table number. The stall owners are alert and eagle-eyed. Back at your table, almost before your bottom hits the seat, steaming portions of your various orders appear.

Among our favorite stalls were the *laksa* makers, who serve a delicious two-noodle seafood soup with elaborate garnishes. Elsewhere in Malaysia, *laksa* is prepared with a creamy base of coconut milk, but in Penang the fish and the delicate homemade rich noodles float in a miraculously scented tamarind broth. The complex, intricate seasonings are an institution in themselves, each version guarded zealously by its maker. *Laksa* comes garnished with an incredible array of different tastes, including a basketful of herbs, pineapple, cucumbers, and a whole palette of sauces.

Another famous local delicacy is *lobak*, a pork sausage that's scented with cinnamon and other spices, wrapped in bean curd, fried to a crisp, and served with sweet and tangy sauces. Along with *lobak*, other deep-fried offerings include crunchy spring rolls; fritters of all shapes and substances; fish cakes; and Indian *rojak*, assorted vegetable and tofu bites.

Most of the seafood served is caught in the deep waters off the island and the selection is enormous. You choose from one of the hundred catches of the day—almost market style—and then your choice is

cooked to order. Sample giant crab, tiny delicate cockles, prawns so large they look like baby lobsters, razor clams, and a showroom of seasonal fish. Anyone who knows their food in Penang will tell you that the best way to have it cooked is Chinese-style: steamed, fried, or baked with black bean, sweet and sour, pepper, or chile sauce.

SEDUCED BY THE FOOD

While seafood is largely the domain of the Hokkiens (the largest ethnic Chinese group in Penang), the Malay vendors seduce eaters with fragrant coconut rice which comes with an assortment of rich, spicy curries,

impeccably crisp, coconut-marinated chicken, and one of our chief favorites, *otak, otak,* seafood loaves spiced with ginger, curry, and lemongrass, and grilled in banana leaves.

Satays—skewers of charcoaled meat cubes served with hot peanut dipping sauce—are everywhere, filling the air with their smoky, slightly sweet aroma. For those who like to approach their foods hands-on, there's *satay celup,* do-it-yourself *satay* making. Eaters choose from dozens of varieties of meats, seafood, and vegetables colorfully laid out, along with bowls of dipping sauces. You thread your pick onto skewers, dip them in a pot of bubbling water, and wait while they cook, holding your own in the friendly competition of elbows.

And, of course, there are the noodle stalls—rice noodles, wheat noodles, egg noodles of all sizes and shapes,

and plump dumplings. These are stir-fried in a flash or served in soup with every conceivable garnish—lacquered roast duck, shrimp balls, crayfish, streaky pork, or bean curd cakes are only a few of the offerings.

After all this, those with enough staying power for dessert congregate around the *pisang goreng* (fried banana) stall or one of the old ladies who make delicious peanut pancakes.

Eating along Gurney Drive is like browsing in a pop-up encyclopedia of the best tastes in Southeast Asia. After a long evening of perfect over-indulgence we looked for the beefiest trishaw driver on the block. All we can say is that our first bicycle-chauffeur was very wise. There was no way on earth he could have pedaled us back to our hotel. Not even at a snail's pace.

**White-Cooked Chicken with
Black Bean Sambal**

....

**David Turner's Crispy
Hoisin Quail**

....

Prosciutto and Fig Handrolls

....

**Duck Spring Rolls with
Roasted Red Pepper Sauce**

....

**Shrimp and Shiitake Ravioli with
Lemongrass-Lime Oil**

....

Poisson Cru Tahitienne

....

Tetsuya's Tuna Tartare

....

Aromatic Mussel Salad

....

**Fried Oysters with
Wasabi Mayonnaise**

....

**Seafood on a Bed of Greens with
Coconut Mayonnaise**

....

**Gingered Salmon Parcels
in Saffron Broth**

....

**Barbecued Tandoori Shrimp over
Spring Greens**

....

**Pepper-Crusted Tataki of Tuna with
Hoisin Vinaigrette**

PACIFIC RIM STARTERS

During our travels in the Pacific, John and I tasted some of the freshest, most imaginative, and most refined food in the world in the elegant restaurants of Australia, Southeast Asia, and New Zealand. The main courses were impressive, the desserts scrumptious, but the beautifully presented first courses are what I remember most. Rather than going for a main course, I would often make up my own meal by ordering a selection of light, elegant appetizers: a tangy salad of herbed Pacific mussels; spicy fried quail on a bed of stir-fried noodles; the freshest yellowfin tuna imaginable, chopped up into a simple tartare, spiked with wasabi and garnished with salmon roe; ethereal shrimp-filled wontons with lemongrass sauce; or an over-size duck spring roll in a pool of vibrant roasted red pepper sauce.

There are times when a tray of finger food or a bowl of soup is not enough. The first course sets the tone for a meal and adds a touch of luxury to your table. As you will find, most of the recipes in this chapter feature seafood. I am traditional in that I like to serve fish as a first course (although not always with white wine). It has the lightness and stylishness we require from a first-rate starter.

Here, you will sample Pacific seafood at its best: fish marinated in an island mixture of lime and coconut; oysters, deep-fried in a flash so they are still briny inside; salmon squares wrapped in bright bok choy leaves and served in a ginger-infused broth; juicy cold seafood accompanied by exotic coconut mayonnaise; spicy seared tuna, drizzled with hoisin vinaigrette. And if your choice is not seafood, you will love the white-cooked chicken with its spiky black bean sauce, or the crisp chili-flavored quail.

With these recipes you will be serving up some of the best food in the Pacific. So make the occasion truly memorable by presenting these first courses on beautiful large plates, on a bed of stylish wild greens, imaginatively garnished and accompanied by a good wine.

WHITE-COOKED CHICKEN

with Black Bean Sambal

The Chinese technique of "white cooking"—immersing poultry in boiling liquid for a short time, then taking it off the heat and letting it sit for a while to finish cooking and absorb the liquid—produces incredibly tender, succulent meat that cannot be achieved with simple poaching. In this recipe the moist, delicate slices of chicken are presented on a bed of peppery watercress and doused with a spicy black bean sauce. You can serve the chicken on individual plates for an appetizer or on a platter as a light luncheon entrée.

6 to 8 cups Chicken Stock (page 384) or
    canned chicken broth (enough to cover
    the chicken completely)
4 slices (½ inch each) fresh ginger, smashed
2 scallions, smashed
Salt
2 whole bone-in chicken breasts (about
    2¼ pounds total), trimmed of all
    fat, rinsed well, and patted dry, at
    room temperature
2 teaspoons peanut oil
1 teaspoon minced garlic
2 teaspoons minced fresh ginger
2 tablespoons fermented black beans,
    chopped
1 tablespoon dry sherry
1 teaspoon dark soy sauce
¼ teaspoon dried red pepper flakes
1 tablespoon rice vinegar
1 teaspoon sugar
2 tablespoons chopped scallions
½ red bell pepper, stemmed, seeded,
    and julienned
1 firm, ripe tomato, seeded and cut into strips
2 small bunches watercress, rinsed and
    patted dry

1. Place the chicken stock and the smashed ginger and scallions in a medium-size saucepan and bring to a boil over medium heat. Season with salt, if necessary. Add the chicken breasts, skin side down, so that they are completely submerged. When the stock returns to a boil, reduce the heat to low, skim off the froth, cover tightly, and cook for exactly 5 minutes. Remove the saucepan from the heat without opening and let stand for 1½ hours. Do not lift the lid at any point.

2. Remove the chicken from the stock and set aside. Strain the stock, then measure and reserve ⅓ cup, saving the rest for another use.

3. When the chicken is cool enough to handle, remove and discard the skin and care-fully remove the meat from the bones without tearing it. Remove the fillet from the underside of each bone. Remove the membrane and tendons from the fillet. Cut the breasts and fillets crosswise into ¾-inch-thick slices. Cover with plastic wrap and set aside.

4. Heat the peanut oil in a medium-size nonreactive saucepan over medium heat and cook the garlic, minced ginger, and black beans, stirring, for 1 minute. Add the sherry and cook for 1 minute more. Add the reserved ⅓ cup stock, the soy sauce, and pepper flakes and simmer over low heat for 5 minutes. Remove from the heat and stir in the vinegar and sugar. Cool to room temperature. Stir in the chopped scallions.

5. To serve, arrange the chicken slices, bell pepper, and tomatoes on a bed of watercress. Drizzle the sauce over the chicken or pass it separately in a bowl.

SERVES 4 TO 6

DAVID TURNER'S CRISPY HOISIN QUAIL

I first met David just a few days after he came to Australia from Hawaii to head the kitchens of a newly opened luxury hotel in Melbourne. I was delighted. Here was a fellow American practicing the art of fusion cuisine who shared my enthusiasm for Oriental flavors and my fascination with the Australian brave new world of food. We spent many hours in David's amazing, high-tech kitchen, exchanging cooking tips, stories, and recipes. After I left Australia,

AUSTRALIAN FUSIONS

*D*uring the last decade or so, Australia has actually given up much of its English heritage and reinvented itself as what it really is—a Pacific country with a European culture. Australia is, in fact, the most convincing point of connection between East and West. Here the concept of Pacific Rim cuisine has reached a culinary high.

The Asian influences are everywhere; you don't just find them in city-center "Chinatowns." Australians travel to Indonesia, Singapore, and Thailand as routinely as Americans visit Mexico and the Caribbean. Floods of Asian immigrants arrive every year as well, bringing with them the newest culinary trends from the cities and hundreds of local shades and colorings from the country; it is remarkable how quickly some of these ideas get tried out in the latest Thai or Indonesian restaurants. Australian chefs do regular stints in the international hotel kitchens of Bangkok, Singapore, and Hong Kong, carefully absorbing the subtleties of the preparations there. The best of the Asian chefs, likewise, bring many Western styles and touches to their most creative menus.

And the restaurant menus really are creative. At an elegant soirée, you might find hot-and-sour soup with Thai prawn cakes next to a spicy chowder; a handsome vegetable terrine wrapped in nori (seaweed); a Malaysian laksa (noodle and seafood dish) next to fettuccine; duck breast with grilled lychees and Japanese peppercorns; an oyster gratin with miso-flavored béchamel; or Thai curried vegetables in puff pastry.

Ginger, chile, coconut milk, lemongrass, and tamarind are common everywhere. Skillfully used, they enhance a dish beautifully, lending an extra depth and dimension to the natural flavors. The best chefs can make them seem like a delicious hint, a mysterious ingredient that hovers in the background of your palate.

Home cooks are just as inventive. At dinner parties in Melbourne, I never knew whether the entrée would be pasta all'Abbruzzi or a Southeast Asian curry; whether the dessert would be a bread-and-butter pudding or a special custard, flavored with coconut milk and plam sugar and served with passion fruit purée.

What most attracted me to the Australian food scene was not "Australian cuisine" per se, but a really appealing attitude toward food and cooking. There is a wonderful ease, grace, and humor in the way boundaries between Eastern and Western approaches to food are crossed and blurred. In fact, it was my Australian experience that inspired me to look much more deeply at the fascinating culinary exchange between cultures.

David became quite a celebrity Down Under, and is regularly profiled on TV and in magazines.

This dish was on David's opening menu, and he suggests serving the crispy, spicy quail on a bed of bright stir-fried greens, such as bok choy or puffy deep-fried rice vermicelli. Halve the recipe, if you are cooking for two.

3 tablespoons hoisin sauce

3 tablespoons oyster sauce

2 tablespoons sambal oelek (page 388) or Chinese chile paste with garlic

1 tablespoon grated fresh ginger

1 tablespoon crushed garlic

8 quail, boned, but with leg bone left intact, and butterflied (ask your butcher to do this for you)

Peanut oil, for deep frying

½ cup all-purpose flour

½ cup rice flour

1 tablespoon ground cayenne pepper

Salt, to taste

1. In a large mixing bowl, combine the hoisin sauce, oyster sauce, chile paste, ginger, and garlic. Add the quail and toss to coat with the mixture. Cover and marinate in the refrigerator for at least 4 hours or overnight.

2. Pour oil to a depth of 2 inches into a deep fryer or wok and heat to 350°F.

3. On a plate, combine the flours, cayenne, and salt. Remove the quail from the marinade and roll them in the flour mixture, shaking off the excess. Deep-fry the quail, in batches, until deep golden and crispy, 8 to 10 minutes, turning once. Make sure the oil temperature returns to 350°F before adding a new batch. Keep the fried quail warm in a low oven.

SERVES 4

PROSCIUTTO AND FIG HANDROLLS

San Francisco's Oritalia was the first restaurant in the Bay Area to combine Italian and Asian flavors. The combination is a hard one to pull off, but thanks to the talent, intelligence, and restraint of young chef Bruce Hill, it was a great success. This is a whimsical dish that you may find yourself serving again and again. Double or triple the amount for a crowd.

1½ teaspoons balsamic vinegar

1½ teaspoons olive oil

Salt and freshly ground black pepper, to taste

6 large slices (9 x 3 inches each) prosciutto

6 arugula leaves, rinsed and patted dry

2 ounces (about ½ package) daikon sprouts or bean sprouts, rinsed and patted dry

3 to 4 fresh figs, preferably Black Mission, cut into thin strips (18 strips total)

1 medium grilled portobello mushroom, sliced into 6 strips (see Note)

1. In a small bowl, whisk together the balsamic vinegar and olive oil. Season with salt and pepper.

2. Lay 1 slice of prosciutto flat on your work surface with a long edge facing you. Place an arugula leaf and some daikon sprouts on the lefthand side of the prosciutto. They should stick out over the top edge of the prosciutto by about 1 inch. Lay 3 fig strips and a mushroom slice on the sprouts. Sprinkle with some of the balsamic vinaigrette and roll up the prosciutto into a cone. Repeat with the remaining ingredients.

3. Arrange the handrolls on a serving platter and serve at once.

SERVES 6

Note: To grill or broil portobello mushrooms, cut off and discard the stem, brush the cap all over with olive oil, and place on a grill over prepared coals or under a preheated broiler. Grill or broil the cap for 5 minutes on each side.

DUCK SPRING ROLLS

with Roasted Red Pepper Sauce

This is a very luxurious, special-occasion spring roll with a tangy Thai-California filling, presented in a bright pool of gingered roasted red pepper sauce. The most convenient way to make it is with purchased Chinese roast duck. Just use what you need for the rolls and eat the rest. If you can't find duck, use shredded roast chicken or turkey, preferably dark meat.

The rolls can be prepared through step 4 the day before you serve them. Place them in one layer on a platter, cover with plastic wrap, and refrigerate.

If you wish to serve the rolls as finger food, accompany them with Vietnamese Tangy Lime Dipping Sauce, Hoisin Dipping Sauce, or Tamarind Dip (see Index).

1½ tablespoons minced fresh ginger
1 tablespoon minced garlic
2 small fresh hot chiles, green or red, stemmed, seeded, and minced
2½ tablespoons peanut oil, plus additional for deep frying the spring rolls
1 cup julienned fennel bulb
¾ cup shredded carrots
1 red bell pepper, stemmed, seeded, and julienned
1¾ cups shredded napa cabbage
2½ cups shredded skinless roast duck, preferably precooked from a Chinese butcher
1½ tablespoons fresh lime juice
1 tablespoon fresh orange juice
1½ tablespoons Asian fish sauce, such as nam pla
1½ teaspoons (packed) light brown sugar
Salt, to taste
3 tablespoons chopped fresh cilantro leaves
3 tablespoons slivered fresh basil leaves
9 spring roll wrappers (8 inches)
1 large egg white, beaten
Roasted Red Pepper Sauce (recipe follows)
Fresh cilantro sprigs, for garnish

1. Using a mortar and pestle or small food processor, pound or process the ginger, garlic, and chiles to a paste.

2. Heat the 2½ tablespoons oil in a wok over high heat until hot but not smoking. Swirl the wok to coat with the oil. Add the ginger paste and stir for 30 seconds. Add the fennel and carrots and stir for 2 minutes. Add the bell pepper and cabbage and stir for 3 more minutes. Reduce the heat to medium-low and cook the vegetables for 2 more minutes.

3. Stir in the duck meat, lime juice, orange juice, fish sauce, sugar, and salt and cook over high heat, stirring for 2 minutes, until the liquid is absorbed. Transfer the mixture to a bowl and stir in the cilantro and basil. Cool.

4. Place a spring roll wrapper on your

When John and I toured Western Hill on Penang Island, in Northeast Malaysia, the seasonal fruits were being gathered by boys dressed in white togalike shifts who arrived on site on Honda 125's. Some of them still carried fruit baskets made of rattan and bamboo.

We passed groves of bananas, some finger-small and lusciously sweet, others as big as your forearm that went by the name of "kings." Nearby were tapioca shrubs, with their symmetrical, closely bunched leaves. In the valley was a row of betel nut palms and a few jackfruit trees, whose bulbous fruits were fancifully covered with newspaper, plastic, or coconut leaves to protect them from insects. Farther along we passed a nutmeg plantation, the trees interspersed with wild rubber trees, then groves of papayas, fiery red rambutans (which taste like lychees), mangosteens, custard apples, Malaysian kiwis (sweeter than the more familiar New Zealand varieties), cloves, pomegranates, pomelos, and special, nutlike fruits called dragon's eyes.

As we watched the boys from the top of Western Hill, we realized there are few places in the world where you can find the sheer variety of fruits and spices that grows on these slopes of inland Penang.

work surface with a corner nearest you. Place about 3 tablespoons of the filling in a compact log diagonally across the bottom third of the wrapper. Fold the bottom corner over the filling and tuck it under the filling. Roll once to enfold the filling, then fold in the sides of the wrapper and continue rolling, gently but tightly, almost up to the end. Brush the top corner with egg white, bring up, and press to seal. Roll up the rest of the rolls in the same fashion.

5. Pour oil to a depth of 1½ inches into a wok or large skillet and heat over medium-high heat to 360°F. Fry the rolls in two batches, turning them several times, until crispy and deep golden, about 4 minutes. Transfer to dry on paper towels.

6. To serve, cut the rolls in half on the diagonal. Place 3 halves on each plate, spoon the sauce around the rolls, garnish with sprigs of cilantro, and serve.

MAKES 9 ROLLS

Roasted Red Pepper Sauce

2 large red bell peppers, left whole but
    stemmed, seeded, and deribbed
1½ tablespoons unsalted butter
¼ cup chopped onion
1½ teaspoons grated fresh ginger
2 tablespoons sliced scallions
1 large clove garlic, sliced
¾ cup Chicken Stock (page 384) or
    canned broth
1 teaspoon grated orange zest
1 tablespoon fresh orange juice
1 teaspoon rice vinegar
1½ tablespoons heavy (or whipping)
    cream
Pinch of sugar
Salt and freshly ground black pepper,
    to taste

1. Preheat the broiler.

2. Broil the peppers until charred and soft, about 12 minutes. Turn at least twice to ensure that they are charred all over. Place in a plastic bag and wrap in a towel. Let stand for 10 minutes. Peel the peppers and cut into strips.

3. Melt the butter in a small saucepan over medium heat. Add the onion and cook for 5 minutes. Add the ginger, scallions, and garlic and cook for 3 minutes. Stir in the stock, orange zest, juice, vinegar, cream, sugar, salt, and pepper.

4. Process the peppers with the stock mixture in a blender or food processor until puréed. Scrape into a bowl and let stand until cooled.

MAKES ABOUT 1½ CUPS

SHRIMP AND SHIITAKE RAVIOLI

with Lemongrass-Lime Oil

Whenever I want to impress guests with a super-elegant dish, I turn to these ethereal ravioli, paper-thin wonton skins filled with a shrimp–shiitake mushroom mixture and drizzled with the fragrant infused oil. This dish, inspired by an outstanding Swiss-born, Sydney-based chef, Dietmar Sawyere, combines the French refinement of presentation with the subtlety and mystique of the East. The original sauce was a classically rich beurre blanc. I opt for a lighter version.

LEMONGRASS-LIME OIL
1 tablespoon plus ½ cup good light olive oil
(do not use virgin or extra-virgin)
1 tablespoon finely chopped shallots
1 tablespoon finely minced fresh lemongrass
(3 inches of the lower stalk, tough outer leaves discarded)
1 tablespoon minced fresh ginger
2½ tablespoons fresh lime juice
1½ teaspoons cracked white peppercorns
1 tablespoon finely minced fresh basil leaves

RAVIOLI
5 dried shiitake mushrooms
¾ cup finely chopped raw shrimp
1½ tablespoons finely diced carrot
2 tablespoons finely diced celery
2 tablespoons finely chopped canned bamboo shoots
2 teaspoons minced ginger
2 tablespoons finely chopped fresh cilantro leaves
1 tablespoon soy sauce
½ teaspoon Oriental sesame oil
2 large egg whites, beaten separately
Salt and freshly ground white pepper, to taste
40 round or square wonton skins
2 teaspoons olive oil
4 large spot prawns or shrimp, peeled and deveined but preferably with heads still on
Snipped fresh chervil or chives, for garnish

1. Make the lemongrass-lime oil: Heat the 1 tablespoon olive oil in a small nonreac-

tive saucepan over medium heat. Add the shallots, lemongrass, and ginger and stir for 1 minute. Add the lime juice and cook to reduce by half, about 2 minutes. Add the ½ cup olive oil and heat for 1 minute. Add the peppercorns and basil and cook for 1 minute more. Remove from the heat and let stand for 2 hours to infuse. Reheat slowly before using.

2. Make the ravioli: Soak the shiitake mushrooms in cold water for 1 hour. Drain, rinse well, and pat dry. Remove and discard the stems and chop the caps fine.

3. In a bowl, mix together the shiitakes, shrimp, carrot, celery, bamboo shoots, ginger, cilantro, soy sauce, sesame oil, and one egg white and season with salt and pepper.

4. Working with 4 at a time, place the wonton skins on your work surface. Brush the edges of the skins with some of the remaining beaten egg white, then place a scant tablespoon of the filling in the middle. Cover with another skin and press with your fingers around the filling to release the air, then around the edges, firmly, to seal. Repeat with the rest of the skins and filling, keeping the finished ravioli covered with a dampened towel. (The ravioli can be made ahead of time and frozen.)

5. Heat the 2 teaspoons olive oil in a large skillet over medium heat, and sauté the whole shrimps until just pink, 3 to 4 minutes, turning once. Reserve for garnish.

6. Bring a large pot of salted water to a gentle boil. Gently lower the ravioli into the water. Cook until they float to the surface, about 45 seconds after the water returns to the boil. With a wire-mesh skimmer, remove the ravioli from the water, gently shaking off the excess.

7. Divide the ravioli among four bowls. Drizzle lemongrass-lime oil over them and garnish each portion with the reserved shrimp and chives.

SERVES 4

P O I S S O N C R U T A H I T I E N N E

A classic Pacific Island preparation: raw fish marinated in a tropical blend of coconut milk and lime juice, which actually cooks it lightly. For the fish you have a choice of salmon, tuna, red snapper, or even small sea scallops—as long as it's impeccably fresh.

12 ounces very fresh fish, cut into ½-inch pieces
⅓ cup fresh lime juice
¾ cup unsweetened coconut milk, well stirred
1 small red bell pepper, stemmed, seeded, and diced
3 tablespoons diced green bell pepper
½ cup chopped red onion
1 fresh hot red chile, stemmed, partially seeded, and minced
1 large firm, ripe tomato, peeled, seeded, and diced
Salt, to taste
1½ tablespoons fresh cilantro leaves

1. In a bowl, toss the fish with the lime juice. Cover and marinate in the refrigerator for at least 1 hour and up to 3 hours, tossing occasionally. Drain.

2. Stir in the coconut milk, red and green peppers, onion, chile, and tomato and toss well. Refrigerate for 1 hour. Season with salt and serve, garnished with cilantro leaves.

SERVES 6

TETSUYA'S TUNA TARTARE

Every dish that comes out of the kitchen of the Sydney chef Tetsuya Wakuda possesses incredible elegance and refinement. Born and trained in Japan, Tetsuya also worked in the best French kitchens of Sydney, becoming a true magician at melding seemingly disparate ingredients and techniques into harmonious wholes. This tartare is a good example of juggling Mediterranean ingredients such as capers, anchovies, and fruity olive oil with such Asian flavors as soy and wasabi. The results are glorious. In keeping with his Japanese origins, Tetsuya has a particularly deft hand when it comes to raw fish. When shopping for the ingredients, keep in mind that you need the freshest, sashimi-quality fish.

12 ounces top-quality, very fresh yellowfin
    or bluefin tuna, finely diced
1½ tablespoons chopped capers
1½ tablespoons finely chopped cornichons
1 tablespoon chopped fresh chives
Pinch of ground cayenne pepper
5 good-quality canned anchovy fillets,
    drained and chopped
2 tablespoons minced shallots
2½ tablespoons extra-virgin olive oil
3 teaspoons light soy sauce
1 large egg yolk, lightly beaten (see Note)
Salt and freshly ground black pepper, to taste
Wasabi Mayonnaise (page 52)
Julienned daikon radish, for garnish
Ogo or other seaweed, if available, for
    garnish
Mizuna or mesclun leaves, for garnish

1. In a large bowl, mix all the ingredients, through the salt and pepper, gently but thoroughly.

2. Divide the tartare among 4 plates, drizzle about 1½ teaspoons of Wasabi Mayonnaise on each portion, and garnish with daikon, seaweed, and mizuna leaves.

SERVES 4

Note: This recipe contains a raw egg, which can contain the bacteria salmonella. If you are unsure of the quality of the eggs you buy, it's best not to prepare recipes that use them raw.

AROMATIC MUSSEL SALAD

This light and tangy salad of mussels tossed with very thinly sliced red onions, julienned cucumbers, cilantro leaves, and lemongrass is a version of a dish I tasted at the restaurant Takrai (which translates as "lemongrass") in the beautiful city of Chiang Mai, in northern Thailand. The Thais serve this kind of salad *(yams),* dressed with a mixture of fish sauce and lime juice, together with other dishes, but its tart, intricate flavors also provide a perfect invitation to a meal. If you wish, serve these mussels on a bed of fancy greens.

2 cloves garlic, crushed through a press

4½ tablespoons fresh lime juice

2½ tablespoons Asian fish sauce, such as
    nam pla

1 tablespoon sugar

2 small fresh very hot chiles, green or red,
    stemmed, seeded, and minced

3 pounds mussels, well scrubbed

4 stalks fresh lemongrass (3 inches of the
    lower stalk, tough outer leaves discarded),
    2 smashed and 2 very thinly sliced

2 cups water

1 small red onion, quartered and very thinly
    sliced

2 small cucumbers, peeled, seeded, and
    julienned

1 large red bell pepper, stemmed, seeded, and
    julienned

⅓ cup fresh cilantro leaves

3 tablespoons slivered fresh basil leaves

Salt, to taste

1. In a bowl, combine the garlic, lime juice, fish sauce, sugar, and chiles and whisk to mix. Let this dressing stand for 30 minutes for the flavors to develop.

2. Beard the mussels right before you are ready to cook them. Combine the smashed lemongrass and water in a large saucepan and bring to a boil over medium-high heat. Let boil for about 3 minutes. Add the mussels, cover, and cook until they open, shaking the saucepan from time to time. Transfer the mussels to a colander, discarding the unopened ones, and drain. Cool to room temperature, then remove the mussels from their shells and discard the shells.

3. In a serving bowl, toss the mussels with the onion, cucumbers, bell pepper, sliced lemongrass, cilantro, and basil, then toss the mixture with the prepared dressing. Serve chilled or at room temperature, on a bed of delicate greens, if you wish.

SERVES 4

FRIED OYSTERS
with Wasabi Mayonnaise

This Japanese-inspired oyster dish is a cosmopolitan rendition of the deep-fried-oysters-with-tartar-sauce theme. Be very careful not to overcook the oysters—the effect is to have them crisp on the outside and a bit slurpy on the inside.

2 cups vegetable oil, for deep frying

¾ cup fine dry bread crumbs

¼ cup finely chopped fresh parsley leaves,
    well dried if rinsed

Salt and freshly ground black pepper, to taste

2 large eggs

2 dozen large oysters, shucked, drained, and
    patted dry

Wasabi Mayonnaise (recipe follows)

1. Heat the oil in a deep fryer to 375°F.

2. Spread the bread crumbs on a plate and mix with the parsley and salt and pepper. Beat the eggs in a separate dish.

3. One at a time, dip the oysters in the egg, then roll in the seasoned bread crumbs, shaking off the excess.

4. Deep-fry the oysters, a few at a time, until just golden, about 45 seconds to 1 minute. (Cover the deep fryer with a mesh, in case the oil splatters.) Drain the oysters on a double thickness of paper towels and serve at once with the Wasabi Mayonnaise.

SERVES 4

Wasabi Mayonnaise

Piquant Wasabi Mayonnaise, besides being a perfect complement to the oysters, is very versatile. It can be served with other deep-fried seafood, tuna or salmon tartare, or a beef carpaccio.

2 tablespoons wasabi powder (Japanese
horseradish), mixed with 2½ tablespoons
water
1 large egg yolk (see Note)
2 teaspoons fresh lemon juice, plus more to
taste
1 tablespoon rice vinegar
1½ tablespoons tamari soy sauce
Pinch of sugar
½ teaspoon freshly ground white pepper
Salt, to taste
1 cup light olive oil or peanut oil

1. Combine all the ingredients except the oil in a food processor and blend quickly. Slowly drizzle in the oil through the feed tube until the mixture is emulsified.

2. Scrape into a bowl and adjust the seasonings, adding more lemon juice, if desired.

MAKES ABOUT 1¼ CUPS

Note: If you are unsure about using raw egg yolks, make this mayonnaise by combining 1 cup best-quality commercial mayonnaise, 2 tablespoons wasabi powder, 2½ tablespoons water, 2 tablespoons rice vinegar, and 1½ tablespoons soy sauce in a blender. It won't be as delicate as home-made, but it is a reliable substitute.

SEAFOOD ON A BED OF GREENS

with Coconut Mayonnaise

This is an ideal beginning to an important dinner, and one that is easily put together, if you prepare the coconut mayonnaise in advance. In the last several years we have been exposed to a vast array of flavored mayonnaises, but this one is truly ahead of its time! I also love to serve it as a dipping sauce with shrimp, lobster, or poached chicken breasts.

If canned coconut milk is not readily available, don't make a special trip to an out-of-the-way grocery; just substitute heavy cream. As the seafood in this recipe is barely cooked, make sure you pick out the freshest there is.

1½ cups dry white wine
1½ cups water
12 large sea scallops, about 7 ounces
12 large shrimp (about 7 ounces total),
shelled and deveined
2 tablespoons virgin olive oil
6 cups peppery salad greens, such as
arugula, mâche, and/or watercress,
rinsed and patted dry
Coconut Mayonnaise (recipe follows)

1. Bring the wine and water in a large nonreactive saucepan to a simmer over medium-low heat. Add the scallops and cook for about 3 minutes. Remove with a slotted spoon to a medium bowl. Bring the liquid back to a simmer, add the shrimp, and cook for 3 minutes. Drain the shrimp and transfer to the bowl with the scallops. Toss with half of the olive oil.

2. Toss the greens with the rest of the olive oil. Divide the greens among 4 plates, arrange the seafood on top, and drizzle with the Coconut Mayonnaise.

SERVES 4

Coconut Mayonnaise

3 tablespoons dessicated (dried) coconut
1 large clove garlic, chopped
1½ tablespoons fresh lime juice
2 tablespoons chopped fresh cilantro
*   leaves*
1 small fresh hot chile, green or red,
*   stemmed, seeded, and chopped*
¼ cup canned unsweetened coconut
*   milk, well stirred, or heavy*
*   (or whipping) cream*
2 large egg yolks (see Note)
½ cup peanut oil
¼ cup light olive oil (do not use
*   virgin or extra-virgin)*
¼ teaspoon sugar
½ teaspoon salt, or to taste
Freshly ground black pepper,
*   to taste*

1. In a small bowl, soak the coconut in warm water to cover for 10 minutes. Drain and squeeze out the excess liquid.

2. Combine the coconut, garlic, lime juice, cilantro, chile, coconut milk, and egg yolks in a food processor and process until blended and minced. With the motor running, slowly drizzle in the oils, through the feed tube until the mixture is emulsified. Add the sugar, salt, and pepper and process to blend. Scrape into a bowl, cover with plastic,

and refrigerate for at least 2 hours for the flavors to blend.

MAKES ABOUT 1½ CUPS

Note: The finished mayonnaise contains raw eggs, which can contain the bacteria salmonella. If you are unsure of the quality of the eggs you buy, it's best not to prepare recipes that use them raw.

GINGERED SALMON PARCELS
in Saffron Broth

Clean, simple, and pristine—rosy slabs of salmon wrapped in bright green Swiss chard leaves, afloat in a saffron-colored, ginger-infused light broth, are accented with colorful julienned vegetables. It's hard to think of a more elegant way to start a meal.

4½ cups Fish Stock (page 385)
Pinch of saffron threads, crumbled
8 large Swiss chard leaves
1¼ pounds skinless salmon fillet, cut into four
*   pieces*
Salt and freshly ground black pepper, to taste
16 paper-thin slices fresh ginger, plus 2
*   tablespoons julienned*
½ large red bell pepper stemmed, seeded, and
*   cut into thin julienne*
6 snow peas, trimmed and cut into thin
*   julienne*
Freshly ground white pepper, to taste
1½ tablespoons fresh lime juice
Fresh cilantro leaves, for garnish

1. Reduce the fish stock to 3 cups in a medium-size saucepan over medium-high heat, about 10 minutes. Add the saffron and cook for 3 more minutes. Remove from the heat and set aside.

2. Carefully trim off the hard outer ribs from the Swiss chard. Blanch the leaves in boiling water for 10 seconds. Refresh under cold running water.

3. Season the salmon with salt and black pepper. Place 2 chard leaves on your work surface side by side, overlapping, with the stem ends to the left. Lay a piece of salmon on the lower third of the leaves. Place 4 slices of ginger on the salmon. Fold in the stem ends of the leaves, and then the top and bottom. Roll up, egg roll fashion, so that the salmon is enclosed in a parcel. Repeat with the remaining salmon.

4. Blanch the julienned ginger, bell pepper, and snow peas in boiling water for 20 seconds. Refresh under cold running water and reserve.

5. Place the salmon parcels in a large, shallow pan. Slowly pour the reserved saffron broth over and bring to a simmer over low heat. Season with salt and white pepper, if needed. Simmer, covered, for about 2½ minutes. Using tongs or two spoons, carefully turn the parcels on the other side and simmer for 2 to 3 more minutes.

6. With a spatula, remove the salmon parcels to 4 soup plates. Add the reserved ginger, bell pepper, and snow peas. Add the lime juice to the broth and ladle some over each portion of salmon. Serve at once, garnished with cilantro.

SERVES 4

BARBECUED TANDOORI SHRIMP
Over Spring Greens

This is what Irene Trias, the proprietor of Appam, a popular San Francisco restaurant, has to say about her recipe for tandoori shrimp: "This is a lighter version of an ancient Indian tandoori barbecue that I created for Appam, where I incorporate fresh California ingredients into my Indian dishes." She suggests serving these tangy shrimp as an appetizer or a light main course.

1 cup low-fat plain yogurt
¼ cup fresh lemon juice
6 cardamom pods, preferably unbleached (green), crushed
2 tablespoons grated fresh ginger
2 tablespoons crushed garlic
1 teaspoon ground turmeric
2 teaspoons paprika
¼ teaspoon ground cayenne pepper
Salt, to taste
1½ pounds jumbo shrimp, peeled and deveined
6 cups mixed young, tender salad greens, rinsed and patted dry
Lemon wedges, for garnish

1. In a large bowl, mix the yogurt, lemon juice, cardamom, ginger, garlic, turmeric, paprika, cayenne, and salt. Add the shrimp and toss to coat with the marinade. Cover and marinate in the refrigerator for 1 hour.

2. Prepare coals for grilling or preheat the broiler.

3. Grill or broil the shrimp until cooked

through and lightly charred, 3 to 4 minutes per side, brushing once with the marinade.

4. Divide the lettuce on individual plates and arrange the shrimp on the lettuce. Squeeze some lemon over the shrimp and lettuce and serve with additional lemon wedges.

SERVES 6 AS A SUBSTANTIAL APPETIZER, OR 4 AS A MAIN COURSE

PEPPER-CRUSTED TATAKI OF TUNA
with Hoisin Vinaigrette

You will love this dish—spicy, seared rare tuna slices, paired with an Oriental-flavored vinaigrette. The method of cooking the tuna (suggested to me by the Sydney chef Dietmar Sawyere) is wonderful and unusual: it's seared very quickly on a grill or under the broiler, wrapped in plastic wrap, and allowed to finish "cooking" to just the right degree of doneness.

1½ tablespoons green peppercorns
1½ tablespoons black peppercorns
1½ tablespoons pink peppercorns
2½ tablespoons virgin olive oil
2 pieces very fresh yellowfin tuna (about 1 pound total), about 1 inch thick
6 cups mixed young, tender salad greens, rinsed and patted dry
Hoisin Vinaigrette (recipe follows)

1. Using a mortar and pestle or small food processor, grind or process the pepper-corns with the oil to a paste. Spread the mixture on the tuna, cover, and refrigerate for 4 hours.

2. Prepare coals for grilling or preheat the broiler.

3. Grill or broil the tuna just to sear, about 1 minute on each side. (Alternatively, you can sear the tuna in a dry cast-iron skillet or wok.) Wrap in plastic wrap, allow to cool, and refrigerate for at least 2 hours. Slice into medium-thin slices.

4. To serve, divide the greens among 4 plates, then fan out the tuna slices on top. Drizzle with the vinaigrette.

SERVES 4

Hoisin Vinaigrette

This sweetish, complexly flavored vinaigrette is also excellent with tender salad greens on their own, asparagus, and sliced grilled steak, at room temperature.

2 teaspoons hoisin sauce
1½ teaspoons soy sauce
1½ teaspoons Dijon or Chinese mustard
2 tablespoons white wine vinegar
1 small clove garlic, crushed through a press
2 teaspoons minced fresh ginger
1½ teaspoons freshly ground white pepper
Salt, to taste
6 tablespoons light olive oil (do not use virgin or extra virgin)

In a bowl, mix together the hoisin sauce, soy sauce, mustard, vinegar, garlic, ginger, pepper, and salt. Slowly drizzle in the oil, whisking until emulsified. Let stand for 30 minutes for the flavors to develop.

MAKES ABOUT ⅔ CUP

THE SPICE TRADE

When Vasco da Gama rounded the Cape of Good Hope in 1498 and sailed as far as the east coast of India, Western taste changed forever. For the great goal of this momentous voyage, the chief reason for Europe's first direct route to the East Indies (as much of Southeast Asia was once known), was a quest: Europeans were searching for the most tangy, heady, fragrant, and aromatic little fragments of the plant kingdom: spices.

spices arrived. They could be used to flavor and invigorate almost anything that the kitchen produced—from sauces, relishes, pickles, and chutneys to beverages, desserts, soups, baked goods, and salads. Of course, their enormous cost reserved spices for the tables of royalty and rich merchants. And they remained an indulgence until the Victorian era.

Derived from the bulbs, roots, bark, fruit, flowers, and seeds of exotic plants and trees, they added zest and pleasure to the consumption of food in the more temperate countries of Europe. Pity the average eaters in northern Europe in the early Middle Ages: Their diet consisted principally of dried, pickled, or salted fish and meat, often of inferior quality. Astonishingly bland, and unvarying, it would be accompanied with a few, most likely sour, half-rotten vegetables.

Imagine the revolution of the senses when

MYSTERIOUS OFFERINGS

But Europe didn't invent the taste for spices. Far from it. For hundreds of years before the Christian era, herbs and spices had been put to medicinal and ritual use, especially by the peoples of Asia. Greek writers such as Hippocrates and Pliny gave rave reviews to the therapeutic qualities of these aromatic delights.

While Asia is home to cardamom, cinnamon, cassia, turmeric, and ginger, it was the clever merchants of southern Arabia (the ancient Arabia Felix, or "Fertile Arabia") who became the first middlemen in one of the world's greatest trades. They added mysterious offerings of their own to the roster of new tastes from the Far East—myrrh, frankincense, and other fragrant resins, which they claimed were cultivated in hidden lakes and forests guarded by mythical beasts and serpents. So originated the long association of spices with exoticism, extravagance, decadence, and danger.

Long before the rise of civilization in the West, Arabs were trading spices and Chinese junks were adventuring in the Straits of Melaka and among the Spice Islands of present-day Indonesia. Situated midway between the two most active trading empires of Asia, Ceylon (today's Sri Lanka) became an important stopover, and eventually a place of cultivation. So, much later, did Hormuz, commanding the narrows of the Persian Gulf. At the height of the Roman Empire, the port of Alexandria, in Egypt, was the world center of the spice trade. Later, in the late Middle Ages, it was the Italian maritime empires of Venice and Genoa that controlled the flow of spices into central and northern Europe.

THE RACE IS ON

By the 1500s the great seafaring nations of Europe—Portugal, Spain, England, and Holland—were competing to find a direct route to the Spice Islands. By the end of the century, they were caught up in a furious rivalry for routes, rights, and monopolies. Christopher Columbus sailed in 1492 on behalf of the Spanish crown (and we know where he mistakenly landed), but it was the Portuguese who led the race for the East Indies. Until they were joined in Southeast Asia by French and Dutch merchant adventurers thirty years later, the Portuguese ran the world's first great waterborne spice trade. For more than 350 years the Spice Route was arguably the most important trading artery in the world. Though long and dangerous in itself, sailing to the Spice Islands of Southeast Asia was much less risky and expensive than the arduous land passage that wound through China and Central Asia.

Sir Francis Drake set off the long fuse of British interests when he pirated his way in the *Golden Hind* (full of treasure plundered from the Spanish New World)

from the tip of South America to the Spice Islands in 1579. There Drake loaded up with cloves and set off for the return trip to England. After a brief stop in Java, he rounded the Cape of Good Hope and reached home in the fall of 1580. Twenty years later, the great East India Company was established in London. Its first voyage was launched in 1601, returning two years later with spices bought in Bantam, in Indonesia, where a "factory" (trading post) was established.

tablishing crucial contacts with India, whose calicoes from the Coromandel (east) coast became more valued in the exchange for spices than money or European goods. Soon

ation of smaller concerns formed in 1602) filled the trade routes of the Indian Ocean. Soon other countries wanted a piece of the action. Ferdinand Magellan sailed from Spain in

With most of the spices of the world readily available to us, it is difficult to believe how precious a commodity they once were.

The records of the voyage show that the *Ascension,* one of four main vessels that formed the group, brought home 210,000 pounds of pepper; 1,100 pounds of cloves; 6,030 pounds of cinnamon; and 4,080 pounds of gum-lac. The East India was to become the most successful of all the English trading companies, eventually es-

trade was raging. Adventure and pirating were replaced by the commerce of a confident merchant empire.

Meanwhile, aggressive Dutch traders were making inroads into the loose monopoly Portugal held over trade in the South Seas. The vessels of the Dutch United East India Company (a feder-

1519, but the Spanish had more than enough on their plates carving out their vast empire in the Americas. It took another 140 years for the French to establish their own East India Company under the Sun King, Louis XIV, in 1664. In the meantime, Siam and the Malay Peninsula were also opened up to trade by the Dutch.

MERE SPECKS

The little islands responsible for changing the taste of Europe are just a few specks on the map, fragrant boulders strewn into a lost corner of the oceans, standing outside time and general knowledge until they made a dramatic appearance on the stage of world history. Ternate and Tidore, the island sultanates to the north of the Banda Sea and the richest source of cloves, were the focus of the Spice Island trade from the earliest Portuguese domination until Pierre Poivre (Peter Pepper) smuggled cloves and nutmegs to Mauritius, and the British set up plantations in India, Africa, and Caribbean Grenada. Today the clove trade is still the mainstay of the islands' economy.

The nine Banda Islands, farther south, are even smaller. Together

they constitute only forty square miles of dry land —and that's at low tide. But these minuscule islets, located at the tip of the long volcanic belt stretching all the way across the Indonesian archipelago, were once the only source of nutmeg and mace on earth. Even today, production from the Banda Islands represents almost 80 percent of the world crop.

With most of the spices of the world readily available to us, it is difficult to believe how precious a commodity they once were and how some were literally worth their weight in gold. It is estimated that each of the many times a spice changed hands on the long route back to Europe its value doubled. Before the direct sea route, this would have made them a thousand times more expensive when bought in London or Paris than they were on the makeshift jetties of the Spice Islands.

Not surprisingly, colossal fortunes were made and lost on the back of this trade. It is no

exaggeration to claim that some of the grandest architectural projects of the Renaissance were built on a foundation of spices. Spices helped form the economies of Europe into something like the capital-driven markets they are today. They spurred on the Western world to rediscovering and then colonizing, Asia, Africa, and the Americas.

Perhaps the best way to sum it up is with the little parable that is often told about the humblest Spice Island of them all, little Run, the western-most of the Bandas, which was stubbornly claimed by the British after decades of competition from the Dutch. So great was Holland's desire to establish a monopoly on the nutmeg trade that its diplomats were instructed to get Run back at all costs. With the Treaty of Breda, in 1667, the Dutch finally persuaded the British to leave their boulder in the Banda Sea in exchange for another, slightly larger, rocky island, not then reckoned to be of much account: Manhattan.

Mussel Soup with a Hint of the East

Penang Fish and Noodle Soup

Thai Spring Soup with Shrimp Dumplings

Bruce Cost's Hot-and-Sour Soup

Hot-and-Sour Shrimp Soup

Singapore Oxtail Soup

Vinny Le's Beef and Noodle Soup

Chicken in Aromatic Coconut Broth

Baliram's Cream of Chicken Soup

Coriander-Flavored Chicken Soup with Rice and Potato Balls

Raffles Mulligatawny Soup

Tart Chicken Soup with Glass Noodles, Lemongrass, and Lime

Coconut Cream of Pumpkin Soup

Peppered Tamarind Broth

Curried Roast Vegetable Soup

Down-Under Spinach and Coconut Soup

Napa Cabbage and Peanut Soup

Mushroom and Star Anise Consommé with Mushroom Dumplings and Prosciutto

Chilled Avocado-Lime Soup

Roast Pepper and Tomato Soup with Chiles and Cilantro

Cucumber and Mango Bisque

Chilled Lemongrass Cream with Pineapple and Kiwi

I have traveled around the world in search of the perfect bowl of soup. This passion (which like any passion is intense, obsessive, and restless) actually had its beginning in a humble Vietnamese *pho* shop in Melbourne. It was love at first taste. I was hooked and couldn't go through a day without a huge bowl of that intensely aromatic broth, whose slurpy rice noodles, juicy succulent meat, and crispy aromatic herbs haunted my food dreams both day and night.

That *pho* was comforting and soothing as only a soup can be, yet it spoke to me of exotic lands, of adventures, of rice fields, and spice routes.

It has led me throughout Southeast Asia and the Pacific collecting recipes for great soups. I found them in markets, back alleys, and fancy restaurants. Amid the colonial splendor of the newly restored tiffin room at Raffles Hotel in Singapore, I had my encounter with a sublime mulligatawny. The street stalls of the enchanted island of Penang lured me with a fish soup to rival the best bouillabaisse. My Singapore mornings inevitably began with a fortifying bowl of soup noodles.

Like many Americans, I was already familiar and in love with the two Thai classics: *tom yum kung*, the tart and spicy shrimp broth, and the *tom kha gai*, also acidic and piquant but based on creamy sweet coconut milk and containing morsels of chicken. I trekked to Bangkok for the most authentic tastes. In Australia, chefs and home cooks taught me to blend some of the best ideas from many continents and cuisines to produce real fusion recipes— a simple cream of spinach soup enhanced with coconut cream and garam masala; a classic mushroom consommé prepared with shiitakes and flavored with star anise.

What it all boils down to is essentially two soup traditions in Asia: One is a "meal-in-a-bowl" containing various meats or seafood and one or several kinds of noodles and furnished with a kaleidoscope of garnishes and sauces. These are usually eaten at stalls or coffee shops for breakfast or a midday snack. You are offered a plastic bowl and then you elbow for the garnishes.

The repertoire of these noodle soups is enormous. The Malaysian classic, *laksa* (chicken and clams in coconut broth), comes replete with two kinds of noodles; then there is the great Vietnamese *pho*, my Melbourne favorite; and the ethereal lime-scented Indonesian chicken soup with delicate rice vermicelli.

Soups from the second great Asian tradition do not begin a meal but are served together with other dishes or even at the end to clear the palate or wash down the meal. These soups are often light, thin, aromatic, and refreshing. But in a Western context, the same soups can happily signal a perfect beginning to a filling meal. Served in small cups, they are a lovely way to whet the appetite and tantalize the palate. Some of the light soups I have collected here include a flavorful tamarind broth, a star anise-flavored mushroom consommé, a ginger-infused salmon broth and two intriguing Thai seafood soups.

Finally, East meets West in a most enchanting encounter—over a classic mussel bisque, enhanced with garam masala and citrus flavors; creamy pumpkin soup with coconut milk, chiles, and rich spices; and a cabbage and peanut soup spiked with lime juice, soy, chiles, and cilantro.

Accompany these soups with bowls of colorful garnishes. Offer spring rolls or papadums, and choice morsels of seafood, dumplings, or strips of grilled meat to float in the fragrant liquid. There is no end to the imaginative use of favorite tastes.

MUSSEL SOUP
with a Hint of the East

A classic French mussel soup is given a cross-cultural rendition—a hint of curry and garam masala, citrus juice, and cilantro—by the brilliant Sydney-based chef Dietmar Sawyere. With Dietmar's background it was only natural for him to turn to "fusion" cuisine. Born in Switzerland, Dietmar started his culinary career in London, working for the Savoy among other places. Subsequent assignments took him to New Zealand and Hong Kong. Then, he virtually pioneered "fusion" cuisine while working at the Regent of Bangkok. "It all started quite simply," he explained. "The local clientele thought they wanted Western food but just couldn't give up the familiar flavors they adored. So we would give them a 'New York steak' but dip it in soy sauce just before grilling." After his highly successful stint in Bangkok, Dietmar settled in Australia, a perfect place for cross-cultural culinary adventures. His thorough training in classical techniques and encyclopedic knowledge of Asian cuisines make his food one of the most successful attempts at combining styles and techniques I have come across.

1½ tablespoons olive oil

½ cup finely chopped celery

⅓ cup finely chopped leeks (white part only)

½ cup finely chopped onion

3 cloves garlic, sliced

2 pounds mussels, scrubbed under cold running water, debearded just before cooking

1¼ cups dry vermouth, preferably Noilly Prat

2 bay leaves

1 sprig fresh thyme, or 1½ teaspoons dried

3 tablespoons unsalted butter

1 fennel bulb, finely chopped (about 1½ cups)

1 tablespoon garam masala, preferably homemade (page 390)

2 teaspoons best-quality mild curry powder

1 large pinch saffron threads, pulverized

2 teaspoons dried laos powder (galangal), if available

¼ cup Pernod

4 cups Fish Stock (page 385) or bottled clam juice

1 cup heavy (or whipping) cream

1½ cups fresh orange juice

2½ tablespoons fresh lemon juice

Salt and freshly ground black pepper, to taste

¼ cup minced fresh cilantro leaves

2 teaspoons finely grated lemon zest

2 tablespoons snipped fresh chives, for garnish

3 tablespoons finely diced, seeded tomato, for garnish

1. Heat the oil in a large heavy pot over medium heat. Add half the celery, half the leeks, and half the onion along with the garlic and cook until wilted, about 5 minutes. Add the mussels and stir for another minute. Add the vermouth, bay leaves, and thyme. Bring to a boil, cover, and cook over high heat, shaking the pan occasionally, until the mussels open, about 5 minutes. Using a slotted spoon, remove the mussels from the cooking liquid.

PLEASE THE KITCHEN GOD

For Chinese cooks, the Kitchen God is the ruler of the household, responsible for blessing and protecting the family. The God is usually represented by a red wooden board inscribed with Chinese characters and a small altar, placed high on the kitchen wall. As patron saint of the household he watches carefully over its goings-on, and sends back reports to the Heavenly Jade Emperor.

The rules of the Kitchen God are well known to everyone in the house. The most important of all is not to tolerate any wastage of rice. Then, there should be no disrespectful behavior in the kitchen, especially toward the written Chinese character. For this reason it is not permitted to use newspaper to ignite the stove. When the God makes his annual sojourn to heaven at the end of the lunar year, the family sends him off well supplied with sweet things, so that he will communicate sweetness and flattery to the Heavenly Jade Emperor. The God is welcomed back home on the fourth day of the year to resume his duties and is again fed honey to sweeten him up for the New Year.

Reserve 6 mussels for garnish. Remove the rest of the mussels from their shells, cover with plastic wrap, and reserve, discarding the shells and any mussels that did not open. Strain the mussel cooking liquid through a double layer of dampened cheese cloth and reserve.

2. Melt the butter in a large heavy pot over medium heat. Add the remaining celery, leeks, and onion, and the fennel. Cover and cook until wilted, about 10 minutes. Add the garam masala, curry powder, saffron, and laos powder and cook, stirring, for 1 minute.

3. Add the Pernod and reduce over high heat for 3 minutes. Add the reserved mussel liquid and Fish Stock, bring to a boil, and reduce by one third, about 10 minutes. Add the cream and reduce again by one third, skimming, about 7 minutes more. Add the orange and lemon juices. Transfer the mixture to a food processor and purée. Pass through a fine strainer into a clean saucepan.

4. Bring the soup to a simmer over low heat. Season to taste with salt and pepper. Stir in the reserved shelled mussels and cook just to heat through. Stir in the cilantro and lemon zest and remove from the heat.

5. Ladle the soup into soup bowls, dividing the mussels evenly. Garnish each portion with a mussel in its shell, chives, and tomato.

SERVES 6

PENANG FISH AND NOODLE SOUP

This soup perfectly captures the tastes of the enchanted island of Penang in northern Malaysia. Penang is a gourmand's dream: It's home to a host of succulent tropical fruits and spices, and its Chinese, Indian, Peranakan, and colonial heritage have blended into fascinating local cuisines.

Best of all, you can enjoy some of the most delicious street food on earth along the bustling boardwalk by the sea.

This recipe is the Penang version of *laksa*, a vigorously aromatic Malaysian seafood noodle soup flavored with an intriguing blend of spices and herbs and lavishly garnished with vegetables, fruit, chiles, and limes. While in most regions the soup is based on coconut milk, in Penang the rich fish broth is flavored by tart tamarind liquid.

The preparation is quite involved, but you will be rewarded with one of the most satisfying one-dish meals in all of Asia. As is the case with complex Asian recipes, the majority of the steps can be prepared in advance. Make the fish stock, squeeze the tamarind liquid, make the spice paste, cook the noodles, and prepare the garnishes at your leisure up to a day ahead.

1 whole red snapper, gutted and cleaned with
    head and tail left on (about 2½ pounds),
    cut into 4 pieces
9 cups water
Salt, to taste
3 tablespoons tamarind pulp, preferably
    from Thailand
12 hot dried red chiles (2 to 3 inches long),
    preferably Asian, stemmed and seeded
¼ cup chopped red onion
5 large cloves garlic, chopped
3 tablespoons chopped fresh ginger
3 stalks lemongrass (3 inches of the lower
    stalk, tough outer leaves discarded)
1½ teaspoons ground turmeric
⅓ cup diced red bell pepper
2 slices fresh or frozen galangal, if available,
    peeled and chopped
2 tablespoons sugar, or more to taste
2½ tablespoons soy sauce
1 pound fresh medium-width rice noodles or
    12 ounces dried rice noodles

GARNISHES

1 cup diced pineapple
2 small cucumbers, peeled, seeded, and finely
    diced
1 cup shredded iceberg lettuce
1 cup fresh mint leaves
4 red cayenne or serrano chiles, seeded and
    sliced
½ cup diced red onion
½ cup fresh cilantro leaves

1. Combine the fish and water in a large heavy pot, and bring to a simmer over medium heat. Add salt and simmer, covered, until the fish is very tender, about 30 minutes. Remove the fish from the stock and strain the stock through a double layer of dampened cheesecloth. When the fish is cool enough to handle, remove and discard the skin and bones, then flake the flesh with a fork and reserve.

2. Soak the tamarind pulp in 1 cup of the hot fish stock off the heat for 15 minutes. While it is soaking, cut the chiles into pieces using scissors. Soak in warm water to cover for 20 minutes.

3. Stir and mash the tamarind pulp with a fork to help it dissolve. Strain through a fine strainer into a bowl, pressing on the solids with the back of a wooden spoon to extract all the liquid.

4. Drain the soaked chiles. In a food processor, combine the chiles, onion, garlic, ginger, lemongrass, turmeric, bell pepper, and galangal and process to a fine paste, adding a little water to assist blending.

5. Combine the chile paste with 1½ cups of the stock and bring to a boil in a large heavy pot. Cook over medium heat, stirring for 5 to 7 minutes.

6. Stir in the rest of the stock, the tamarind liquid, sugar, soy sauce, and the reserved fish. Simmer the soup, uncovered, for 5 minutes.

7. While the soup is simmering, bring a large pot of salted water to a boil. Plunge the noodles into the water for about 20 seconds. If using dried noodles, soak in hot water for 20 minutes and then cook them in boiling water for 30 seconds. Drain and rinse under cold running water.

8. To serve, place the garnishes in serving bowls and set on the table. Place some noodles in each bowl, ladle the soup over them, and serve at once.

SERVES 8

THAI SPRING SOUP
with Shrimp Dumplings

An intense herby freshness sets Thai cuisine apart from the other cuisines of Southeast Asia. This soup, adapted from a recipe I learned at the Oriental Hotel Cooking School in Bangkok, is the perfect example—it practically makes your mouth explode with sprightly flavors of herbs and aromatics.

You can use any combination of baby vegetables available at the market. If you can find them, use long (snake) beans, instead of the string beans. Blanch them in boiling water until almost soft, refresh under cold running water, fold them in half, and tie a knot in each. It's very Thai! Also, look for fresh baby corn. If you can't find it, substitute fresh corn kernels rather than using canned baby corn. I especially love the tingle of the crushed fresh green peppercorns, added at the end. Jarred green peppercorns in brine can be found at most specialty or Thai grocery stores. Make an effort to get them.

10 ounces large shrimp
6 cups water
Salt, to taste
1½ tablespoons chopped shallots
1 clove garlic, chopped
1½ teaspoons black peppercorns
1 large egg white, lightly beaten
1 teaspoon cornstarch
1 cup trimmed and halved string beans
2½ to 3 cups baby spring vegetables (use baby corn, tiny button mushrooms, baby squash, baby carrots)
1½ cups baby or regular spinach leaves, rinsed
1 cup shredded fresh basil leaves, preferably Thai
½ cup lemon balm leaves, if available
3 tablespoons Asian fish sauce, such as nam pla
2 tablespoons fresh lime juice
2 tablespoons fresh green peppercorns, crushed

1. Shell the shrimp, reserving the shells, and devein. Chop the shrimp coarsely and mince in a food processor.

2. Combine the shrimp shells in a medium-size saucepan with the water, bring to a boil, season with salt and simmer for 15 minutes. Strain the stock into a large heavy pot.

3. Using a mortar and pestle or a small food processor, pound or process the shallots, garlic, ½ teaspoon salt, and the black peppercorns to a paste. In a bowl, combine the paste with the minced shrimp, egg white, and cornstarch. Mix well in one direction until you have a smooth paste.

4. Bring the shrimp stock to a boil, add the string beans and baby vegetables, and cook over medium-high heat for 5 minutes. (If some of the vegetables are bigger than the others, they may take longer to cook. Add them a minute before adding the smaller vegetables.) With wet hands, shape the shrimp mixture into balls the size of walnuts and add to the soup. Wet your hands as needed to keep the mixture from sticking to them. Cook until the balls float to the surface, about 4 minutes.

5. Add the spinach and cook for 30 seconds. Stir in the basil, lemon balm, fish sauce, lime juice, and green peppercorns and remove from the heat. Adjust the seasoning, if necessary. Serve at once.

SERVES 4

BRUCE COST'S HOT-AND-SOUR SOUP

Bruce Cost, a San Francisco chef, scholar, and author, possesses a staggering knowledge of Chinese gastronomy. In China, food is often valued for its medicinal properties, and according to Bruce, this classic soup is a true panacea for various ailments. The white pepper is invigorating and helps combat colds, tree ears and lily buds improve circulation, bean curd and eggs lend protein, vinegar cleanses the system, cilantro attacks bodily toxins, and sesame oil is a digestive aid. But above all, it is a deliciously simple dish to prepare, resulting in soup far superior to anything one might encounter in a restaurant.

3 dried shiitake mushrooms
1 piece (2 inches) tree ear mushroom
20 dried tiger lily buds, if available
1 boneless center-cut pork chop (4 ounces), sliced into thin strips
1½ teaspoons dark soy sauce
5 cups Chicken Stock (page 384) or canned broth
1 tablespoon peanut oil
¼ cup shredded canned bamboo shoots
1½ tablespoons light soy sauce
¼ cup distilled white vinegar
Salt, to taste (optional)
1½ cakes soft tofu, cut into thin strips
3 tablespoons cornstarch, mixed with ¼ cup cold water
1 large egg, beaten
1 teaspoon freshly ground white pepper
1 tablespoon Oriental sesame oil
2 tablespoons chopped fresh cilantro leaves
2 tablespoons chopped scallions

1. In separate bowls, soak the shiitakes, tree ear, and lily buds in cold water to cover for 1 hour.

2. In another bowl, marinate the pork in the dark soy sauce for 30 minutes, tossing occasionally.

3. Bring the stock to a boil in a large heavy pot. Lower the heat and keep the stock at a simmer.

4. Stem the shiitakes and cut the caps into thin slices. Cut the tree ear into strips. Shred the lily buds by hand.

5. Heat the oil in a wok or large skillet until almost smoking. Add the pork and stir-fry until opaque, about 1 minute. Add the shiitakes, tree ear, lily buds, and bamboo shoots and stir-fry for 1½ minutes.

KUALA LUMPUR

The bustling capital of Malaysia was founded in the 1860s as a tin city at the confluence of the Klang and Gombak rivers. Its name, Kuala Lumpur, literally means "muddy estuary." During the second half of the nineteenth century it sprung into life as a brash mining boomtown—like Ballarat in Australia or San Francisco in California, which flourished at much the same time. You can still see the remnants of Kuala Lumpur's glory days in the millionaires' mansions that line the elegant Jalan Ampang (Ampang Street), many of them now serving as embassies or fine restaurants.

The ceremonial center of the city is focused on Merdeka Square, a flat, grassy field that used to be called the Padang, where cricket matches have been played for over a century and independence was declared in 1957. It is overlooked by the Royal Selangor Club, whose facade is as giddy as the tin-rush 1890s when it was built.

Shopping, old-style and new, is going to make Kuala Lumpur the Singapore of the 1990s. The great neo-Moorish Sultan Abdul Saman building, opposite Merdeka Square, is being converted into what is claimed will be the largest covered bazaar in Asia. In the meantime, there's virtually nothing you might consider buying on a visit to Paris or Tokyo that you can't find at the pristine post-modernist Ishetan complex, a stone's throw from the Regent Hotel. But Kuala Lumpur also guards its traditions and culture: Here the local McDonald's dispenses sugarcane and durian juice and sells as many rendang-flavored burgers as ketchup-coated Big Macs.

Colonial, modern, postmodern, and revivalist—Kuala Lumpur is all of these things at once. In fact, the most delightful thing about Malaysia in the 1990s is that none of its many styles has yet become so dominant that the others are eclipsed. It's the same on the streets, where the local Tower of Babel has four sides—Malay, Chinese (in its many dialects), English, and various Indian languages (with Tamil predominating). Almost everyone we met could speak two of these languages well, one passably, and a fourth with gusto and invention.

ON THE TOWN

We took an upbeat taxi ride through the districts of the Malaysian capital with a driver who was just our kind of guide. He pointed things out left and right, with no concession to rank or hierarchy. He was more enthusiastic about his local drive-in fast food joint, the A & W (the driver's boyhood hangout in the sixties) than he was about the chic boutiques and the spectacular new hotels of the city's vibrant downtown. But when he turned into Jalan Sultan, the Madison Avenue of Kuala Lumpur, our chameleon driver negotiated it with the finesse of an ambassador.

Then we visited the glorious old railway station. Only the British could build their stations on a grander scale than their palaces. And this is a station that could take the steam out of all the railways in the world. Along with the Railway Administration building and the old Majestic Hotel (now a modern art gallery), it's one of a trio of colonial curios, decked with pinnacles, spires, and domes, that look as if they were follies imagined in the tales of the Arabian Nights.

SOUL AND HEART

But Kuala Lumpur is more than colonialism and commerce. The city also has its religious side, and mosques and temples are scattered here and there, including the giant modern National Mosque, not far from the station, with its forty-eight domes and acres of pools and terracing. A park beyond the mosque is home to the Lake Gardens, the Malaysian Parliament, and the National Museum and Monument.

At night, the central section of Kuala Lumpur's Chinatown is closed to traffic and becomes a pasar malam—an evening bazaar. These neighborhood markets are one of the great institutions of Malaysia. Their thoroughfares and the side streets around them teem with shoppers, browsers, and hangers-on. Everyone goes there, and the night bazaars serve the same purpose as an American mall. They combine the functions of an inexpensive department store, crafts shop, restaurant row, and entertainment center. It's here that you find the heart of the city.

6. Add the light soy sauce and vinegar to the simmering stock. Season with salt, if needed. Add the pork mixture and bring to a boil. Gently stir in the tofu and let cook for 1 minute. Slowly drizzle in the cornstarch mixture, stirring gently. Cook until the soup thickens, about 2 minutes.

7. Turn off the heat and slowly swirl in the beaten egg. Transfer the soup to a tureen, sprinkle with pepper, and swirl in the sesame oil. Sprinkle with cilantro and scallions before serving.

SERVES 4 TO 6

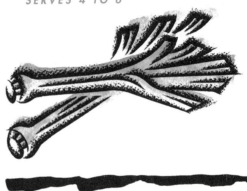

HOT-AND-SOUR SHRIMP SOUP

Thai food aficionados in this country are familiar with *tom yum kung*, a fragrant spicy-sour shrimp soup that appears on every Thai restaurant menu (alas, all too frequently in its instant package incarnation). This recipe comes from the luxurious restaurant Benjarong in Bangkok, which serves up the best version of this bewitching potage I have tasted.

At a Thai meal, soups are served hot or at room temperature together with the rest of the dishes, but I have seen *tom yum kung* actually appear at the end, its tart, refreshing flavor rightly considered a perfect way to aid the digestion of the meal. Although

Thai soups are usually based on water, it makes sense here to use the shrimp shells to prepare a light stock.

1 pound large shrimp

2 teaspoons peanut oil

3 tablespoons chopped shallots

7 cups water

1 stalk fresh lemongrass, smashed, plus 3 tablespoons thinly sliced (use 3 inches of the lower stalk, tough outer leaves discarded for both)

3 sprigs fresh cilantro

1 kaffir lime leaf (if available), smashed

2 teaspoons white peppercorns

3 cloves garlic, chopped

2½ tablespoons chopped cilantro roots and/or stems

2 to 3 small fresh hot chiles, green or red, stemmed, seeded, and thinly sliced

4 slices fresh or frozen galangal, (if available), peeled and smashed

¼ cup fresh lime juice

3 tablespoons Asian fish sauce, such as nam pla

1 teaspoon sugar

1 cup straw mushrooms, fresh or canned, drained if canned

½ cup red bell pepper strips

Salt, to taste (optional)

¼ cup fresh cilantro leaves, for garnish

1. Shell the shrimp, reserving the shells, devein, and set aside.

2. Heat the oil in a large heavy pot over medium heat. Add the shallots and shrimp shells and sauté, stirring, for 5 minutes. Add the water, lemongrass stalk, cilantro sprigs, and kaffir lime leaf and bring to a boil. Reduce the heat to low and cook for 15 minutes. Strain the stock into a second large pot.

3. Using a mortar and pestle or a small food processor, pound or process the peppercorns, garlic, and cilantro roots to a paste.

4. Bring the shrimp stock to a simmer. Add the peppercorn paste, chiles, lemongrass slices, and galangal and simmer for 5 minutes. (If you don't like the bits of aromatics floating in the soup, you can strain it again at this point, but the stock will lose some of its flavor.)

5. Add the shrimp and cook until they turn pink, about 2 minutes. Stir in the lime juice, fish sauce, sugar, mushrooms, and bell pepper and simmer for 2 more minutes. Season with salt, if desired. Serve in decorative bowls, garnished with cilantro.

SERVES 6 TO 7

SINGAPORE OXTAIL SOUP

Singapore is a veritable bazaar of culinary styles. In addition to the obvious Indian overtones in this soup, I also suspect a hint of Portuguese influence. The recipe hails from the multiethnic kitchens of the Nutmeg Restaurant at the luxurious Hyatt Regency Hotel in Singapore. The flavorful stock for this soup is best prepared a day, or at least a few hours, ahead so that you can refrigerate it and easily skim off the fat. A splash of dry sherry will enliven the soup's flavor, so pass some separately to your guests.

3 pounds meaty oxtails

9 cups water, or more as needed

Salt, to taste

2 tablespoons unsalted butter

1 tablespoon olive oil

3 medium onions, thinly sliced

2 large cloves garlic, sliced

1 tablespoon julienned fresh ginger

½ teaspoon ground turmeric

½ teaspoon ground ginger

*1 serrano chile, stemmed, seeded,
    and chopped*

*2 medium firm, ripe tomatoes, peeled, seeded,
    and cut into thin wedges*

Freshly ground black pepper, to taste

*1 tablespoon slivered fresh basil leaves, for
    garnish*

*1 tablespoon coarsely chopped celery leaves,
    for garnish*

Dry sherry, to taste

1. Combine the oxtails with enough water to cover them in a large heavy pot and bring to a boil over medium-high heat. Skim off the froth that rises to the surface, reduce the heat to low, season with salt, cover, and simmer until the oxtails are tender, about 2 hours, skimming from time to time. Cool the stock with the meat in it. After it cools, refrigerate it until the fat solidifies on the surface. Skim off the fat.

2. With a slotted spoon, remove the oxtails from the stock to a bowl or platter. Remove the meat from the bones and set aside, discarding the bones and gristle. Melt the butter in the oil in a large heavy pot over medium heat. Add the onions, garlic, and julienned ginger and cook until the onion is translucent, about 7 minutes. Stir in the turmeric, ground ginger, and the chile and cook, stirring, for 1 more minute.

3. Stir in 7 cups of the oxtail stock, reduce the heat to low, and simmer for about 10 minutes. Add the oxtail meat and tomatoes and cook until heated through, about 2 minutes. Season to taste with salt and pepper. Serve garnished with chopped basil and celery leaves. Pass some dry sherry separately.

SERVES 4 TO 6

VINNY LE'S BEEF AND NOODLE SOUP

Vinny Le is the proprietor of a tiny noodle-soup shop in a Vietnamese suburb of Melbourne. Her addictively delicious soup sustained John and me, body and soul, through our Australian sojourn. The long-simmered broth was wonderfully rich, redolent of ginger and star anise, and the sliced brisket was perfectly moist and flavorful. The slurpy wide rice noodles were the freshest possible. And when the soup arrived at the table, it was garnished with a virtual garden of fragrant herbs, chiles, and crispy bean sprouts. I can't think of anything more satisfying, and I cook this soup as often as I can, just for myself, for family, for friends, and for important guests. When you try it, so will you!

The name of the soup is *pho* (pronounced "far") and it is derived from the name of the wide rice noodles it contains. In Vietnam it is a favorite one-dish breakfast or lunch. Some establishments serve nothing but *pho*, either chicken or meat. Serve it in large bowls and let guests add their own garnishes. If you can't find fresh rice noodles, then use dried ones—but only if you have to.

SOUP

2 pounds beef marrow bones

4 slices (each 1 inch thick) fresh ginger,
    smashed

3 quarts water

Salt, to taste

1½ pounds first-cut beef brisket, trimmed

1 piece star anise and 1 piece (1 inch long)
    cinnamon stick, tied in a
    cheesecloth bag

¼ cup Asian fish sauce, such as nam pla,
    plus more for serving with the soup

2 medium onions, thinly sliced

1 pound fresh wide rice noodles, or
    12 ounces dried

GARNISHES

2 scallions, finely chopped

2 tablespoons chopped fresh cilantro leaves

1 cup fresh bean sprouts

2 small fresh hot chiles, green or red,
    stemmed, seeded, and sliced

1 lime, cut into wedges

6 to 8 sprigs fresh basil, preferably Thai

6 to 8 sprigs fresh mint

Sambal oelek or Chinese chile paste with
    garlic

Hoisin sauce (optional)

1. Make the soup: Combine the marrow bones, ginger, water, and salt in a large, heavy pot and bring to a boil. Cook over medium heat, uncovered, for 10 minutes, skimming off the froth that rises to the surface.

2. Add the brisket, reduce the heat to low, and cook, skimming often, until the stock is completely clear, another 10 minutes. Reduce the heat to low, cover, and simmer until the brisket is tender, about 2 hours.

3. Remove the brisket and marrow bones from the stock and set aside. Remove and discard the bones. Continue to simmer the stock, covered, for another hour.

4. If the stock does not look clear, strain it through a double layer of dampened cheesecloth into a clean pot.

5. Return the stock to the heat, add the cheesecloth bag with the star anise and cinnamon, the ¼ cup fish sauce, and onions, and simmer for another 30 minutes.

6. Meanwhile, prepare the noodles: In a large pot, bring about 3 quarts of water to a boil. Separate fresh noodles with a fork to untangle. Plunge the noodles into the water for about 30 seconds, just until heated through. Do not allow them to cook longer. (If using dry noodles, soak them in hot water for 20 minutes and then plunge into boiling water for 30 seconds.) Drain in a colander and rinse under cold water.

7. To serve, cut the reserved brisket across the grain into thin slices. Divide the noodles among 6 or 8 large soup bowls, add a few slices of brisket, and ladle some broth over the top. Sprinkle with scallions and cilantro. Arrange the remaining garnishes in individual plates and bowls and place them on the table, along with extra fish sauce, if desired.

SERVES 6 TO 8

CHICKEN IN AROMATIC COCONUT BROTH

This soup, called *tom kha gai,* which literally means "chicken and galangal soup," is one of the best-known Thai dishes in this country. When made at home with fresh aromatics and fresh coconut milk, its taste can not be surpassed for sophistication and fragrance.

As is evident from the soup's name, *kha*, or galangal, the aromatic rhizome with a soda-pop taste, is the crucial element in the flavor. Galangal is usually sold frozen at Thai markets. For those who can't find it, an acceptable substitute is fresh ginger, although the distinctive galangal taste will be missing.

I like to infuse the soup twice with the aromatics. The first run achieves a hovering background taste. Then I strain the soup and add more aromatics at the end for a splash of freshness.

¼ cup finely chopped peeled fresh or frozen
    galangal (if unavailable, substitute
    2 tablespoons finely chopped fresh ginger)
¼ cup chopped cilantro roots and/or stems
2 serrano chiles, seeded, stemmed, and
    chopped
½ teaspoon freshly ground white pepper
3 stalks fresh lemongrass (3 inches of the
    lower stalk, tough outer leaves discarded),
    chopped
2 tablespoons chopped garlic
3 tablespoons chopped red onion
4 cups canned unsweetened coconut milk,
    well stirred
2 cups Chicken Stock (page 384) or canned
    broth
8 ounces skinless, boneless chicken breast, cut
    into strips
5 tablespoons fresh lime juice
3 tablespoons Asian fish sauce, such as
    nam pla
2 cayenne or serrano chiles, stemmed, seeded,
    and sliced
5 kaffir lime leaves, if available, shredded
Salt, to taste (optional)
¼ cup fresh cilantro leaves, for garnish
¼ cup red bell pepper strips, for garnish

1. In a food processor, combine the galangal, cilantro roots, chiles, pepper, lemongrass, garlic, and onion and process to a paste, adding a little water to assist blending. Scrape into a small bowl.

2. Combine half of the galangal paste with 3 cups of the coconut milk in a medium-size saucepan and bring to a boil over medium heat. Cook for 10 minutes. Strain through a fine strainer into a large, heavy pot, pressing on the solids with the back of a spoon to extract as much liquid as possible.

3. Return the soup to the heat, add the remaining coconut milk and the stock and bring to a simmer over low heat. Add the remaining galangal paste and the chicken, and simmer until the chicken is cooked, about 7 minutes.

4. Stir in the lime juice, fish sauce, chiles, and kaffir lime leaves. Season with salt, if necessary. Heat for 1 minute. Serve garnished with cilantro leaves and bell pepper strips.
SERVES 6

BALIRAM'S CREAM OF CHICKEN SOUP

Baliram Sangkaran, one of Singapore's Indian cooking stars, oversees the tiffin room at the Raffles Hotel and has recreated many of the dishes from the original Raffles menu. I imagine that this soothing colonial soup, enlivened with lime juice and soy sauce, must have been especially welcomed by the original Raffles clientele—the mild-mannered British clerks eking out a living in their "messes" (shared bachelor flats) in an unfamiliar tropical land.

1 whole large bone-in chicken breast
(about 1½ pounds), well rinsed and
patted dry
4½ cups water
1 small onion
1 carrot, peeled
1 parsnip, peeled and halved
3 star anise points, 4 crushed cardamom
pods, and 3 whole cloves, tied in a
cheesecloth bag
2 tablespoons unsalted butter
1½ cups finely chopped leeks, white
part only
1 large carrot, peeled and diced
1 tablespoon chopped garlic
1 heaping tablespoon all-purpose
flour
1 large baking potato, cooked and
mashed
½ cup half-and-half
1 teaspoon grated lime zest
1 tablespoon fresh lime juice, or more
to taste
1½ teaspoons soy sauce
Salt and freshly ground black pepper,
to taste
¼ cup sliced almonds, toasted (page 389)
for garnish
Fresh cilantro leaves, for garnish

1. Combine the chicken, water, the whole onion and carrot, the parsnip, and the spice bag in a large heavy pot and bring to a boil over medium heat. Skim off the froth,

then reduce the heat to low and simmer, covered, until the chicken is cooked, about 20 minutes.

2. Remove the chicken from the stock. Strain the stock and reserve. When the chicken is cool enough to handle, discard the skin and bones and shred the meat. Set aside.

3. Melt the butter in the cleaned pot over low heat. Add the leeks, diced carrot, and garlic, then cover and cook until the vegetables are soft, about 10 minutes.

4. Add the flour and cook, stirring for 1 minute. Gradually stir in the strained stock and bring to a simmer. Place the mashed potato in a large bowl and whisk in ½ cup of the hot stock. Whisk back into the soup. Stir in the half-and-half and bring to a simmer.

5. Add the lime zest and juice, soy sauce, and salt and pepper to taste. Replace the chicken in the soup and cook until heated through.

6. Ladle the soup into bowls and garnish with almonds and cilantro leaves.

SERVES 4 TO 6

CORIANDER-FLAVORED CHICKEN SOUP

with Rice and Potato Balls

Elaborate garnishes are one of the trademarks of Southeast Asian cooking. This heady, coriander-infused Malaysian broth is garnished with crispy fried rice vermicelli, herbs, fried shallots, and potato balls. The balls, I suspect, are a colonial touch.

I like to prepare steps 1 through 4 a day in advance. I keep all the solids in the stock, then skim the fat off, and strain it before reheating.

1½ tablespoons
*   coriander seeds*
1 teaspoon cumin seeds
1 teaspoon black peppercorns
6 shallots, finely chopped
1½ tablespoons chopped garlic
1 tablespoon chopped fresh ginger
2½ tablespoons peanut oil, plus more for
*   frying the potato balls and the garnishes*
1½ cups chopped onions
10 cups Chicken Stock (page 384) or
*   canned broth*
2 ribs celery, with leaves
2 carrots, peeled
2 teaspoons light soy sauce
4 Chinese dried black mushrooms or
*   dried shiitakes*
Salt, to taste
2 whole bone-in chicken breasts, about
*   1 pound each*
2 large baking potatoes, cooked and
*   mashed*
½ ounce rice vermicelli, broken into pieces
1½ cups cooked long-grain rice
Fried Shallots (page 389), for garnish
3 tablespoons chopped scallions,
*   for garnish*
2 tablespoons fresh cilantro leaves, for
*   garnish*

1. Heat a small skillet over medium-high heat. Add the coriander seeds, cumin seeds, and peppercorns and toast, stirring, until fragrant and several shades darker, about 1 minute. Grind in a spice grinder or coffee grinder until fine.

2. Using a mortar and pestle or a small food processor, pound or process the shallots, garlic, ginger, and ground spices to a paste. Set aside.

3. Heat 2½ tablespoons oil in a large heavy pot over medium heat. Add the onions and cook until lightly browned, about 10 minutes. Add the shallot paste and cook over low heat, stirring until the mixture is fragrant and no longer tastes raw, about 5 minutes. Add the stock, celery, carrots, soy sauce, mushrooms, salt, and chicken and bring to a boil, skimming off the froth that rises to the surface. Cook, partially covered, over low heat, until the chicken is tender and the soup is suffused with the flavor of spices, about 20 minutes.

4. Remove the chicken from the liquid. When cool enough to handle, remove and discard the skin and bones and cut the meat into bite-size pieces. Set aside, keeping it warm.

5. Strain the liquid through a fine strainer into a clean large pot, pressing on the solids to extract as much liquid as possible, and discard the solids (including the mushrooms). Keep the soup warm while preparing the garnishes.

6. To make the potato balls, shape the mashed potatoes into balls the size of a walnut. Pour oil to a depth of 1½ inches into a large, deep skillet. Heat to 360°F over medium heat and fry the potato balls on all sides until golden, about 5 minutes. Drain on paper towels.

7. Reheat the oil to 360°F. Add the rice vermicelli and fry until puffed and crispy, about 15 seconds. Drain on paper towels.

8. To serve, ladle some hot soup into

soup bowls, add some chicken meat, rice, scallions, cilantro, and potato balls and sprinkle with Fried Shallots and crispy noodles. Serve immediately.

SERVES 8

RAFFLES MULLIGATAWNY SOUP

This classic Indian soup is presented as a part of the spectacular tiffin buffet at the fabled Raffles Hotel in Singapore. To come up with the perfect recipe, the team of chefs, led by the estimable Baliram Sangkaran, went through six versions of the soup a day until they finally captured the true splendor of Raffles colonial past. Their mulligatawny, rich with chicken, spices, and rice, is the best I have ever tasted.

Plan to make the soup several hours before serving so you can refrigerate it and skim off the fat. If you plan to make the soup a day ahead, add the rice before reheating. The rice expands and becomes mushy when left in the soup for too long.

4 large cloves garlic, chopped
6 to 7 medium shallots, chopped
2½ teaspoons grated fresh ginger
3 tablespoons vegetable oil, or more as needed
2 medium onions, thinly sliced
¼ teaspoon ground cinnamon
¼ teaspoon ground cloves
¼ teaspoon grated star anise
1 tablespoon best-quality curry powder, preferably homemade (page 390)
¾ teaspoon ground turmeric
2 teaspoons paprika
½ teaspoon pure chile powder
1 teaspoon freshly ground black pepper
3 tablespoons tomato paste
9 cups Chicken Stock (page 384) or canned broth
2½ tablespoons mango chutney
2 tablespoons heavy (or whipping) cream
1½ tablespoons cornstarch, mixed with 2 tablespoons cold water
2 tablespoons fresh lime juice, or more to taste
Salt, to taste
2 cups bite-size pieces cooked chicken breast
1½ cups cooked long-grain rice
Fresh cilantro leaves, for garnish
Fried Shallots (page 389), for garnish (optional)

1. In a food processor, combine the garlic, shallots, and ginger and process to a paste, adding a little oil to assist blending. Set aside.

2. Heat the 3 tablespoons oil in a large heavy pot over medium-low heat. Add the onions and cook until limp, about 5 minutes. Add the garlic paste and continue cooking, stirring frequently, until the mixture no longer tastes raw, about 7 minutes. Add more oil, a teaspoon at a time, if the mixture begins to stick to the bottom of the pot. Add the cinnamon, cloves, star anise, curry powder, turmeric, paprika, chili powder, and black pepper and stir for 1 minute.

3. Stir in the tomato paste and stock. Bring to a simmer and cook over medium-low heat for 10 minutes. Add the mango chutney to the soup and simmer, uncovered, for 10 minutes. Add the cream and the cornstarch mixture and cook until the soup thickens slightly, 2 to 3 minutes. Add lime juice to taste, adjust the seasoning for salt, and remove from the heat. Cool and refrigerate the soup, and skim off the fat after it solidifies.

4. Slowly reheat the soup and add the chicken and rice and cook just to heat through. Serve garnished with cilantro leaves and Fried Shallots, if desired.

SERVES 6 TO 8

TART CHICKEN SOUP
with Glass Noodles, Lemongrass, and Lime

Believe it or not, most Southeast Asian recipes are quite easy to re-create once you learn a thing or two about ingredients and techniques. This soup is the proof. When I first tasted Indonesian, Thai, and Vietnamese dishes, everything about them seemed secret and mysterious. But after only a few trips to Asian markets, one cooking class, and several afternoons with my ethnic cookbooks, I was able to reproduce a tasty, tart soup I once sampled at an Indonesian home.

A small bowl of this deliciously refreshing soup can precede almost any entrée. A larger portion will make a lovely light lunch.

2 ounces glass noodles (bean threads)
8 cups Chicken Stock (page 384) or canned broth
2 stalks fresh lemongrass (3 inches of the lower stalk, tough outer leaves discarded), chopped
3 cloves garlic, chopped
1 tablespoon chopped fresh ginger
1 small fresh hot chile, green or red, stemmed, seeded, and chopped
1 tablespoon chopped cilantro stems
3 tablespoons unsalted butter
Grated zest of 1 lime
2½ tablespoons fresh lime juice
1½ teaspoons soy sauce
Pinch of sugar, or more to taste
8 ounces firm tofu (preferably silken), cut into ½-inch cubes
Salt and freshly ground white pepper, to taste
2 cups shredded cooked chicken breast
¼ cup chopped scallions
¾ cup bean sprouts
3 tablespoons shredded fresh mint leaves, plus additional for garnish

1. Soak the glass noodles in hot water to cover for 10 minutes. Drain and cut into 2-inch lengths. In a medium-size saucepan bring 1½ cups of stock to a simmer. Add the noodles and cook over low heat until most of the liquid has been absorbed, about 5 minutes.

Set the noodles aside. (The noodles can be prepared up to a day ahead.)

2. Using a mortar and pestle or a small food processor, pound or process the lemongrass, garlic, ginger, chile, and cilantro stems to a paste.

3. Melt the butter in a large heavy pot over low heat. Add the lemongrass paste and stir for 2 minutes.

4. Add the remaining stock, bring to a simmer, and cook for 5 minutes. Strain through a fine strainer into a clean pot and return to the heat. Add the lime zest, lime juice, soy sauce, sugar, tofu, and salt and pepper to taste. Heat for 1 minute.

5. To serve, place some noodles, chicken, scallions, bean sprouts, and mint into soup bowls and ladle some liquid and tofu over them.

SERVES 4 TO 6

COCONUT CREAM OF PUMPKIN SOUP

Pumpkin soup is a favorite both in America and in Thailand. The American version is usually creamy and quite bland, while Thais make it with pumpkin cubes floating in a scented, spicy coconut broth. Here I have combined the two ideas. The nutty richness of coconut milk blends perfectly with the velvety texture of pumpkin, while chiles, cilantro, soy sauce, and lemon juice provide the needed jolt to bring the silky purée to life. I like to pass small colorful bowls of garnishes—minced red onion, finely diced fresh pineapple and red bell pepper, cilantro leaves, chopped roasted peanuts, or toasted shredded coconut—for the guests to help themselves.

2½ pounds fresh pumpkin, butternut squash, or calabaza, peeled and cut into 2-inch cubes

4½ cups Chicken Stock (page 384) or canned broth

3 tablespoons unsalted butter

1 cup finely chopped leeks, white part only

3 large cloves garlic, crushed through a press

1 teaspoon best-quality curry powder

2 teaspoons ground ginger

1½ teaspoons ground coriander

2 teaspoons paprika

3½ cups canned unsweetened coconut milk, well stirred

2 tablespoons soy sauce, or more to taste

½ cup chopped fresh cilantro leaves, plus additional for garnish

2 teaspoons minced garlic

2 small fresh hot red chiles, stemmed, seeded, and chopped

3 tablespoons fresh lemon juice

Salt, to taste

Garnishes suggested in headnote above

1. Combine the pumpkin and the broth in a large heavy pot and bring to a boil over medium heat. Cook, covered, until the pumpkin is tender, about 15 minutes. Purée the pumpkin and the liquid, in batches, in a blender or food processor until smooth. Set aside.

2. Melt the butter in the cleaned pot over medium heat. Add the leeks and cook until soft, about 7 minutes. Reduce the heat to low and stir in the crushed garlic, curry powder, ginger, coriander, and paprika. Cook, stirring, over low heat until fragrant, about 2 minutes. Add the coconut milk, bring to a boil, and simmer for 5 minutes. Stir in the puréed pumpkin and cook over low heat for 5 more minutes. Stir in the soy sauce.

3. Using a mortar and pestle or small food processor, pound or process the cilantro, minced garlic, and chiles with the lemon juice to a paste. Stir the mixture into the soup, adjust the salt, and cook for 1 minute. (If making the soup ahead of time, stir in this mixture right before serving.)

4. Ladle the soup into bowls and sprinkle with the suggested garnishes.

SERVES 6

P E P P E R E D
T A M A R I N D
B R O T H

Asians believe there is nothing like a tart, spicy beginning to a meal to tease the appetite, tantalize the palate, and aid digestion. This spiky tamarind broth, called *rassam* (which simply means "broth") is of South Indian provenance. The recipe was given to me by a dignified elderly Tamil man we encountered on an afternoon stroll through the Indian quarter of the island of Penang. This is a soup that is supposed to be drunk rather than eaten with a spoon, so offer small cups of this delicious brew to your guests before proceeding to dinner.

2½ tablespoons tamarind pulp, preferably from Thailand
5 cups Chicken Stock (page 384) or canned broth
2 teaspoons coriander seeds
2 teaspoons cumin seeds
2 tablespoons unsalted butter
7 shallots, minced
3 cloves garlic, crushed through a press
1 tablespoon grated fresh ginger
1½ teaspoons freshly ground black pepper
¼ teaspoon ground fenugreek
Salt, to taste
¾ teaspoon sugar, or to taste
1 teaspoon vegetable oil
1 to 2 dried red chiles (2 to 3 inches long), preferably Asian, seeded and cut into ½-inch pieces
¾ teaspoon mustard seeds
Fresh cilantro leaves, for garnish

1. Soak the tamarind pulp in ¾ cup boiling stock off the heat for 15 minutes. Stir and mash it with a fork to help it dissolve. Strain through a fine strainer into a bowl, pressing on the solids with the back of a wooden spoon to extract all the liquid. Set aside.

2. Toast the coriander and cumin seeds in a small skillet over medium heat for about 2 minutes. Grind in a spice grinder or coffee grinder to a somewhat coarse grind.

3. Melt the butter in a medium-size saucepan over medium heat. Add the shallots and cook until translucent, about 3 minutes. Add the garlic and ginger and cook for 2 minutes. Add the ground coriander and cumin, black pepper, and fenugreek and stir for 1 minute. Add the tamarind liquid and the remaining stock and bring to a simmer. Simmer for 5 to 7 minutes. Remove from the heat and season to taste with salt and sugar.

4. Heat the oil in a small skillet over medium heat. Add the chiles and mustard seeds and cook, covered, until the mustard seeds pop, about 2 minutes. Stir into the soup and simmer for 2 more minutes. Remove from the heat and let stand for 10 minutes. Serve in small cups, garnished with cilantro.

SERVES 4 TO 6

CURRIED ROAST VEGETABLE SOUP

A thick and creamy autumnal soup, loosely inspired by Indian flavors but one that can happily precede a Mediterranean meal. Try to use tender Japanese eggplants which need no salting in the preparation, for they are sweet, not bitter. For an Asian touch, serve this soup accompanied by pappadums, the crisp Indian wafers. Otherwise, serve it with grilled crusty country bread, brushed with good olive oil and rubbed with garlic. Garnish the soup with fresh herbs of your choice. Flatleaf parsley, cilantro, basil, or mint, or a combination, all provide a flourish of freshness.

The soup tends to thicken as it stands, so if you are making it ahead, you might want to add some stock when reheating.

1½ pounds Chinese or Japanese eggplants, stemmed, peeled, halved lengthwise, and cut into 3-inch pieces
4 medium firm, ripe tomatoes, quartered
2 medium red bell peppers, stemmed, seeded, and halved
1 large green bell pepper, stemmed, seeded, and halved
4½ to 5 tablespoons light olive oil (do not use virgin or extra-virgin)
2 tablespoons unsalted butter
2 medium onions, sliced thin
4 cloves garlic sliced thin
2 fresh mild green chiles, such as Anaheim, seeded and finely chopped
1½ tablespoons minced fresh ginger
1½ teaspoons best-quality curry powder
¾ teaspoon pure chile powder
1 teaspoon ground cumin
1 teaspoon ground coriander
¼ teaspoon ground fenugreek
4 cups Chicken Stock (page 384) or canned broth
Salt and freshly ground black pepper, to taste
¾ cup heavy (or whipping) cream
¼ cup chopped fresh herbs, for garnish

1. Preheat the oven to 450°F.

2. Arrange the eggplants, tomatoes, and peppers on a baking sheet (use 2 sheets, if necessary) and brush with 1½ tablespoons of the oil. Bake until the vegetables are soft and lightly browned, about 25 minutes, brushing the eggplant with additional oil if it seems dry. Wrap the roasted bell peppers in a plastic bag and cover with a towel.

3. Melt the butter in the remaining 3 tablespoons oil in a large heavy pot over medium-low heat. Add the onions, garlic, chiles, and ginger and cook, stirring, until the onion is softened, about 7 minutes. Add the curry powder, chile powder, cumin, coriander, and fenugreek and cook, stirring, for 2 more minutes.

4. Stir the roasted tomatoes and eggplants into the onion mixture and cook for 5 minutes. Add the stock and bring to a boil. Season with salt and pepper. Reduce the heat to low and simmer, uncovered, for 10 minutes.

5. Peel the roasted peppers and cut into thin strips.

6. Purée half of the soup in a food processor and return to the pot. Add the cream and bring to a simmer. Stir in the pepper strips and simmer for 5 more minutes. Serve garnished with fresh herbs.

SERVES 6

D O W N - U N D E R
S P I N A C H   A N D
C O C O N U T   S O U P

The newsagent down the street from where I lived in Australia carried a large selection of cookbooks, including a wonderful illustrated series published by Australian *Women's Weekly*. Mass market publications like this really reveal the culinary tastes of a country, and I was startled to discover that the Australian palate is in many ways more sophisticated than ours, and certainly more attuned to foreign influences. A further surprise awaited me at the neighborhood "milk bar," an Australian corner grocery store, which carried several brands of coconut milk, instant Thai soups, jars of satay peanut sauce, and curry powders for every occasion. All this was cheek by jowl with marinara sauces and jars of hummus.

This soup, inspired by the *Women's*

Weekly series, was one of the first Australian "East/West" recipes I made—just a basic cream of spinach soup, but with coconut milk replacing the cream. I like the smooth, creamy texture of this soup, but if you want a bit of excitement, garnish it with finely diced cooked or raw vegetables or with croutons or papadums.

> 3½ tablespoons unsalted butter
> 1 tablespoon chopped garlic
> 1½ cups chopped leeks, white part only
> 1½ pounds fresh spinach, trimmed, rinsed, and dried
> 4½ cups Chicken Stock (page 384) or canned broth
> 1 medium all-purpose potato, cooked, peeled, and diced
> 1¼ cups canned unsweetened coconut milk, well stirred
> ¾ teaspoon ground coriander
> ½ teaspoon paprika
> ¼ to ½ teaspoon ground cayenne pepper
> 2 teaspoons fresh lemon juice, or more to taste

1. Melt 2 tablespoons of the butter in a large heavy pot over medium-low heat. Add the garlic and leeks and cook, covered, for 10 minutes, stirring from time to time. Add the spinach and stir for 3 minutes. Stir in the stock, add the potato, and simmer the soup for about 5 minutes.

2. Transfer the soup to a food processor and process briefly, in batches if necessary. Pour the soup back into the pan, add the coconut milk, and bring to a simmer.

3. Melt the remaining 1½ tablespoons of butter in a small skillet over low heat. Add the coriander, paprika, and cayenne and stir for 30 seconds. Stir in the lemon juice.

4. Ladle the soup into bowls and swirl a small spoonful of the spice-lemon butter into each bowl.

SERVES 6

NAPA CABBAGE AND PEANUT SOUP

Peanut lovers will be pleased with this soup, which is mild and sweet from the peanuts and pungent from spices, lemon, and soy sauce. It's certainly unusual, but also disarmingly homey.

2 tablespoons peanut oil
1 cup chopped onion
1 large clove garlic, minced
2 teaspoons grated fresh ginger
1½ teaspoons ground turmeric
1½ teaspoons best-quality curry powder
½ teaspoon ground cayenne pepper, or more to taste
1 teaspoon ground coriander
6½ cups Chicken Stock (page 384) or canned broth
3 medium all-purpose potatoes, peeled and cut into small cubes
1 large sweet potato, peeled and cut into small cubes
1 cup smooth unsalted, unsweetened peanut butter
3 tablespoons fresh lemon juice
2½ tablespoons soy sauce
2 cups shredded napa cabbage
½ cup heavy (or whipping) cream or canned unsweetened coconut milk, well stirred
Sugar, to taste (optional)
Chopped roasted peanuts, for garnish
Julienned red bell pepper, for garnish
Fresh cilantro leaves and snipped fresh chives, for garnish

1. Heat the oil in a large heavy pot over medium-low heat. Add the onion, garlic, and ginger and cook until the onion is translucent, about 5 minutes. Add the turmeric, curry powder, cayenne, and coriander and cook, stirring often, for another 2 minutes.

2. Stir in the stock and bring to a boil. Add the potatoes and sweet potato and simmer over low heat until almost cooked, about 10 minutes.

3. Place the peanut butter in a bowl and whisk in about 1 cup of the hot stock from the soup. Add the lemon juice and soy sauce and stir well. Whisk the mixture back into the soup and simmer for 5 minutes.

4. Stir in the cabbage and cook until tender but not overcooked, about another 3 minutes.

5. Add the cream and cook until heated through. Adjust the seasoning, adding sugar, if desired. Ladle the soup into bowls and garnish with peanuts, red pepper julienne, cilantro, and chives.

SERVES 6

MUSHROOM AND STAR ANISE CONSOMME

with Mushroom Dumplings and Prosciutto

The idea for this suave soup came from a kitchen cleanup. I was leaving for the summer, and the half-empty bags of dried mushrooms, a few forsaken fresh shiitakes, leftover chicken and prosciutto, and a dozen unused wonton skins in the freezer had to go. In half an hour they were transformed into an intensely flavored mushroom broth with a sweet suggestion of star anise, a few plump dumplings filled with the chicken and mushrooms used in the broth, shreds of prosciutto (which suggests Chinese ham), and a splash of sherry to bind the flavors. The inspiration was furnished by Barbara Tropp's *The Modern Art of Chinese Cooking*, a treasured tome that at the time followed me wherever I went.

The recipe looks long, but is actually quick and simple to put together.

½ ounce dried porcini mushrooms

10 dried shiitake mushrooms

4 cups Chicken Stock (page 384) or
*   canned broth*

2 cups water

1 whole star anise, broken up, and
*   8 coriander seeds, lightly crushed,*
*   tied in a cheesecloth bag*

3 ounces fresh shiitake mushrooms, stems
*   discarded*

1 tablespoon peanut or vegetable oil

1½ teaspoons minced fresh ginger

1½ teaspoons minced garlic

½ cup finely chopped onion

¼ cup minced cooked chicken breast, plus
*   ¼ cup diced for garnish*

2 tablespoons thinly sliced scallion greens,
*   plus more for garnish*

Salt and freshly ground black pepper,
*   to taste*

1½ tablespoons soy sauce

½ teaspoon Oriental sesame oil

2 large egg whites, lightly beaten

16 round wonton skins

2 tablespoons dry sherry

½ teaspoon rice vinegar

2 tablespoons diced prosciutto,
*   for garnish*

1. Rinse the dried porcinis and shiitakes under cold running water and soak in 1 cup cold stock until softened, about 1 hour. The shiitakes might take less time than the porcinis.

2. Remove the mushrooms from the soaking liquid and strain the liquid through a coffee filter into a large heavy pot. Add the mushrooms, remaining 3 cups stock, water, and the cheesecloth bag. Bring to a boil and simmer until the mushrooms are tender, about 20 minutes. With a slotted spoon, remove the mushrooms and gently squeeze the excess liquid from the mushrooms back into the pot. Set the pot aside, off the heat.

3. Slice half of the mushrooms thin and reserve. Finely mince the other half.

4. Slice half of the fresh shiitakes thin and reserve. Finely mince the other half and add to the minced dried mushrooms.

5. Make the dumpling filling: Heat half of the peanut oil in a small skillet. Add half the ginger, half the garlic, and half the onion and stir for 30 seconds. Add the finely minced dried and fresh mushrooms and cook, stirring, for 3 minutes. Transfer to a bowl and let cool slightly. Add the minced chicken, scallions, 1 teaspoon of the soy sauce, the sesame oil, salt and pepper to taste, and half of the egg whites.

6. Place a wonton skin on your work surface. Place 1 teaspoon of the filling on the lower half. Brush the edges with some of the remaining egg white and fold over to form a semicircle. Pleat the edges toward the center, if you wish. Repeat with the rest of the skins. Place the filled dumplings on a plate and cover with a damp cloth until ready to cook.

7. Heat the remaining peanut oil in a small skillet over medium-high heat. Add the remaining ginger, garlic, and onion and stir for 30 seconds. Add the sliced dried and fresh mushrooms and cook, stirring, for 3 minutes.

8. Bring the soup to a simmer and stir in the seasoned mushroom mixture. Add the remaining soy sauce, the sherry, and the vinegar to the soup.

9. Bring a medium-size pot of water to a simmer for boiling the dumplings. Boil the dumplings until they float to the surface, about 1 minute. Remove with a wire-mesh skimmer or a large slotted spoon, gently shaking off the excess water, and divide among 4 serving bowls. Ladle the soup over the dumplings and garnish each portion with diced chicken, scallions, and prosciutto.

SERVES 4

CHILLED AVOCADO-LIME SOUP

Sometimes I like this soup simple and silky, on other occasions I serve it studded with colorful diced vegetables, such as ripe tomatoes, cucumbers, red onion, bell peppers, or radishes. Its lovely, light green smoothness invites all kinds of inventive garnishes.

3 medium-large avocados, preferably Hass, pitted, peeled and, coarsely chopped
3½ tablespoons fresh lime juice
¾ cup low-fat plain yogurt
3½ cups canned low-salt chicken broth
2 teaspoons Ginger Juice (page 390)
2 cloves garlic, crushed through a press
2 tablespoons chopped fresh mint
1 small fresh hot green chile, stemmed, seeded, and chopped
1½ teaspoons grated lime zest
Fresh mint leaves, for garnish
Julienned red bell pepper, for garnish
1 tablespoon finely chopped red onion, for garnish

1. In a blender or food processor, combine the avocado, lime juice, yogurt, broth, ginger juice, garlic, mint, chile, and lime zest. You might have to do it in two batches. Transfer the purée to a serving bowl and chill until cold, about 1 hour.

2. Ladle the soup into bowls and serve, garnished with mint leaves, bell pepper julienne, chopped red onion, or any other garnish suggested in the headnote.

SERVES 4 TO 6

ROAST PEPPER AND TOMATO SOUP

with Chiles and Cilantro

In this soup, roasting the peppers and tomatoes produces a vividly concentrated flavor, which is then suffused by the zest of chiles, cilantro, ginger, and a touch of orange. This soup is also delicious served chilled.

2 large red bell peppers, stemmed, seeded, and cut into chunks

10 medium ripe, meaty plum tomatoes, cored and halved

Salt, to taste

3 tablespoons olive oil

1 cup chopped onion

3 cloves garlic, crushed through a press

1 tablespoon grated fresh ginger

2 tablespoons finely minced cilantro stems

3 cups Chicken Stock (page 384) or canned broth, or more as needed

½ cup dry white wine

½ cup fresh orange juice

¼ cup heavy (or whipping) cream

Freshly ground black pepper, to taste

1½ tablespoons finely chopped fresh cilantro leaves, for garnish

1 teaspoon finely grated orange zest, for garnish

1. Preheat the oven to 350°F.

2. Place the peppers and tomatoes in a roasting pan. Sprinkle with salt and drizzle with 1 tablespoon of the oil. Roast, turning once, until the vegetables are soft but not charred, about 35 minutes.

3. Heat the remaining 2 tablespoons oil in a large heavy pot over medium-low heat. Add the onion and cook until softened, about 5 minutes. Add the garlic, ginger, and cilantro stems and cook, stirring, for 2 minutes. Add the peppers and tomatoes, stock, wine, and orange juice and bring to a simmer. Cover and simmer for 10 minutes.

4. Let the soup cool a little and purée in a food processor.

5. Return the soup to the saucepan and add the cream. If the soup seems too thick,

add more stock to taste. Season with salt and pepper and bring to a simmer.

6. In a small bowl, mix together the chopped cilantro leaves and orange zest. Ladle the soup into bowls and garnish with the cilantro–orange zest mixture.

SERVES 4

CUCUMBER AND MANGO BISQUE

This easy, delicious cucumber and mango purée, with its accent of basil, is a great way to begin an *al fresco* luncheon. Choose ripe, but firm mangoes, and very firm fresh cucumbers, otherwise you might end up with a watery taste. Follow this soup with a light salad, such as Vietnamese Minted Lemon Beef Salad (see Index).

1 cup buttermilk

1 cup canned low-salt chicken broth

⅓ cup low-fat plain yogurt

2 cups peeled, seeded, and chopped firm cucumbers

2 cups chopped fresh mango pulp

¼ cup chopped fresh basil leaves

1 teaspoon chopped garlic

1 serrano chile, stemmed, seeded, and chopped

2 tablespoons fresh lemon juice

1 teaspoon rice vinegar

Salt, to taste

Diced mango, for garnish

Fresh basil leaves, for garnish

1. Working in batches if necessary, purée all the ingredients except the salt and garnishes in a blender. Do not over-purée.

2. Transfer to a bowl, add salt to taste, and chill for at least 1 hour. Serve garnished with diced mangoes and basil leaves.

SERVES 4

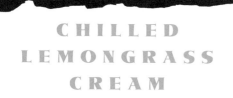

CHILLED LEMONGRASS CREAM

with Pineapple and Kiwi

This exotic soup, perfumed with spices and aromatics, is adapted from a recipe by Ken Oringer, executive chef at the restaurant Silks in San Francisco's Mandarin Oriental Hotel. He suggests serving it in decorative glass bowls, as an intermezzo between courses, or as dessert. I have also served it as an opening to a summer meal. The final amount of sugar depends on the context in which you will be serving the soup, but even as a dessert, it shouldn't be too sweet.

2 cups canned evaporated milk (not sweetened condensed milk)

1 cup half-and-half

1 cup milk

¼ cup finely sliced fresh lemongrass (3 inches of the lower stalk, tough outer leaves discarded)

1 slice fresh ginger, smashed

1 teaspoon crushed white peppercorns

9 cardamom pods, preferably unbleached (green), crushed

1 tablespoon fennel seeds, lightly crushed

1½ teaspoons to 1½ tablespoons sugar, to taste

¾ cup finely diced fresh pineapple, for garnish

¾ cup finely diced firm, ripe kiwi, for garnish

1. Combine the evaporated milk, half-and-half, and milk in a medium-size nonreactive saucepan and bring to a simmer over low heat. Add the lemongrass, ginger, peppercorns, cardamom pods, fennel seeds, and sugar to taste, and simmer for 1 minute.

2. Transfer the soup to a bowl and place a layer of plastic wrap on the surface of the soup to prevent a skin from forming. Refrigerate the soup for 6 hours or overnight.

3. Strain the soup and discard the aromatics. Ladle the soup into small decorative bowls and add 1½ tablespoons each of diced pineapple and kiwi to each portion.

SERVES 8

TRUE THAI TASTES

⊙

Thailand is the only nation in Southeast Asia that escaped colonization; its name means "land of the free." Originally from the Yunnan province of southern China, the Thai people began migrating 2,000 years ago into present-day northern Thailand, Burma, and Laos. The great Khmer kingdom, with its glorious capital of Angkor Wat, dominated the region at the time, but the Thais established their own capitals, first at Sukhothai and then at Ayutthaya in the middle of the fourteenth century.

the mysterious Siam, the heart of the unknown Orient.

In the age of colonization (the eighteenth century), Thailand's greatest rival came not from Europe but from the kingdom of Burma, across its western border. The clash of the two armies, both led by swaying ranks of battle-ready elephants decked out in glittering costumes, are famous in Thai legend.

Ayutthaya was at the height of its richness and power when the first European ships appeared in Southeast Asia, spearheaded by the Portuguese, who arrived in 1511. At first the Thais were content to pit the rival powers against each other to protect their interests, but gradually, as plots were hatched against them from every direction, they resolved to keep all Westerners out of their country, a policy that lasted until the middle of the nineteenth century and was instrumental in preserving local tastes and traditions. Thailand was

Twice the Burmese army took control of Ayutthaya, and during the second occupation, the city was razed. The Thais regrouped and formed a new capital, further south again, in Bangkok (the City of Angels), on the Chao Phraya river. From this capital, modern Thailand was born, gradually opening up to outside trade and foreign interests and finally establishing a constitutional monarchy in 1932.

Many influences have contributed to the evolution of Thai cuisine, but its roots can be traced back to China. When the Thai tribes descended from the slopes of southern Yunnan, they brought with them the penchant for spicy seasoning that defines the cooking of China's southernmost province. And sustained contact with the Chinese brought many staple foods without which Thai cuisine would be unimaginable. These include

noodles of many kinds, dumplings, soy sauce, oyster sauce, and numerous soybean by-products. They also introduced the important techniques of stir frying and deep frying in a wok. But the most important inheritance from the Chinese was the philosophy of blending the "five flavors": salty, sweet, sour, bitter, and hot. This melding and juxtaposing of tastes became the cornerstone of true Thai tastes—Chinese in origin, Thai in execution, and always performed with inimitable brilliance and daring originality.

India also contributed notably to the shaping of Thai cuisine, although its most significant contribution was cultural—Theravada Buddhism and the epic *Ramayana*. In their many waves of migration, Indians brought a spice chest of aromatic seasonings, such as cumin, coriander, and cardamom, and introduced their adopted country to curries. The Thais took to curry with the same originality that characterized all their borrowing of tastes and techniques.

To round out the picture, the Malays, just to the south, contributed the penchant for luscious hot and sweet seasonings and the love of coconut and *satay*. The cuisine of southern Thailand is, in fact, closely related to the cooking of Penang Island, of the northwest coast of Malaysia.

Many of those familiar with only the American restaurant incarnation of Thai food might think of it as simply perfumy, just sweet, or plain hot. But at its best, Thai cooking is one of the most multidimensional and exciting of the world's cuisines. The flavors are so bold, radiant, and alluring they keep your taste buds on full alert—perplexed, bewildered, sometimes challenged or overwhelmed, but always charmed and seduced by turns.

If the effort of most European and even Asian cuisines is directed at melding and homogenizing diverse flavors, Thai cuisine is characterized by the drama of heterogeneity. There is always a certain crispness and transparency to the food; no sauce is ever enough to mask other flavors; no single element is allowed to predominate. Chinese stir-fries are often coated with a cornstarch-thickened, soy-based sauce. Thai stir-fries, on the other hand, are a whole range of complex flavorings beautifully

. . . true Thai tastes—Chinese in origin, Thai in execution, and always performed with inimitable brilliance and daring originality.

subtle whole. In most Thai curries, the spice base is mellowed by the creamy sweetness of coconut milk only to be disrupted at the very last minute by crunchy, bitter tiny eggplants, the powerfully fragrant boost of the

sweet with sour, crispy with soft. All these counterpoints may appear in one dish, yet always with a sense of balance. As you bite into such dishes, you'll experience revolutions of flavor with each mouthful.

THE SEASONINGS

One of the most unmistakable Thai tastes is that of the intensely perfumed kaffir lime, which looks like a knobby common lime. Its grated zest is mixed with other aromatics as a base for curry, its juice used to perfume soups and dips, and its bright green leaves (which are bought separately) are finely shredded and tossed into

layered, one on top of the other. And while Indian curries are a thick paste of spices and aromatics, Thai curries are herby, light, and fragrant. In an Indian or Malay curry, all the ingredients are painstakingly blended and tamed to produce a

kaffir lime and holy basil, and the saltiness of fish sauce.

The same innovative diversity characterizes a Thai *yam* (salad). It may pair something hot with something cold, fiery with bland, devilishly pungent with delicately aromatic, finished dishes, adding a heady, mysterious scent. Other unique flavorings include galangal, a cousin of ginger with a tingling aftertaste of bubblegum, which is used in curries and soups, and its cousin, lesser galangal, similar in taste to fresh turmeric root and favored in fish curries.

One of the most crucial ingredients in Thai cooking is the amber *nam pla* (*nam* means "water," *pla* "fish")—fish sauce made from small, anchovylike fish that are fermented in enormous stone jars, from which the liquid is then filtered. This is the salt of Thailand, and it is added to virtually every dish to heighten the flavor.

Another salty and

pungent element is *kapi*, fermented shrimp paste. On its own, it smells like nothing else on earth (although Thais actually love its smell and the taste, don't count on your own pleasure), but when roasted and blended with other flavors, it gives Thai dishes that unmistakable piquancy so essential to counterbalance the sweet richness of coconut milk and palm sugar.

The tang that is so important to Thai food

to produce a similar sensation.

The notorious heat of Thai food comes from fresh or dried chiles. In fact, refined royal Thai cuisine is not supposed to be blisteringly hot, but a bowl of thinly sliced hot red or green chiles lets the diner control the degree of fire. Chiles,

The royal Thai table is always adorned with orchids, set with exquisite porcelain or ceramics, and catered by servants in silk.

comes from fresh lime juice or tamarind pulp. A blend of tamarind and palm sugar is often used to achieve sweet-and-sour effects, a combination much more noble and authentic than the mix of vinegar and sugar often used in Thai restaurants

synonymous as they are with Thai cuisine, were not introduced to Thailand until the sixteenth century by Portuguese spice traders. Before that peppercorns, called *prig Thai* (Thai pepper), were used for heat. The Thais prefer white peppercorns, and with their love of heady fresh flavors, they also adore young green peppercorns, which are lightly crushed and added to dishes at the last minute.

Many Thai dishes, from curries to soups to stir-fries, begin with a mixture of cilantro roots, hot red or green chiles, lemongrass, garlic, and galangal. Here is the nucleus of Thai taste. These are crushed and pounded in large granite mortars to release their aromatic properties. To this mixture, depending on the dish, one might add spices or shrimp paste, ground white peppercorns, coriander, or cumin. If the aromatic mixture is the initial flavoring for cooked dishes, the next layering of flavors comes from the fish sauce, fresh lime juice, comfortingly sweet palm sugar, and herbs—added toward the end of cooking. Garnishes are also crucial to Thai cuisine, since they are relied on to contribute texture and taste. The garnishes are almost endless—a dish might be topped with crunchy roasted peanuts; pungent, crisp deep-fried garlic, shallots, red onions, and herbs; shreds of fresh ginger or turmeric root, toasted coconut, or red bell pepper; or cream of coconut.

Thai cuisine rarely relies on slow cooking. The ingredients for a dish might take a while to pound, chop, or blend, but the actual cooking time rarely exceeds ten minutes. Soups and curries are simmered briskly and quickly infused with aromatics at the end, salads are assembled just before serving, and noodles are fried in a matter of minutes. The favorite

cooking methods are deep frying, steaming, and stir frying, which is traditionally done in beautiful brass woks. Grilling is also incredibly popular, and the aroma of burning charcoal fills the streets as the vendors produce satays of lime- and coriander-scented chicken and sweet and spicy grilled pork strips.

FOOD FOR COURT AND COUNTRY FOLK

As with other cuisines around the world, Thai has two faces—that of the nobility, refined in the Sukhothai and Ayutthaya courts, and that of the peasants, farmers, and laborers. Royal Thai cuisine, sophisticated and subtle, like Thai culture itself, is characterized by elaborate, painstakingly prepared dishes and artistry in presentation: dumplings dyed blue using natural food coloring and formed into flowers or birds; stuffed peppers encased in a lacy egg net; a salad made into a pyramid of carved blossoms. The royal Thai table is always adorned with orchids, set with exquisite porcelain or ceramics, and catered by servants in silk. All in all, the everyday Thai aesthetic rivals that of the Japanese.

Up-country cooking is surely less refined, but it is still interesting and imaginative. A nurturing bowl of *khao tom*, a warming rice soup, often begins the day, and an afternoon meal might be a fiery, pungent dip served with raw vegetables, a curry with morsels of chicken, or a seafood or noodle dish. Workers might enjoy a quick snack bought at a stall— perhaps some shredded, chile-laden green papaya with rice, satays with peanut sauce, or succulent grilled marinated chicken.

AT TABLE

A complete Thai meal follows the same principle of carefully orchestrated heterogeneity that stands as the basis of the cuisine. Each bite you take contributes its own special effect. A full formal meal has several mandatory components: small dishes, a curry, a soup, a dip, a salad, and a stir-fried, grilled, or steamed dish, followed by dessert. The stir-fry might be chicken or seafood enlivened with crispy garlic or purple basil, or perhaps pork strips and colorful vegeta-

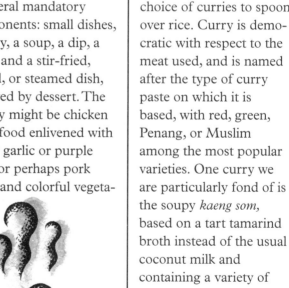

bles coated with a vibrant chile-lemongrass sauce. One might opt for grilled or fried whole fish or spiced slices of meat. On the lighter side, there might be a steamed dish such as *har mok pla*, a delicate fish pudding scented with coconut milk and kaffir lime, a whole steamed fish with a spirited sauce of chiles and lime, or steamed squid stuffed with spicy ground pork.

There is a large choice of curries to spoon over rice. Curry is democratic with respect to the meat used, and is named after the type of curry paste on which it is based, with red, green, Penang, or Muslim among the most popular varieties. One curry we are particularly fond of is the soupy *kaeng som*, based on a tart tamarind broth instead of the usual coconut milk and containing a variety of vegetables and grilled seafood.

Soup is often served in the middle, or even at the end, of the meal to clear the palate. The best-known masterpieces of the

Thai soup kitchen are *tom yum kung*, the hot-and-sour shrimp soup, and *tom kha gai*, a cakes, stuffed vegetables, or *satays* served with spicy dipping sauces. To temper the spiciness and are served together. It's the same at home, though here the food is served casually and at room temperature, with the various dishes eaten in no particular order. But the heart of the meal is always a large bowl of fragrant jasmine rice. As the Thais say, a meal without rice leaves the stomach empty. Platters of luscious tropical fruit are the most common way to conclude the meal. For a more formal occasion, slices of ripe mango might be accompanied by a bowl of sweet sticky rice sprinkled with sesame seeds, or a coconut custard would be baked and presented in a small pumpkin.

. . . the heart of the meal is always a large bowl of jasmine rice. As the Thais say, a meal without rice leaves the stomach empty.

creamy, tart concoction of coconut milk, chicken, and galangal. Thai dips can be a meal in themselves. They are usually based on the pounded mixture of chiles and smoky shrimp paste, with other ingredients added at whim, and surrounded by meats, fried fish, omelet strips, and raw and deep-fried vegetables.

Interspersed with larger dishes are toothsome snacks: fritters, dumplings, fish balance the rich sweetness of coconut curries, a Thai meal often includes a *yam*, an artfully composed herbed salad dressed with a tangy mixture of fish sauce, lime juice, and palm sugar.

Even at the poshest restaurants, all the dishes

There's no better way to capture some of the mysterious sense of charm and well-being that strikes one in Thailand than by cooking a Thai meal in your home. In this way you will experience *sanuk*, the Thai word for their own exotic pleasures. An almost untranslatable term, it comes as close as any other to what the French call *joie de vivre*.

Tuna Poke Salad with Nashi Pear

Thai Seafood and Rice Noodle Salad

Shrimp and Pineapple Salad with
Cashews in Pineapple Boats

Chile Squid Salad with Chinese Noodles

Spice Market Pomelo Salad with
Grilled Shrimp and Crispy Shallots

Grilled Chicken and Shrimp Salad with
Tamarind-Honey Dressing

Grilled Chicken Salad

Thai Roast Pork Salad with Peanuts
and Herbs

Grilled Beef Salad

Vietnamese Minted Lemon Beef Salad

Potato Salad with Japanese Dressing

Irene's Potato Salad with Indian Spices

Pasta Salad with Peanut-Lime Vinaigrette

Herbed Eggplant Salad with
Pickled Garlic

Heirloom Tomato Salad with
Miso Vinaigrette and Basil Oil

Chick-pea, Tomato, and Cilantro Salad
with Toasted Cumin Vinaigrette

Raita

Papaya Salad with Palm Sugar Dressing

Green Papaya Slaw

Gingered Beet Slaw with
Citrus Vinaigrette

Carol Selvarajah's Vegetable Salad
with Kiwi and Pickled Ginger

SALADS

Healthful, imaginative, vibrant with the colors and flavors of the Pacific, the salads in this book continue to seduce me with their wonderful orchestration of tastes and textures. Sweet, succulent seafood, spiced grilled rare beef, a variety of Asian noodles, garden-fresh vegetables, a cornucopia of nuts, fragrant herbs—each drizzled with a light dressing that accentuates rather than masks the flavor of the food. What a way to showcase unforgettable tastes!

Salads are allocated diverse roles in the theater of an Oriental meal. Sometimes they appear as a part of a chorus of dishes, at other times they act as palate refreshers between courses, or are served strictly as accompaniment to help extinguish the fire of the spices or to punctuate the rich sweetness of coconut curries. A bowl of crunchy green mango, papaya, or other diced fruit tossed with a tamarind dressing is eaten to assuage an afternoon hunger. Whatever else the Southeast Asian salad might be, it must appeal to all the senses. Red peppers mingle with purplish onion, golden peanuts, and jade-colored herbs to produce beautiful still lifes good enough to eat.

Oriental salads have become the core of my summer menus. When the heat or the pressure of life make cooking a serious meal out of the question, I bring together various combinations of vegetables, meats, and noodles with astonishing effortlessness and speed. Yesterday's barbecued steak is cut into thin slices, tossed with crunchy vegetables, aromatic herbs, and a piquant lime dressing; inexpensive squid combines with Oriental noodles and an aromatic sauce; ordinary potato salad puts on a glamorous

Asian guise when drizzled with a soy and ginger-laced dressing; juicy grilled chicken breast is set atop fresh greens and sparkled with jade kiwi vinaigrette.

TRUE THAI TASTES DINNER

If you wish to serve the meal in an authentically Thai fashion, serve all the dishes together.

CRISPY CRESCENTS
filled with Herbed Shrimp and Pork

HOT-AND-SOUR SHRIMP SOUP

ROAST DUCK WITH PINEAPPLE
in a Red Curry Sauce

HERBED EGGPLANT SALAD
with Pickled Garlic

STEAMED JASMINE RICE

THAI-INSPIRED PUMPKIN TART

The salads in this book have the added advantage of being light and low in calories. At first, Asian dressings, which usually contain none or very little oil, might seem to lack the complexity of a vinaigrette. But by continuing to taste them you will see just how the saltiness of the fish sauce, the acidity of lime juice or rice vinegar, the fire of the chiles, all balance with the sweetness of the palm or brown sugar to create a very special depth of flavor.

TUNA POKE SALAD

with Nashi Pear

Poke is a classic Hawaiian salad of raw fish marinated in a flavorful mixture of soy sauce, scallions, ginger, and sesame seeds, which also cooks it slightly. Inspired by an idea from San Francisco chef Bruce Hill of the Oritalia restaurant, I also add diced nashi (also known as Asian or Japanese) pears for a touch of sweetness and crunch. Needless to say, a successful *poke* requires impeccable, sparklingly fresh tuna. Ahi is best.

1½ teaspoons coarse (kosher) salt
1 tablespoon grated fresh ginger
1 clove garlic, crushed through a press
½ small fresh hot green chile, stemmed,
    seeded, and minced, or more to taste
10 ounces very fresh ahi, yellowfin, or
    bluefin tuna, cut into ¼-inch dice
⅓ cup minced red onion, plus more for
    garnish
¼ cup thinly sliced scallions, plus more for
    garnish
½ cup chopped, seeded firm, ripe tomato,
    plus more for garnish
1 tablespoon lightly toasted sesame seeds,
    plus more for garnish
2 tablespoons plus 2 teaspoons soy sauce,
    preferably Japanese shoyu
1½ teaspoons rice vinegar
Pinch of sugar
1½ teaspoons Oriental sesame oil
½ cup diced peeled nashi pear
1 small bunch arugula or watercress,
    rinsed and patted dry
Lemon wedges, if desired, for garnish

1. In a large bowl, combine the salt, ginger, garlic, and chile. Add the tuna and gently massage the salt mixture into the fish.

2. Sprinkle in the onion, scallions, tomato, sesame seeds, the 2 tablespoons soy sauce, the vinegar, and sugar and toss well to combine. Cover with plastic wrap and refrigerate for 2 hours.

3. Stir in the remaining 2 teaspoons soy sauce, the sesame oil, and nashi. To serve, arrange arugula or watercress leaves on appetizer plates and spoon equal portions of the salad on top. Garnish each portion with additional red onion, scallions, and tomato and sprinkle with sesame seeds.

SERVES 4 TO 6 AS AN APPETIZER

THAI SEAFOOD AND RICE NOODLE SALAD

Make this Thai salad of herbed seafood, set atop a bed of rice noodles and dressed with a refreshingly tart lime sauce, with any combination of seafood that strikes your fancy. Lobster or crabmeat, shelled clams or mussels, or chunks of firm fish can all be used—although I wouldn't combine more than three kinds.

I have brought this salad to potluck picnics as a refreshing alternative to the cold pasta salad standbys. To save wear and tear

on my answering machine when friends call for the recipe, I usually bring a stack of typed recipes along as well.

6 to 7 ounces rice vermicelli

⅓ cup fresh lime juice

¼ cup Asian fish sauce, such as nam pla

1 tablespoon hot water

1 teaspoon light soy sauce

2 dried hot red chiles (2 to 3 inches long), partially seeded and crumbled

1 large clove garlic, crushed through a press

2 tablespoons sugar

8 ounces large shrimp, peeled, deveined, cooked

6 ounces squid (calamari), cleaned and poached bodies cut into ¼-inch rings, tentacles halved, if large (for poaching instructions, see step 2, page 100)

6 ounces bay scallops, poached and halved

1 cup bean sprouts

½ cup finely chopped red onion

3 medium firm, ripe tomatoes, cut into thin wedges

¾ cup torn fresh mint leaves (or a combination of mint, basil, and cilantro)

Salt, to taste

1 head green leaf lettuce, separated into leaves, rinsed and patted dry

3 to 4 tablespoons chopped roasted peanuts, for garnish

Fresh cilantro leaves, for garnish

2 limes, cut into wedges, for garnish

1. Soak the vermicelli in a bowl of warm water for 20 minutes. Drain well. Bring a large pot of water to a boil. Cook the noodles for 30 seconds. Drain in a colander, rinse with cold water, and drain again until completely dry. Using scissors, cut the noodles into 3-inch lengths.

2. In a small bowl, whisk the lime juice, fish sauce, hot water, soy sauce, chiles, garlic, and sugar until the sugar is dissolved.

3. In a large bowl, toss the noodles with half of the dressing. In another bowl, combine the shrimp, squid, and scallops with the bean sprouts, onion, tomatoes, and mint, and toss with the rest of the dressing. Season lightly with salt.

4. Line a salad platter with the lettuce leaves. Arrange the noodles on the lettuce and the seafood mixture on top. Sprinkle the salad with peanuts and cilantro right before serving. Arrange the lime around the platter.

SERVES 6 TO 8

SHRIMP AND PINEAPPLE SALAD

with Cashews in Pineapple Boats

The refreshing acidity of the pineapple, the coolness of the cucumber, and the bite of chiles create a perfect counterpoint to the sweet plumpness of the shrimp. The herbs and red pepper impart a splash of color, the cashews provide crunch, and the gingery soy-based dressing rounds off this lovely play of flavors. The presentation in pineapple boats adds a visual touch of the tropics.

In Asia, where pineapples are sweet, juicy, and impart a heady fragrance, it is customary to use slightly underripe ones for anything but dessert. Choose a pineap-

THAI YAMS

There is hardly any culinary invention more original than Thai yams, composed salads in which various textures and tastes are brought together with incredible skill and finesse. To me these are some of the very best offerings from the Thai kitchen.

Yam means to blend or mix together, and the principle of Thai yams is based on exactly that. A polyphony of contrasting colors, flavors, and textures: cool and hot, soft and crunchy, pungent and sweet, come together under the foil of a classic Thai dressing that features different combinations of chiles, lime juice, fish sauce, and sugar. Simple as this dressing is, the magic blend will taste completely different with whatever it dresses. Imagine sweet crabmeat, chewy clams, fragrant lemongrass, and crispy fried garlic; or the mysterious sweet and tart pomelo; delicate shrimp and toasted coconut; or rice noodles, an assortment of seafood, the crispness of the cucumbers, the aroma of the herbs, and the crunch of roasted peanuts. These are deliciously refreshing in the scorching heat and humidity of Thailand, and show off the culinary imagination of the region at its best.

ple whose flavor and aroma will not overpower the other tastes.

- 1 small pineapple with the leaves on
- 1 small firm cucumber, peeled, seeded, and diced
- ½ cup diced red bell pepper
- ½ cup diced jicama
- ¾ cup chopped red onion
- 2 fresh medium-hot red chiles (such as fresno), seeded and chopped
- 1½ pounds medium shrimp, peeled, deveined, and cooked
- 3 tablespoons soy sauce
- 3 tablespoons sherry vinegar
- 3 tablespoons unsweetened pineapple juice
- 2½ teaspoons sugar, or more to taste
- 1 tablespoon peanut oil
- 2 cloves garlic, crushed through a press
- 2 teaspoons minced fresh ginger
- 3 tablespoons torn fresh cilantro leaves
- 3 tablespoons torn fresh mint leaves
- 3 tablespoons chopped roasted cashew nuts, for garnish

1. With a large, sharp knife, cut the pineapple in half lengthwise, cutting through the leaves. With a small, sharp knife, carefully remove the flesh from the shell, then dice the flesh away from the core. Measure 1 cup diced pineapple and reserve the rest for another use. Set the pineapple boats aside.

2. In a large bowl, combine the pineapple, cucumber, bell pepper, jicama, onion, chiles, and shrimp and toss until mixed.

3. Heat the soy sauce, vinegar, pineapple juice, and sugar in a small, nonreactive saucepan over medium heat, stirring until the sugar is dissolved. Allow to cool to room temperature, then whisk in the oil, garlic, and ginger.

4. Toss the salad with this dressing and stir in the cilantro leaves and mint.

5. To serve, arrange the salad in the reserved pineapple boats and garnish with chopped cashews.

SERVES 4 TO 6

CHILE SQUID SALAD

with Chinese Noodles

Squid devotees, of whom I am happy to observe, there are an increasing number, will delight in this wonderful salad. Here just the squid bodies (no tentacles) are cooked by quickly blanching them in boiling water and then marinating them in a mixture of chiles and herbs. This method leaves the texture of the squid tender and delicate and imbues its sweet flesh with spicy, herby flavors. If you like this squid as much as I do, you can also serve it on its own, on a bed of greens or tossed with some cold pasta or rice. If Chinese noodles are not readily available, you can use capellini or other thin pasta.

1 pound large squid (calamari), bodies
    cleaned, tentacles reserved for another use
2½ tablespoons fresh lemon juice
2 tablespoons minced fresh basil leaves
2 tablespoons minced fresh cilantro leaves
1½ teaspoons Chinese chile paste with garlic
Salt, to taste
8 ounces thin fresh Chinese egg noodles
1 tablespoon soy sauce
1 tablespoon plus 4 teaspoons peanut oil
1½ cups sliced fresh shiitake mushroom caps
1 large bunch watercress, rinsed and patted
    dry, tough stems removed
1 large red bell pepper, stemmed, seeded, and
    julienned
8 to 10 firm, ripe cherry tomatoes, halved

MIRIN AND SOY DRESSING
2 teaspoons finely chopped fresh ginger
2 cloves garlic, chopped
1 tablespoon chopped scallions
2½ tablespoons mirin or medium-dry sherry
2 tablespoons white wine vinegar
½ teaspoon sugar, or more to taste
2½ tablespoons light soy sauce
1½ teaspoons Oriental sesame oil
2½ tablespoons canola or peanut oil

1. Cut the squid bodies lengthwise along one side to open them like a book. Lay the squid on a work surface, inner side up, and using a small, sharp knife, score a ¼-inch diamond pattern on it. Cut the scored squid into 1¾ x ¾-inch rectangles. Rinse well and place in a large heatproof bowl.

2. Bring a pot of water to a boil. Pour enough water on the squid to cover. Let stand until the squid just begins to turn opaque, about 40 seconds. Drain and rinse thoroughly under cold running water.

3. In a bowl, combine the lemon juice, basil, cilantro, chile paste with garlic, and salt. Stir in the squid, cover, and let stand for at least 30 minutes.

4. While the squid is marinating, prepare the noodles. Separate the noodle strands with a fork to untangle. Bring a pot of salted water to a boil. Add the noodles and cook until tender but still slightly al dente, about 3 minutes. Place in a colander, drain well, and rinse under cold running water. Drain again, then place the noodles in a bowl and toss with the soy sauce and 1 tablespoon of the oil.

5. Heat 2 teaspoons of the oil in a medium-size skillet over medium heat. Cook the shiitake mushrooms, stirring occasionally, for 5 minutes. Remove them from the skillet and set aside. Heat the remaining 2 teaspoons oil. Add the watercress and cook until just wilted, about 1½ minutes.

6. In a large bowl, toss the noodles with

the squid, mushrooms, watercress, bell pepper, and tomatoes.

7. Make the dressing: Combine the ginger, garlic, scallions, mirin, vinegar, and sugar in a small nonreactive saucepan. Bring to a boil and cook until reduced by half, about 3 minutes. Pour into a bowl and cool.

8. To the cooled mirin mixture, add the soy sauce and sesame and vegetable oils; whisk. Toss the salad with the dressing and serve.

SERVES 6

SPICE MARKET POMELO SALAD

with Grilled Shrimp and Crispy Shallots

Among the many remarkable dishes I tasted at the enchanting Spice Market Restaurant in Bangkok, one of the most memorable was *yam som*, a salad of shredded pomelo—a large fruit that resembles a grapefruit—grilled shrimp, toasted coconut, and crispy fried shallots. Like the best of Thai food, the dish possessed an eye-opening contrast of flavors that was bold yet incredibly refined.

Pomelo, a fruit of Chinese origin, looks like an overgrown, slightly pear-shaped, greenish grapefruit, and its flesh is ideal for using in salads, as it is quite dry and separates very easily into strands. It is often available on the West Coast, and sometimes on the East Coast, too. Look for it in winter at good fruit and vegetable shops or in eth-

nic markets. If you can't find it, substitute grapefruit, which you should drain in a colander of excess juice before using. The amount of lime juice and sugar in the dressing should be adjusted, depending on the sweetness of the pomelo or grapefruit. The salad should maintain a good balance of tartness and sweetness, so let your palate be the judge.

Serve this salad as an unusual and sophisticated appetizer or as part of a multicourse Thai meal.

1½ teaspoons vegetable oil
¼ cup Asian fish sauce, such as nam pla
4 to 5 tablespoons fresh lime juice, or to taste
2½ tablespoons palm sugar or (packed) light brown sugar, or more to taste
12 ounces large shrimp, peeled and deveined
1 large pomelo, about 1½ pounds, or 2 not-very-sweet medium grapefruits
Peanut oil, for deep frying shallots and garlic
¼ cup sliced shallots
¼ cup sliced garlic
1 small fresh hot chile, green or red, stemmed, partially seeded, and chopped
½ cup desiccated (dried) or unsweetened shredded coconut, toasted (see page 389)
⅓ cup fresh cilantro leaves
6 to 8 Boston lettuce leaves, rinsed and patted dry

1. Prepare coals for grilling or preheat the broiler. Soak 6 to 8 long bamboo skewers in water to cover for 30 minutes.

2. In a medium-size bowl, combine the oil, 1 tablespoon of the fish sauce, 1 tablespoon of the lime juice, and 1 tablespoon of the sugar. Add the shrimp and toss to coat with this mixture. Thread the shrimp on skewers. Grill or broil until the shrimp are golden and just cooked through, 2 to 3 minutes per side. Set aside.

3. Peel the pomelo or grapefruits so that

no white pith remains. Cut into segments, remove the thin membranes, and separate the flesh into shreds or small pieces. If using grapefruit, let it drain in a colander to get rid of the excess juice. Place in a bowl.

4. Pour the peanut oil to a depth of 1 inch into a small skillet and heat to 375°F over medium-high heat. Add the shallots and cook until golden brown and crispy, 1 to 1½ minutes. Without turning off the heat, use a slotted spoon to transfer the shallots to paper towels to drain. Add the garlic to the skillet and cook until deep golden and crispy, about 1 minute. Drain on paper towels.

5. Heat the chile and the remaining fish sauce, lime juice, and sugar in a small nonreactive saucepan over medium heat, stirring until the sugar is just dissolved. Cool completely, then toss with the pomelo. Remove the shrimp from the skewers and add, along with the toasted coconut and cilantro leaves, into the salad. Toss to combine.

6. Line a serving platter with the lettuce leaves. Arrange the salad on top and scatter the fried shallots and garlic on top.

SERVES 4

GRILLED CHICKEN AND SHRIMP SALAD

with Tamarind-Honey Dressing

This is an extraordinary salad of grilled large shrimp and chicken breasts, papaya, vegetables, and herbs tossed in a fragrant dressing that combines my favorite sweet and sour flavors: tamarind and honey. You can serve it either cold or warm. In the latter case I find it tastier to mound the chicken and shrimp on the vegetables and papaya and drizzle it with the dressing.

TAMARIND-HONEY DRESSING
2 tablespoons tamarind pulp, preferably from Thailand
½ cup boiling water
3 tablespoons fresh lime juice
1½ tablespoons soy sauce, or more to taste
2½ teaspoons ketchup
2 tablespoons honey, or more to taste
1½ teaspoons grated fresh ginger
2 cloves garlic, crushed through a press
1 to 2 dried hot red chiles (2 to 3 inches long), preferably Asian, crumbled
1 tablespoon finely sliced fresh lemongrass (3 inches of the lower stalk, tough outer leaves discarded)
Salt and freshly ground white pepper, to taste

12 ounces large shrimp, peeled, deveined, and butterflied
2 teaspoons olive oil
Salt and ground cayenne pepper, to taste
1 tablespoon fresh lime juice
12 ounces skinless, boneless chicken breasts, rinsed well and patted dry
2 cups bite-size pieces romaine lettuce hearts
1 large Kirby cucumber, seeded, halved lengthwise, and cut into ½-inch slices
2 firm, ripe plum tomatoes, seeded and cut into large dice
⅔ cup diced red onion
1 cup diced papaya, plus 2 tablespoons for garnish
1 cup torn fresh cilantro leaves
½ cup torn fresh basil leaves, plus additional for garnish
Chopped roasted peanuts, for garnish

1. Make the dressing: Soak the tamarind pulp in the boiling water off the heat for 15 minutes. Stir and mash it with a fork to help it dissolve. Strain through a fine strainer into a bowl, pressing on the solids with the back of a wooden spoon to extract all the liquid.

2. In a bowl, combine the tamarind juice, lime juice, soy sauce, ketchup, honey, ginger, garlic, chiles, and lemongrass. Stir well to dissolve the honey. Season with salt and pepper. Set aside.

3. Prepare coals for grilling or preheat the broiler.

4. Toss the shrimp with half of the oil and season with salt and cayenne. Grill or broil until just done, about 6 minutes, turning once. Place in a bowl and toss with half of the lime juice.

5. Brush the chicken with the remaining oil and rub with salt. Grill or broil until done, about 5 minutes per side. When cool enough to handle, cut the chicken into bite-size pieces, place in a bowl, and toss with the remaining lime juice.

6. In a large bowl, combine the chicken, shrimp, lettuce, cucumber, tomatoes, onion, 1 cup papaya, cilantro, and ½ cup basil. Toss with the dressing.

7. To serve, transfer to a serving platter and garnish with peanuts and additional papaya and basil.

SERVES 6 TO 8

GRILLED CHICKEN SALAD

This recipe takes its inspiration from my visit to New Zealand. During my stay, I took a "fresh" look at the country's national export, the kiwi, which I have tasted and prepared in more wonderful ways than one can imagine. Needless to say, my kitchen has never been without a stock of these fuzzy emeralds ever since.

MARINADE AND CHICKEN
2 tablespoons soy sauce
1½ tablespoons fresh lime juice
2 tablespoons (packed) light brown sugar
1 tablespoon minced garlic
2 teaspoons Ginger Juice (page 390)
4 skinless, boneless chicken breast halves, well rinsed and patted dry

KIWI VINAIGRETTE
2 firm, ripe kiwis, peeled and chopped
1 clove garlic, chopped
1 teaspoon grated fresh ginger
½ teaspoon minced, seeded fresh hot red chile
1½ teaspoons Dijon mustard
3 tablespoons white wine vinegar
½ cup light olive oil (do not use virgin or extra-virgin)
Salt and freshly ground black pepper, to taste

SALAD
8 cups mixed greens (such as Bibb lettuce, arugula, red-leaf lettuce, mizuna), rinsed, patted dry, and torn into bite-size pieces
2 medium Belgian endives, thinly sliced crosswise
¼ cup alfalfa sprouts
8 firm, ripe cherry tomatoes, halved

1. In a shallow dish, combine the soy sauce, lime juice, sugar, garlic, and ginger juice and stir well to dissolve the sugar. Add the chicken and turn to coat. Cover with plastic wrap and refrigerate for 2 to 6 hours.

2. Prepare coals for grilling or preheat the broiler.

3. Grill or broil the chicken until cooked through but still moist inside, about 4 to 5 minutes per side. Cool to room temperature. Slice into ½-inch thick slices.

4. Make the vinaigrette: In a food processor combine the kiwis, garlic, ginger, chile, mustard, and vinegar and process to a coarse purée. With the motor running, drizzle in the oil through the feed tube until the mixture is emulsified. Transfer to a bowl and season with salt and pepper.

5. In a large bowl, toss the salad greens with the endives, alfalfa sprouts, and tomatoes. Divide the salad among 6 plates. Arrange the chicken slices in a fan on the salad, then drizzle the vinaigrette on each portion and serve.

SERVES 6

THAI ROAST PORK SALAD

with Peanuts and Herbs

It's difficult to stay away from Thai *yams* (salads), especially those enlivened by the crunch of fried garlic and shallots and chopped nuts. This dish transforms leftover roast pork or Thanksgiving turkey into an exotic feast.

You can serve it as a light lunch or sup-

per entrée, accompanied by steamed rice; or as an appetizer on a bed of greens.

If you don't have any leftover roast meat at hand, make this salad with grilled or sautéed boneless loin pork chops.

Peanut oil, for deep frying the onion and garlic
½ cup thinly sliced shallots
½ cup thinly sliced garlic
1 pound roast pork or turkey (warm or at room temperature), thinly sliced
1¼ cups shredded carrots
4 medium firm, ripe tomatoes, seeded and cut into strips
5 scallions, trimmed, cut lengthwise into strips, then crosswise into 2½-inch lengths
1 cup thinly sliced red onion
⅓ cup finely chopped fresh mint leaves
¼ cup finely chopped fresh cilantro leaves
⅓ cup fresh lime juice
¼ cup Asian fish sauce, such as nam pla
2 tablespoons sugar
2 small dried red chiles, crumbled
Romaine lettuce leaves, rinsed and patted dry
⅓ cup finely chopped roasted cashew nuts, for garnish

1. Pour oil to a depth of 1 inch into a small skillet and heat to 375°F over medium-high heat. Add the shallots and cook until golden and crispy, 1 to 1½ minutes. Without turning off the heat, remove the shallots from the skillet with a slotted spoon and drain on paper towels. Add the garlic to the oil and cook until deep golden and crispy, about 1 minute. Transfer to paper towels to drain. Reserve the shallots and garlic.

2. In a large bowl, toss together the pork, carrots, tomatoes, scallions, onion, mint, and cilantro.

3. In a small bowl, whisk together the lime juice, fish sauce, sugar, and chiles. Then toss the salad with the dressing.

4. Line a serving platter with the lettuce leaves. Arrange the salad on the leaves and sprinkle with the cashew nuts. Scatter the reserved fried shallots and garlic on the salad and serve.

SERVES 4 TO 6

GRILLED BEEF SALAD

This stylish salad artfully and elegantly combines the flavors of the Orient—slices of grilled spiced beef, crispy bean sprouts, and chived omelet strips on a bed of greens, all dressed in a sweet and tangy plum sauce vinaigrette. Prepare the beef, omelet strips, and vinaigrette beforehand, so all you have to do is toss everything together and enjoy a lovely light lunch.

2 teaspoons Oriental sesame oil
1 teaspoon dark soy sauce
2 cloves garlic, crushed through a press
1½ teaspoons crushed black pepper
1 teaspoon Chinese plum sauce
1 small serrano chile, stemmed, seeded, and
*   minced*
1½ pounds beef fillet
3 cups torn red-leaf lettuce, rinsed and
*   patted dry*
3 cups torn butter lettuce, rinsed and
*   patted dry*
1 bunch arugula, rinsed and patted dry
¾ cup bean sprouts
Plum Vinaigrette (recipe follows)
Omelet Strips (recipe follows)
Fresh cilantro leaves, for garnish

1. In a shallow bowl, combine the sesame oil, soy sauce, garlic, black pepper, plum sauce, and chile. Brush the beef with this mixture, place in a glass baking dish, and let stand for 2 hours.

2. Prepare coals for grilling or preheat the broiler.

3. Grill or broil the meat on both sides until medium-rare, about 3 to 4 minutes per side. Refrigerate until cold, about 2 hours, then cut across the grain into thin slices.

4. In a bowl, toss the lettuces, arugula, and bean sprouts with half of the vinaigrette. Arrange on a large serving platter. Arrange the omelet strips and beef slices decoratively on top and drizzle with the remaining vinaigrette. Garnish with cilantro leaves.

SERVES 6

Plum Vinaigrette

1 clove garlic, crushed through a press
1½ teaspoons Dijon mustard
1 tablespoon Chinese plum sauce
1 teaspoon Ginger Juice (page 390)
2½ tablespoons red wine vinegar
2 tablespoons fresh lime juice
1 tablespoon finely minced fresh cilantro
*   leaves*
½ cup light olive oil (do not use virgin or
*   extra-virgin)*
1 teaspoon freshly ground black pepper
Salt, to taste

In a bowl, whisk together the garlic, mustard, plum sauce, ginger juice, vinegar, lime

juice, and cilantro. Slowly drizzle in the oil, whisking until emulsified. Add the pepper and salt and let stand for 30 minutes for the flavors to develop.

MAKES ABOUT ¾ CUP

Omelet Strips

2 large eggs
2 tablespoons snipped fresh chives
Salt and freshly ground black pepper, to taste
1 teaspoon peanut oil

In a large bowl, beat the eggs with the chives and salt and pepper to taste. Heat the peanut oil in a large omelet pan over medium heat. Add the egg mixture and cook until almost set, about 2 minutes. Flip over and cook on the other side for 1 minute. Cool. Roll up the omelet and cut into thin strips. Set aside.

VIETNAMESE MINTED LEMON BEEF SALAD

I can't think of a more refreshing, exotic, and pretty dish to serve on a blistering day than this Vietnamese-inspired main-course salad of thinly sliced marinated beef served over a bed of crispy, colorful shredded vegetables and aromatic herbs.

Shredded chicken breast meat or seafood can be substituted for the beef. Traditionally the salad is garnished with Shrimp Chips. Serve with Steamed Jasmine

Rice (see Index) as a light summer meal or as part of a buffet.

1 pound beef sirloin, about ¾ inch thick
¼ teaspoon ground cayenne pepper
5 tablespoons Asian fish sauce, such as nam pla
2½ tablespoons plus 2 teaspoons (packed) light brown sugar, or more to taste
1 small fresh hot chile, green or red, stemmed and chopped
1½ teaspoons minced fresh ginger
1 large clove garlic, chopped
½ teaspoon salt
7 tablespoons fresh lemon juice
2 tablespoons hot water
2 medium lemons, skin and white pith removed, sliced very thin

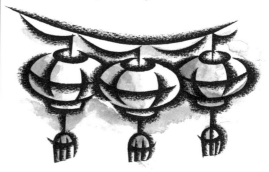

COLE SLAW
1 cup julienned or shredded carrots
2 medium cucumbers, peeled, seeded, and julienned or shredded
½ small red onion, halved, sliced very thin, and separated into rings
2¼ cups shredded red cabbage
1 cup bean sprouts
1 cup slivered fresh mint leaves
½ cup slivered fresh basil leaves, preferably Thai
Salt, to taste

⅓ cup roasted peanuts, for garnish
Shrimp Chips, for garnish (page 5), if desired

1. Place the beef in a shallow dish, rub with cayenne, and sprinkle on both sides with 1½ tablespoons of the fish sauce and 2 teaspoons of the sugar. Let stand at room temperature for 30 minutes.

2. Prepare coals for grilling or preheat the broiler.

3. Grill or broil the meat until medium-rare, about 4 minutes per side. Cover with aluminum foil and let stand for 10 minutes.

4. Meanwhile, using a mortar and pestle, or in a ceramic bowl, using the back of a spoon, crush the chile, ginger, and garlic to a paste with ½ teaspoon salt. Add the lemon juice, the remaining fish sauce, the remaining sugar and the hot water. Stir well to dissolve the sugar.

5. Cut the meat, across the grain and at an angle, into thin slices. Place in a bowl and toss with the lemon slices and 2 tablespoons of the dressing. Let stand for 30 minutes. The meat can also be covered and left to marinate overnight in the refrigerator.

6. Make the slaw: In a large bowl, toss the carrots, cucumbers, onion, cabbage, bean sprouts, mint leaves, and basil together. Season very lightly with salt. Toss with the remaining dressing.

7. When ready to serve, arrange three fourths of the slaw on a large serving platter. Scatter the meat with the lemon slices on top of the slaw, then cover with the remaining slaw. Sprinkle with peanuts and serve. If using shrimp chips, place them on the platter around the salad.

SERVES 4 AS A MAIN COURSE, 6 TO 8 WITH OTHER DISHES

POTATO SALAD
with Japanese Dressing

This recipe was inspired by my friend, Japanese food writer Nekko Edamoto. She served this creamy-rich dressing of peanut butter, soy sauce, rice vinegar, and oyster sauce over a delicate salad of diced tofu, tomatoes, scallions, cilantro, and salted duck eggs. I, in turn, added an American twist by tossing it into a salad of tender new red potatoes. Nekko was so impressed with the results that she wrapped up the leftovers to take as a gift for Japanese friends in San Francisco.

The healthy dressing is delicious with almost any cooked vegetable, tofu, eggs, or avocado; and Nekko suggests that the peanut butter can be replaced by tahini or ground walnuts. Be sure to allow it to stand for 30 minutes before mixing it into the salad.

3½ pounds small red-skin potatoes, scrubbed
1 cup sliced scallion greens, plus additional
for garnish
¾ cup chopped fresh cilantro leaves, plus
additional for garnish
Japanese Dressing (recipe follows)

1. Cook the potatoes until tender in a large pot of salted water, about 25 minutes. Drain. When cool enough to handle halve the potatoes.

2. In a large bowl, toss the potatoes with 1 cup scallions, ¾ cup cilantro, and the dressing. Chill until ready to serve. Serve garnished with additional scallions and cilantro.

SERVES 10

Japanese Dressing

2 teaspoons finely minced garlic
1 tablespoon grated fresh ginger
1/4 teaspoon dried red pepper flakes
1/4 cup smooth unsalted, unsweetened
    peanut butter
1/4 cup tamari soy sauce
6 1/2 tablespoons oyster sauce
1/4 cup rice vinegar
1/2 cup Chicken Stock
    (page 384) or
    spring water, plus more
    if needed
Salt, to taste

In a bowl, whisk all the dressing ingredients until well combined. If the dressing seems too thick, add some additional stock or water. Let stand for 30 minutes before using.

MAKES ABOUT 1 3/4 CUPS

IRENE'S POTATO SALAD
with Indian Spices

Irene Trias is a beautiful, vivacious San Francisco restaurateur. At her two restaurants, Appam and Indian Oven, she serves up some of the freshest and most imaginative Indian food in America, adding a California touch of baby vegetables, baby greens, and luxurious fish and game. This is Irene's summertime version of potatoes, jazzed up with mustard seeds, cayenne, and cilantro.

2 1/2 pounds baby new potatoes, scrubbed
3 tablespoons canola oil
1 tablespoon mustard seeds, either all yellow
    or a mixture of yellow and black
1/2 teaspoon ground turmeric
1/2 teaspoon ground cayenne pepper
1/3 cup finely chopped scallions
3 tablespoons fresh cilantro leaves, for
    garnish
Salt, to taste

1. Cook the potatoes until tender, about 20 minutes. Drain. When cool enough to handle, halve the potatoes.

2. Heat the oil in a small, heavy skillet over high heat until it begins to shimmer. Add the mustard seeds and cook, covered, until they begin to pop, 15 to 30 seconds. Allow the seeds to pop for 30 more seconds to release their fragrance. Remove the skillet from the heat at once and stir in the turmeric and cayenne.

3. In a large bowl, combine the potatoes, spiced oil, and scallions. Season with salt to taste. Toss gently but thoroughly. Sprinkle with the cilantro and serve warm.

SERVES 4

PASTA SALAD
with Peanut-Lime Vinaigrette

The vinaigrette is delicious when tossed on cooked vegetable salads, or a salad of spinach and tofu; or when used as a dipping sauce with sliced chicken breast, shrimp, strips of grilled beef, or asparagus. I am not wild about overly sweet peanut sauces, but you can adjust the amount of sugar here to suit your own taste.

1 pound thin pasta, such as capellini or Chinese noodles, cooked al dente and cooled

1 cup julienned red bell pepper, plus more for garnish

⅔ cup sliced scallion greens, plus more for garnish

Peanut-Lime Vinaigrette (recipe follows)

Chopped roasted peanuts, for garnish

In a very large bowl, toss the pasta with 1 cup bell pepper, ⅔ cup scallions, and the vinaigrette. Transfer to a serving bowl or platter and garnish with additional bell pepper and scallions, and peanuts.

SERVES 8

Peanut-Lime Vinaigrette

1 tablespoon grated fresh ginger

2 cloves garlic, minced

1 serrano chile, stemmed, seeded, and chopped

3 tablespoons chopped fresh cilantro leaves

1½ tablespoons smooth unsalted, unsweetened peanut butter

3 tablespoons fresh lime juice

1½ tablespoons rice vinegar

1½ tablespoons soy sauce

1½ teaspoons (packed) light brown sugar, or more to taste

¾ cup canola oil

Salt, to taste (optional)

In a food processor, process the ginger, garlic, chili, cilantro, peanut butter, lime juice, vinegar, soy sauce, and sugar. With the motor running, slowly drizzle in the oil through the feed tube until emulsified. Scrape into a bowl and season with salt, if needed. Let stand for 30 minutes for the flavors to develop.

MAKES ABOUT 1½ CUPS

HERBED EGGPLANT SALAD
with Pickled Garlic

I learned the recipe for this striking, intensely flavored salad at the Oriental Cooking School in Bangkok, and it has since become one of my favorite Thai *yams* (salads). In Thailand, the traditional version called *yam makheua yow,* would usually include whole or pounded dried shrimp—an acquired taste for some Occidental diners—to add smoky saltiness to the dish. I opt for a more delicate flavor and omit the shrimp.

Another variation contains cooked minced meat. If you desire a more substantial dish, you can add about 1½ cups of cooked lean ground pork, chicken, or turkey to the salad. If adding the meat, increase the amount of dressing.

Apropos the dressing, for those unaccustomed to Thai tastes, the suggested amount of chile- and garlic-laden dressing might seem a bit overpowering, so do not add all the dressing at once, but keep tossing and tasting until you reach your desired flavor level. The thing to remember about

the pungent Thai salads is that they are designed to be served as part of a meal in which all the tastes—sour, salty, sweet, and mild—mingle and blend to achieve a perfect harmony.

2 pounds Chinese or Japanese eggplants,
    trimmed and halved lengthwise
2 teaspoons olive oil
1 medium red onion, finely chopped
3 orange Italian (frying) peppers or
    wax peppers, stemmed, seeded, and
    cut into strips
¾ cup coarsely chopped fresh cilantro
    leaves
½ cup slivered fresh basil leaves,
    preferably Thai

DRESSING
2 tablespoons chopped garlic
1½ tablespoons chopped cilantro roots
    and/or stems
6 small fresh hot chiles, green or red,
    stemmed, partially seeded, and chopped
3 tablespoons sweet Asian pickled garlic
⅓ cup fresh lime juice
¼ cup Asian fish sauce, such as nam pla
2 teaspoons sugar
3 tablespoons brine from the pickled garlic
Salt, to taste (optional)

1. Preheat the broiler.

2. Brush the eggplants with oil and broil on both sides until the skin is lightly charred and the eggplants are soft but still hold their shape, about 10 minutes. Cool and cut crosswise into 2-inch slices.

3. In a serving bowl, toss the eggplant slices with the onion, peppers, cilantro, and basil.

4. Make the dressing: Combine all the dressing ingredients except the salt in a food processor and process until minced but not puréed.

5. Toss the salad with the desired amount of dressing and season to taste with salt, if needed. Allow the salad to stand at room temperature for at least 1 hour for the flavors to develop. You can also refrigerate it for several hours or overnight.

SERVES 6

HEIRLOOM TOMATO SALAD
with Miso Vinaigrette and Basil Oil

Come summer, the San Francisco farmers' markets are ablaze with ripe, juicy tomatoes of all shapes and colors. This salad created by San Francisco chef Bruce Hill, uses Heirloom tomatoes but you can substitute with any other meaty, vine-ripened tomatoes.

MISO VINAIGRETTE
⅓ cup virgin olive oil
1 tablespoon minced garlic
2 tablespoons mirin or medium-dry sherry
1 tablespoon rice vinegar
1 tablespoon yellow miso (shiro miso)
Salt and freshly ground black pepper,
    to taste

4 cups arugula leaves, rinsed, patted dry, and
    sliced thin
½ cup thinly sliced red onion
4 medium firm, ripe meaty tomatoes, sliced
    ½ inch thick
Basil Oil (recipe follows)

1. Make the vinaigrette: Heat the oil in a medium-size skillet over medium-low heat. Add the garlic and sauté, stirring, until light golden, about 1½ minutes. Stir in the mirin and remove the skillet from the heat. In a mixing bowl, whisk the vinegar with the miso. Strain the oil and slowly whisk it into the vinegar mixture until emulsified. Add salt and pepper to taste and set aside.

2. In a large bowl, combine the arugula and onion. Toss with ¼ cup of the vinaigrette. Arrange the tomato slices around the edges of 4 plates. Place a pile of arugula in the center of each plate, then drizzle the entire plate with some of the basil oil and remaining vinaigrette. Serve at once.

SERVES 4

Basil Oil

The recipe here makes more basil oil than you will need for the salad, but you will find many uses for it in your kitchen. You can double or triple the recipe, as it will keep for a long time in the refrigerator in a clean bottle or jar.

2 cups fresh basil leaves
¾ cup virgin olive oil

1. Blanch the basil in boiling water for 15 seconds. Drain and plunge the leaves into a bowl of ice water for 1 minute. With your hands, squeeze out as much moisture as pos-sible from the basil, then pat dry with paper towels.

2. Combine the basil and oil in a blender and blend until smooth. Let stand for 1 hour. Strain through a fine-mesh strainer lined with cheesecloth. Discard the basil and transfer the oil to a clean jar.

MAKES ABOUT ¾ CUPS

CHICK-PEA, TOMATO, AND CILANTRO SALAD

with Toasted Cumin Vinaigrette

Healthy, simple, and faintly exotic, this salad is wonderful to serve *al fresco* next to an Asian-inspired grill. Ripe, flavorful tomatoes will make all the difference.

1 can (19 ounces) chick-peas, drained well
2 cups diced firm, ripe tomatoes
¾ cup chopped red onion
½ cup chopped fresh cilantro leaves
2 to 3 serrano chiles, stemmed, seeded, and sliced thin
1 teaspoon ground cumin
½ teaspoon ground cayenne pepper
3 cloves garlic, chopped
½ teaspoon salt
3 tablespoons fresh lemon juice
1½ tablespoons red wine vinegar
3 tablespoons light olive oil (do not use virgin or extra-virgin)

1. In a salad bowl, toss together the chick-peas, tomatoes, onion, cilantro, and chiles.

2. Stir the cumin and cayenne in a small skillet over medium heat until fragrant, about 30 seconds.

3. Using a mortar and pestle, or a ceramic bowl and the back of a spoon, mash the garlic to a paste together with the salt. Transfer to a small bowl and add the lemon juice and vinegar. Whisk in the oil, cumin, and cayenne.

4. Toss the salad with the dressing to combine well.

SERVES 6

RAITA

(Indian Cucumber, Tomato, and Yogurt Salad)

No curry meal is imaginable without the soothing companionship of a raita, a cooling concoction of fresh vegetables and yogurt designed to punctuate the richness of sauces and extinguish the fire of spices. This recipe makes a rather thick raita. If you like it thinner, don't drain the yogurt.

2 cups low-fat plain yogurt
⅔ cup diced, seeded cucumber
½ cup diced, seeded firm, ripe tomato
¼ cup chopped red onion
2 mild fresh green chiles, stemmed, seeded, and chopped
2 tablespoons chopped fresh cilantro leaves
Salt and freshly ground black pepper, to taste
1 large clove garlic, crushed through a press
1½ tablespoons fresh lemon juice
½ teaspoon pure chile powder
½ teaspoon ground cumin

1. Place the yogurt in a fine-mesh sieve lined with a double layer of cheesecloth and set over a bowl. Place in the refrigerator and let drain for 2 hours.

2. In a bowl, combine the cucumber, tomato, onion, chiles, and cilantro and season with salt and pepper.

3. Place the yogurt in another bowl and toss with the garlic and lemon juice. Toss the vegetables with the yogurt.

4. Stir the chile powder and cumin in a small skillet over medium heat until fragrant, about 30 seconds. Stir into the salad.

SERVES 4 TO 6 AS AN ACCOMPANIMENT TO CURRIES AND STEWS

PAPAYA SALAD

with Palm Sugar Dressing

This delicious Indonesian dish of thinly sliced marinated papaya, whose sweet-

RAITAS

Raitas, Indian yogurt salads, add a cooling tangy note to a spicy meal. The recipe given here is for the most basic of all raitas, but it doesn't have to stop with that one. Here are some more ideas. There is no real rule for the proportions of vegetables and yogurt—raitas can be thick or runny—but the accent of toasted spices added at the end is essential. Here are some of my favorite combinations to mix into yogurt:

DICED COOKED RED POTATOES AND TOASTED MUSTARD SEEDS

GRILLED EGGPLANT AND TOMATO AND TOASTED CORIANDER

BANANA AND GRATED COCONUT WITH A TOUCH OF GARAM MASALA

FRESH MINT AND RED ONION

LIGHTLY TOASTED CHOPPED WALNUTS AND CILANTRO

DICED PAPAYA AND CUCUMBER

CHICK-PEAS, TOMATOES, AND TOASTED CUMIN

ness is accented with palm sugar and then offset by the heat of the chile and the pucker of lime, is best when served as a condiment with grilled poultry or meat, rather than as an individual salad.

2½ tablespoons distilled white vinegar
2½ tablespoons fresh lime juice
3 tablespoons palm sugar or (packed) light
    brown sugar
2 small fresh hot red chiles, stemmed,
    partially seeded, and minced
Salt, to taste
1 large papaya, not too ripe, peeled, seeded,
    and thinly sliced lengthwise
⅓ cup finely sliced red onion

1. Heat the vinegar, lime juice, and palm sugar in a small nonreactive saucepan over medium heat, stirring until the sugar is dissolved. Remove the saucepan from the heat, add the chiles and salt, and let stand for 15 minutes.

2. Place the papaya and onion in a glass bowl and toss with the dressing. Refrigerate for 1 hour and up to 6 hours, tossing occasionally.

SERVES 4 TO 6 AS A CONDIMENT

GREEN PAPAYA SLAW

In Thailand, where the native fruits are lush, soft, and intoxicatingly fragrant, eventually one will get nostalgic for something hard, tart, and crunchy—like, say, an apple. Green, underripe fruit such as mango or papaya is the Thai answer to this craving. Mention *som tum,* green papaya pounded with garlic and chiles, to any expatriate Thai, and their polite, serene smile will turn into an enthusiastic glow. In Thailand this is the midday snack of choice and is usually turned out right on the spot by roadside vendors who grate, pound, and toss it with astonishing speed. The authentic presentation also includes pieces of pickled crab, with claws and all. But I usually omit this Thai delicacy.

Green papaya can be found in Southeast Asian, Indian, and Hispanic markets. The tart spicy salad is great to serve as a relish with a rich fragrant coconut curry or spoon atop barbecued meat or fish.

4 cups grated green papaya
4 cloves garlic, chopped
4 to 5 small fresh hot chiles,
    preferably red, stemmed
    and seeded according
    to the desired degree of
    heat
½ teaspoon salt
2½ tablespoons fresh lime juice
3 tablespoons Asian fish sauce,
    such as nam pla
1 tablespoon sugar
2 medium firm, ripe tomatoes, seeded and
    cut into strips
¼ cup roasted peanuts, crushed with a
    rolling pin

1. Soak the papaya in cold water to cover for 30 minutes. Drain well and gently squeeze out the excess water. Refrigerate in the colander until dry.

2. Using a mortar and pestle or a small food processor, pound or process the garlic and chiles together with the salt to a paste. Place the green papaya on a platter and massage the chile garlic mixture into it with your fingers.

3. In a small bowl, whisk the lime juice, fish sauce, and sugar until the sugar is completely dissolved.

4. In a salad bowl, toss together the green papaya, tomatoes, and dressing. Sprin-

kle with peanuts and serve. You can make and dress the salad several hours ahead of time. Garnish with the peanuts right before serving.

SERVES 4

GINGERED BEET SLAW
with Citrus Vinaigrette

Beets, shredded and dressed with a light vinaigrette that is perfumed with ginger and orange, can serve as a colorful relish to many of the curries, roasts, and grills in this book. The recipe is authentically Californian.

2 pounds beets, trimmed, leaving 2 inches of
    stem attached
⅔ cup minced shallots
1½ tablespoons grated fresh ginger
⅓ cup slivered fresh basil leaves
2 teaspoons grated orange zest
1 tablespoon fresh orange juice
2 tablespoons fresh lime juice
2½ tablespoons white wine vinegar
½ teaspoon sugar
¼ cup canola or peanut oil
Salt and freshly ground black pepper,
    to taste

1. Combine the beets with cold water to cover in a large saucepan and bring to a boil. Reduce the heat to low and simmer, covered, until the beets are tender, 35 to 40 minutes. Drain the beets (you can reserve the cooking liquid for making borscht) and place in a bowl of cold water until cool. Slip the skins off. Pat dry with paper towels.

2. Grate or shred the beets in a food processor. Transfer to a bowl. Toss with the shallots, ginger, basil, and orange zest.

3. In a small bowl, whisk together the orange juice, lime juice, vinegar, and sugar. Slowly whisk in the oil until emulsified. Add the dressing to the beets and toss well. Season with salt and pepper. Chill, covered, for 2 to 6 hours.

SERVES 6

CAROL SELVARAJAH VEGETABLE SALAD

with Kiwi and Pickled Ginger

This cooling, colorful salad is an all-purpose palate refresher that can be served alongside any Southeast Asian or Indian meal, whether a curry, a roast, or a grill. I had it at the house of Carol Selvara-jah, a food writer who is Sri Lankan by origin, but who was born in Malaysia, and is now based in Sydney.

2 firm, slender cucumbers, peeled, halved lengthwise, and sliced on the diagonal into ½-inch slices

3 firm, ripe tomatoes, seeded and cut into thin wedges

1 small red onion, quartered and thinly sliced

2 serrano chiles, stemmed, seeded, and thinly sliced

3 firm, ripe kiwi, peeled, halved lengthwise, and thinly sliced

2½ tablespoons Japanese pink pickled ginger, drained and coarsely chopped

Salt and freshly ground black pepper, to taste

⅓ cup seasoned rice vinegar

On a platter, arrange the vegetables and kiwi in layers, sprinkling each layer with pickled ginger, salt, pepper, and the vinegar. Let stand for 1 hour before serving.

SERVES 4 TO 6 WITH OTHER DISHES

SYDNEY AND MELBOURNE

Australia's largest cities, Sydney and Melbourne, are two of the most livable—and dinable—cities in the world. Between them they boast every color in the bright rainbow of innovative fusion cuisine at gorgeous hotel dining rooms, waterside restaurants, and elegant mansions that can rival Paris or Milan. Even the diversity of local wines is thrilling.

It's often said that if Sydney is the New York City of Australia, Melbourne is its Los Angeles. The city certainly has some of the sheer scale, that feeling of suburban infinity that is conjured from the L.A. basin. But Melbourne is first and foremost a Victorian city. Wandering around the downtown shops, arcades, and houses, and among the turn-of-the-century streets of the inner suburbs, you might think that some enlightened town planner stole all the brightest ideas from nineteenth-century Britain and ferried them Down Under, where they emerged on the streets of Melbourne, changed and brilliant.

The best expression of this transplanted style is the splendid Exhibition Buildings, set in their own gardens to the north of the city. Built for the Great Exhibition of 1880 and still used today for major trade shows and spectaculars, they also served as the parliament building for nearly three decades, until a national legislature was established in Canberra. But Melbourne blooms all over with the flowers of Victorian architecture—the ornate Flinders Street train station, which stretches like a fairy-tale castle wall for three blocks along the Yarra River at the bottom of the inner-city grid. Crisscrossing the town is one of the most extensive systems of still-functioning tram lines in the world.

Melbourne may look like a Victorian city, but it definitely doesn't eat like one. A patchwork of vibrant ethnic communities has made Melbourne one of the best eating places anywhere. There are so many Greeks living here that Melbourne ranks as the third largest Greek city in the world. Victoria Street, in the Richmond neighborhood, is buzzing with inexpensive Vietnamese restaurants. Carlton is home to dozens of Italian pastry and coffee shops and regional trattorias. There are both Turkish (Sydney Road, Brunswick) and Spanish (Johnston Street, Fitzroy) restaurant rows, and a buoyant Chinatown along little Bourke Street in the city. By the bay, slightly south of down-

town, St. Kilda is a miniature version of Manhattan's Lower East Side, with Jewish delis, Hungarian pastry shops, and a slew of bohemian tearooms and groovy hangouts.

In Melbourne the restaurant scene is polarized. The cream of the crop have a traditional European, mostly French-influenced attitude toward food and wine. At Mietta's famous upstairs restaurant in the heart of the city or under the spectacular glass dome in the Windsor Hotel, you can lose yourself in a dining fantasy that would make even Parisians sit up and take notice. Stephanie Alexander, who presides over a restaurant bearing her name, located in a lavishly appointed Victorian mansion east of town, adds an Australian flourish to her European kitchen with top-quality local produce.

At the humble end of the scale, Melbourne is the home of the BYO (bring your own alcoholic beverage of choice) restaurant. We loved this

concept, which enabled us to drink through the extraordinary diversity of top-notch Australian wines without relying on the restaurants' list and without emptying our wallets.

FAR AND AWAY

M elbourne is so far from anywhere in the Western world that its European immigrants have made it over, with passion, into a home away from home. The tyranny of distance

has preserved wonderful aspects of the past. The Italian joints have 1930s coffee machines that turn out some of the best coffee we've ever tasted. Old syrup bottles flank the counters. The streets are lined with comforting English pubs serving ales and Cornish pasties. There are cavelike Italian groceries and Egyptian spice stores with aromatics lying around in open sacks as they would in the bazaars of Cairo.

Immigrant culture in Australia has not been subject to the same standardizing social demands as in New York or Chicago, and the city remains multicultural to the core. The best of culinary Melbourne comes together at the incomparable Victoria Market. If volume is your guide, you will gravitate first to the meat section, which has the loudest shouts and is dominated by Australian butchers barking prices and special offers. These burly, red-faced men sell some of the best-quality meat in the world for what must be the best prices on earth. Australians happily spit-roast a whole side of lamb for their unending summer barbecues. But there's also plenty at the more delicate end of the scale—succulent baby lamb chops, plump free-range chickens, and rabbits at three for a dollar.

Such is the mercantile infectiousness of the Victoria Market that the Chinese and Vietnamese vegetable sellers try to imitate the vocal pyrotechnics of the Aussies. The result is a remarkable babble that couldn't possibly be understood by a non-Melbournian without three months of intensive training.

"Well, gud on'ya, mate, here's a deal."

"That's a beaut bargain . . . no worries, luv. . . ."

"Four fer-a-dollaw . . . ," yells an old Chinese woman selling passion fruit in season.

Best of all, though, is a deli section to die for, a place where the many hearts of the city really beat together. The very best of Italian, Greek, and Middle Eastern specialties are allied with premium produce from all over Australia—Tasmanian brie and blue cheeses, smoked fish, local sun-dried tomatoes, and exotic preserves from the Northern Territories. We counted ten different kinds of foccacia and were dizzied by the variety of olives—Greek, Lebanese, Italian, Spanish, Australian.

You want the best souvlaki, spinach pies, Croatian steak, or Ukrainian borscht? You want a vintage Barolo, or the finest tuna steaks, or fresh truffles lightly infused with eucalyptus, or a dessert wine to quicken the pulse? Well, try New York City, then fly down to Melbourne.

SPECTACULAR SYDNEY

When the earth was created, the chief designer took special care of Sydney, blessing it with one of the most spectacular settings of any city in the world. At its center is the Sydney Harbor, a gorgeous, many-fingered lagoon that focuses the entire life of the metropolis.

The futuristic opera house sits on… land at the most visible point of the harbor, like a guardian of the waters.

Sydney's great monuments are studded like glittering jewels into this natural tiara. The 1930s-style Harbor Bridge, as famous in Australia as the Brooklyn or Golden Gate is in the United States, links the two sides of Sydney at the harbor's narrowest point. It looks as if it has been forged by an other worldly blacksmith, and the locals call it the coat hanger.

Nearby, the futuristic opera house sits on a little spit of land at the most visible point of the harbor, like a guardian of the waters. Behind it rise the luxurious

Botanical Gardens, flowing over a series of lush green hills around Farm Cove, one of the bay's innumerable

picturesque inlets. The upbeat business district fronts the harbor in a grand finale at Circular Quay. And as in Hong Kong and Istanbul, commuter ferries frisk about on their zigzag runs, and a never-ending flotilla of pleasure boats catches the afternoon breeze.

Sydney shares a

colonial history similar to Victorian Melbourne, but has emerged in the last two decades as the capital of the Southern Hemisphere—a reign that will be crowned by the Olympic Games in the year 2000. Long open to Asian influence, Sydney manages to be casual, serious, and cosmopolitan all at once. English wit and eccentricity are combined with

a laid-back, California-style beach culture and the great Australian knack for taking it easy.

Sydney is unbeatable for casual fusion cuisine. Naturally situated on the crossroads of the East and West, Sydney has a dining scene that is dynamic and bubbling with the kind of energy that can be found only in a youthful culture blessed with the finest ingredients imaginable. If the East/West culinary convergence in America is a budding love affair, Down Under it's been in a state of marital bliss and harmony for years. Many people have contributed to the great Australian food revolution, but in Sydney it sometimes seems there's innovation on every street. Here, perhaps, is the only place in the world where one can find on the same menu spectacular lamb served up with Mediterranean flair, sparkling seafood prepared with Japanese finesse, a Thai curry to match the best in Bangkok, puddings that would make the English commute, and sauces that overshadow the preparations in France. There are dozens of wonderful local wines to match all these, and others left over for the

imagination. To top it all, the price for this sheer quality and

indulgence is a fraction of the outlay in Tokyo, Los Angeles, or London.

MEET THE CHEFS

The skill of Sydney chefs have made a very special contribution to this book. Their recipes sparkle with talent, enthusiasm, and that perfect combination of style and comfort. Here are a few introductions.

One of our very favo-

rite Sydney restaurants is Tetsuya's. Inside Tetsuya's, the only images that compete for attention with the exquisitely crafted food are the brilliant Aboriginal

Inside Tetsuya's, the only images that compete for attention with the exquisitely crafted food are the brilliant Aboriginal works that adorn the walls.

works that adorn the walls. Chef Tetsuya Wakuda's Japanese background, French training, and relentless pursuit of the region's finest ingredients combine to produce refined, light, and harmonious flavors. A tasting menu might include a terrine of venison with chestnuts and morels, whose richness is punctuated by a refreshing mizuna salad; glazed strips of eel on rounds of sushi rice; corn-fed squab with a marvelous sauté of shimeji mushrooms (grown especially for Tetsuya by a botany professor) with arugula pesto; and a stunning pumpkin terrine with pistachio crème anglaise and ginger ice cream.

The best of Sydney's chefs somehow manage to instill each dish with an almost magical dimension of extra taste, which lingers mysteriously, challenging, teasing, and bewildering. Chris Manfield is one of the city's most lauded younger chefs and one of the chief magicians. She weaves Asian and Western flavors into a style so bold and original it approaches wizardry. Yet her preparations are rarely overworked or excessive.

Neither of us will forget our first taste of this alchemy for the palate. Her version of a bewitching Thai coconut broth was infused with aromatics at various stages of cooking. The result was a beguiling layering of tastes.

She cooked baby chicken at a low temperature in a broth flavored with rock sugar, cassia bark, and soy. The bird was then hung out to dry, fried to a crisp and served with a mandarin-scented black rice timbale and a chile jam that required eight hours in a slow oven to meld the flavors. A fillet of delicate pink ocean trout enclosing a light mousse of prawns and toasted nori appeared in a pool of prawn sauce so reduced it tasted of toasted almonds. Then our taste buds were elevated even farther by her combination of roasted coconut ice cream and intensely flavored mango sorbet sculpted together in a perfect geometric design. This is the kind of food that leaves you wondering "just how did it all happen?"

After stints at several

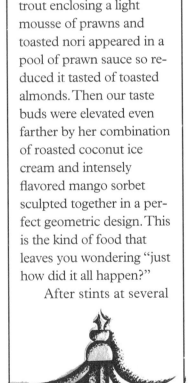

restaurants Chris has finally opened the Paramount, a knockout restaurant where Sydney's trendy set spend their nights entranced by her New Age tastes. As one Australian reviewer put it "if Sydney were a restaurant it would look very much like The Paramount."

When it comes to ethnic dining, Sydney has much to offer. But the Thai food at Darley Street Thai is in a class of its own. The chef/owner David Thompson, who has lived in Thailand and speaks the language, creates dishes that are bold and vibrant with flavors that can come only from the kind of passionate research and lengthy, painstaking preparation the cuisine requires. The crispy fried chicken in pandanus leaf, beautifully textured salads, intriguing curries, and perfectly cooked seafood dishes testify to one of the subtlest knowledges of Thai cuisine in the English-speaking world. We learned as much about it from David as we did on our trips to Thailand.

121

Pan-Fried Salmon with Sesame Crust

Grilled Salmon with Spiced Butter

Grilled Salmon Steaks with Cilantro Pesto

Miso-Poached Salmon with Pearl Onions

Sautéed Halibut with Peanut and Herb Vinaigrette

Grilled Ahi with Toasted Curry Oil

Grilled Swordfish with Sesame-Scallion Relish

Grilled Tuna...with Thai Dressing

Barbecued Flounder in Hot and Pungent Sauce

Fried Flounder in Sri Lankan Spices

Steamed Black Sea Bass with Black Vinegar Sauce

Goodwood Park Sea Bass with Plum Wine Sauce

Tamarind-Honey Glazed Baked Snapper

Grilled Snapper in a Tangy Infusion

Red Snapper Cakes Orientale

Steamed Fish with Chile-Lime Sauce

Balinese Baked Fish with Macadamia-Turmeric Sauce

Broiled Bluefish with Caramelized Lemons

Seared Snapper with Passion Fruit Sauce

Thai-Style Stir-Fried Squid

Coconut Scallop Tempura with Mango-Mustard Sauce

Pan-Fried Scallops with Orange-Basil Sauce

Elizabeth's Shrimp in Chile-Onion Sambal

Fragrant Shrimp with Crispy Basil and Shiitakes

Pulau Ubin Garlic Prawns

Nonya Pineapple Shrimp

Almond-Coated Shrimp Cakes

Singapore Chile Crab

Grilled Sesame Crab Hash

Black Pepper Soft-Shell Crabs

Double-Prosperity Clams

Mussels with Lemongrass Herb Butter

Summery New Zealand Mussels

Luck and Prosperity Oyster Stew

FISH
AND
SEAFOOD

Let's begin at The End of the World. This is neither a street sign nor the title of a sermon in an evangelical chapel. It is in fact the name of a restaurant located at the far northwestern tip of Penang Island, in northwestern Malaysia, where you can get one of the best fresh fish feasts in Southeast Asia.

The setting is magnificent, especially if you go—as you should—in time for the sunset. The restaurant has indoor and outdoor sections spread along the beach. Opposite is a creaking wooden jetty that stretches far into the tranquil shallows of the bay. Tied up to great wooden piles along it are a score of gaily painted fishing boats. Those in the "mud dock" nearest the shore are stranded at fantastic angles, like beached whales caught in mid somersault. At the end of the day the crews often lounge in their rope hammocks or stretch out on the decks. Beyond the boats the intricate coastal profile of the island, dotted with fruit and spice trees and framed by grainy patterned rocks, blends with the horizon and the haze. The beach, the boats, the pier, lush, tropical vegetation and deep purple-blue water: What more could you want from your dinnertime view?

You settle into your chair, sipping tinglingly cold beer, and watch the ocean recede into the sunset. Interrupted from your reverie, you look around you and see large Chinese families devouring huge plates of crabs and giant prawns. Waiters are rushing to and fro carrying platters of steamed fish with ginger and scallion sauce. A briny aroma of oysters is punctuated by the fragrance of the black bean sauce. Fried fish still crackles from the sizzling oil. You order some giant chile crab and grilled sting ray, smothered with a fiery *sambal* and packaged in a banana leaf. The vibrant green bok choy comes redolent with garlic. You are in heaven.

Besides the sensual thrill of it all, what makes a Pacific seafood experience so special? The first answer is the Asian dedication to freshness and quality. Asians are obsessed with seafood and will pay anything for a prize catch. To the Asian palate fresh fish is live fish, hence the popular Chinese restaurant practice of keeping live fish in tanks for the diners to choose. At Asian fish markets, the fish is delivered within hours of being caught, and by the end of the market day it can be had for a song, as its price decreases by the hour.

The seasonings and preparation methods are dictated by this drive for quality. Once you have gorgeous seafood, you won't want to mask its flavor with a heavy sauce or complex preparation. Stir frying over very high heat with a flash of flavor from garlic or black beans is one option, which works especially well with shellfish. For a firmer fish with delicate taste, nothing beats steaming—it cooks the fish gently, bringing out its sweet natural flavor, which should be complemented with a quickly prepared, lightly spicy sauce. For a robust fish such as tuna or swordfish, pan frying and wok searing are a great option, especially if you serve the finished fish on a bed of greens or a colorful vegetable stir-fry, doused with a light aromatic sauce. And when barbecue is the order of the day, your fish will benefit from a flavorful marinade and a refreshing herb-based sauce or side dish of caramelized grilled lemons. These dishes are a step beyond the end of the world—they are truly heavenly.

PAN-FRIED SALMON

with Sesame Crust

This crispy-skinned salmon, with its mix of Chinese-Japanese sweet and spicy flavors, is wonderful and simple to prepare. For a beautiful presentation, serve it on a bed of colorful stir-fried vegetables or Chinese greens.

4 salmon fillets (6 to 7
ounces each), with skin on
¼ cup sake or medium-dry
sherry
1½ teaspoons grated fresh ginger
1 teaspoon minced garlic
3½ tablespoons tamari soy sauce
3 teaspoons Oriental sesame oil
2 scallions, smashed
2½ teaspoons hot Chinese mustard
1½ teaspoons (packed) light brown sugar,
plus more to taste
2 tablespoons peanut or canola oil
3 tablespoons Fish Stock (page 385)
or water

1. Rinse the salmon fillets and pat dry with paper towels.

2. In a shallow dish, whisk together the sake, ginger, garlic, 2½ tablespoons soy sauce, 1 teaspoon of the sesame oil, and scallions. Add the salmon fillets and turn to coat with the marinade. Cover and refrigerate for 2 to 4 hours, turning occasionally.

3. In a small bowl, whisk together the remaining soy sauce, the remaining sesame oil, the mustard, and 1½ teaspoons sugar. Remove the salmon from the marinade and shake off the excess. Strain and reserve the marinade. Brush the skin of the salmon with the mustard glaze.

4. Heat the peanut oil in a large, nonstick skillet over medium-high heat until almost smoking. Add the salmon, glazed side down, and cook until the skin is deep golden and crispy, about 4 minutes. Brush the skinless side of the salmon with mustard glaze and turn over. Cook until the salmon is opaque and just begins to flake, 2 to 3 minutes more. Carefully remove the salmon to a heatproof platter and keep warm in a 200°F oven while making the sauce. (If you simply cover the salmon with aluminum foil to keep warm, the skin will get soggy.)

5. Add the reserved marinade and stock to the skillet and reduce over high heat for about 3 minutes. Adjust the amount of sugar to taste. Divide the salmon among 4 plates and spoon the sauce around it.

SERVES 4

GRILLED SALMON

with Spiced Butter

The amount of Spiced Butter in the recipe below is about double what you will need for 4 people. You can freeze the leftover and serve it with other firm fish—mahi-mahi, tuna, or swordfish—or shellfish or steak. It will keep in a freezer for up to 2 months; just let it stand at room temperature for 2 to 3 hours before serving.

4 salmon steaks (8 ounces each)
Peanut oil, for brushing salmon
Salt and freshly ground black pepper, to taste
Spiced Butter (recipe follows)

1. Prepare coals for grilling or preheat the broiler.

2. Rinse the salmon steaks and pat dry with paper towels. Brush the salmon lightly with oil and season with salt and pepper. Grill or broil the fish until slightly charred and the flesh flakes easily when tested with a fork, 4 to 5 minutes per side.

3. Unwrap the butter and cut off four ½-inch slices. Place the fish on serving plates and top with a slice of the butter. Serve at once.

SERVES 4

Spiced Butter

7 tablespoons unsalted butter, at room
    temperature
1 teaspoon grated fresh ginger
2 cloves garlic, crushed through a press
2 teaspoons sambal oelek (page 388) or
    Chinese chile paste with garlic
3 tablespoons finely chopped fresh cilantro
    leaves
¼ teaspoon ground coriander
¼ teaspoon ground turmeric
1 tablespoon fresh lime juice
1 tablespoon fresh orange juice
3 tablespoons coarsely ground roasted
    peanuts

Combine all the ingredients in a food processor and process until blended. Place a sheet of waxed paper on your work surface. Using a rubber spatula, scrape the butter onto

the paper and form into a 3½ x 1-inch log. Roll up tightly, twist the ends of the paper, and chill until firm, at least 2 hours.

MAKES ABOUT ⅔ CUP

GRILLED SALMON STEAKS
with Cilantro Pesto

The delicate taste of the salmon is accented by the sprightly pesto flavor, and their pink and green colors are visually pleasing as well.

CILANTRO PESTO
¾ cup tightly packed fresh cilantro leaves
2 serrano chiles, stemmed, seeded
    to taste, and chopped
2 cloves garlic, minced
½ cup coarsely chopped raw cashews
1 teaspoon grated lime zest
1 teaspoon grated orange zest
2½ tablespoons fresh lime juice
½ teaspoon sugar, or more to taste
1 teaspoon freshly ground white pepper
5 tablespoons light olive oil (do not use
    virgin or extra-virgin)
1 tablespoon rice vinegar
1½ teaspoons tamari soy sauce
Salt, to taste

4 salmon steaks (8 ounces each), 1 inch
    thick

1. Combine the cilantro, chiles, garlic, cashews, lime and orange zests, lime juice, sugar, and pepper in a food processor and process until finely minced. With the processor running, pour in the oil through the feed tube and process until emulsified. Scrape the mixture into a bowl and add the vinegar, soy sauce, and salt to taste, if needed.

2. Prepare coals for grilling or preheat the broiler.

3. Rinse the salmon steaks and pat dry with paper towels. Season the steaks with salt and brush them lightly with some of the pesto. Reserve the rest.

4. Grill or broil the fish until lightly charred and the flesh flakes easily with a fork, 4 to 5 minutes per side. Serve at once with the remaining pesto on the side.

SERVES 4

MISO-POACHED SALMON

with Pearl Onions

This dish was created by San Francisco chef Bruce Hill as an entry in the regional finals of the Evian Healthy Menu Award. In its full presentation, the salmon

was served on a purée of celery root and Yukon Gold potatoes, accompanied by red and white pearl onions and wild baby leeks, and topped with oven-crisped julienned leeks. The result was perfect, a healthy dish, full of flavor. I have simplified the recipe for home use, but it remains one of my favorites. You can serve it with either its original accompaniment of the Celery Root Purée, simple mashed potatoes, or steamed rice.

*2¼ pounds skinless salmon fillet, cut
    into 6 pieces*
¾ cup yellow miso paste (shiro miso)
*4 cups Chicken Stock (page 384) or
    low-salt canned broth*
*½ cup mirin or sake (if using sake, add
    1 tablespoon sugar to the poaching liquid)*
3½ tablespoons tamari soy sauce
*18 pearl onions, preferably a mix of
    white and red, blanched and peeled*
Celery Root Purée (recipe follows, optional)

1. Rinse the salmon pieces and pat dry with paper towels.

2. Place the miso paste in a medium-size bowl and slowly add about 1 cup of the stock, stirring until smooth. Combine the miso mixture, remaining stock, mirin, and soy sauce in a large shallow saucepan and bring to a boil over medium heat. Add the onions and cook, covered, until tender, about 8 minutes, stirring occasionally.

3. Add the salmon and poach, covered, until just cooked through, about 2½ minutes per side.

4. To serve, place some of the celery root purée on each plate, top with a piece of salmon, add some onions and drizzle with some poaching liquid. You can also serve the salmon and onions, sprinkled with the poaching liquid, on a serving platter accompanied by the purée.

SERVES 6

Celery Root Purée

3 cups peeled, 1-inch cubes fresh celery root
1 cup peeled and diced Yukon Gold potatoes
2 tablespoons unsalted butter, at room
    temperature
Salt, to taste
Freshly ground white pepper, to taste

1. Boil the celery root and potatoes in a large pot of salted water until tender, about 12 minutes. Drain well.

2. Place the celery root, potatoes, and butter in a food processor and purée until smooth. To remove any lumps and tough fibers, press through a strainer into a bowl. Season to taste with salt and pepper.

SERVES 6, AS AN ACCOMPANIMENT TO THE SALMON

SAUTEED HALIBUT

with Peanut and Herb Vinaigrette

The extraordinary vinaigrette served in this halibut dish is based on the flavors of the typically Vietnamese garnish of chopped roasted peanuts, cilantro, and Asian basil. It beautifully complements the sweet taste and firm texture of the halibut, making the dish one of my all-time favorites.

PEANUT AND HERB VINAIGRETTE

3 tablespoons roasted peanuts
1 tablespoon chopped shallot
2 cloves garlic, chopped
2 teaspoons chopped fresh ginger
1 small fresh hot chile, green or red, stemmed
    seeded, and chopped
3 tablespoons chopped fresh cilantro leaves
2 tablespoons chopped fresh basil leaves,
    preferably Thai or purple
1 tablespoon rice vinegar
2 tablespoons red wine vinegar
1 tablespoon fresh lime juice
½ cup walnut or peanut oil
Salt and freshly ground black pepper,
    to taste

4 halibut steaks (6 ounces each), about
    ¾ inch thick
1 tablespoon peanut oil
2 roasted red bell peppers, cut into strips

1. Make the vinaigrette: Place the peanuts in a food processor and process for several pulses until chopped but not ground. Add the shallot, garlic, ginger, chile, cilantro, and basil and process until finely minced. Add the vinegars and lime juice, then, with the processor running, slowly drizzle in the oil through the feed tube until emulsified. With a rubber spatula, scrape the mixture into a bowl and add salt to taste and ½ teaspoon black pepper. Set aside for at least 30 minutes to allow the flavors to develop.

2. Rinse the halibut steaks and pat dry with paper towels. Rub the steaks on both sides with salt and pepper. Heat the peanut oil in a large skillet over high heat until hot but not smoking. Add the fish and cook until just opaque throughout, about 3 minutes per side.

3. Set one fish steak on each dinner plate, spoon the vinaigrette over the fish and top with the roasted peppers. Serve at once.

SERVES 4

GRILLED AHI

with Toasted Curry Oil

This contemporary California dish hails from the kitchen of the San Diego-based chef Jeff Tunks—who cooks at the Azzura Point Restaurant in Coronado, known for its imaginatively prepared seafood and the spectacular nighttime view of the bay. The clever interplay of the dense, intensely flavored curry oil, which lingers on the back of the palate, and the burst of tangy freshness in the mango is a great success, and the dish is both innovative and simple to prepare.

The tuna here must be grilled over very high heat so that it is slightly charred on the outside and rare on the inside. If you're making the tuna indoors, don't broil it unless your broiler heat is very intense. Instead, sear it in a well-heated wok or cast-iron skillet to achieve the right effect.

FISH AND MARINADE

4 top-quality boneless tuna steaks (5 to
   6 ounces each), preferably ahi

3 tablespoons soy sauce

3 tablespoons virgin olive oil

1 tablespoon oyster sauce

1 tablespoon minced scallions

2 cloves garlic, crushed through a press

1 tablespoon grated fresh ginger

1 teaspoon (packed) light brown sugar

TOASTED CURRY OIL

3½ tablespoons best-quality curry powder,
   preferably homemade (page 390)

⅓ cup virgin olive oil

3½ tablespoons fresh lime juice

Mango Relish (recipe follows)

1. Rinse the tuna steaks and pat dry with paper towels.

2. Combine all the marinade ingredients in a shallow bowl, add the fish, and toss to coat. Refrigerate for 2 to 4 hours, turning occasionally.

3. Make the curry oil: Stir the curry powder in a small skillet over medium-low heat until very fragrant, about 1½ minutes. Add the oil and heat for 2 minutes. Remove from the heat and let stand in the skillet for 2 hours, stirring once. Strain into a clean jar through a small strainer lined with cheesecloth. Stir in the lime juice.

4. Prepare coals for grilling or preheat the broiler.

5. Grill the fish until lightly charred on the outside and rare inside, about 2½ minutes on each side. (Alternatively, shake off the excess marinade and sear the tuna for 1 to 2 minutes on each side in a hot wok or cast-iron skillet.)

6. To serve, cut each piece of fish into medium-thick slices. Arrange the slices in a fan fashion on 4 plates, spoon some Mango Relish in the center of the fan, and spoon some curry oil around the fish.

SERVES 4

Mango Relish

¾ cup diced fresh mango

¼ cup minced red onion

¼ cup diced red bell pepper

¼ cup chopped fresh cilantro leaves

1 teaspoon minced jalapeño pepper

1 tablespoon minced fresh ginger

5 tablespoons fresh lime juice

Salt, to taste

Combine all the ingredients in a small bowl and let stand at room temperature for 30 minutes to meld the flavors.

MAKES ABOUT 1¾ CUPS

GRILLED SWORDFISH

with Sesame-Scallion Relish

In the American food scene of the 1980s and 90s, grilled swordfish, served with a lively exotic salsa or relish of some kind, has replaced sole meunière and trout almondine (remember them?) as the most frequently ordered and prepared seafood classics. Before we move on to something else (Amazonian seafood, perhaps), here is another delectable addition to your swordfish recipe collection. And if you are suffering from a swordfish overkill, try mako shark, tuna, or mahi-mahi.

SESAME-SCALLION RELISH

¼ cup sesame seeds

¾ cup chopped scallions

1 clove garlic, chopped

2 teaspoons chopped fresh
    ginger

1½ tablespoons tamari
    soy sauce

1 teaspoon rice vinegar

1 teaspoon Oriental
    sesame oil

¼ teaspoon sugar

Salt, to taste

SWORDFISH

4 swordfish steaks (about 7 ounces each),
    ½ inch thick

1½ tablespoons soy sauce

1 teaspoon (packed) light brown sugar

1 tablespoon peanut oil

Salt and freshly ground black pepper,
    to taste

1. Prepare coals for grilling or preheat the broiler.

2. Make the relish: Combine all the ingredients (through the salt, to taste) in a food processor and process until minced. Do not over-purée.

3. Rinse the swordfish steaks and pat dry with paper towels.

4. In a small bowl, whisk together the soy sauce, sugar, and oil. Rub the fish with salt and pepper and brush with the soy mixture. Grill or broil until just cooked through, about 4 minutes on each side. Serve with the relish.

SERVES 4

GRILLED TUNA ON A BED OF BOK CHOY

with Thai Dressing

In this recipe, the grilled tuna is presented on a bed of stir-fried bok choy, with its bright green leaves, which soaks up the tangy Thai dressing of lime, sugar, lemongrass, and chile. Try to get the tender baby bok choy, and be sure to put some fish and some bok choy on the same forkful.

2 small fresh hot chiles, green or red,
   stemmed, seeded and chopped
1 stalk fresh lemongrass (3 inches of the
   lower stalk, tough outer leaves
   discarded), sliced very thin
1½ to 2 tablespoons palm sugar or (packed)
   light brown sugar, or to taste
⅓ cup fresh lime juice
2 tablespoons Asian fish sauce, such as
   nam pla
2 teaspoons water
5 tablespoons finely chopped fresh
   cilantro leaves
6 tuna steaks (6 ounces each), 1 inch thick
2 teaspoons light olive oil (do not use virgin
   or extra-virgin)
2 teaspoons freshly ground black pepper
1 tablespoon vegetable oil
2 medium heads bok choy, trimmed, white
   stems sliced thin, leaves coarsely shredded
4 large cloves garlic, chopped

1. Combine the chiles, lemongrass, sugar, lime juice, fish sauce, and water in a small nonreactive saucepan. Bring to a simmer, stirring to dissolve the sugar, then remove from the heat. Cool to room temperature and add the cilantro.

2. Prepare coals for grilling or preheat the broiler.

3. Rinse the tuna steaks and pat dry with paper towels. Brush the steaks with the olive oil and sprinkle with black pepper.

4. Grill the tuna until charred on the outside and still pink inside, about 4 minutes per side.

5. In a wok or skillet, heat the vegetable oil over high heat until almost smoking. Add the bok choy and garlic and cook, stirring, until the leaves are just wilted.

6. Divide the bok choy among 6 plates. Place a tuna steak on top of each portion and drizzle with the dressing.

SERVES 6

BARBECUED FLOUNDER

in Hot and Pungent Sauce

At street stalls and markets in Malaysia and Singapore, vendors hawk flounder or stingray smouldered with a fiery pungent sauce of red chiles and shrimp paste, wrapped in banana leaves and barbecued over an open fire. The idea of brushing the fish with the intense chile sauce does not have to be limited to flounder. I have tasted it with many other fish and it was almost as good. Try it with grilled sea bass, swordfish steaks, or any whole fish you want to throw on the grill.

8 dried hot red chiles (2 to 3 inches long),
   preferably Asian
1 tablespoon anchovy paste
1½ tablespoons chopped fresh lemongrass
   (3 inches of the lower stalk, tough outer
   leaves discarded)
3 tablespoons chopped red onion
1 small red bell pepper, stemmed, seeded,
   and chopped
2 large cloves garlic, chopped
1 tablespoon peanut oil, plus more if needed
1 whole flounder (about 2 pounds), gutted
   and cleaned but head and tail left on
Salt, to taste

1. Stem the chiles and shake out the seeds. Using scissors, cut the chiles into pieces. Soak in warm water to cover for 10 minutes. Drain well.

2. Prepare coals for grilling or preheat the broiler.

THE SARAWAK CULTURAL VILLAGE

Terrific Pacific • *Fish and Seafood*

In order to understand something about the way people live on the great island of Borneo, we were advised to visit the Sarawak Cultural Village. So, Anya and I left Kuching, the capital of Sarawak on a road parallel to the wiry old suspension bridge on the northern exit route. The bridge is the butt of much local humor. Begun in 1902, it wasn't completed until twenty-four years later. The Dayak construction workers were convinced that the spirits of the bridge needed a blood sacrifice to appease them. Their superstition gave rise to a penya-mun, or headhunting scare, and plagued the project for years until a worker happened to fall into the river from the makeshift scaffolding and never resurfaced. Its appetite thus satisfied, the bridge was finally opened in 1926 and is now known, with a deferential nod to San Francisco, as the Silver Gate Bridge of Sarawak.

We made our way through countryside thick with versatile atap palms—the fronds are used for thatch, and the sap is made into sugar. We wound through some gentle hills, past an eighteen-hole golf course designed by Arnold Palmer, glimpsed the turtle islands a short distance off-shore, and arrived at the Kampung Budaya (the Sarawak Cultural Village). Although the village is a composed rather than natural one, it is emphatically not an ethnic Disneyland. In a spectacular lakeside setting under the shadow of the steepest side of the mountain, an authentic dwelling from each of the seven major indigenous peoples of Borneo has been built. Each is fully furnished with uten-sils and ritual objects and occupied during the day by native people who demonstrate their crafts, cuisine, dances, and daily routines.

THE INDIGENOUS ROUTE

The tour of the village starts at a wonderful bamboo bridge that leads to an elevated Bidayuh Round House. The Bidayuh, called land Dayaks by the European settlers, lived mainly in the high limestone mountains in western Sarawak. Their bamboo work, which they use for construction, cooking, and even for pipes, is famous. Outside the house is a homemade sugarcane press with hardwood rollers to crush the cane.

The nearby Iban longhouse represents the culture of the largest native group in Sarawak. These longhouses were traditionally sited close to a river and were built to last for about eighteen years, the time it took to exhaust adjacent agricultural land. Some of the longhouses are massive. A common covered walkway runs the length of the dwelling, with the individual "family" rooms leading off it. Each family room has an upstairs "attic" used for storage, sleeping, or weaving the pau kumbu, the Iban's colorful, tie-dyed, ceremonial textiles.

Behind the longhouse are a few temporary shelters made from saplings, bark, and palm leaves in the style of the nomadic Penan people, who still inhabit the jungles of central Borneo. These would normally be situated next to a thick stand of wild sago palms, the source of the

Penans' staple food. Here we were given a lesson on making and using blowpipes fashioned from ironwood. In the jungle the darts would be cunningly dosed with poison from the sap of the upas tree. The Penan boys laughed at Anya uproariously as her dart flew a measly few yards on the first attempt at blowing, and applauded wildly when she actually managed to hit the large makeshift target (well off-center) after a few tries.

The other dwellings in the village include an Orang Ulu ironwood longhouse (built to last) and a twelve-yard-high Melanau house with an adjacent sago-processing hut. The coastal Melanau prefer sago to rice and are expert at grinding it into flour, and then cooking up biscuits, grits, and other delicacies on a huge clay griddle.

The tour winds down with two houses representing the dominant sedentary cultures of Sarawak. There is a traditional urban Malay dwelling, built on stilts with decorative stairs, railings, and fascia boards. And the final stop was a Chinese farmhouse typical of the Hakka and Foochow people, who were invited by the white rajahs at the turn of the century to develop market agriculture and work the tin mines.

When we returned to the wooden terrace of the visitor center, we looked back over the village. Clouds floated around the midriff of Mount Santubong, and we could hear the percussive sounds of some of the local dances. We felt a sense of peace and a sense of the real Borneo.

3. In a food processor, combine the chiles, anchovy paste, lemongrass, onion, pepper, and garlic. Process to a paste, adding a little oil to assist blending, if necessary.

4. Heat the 1 tablespoon oil in a small skillet over low heat. Add the chile paste and cook, stirring, until it is fragrant and no longer tastes raw, about 5 minutes.

5. Rinse the flounder inside and out and pat dry with paper towels. Brush the fish on both sides with the chile mixture.

6. Grill or broil, as close as possible to the heat, until the fish is lightly charred and opaque, about 5 minutes per side.

SERVES 2, OR 6 WITH OTHER COURSES

FRIED FLOUNDER
in Sri Lankan Spices

Matthew Moran, the young chef-proprietor of a popular Sydney bistro, served me this dish upon his return from a holiday in Sri Lanka. He suggested making it with thin, mild-flavored fish fillets, which would really absorb the haunting, sweet and hot marinade. It is important to heat the ghee (available at Indian markets), or clarified butter, very well, so that the fish is just seared, crispy on the outside and juicy inside. The side salad of tomatoes, cucumbers, and red onion, which adds a piquant crunch to the gentle sweetness of the fish, is a sign of Portuguese influence on Sri Lankan cuisine.

MARINADE

Generous pinch of pulverized saffron
threads

½ teaspoon ground cayenne pepper

1½ teaspoons best-quality curry powder

1 tablespoon grated fresh ginger

2 cloves garlic, crushed through a press

3 tablespoons mango chutney, strained
through a strainer

Salt and freshly ground black pepper,
to taste

8 thin flounder fillets (about 4 ounces
each)

2 small, firm cucumbers, peeled, halved
lengthwise, and cut into ½-inch-thick
slices

3 firm, ripe tomatoes, seeded and cut into
strips

½ cup sliced red onion

1 fresh hot green chile, stemmed, seeded,
and minced

1½ tablespoons red wine vinegar

1 tablespoon olive oil

¼ cup (packed) coarsely chopped fresh
flat-leaf parsley leaves

6 tablespoons clarified butter (page 390)

1. In a small bowl, combine the marinade ingredients and stir well.

2. Rinse the flounder fillets and pat dry with paper towels.

3. Arrange the fish fillets in a single layer in a large shallow dish and brush on both sides with the marinade. Cover with plastic wrap and refrigerate for 2 to 6 hours.

4. In a medium-size bowl, mix together the cucumbers, tomatoes, onion, and chile. Sprinkle on the vinegar and oil, season with salt and pepper, and toss. Let stand at room temperature for 1 hour to marinate lightly.

5. Divide the clarified butter between two heavy skillets and heat over medium-high heat until very hot. Add 4 fish fillets to each

skillet and cook until golden and crispy on the outside and just opaque inside, about 2 minutes on each side. Divide the fish among 4 plates and arrange the salad on the side. Serve at once.

SERVES 4

STEAMED BLACK SEA BASS

with Black Vinegar Sauce

Just the right dish for a special occasion, this beautifully prepared fish, on its bed of bright greens, deserves your best china. As is always the case with steaming, the fish has to be absolutely impeccably fresh. When at the fish market, take advantage of what looks best, rather than pursuing a particular fish. Substitute salmon, rock cod, or other firm, clean-tasting fish fillets for the black sea bass.

6 skinless black sea bass fillets (about
6 ounces each)

2 tablespoons Chinese rice wine

4½ tablespoons light soy sauce

1 tablespoon Asian fish sauce, such as
nam pla

2 small bunches spinach (about
1 pound), trimmed

Black Vinegar Sauce (recipe
follows)

Julienned fresh ginger, for garnish

Scallion flowers, for garnish
(see Note)

1. Rinse the sea bass fillets and pat dry with paper towels.

2. In a small bowl, whisk together the rice wine, soy sauce, and fish sauce. Arrange the fish fillets in a single layer in a large, shallow dish and pour the marinade over them. Turn the fillets to coat them with the marinade, then cover and refrigerate for 2 hours. Bring to room temperature before steaming.

3. Pour water to a depth of 2 inches in a wok or on the bottom of a regular steamer and bring to a boil. Line a steamer insert with baking parchment. Place the fish in one layer on top of the parchment. Set the steamer insert over the boiling water, cover tightly, and steam over high heat until the fish is opaque throughout, about 8 minutes.

4. Rinse the spinach well, but do not drain. Place it in a skillet and cook over medium-high heat, stirring, in the liquid clinging to the leaves until wilted, 2 to 3 minutes.

5. Drain the spinach and divide it among 6 plates. Arrange a fish fillet on top. Pour the vinegar sauce on and around the fish and garnish with julienned ginger and scallion flowers.

SERVES 6

Note: To make scallion flowers, trim the scallions to about 3 inches long. Using a small sharp knife, cut the top 1½ inches of remaining green stem into thin fringe, then place the scallions in ice water to curl the fringe. Shake out the excess water before serving.

Black Vinegar Sauce

This dark, mild vinegar, made from wheat, millet, or sorghum, is available at Chinese markets. The Chinese believe in its healing properties, so Chinese women who adhere to traditions often take it as an energy restorer after childbirth. If unavailable, substitute 1 part rice vinegar to 2 parts balsamic vinegar.

Young, green ginger is available in the early fall in Asian and specialty produce markets in the United States.

2 teaspoons peanut oil
1 teaspoon Oriental sesame oil
2 teaspoons finely minced fresh ginger, preferably young, green ginger
¼ cup sliced scallions
3½ tablespoons Chinese black vinegar
4 tablespoons dark soy sauce
1¼ cups Fish Stock (page 385) or bottled clam juice
1½ to 2 tablespoons palm sugar or (packed) light brown sugar, to taste
1 tablespoon cornstarch, mixed with 1½ tablespoons cold water

Heat the peanut and sesame oils in a medium-size skillet over medium heat and cook the ginger and scallions, stirring, until soft and aromatic, about 1 minute. Add the black vinegar, soy sauce, fish stock, and sugar and bring to a boil. Reduce the heat to low and simmer for 10 minutes. Slowly drizzle in the cornstarch mixture and cook, stirring, until the sauce is glossy and slightly thickened.

MAKES ABOUT 1½ CUPS

GOODWOOD PARK SLICED SEA BASS

with Plum Wine Sauce

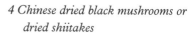

As you will see from this delicate sea bass in a sauce perfumed with plum wine and ginger, the quality of the food in the Goodwood Hotel's Chang Jiang Shanghai restaurant perfectly matches the opulence of the setting.

4 Chinese dried black mushrooms or dried shiitakes

1¼ pounds skinless sea bass fillet, at least 1 inch thick

1 tablespoon peanut oil

½ teaspoon minced garlic

½ teaspoon minced fresh ginger

2 scallions, trimmed and sliced

3 tablespoons Chinese plum wine (hua tiao chiew)

½ cup Chicken Stock (page 384) or canned broth

½ cup fresh or frozen green peas, thawed if frozen

¼ teaspoon sugar

1 teaspoon cornstarch, mixed with 2 teaspoons cold water

Salt and freshly ground black pepper, to taste

1½ teaspoons snipped fresh chives, for garnish

GOODWOOD PARK IN SINGAPORE

If you love hotels packed with history, then you'll love the Goodwood Park in Singapore. Located on leafy Scotts Road about ten minutes from the city center, the Goodwood was originally built as the Teutonia Club for local German residents. The main facade looks like a cross between a Rhineland castle and a Byzantine cathedral. After World War I it served as an electricity station, before being converted into a luxury hotel in 1929.

The Japanese knew a good hotel when they saw it and used the property as their headquarters and residence from 1942 to 1944. This accident of history aside, the Goodwood has served as a world-class hotel without interruption since then. Today there are no fewer than seven different restaurants at the hotel, including the excel-

lent Gordon Grill (specializing in high-quality meat and game dishes), the Japanese restaurant Shima, and the Min Jiang Sichuan restaurant.

Outstanding, though, is the Goodwood's Chang Jiang Shanghai. The interior is long and narrow, a fact reflected in the restaurant's name—Chang Jian means "long river," referring to China's longest river, the Yangtze. The decor is animated by maroon, gold, and ivory, and the walls are of curved onyx, the furnishings bleached teak. As a final touch, the chopsticks are plated in 24-carat gold. Here you can taste the very best of traditional Shanghai fare in combination with the fine dining service. I was fortunate to have the chef share with me his recipe for a lovely sea bass. It's pure 24-carat gold.

1. Rinse the mushrooms well and soak in hot water for 30 minutes. Remove and discard the stems and slice the caps thin.

2. Rinse the sea bass fillet and pat dry with paper towels. Holding a large, sharp knife at an angle, cut the fish crosswise into 8 slices.

3. In a large skillet or wok, heat half the oil until hot but not smoking. Add the fish and sauté on both sides until opaque and light golden, about 3 minutes total. Remove from the skillet and keep warm.

4. Add the remaining oil to the skillet and heat over high heat. Add the garlic, ginger, and scallions and stir, until aromatic, about 30 seconds. Add the mushrooms and stir for 3 more minutes. Stir in the wine and cook until reduced by half, about 1 minute. Add the stock, peas, and sugar and bring to a boil. Stir in the cornstarch mixture, reduce the heat and cook until the sauce thickens, about 1 minute. Season with salt and pepper.

5. Return the fish to the skillet and turn gently to coat with the sauce. Serve at once, garnished with chives.

SERVES 4

TAMARIND-HONEY-GLAZED BAKED SNAPPER

Fish, deep-fried or baked and served with some manner of sweet-and-sour sauce, is one of the most-ordered dishes in Thai restaurants in the U.S. While at many restaurants the sauce is purveyed from bottles and jars, here the authentic glaze for the crispy fish is a delicate combination of honey and fruity-tart tamarind. The versatile glaze is delicious with grilled or baked poultry, fish, or meat. Give it a try next time you are roasting a duck.

The fish will look great with a simple and colorful vegetable stir-fry, such as Orangey Fennel and Red Pepper Stir-fry (see Index).

*1 whole red snapper (5 to 6 pounds), gutted
and cleaned, with head and tail left on
2 teaspoons chopped fresh mint
Salt and freshly ground black pepper, to taste
Tamarind Glaze (recipe follows)*

1. Preheat the oven to 400°F.

2. Rinse the fish, inside and out, and pat dry with paper towels. Make 4 slits about ½ inch deep and 2 inches long on each side of the fish. Rub the slits with salt and pepper and stuff with the mint. Season the cavity of the fish with salt and pepper.

3. Place the fish in a roasting pan and brush all over with the Tamarind Glaze. Bake until the thickest part of the fish flakes easily when tested with a fork and the skin is crisp. This should take 45 minutes to 1 hour, depending on the size of the fish. Brush several times with the remaining glaze while baking. Serve at once.

SERVES 6 WITH OTHER DISHES

When it comes to steaming fish, freshness is all; and, as any Asian cook would tell you, the only fresh fish is live fish. If you know of a good Chinese fish market with a live fish tank, you should make every effort to get your fish there. The experience of shopping at Chinese fish markets, jam-packed with aggressive customers and strange-looking fish, is certainly intimidating, but nothing beats it for quality and prices. Act boldly and confidently—the worst policy is to linger and ask questions. Pick the fish that looks best to you, ask for the price (this question is universally understood), and give precise instructions as to how you want the fish cleaned. You are guaranteed the respect of the fishmonger, and you might even get a smile.

Tamarind Glaze

1½ tablespoons tamarind pulp, preferably from Thailand
⅓ cup boiling water
2 teaspoons pressed, crushed garlic
1½ teaspoons ginger juice (page 390)
½ teaspoon dried red pepper flakes
1 tablespoon distilled white vinegar
1½ tablespoons honey
2 teaspoons ketchup
1 teaspoon soy sauce
Salt, to taste

1. Soak the tamarind pulp in the boiling water off the heat for 15 minutes. Stir and mash it with a fork to help it dissolve. Strain through a fine strainer into a bowl, pressing on the solids with the back of a wooden spoon to extract all the liquid.

2. Combine the tamarind liquid with the remaining ingredients in a small nonreactive saucepan before using and heat, stirring until the honey is dissolved. Cool slightly.

MAKES ABOUT ⅓ CUP

GRILLED SNAPPER

in a Tangy Infusion

Grilled or poached seafood and vegetables afloat in a bewitchingly fragrant broth, tart with the flavors of tamarind or lime, is a customary offering at a Thai meal, classified somewhere between curry and soup. This preparation also fits in with the recent trend of serving fish or meat in intensely flavored aromatic liquids, known as "infusions."

You can serve this as a first course or a light luncheon or supper entrée, accompanied by steamed rice. Prepare the tamarind liquid and the chile paste up to several days ahead, if you wish. Thais usually don't use stock, preferring water infused with aromatics, but if you desire an extra dimension of taste, use Aromatic Shrimp Stock (see Index), if you have it at hand. The aromatic paste which infuses the liquid is essentially a red curry paste, so if you have already tried a red curry dish from this book and have homemade Red Curry Paste (see Index) in your freezer, you can use that instead of making the mixture all over again. Use about 2½ to 3 tablespoons and omit steps 2 to 4.

1½ tablespoons tamarind pulp, preferably from Thailand

½ cup boiling water

5 dried red chiles (2 to 3 inches long), preferably Asian

6 shallots, sliced

5 cloves garlic, sliced

2 teaspoons chopped fresh or frozen galangal, or fresh ginger

1 tablespoon chopped cilantro roots and/or stems

1 teaspoon freshly ground white pepper

1½ pounds thick red snapper fillets, cut into 4 pieces

2 teaspoons vegetable oil

Salt and freshly ground black pepper, to taste

5 cups water or Light and Aromatic Shrimp Stock (page 385)

¼ cup thinly sliced fresh lemongrass (3 inches of the lower stalk, tough outer leaves discarded)

2 tablespoons Asian fish sauce, such as nam pla

4 teaspoons sugar, or more to taste

1 tablespoon fresh lime juice

1 medium onion, halved and thinly sliced

½ cup sliced white mushroom caps

12 slender asparagus tips (each 2 inches long)

1 medium red bell pepper, stemmed, seeded, and julienned

16 snow peas, trimmed

3 small firm, ripe plum tomatoes, seeded and cut into strips

½ cup fresh basil leaves, preferably Thai

Fresh cilantro leaves, for garnish

1. Soak the tamarind pulp in the boiling water off the heat for 15 minutes. Stir and mash it with a fork to help it dissolve. Strain through a fine strainer into a bowl, pressing on the solids with the back of a wooden spoon to extract all the liquid. Reserve the liquid.

2. Stem the chiles and shake out the seeds. Using scissors, cut the chiles into pieces. In a small bowl, soak the chiles in warm water to cover for 10 minutes. Drain well.

3. Heat a heavy skillet or wok over medium heat. Add the shallots and garlic and dry-roast, stirring, until lightly charred, 5 to 7 minutes. Remove from the heat.

4. Combine the chiles, roasted shallots and garlic, galangal, cilantro, and ground white pepper in a food processor and process to a paste, adding a little water to assist the blending.

5. Prepare coals for grilling or preheat the broiler.

6. Rinse the red snapper pieces and pat dry with paper towels. Brush the fish with oil and season with salt and black pepper.

7. Grill or broil the fish until opaque and firm, 3 to 4 minutes per side. Remove from the grill or broiler and keep warm.

8. Bring the water to a boil in a medium-size saucepan. Add the chile paste and lemongrass and simmer over medium heat for about 7 minutes. Strain through a fine strainer and return to the saucepan. Add the tamarind liquid and bring to a simmer. Stir in the fish sauce, sugar, and lime juice.

9. Add the onion, mushrooms, asparagus, bell pepper, snow peas, and tomatoes

and simmer over medium heat until the vegetables are just tender, about 3 to 4 minutes. Stir in the basil.

10. To serve, place a piece of fish in a soup plate and ladle some broth and vegetables around it. Garnish each portion with cilantro leaves.

SERVES 4

RED SNAPPER CAKES ORIENTALE

These tasty fish cakes, laced with lemon grass, ginger, and garlic, are an amalgamation of two concepts—the wonderful chewy and spicy Thai fish cakes called *tord mun pla* and traditional American fish cakes, fluffy with cream and bread crumbs. The result is a perfect blend: exotic tastes nestled in familiar, nostalgic texture.

You can serve these with lemon wedges, or for a more formal presentation, in individual portions in a pool of bright orange Roasted Red Pepper Sauce (see Index). You can also make them any size you wish—bite-size to pass around as an hor d'ouevre, medium size for an elegant first course, and full size for the main meal.

Leftovers will taste great cold, dabbed with some spicy mayonnaise.

> 2 tablespoons chopped fresh lemongrass
>   (3 inches of the lower stalk, tough
>   outer leaves discarded)
> 3 cloves garlic, chopped
> 1½ teaspoons chopped fresh ginger
> 1½ teaspoons paprika
> ¼ to ½ teaspoon ground cayenne pepper
> ⅓ cup chopped onion
> 1 teaspoon ground turmeric
> 1 teaspoon freshly ground white pepper
> ½ cup heavy (or whipping) cream
> 1 pound red snapper fillets, skinned
>   and boned
> 2 large eggs, lightly beaten
> 2 cups fresh bread crumbs
> 1 teaspoon salt
> ⅓ cup finely diced red bell pepper
> ⅓ cup finely chopped red onion
> 3 tablespoons thinly sliced fresh
>   green beans
> ¼ cup chopped fresh cilantro
>   leaves
> 2 tablespoons vegetable oil
> 1 tablespoon unsalted butter
> Lemon wedges, for garnish
>   (optional)
> Roasted Red Pepper Sauce (page 47;
>   optional)

1. Combine the lemongrass, garlic, ginger, paprika, cayenne, onion, turmeric, white pepper, cilantro, and cream in a food processor and process to a paste. Scrape into a large bowl.

2. Rinse the red snapper fillets and pat dry with paper towels.

3. To the processor, add the fish and process until finely ground, then transfer to the bowl with the lemongrass paste. Stir in the eggs, 1¼ cups of the bread crumbs, and salt. Stir to combine. Add the bell pepper, red onion, beans, and cilantro and stir well. Cover the bowl with plastic wrap, and refrigerate for 2 hours.

4. Heat the oil and butter in a large skillet over medium heat. Lightly wet your hands and shape the fish mixture into 12 cakes. Roll in the remaining bread crumbs and fry, in batches, until golden, crispy, and cooked through, about 4 minutes per side. Drain on paper towels. Serve at once, accompanied by lemon wedges or Roasted Red Pepper Sauce.

SERVES 6

STEAMED FISH

with Chile-Lime Sauce

Accented with a sweet and tangy Thai sauce, this steamed fish will delight garlic and chile lovers. I have eaten this dish many times in Thailand, where it is prepared in two ways: the fish is either steamed *au naturel* and then served with the sauce, or the sauce is poured on the fish before steaming, which softens the effect of the garlic and chiles. I prefer the first option, as I like the contrast of a delicate steamed fish with the intense herbiness of the sauce. The sauce also provides just the right counterpoint to crispy deep-fried whole fish.

It is not worth seeking out a Thai grocery store just to stuff the fish with galangal, lemongrass, and kaffir lime, but certainly do it if you have them at hand. I am not a Lud-

dite, but using a mortar and pestle makes all the difference in this dish. I cannot stress enough how dramatically the food processor alters the taste of puréed pastes. If you absolutely have to use the processor, process the chile mixture in quick pulses so that it is just crushed, and not reduced to a liquidy purée.

3 cloves garlic, chopped

3 to 5 small fresh hot chiles, green or red, stemmed, seeded according to taste, and chopped

3 tablespoons chopped cilantro roots and/or stems

Salt, to taste

⅓ cup fresh lime juice

1½ tablespoons sugar

1 tablespoon Asian fish sauce, such as nam pla

1 impeccably fresh whole fish (about 2 pounds), such as black sea bass, red snapper, flounder, or catfish, gutted and cleaned but with head and tail left on

2 stalks fresh lemongrass (3 inches of the lower stalk, tough outer leaves discarded), smashed, if available

3 to 4 fresh kaffir lime leaves, smashed, if available

3 slices fresh or frozen galangal, smashed, if available

1. Crush the garlic, chiles, cilantro, and ½ teaspoon salt to a paste, preferably using a mortar and pestle. In a small bowl, whisk together the lime juice, sugar, and fish sauce. Add the garlic paste and set the sauce aside.

2. Rinse the fish, inside and out, and pat dry with paper towels. Make 4 slits about ½ inch deep and 2 inches long on each side of the fish. Rub the fish all over with salt. Season the cavity of the fish with salt and stuff with the lemongrass, kaffir lime leaves, and galangal.

3. Pour water to a depth of 2 inches into a wok or the bottom of a regular steamer and bring to a boil. Place the fish on a heatproof plate 1 inch smaller than the diameter of the steamer insert you are using. Place the plate on the steamer insert and set the insert over the boiling water. Cover tightly and steam the fish over high heat until just cooked through, 15 minutes. Do not open the steamer to check the fish before 15 minutes are up.

4. Pour some of the sauce over the fish and serve the rest in a small bowl. Serve at once.

SERVES 2, OR 6 AS A PART OF A MULTI-COURSE MEAL

BALINESE BAKED FISH PARCELS

with Macadamia-Turmeric Sauce

I n Southeast Asia one of the most popular and traditional methods of preparing fish is to wrap it, together with a flavorful sauce, in a *papillote* of banana leaf and bake it over hot coals. In the West we can wrap the fish in aluminum foil and bake it in the oven to achieve a similar effect. If you are after authenticity, however, look for banana leaves at Southeast Asian or Hispanic grocery stores. They will impart a nice greenish, sappy flavor to the fish and certainly make for a dramatic presentation. If you are using a banana leaf, first pass it over a gas flame to soften it.

The yellow-hued coconut sauce, thickened with macadamia nuts (which are a stand in for the candlenuts used in Asia), is typical of Indonesia, whose food is somewhat milder and more delicate than the cuisines of neighboring Thailand and Malaysia. The preparation is both simple and exotic, and you should let the guests open the packages themselves so they'll be teased by the seductive aroma of coconut, spices, and fish.

You can replace the sea bass in this recipe with any delicate but firm white fish fillets.

BANANA APPEAL

A ccording to an old Malaysian belief, pregnant women should under no circumstances put banana leaves in front of the fire to soften. If they do their child will be born with spots, just like the leaf. Luckily, modern women have found a way out of this difficult dilemma—they iron their banana leaves soft instead.

After a banana leaf meal, folding the leaf away from you means that you didn't enjoy your food. To compliment your hostess, make sure to fold the leaf toward you.

4 skinless sea bass fillets (6 to 7 ounces
each), about 1 inch thick, each fillet
cut in 2
2 tablespoons unsalted butter
1 large onion, cut into rings
1 small green bell pepper, stemmed, seeded,
and cut into strips
1 small red bell pepper, stemmed, seeded, and
cut into strips
¾ teaspoon ground turmeric
1½ cups canned unsweetened coconut milk,
well stirred
1¼ cups ground unsalted macadamia nuts
1 teaspoon Chinese chile paste with garlic
1½ tablespoons fresh lemon juice
Salt, to taste
Fresh cilantro leaves, for garnish
Freshly ground black pepper, to taste

1. Rinse the sea bass fillets and pat dry
with paper towels.

2. Melt the butter in a large skillet over
medium heat. Add the onion and bell peppers
and sauté until they begin to soften, about 3
minutes. Add the turmeric and stir for 1
minute. Add the coconut milk and bring to a
boil. Add the macadamia nuts and chile paste
and cook over medium heat until the mixture
thickens a little, about 5 minutes. Off the heat,
stir in the lemon juice and salt to taste.

3. Preheat the oven to 425°F.

4. Rub the fish with salt. Tear off four
sheets of aluminum foil, each sheet slightly
more than double the size of the two fillet
pieces laying side by side. Place two fillet
pieces on each piece of foil. Spoon about one
fourth of the sauce over each portion of fish
and tightly seal the foil by bringing together
the edges over the center of the fish and folding them over twice. Place the packets on a
baking sheet and bake for 10 minutes. Transfer the packets to plates, open, sprinkle with
cilantro and pepper, and serve at once.

SERVES 4

BROILED
BLUEFISH
with Caramelized Lemons

I love to grill slices of lemon with fish but
this particular idea came to me quite
spontaneously. As I was about to slide some
great, just-caught bluefish under the broiler,
I glanced at the Asian shelf of my cupboard,
and in a fit of inspiration, dipped the lemon
slices into a mixture of palm sugar, soy
sauce, and balsamic vinegar, then placed
them on top of the fish as it grilled. When I
tasted the results, I knew I'd hit the jackpot.
The marinade and lemons worked particularly well with bluefish, as the acidity helped
cut through the fish's rich oily texture, but
I have subsequently tried caramelized
lemons with salmon, swordfish, and shark
with equal success.

1 thick skinless bluefish fillet (about
1 pound), cut into 2 equal pieces
1 large lemon
3½ tablespoons fresh lemon juice
2 teaspoons plus 1 tablespoon soy sauce
2 tablespoons light olive oil (do not use virgin
or extra-virgin)
1 tablespoon chopped fresh parsley leaves
1½ tablespoons chopped fresh mint leaves
½ teaspoon freshly ground black pepper
Salt, to taste
2 tablespoons palm sugar or (packed) light
brown sugar
1 tablespoon Chinese black vinegar or
balsamic vinegar

1. Rinse the bluefish pieces and pat dry
with paper towels.

2. Peel the lemon so that no white pith

Terrific Pacific Fish and Seafood

remains. Cut the fruit into six ½-inch-thick slices.

3. In a shallow bowl, combine the lemon juice, 2 teaspoons soy sauce, the oil, parsley, mint, pepper, and lemon slices. Rub the fish with salt, add the fish to the bowl and turn to coat with the marinade. Cover and refrigerate for 30 minutes to 1 hour, turning once.

4. Preheat the broiler.

5. Remove the fish from the marinade, reserving the lemon slices. Place the fish on a rack in a broiler pan and broil on one side until opaque, about 3 minutes.

6. While the fish is broiling, whisk the sugar, 1 tablespoon soy sauce, and the vinegar together in a small bowl. Dip the reserved lemon slices in this mixture.

7. Carefully turn the fish over. Top each piece with 3 lemon slices and broil until the fish is opaque and the lemon is lightly caramelized, 4 to 5 minutes. Serve at once.

SERVES 2

SEARED
SNAPPER
with Passion Fruit Sauce

If a classically trained French chef were transplanted to a tropical country, this is a dish I imagine he (and in most cases it would be a he) would come up with. In recent years I have grown tired of traditional butter sauces, usually opting for vinaigrettes and vegetable or fruit reductions. Here, though, the exquisite fragrance and the intense acidity of passion fruit plays off against the silky richness of the sauce so successfully that I would certainly recommend this dish for any occasion that calls for luxury and indulgence. The *beurre blanc* works with any delicate fish, and is absolutely sensational with lobster or sweet New England scallops.

If you can't find fresh passion fruit, go to a nearby Hispanic market and ask for frozen *maracuya* or *parcha* (Spanish for passion fruit) pulp.

2 teaspoons fennel seeds
2 teaspoons coriander seeds
1 teaspoon best-quality curry powder
¼ teaspoon ground cayenne pepper
Salt
1 tablespoon plus 2 teaspoons peanut oil
4 red snapper fillets (6 to 7 ounces each), with skin on
1 tablespoon chopped shallots
¼ cup passion fruit pulp (4 passion fruit)
1½ teaspoons finely grated orange zest
2 tablespoons fresh orange juice
½ teaspoon sugar, or to taste
3 tablespoons heavy (or whipping) cream
7 tablespoons unsalted butter, cut into small pieces, chilled

1. In a mortar and pestle or small food processor, pound or process the fennel seeds, coriander seeds, curry powder, cayenne, ½ teaspoon salt, and 1 tablespoon of the oil to a coarse paste.

2. Rinse the red snapper fillets and pat dry with paper towels. Rub the fillets on all sides with the spice paste and let stand while preparing the sauce.

3. Combine the shallots, passion fruit pulp, zest and orange juice, and sugar in a

*S*quid and octopus are two of the most delicious, inexpensive, and readily available seafood around. High in protein, low in calories and cholesterol, they cost just a fraction of what shrimp and scallops cost. In addition, squid is readily available on the East and the West coasts all year round. It takes just minutes to cook, and its delicate, sweet taste can be paired with a wide range of ingredients.

Despite these obvious advantages, it was only when ethnic cuisines caught on in the United States that Americans began to pay serious attention to this wonderful mollusk. I suspect many people were intimidated by misconceptions about how to clean and prepare squid and octopus. Fortunately, most fishmongers these days sell the mollusks already cleaned. Another problem was the cooking, since when overcooked squid and octopus will become as tough as the proverbial piece of rubber. As a general rule, squid should be cooked for no more than 1 to 2 minutes in quick-cooked dishes, or long braised (40 minutes or more), which tenderizes it again. The best thing is to taste the squid once it turns opaque; when the squid is tender but still slightly springy to the bite, you know it is done.

medium-size heavy saucepan, and cook over medium heat until reduced by half, about 5 minutes.

4. Off the heat, whisk in the cream, then return to the heat and bring to a simmer, stirring. Do not allow the mixture to boil. Remove from the heat again and quickly whisk in the butter, 1 piece at a time, working on and off a low heat, to keep the sauce at an even, butter-melting temperature. Whisk constantly, until all the butter is emulsified. Season the sauce with salt and keep warm.

5. Heat the remaining oil in a large heavy skillet over high heat until almost smoking. Cook the fish, skin side down, pressing it down with a metal spatula, about 2 minutes. Turn the fish and cook until it flakes easily when tested with a fork, about 2 minutes more.

6. Transfer the fish to four plates, spoon the sauce over it and serve at once.

SERVES 4

THAI-STYLE STIR-FRIED SQUID

*S*quid is a perfect candidate for stir frying. It cooks in a flash, and its sweet nuttiness marries beautifully with the pungent and aromatic Asian flavorings. Here is a dish you can have on your table virtually in minutes, provided everything is chopped, mixed, and ready to go before you heat your wok. Try, if you can, to get Thai basil for this dish, as it will lend a special perfume. If it's not available, try a combination of Italian basil and mint.

You can serve this squid either as an appetizer or as a light main course with pasta, such as capellini, or Steamed Jasmine Rice (see Index).

3 tablespoons chopped shallots

3 cloves garlic, chopped

2 teaspoons grated fresh ginger

3 small fresh hot chiles, green or red,
    stemmed, seeded, and chopped

1 tablespoon chopped cilantro roots
    and/or stems

1/2 teaspoon freshly ground white
    pepper

3/4 teaspoon salt

1 1/2 pounds squid, cleaned

2 1/2 tablespoons peanut oil

5 teaspoons Asian fish sauce, such as
    nam pla

1 tablespoon fresh lime juice

1 1/2 teaspoons (packed) light brown
    sugar

1/2 cup shredded fresh Thai basil leaves,
    or 1/4 cup each fresh Italian
    basil leaves and mint leaves

3 tablespoons chopped fresh cilantro
    leaves

1. In a mortar and pestle or small food processor, pound the shallots, garlic, ginger, chiles, cilantro roots or stems, pepper, and salt to a coarse paste. Set aside.

2. Cut the squid bodies into 1/4-inch rings and cut the tentacles in half, if large. Rinse well and pat dry with paper towels.

3. Heat the oil in a wok or a large cast-iron skillet over high heat until almost smoking. Reduce the heat to medium, add the shallot mixture, and cook, stirring, for about 2 minutes. Add the squid, and cook, stirring, until tender, about 3 minutes. (Keep tasting the squid, as you would pasta, to determine its doneness). Stir in the fish sauce, lime juice, and sugar and toss to coat the squid with the sauce. Stir in the basil.

4. Transfer the squid to a pretty serving platter, garnish with chopped cilantro, and serve at once.

SERVES 4 TO 6

COCONUT SCALLOP TEMPURA

with Mango-Mustard Sauce

Terrifically tasty, this scallop dish is always a hit as an appetizer or light entrée. You can also use the tropical batter to coat shrimp, nuggets of chicken, or firm white fish. If serving as an entrée, accompany the scallops with a colorful pilaf and a big green salad.

1 pound sea scallops, halved horizontally

1 cup plus 1 tablespoon all-purpose flour

2 teaspoons baking powder

1 teaspoon paprika

1 teaspoon freshly ground black pepper

1/4 teaspoon ground turmeric

1/4 teaspoon ground cayenne pepper

Salt, to taste

1 cup club soda

Peanut oil, for deep frying

About 3 cups dessicated (dried) coconut

Mango-Mustard Sauce (recipe follows)

1. Rinse the scallops and pat dry thoroughly with paper towels.

2. In a medium-size bowl, sift together the flour, baking powder, paprika, pepper, turmeric, cayenne, and salt. Whisk in the club soda and let stand for 10 minutes.

3. Pour oil to a depth of 1 1/2 inches into a deep fryer and heat to 350°F over medium heat.

4. Spread the coconut on a cutting board covered with waxed paper. (You might want to use the coconut in batches). Season the scallops lightly with salt, then dip each in the batter, letting the excess drip off. Roll the scallops in the coconut, pressing with your fingers to help it adhere. Fry the scallops, in batches, until crisp and golden, 4 to 5 minutes, turning once. Drain on paper towels and serve at once, accompanied by the sauce.

SERVES 4

Mango-Mustard Sauce

½ cup puréed fresh mango pulp
5 teaspoons Dijon mustard
2 teaspoons white wine vinegar
1 tablespoon fresh lime juice
1 clove garlic, crushed through a press
⅓ cup light olive oil (do not use virgin or
*   extra-virgin)*
Pinch of ground cayenne pepper
⅛ teaspoon best-quality curry powder
Salt, to taste

In a bowl, stir together the mango purée, mustard, vinegar, lime juice, and garlic. Slowly whisk in the oil, until emulsified. Stir in the cayenne and curry powder and season with salt to taste.

PAN-FRIED SCALLOPS
with Orange-Basil Sauce

In Singapore we indulged in all manner of street food, had fun eating with our fingers at "banana leaf" Indian curry dives, and feasted like emperors at lavish Chinese banquets. But our final lunch in this city was French, at a great bistro called the Marco Polo. These scallops, accented with the tang of citrus and perfumed with basil, were one of the dishes we sampled there, and its fresh, bright flavors seemed right at home on this exotic island.

½ cup Fish Stock (page 385), bottled clam
*   juice, or water*
⅓ cup dry vermouth, preferably Noilly Prat
3 tablespoons dry white wine
2 tablespoons fresh orange juice
8 tablespoons (1 stick) unsalted butter,
*   chilled*
1¼ pounds sea scallops, halved lengthwise,
*   if large*
1 tablespoon whole green peppercorns in
*   brine, drained*
1½ tablespoons fresh lemon juice
1 small seedless orange, peel and all the white
*   pith removed, cut into medium dice*
3 tablespoons shredded fresh basil leaves
Salt and freshly ground black pepper, to taste

1. In a medium-size nonreactive saucepan, combine the fish stock, vermouth, wine, and orange juice and reduce over medium heat to ¼ cup, about 15 minutes.

2. Meanwhile, melt 2½ tablespoons of the butter in a large skillet over medium heat.

Add the scallops and cook until opaque throughout, about 2 minutes per side. Remove from the heat and keep warm while preparing the sauce.

3. Cut the remaining 5½ tablespoons of butter into small pieces. Remove the stock mixture from the heat and quickly whisk in the butter, 1 piece at a time, working on and off low heat, to keep the sauce at an even, butter-melting temperature. Whisk constantly until all the butter is emulsified. Stir in the peppercorns, lemon juice, orange, and basil and season with salt and pepper to taste.

4. To serve, divide the sauce among 4 plates and top with the scallops.

SERVES 4

ELIZABETH'S SHRIMP IN CHILE-ONION SAMBAL

Elizabeth lives in the Portuguese settlement in Melaka, a city in Malaysia. Her mother is a chef and her father fishes for prawns in the Straits of Melaka. When we came to lunch at her house one blistering afternoon, she served us a small dish of large prawns—which her father had brought home just an hour before we arrived—in a fiery *sambal* sauce of chiles and tomatoes. We sat on the floor, eating the juicy prawns with our fingers, the sauce dripping on our chins. She laughed when she saw us spit out the heads. "Eat, can, can," she said in a typical patois. In the Portuguese colony "can" is one of the staple words of seaside life, denoting a vast range of possibilities from "this is quite possible to do" to "you absolutely should." Medium-size shrimp make a fine substitute for the prawns.

6 medium dried red chiles, preferably Asian
½ cup chopped red bell pepper
1 small onion, chopped
1½ teaspoons anchovy paste or finely mashed anchovies
5 cloves garlic, chopped
1 tablespoon peanut oil, or more as needed
1 medium onion, quartered and sliced
1 cup Fish Stock (page 385), bottled clam juice, or water
1 large firm, ripe tomato, peeled and chopped
2 tablespoons fresh lime juice, or more to taste
½ teaspoon sugar, or more to taste
Salt, to taste
1 pound medium shrimp, shelled and deveined
Snipped fresh chives or chopped scallions, for garnish

1. Stem the chiles and shake out the seeds. Using scissors, cut the chiles into pieces. Soak in warm water to cover for 10 minutes. Drain well.

2. Process the chiles, bell pepper, chopped onion, anchovy paste, and garlic to a paste in a food processor, adding a little oil to assist the blending if necessary.

3. Cook the sliced onion in the 1 tablespoon oil in a nonreactive skillet over medium heat until softened, about 5 minutes. Turn the heat down to low, add the chile paste, and cook, stirring often, until the mixture no longer tastes raw, about 7 minutes. Add oil, a little at a time, if the mixture begins to stick.

4. Add the stock and tomato, bring to a boil, and cook over medium heat until the sauce is reduced, about 5 minutes. Stir in the lime juice, sugar, and salt to taste.

5. Add the shrimp, stir to coat with the sauce, and cook until the shrimp turn pink, about 4 minutes. Serve garnished with chives or scallions.

SERVES 4

FRAGRANT SHRIMP

with Crispy Basil and Shiitakes

The dramatic "crispy basil" dishes are always a hit at Thai restaurants in America. This richly perfumed stir-fry will practically set your table on fire with its adventurous flavors. Here is a dish that manages to be both trendy and authentic. As with most stir-fries worth their wok, it requires a bit of work, but almost all of it can be done ahead of time, when you have the opportunity. You can prepare the spice paste, and deep-fry the garlic and basil up to a day ahead. This will take you to step 4. If you already have homemade or purchased Thai red curry paste on hand, use 2 tablespoons of that instead of making it fresh (omit all the ingredients through the salt and skip to step 3). For a fun presentation, serve with Coconut Rice or Zucchini and Red Peppers Pilaf (see Index).

5 hot dried red chiles (2 to 3 inches long), preferably Asian
3 tablespoons chopped red bell pepper
4 teaspoons finely minced fresh ginger
3 cloves garlic, chopped
1½ tablespoons chopped cilantro roots and/or stems
Salt, to taste
3 to 4 tablespoons peanut or canola oil, plus more for deep frying the basil and garlic
1 cup fresh basil leaves, preferably Thai (the basil should be completely dry)
10 cloves garlic, sliced
1 pound large shrimp, peeled and deveined but with tails left on
1 small onion, sliced
1½ cups sliced fresh shiitake mushroom caps
1 medium red bell pepper, stemmed, seeded, and cut into strips
¾ cup chopped, seeded firm, ripe tomato
1½ tablespoons Asian fish sauce, such as nam pla
1½ teaspoons (packed) light brown sugar

1. Stem the chiles and shake out the seeds. Using scissors, cut the chiles into pieces. Soak in warm water to cover for 10 minutes. Drain well.

2. Using a mortar and pestle or a small food processor, pound or process the chiles, chopped pepper, ginger, chopped garlic, cilantro, and ¾ teaspoon salt to a paste, adding a little oil to assist the process if necessary. Set aside.

3. Pour oil to a depth of 1 inch into a deep skillet and heat to 350°F over medium heat.

4. Fry the basil leaves, in batches, until crispy, about 20 seconds. (Stand back as the oil will splatter). With a slotted spoon, transfer the leaves to paper towels to drain. In the same oil, fry the sliced garlic cloves until golden and crispy, about 1 minute. With a slotted spoon, transfer to paper towels to drain. Reserve the basil and garlic.

5. Heat 3 tablespoons oil in a wok over high heat until hot but not smoking. Swirl the wok to coat with the oil. Add the shrimp and stir-fry them until just pink, about 3 minutes. Remove the shrimp from the wok with a slotted spoon. Add more oil if necessary, then add the onion and chile paste and stir over medium-high heat for 2 minutes. Add the shiitakes and pepper strips and stir for another 3 minutes. Return the shrimp to the wok, add the tomato, and cook, stirring, for 1 minute more. Stir in the fish sauce and sugar and toss well.

6. Toss the shrimp with half of the reserved crispy basil and garlic and transfer to a serving platter. Garnish with the remaining fried garlic and basil and serve at once.

SERVES 4, OR 6 TO 8 WITH OTHER DISHES

PULAU UBIN GARLIC PRAWNS

On our last evening in Singapore, our friend Juliet David, a famous culinary personality on the island, sprang a surprise. She gathered together a group of friends and drove us at dusk to a little port half an hour from downtown. There was a rented boat waiting to whisk us away to the island of Pulau Ubin. Malaysia was a stone's throw to our left, and another half hour on the balmy coastal waters whetted our appetites perfectly for what turned out to be the best seafood experience we had in Southeast Asia.

We docked at a tiny jetty and made our way up a wooden walkway to a simple canopied dining terrace lit by fairy lanterns. The fish and seafood were so fresh, the salt air so crisp, the beer so chilled that we thought we were dining under water. Ervin Chua, the chef, who looked as if he hadn't yet made it into his twenties, prepared many delicious dishes for us during a long, delightful evening. One—enormous prawns in their shells, quickly stir-fried with salt and garlic over intense heat—seemed to me simply the best way to prepare this shellfish.

The crispy, garlic-infused shells are certainly good enough to eat. The etiquette in the seaside havens of Asia is to loudly suck and chew on the shells and heads and spit the tough bits right on the plastic-covered tables. Although this may not be up your alley, you should at least eat the tails and provide plenty of bowls for the shells, plus finger bowls for rinsing fingers. For an accompaniment I like to serve cooked pasta or noodles, which I quickly stir-fry in the oil remaining from the prawns.

5 tablespoons peanut oil
1½ pounds jumbo shrimp in their shells,
*   dried well with paper towels*
2 teaspoons salt
2 teaspoons garlic powder
⅓ cup minced garlic

1. Heat the wok over high heat for 3 minutes. Being careful to avoid hot splatters, add the oil and heat until almost smoking, about 3 minutes. Swirl the wok to coat with the oil.

2. Working in batches of about 8 shrimp, fry the shrimp with some salt and garlic powder, tossing constantly until the shells are pink and crisp 3, to 4 minutes. With a slotted spoon, transfer the cooked shrimp to a bowl. Repeat with all the shrimp, making sure the oil reheats after every batch. Stir in the garlic and cook for another minute. Return the shrimp to the wok and toss until they are reheated and the garlic is crispy, about 1 more minute. With a slotted spoon, remove the shrimp and the bits of garlic to a serving platter, shaking off excess oil. Serve at once.

SERVES 4

NONYA PINEAPPLE SHRIMP

"This dish of pineapple prawns," insisted Mr. Guih, a historian of Straits Chinese culture who prepared it for us at his house in a Singapore suburb, "maintains youthfulness, streams down the belly, serves as an aphrodisiac, eliminates the effect of alcohol, and is fed to ladies after childbirth to tighten the stomach." If these benefits don't convince you to try this recipe, then perhaps you would like to do so for its absolutely exquisite taste.

To save time and allow the flavors to ripen, it is a good idea to prepare the sauce through step 3 ahead of time. Reheat the sauce by bringing it to a simmer, and add the shrimp and pineapple right before serving. Serve with rice.

3 red or green hot fresh chiles, stemmed, seeded, and chopped
½ red bell pepper, stemmed, seeded, and chopped
6 shallots, chopped
4 cloves garlic, chopped
1 tablespoon grated fresh ginger
2 teaspoons grated lemon zest
3 tablespoons ground raw macadamia or cashew nuts
1¼ cups canned unsweetened coconut milk, well stirred
2½ tablespoons peanut oil, or more as needed
1 teaspoon ground turmeric
1 teaspoon paprika
1¾ cups Fish Stock (page 385), bottled clam juice, or water
2 cups neat, triangular pieces sliced firm, ripe pineapple
1 teaspoon sugar, or more to taste
1 teaspoon fresh lemon juice, or more to taste
Salt, to taste
1½ pounds medium shrimp, peeled and deveined
Julienned red bell pepper, for garnish
Snipped fresh chives or chopped scallions, for garnish

1. Process the chiles, bell pepper, shallots, garlic, ginger, lemon zest, and nuts to a fine paste in a food processor, adding a little coconut milk to assist the blending if necessary.

2. Heat the oil in a heavy medium-size saucepan over low heat. Add the turmeric and paprika and stir for 30 seconds. Add the chile paste and cook, stirring, until the mixture no longer tastes raw, 8 to 10 minutes. Add a little more oil if the mixture begins to stick.

3. Stir in the remaining coconut milk and bring to a simmer over medium heat. Simmer for 5 minutes. Add the fish stock and cook, stirring several times, until the mixture thickens and reduces, 10 minutes. Stir in the sugar, lemon juice, and salt.

4. Add the shrimp and pineapple and cook until the shrimp are pink, 3 to 5 minutes, taking care not to overcook them. Adjust the amounts of sugar, lemon juice, and salt, if necessary. Transfer the mixture to a serving bowl and garnish with julienned red pepper and chives or scallions.

SERVES 6

ALMOND-COATED SHRIMP CAKES

The versatile shrimp paste—a mixture of ground shrimp, cornstarch, and aromatics—has many uses in a Chinese kitchen. This version comes from the venerable Master Law, a *dim sum* chef at the Harbor Village restaurant in San Francisco, who began his culinary career as a fish cake master. In his *dim sum* empire, where he presides over a large staff of dumpling makers, Master Law initiated me into the intricacies of making fish and shrimp paste. The perfect fish or shrimp ball is ethereally light, yet springy and resilient. The secret, he insisted, is very fresh shrimp (he uses gulf prawns), scrupulously washed to get rid of the fishy taste and well dried. Then the shrimp are minced in a food processor, the other ingredients being added in strict order. The pork fat imparts juiciness to the paste, but the calorie conscious can certainly omit it.

These shrimp cakes, rolled in almond flakes, are just one example of the many things that can be done with shrimp paste. It can be used to make shrimp toasts, stuffed into vegetables and dumplings, or made into walnut-sized balls and floated in a soup.

1 pound very fresh shrimp (any size), peeled and deveined
1½ tablespoons minced pork fat (optional)
1 teaspoon salt
½ teaspoon sugar
1 tablespoon cornstarch
½ teaspoon freshly ground white pepper
1 teaspoon Oriental sesame oil
2 tablespoons minced water chestnuts, patted dry
2 tablespoons finely minced scallions (white part only)
1½ tablespoons minced celery
About ½ cup sliced almonds
Peanut oil, for deep frying

1. Rinse the shrimp well under cold running water. Squeeze batches of shrimp between paper towels or kitchen towels to get rid of as much moisture as possible. Chop the shrimp.

2. Place the shrimp and the pork fat in a food processor and process to a paste. Add the salt and process for 15 seconds. Add the cornstarch and sugar and process for 1 minute. Add the pepper, sesame oil, water chestnuts, scallions, and celery and process to combine. You should have an opaque, pasty mixture. Scrape the mixture into a bowl.

3. With oiled hands, shape the mixture into twelve 2½-inch patties. Flatten them slightly with the palms of your hands.

4. Pour peanut oil to a depth of 2 inches into a wok and heat to 350°F over medium heat.

5. In batches spread the almonds in one layer on a plate. Dip the shrimp cakes in almonds to coat on both sides. The almond

Singapore is a Mecca for food lovers, and everywhere you go you are accosted by vibrant tastes and seductive smells. Deep knowledge of and respect for the culinary scene runs throughout the culture. The latest gossip about food is the constant focus of street chatter, and no subject arouses more enthusiasm and elicits more debate than chile crab, one of Singapore's national dishes. So important is the dish, chances are that the first question you'll be asked in the taxi from the airport is: "Have you tasted our chile crab yet?" And if you admit to never having had the pleasure, you'll be showered with restaurant suggestions and recipes for this delicate wok-fried crab, smothered in an addictive sweet-and-sour, tomato-chile-garlic-ginger sauce.

The debates are endless. Which are the best crabs—the giant two-pound ones from Sri Lanka or the smaller blue swimmers, caught right off the island? Should the sauce be thickened with cornstarch or beaten eggs, flavored with pure Chinese chile sauce or a homemade concoction of pounded chiles, shallots, and lime juice? And not the least of all, should the crab be immersed in boiling water to kill it or put to sleep in a freezer? The recipe below is an amalgamation of tastes and recipes John and I enjoyed throughout the island.

One of the joys of chile crab is that it is such a messy, fun, hands-on affair. Cracking the claws with your teeth, sucking, slurping, finger licking are all part of chile crab etiquette. Don't even think of setting out knives and forks—but don't forget to provide finger bowls, bibs, nutcrackers, bowls for the wreckage, and baskets of crusty bread or bowls of rice to sop up the sauce.

Terrific Pacific Fish and Seafood

153

coating should not be too thick. Deep-fry the shrimp cakes, 4 to 6 at a time, until golden, about 3 minutes, turning once. Reduce the heat a little if the almonds begin to burn. With a slotted spoon, transfer the finished shrimp cakes to dry on paper towels. Serve at once.

SERVES 6 TO 8 WITH OTHER DISHES

SINGAPORE CHILE CRAB

Intimidated by the thought of combating a giant live crab, I put off testing this recipe as long as I could. When the time finally came, I decided to take the easy route and asked my Chinese fishmonger to kill and clean the crab for me. He obliged without a word, but as he performed the operation I became aware of the strange silence that had fallen over the usually noisy store. The dish was a hit with my Western friends, and I sighed a sigh of relief.

The following evening I had dinner with a refined lady from Hong Kong, and the conversation inevitably turned to seafood. "Imagine, I was recently served a dead crab in a San Francisco restaurant," she exclaimed, as her composed face convulsed with horror and disgust at the graveness of the offense. I blushed (from indignation, she must have thought), rolled my eyes in disbelief, and muttered my condolences. From that day on I have never served a dead crab again.

2 large live crabs (preferably Dungeness), about 1½ pounds each

5 dried chiles (2 to 3 inches long), preferably Asian

1 tablespoon chopped garlic

2 tablespoons finely chopped shallots

1½ tablespoons chopped fresh ginger

2 tablespoons vegetable oil, plus more as needed

7 tablespoons ketchup

6 tablespoons Thai or Chinese sweet chile sauce

1½ cups water

3 tablespoons fresh lime juice

1 tablespoon Asian fish sauce, such as nam pla

1½ tablespoons Worcestershire sauce

1½ tablespoons cornstarch, mixed with 2 tablespoons cold water

2 large eggs, beaten

3 tablespoons thinly sliced scallions, for garnish

1. Bring a large pot of water to a boil. Drop the crabs into the water and cook until they stop moving, about 1 minute. Drain and set aside until cool enough to handle.

2. To clean the crabs, lay them on their stomachs and pull off each top shell. Turn the crabs over. Pull and twist off each apron. Remove the viscera and the gills. With a sharp knife, cut the crabs into quarters. Rinse thoroughly, drain, and set aside.

3. Stem the chiles and shake out the seeds. Using scissors, cut the chiles into pieces. Soak in warm water to cover for 10 minutes. Drain well.

4. Using a mortar and pestle or a small food processor, pound or process the chiles, garlic, shallots, and ginger to a paste. If using a food processor, add a little vegetable oil to assist the blending.

5. In a large wok, heat 2 tablespoons oil over medium heat. Add the chile paste and cook, stirring, until fragrant, about 3 minutes. Add the ketchup, chile sauce, water, lime juice, fish sauce, and Worcestershire sauce. Stir well and bring to a boil.

6. Add the crabs and toss well to coat with the chile mixture. Cook over high heat, stirring, for 5 minutes. Cover the wok, reduce the heat to medium low, and cook for another 5 to 6 minutes.

7. Remove the crabs to a platter and keep warm. Stir the cornstarch mixture into the mixture in the wok and cook until the sauce thickens, about 1 minute. Pour in the beaten eggs in a slow steady stream, whisking constantly. Cook, stirring, for 1 minute. Pour the sauce over the crabs, garnish with scallions, and serve at once.

SERVES 4

GRILLED SESAME CRAB HASH

with Black Bean and Tomato Sauces

This recipe comes from Gary Strehl, a Honolulu chef who cooks at the Hawaiian Princess Hotel. After a stint as a sous-chef at the Lafayette, a restaurant in New York City, Gary took off for the Orient, where he worked and trained in Bangkok and Hong Kong, and finally settled in Honolulu. His crab hash—served with both an Asian and a European sauce—was a rapturous experience from the very first bite.

12 ounces lump crabmeat, picked over and
    shredded by hand
1½ cups finely diced cooked red-skin potatoes
2 roasted red bell peppers, diced
1 large egg, lightly beaten
1 tablespoon Dijon mustard
1 teaspoon Worcestershire sauce
1 teaspoon pure chile powder
¼ cup heavy (or whipping) cream
1 tablespoon chopped fresh cilantro leaves
2½ tablespoons fresh lime juice
Salt and freshly ground black pepper,
    to taste
¼ cup fresh bread crumbs
3 tablespoons sesame seeds, ground in a coffee
    or spice grinder
1 teaspoon Oriental sesame oil
Salt and freshly ground black pepper, to taste
1 tablespoon light olive oil (do not use virgin
    or extra-virgin)
Black Bean Sauce (recipe follows)
Tomato Sauce (recipe follows)

1. Preheat the broiler.

2. In a large bowl, combine the ingredients through the salt and pepper and toss gently with 2 forks until well mixed.

3. Shape the crab mixture into 6 large patties. Place on a rack in a broiler pan, brush with the olive oil, and broil until golden, about 5 minutes. Carefully turn on the other side and broil for 5 minutes more.

4. Place each patty on a plate and spoon one sauce to the left of the patty and the other sauce to the right.

Black Bean Sauce

1 tablespoon peanut oil
2 teaspoons minced garlic
½ teaspoon dried red pepper flakes
1 teaspoon minced fresh ginger
¼ cup fermented black beans, well rinsed
    and chopped
1 cup Fish Stock (page 385), bottled clam
    juice, or water
1 teaspoon oyster sauce
1 teaspoon dark soy sauce
½ teaspoon sugar, or more to taste
2 teaspoons cornstarch, mixed with
    1 tablespoon cold water

1. Heat the oil in a medium-size saucepan over medium heat and cook the garlic, pepper flakes, ginger, and black beans, stirring, for 1 minute.

2. Add the fish stock, soy and oyster sauces, and sugar and simmer over low heat for 5 minutes. Add the cornstarch mixture and stir over low heat until the sauce thickens, about 1 minute.

MAKES ABOUT 1½ CUPS

Tomato Sauce

2 tablespoons olive oil
¼ cup chopped shallots
1 clove garlic, minced
4 large firm, ripe, meaty tomatoes, peeled,
    seeded, and finely chopped
2 tablespoons slivered fresh basil leaves

1. Heat the oil in a large skillet over medium heat. Add the shallots and garlic and cook for 2 minutes, stirring.

2. Add the tomatoes and cook, uncovered, until the tomatoes are soft, about 7 minutes. Stir in the basil and cook for 1 more minute.

MAKES ABOUT 1½ CUPS

156

BLACK PEPPER SOFT-SHELL CRABS

To me, no seafood meal is more enchanting than those served in the Chinese waterfront restaurants of Asia. These establishments—often just a simple hut on stilts in the water—usually don't have a menu, simply offering the seasonally priced catch of the day, prepared to order, steamed, grilled, or wok-seared and accompanied by garlic-laced Chinese greens. When it comes to shellfish, the locals prefer them unshelled, quickly stir-fried in a wok over intense heat, perhaps just with garlic and chile, black pepper, or black bean sauce. We

SAINTLY CRAB

St. Francis Xavier was said to have dropped his rosary into the Melaka Straits, where it was miraculously retrieved by a crab. He solemnly blessed the crustacean, and from then on, all species of crab had a cross etched on their shells.

enjoyed the most spectacular black pepper crab on the island of Pulau Ubin in Singapore. It is a simple, intense, and flavorful preparation that works even better with soft-shell crab, as the pepper-garlic crust on the shell can actually be eaten.

Intense heat is the secret to this preparation. It's difficult to maintain with a regular stove burner, but at least heat your wok really well. Tasting of fire and crab, the garlic and pepper bits are the really delicious part of the meal. Serve with Chinese Greens with Oyster Sauce (see Index).

1½ cups peanut or other light
    vegetable oil
4 tablespoons cracked black
    peppercorns
2 teaspoons coarse (kosher) salt
8 cleaned soft-shell crabs, patted thoroughly
    dry with paper towels
½ cup minced garlic

1. Heat the oil in a wok to 375°F over high heat.

2. Being careful to avoid hot splatters, add 2 tablespoons of the pepper and 1 teaspoon of the salt and stir for 15 seconds. Stir in 4 crabs and toss until red and crisp, about 5 minutes. Make sure you maintain the heat at 375°F. Stir in ¼ cup of the garlic and stir for 30 seconds.

3. With a skimmer, remove the crabs, along with as many pepper and garlic bits as you can, to paper towels to drain off the excess oil.

4. Repeat with the remaining salt, pepper, crabs, and garlic, making sure the oil returns to 375°F. Serve at once.

SERVES 4

DOUBLE-PROSPERITY CLAMS

Presented as a part of the Chinese New Year banquet, this dish of clams in black bean sauce is destined to bring twofold prosperity to anyone who feasts on it. Perceived as quintessentially Chinese (it's full of garlic and strong flavors), clams in black bean sauce is certainly one of the most heavily ordered Chinese restaurant dishes in this country. "When done right," says Clifford Chow, the manager of Harbor Village restaurant in San Francisco, "black bean dishes should be saucy and delicate, with just a whiff of garlic and black beans." This recipe is adapted from the recipe of Andy Wai, Harbor Village's executive chef. Serve over rice.

1½ pounds small littleneck clams (about 1½ dozen)
2 tablespoons rock salt
1 tablespoon fermented black beans, well rinsed
1 clove garlic, crushed through a press
2½ teaspoons peanut oil
⅔ cup Chicken Stock (page 384) or canned broth
1 tablespoon Chinese rice wine or dry sherry
1 tablespoon soy sauce
1 teaspoon oyster sauce
½ teaspoon sugar, or more to taste
1 teaspoon Oriental sesame oil
1 tablespoon thinly sliced scallions
2 tablespoons finely diced red bell pepper
1 small fresh hot green chile, stemmed, seeded, and diced
1 teaspoon cornstarch, mixed with 2 teaspoons cold water
Salt, to taste

1. Rinse and scrub the clams thoroughly. Place in a large bowl with cold water to cover and add the salt. Let stand for 30 minutes. Drain and pat the clams dry with paper towels.

2. In a small bowl, crush the black beans, garlic, and 1 teaspoon of the peanut oil with the back of a spoon.

3. In another bowl, stir together the stock, rice wine, soy sauce, oyster sauce, and sugar.

4. Heat the remaining peanut oil and the sesame oil in a wok over medium-high heat until almost smoking. Being careful to avoid hot splatters, add the black bean mixture and stir for 15 seconds. Add the scallions, bell pepper, and chile and stir for another 30 seconds. Add the clams and stir for 1 minute. Stir in the stock mixture, cover, and cook until the clams open, about 4 minutes, shaking the wok several times.

5. With a large slotted spoon, push the clams to the side of the wok and slowly drizzle in the cornstarch mixture. Cook until the sauce thickens, about 30 seconds.

6. Discard any unopened clams, then transfer the opened clams and the sauce to a serving platter and serve at once.

SERVES 2 AS A MAIN COURSE, 4 TO 6 AS PART OF A MULTICOURSE MEAL

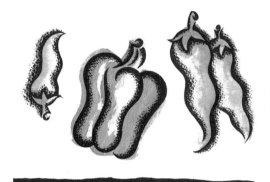

MUSSELS

with Lemongrass Herb Butter

I enjoyed this delicate mussel dish at Thien Doung, an outstanding Vietnamese restaurant in the plush Dusit Thani Hotel in Bangkok. I was especially impressed with the combination of impeccably authentic tastes and the elegant atmosphere, which befits this sophisticated cuisine.

This dish of gratinéed mussels, called *so ham beurre*, is obviously influenced by the years of French colonial rule. At Thien Doung it is served with French bread to sop up the spicy lemongrass-flavored butter. You can serve the mussels either as a light entrée, or as an hors d'oeuvre, in which case two pounds of mussels will stretch a long way. Any leftover butter can be shaped into a log and frozen. It's delicious dabbed on grilled fish steaks or chicken breasts.

8 tablespoons (1 stick) unsalted butter, softened

1 tablespoon finely minced fresh parsley leaves

3 tablespoons finely minced fresh cilantro leaves

1 serrano chile, stemmed, seeded, and minced

2 tablespoons minced fresh lemongrass (3 inches of the lower stalk, outer leaves discarded)

4 teaspoons minced garlic

1 teaspoon freshly ground white pepper

1½ tablespoons fresh lemon juice

1 tablespoon Asian fish sauce, such as nam pla

¾ teaspoon sugar

2 pounds mussels, well scrubbed

1. Prepare the butter: Combine all the ingredients through the sugar in a food processor and process until just blended. Scrape the mixture into a bowl and let stand for 30 minutes for the flavors to develop. (The butter can be prepared the day before, chilled, and brought to room temperature before using).

2. Debeard the mussels just before you are ready to cook them. Pour water to a depth of 1 inch in a large pot and bring to a boil over medium-high heat. Add the mussels, cover, and cook, shaking the pot occasionally, until they open, about 5 minutes. Transfer to a colander and drain. When the mussels are cool enough to handle, remove and discard one shell from each mussel, as well as any mussels that have not opened.

3. Preheat the broiler.

4. Arrange the mussels on a rack in a broiler pan. (You might have to broil the mussels in 2 batches if they don't all fit.) Using a dinner knife, spread about ½ teaspoon of the butter over each mussel. Pass the mussels under the broiler until the butter is bubbly, 1 to 2 minutes. Serve at once.

SERVES 4 AS A LIGHT MEAL

SUMMERY NEW ZEALAND MUSSELS

In this recipe developed by New Zealand's Kiwifruit Marketing Board, who do wonders for promoting kiwi at home and abroad, the huge, succulent, green-lipped New Zealand mussels are served in their shells topped with a cooling colorful Mediterranean salsa of olives, peppers—and tangy kiwi.

1 cup finely diced firm, ripe New Zealand kiwi
1½ tablespoons fresh lemon juice
¼ cup finely diced red bell pepper
¼ cup finely diced red onion
¼ cup chopped black olives
2½ teaspoons chopped fresh parsley
1 tablespoon sherry vinegar
1 tablespoon virgin olive oil
Salt and freshly ground black pepper, to taste
24 large mussels, preferably green-lipped New Zealand mussels, well scrubbed
⅔ cup dry white wine
2 bay leaves
Lemon wedges, for garnish

1. In a bowl, toss the kiwi with the lemon juice. Add the bell pepper, onion, olives, parsley, vinegar, oil, salt, and pepper; toss gently.

2. Debeard the mussels just before you are ready to cook them. Bring the wine with the bay leaves to a boil in a large saucepan over medium-high heat. Add the mussels and cook, covered, shaking the pan occasionally, until they just open, 6 to 7 minutes. Remove the mussels with a slotted spoon and set aside to cool.

3. Remove and discard the empty top shell from each mussel, as well as any mussels that have not opened. Arrange the mussels on a serving platter. Spoon some kiwi mixture over each mussel in its shell and garnish the platter with lemon wedges.

SERVES 4

POT LUCK

For the Chinese, oysters symbolize all the good things in life, and are invariably present at special-occasion dinners. In fact, the Cantonese word for oyster, ho see, also means "good business."

Pig's trotters betoken a windfall, while it is always bad luck to spill rice. On the other hand, it is said that as long as a patient can still eat rice, there is always hope for his health.

LUCK AND PROSPERITY OYSTER STEW

Oysters, in one form or another, are essential at the Chinese New Year table, if not always for their taste then certainly for their name, *ho see*, which closely resembles the phrase "good business." Those who do not look to their plates for omens of fortune will at least enjoy the briny, delicate taste of the oysters, enlivened by crispy vegetables and the heady aroma of the sauce.

SAUCE

1½ tablespoons dark soy sauce

2 teaspoons Chinese rice wine or dry sherry

1 teaspoon Oriental sesame oil

¼ teaspoon sugar

Salt, to taste (optional)

2 teaspoons cornstarch, mixed with
    1 tablespoon cold water

⅓ cup bottled clam juice

5 Chinese dried black mushrooms or dried
    shiitakes

1 tablespoon peanut oil

2 teaspoons finely chopped fresh ginger

2 cloves garlic, minced

1 tablespoon chopped scallions

¾ cup very thin carrot strips

½ cup very thin celery strips

1½ cups shredded napa cabbage

¾ cup snow pea strips, sliced on the
    diagonal

24 small oysters, shucked

Salt, to taste (optional)

1. Make the sauce: Combine the soy sauce, rice wine, sesame oil, sugar, and salt, if needed, in a bowl. Whisk in the cornstarch mixture and the clam juice. Set aside.

2. Soak the mushrooms in hot water for 30 minutes. Drain, discard the stems, and thinly slice the caps. Set aside.

3. Heat the oil in a wok over high heat until almost smoking, then reduce the heat to medium. Add the ginger, garlic, and scallions and stir for 30 seconds. Add the carrots and stir for 30 seconds. Add the reserved mushrooms, celery, cabbage, and snow peas and stir for 2 minutes.

4. Add the oysters and the sauce and bring to a boil, stirring. Reduce the heat to low and simmer for about 3 minutes. Season with salt, if desired, and serve immediately.

SERVES 2 OR 4
WITH OTHER DISHES

THE KRETA AYER WET MARKET

No visit to Southeast Asia is complete without a trip to one of the fabulous "wet markets" that are the very lifeblood of the regional culture. So named because the floors are constantly being hosed down—to remove debris and keep things cool—wet markets are completely different from anything we associate with food buying in the West. We visited the Kreta Ayer in Singapore, and even though Anya and I arrived relatively late in the day, the bustle and commotion were unbelievable.

It was like being in a petting zoo for produce; everything is touched and examined, with buyers routinely testing ninety-nine jade radishes before making an offer on the hundredth. The cacophony of shrieks and yells made a Middle Eastern bazaar sound like a Buddhist retreat. Add to this water cannons firing randomly at your ankles (rubber boots are a must) and a menagerie of dangerous animals (see the next page) and spirited grandmothers coming at you from all sides, and you'll get some idea of what a wet market is really like.

A GOOD PLACE TO START

We started at the vegetable stalls, the real stars of any good Chinese market, and our food-obsessed guide was quick to offer culinary comments on everything we saw. Huge piles of fresh lotus roots, still covered with mud, would be used in a long-cooked soup with dried red dates, ginger, and pork, she said. The leaves of the lotus are used for wrapping dumplings or rice.

"This is our cooking at its very best," she continued as she smacked her lips. Lip smacks are as good a way as any to measure a wet market, and it seemed as if we were a thousand smacks from the end.

At the next stand a small army of determined shoppers were furiously grabbing for bitter melon, which is referred to by the locals as "gentleman vegetable," since its slight bitterness doesn't affect the other foods it's cooked with. The selection of tender, bright greens before us was vast and vibrantly colored: mustard greens, water convulvus (or morning glory), many varieties of crispy bok choy, Chinese broccoli, delicate, buttery jungle ferns from Malaysia, baby asparagus, and the especially tender purple-stemmed spinach. And this was just a fraction of the pickings.

SNIFFS AND SOUNDS

Next we stopped at the aromatic shops, referred to by Malays as *ulam-ulam*. As we could tell from the serious expressions of a dozen sniffers, curiously lined up with their noses to the produce, aromatics hold the key to the flavors of Straits Chinese cooking. Colorfully arranged on marble slabs were the heart and soul of the local cuisine: garlic, tender, light green stalks of lemongrass, sturdy old gingerroots—good with braised meats—and delicate young ginger, which is best for pickling. Turmeric is used by Singaporean cooks fresh rather than in its powdered state.

Other, more recognizable palate stimulants included cilantro, mint, and several varieties of basil.

But what really got our attention was the extraordinary range of exotica—including rhizomes like galangal, both whole and grated, fragrant ginger flowers, sweet-potato leaves, fern fronds, aromatic kaffir limes, and pandanus leaves, which impart a sweet, vanilla-like aroma to dishes and are also used for a natural green coloring in dainty local desserts. Next to all this, chiles of every size, color, and hotness were piled on the floor in dense red and green mountains.

The live produce area was more like a miniature zoo than a meat section. There were fluttering pigeons, jumping frogs (best in a Cantonese soup redolent of ginseng), turtles, flying foxes, and various snakes (which taste like a cross between chicken and tuna, and can be simply stewed or red-braised), including an open cage of huge live pythons being prodded and poked by gaggles of fearless grannies testing their meatiness. One of the most curious sights— and there were many contenders—was the black chicken, the feathers of which are white but the skin, black, making the legs look like socks. This chicken is considered a delicacy for its very tender sweet meat, which doesn't dry out with clay cooking. The Chinese prefer it for a tonic soup:

The chicken is simmered with ginseng in a double boiler until the bones become soft enough to eat. As if the market were not theatrical enough, the freshness-obsessed locals still long for the days when live produce was slaughtered to order right in front of the customer. But this practice has been banned by the Singaporean health officials.

Near the live produce, were the fish stalls, packed with the day's catch from the South China Sea, which vendors buy at auction at the Jurong Fishery Port. When we visited, varieties included snapper, several kinds of pomfret, trevally, mackerel, and a slew of small fish such as sardines and anchovies. We also saw sea cucumbers, shark's fin, prawns of every size, mussels, cockles, and clams—all beauti-

fully arranged and displayed.

Live crabs are a specialty—the blue swimmer crabs and the "serrated" crab, which lives in the mangrove swamps. Eel also seemed to have plenty of buyers.

One of the knowledgeable fishmongers helpfully informed us that it was favored by construction workers, as it did wonders for the circulation.

Other sections of the market were devoted to tofu and fish-paste products. The Hakkas of southern China sold delicate chewy balls for soups and hot pots and lovely baby vegetables stuffed with the fish paste, which could be steamed and savored on the spot or taken home to the family. To compete with canned coconut milk and instant powder (which has taken Southeast Asia by storm), there were rows of coconut graters who have invested in expensive machines that make the flawless coconut milk and

cream so essential for the rich Malay curries.

Finally, we threaded our way through rows of cooked delicacies dangling from the ceiling: lacquered roast ducks, sweet roast pork with its bright red exterior, sausages, and chickens. By this time we had learned how to keep our feet dry, dodging the water hoses as if they were jump ropes, but now we were in danger of getting hit in the head, and had to shuffle through the aisles hunched over (which made it impossible to jump clear of the shooting water).

The market had overwhelmed every sense, and our guide, noting our exhaustion with a little more satisfaction than we thought the occasion merited, offered us a remedy. "Why don't we go back and pick up a winter toad," she said cheerfully. "They're perfect restoratives for all-over fatigue!"

Roast Chicken with Honey-Lime BBQ Sauce

Roast Chicken
with Chinese Sausage Stuffing

Hainanese Chicken Rice with Condiments

Chicken Poached in a Fragrant Broth

Fried Chicken in Tamarind Sauce

Penang Fried Chicken

Yin Yang Chicken and Shiitake Stew

Sweet Soy and Citrus Baked Chicken

Best-Ever Broiled Chicken

Thai-Style Drumsticks for a Crowd

Chicken Nuggets in
Sweet-and Tangy Chile Sauce

Chutney-Glazed Grilled Chicken
with Mint Relish

Cold Poached Chicken
with Asparagus and Honey-Miso Dressing

Aromatic Steamed Chicken Pudding

Chicken Breasts with Tropical Fruit Sauce

Crispy "Twice-Cooked" Cornish Hens
with Black Rice Timbales

Balinese Grilled Cornish Hens with
Wild Rice and Greens in a Fragrant Broth

Grilled Cornish Hens in Coconut-Lime Sauce

Roast Turkey with Thai Curry Gravy

Hoisin-Glazed Turkey Burgers
with Sizzling Scallions

Roasted Duck Breast with
Lychees and Sancho and Honey Sauce

Roast Garlic Quail with Maple Glaze

Outback Rabbit and Prune Pie

Seared Venison
with Spicy Masala Sauce and
Sweet Potato Purée

New Zealand Venison Steaks with
Tamarillo Coulis

POULTRY
AND
GAME

Muslims would not even look in the direction of a pig, Hindus are prohibited from eating the cows sacred to their religion, Jewish law forbids shellfish, and the Great Diet God of the West outlaws all manner of fatty meats. There's so much that so many people can't eat, that it's a relief to find a meat that everybody loves—and the whole world adores a good plump chicken. It has tender, delicate meat, it's easy on the purse, and pretty good for the health. What more could one ask for! I think it was Brillat-Savarin who remarked that chicken to a chef was like a blank canvas to a painter. And to my mind, no culinary artist treats the bird with more imagination and respect than the cooks of Asia, be they Chinese, Indian, or Thai.

We have much to learn from the Orient with regard to cooking poultry, not just the infinite play of flavorings but also techniques and preparations. Stir frying is probably the best known of all Asian methods. Quick and easy, it seals in the juices and vitamins of meat or poultry over high heat, and then, if the cook adds colorful and flavorful spices and vegetables, it produces healthy, mouth-watering results.

Asian subtleties and skills are endless. With the Chinese "white cooking" method, you first submerge the bird in boiling liquid, then take it off the heat and let it sit there to plump up and finish cooking. This produces incredibly white, succulent meat that no Western technique can achieve. The famous "twice cooking" method, which I turn to often in this chapter, can be a combination of braising and grilling (in either order) or poaching and deep frying, or deep frying and braising. The techniques here are many, and they produce tantalizing variations in the texture of the bird. From India comes the curry method, where the bird is stewed in the thick of aromatics. None of these methods, by the way, are reserved for chicken, but time and again cooks turn to chicken for the best results.

And the seasoning! Again the possibilities here are manifold. Try the wonderfully fragrant *rempeh*, a pounded mixture of ginger, shallots, lemongrass, and chiles from the Straits of Melaka; the zingy, typically Chinese blend of garlic, scallions, rice wine, and soy; a special Thai blend of herbs, lime, fish sauce, and rich palm sugar; the magical Indian combination of coriander, cumin, turmeric, and chile powder. Add to this the penchant for tropical fruit, such as coconut, tamarind, and lime, which defines contemporary Pacific haute cuisine; and a whole palate of wonderful Asian marinades, which tenderize and often act as a glaze for the bird.

These are just a few of the beguiling ways with poultry—and rabbit, quail, and venison—that are explored in this chapter. Use the recipes as suggestions and jumping-off points to create your own combination of tastes. When it comes to poultry, no experiment is too wild. You'll see.

ROAST CHICKEN
with Honey-Lime BBQ Sauce

The ginger-laced barbecue sauce acts both as a marinade and glaze for the bird. It will also work magic with Cornish hens, duckling, or ham. I like to serve Fried Spinach in a Pungent Sauce (see Index) alongside to balance the sweetness of the chicken.

1 roasting chicken (about 4½ pounds)
Salt, to taste
2 tablespoons dark soy sauce
¼ cup ketchup
¼ cup fresh lime juice
1½ tablespoons honey
2½ tablespoons grated fresh ginger
1 tablespoon minced garlic
Grated zest of 1 lime
1 cup Chicken Stock (page 384) or canned
    broth

1. Rinse the chicken well, inside and out, and pat dry with paper towels. Rub inside and out with salt.

2. In a bowl, combine the soy sauce, ketchup, lime juice, honey, ginger, garlic, and lime zest. Stir well to mix. Place the chicken in a bowl and brush with some of the sauce, then refrigerate for 6 hours or overnight. Cover the unused sauce and refrigerate. Bring the chicken to room temperature before roasting.

3. Preheat the oven to 425°F.

4. Place the chicken in a roasting pan and brush with some of the remaining unused sauce. Roast for 15 minutes. Reduce the oven temperature to 350°F, pour the stock into the pan, and roast the chicken until the juices run clear when you test the thickest part of the thigh with a skewer, about 1 hour, brushing once or twice with the sauce. (If all the sauce is not used up, pour the rest into the pan.)

5. Remove the chicken to a carving board and let rest covered with aluminum foil for 10 minutes. Skim off the fat from the pan juices and reheat the juices, if necessary. Cut the chicken into serving pieces, arrange on a serving platter, and pour the juices over.

SERVES 4

ROAST CHICKEN
with Chinese Sausage Stuffing

In Southern China, wax sausage and bacon were prepared and stocked for the winter at the beginning of the cold months, the preparations having to be completed by the Lunar New Year. Chinese wax sausages get their name and shiny surface from being soaked in oil, which acts as a kind of preservative. The sausage casings are known to the Chinese as "intestinal clothing." These sausages are very sweet, so if you don't have access to them, substitute honey-roasted ham rather than another kind of sausage. If you can, try to get Chinese wax bacon; otherwise, use regular bacon. This is a good wholesome winter dish, and I recommend serving it with a stir-fried green vegetable such as Chinese Greens with Oyster Sauce or Fried Spinach in a Pungent Sauce (see Index).

6 large dried shiitake mushrooms, well rinsed

3½ cups warm Chicken Stock (page 384), or canned broth, plus additional as needed

2 tablespoons unsalted butter

1½ cups long-grain rice

¾ cup water

½ cup chopped bacon, preferably Chinese wax

1 cup diced onion

¾ cup diced celery

3 links Chinese wax sausages, chopped, or ¾ cup diced honey-roasted ham

¾ cup diced red bell pepper

¾ cup sliced scallions

3½ tablespoons dark soy sauce

Salt, to taste

1 roasting chicken (about 5½ pounds)

Freshly ground black pepper, to taste

Large pinch of five-spice powder

1½ tablespoons maple syrup or honey

1. Soak the mushrooms in the warm stock for 30 minutes. Remove the mushrooms with a slotted spoon and pat dry with paper towels. Remove and discard the stems and slice the caps thin. Measure 2 cups of the soaking liquid and reserve the rest.

2. Melt the butter in a heavy saucepan over medium heat and sauté the shiitakes for about 5 minutes. Add the rice, the 2 cups mushroom soaking liquid, and the ¾ cup water and bring to a boil. Reduce the heat to low and simmer, covered, until all the liquid has been absorbed and the rice is tender but still slightly al dente, about 15 minutes.

3. Cook the bacon in a large skillet over medium heat until it renders its fat. If there is more than 2 tablespoons of the fat in the skil-let, remove the excess. Add the onion and celery to the skillet and cook until softened, about 5 minutes. Add the sausage and bell pepper and cook for 5 more minutes.

4. Preheat the oven to 350°F.

5. In a bowl, combine the rice with the bacon-sausage mixture and scallions. Add 1½ tablespoons of the soy sauce, stir well and season with salt, if needed.

6. Rinse the chicken well, inside and out, and pat dry with paper towels. In a small bowl, combine salt, pepper, and five-spice powder, then rub the chicken, inside and out, with the mixture. Stuff with as much of the rice stuffing as will comfortably fit. Close the cavity opening with skewers and truss the bird. Place any remaining stuffing in an ovenproof dish and drizzle with a little of the reserved mushroom soaking liquid. Set aside.

7. Place the chicken in a roasting pan. Stir together the remaining soy sauce and the maple syrup or honey, and brush the chicken with some of the glaze. Roast for 30 minutes.

8. Pour the remaining mushroom soaking liquid into the roasting pan and brush the chicken with some more of the glaze. Continue roasting the chicken until the skin is golden and a skewer inserted in the thickest part of a thigh comes out clean, 1¼ to 1½ hours, basting occasionally with the pan juices.

9. Twenty minutes before the chicken is ready, place the dish with the additional stuffing, covered with aluminum foil, in the oven to heat.

10. Place the chicken on a cutting board and remove the trussing string and skewers. Spoon the stuffing from the chicken into a serving dish. Sprinkle the additional stuffing with some pan juices. Let the chicken stand loosely covered with aluminum foil for 10 minutes. Carve the chicken, arrange on a serving platter and pour the remaining pan juices over it.

SERVES 4 TO 6

HAINANESE CHICKEN RICE

with Condiments

In Malaysia and Singapore snacking is a national obsession, and no other culture in the world can boast a better variety of street food. One of the treats most in demand is this chicken rice dish. Introduced to the Straits by Hainanese immigrants, it's a simple, addictively nourishing meal of chicken poached in a ginger-infused broth, cut into bite-size pieces, and served with ginger, soy, and chile condiments. Flavorful rice, cooked in the fragrant chicken broth, accompanies the chicken.

Unlike Western-style poaching, which invariably produces a somewhat mushy texture, the Chinese "white-poaching" method (immersing the bird in boiling liquid, switching the heat off, and letting it finish cooking slowly and evenly) results in flesh that is miraculously luscious and firm at the same time. Plunging the chicken into cold water at the end makes the skin tight and silky. It is a preparation truly remarkable in its goodness and simplicity.

As any Asian will tell you, the quality of the chicken is all. The best choice by far is a white, head-and-feet-on Chinatown chicken. Your next choice is a kosher bird. If you can't find either, use a free-range chicken; it will be less flavorful than the first two options, but at least you can be assured of the quality. I would not bother with a yellow, fatty supermarket chicken for this dish.

1 good-quality chicken (3½ to 4 pounds)
    preferably Chinese or Kosher
10 cups water
8 cloves garlic in their skins, smashed,
    plus 1 teaspoon minced
5 slices fresh ginger, smashed,
    plus 2 teaspoons minced
Salt, to taste
1 tablespoon peanut oil
2 cups long-grain rice
2 Kirby cucumbers,
    peeled and sliced,
    for garnish
2 firm, ripe tomatoes, peeled
    and quartered, for garnish
3 tablespoons chopped scallions,
    for garnish
Fresh cilantro leaves, for garnish
Chile Sauce (recipe follows)
Ginger Sauce (recipe follows)
Oyster Sauce (recipe follows)

1. Rinse the chicken well, inside and out, and pat dry with paper towels.

2. Combine the water, garlic cloves, ginger slices, and salt in a tall stockpot and bring to a boil over high heat. Rub the chicken generously with salt inside and out (If you are using a kosher chicken you won't need to salt it.) Lower the chicken into the water, breast side down. If the chicken isn't completely submerged in the liquid, weight it down with a plate. Cover the pot tightly, reduce the heat to medium, and cook the chicken for exactly 10 minutes. Without uncovering the pot, remove it from the heat, and let stand, tightly covered, for 2 hours. Do not open at any time.

3. Fill a large bowl with ice-cold water. Remove the chicken from the stock and plunge it into the cold water for 10 minutes. Drain well.

4. Strain the stock. Measure 4 cups and save the rest for another use. Heat the oil in a saucepan over medium heat. Add the minced garlic and ginger and stir for 1 minute. Add the rice and stir until the grains are translucent. Add the stock and bring to a boil. Reduce the heat to low, cover, and simmer until the rice is tender and all the liquid has been absorbed, about 20 minutes. Let the rice stand, covered, for 10 minutes.

5. To serve, cut the chicken into serving pieces. (If you have a cleaver and the know-how, hack the chicken through the bone, Chi-

nese style.) Place a portion of rice in a small cup or an individual mold and turn out on each dinner plate. Place some chicken on the plate and garnish with cucumber slices, tomato wedges, scallions, and cilantro. Alternatively, you can arrange the rice and the chicken on a serving platter. Serve the Chile Sauce, Ginger Sauce, and Oyster Sauce alongside.

SERVES 4

Chile Sauce

5 fresh medium-hot red chiles, such as
*   fresnos, stemmed, seeded, and chopped*
1/3 cup chopped red bell pepper
4 cloves garlic, chopped
1 tablespoon chopped fresh ginger
1 1/2 teaspoons sugar
2 tablespoons fresh lime juice
1 tablespoon distilled white vinegar
2 tablespoons vegetable oil
Salt, to taste

Combine all the ingredients in a blender or food processor and process until minced. Do not overmix.

MAKES ABOUT 1/2 CUP

Ginger Sauce

1/4 cup grated fresh ginger
4 1/2 tablespoons vegetable oil
Salt, to taste

In a small bowl, toss together all the ingredients and let stand at room temperature for 30 minutes.

MAKES ABOUT 1/2 CUP

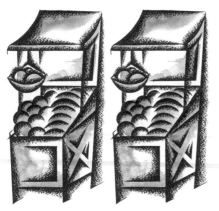

Oyster Sauce

2½ tablespoons light soy sauce
3 tablespoons oyster sauce
1 tablespoon Oriental sesame oil
Pinch of sugar, to taste

In a small bowl, whisk together all the ingredients.

MAKES ABOUT ⅓ CUP

CHICKEN POACHED

in a Fragrant Broth

Poultry cooked in a liquid of soy sauce, water, rice wine, rock sugar, and numerous aromatics (referred to as the "master sauce") is to me the most addictive offering of the Chinese table. The sauce imparts a lovely dark color and wonderfully fragrant taste to the bird, and the cooking procedure of immersing the bird in boiling liquid and letting it steep for a long time produces excellent texture.

The master sauce is meant to be used and reused, becoming richer and richer with time by picking up the flavor of whatever's cooked. The older the sauce, the better the result. For this reason, Chinese cooks rarely make master sauce dishes at home, relying instead on a well-tested old barbecue shop—some of which have had their sauces simmering since the shop first opened. Often when a barbecue chef leaves a restaurant or takeout shop, the sauce goes with him. Traditionally after the chicken is cooked, it's covered with a sweet sheen of maltose and hung up by its neck to air-dry.

As with many Chinese dishes, the classic result is difficult to achieve at home, but this chicken is an excellent and simple compromise. The only requirement is a Chinese, kosher, or free-range, impeccably fresh bird. An ordinary supermarket chicken won't do. Once you've prepared the sauce, you should use it again and again. Store it in the freezer or refrigerator, and bring to a boil each time you have finished cooking the chicken. This way it can be stored indefinitely. Just replenish it with some water, soy, and aromatics, and skim off all the fat.

8½ cups Chicken Stock (page 384) or
canned broth
2½ cups dark soy sauce
⅔ cup light soy sauce
⅔ cup Chinese rice wine or dry sherry
¾ cup Chinese yellow rock sugar, broken into
small pieces with a hammer, or ½ cup
granulated sugar
1 large star anise, broken into points
2 pieces (3 inches each) dried tangerine peel
or fresh tangerine zest
6 thick slices fresh ginger, smashed
3 scallions, smashed
1 piece cassia bark or 1 cinnamon stick
(3 inches), broken into 1-inch lengths
1 tablespoon Szechuan peppercorns, lightly
crushed
1 good-quality chicken (3½ to 4 pounds),
preferably Chinese or kosher, at room
temperature
Oriental sesame oil, for serving

1. Place all the ingredients except the chicken and sesame oil in a tall pot that will fit the chicken snugly and bring to a boil. Reduce the heat to low and simmer, uncovered, for 10 minutes. This will be your "master sauce."

2. Meanwhile, bring another large pot of water to a boil. Rinse the chicken well and drain, then lower into the boiling water and scald for 1 minute. Carefully remove the chicken to a colander and rinse under cold running water.

3. Bring the master sauce to a rolling boil. Lower the chicken into the liquid, breast side down. Lower the heat and cook, partially covered, at a medium boil for 15 minutes. Turn the chicken on the other side and cook for another 10 minutes. If the chicken is not submerged in the liquid, weight it down with a plate. Turn off the heat and let the chicken stand, tightly covered, for 2 hours, without opening the lid.

4. Carefully remove the chicken from the liquid and let drain in a colander. Bring the master sauce to a boil, then remove from the heat, strain, and degrease. If you store it in the refrigerator, bring it to a boil every 4 to 5 days and replenish with water, soy, and aromatics, (keeping roughly to the proportion of the original recipe) as necessary. This way it will store for several months in the refrigerator and indefinitely in the freezer. Use it to cook chickens, ducks, pork, lamb shanks, or tofu.

5. Brush the chicken with sesame oil, then cut into serving pieces or hack Chinese-style. Serve as a light main course or as part of a multicourse meal. If you would like to serve the chicken hot, reheat it gently in the poaching liquid.

SERVES 4 TO 6

SOUTHWEST ASIAN
BUFFET FOR EIGHT
. . . .

SEAFOOD RICE PAPER ROLLS
with Two Dipping Sauces

FRIED CHICKEN
in Tamarind Sauce

VEGETABLE COCONUT CURRY

HERBED EGGPLANT SALAD
with Pickled Garlic

STEAMED JASMINE RICE

SPICE ROUTE COCONUT CAKE

FRIED CHICKEN

in Tamarind Sauce

This and the Grilled Cornish Hens in Coconut-Lime Sauce (see Index) are part of the fascinating tradition of Straits Chinese, or Nonya, cookery, which combines Chinese and Southeast Asian culinary heritages. Nonya dishes are based on fragrant, aromatic spice pastes called *rempeh*, which are then blended into intricate sauces made sweet with coconut milk or tangy with tamarind, and often thickened with pounded nuts. In this recipe the chicken is first fried to a crunch and then finished in an intriguing hot and sour sauce. To save time, prepare the spice mixture beforehand. You can also grill the chicken instead of frying it.

MARRIAGE MATERIAL

In the Straits Chinese culture, dedicated above all to its own survival and regeneration, Nonya cuisine is a symbol of difference and excellence.

At one time, the ideal Nonya woman was supposed to embody decorum and domesticity. Safely tucked away behind the decorated lattice door of the traditional Chinese shop house, a true Nonya lady was allowed to peep out onto the street but almost never to appear. Her main duty was to oversee a large and elaborate household in a culture where culinary skills were de rigueur. In fact, much of the cooking was performed by various members of the household staff, but every young girl was still expected to have mastered Nonya cuisine by the time she came of age. So important was cooking to the Peranakan household that matchmakers purportedly listened outside the kitchen door for the right sounds of the mortar and pestle to determine a girl's suitability for marriage.

5 hot dried red chiles (2 to 3 inches),
    preferably Asian
¼ cup chopped red bell pepper
2 teaspoons chopped garlic
2 tablespoons chopped shallots
1 tablespoon chopped fresh ginger
2 stalks fresh lemongrass (3 inches of the
    lower stalk, tough outer leaves discarded),
    finely chopped
1 tablespoon chopped fresh or thawed frozen
    galangal
1½ tablespoons ground macadamia nuts
1 teaspoon ground turmeric
Peanut oil, for deep frying the chicken, plus
    more as needed
1 tablespoon tamarind pulp, preferably from
    Thailand
1½ cups boiling Chicken Stock (page 384)
    or canned broth
3 pounds chicken pieces (breasts halved
    if whole, thighs and drumsteaks
    separated)
Salt, to taste
1 teaspoon tomato paste
1 tablespoon palm sugar or (packed) light
    brown sugar
Fresh cilantro leaves, for garnish

1. Stem the chiles and shake out the seeds. Using scissors, cut the chiles into pieces. Soak in warm water to cover for 10 minutes. Drain well.

2. Combine the chiles, bell pepper, garlic, shallots, ginger, lemongrass, galangal, macadamias, and turmeric in a food processor and process to a paste, adding a little oil to assist blending if necessary. Set aside.

3. Soak the tamarind pulp in the boiling stock off the heat for 15 minutes. Stir and mash it with a fork to help it dissolve. Strain through a fine strainer, into a bowl, pressing on the solids with the back of a wooden spoon to extract all the liquid.

4. Rinse the chicken pieces well and pat dry with paper towels. Rub the pieces with salt and let stand for 10 minutes.

5. Pour oil to a depth of 2 inches into a wok and heat to 350°F over medium-high heat.

6. Fry the chicken pieces, a few at a time, until golden and almost cooked through, about 15 minutes. Drain on paper towels.

7. Pour off all but 1 tablespoon oil from the wok. Add the chile paste and cook over low heat, stirring, until it no longer tastes raw, about 7 minutes. Add oil, a little at a time, if the mixture begins to stick to the bottom. Add the tamarind liquid, tomato paste, sugar, and salt to taste, then bring to a simmer and cook until the sauce is thickened and reduced, about 7 minutes.

8. Add the chicken, stir to coat with the sauce, and cook over low heat until the sauce thickens and the chicken is cooked through, about 10 minutes. Garnish with cilantro and serve at once.

SERVES 4 TO 6

PENANG FRIED CHICKEN

Crispy fried, marinated chicken, called *inchee kabin,* is as ubiquitous a snack in Malaysia as Colonel Sanders' creation is on Route 66. But nowhere is the skin crunchier, the flesh more succulent, and the marinade more pungently penetrating than in Penang, the street-food capital of Southeast Asia. The secret to crispy skin is letting the chicken parts dry before frying, without wiping off all the marinade. To perform this trick, the cooks of this newly technologized nation often resort to a hair drier. Keep in

mind that the longer you marinate the chicken, the more flavorful it will be.

Colonial touches are to be found all over Malaysia, and this very traditional chicken is usually eaten Western style, with toasted white bread triangles and Worcestershire sauce.

3 pounds chicken pieces (breasts halved if
*   whole, thighs and drumsticks separated)*
Salt, to taste
¼ cup dark soy sauce
1 tablespoon best-quality curry powder,
*   preferably homemade (page 390)*
2 teaspoons dry mustard powder
2 tablespoons Ginger Juice (page 390)
3 tablespoons canned unsweetened coconut
*   milk, well stirred*
1½ tablespoons (packed) light brown
*   sugar*
Canola or peanut oil, for deep frying
½ cup all-purpose flour
½ cup rice flour or cornstarch
Worcestershire sauce, for serving

1. Rinse the chicken parts well and pat dry with paper towels, then rub with salt.

2. Place the chicken pieces in a large dish. In a small bowl, whisk together the soy sauce, curry and mustard powders, ginger juice, coconut milk, and sugar. Pour the mixture evenly over the chicken and marinate, covered in the refrigerator, overnight, tossing occasionally. The chicken can be marinated for up to 2 days.

3. Drain the chicken pieces, shaking off the excess marinade, place on a baking sheet, and let dry completely, about 3 hours. Alternatively, dry with a hair dryer.

4. Pour oil to a depth of 2 inches into a deep fryer and heat to 350°F over medium-high heat.

5. Sift the flour, rice flour, and salt together into a large bowl. Working in batches,

There are two things that seem to obsess the Chinese—money and health. Both passions frequently make their way (at least symbolically) to the Chinese table. If the color, look, or name of a dish will not bring you a financial windfall, it's sure to relieve you of stomach winds, give you a glowing complexion, improve your sex drive, or purify your blood. If finances govern the healthy spirit department, the secret to a healthy body lies in maintaining a harmonious balance of yin and yang, the negative and positive forces of life. If you are a pallid creature who suffers from cold spells and easily falls ill, the chances are you're under the influence of yin. If, on the other hand, your cheeks are rosy and you are bursting with excess energy, you are probably the yang type (usually associated with businessmen by the Chinese). If you fit one of the above descriptions, keep in mind that you should be eating food of the opposite type to restore the balance.

dust the chicken pieces with the flour mixture. Fry the chicken, a few pieces at a time, until deep golden and cooked through, about 15 minutes. Drain the chicken pieces as they are fried on paper towels. Reduce the heat if the chicken browns too quickly and bring the oil back to 350°F before adding each batch. (You can keep the cooked chicken warm in a low oven).

6. Serve accompanied by Worcestershire sauce.

SERVES 4 TO 6

YIN YANG CHICKEN AND SHIITAKE STEW

Although the Chinese believe in restorative yin yang eating (see box, above), there are occasions when a perfectly balanced dish—possessing both elements in equal measure—is required. And here it is, an attractive adaptation of a recipe I found in a medicinal Chinese cookbook. The yin is represented by the mushrooms and the yang by the chicken, and the dish, the Chinese author suggests, is a godsend for combating fatigue. Medicinal properties aside, it's a wonderfully satisfying, homey chicken stew, redolent of ginger, scallions, and rice wine and teeming with delicious chewy shiitakes.

Unlike the colorful and dramatically presented restaurant stir-fries, Chinese home-cooked stews are not meant to look either pretty or elegant—which is just fine, as far as I am concerned. However, if you have an aversion to an overall brown-color dish, you can remedy the situation with a simple garnish of julienned red bell peppers and scallion flowers.

If further elegance is required, you can use boneless, skinless chicken breasts for this dish. Since the breasts will take less time to cook, simmer the sauce first for about 10 minutes to allow the mushrooms to cook through before adding the chicken. I like serving this stew over mashed potatoes, instead of the traditional rice, to sop up the fragrant sauce.

3 pounds chicken pieces, cut into smallish pieces

2 tablespoons light soy sauce

⅓ cup Chinese rice wine or dry sherry

1½ tablespoons oyster sauce

1 tablespoon grated fresh ginger, plus 2 tablespoons julienned

Salt, to taste

10 to 12 dried shiitake mushrooms

2 cups warm Chicken Stock (page 384) or canned broth, plus more as needed

3 tablespoons peanut or canola oil

1 medium onion, chopped

3 slender carrots, peeled and sliced crosswise on the diagonal

2 teaspoons rice vinegar

1½ tablespoons dark soy sauce, or more to taste

¾ teaspoon sugar, or more to taste

3 tablespoons chopped scallions, plus more for garnish

2 teaspoons cornstarch, mixed with 1 tablespoon cold water

1. Rinse the chicken pieces well and pat dry with paper towels.

2. Place the chicken in a large bowl. In a small bowl, whisk together the light soy sauce, 1½ tablespoons of the rice wine, oyster sauce, the grated ginger, and the salt. Pour the marinade over the chicken and toss to coat. Cover and refrigerate from 2 to 6 hours, turning the pieces occasionally.

3. Soak the mushrooms in the warm stock for 30 minutes. Drain and reserve the soaking liquid. Discard the stems from the shiitakes and slice the caps.

4. Remove the chicken pieces from the marinade and shake off the excess, reserving any marinade remaining in the bowl. Heat the oil in a heavy flameproof casserole over medium heat and brown the chicken pieces a few at a time. Transfer the pieces as they are browned to a plate lined with paper towels.

5. If there is too much oil in the casserole, drain off all but 1 tablespoon and heat over medium heat. Add the onion and cook it, stirring, until translucent. Add the carrots, mushrooms, and julienned ginger and cook for another 5 minutes.

6. Stir the remaining rice wine and the vinegar into the casserole, turn the heat up to high and cook about 1 minute to reduce the liquid by half, scraping the bottom of the casserole with a wooden spoon. Return the chicken to the casserole, add the mushroom soaking liquid, dark soy sauce, sugar, and enough additional stock to barely cover the chicken. Reduce the heat to low, cover, and simmer until the chicken is tender, 20 to 25 minutes.

7. With a slotted spoon, remove the chicken and other solids to a heated serving bowl and keep warm. Raise the heat to high and reduce the liquid by one third, about 5 minutes. Reduce the heat to low, add the scallions, and slowly whisk in the cornstarch mixture. Adjust the amount of soy sauce and sugar, if desired, and simmer the sauce until it thickens, about 1½ minutes.

8. Pour the sauce over the chicken, garnish with additional scallions, and serve at once.

SERVES 4

SWEET SOY AND CITRUS BAKED CHICKEN

To me, Asian marinades are the most flavorful option for grilling or roasting poultry. Usually they don't just tenderize the bird, but impart tantalizing flavor and provide a delicious glaze as well. In this dish, inspired by the stall food of Indonesia, the marinade is based on a thick, syrupy sweet Indonesian soy sauce, called *ketjap manis,* and citrus zest and juice. Serve with Tomato-Flavored Basmati Rice with Sweet Spices (see Index) and a stir-fried green.

3½ pounds chicken pieces (breasts halved if whole, thighs and drumsticks separated)

2 teaspoons ground coriander

1 teaspoon ground cayenne pepper

Salt, to taste

⅓ cup Ketjap Manis (page 388) or sweet soy sauce

2 tablespoons dark soy sauce

1 small seedless orange, peeled and chopped

4 cloves garlic, chopped

1 tablespoon grated orange zest

1 teaspoon grated lime zest

1 tablespoon white wine vinegar

2 tablespoons fresh lime juice

1½ tablespoons maple syrup

¼ cup chopped fresh mint leaves

¼ to ½ teaspoon dried red pepper flakes

½ cup Chicken Stock (page 384) or canned broth, or more as needed

1. Rinse the chicken pieces well and pat dry with paper towels. Prick the skin all over with tines of a fork.

2. In a small bowl, combine the coriander, cayenne, and salt. Rub the chicken pieces with the mixture. Set aside.

3. Combine the soy sauces, orange, garlic, orange and lime zests, vinegar, lime juice, maple syrup, mint, and pepper flakes in a food processor and process to a purée.

4. Place the chicken in a large shallow dish, add the marinade, and turn the pieces to coat well. Cover and refrigerate for 4 to 6 hours, or overnight.

5. Preheat the oven to 400°F.

6. Place the chicken and marinade in a roasting pan. Roast until the chicken begins to brown, about 15 minutes, then reduce the oven temperature to 350°F. Pour the stock into the pan and roast the chicken until cooked through, about 25 more minutes, basting with the pan juices. Add some more stock if the bottom of the pan looks dry.

7. Transfer the chicken to a serving platter, spoon the pan juices over it, and serve.

SERVES 4 TO 6

BEST-EVER BROILED CHICKEN

I love grilled chicken in just about any form, but none more than this. Its secret is the marinade (also used as a basting liquid), which is made from a heady mixture of shallots, garlic, lemongrass, ginger, and red chiles, combined with the refreshing acidity of tamarind, the pungency of soy, and the sweetness of brown sugar. Broiling is preferable to grilling here because the chicken needs to be placed in a shallow pan together with the marinade. If, however, you want to cook it on the grill, baste it often and then heat the marinade through and pour over the chicken.

The marinade will work with just about any meat, poultry, or fish you decide to throw on the grill. Besides chicken, I especially like it with lamb or pork chops.

For a great summer party dish, serve the chicken with Cold Noodles with Asian Pesto (see Index).

3½ pounds chicken pieces (breasts halved if whole, thighs and drumsticks separated)

2 teaspoons ground coriander

1 teaspoon freshly ground black pepper

1 teaspoon salt

1½ tablespoons tamarind pulp, preferably from Thailand

⅓ cup boiling Chicken Stock (page 384) or canned broth

6 dried red chiles (2 to 3 inches), preferably Asian

4 large cloves garlic, chopped

3 tablespoons chopped shallots

2 teaspoons chopped fresh ginger

1 tablespoon chopped fresh lemongrass (3 inches of the lower stalk, tough outer leaves discarded) or 2 teaspoons grated lime zest

1½ tablespoons vegetable oil

3 tablespoons dark soy sauce

3 tablespoons (packed) light brown sugar

1½ tablespoons rice vinegar

1½ tablespoons ketchup

½ cup finely chopped fresh basil leaves

1. Rinse the chicken pieces well and pat dry with paper towels. Prick the skin all over with tines of a fork.

2. In a small bowl, combine the coriander, pepper, and salt and rub into the chicken pieces. Set aside.

3. Soak the tamarind pulp in the boiling stock off the heat for 15 minutes. Stir and mash it with a fork to help it dissolve. Strain through a fine strainer into a bowl, pressing on the solids with the back of a wooden spoon to extract all the liquid. Set aside.

4. Stem the chiles and shake out the seeds. Using scissors, cut the chiles into pieces. Soak in warm water to cover for 10 minutes. Drain well.

5. Combine the chiles, garlic, shallots, ginger, lemongrass, tamarind liquid, oil, soy sauce, sugar, vinegar, ketchup, and basil in a food processor and process to a purée. Arrange the chicken in a large shallow dish and pour the marinade over. Cover and refrigerate 2 hours or overnight.

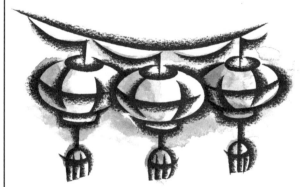

6. Preheat the broiler.

7. Remove the chicken pieces from the marinade and arrange in a baking dish deep enough to later accommodate the marinade. Broil the chicken until browned and half cooked, about 10 minutes. Pour the marinade over the chicken, turn the pieces on the other side, and broil until cooked through, another 10 to 15 minutes. If the chicken is browning too fast, move the baking dish further away from the broiling element. If your oven and broiler are controlled by the same dial, reduce the temperature from broil to about 375°F.

8. Remove the chicken pieces to a serving dish and pour the pan juices over it. Serve at once.

SERVES 4 TO 6

THAI-STYLE DRUMSTICKS FOR A CROWD

By now I am so familiar with the basic combination of flavors that define Thai taste—the tang of lime juice, sweetness of palm sugar, saltiness of fish sauce, bite of chiles, and the intense herbiness of cilantro—that I put them together almost without thinking (not that they can ever become routine). This recipe for baked chicken drumsticks, marinated in these essential Thai ingredients, is so basic, it would have never occurred to me to put it on paper, if it weren't for the inevitable requests that follow whenever anyone tastes them. So, here it is, an easy, economical dish, bursting with the exotic flavors that make Thailand one of the world's great culinary cultures.

Since I serve these for large cocktail parties or buffets, I find it easier to bake rather then grill the chicken (which would have to be done in several batches) and finish it under a broiler to give it a charred flavor. The marinade is great for any cut of chicken or for flank steak. Skin the drumsticks for a healthier dish, if you wish.

4½ pounds chicken drumsticks
6 small fresh hot chiles, green or red,
    stemmed, seeded, and chopped
½ cup chopped cilantro roots
    and/or stems
10 cloves garlic, chopped
Salt
¾ cup fresh lime juice
5 tablespoons Asian fish sauce, such
    as nam pla
¼ cup palm sugar or (packed)
    light brown sugar
2 tablespoons vegetable oil
1 tablespoon white peppercorns,
    crushed

1. Rinse the chicken drumsticks well and pat dry with paper towels. Prick the skin all over with the tines of a fork.

2. In a food processor, process the chiles, cilantro stems, garlic, 1½ teaspoons salt, lime juice, fish sauce, sugar, and oil until finely minced.

3. Rub the chicken all over with salt and the peppercorns. Arrange the chicken in a large shallow dish and pour the marinade over it. Cover with plastic wrap and refrigerate for 6 hours or overnight, tossing the drumsticks occasionally. Bring the chicken to room temperature before proceeding.

4. Preheat the oven to 425°F.

5. Choose a baking dish large enough to accommodate all the drumsticks in one layer, or use two baking dishes. Arrange the drumsticks in the dish or dishes and reserve the marinade. Bake for 15 minutes.

6. Reduce the oven temperature to 350°F. Turn the drumsticks and bake for another 15 minutes. Pour in the marinade and continue baking until the juices run clear when you pierce a drumstick with a skewer, about 10 minutes more.

7. Preheat the broiler.

8. Pass the chicken under the broiler

DANCING ELEPHANTS

*T*hais have been captivated by elephants for more than a millennium, and the highlight of every elephant lover's year is the great Round-Up in Surin, which takes place in mid-November. Determined not to miss out, Anya and I boarded a train chartered for the occasion in downtown Bangkok. After a comfortable night's sleep, we arrived to an orchard-filled greeting and full breakfast.

By 8:15 we had found our reserved places in the massive grass amphitheater. Most of the 120 or so elephants brought together for the occasion—towering 60-year-olds with gleaming tusks, diminutive toddlers, sprightly adolescents—had already assembled for the opening ceremony. From their flower-bedecked booth, the governor of the province and his entourage of dignitaries opened the Round-Up, and the show was on.

Four streams of colorfully attired dancers flowed into the arena. Each group of male and female couples gathered around a pair of rhythm makers wielding two long, dry sticks with which they eloquently marked the time and the mood of some half a dozen dances. Then a small wooden kiosk with a leaf roof was moved to center stage for the reenactment of a ritual elephant hunt. A dozen elephants and riders loped out and formed a semicircle around the booth. They brought gifts for the priest and presented their ropes and long spears for blessing. Prayers were uttered and coded messages exchanged.

There was a time when the hunt was the most important event for the elephant communities of northern Thailand. It could last up to three months and was attended by the strict observance of various complicated rules and subtle taboos. For instance, the village wives left behind were not to entertain guests, cut their hair, or sweep up outside the house. And the hunters were forbidden to quarrel or even to raise their voices while the hunt was on. Chasing elephants was a serious business.

We visitors didn't see anything too serious, of course. In fact, the next "event" was splendidly comical. After the haunting music of the dedication ritual had faded away, a select group of elephants showed off their tricks. They responded to their names, bowed, curtsied, stood on two legs. They even wagged their trunks and flapped their ears in unison. Then the beat changed to disco, and one especially talented creature boogied with such agility that he wouldn't have looked (much) out of place at a high school prom. This episode was rounded off by half a dozen elephant couples smooching, trunk to trunk, to a sappy fifties ballad.

LET THE GAMES BEGIN

The ambience changed swiftly as more brightly clad dancers assembled to perform a twelve-rhythmed rain dance. Then it was back to elephants. After the two-hundred-meter dash, neat ranks of Thai army boys jogged out in military high step, carrying their portion of an impressively long, thick rope. The other end was attached to a beefy-looking mature elephant renowned for his strength. First he up-ended sixty cadets, then eighty, and finally he pulled out all one hundred in a herculean display.

One cocky elephant and a platoon of dusty troops scampered off, clearing the way for a makeshift soccer pitch. Two six-player teams went at it with enormous skill. The elephants kicked and dribbled an over-size ball by any and all means possible—including their trunks—urged on all the while by yells, slaps, and prods from their sinewy, turbaned riders. It was a riotous spectacle and a fitting event before the grand finale.

At midday two elephant armies assembled to act out a conflict modeled on legendary sixteenth-century battles between Thailand and Burma. Fifteen or so of the finest creatures were outfitted in beautifully decorated silks and dyed cloths. The canopied platforms on the elephants' backs were manned by crews of "pilots" and "rear gunners," and the elephants with the most important riders were protected by a foot-soldier. Then the cannon sounded and the armies charged, led by saber-wielding runners. The battlefield was ablaze with tusks and eyes and metal and silk. Spears and peacock feathers flew.

Then suddenly the war was over, and the Round-Up changed gear for the last time, as the entire arena gradually filled with a hundred handsome elephants milling around, taking the audience for rides two, four, or six at a time.

until the skin is lightly charred, about 5 minutes. Arrange on a serving platter and pour the juices over.

SERVES 8 TO 10 AS A PART OF A BUFFET

CHICKEN NUGGETS
in Sweet-and-Tangy Chile Sauce

Lightly battered chicken chunks are tossed with a delicate homemade Thai-style chile sauce and cilantro to produce this incredibly tasty dish, which can be served either slightly warm, at room temperature, or cold. Add as much chile sauce as you feel you'd like. Leftover sauce will keep in a refrigerator for a week and is delicious with fried calamari or grilled chicken. This recipe was inspired by Japanese food writer Nekko Edamoto.

1 pound skinless, boneless chicken breast
    or thigh meat, cut into 1½-inch
    nuggets
2 tablespoons soy sauce
¼ cup all-purpose flour
¼ cup cornstarch
1 large egg, beaten
5 tablespoons cold water
Peanut or canola oil, for deep frying
Sweet-and-Tangy Chile Sauce (recipe
    follows)
1 tablespoon fresh lemon juice, or
    more to taste
3 tablespoons fresh cilantro leaves

1. Place the chicken in a bowl and sprinkle the soy sauce over it. Cover and refrigerate for 1 hour.

2. Sift together the flour and cornstarch into a bowl. Whisk in the egg and water until smooth. Let the batter stand for 10 minutes.

3. Pour oil to a depth of 2 inches into a deep fryer or wok, and heat to 350°F over medium heat. Working in batches, dip the chicken in the batter and gently shake off the excess. Deep-fry the chicken, a few pieces at a time, until light golden and cooked through, 4 to 5 minutes. Reduce the heat if the chicken browns too quickly. With a slotted spoon, remove the chicken to drain on paper towels. Cool to warm or to room temperature.

4. Before serving, place the chicken in a serving bowl and gently toss with the desired amount of Sweet-and-Tangy Chile Sauce, lemon juice, and cilantro leaves. Serve at once.

SERVES 4

Sweet and Tangy Chile Sauce

½ red bell pepper, stemmed,
*   seeded, and chopped*
2 large cloves garlic, chopped
7 tablespoons rice vinegar
3½ tablespoons sugar
¼ cup water
2 dried red chiles (2 to 3 inches),
*   preferably Asian, crumbled*
*   (seed the chiles for a milder sauce)*
1¼ teaspoons cornstarch, mixed
*   with 1½ teaspoons cold water*

1. Process the bell pepper, garlic, vinegar, sugar, water, and chiles in a food processor until smooth.

2. Transfer the mixture to a small nonreactive saucepan and cook over low heat for about 7 minutes, skimming once or twice. Slowly whisk in the cornstarch mixture and cook for another minute. Cool to room temperature.

MAKES ABOUT 1 CUP

CHUTNEY-GLAZED GRILLED CHICKEN

with Mint Relish

When I am short of time I often turn to bottled sweet mango chutney as a delicious glaze for grilled chicken breasts. Major Grey from a supermarket is fine, but if you know of an Indian grocery store, get your chutney there.

2 whole chicken breasts with skin and bones
*   (about 12 ounces each)*
½ teaspoon paprika
¼ teaspoon ground turmeric
¼ teaspoon ground cayenne pepper
¼ teaspoon ground cumin
Salt, to taste
2 tablespoons mango chutney, lumpy bits
*   removed*
1 tablespoon fresh lime juice
1 clove garlic, crushed through a press
1 teaspoon grated fresh ginger
Fresh cilantro leaves, for garnish
Mint Relish (recipe follows)

1. Prepare coals for grilling or preheat the broiler.

2. Rinse the chicken breasts well and pat dry with paper towels.

3. In a small bowl, combine the paprika, turmeric, cayenne, cumin, and salt, then rub the chicken breasts with the mixture.

4. In a second bowl, stir together the mango chutney, lime juice, garlic, and ginger. Brush the chicken with the glaze. Grill or broil the chicken, skin side first, until slightly charred and just cooked through, about 5 minutes on each side. Transfer to a cutting board and let stand for 5 minutes.

5. Cut the chicken off the bone into ¾-inch slices and arrange on 4 plates. Drizzle some Mint Relish over each serving and garnish with cilantro. Serve with the remaining relish on the side.

SERVES 4

Mint Relish

The addition of chile to this relish gives a bit of fire to the fresh herbs.

1 cup (tightly packed) fresh mint leaves
½ cup (tightly packed) fresh cilantro
    leaves
1 clove garlic, minced
½ serrano chile, stemmed, seeded, and
    minced
¼ cup buttermilk
3 tablespoons low-fat plain yogurt
1 tablespoon fresh lemon juice
Pinch of sugar

Process all the ingredients in a food processor until finely minced. Transfer to a bowl and let stand at room temperature for 30 minutes.

MAKES ABOUT 1 CUP

COLD POACHED CHICKEN

with Asparagus and Honey-Miso Dressing

Here is a dish that will gladden the heart of any dieter, a colorful healthy mélange of poached chicken breasts, tofu, and asparagus, dressed with a rich, flavorful sauce made with only half a teaspoon of oil.

2 whole chicken breasts, bone in but
    skinned (about 1½ pounds total)
1 bunch (about 16) slender asparagus,
    trimmed
Salt, to taste
Red-leaf lettuce leaves
1 small red bell pepper, stemmed,
    seeded, and cut into strips
Half of an 8-ounce cake soft tofu, cut into
    strips
3 scallions, cut on the diagonal into
    1½-inch lengths
Honey-Miso Dressing (recipe follows)

1. Rinse the chicken breasts well and pat dry with paper towels.

2. Place the chicken in a medium-size saucepan with enough water to cover it by 1 inch and bring to a boil. Skim off the froth, reduce the heat to low, and simmer until the chicken is just tender, about 15 minutes. Let the chicken cool in the liquid. Bone the chicken and cut into strips.

3. Cook the asparagus in boiling salted water until bright green and crisp-tender, 2 to 3 minutes. Refresh under cold running water and pat dry.

4. Line a platter with lettuce leaves.

Arrange the chicken, asparagus, red pepper strips, tofu, and scallions on the lettuce and drizzle with the Honey-Miso Dressing.

SERVES 4

Honey-Miso Dressing

2½ to 3 tablespoons red miso (aka miso), or
to taste
2 tablespoons honey
2 teaspoons Chinese or Dijon mustard
3 tablespoons Chicken Stock (page 384),
canned broth, or spring water
1 tablespoon soy sauce
1 tablespoon cider vinegar
½ teaspoon Oriental sesame oil
1 teaspoon grated fresh ginger
1 clove garlic, minced
1 tablespoon finely chopped scallions

In a bowl, whisk together the miso, honey, and mustard. Add the remaining ingredients, whisking until the dressing is smooth. Let stand for 15 minutes for the flavors to ripen.

MAKES ABOUT ½ CUP

AROMATIC STEAMED CHICKEN PUDDING

When I take friends to Thai restaurants, I make sure they order *har mok,* one of my favorite offerings of the Thai kitchen. It's a fragrant, steamed fish pudding, perfumed with lemongrass, coconut, and kaffir lime leaves. Here is a version using delicate minced chicken breast. Those who prefer it with fish can substitute 1 pound of white fish fillets such as snapper for the chicken.

Serve *har mok* as you would individual savory soufflés—as an elegant first course or a light meal, with steamed rice and a green salad.

⅓ cup chopped red onion
4 cloves garlic, minced
3 small fresh hot red chiles, stemmed,
seeded, and chopped
1 stalk fresh lemongrass (3 inches of the
lower stalk, tough outer leaves discarded),
chopped, or ¾ teaspoon grated lime zest
½ teaspoon freshly ground white pepper
½ teaspoon salt
1 cup canned unsweetened coconut milk, well
stirred, or more as needed
1 pound skinless, boneless chicken breasts
1 large egg, lightly beaten
1 tablespoon Asian fish sauce, such as
nam pla
½ teaspoon sugar
⅓ cup (tightly packed) fresh basil leaves,
preferably Thai
1 teaspoon cornstarch, mixed with
1½ teaspoons cold water
½ small red bell pepper, stemmed, seeded, and
cut into fine julienne
3 kaffir lime leaves, finely shredded
(optional)

1. Using a mortar and pestle or a small food processor, grind or process the onion, garlic, chiles, lemongrass, pepper, and salt to a paste. If using the processor, add a little coconut milk to assist the blending. Scrape the mixture into a bowl.

2. Rinse the chicken fillets well and pat

dry with paper towels. Chop into smaller pieces, then grind in a food processor until minced.

3. In a large bowl, combine the ground chicken, the onion paste, ½ cup of the coconut milk, the egg, fish sauce, and sugar. Mix well with a wooden spoon.

4. Preheat the oven to 325°F.

5. Line the bottom and sides of six 1-cup soufflé molds with basil leaves. Distribute the chicken mixture evenly among the molds. Place the molds in a large baking pan and add enough hot water to reach two thirds of the way up the sides of the molds. Cover the molds tightly with aluminum foil.

6. Bake until the puddings are set, 10 to 15 minutes.

7. While the puddings are baking, bring the remaining coconut milk to a simmer over medium heat. Slowly whisk in the cornstarch mixture and stir over low heat until it thickens.

8. Carefully remove the pan with the molds from the oven. Uncover the molds, then drizzle the puddings with the coconut milk mixture and sprinkle with julienned red pepper and kaffir lime leaves. Return the pan to the oven and bake, uncovered, for another 5 to 7 minutes.

9. Remove the molds from the pan and let cool slightly. Place on plates and serve.

SERVES 6

CHICKEN BREASTS
with Tropical Fruit Sauce

We are blessed with a good selection of tropical fruit all year round, and I like to cook this chicken, with its rich sauce of rum, coconut, and tropical fruit, on one of those gray winter days when I'm suddenly hit by a craving for palm trees and azure waters.

4 skinless, boneless chicken breast halves
1 teaspoon paprika
Salt and freshly ground black pepper,
 to taste
2 tablespoons canola oil
½ cup chopped onion
2 teaspoons grated fresh ginger
1 small fresh hot chile, green or red, stemmed,
 seeded, and minced
⅓ cup unsweetened pineapple juice
4 tablespoons dark rum
½ cup plus 2 tablespoons fresh or canned
 unsweetened coconut milk
1 cup Chicken Stock (page 384) or canned
 broth
3 tablespoons puréed fresh mango
1 teaspoon grated orange zest
2 teaspoons soy sauce
1 teaspoon rice vinegar
1 tablespoon unsalted butter
¼ cup diced fresh pineapple
¼ cup diced fresh papaya
1½ teaspoons fresh lime juice, or more
 to taste
Pinch of sugar

1. Rinse the chicken breasts well and pat dry with paper towels. Remove the fillets (the finger-sized muscle on the back of each half) and reserve for another use. Flatten each breast with the flat side of a meat cleaver until thin.

2. In a small bowl, combine the paprika, salt, and pepper. Rub the chicken breasts with the mixture.

3. Heat the oil in a large skillet over medium heat. Add the chicken breasts and cook until they are cooked through and lightly colored, about 3 minutes per side. Remove from the skillet and keep warm.

4. Add the onion, ginger, and chile to the skillet and cook until the onion is translucent, about 5 minutes. Add the pineapple juice and 3 tablespoons of the rum and cook until reduced and syrupy, about 7 minutes. Add the ½ cup coconut milk and all of the stock and cook until thickened and reduced, about 10 minutes. Strain through a fine strainer and return to the skillet. Add the 2 tablespoons coconut milk, the puréed mango, orange zest, soy sauce, and vinegar and cook over low heat until the mixture reduces to a saucelike consistency and coats the back of a spoon, about 7 minutes.

5. Melt the butter in a small skillet over medium heat. Sauté the pineapple and papaya until just heated through. Stir in the remaining rum, the lime juice, and sugar and cook over high heat for 1 minute.

6. Arrange the chicken on 4 plates. Spoon some sauce around each serving and top with the sautéed fruit.

SERVES 4

CRISPY "TWICE-COOKED" CORNISH HENS
with Black Rice Timbales

This dish exemplifies the finesse and sophistication the East-meets-West culinary experiment has achieved in Australia. For Australian chefs—who have been traveling to the Orient for decades and are surrounded by Asian immigrants at home—"fusion cuisine" comes from years of experimentation with textures and flavors, and longstanding familiarity with classic Oriental techniques and ingredients.

In this recipe, based on the Chinese concept of "twice cooking," the Cornish hen is first cooked in an aromatic licorice-scented infusion, then dried and deep-fried to crispy perfection. The finished bird is dramatically presented with a mandarin-scented black rice timbale. This dish might be a bit overwhelming for a novice cook, but those already initiated into Oriental cooking or serious cooking in general will achieve startling results. The recipe was given to me by Chris Manfield of the Paramount restaurant in Sydney.

The hens should be prepared ahead through step 4, and the rice, which needs a long soaking time, can be made a day ahead through step 3. All the ingredients should be readily available in a good Chinese grocery store. The poaching liquid can be frozen and reused for poaching chicken, duck, or for braising meats.

Both the hens and the black rice timbales can be served on their own or with other accompaniments.

2 quarts Chicken Stock (page 384) or
    canned broth
1½ cups dark soy sauce
1½ cups light soy sauce
1½ cups Chinese rice wine
10 tablespoons Chinese yellow rock sugar,
    broken into small pieces with a hammer,
    or ½ cup granulated sugar
4 pieces cassia bark, or 4 pieces (1½ inches
    each) cinnamon stick
1 cardamom pod, preferably unbleached
    (green), cracked open
1 tablespoon dried tangerine peel
4 pieces dried licorice root (see Note)
1 tablespoon fennel seeds
3 whole star anise
1 tablespoon Szechuan peppercorns
3 Rock Cornish game hens (about 2 pounds
    each), wing tips removed, butterflied
    (breastbone removed)
1 tablespoon cornstarch, mixed in
    2 tablespoons cold water
Peanut oil, for deep frying
Black Rice Timbales (recipe follows)
Spiced Salt (recipe follows)

1. Combine the ingredients through the Szechuan peppercorns in a large stockpot. Bring to a boil and simmer, uncovered, over low heat for 30 minutes. Strain this stock through a fine strainer into a large flameproof casserole or Dutch oven and discard the solids.

2. Meanwhile, rinse the hens well and pat dry with paper towels.

3. Reduce the heat to low so that the stock barely simmers without bubbling. Carefully lower the hens into the liquid and poach, partially covered, for 25 minutes, stirring gently every 5 minutes to make sure the hens are properly submerged in the liquid.

4. With a large slotted spoon, remove the hens from the stock, taking care not to damage the skin. Drain the hens of all the liq-

uid. Ideally this should be done by hanging the hens to dry, but you can do it by placing the hens, uncovered, on a clean refrigerator rack, with a tray underneath to catch the liquid. Leave the hens in the refrigerator until completely dry, at least 2 hours or overnight. Degrease the poaching liquid, reserve 2 cups, and save the rest for another use.

5. Reduce the reserved poaching liquid over high heat to 1 cup, about 10 minutes. Reduce the heat to low, whisk in the cornstarch mixture, and simmer until thickened, 1 minute. Set the sauce aside.

6. Pour oil to a depth of 2 inches in a deep fryer and heat to 360°F over medium heat. Deep-fry the hens, 1 at a time, until well browned and crispy, about 6 minutes. Bring the oil back to 360°F before each batch. Drain on paper towels. Keep the cooked hens warm in a low oven. Cut each hen in half with a sharp knife or shears.

7. To serve, unmold a Black Rice Timbale on each of 6 large dinner plates and put a hen half next to it. Sprinkle the hens with Spiced Salt, spoon some sauce around it, and serve at once.

SERVES 6

Note: Licorice root imparts a strong anise flavor to poached and braised Chinese dishes. It can be found dried and sliced at Chinese herbal shops and pharmacies.

Black Rice Timbales

If you are short of time, you don't have to steam the rice in molds as suggested in steps 2 and 3. Just mound it attractively on each plate.

1¼ *cups black sticky rice*

1 teaspoon peanut oil

1 teaspoon Oriental sesame oil

1 onion, finely chopped

4 small fresh hot chiles, green or red,
*   stemmed, seeded, and chopped*

2 cloves garlic, minced

2 teaspoons minced fresh ginger

1 teaspoon minced, dried orange peel, soaked
*   for 30 minutes and drained before*
*   mincing, or 1 teaspoon minced fresh*
*   orange zest*

2 black dates, pitted and minced

1 teaspoon ground fennel seeds

2 cups warm Chicken Stock (page 384) or
*   canned broth*

Salt, to taste

1. Place the rice in a bowl and rinse in several changes of cold water. Drain, return it to the bowl, and add water to cover by 2 inches. Soak for at least 6 hours or overnight, then drain.

2. Heat the oils in a heavy flameproof casserole or Dutch oven over medium-low heat. Add the onion, chiles, garlic, ginger, orange peel, black dates, and fennel and cook, stirring, until the ingredients are softened and aromatic but not browned, 5 minutes. Add the rice and stir for 2 minutes. Stir in the stock and cook, covered, over low heat until the rice is tender and all the liquid is absorbed, about 25 minutes. The rice should appear sticky, similar in texture to a risotto. If it is too liquidy, reduce the liquid over medium heat, stirring continuously. Remove from the heat and let cool.

3. Oil 6 heatproof molds, about 3 inches wide and 2½ inches deep. (You can use soufflé or custard cups.) Spoon the rice into the molds and press down firmly. Cover with plastic wrap and let stand, at room temperature, until ready to use. (If making this the day before, store in the refrigerator.)

4. Remove the plastic wrap. In a steamer set over boiling water, steam the rice in the molds for 10 minutes. Run a knife around the edge of the molds and invert onto the plates.

SERVES 6

Spiced Salt

1 tablespoon coarse (kosher) salt

¼ *teaspoon five-spice powder*

1 teaspoon toasted and ground Szechuan
*   peppercorns*

Mix all the ingredients together well. Store in an airtight container.

ABOUT 1½ TABLESPOONS

BALINESE GRILLED CORNISH HENS

with Wild Rice and Greens in Fragrant Broth

Many Melbourne residents consider Stephanie Alexander, a celebrated restaurateur, author, and teacher, something of an Australian national treasure. In her relentless pursuit of perfect tastes, Stephanie travels and tours high and low to explore the natural bounty of her native country. Her name is synonymous with Australian haute cuisine, a vibrant blend of the world's culinary cultures, based on the spectacular local produce.

This recipe for a Balinese dish called *ayam tutu* is adapted from her book, *Stephanie's Feasts and Stories*. It is a whole meal consisting of spiced grilled Cornish hens served in a richly flavored broth together with wild rice (a substitute for black rice) and a bright stir-fried green.

If you have black rice at hand, it will make the presentation even more dramatic. Rinse and soak it overnight and then cook it in 1⅔ cups water per each cup rice until tender, about 20 minutes.

1 cup wild rice
7 cups Chicken
    Stock (page 384)
    or canned broth
4 tablespoons (½ stick)
    unsalted butter
1 tablespoon grated fresh ginger
4 cloves garlic, crushed through a press
2 stalks fresh lemongrass (3 inches of the
    lower stalk, tough outer leaves discarded),
    finely chopped
2 small fresh hot chiles, green or red,
    stemmed, seeded, and finely chopped
2 teaspoons ground turmeric
2 tablespoons finely chopped cilantro
    stems
4 fat scallions, thinly sliced
1 tablespoon fresh lime juice
3 Rock Cornish game hens
    (about 1¼ pounds each)
2 tablespoons unsalted butter, melted
Salt, to taste
2 teaspoons peanut oil
1 large head bok choy, choy sum, or
    other Chinese greens
Finely julienned red bell pepper,
    for garnish
Fresh cilantro leaves, for garnish
Roasted peanuts, for garnish

1. Make the wild rice: Rinse the rice well under cold running water and drain in a colander. Combine the rice and 3 cups of the stock in a heavy medium-size saucepan, cover, and bring to a boil over medium-high heat. Reduce the heat to low and simmer until the rice is tender. This should take anywhere from 40 minutes to an hour, depending on the rice. Don't worry if all the liquid has not been absorbed; you will be serving the rice in broth anyway. Keep warm.

2. Melt the butter in a small skillet over low heat. Add the ginger, garlic, lemongrass, chiles, turmeric, cilantro stems, and scallions and stir for 1 minute. You should have a fairly thick paste. Stir in the lime juice. Set aside.

3. Preheat the broiler.

4. Rinse the hens well, inside and out, and pat dry with paper towels. Cut out the backbone from each, and make a cut on either side of the breastbone, so that the hens open flat like a book. Place the hens between two sheets of waxed paper and pound lightly with a mallet to flatten. With your fingers, loosen the skin around the breast and the upper part of the legs. Rub all but 2 tablespoons of the spice paste over the breasts and thighs of the hens, under the loosened skin.

5. Brush the skin of the hens with the melted butter and broil, split side down, until cooked through and golden, about 20 minutes.

6. While the birds are cooking, prepare the sauce: Bring the remaining chicken stock to a boil over medium-low heat. Add the reserved 2 tablespoons spice paste and simmer for 45 seconds. Remove from the heat, season with salt to taste, and keep warm.

7. Heat the oil in a wok over medium-high heat. Add the bok choy and stir-fry until it turns bright green, 2 to 3 minutes.

8. To serve, cut each hen in half. Divide the greens among 6 large soup bowls. Mound a portion of wild rice in the middle of each

bowl and place a hen on the rice. Ladle some seasoned stock on each portion. Garnish with julienned red pepper, cilantro leaves, and peanuts. Serve at once.

SERVES 6

GRILLED CORNISH HENS
in Coconut-Lime Sauce

Here the hens are marinated in a zesty lime-sugar mixture, grilled, and finished off in an extraordinarily fragrant coconut sauce, with a lively crunch of roasted peanuts and exotic scent of kaffir lime. The marinating and grilling give the hens a firm but juicy texture and imparts a smoky flavor to the beguiling sauce. This curious combination of grilling and braising, inherited from the Chinese concept of twice-cooking, is very common in Southeast Asian cooking and is a highlight of the cuisine.

3 Rock Cornish game hens
(about 1¼ pounds each)
Salt, to taste
¼ cup fresh lime juice
1½ tablespoons palm sugar or (packed) light
brown sugar
2 teaspoons peanut oil
Coconut-Lime Sauce (recipe follows)
½ cup roasted peanuts, chopped in a food
processor
4 kaffir lime leaves, finely shredded,
if available
¼ cup chopped fresh cilantro leaves

1. Rinse the hens well, inside and out, and pat dry with paper towels. Cut in half with a sharp knife or shears and flatten with the flat side of a cleaver.

2. Rub the hens with 1 teaspoon salt and arrange in a large shallow dish. In a small bowl, whisk together the lime juice and sugar. Pour this marinade over the hens and turn to coat. Marinate at least 2 hours or overnight in the refrigerator, turning several times.

3. Prepare coals for grilling or preheat the broiler.

4. Remove the hens from the marinade and shake off the excess. Brush with the oil. Grill or broil the hens until almost cooked through and slightly charred, turning several times, 15 to 20 minutes.

5. Add the hens to the Coconut-Lime Sauce and turn to coat. Cook over medium-high heat, turning the hens several times, until the sauce thickens and coats the hens, about 7 minutes. Stir in the peanuts, kaffir lime leaves and cilantro. Transfer to a serving platter and serve at once.

SERVES 6

Coconut-Lime
Sauce

3 dried red chiles (2 to 3 inches), preferably
    Asian, seeded
1 small fresh hot red chile, seeded and
    chopped
¼ cup chopped red bell pepper
2 large cloves garlic, minced
4 shallots, chopped
4 stalks fresh lemongrass (3 inches of the
    lower stalk, tough outer leaves discarded),
    chopped
½ teaspoon freshly ground white
    pepper
1 teaspoon paprika
½ teaspoon ground turmeric
1½ tablespoons peanut oil, plus more as
    needed
¾ cup fresh or canned unsweetened
    coconut milk, well stirred
¾ cup Chicken Stock (page 384) or
    canned broth
2 teaspoons grated lime zest
1 tablespoon fresh lime juice
2 teaspoons palm or (packed) light
    brown sugar
Salt and freshly ground black pepper,
    to taste

1. Cut the dried chiles into pieces using scissors. Soak in warm water to cover for 20 minutes. Drain well.

2. Combine the fresh and dried chiles, bell pepper, garlic, shallots, lemongrass, white pepper, paprika, and turmeric in a food processor and process to a paste, adding a little oil to assist blending if necessary.

3. In a wok, heat 1½ tablespoons of the oil over low heat. Add the chile paste and cook, stirring often, until it no longer tastes raw, about 5 minutes. Add the coconut milk and cook over medium heat for 5 minutes.

Add the stock and cook for another 7 minutes, stirring occasionally. Stir in the lime zest, lime juice, and sugar, and season with salt and pepper to taste.

MAKES ABOUT 2¼ CUPS

ROAST TURKEY
with Thai Curry Gravy

It may be a touch too adventurous for a Thanksgiving meal, but this turkey with its aromatic Thai coconut gravy, basil, and pineapple is nevertheless a spectacular centerpiece for a large dinner party or buffet. It is highly unusual, takes almost no time to put together, and will handily feed a crowd.

1 young turkey (10 to 12 pounds),
    giblets removed
Salt and freshly ground black pepper,
    to taste
1 tablespoon paprika
8 tablespoons (1 stick) unsalted butter,
    melted
2 cups Chicken Stock (page 384) or
    canned broth
1 can (13½ ounces) unsweetened coconut
    milk, well stirred
2 tablespoons Thai red curry paste, preferably
    homemade (page 268)
2 cups diced fresh pineapple
2½ tablespoons Asian fish sauce, such as
    nam pla
1½ teaspoons sugar
¾ cup julienned red bell pepper
¾ cup (tightly packed) fresh basil leaves,
    preferably Thai

1. Preheat the oven to 425°F.

2. Rinse the turkey well, inside and out, and pat dry with paper towels.

3. In a small bowl, combine the salt, pepper, and paprika and rub the turkey, inside and out, with the mixture.

4. Place the turkey in a roasting pan and brush generously with the melted butter. Roast for 30 minutes. Reduce the temperature to 325°F and pour the stock into the pan. Roast the turkey for 2 to 2½ hours longer, brushing with the melted butter and basting with pan juices every 20 minutes. The turkey is ready when the juices run clear when you pierce the thickest part of the thigh.

5. Remove the turkey from the oven, cover loosely with aluminum foil, and let stand for 15 minutes.

6. While the turkey is standing, prepare the gravy. Skim the fat off the pan juices and measure 2 cups. If there isn't enough liquid, add water. Set aside. Heat the coconut milk in a heavy saucepan over high heat, covered with a lid or splatter screen. Add the curry paste and cook, gently breaking it up with a wooden spoon, for 5 minutes. Add the 2 cups pan juices and cook for 5 minutes more. Add the pineapple, fish sauce, sugar, bell pepper, and basil and cook for 2 minutes more.

7. Carve the turkey and arrange on a serving platter. Pour some of the gravy on and around the turkey and serve the rest in a deep bowl.

SERVES 8, OR 12 AS PART OF A BUFFET

HOISIN-GLAZED TURKEY BURGERS

with Sizzling Scallions

With the Asianization of the American palate, it hasn't taken long for burgers to take on an Oriental guise. While certainly healthy, turkey burgers are usually bland, uninspired fare. But in this simple recipe the rich, spicy hoisin-Chinese mustard glaze provides such a delicious accent of flavor that you won't even need to reach for the ketchup bottle. Serve these with seared scallions and good sesame buns. The glaze is also excellent on grilled or broiled lamb burgers.

1¼ pounds ground turkey
⅓ cup finely chopped onion
2 tablespoons fresh bread crumbs
2 cloves garlic, crushed through a press
¼ cup finely chopped scallions
¼ teaspoon ground cayenne pepper
Salt and freshly ground black pepper,
*   to taste*
2 tablespoons hoisin sauce
2½ teaspoons Chinese or Dijon mustard,
*   plus additional for serving*
1 tablespoon soy sauce
1½ teaspoons rice vinegar or cider vinegar
1½ teaspoons Oriental sesame oil
8 scallions, trimmed and cut into 2½-inch
*   lengths*
4 sesame buns, halved and toasted

1. Prepare coals for grilling or preheat the broiler.

2. In a large bowl, mix the ground tur-

key with the onion, bread crumbs, garlic, chopped scallions, cayenne, salt, and black pepper.

3. In a small bowl, whisk together the hoisin sauce, mustard, soy sauce, vinegar, and 1 teaspoon of the sesame oil.

4. Shape the ground turkey mixture into 4 patties. Brush the burgers on one side with the hoisin glaze, then grill or broil for 4 minutes. Turn on the other side, brush with the remaining glaze, and cook until the juices run clear, about 4 more minutes.

5. While the burgers are cooking, sear the scallions. Brush a wok or cast-iron skillet with the remaining sesame oil and heat over medium-high heat until almost smoking. Add the scallions and stir until lightly charred and soft, about 1 minute.

6. Serve the burgers on the buns, topped with the scallions. If the you wish, pass some Chinese mustard as an accompaniment.

SERVES 4

JAPANESE-INSPIRED ELEGANT SUPPER FOR FOUR

· · · · · · · · · · · · · ·

FRIED OYSTERS
with Wasabi Mayonnaise

ROASTED DUCK BREAST
with Lychees and Sansho and
Honey Sauce

ASPARAGUS AND SNOW PEAS
with Mirin Dressing

GINGER CREME BRULEE

ROASTED DUCK BREAST

with Lychees and Sansho and Honey Sauce

Serve this very chic East-meets-West *à la minute* entrée for an evening when you want to impress without spending much time in the kitchen. Ideally, duck stock should be used for the sauce, so next time you are roasting a duck, save the neck and giblets, make about 1½ cups stock and freeze. Otherwise, use well-reduced good homemade chicken stock. Turn to canned broth only as a last resort.

The combination of rich, rare duck meat and delicate fresh lychees is sensational. While I don't have an aversion to canned lychees, using canned fruit in a dish as refined as this one is like takeout Chinese meets three star cuisine. But if you can't get fresh lychees—the duck will still be great.

1 tablespoon light olive oil (do not use
    virgin or extra-virgin)
4 duck breast halves (about 2 pounds
    total)
Salt, to taste
3 tablespoons honey
¾ cup rich duck stock, well-reduced Chicken
    Stock (page 384), or canned broth
2½ tablespoons rice vinegar
1 teaspoon cornstarch, mixed with
    1½ teaspoons cold water
1 tablespoon fresh lime juice
1½ teaspoons dark soy sauce
8 lychees, preferably fresh, peeled
1 tablespoon sansho pepper (available in
    Japanese and specialty food stores)

1. Preheat the oven to 375°F.

2. Rinse the duck breasts well and pat dry with paper towels.

3. Heat the oil over high heat in a large nonstick ovenproof skillet. Rub the duck breasts with salt. Cook the duck breasts, skin side down first, about 3 minutes on each side. Transfer to the oven in the skillet and cook until golden on the outside and rare inside, 6 to 7 minutes. Remove from the oven, cover with aluminum foil, and let stand for 10 minutes while you prepare the sauce.

4. Place the honey in a small nonreactive saucepan and cook over low heat, stirring, until it is frothy and darkens in color, about 3 minutes. Stir in the stock and vinegar and reduce over high heat by half, about 12 minutes. Slowly whisk in the cornstarch mixture and cook over low heat until thickened, about 30 seconds. Stir in the lime juice and soy sauce and season with salt, if necessary.

5. To serve, cut the duck breasts crosswise into thin slices, arrange in a fan on dinner plates, and place 2 lychees at the base of each fan. Sprinkle the duck with *sansho* pepper and spoon some sauce over and around each portion.

SERVES 4

R O A S T   G A R L I C
Q U A I L
with Maple Glaze

This simple, spicy quail dish will be elegant and festive if you present it with Pineapple Fried Rice (see Index) and a cheerful vegetable stir-fry. The preparation also works nicely with tiny Cornish hens.

6 quail
3 tablespoons maple syrup
3 tablespoons soy sauce
1 tablespoon rice vinegar or white wine vinegar
1½ tablespoons Sambal Oelek (page 388) or Chinese chile paste with garlic
7 cloves garlic, crushed through a press
Salt and freshly ground black pepper, to taste

1. Rinse the quail well, inside and out, and pat dry with paper towels.

2. In a small bowl, whisk together the maple syrup, soy sauce, vinegar, *sambal oelek*, and garlic. Rub the quail inside and out with salt and pepper and place in a shallow bowl. Pour the maple mixture over and turn to coat. Cover and refrigerate at least 6 hours or overnight.

3. Preheat the oven to 450°F.

4. Place the quail on a baking sheet with sides and roast for 10 minutes. Reduce the temperature to 375°F and continue roasting, basting frequently with the marinade, until the quail are crispy and dark golden, about 15 more minutes. Serve at once.

SERVES 6 AS AN APPETIZER, 3 AS A MAIN COURSE

OUTBACK RABBIT AND PRUNE PIE

When rabbits were introduced to Australia in the last century, they multiplied in such proportions that they soon became a serious menace to the country's agriculture. As a result, rabbit became the unofficial Australian national meat, and rabbit pie a symbol of outback home cooking.

Recently rabbit pie has come into its own as a comfort food. This wonderful pie is an amalgamation of rabbit pie recipes I collected during my Australian stay. You can prepare the rabbit stew filling (steps 1 through 7) ahead of time.

2 rabbits (2¼ to 2½ pounds each), cut into serving pieces
Salt and freshly ground black pepper, to taste
4⅔ cups dark beer
4 slices lean bacon, chopped
3 tablespoons unsalted butter
1 cup sliced onion
2 teaspoons chopped garlic
1 rib celery, diced
1 small carrot, peeled and diced
8 ounces mushrooms, cleaned and sliced
1 heaping tablespoon all-purpose flour
½ cup medium-dry sherry
1 can (14 ounces) plum tomatoes, chopped, juice reserved
1½ tablespoons finely chopped fresh parsley leaves
1 tablespoon chopped fresh tarragon leaves
8 pitted prunes, coarsely chopped
Salt and freshly ground black pepper, to taste
2 sheets frozen puff pastry, thawed
1 large egg yolk, mixed with 1 teaspoon milk, for egg wash

1. Rinse the rabbit pieces well and pat dry with paper towels.

2. Rub the rabbit pieces with salt and pepper, place in a large bowl, and pour 4 cups of the beer over them. Cover and refrigerate for 6 hours or overnight, turning occasionally.

3. Cook the bacon in a large Dutch oven over medium-low heat until crisp. Transfer to paper towels to drain. Pour off all but 3 tablespoons of the fat.

4. Remove the rabbit pieces from the marinade and shake off the excess. Brown the rabbit pieces, in batches, in the bacon fat over medium-high heat. Drain on paper towels.

5. Add the butter to the Dutch oven and melt over medium heat. Add the onion and garlic and cook until the onion is translucent, about 5 minutes. Add the celery, carrot, and mushrooms and cook, stirring, until soft, 10 to 12 minutes.

6. Add the flour and stir for 30 seconds. Stir in the remaining beer, the sherry, and the tomatoes with their juice. Stir until the mixture thickens. Add the rabbit, the reserved bacon, the parsley, tarragon, prunes, and salt and pepper to taste. Simmer, covered, over low heat, stirring occasionally, until the rabbit is tender, 45 to 50 minutes.

7. With a slotted spoon, remove the rabbit from the sauce. When cool enough to handle, remove the meat from the bones and cut into bite-size pieces. Discard the bones.

8. Reduce the sauce over medium-high heat until thickened, stirring occasionally, about 15 minutes. Return the rabbit to the sauce and toss to coat. Cool to room temperature before filling and baking the pie.

9. Preheat the oven to 425°F.

10. On a lightly floured surface, lightly roll out 1 sheet of pastry and cut out an 11-inch round. Line a 9-inch pie plate with the pastry round. Roll out the other piece of pastry lightly and cut into a 12-inch round. Set aside.

11. Spoon the rabbit stew into the pastry-lined pie plate. Fit the top crust over the mixture and press the edges gently but firmly to the edges of the bottom crust to seal them. Trim the pastry and crimp the edges decoratively. With a sharp knife make several slits on the top of the pie to allow steam to escape. Brush the crust with the egg wash. Place the pie in the oven and bake until the crust is deep golden, about 25 minutes.

12. Remove from the oven and let stand for 5 minutes before serving.

SERVES 6

S E A R E D
V E N I S O N
with Spicy Masala Sauce and Sweet Potato Purée

An exquisitely balanced and sophisticated dish, this venison requires some specialty ingredients and careful preparation, but the results are truly worth the effort. The East-meets-West sauce tastes sensational with the gamey venison and is perfectly complemented by the sweet potato purée. The recipe is the creation of one of my favorite Australian chefs, Chris Manfield, of the Paramount restaurant in Sydney.

Do not be put off by the long list of sauce ingredients, since most of them are spices. If you are looking for a real restaurant effect, use demiglace (which can be purchased in many specialty grocery stores) instead of the stock. You will need about

1½ cups. If using demiglace, reduce it just enough to thicken slightly.

3 tablespoons light olive oil (do not use
    virgin or extra-virgin)
Freshly ground black pepper, to taste
1 teaspoon garam masala
2¼ pounds venison fillets (from the saddle),
    cut into 6 pieces
2 pounds sweet potatoes, peeled and diced
4 tablespoons (½ stick) unsalted butter, at
    room temperature
¼ cup heavy (or whipping) cream
Salt, to taste
Spicy Masala Sauce (recipe follows)

1. Whisk the oil with 1 teaspoon black pepper and the garam masala. Arrange the venison pieces in a shallow dish, then drizzle with the oil and toss to coat. Cover and refrigerate for 3 hours. Bring to room temperature before cooking.

2. Cook the sweet potatoes in salted water until tender, 15 minutes, and drain. Transfer to a food processor and puree, adding the butter and cream. Scrape into a bowl and season with salt and pepper to taste. Keep warm.

3. Preheat the oven to 400°F.

4. Add 2 teaspoons of the marinade from the venison to a heavy ovenproof skillet and heat over high heat. Add the venison and sear until rare, about 3 minutes per side. Place the skillet in the oven for 2 minutes. Remove, cover with aluminum foil, and let stand for 10

minutes. Transfer the venison to a cutting board and cut each piece into 5 slices.

5. To serve, spoon some sweet potato purée over the center of each of 6 plates. Arrange the sliced meat in a fan next to the purée and spoon some sauce over the meat.

SERVES 6

Spicy Masala Sauce

This flavorful sauce will also taste delicious on roast chicken, seared steak, or roast lamb.

1 teaspoon shrimp paste
1 teaspoon coriander seeds
1 teaspoon cumin seeds
1 teaspoon Szechuan peppercorns
1 small onion, chopped
3 cloves garlic, chopped
1 tablespoon chopped fresh ginger
2 tablespoons chopped cilantro roots
    and/or stems
3 small fresh hot red chiles, stemmed,
    seeded, and chopped
2 teaspoons ground turmeric
2 pinches freshly ground nutmeg
2 tablespoons Chinese yellow rock sugar,
    broken into small pieces with a hammer,
    or 2 tablespoons granulated sugar
5 tablespoons Chinese rice wine or dry sherry
3 cups Beef Stock (page 384) or canned
    broth
1 cinnamon stick (3 inches), 2 slices dried
    galangal, and 6 fresh or dried curry leaves
    tied in a piece of cheesecloth
1 tablespoon Asian fish sauce, such as nam
    pla, or soy sauce

1. Wrap the shrimp paste in a double layer of aluminum foil and toast over high heat in a small skillet, about 2 minutes per side. Remove from the skillet and set aside.

2. To the skillet add the coriander and cumin seeds and the peppercorns. Toast, shaking the pan often, until fragrant, about 2 minutes. Grind in a spice grinder until fine.

3. Combine the onion, garlic, ginger, cilantro roots and/or stems, chiles, turmeric, nutmeg, and the toasted shrimp paste and ground spices in a food processor and process to a paste, adding a little water to assist the blending if necessary.

3. Place the rock sugar in a heavy saucepan and stir over low heat until dissolved. Add the spice paste and cook over low heat, shaking the pan often to prevent sticking, until the paste begins to color and becomes fragrant, about 2 minutes. Slowly add the rice wine, standing back, as the mixture will splatter. Cook, stirring, for 1 minute.

4. Slowly add the stock, then add the cheesecloth bag and cook over medium heat until the sauce reduces to 1 cup, 20 to 25 minutes. Strain the sauce through a strainer. Season with fish sauce or soy sauce.

MAKES 1 CUP

NEW ZEALAND VENISON STEAKS
with Tamarillo Coulis

Besides lamb and kiwis, New Zealand boasts some of the best farm-raised venison in the world, and it is also home to a thriving tamarillo industry.

So this culinary pairing is typically New Zealand and very delectable. Look for tamarillos (which look and taste like very sour plums) at gourmet groceries or specialty sections of supermarkets.

3 tamarillos
1/4 cup chopped onion
2 tablespoons red currant jelly
3 tablespoons Marsala wine
Salt, to taste
1½ tablespoons chopped fresh
    mint leaves
4 venison steaks (about 8 ounces each)
½ teaspoon paprika
1½ teaspoons cracked black pepper
2 teaspoons light olive oil (do not use
    virgin or extra-virgin)

1. Make the tamarillo coulis: Blanch the tamarillos in boiling water for 20 seconds, drain, and plunge into cold water. Remove the skins.

2. Purée the peeled tamarillos in a food processor together with the onion and currant jelly. Transfer the puréed mixture to a small nonreactive saucepan. Bring to a simmer and cook over low heat for 5 minutes. Add the Marsala, turn the heat up to high, and cook until the mixture is slightly reduced, about 3 minutes. Add salt to taste. Transfer to a serving bowl and cool to room temperature. Stir in the mint.

3. Rub the venison steaks with salt, paprika, and black pepper. In a heavy, preferably cast-iron skillet, heat the oil over medium-high heat until hot but not smoking. Add the venison steaks and sear them quickly on both sides. Then cook an additional 3 to 4 minutes per side, for medium-rare meat.

4. Place each steak on a serving plate and spoon some tamarillo sauce on the side.

SERVES 4

NONYA COOKERY
A MARRIAGE OF CUISINES

The legend goes that when, in 1459, the sultan of Melaka, Mansur Shah, married the beautiful Chinese princess Han Li Po to strengthen relations between China and Malaysia, she arrived with five hundred maidens, who all married local men. Their descendants became the first Peranakans (literally "born of the soil"), or Straits Chinese, whose men were referred to as *Babas* and women as *Nonyas*.

Sino-Malay interchange prospered further in the nineteenth century as Chinese working men migrated to the Straits settlements of Penang, Melaka, and Singapore in search of spoils from the British Empire and settled down with Malay women.

The Straits Chinese flourished in the former British colonies along the Straits of Melaka, and by the end of the nineteenth century, the Peranakans, some of whom made a fortune in the Malaysian tin mines, were prospering both culturally and financially. Living in closed communities and zealously preserving their identity through adopted Chinese rituals and traditions, they surrounded themselves with luxury: heavy, ornately carved wooden furniture, costly imported Chinese porcelains, and European finery. As a result, their costumes, traditions, and celebrations are among the most elaborate in the region.

The Nonya style of cooking is an extraordinary blend of carefully guarded Chinese traditions combined with an inspired use of tropical produce. When the Chinese men took Malay wives, they taught them to cook the foods of their homeland. But to the women, used to the intricate seasonings and vibrant tastes of their spice-blessed land, Chinese cooking seemed unbearably bland. Little by little they began smuggling familiar tastes into the new food. The men could do nothing but accept the inevitable. The Nonyas, however, had to make greater sacrifices. Their Chinese husbands, for example, insisted on pork as the predominant meat of the household, so the Muslim Malay women had to relinquish their dietary taboos.

FUSION AT ITS BEST

My first experience with Nonya cuisine began with coriander-infused chicken soup accompanied by a dizzying array of garnishes; prawns seductively cloaked in spiced coconut milk, nuts, and pineapple; *nasi ulam,* rice studded with pickled vegetables and greens; fried chicken in a fragrant tart and sweet tamarind gravy, and a selection of diminutive cakes. I was stunned at the intricacy and imagination of this unfamiliar cuisine. I wanted to know more. The feast I sampled had been prepared by Christobelle Savage, or

Auntie Belle—one of Malaysia's celebrity chefs—who came to demonstrate Nonya food at a top hotel in Melbourne.

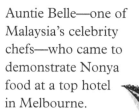

Auntie Belle is far from being a refined and aristocratic "true blue" Nonya. Born into an impoverished fishing family in Melaka, she was sent as a cooking apprentice at the age of ten to a wealthy Nonya household. It was there, under the watchful eye of the family's matriarch and the strictures of innumerable *pantang* (Nonya superstitions), that she mastered the elaborate art of cooking the traditional Straits Chinese delicacies.

She recalled her cooking debut. Instructed to prepare a huge pot of *ayam pongtee* (chicken in rich, dark soybean sauce) for a Christmas feast, she accidentally used a pinch of the wrong spice. The difference in taste was minute, but the lady of the house tasted it and without a word threw the whole pot into a ditch. "I just sat there and cried all night," remembered Auntie Belle. But the Cinderella story had its happy ending. Auntie Belle started her own restaurant in Melaka, becoming the city's unofficial culinary queen. A posh Hyatt resort near Kuala Lumpur, about to open a Nonya Melakan restaurant, heard of Auntie Belle through the grapevine and whisked her away to cook for sultans and Japanese golf professionals, and fly around the world promoting her adopted cuisine.

A NONYA CELEBRATION

Next, my quest for Nonya culture and cuisine took me to the Peranakan communities of Penang and Singapore. In Penang John and I were looked after by the Khor family, members of an important Baba-Nonya clan. They took us to the Dragon King restaurant—which specializes in Nonya home cooking. As soon as we walked in the door, it was obvious that something special was going on. It turned out to be a celebration of a child's "first month." The long tables were laden with dozens of dishes decorated with symbolic red

orated batik sarongs and beaded slippers.

John and I could scarcely take our eyes off the proceedings, but were eventually seated for lunch with our new friends, who continued to educate us about their culinary heritage. The

The women looked like butterflies in their traditional kabayas, *the lavishly embroidered lacy blouses worn with intricately decorated batik sarongs . . .*

fruit, traditional Malay mounds of yellow rice, a red Chinese molded cake, and decorative stacks of longevity noodles. The women looked like butterflies in their traditional *kabayas,* the lavishly embroidered lacy blouses worn with intricately dec-

aromatic *ulam,* they explained, is the key to Nonya flavors. Nonya cuisine, they insisted, has much more kick and variety than Malay or Chinese. The aromatics—copious amounts of garlic, chiles, ginger, lemongrass, galangal, and turmeric

root—are pounded into a paste called *rempeh.* This is the foundation of Nonya cooking.

"Much of the attention of the Nonya cook," they continued, "is centered on blending and harmonizing the spices." The aromatics are combined with sweet, lush coconut or tangy tamarind- flavored liquid as a base for curries, which are thickened with pounded candlenuts (somewhat similar to macadamias). The *rempeh* is used to spice up marinades, stir-fries, soups, grilled foods, and sauces. Dishes come with a selection of tongue-teasing *sambals,* hot and tangy condiments, or tart lime-scented, shredded salads that punctuate the blended richness of the sauces.

There is a strong Chinese accent, too, particularly in the huge assortment of Hokkien noodle dishes, usually served at street stalls: Soy- and other bean-paste-based sauces flavor pungent stir-fries, as well as dishes prepared with other Chinese techniques, like steaming, double boiling, and twice-cooking.

ACCEPT NO SUBSTITUTES

"What is the real hallmark of Nonya cooking?" I asked my friends.

"No shortcuts and no substitutes," they were quick to reply.

In the Nonya kitchen, everything has to be done right: vegetables cut to precise miniature shapes (otherwise the results are dismissed as *masuk medan,* "not fit for a banquet hall") and often carved into flowers; curries cooked to an exact consistency; and spices ground to the finest powders. Everything must be meticulously prepared from scratch. Rice flour is ground by hand, coconut painstakingly grated on a wooden grater to extract milk, spices ground on huge granite slabs. Fresh tamarind is bought in season and dried for later use. And whenever possible, ingredients are expensive and refined.

As John and I listened

to our friends, we were tucking into *itek tim,* the classic tangy soup with steamed duck, preserved vegetables, and pickled plums—Szechuan in origin, Nonya in execution.

Then we tried some of the other dishes on the table: crispy *lobak,* a roll made of bean curd skin stuffed with a mixture of ground pork and served with sweet-and-sour

chile sauce; and *kerabu,* a salad of prawns, chicken, shallots, and black mushrooms tossed in a lime-chile dressing. We loved the *otak otak,* an aromatic fish pudding steamed in a banana leaf. But it took us a while to figure out whether we liked *perut ikan,* dried fish intestines that came almost concealed in a mixture of vegetables and exotic greens.

Our education in this elaborate and unusual cuisine continued in Singapore, where we met Mr. Guih, one of the

chief historians of Peranakan culture in this great port city. He invited us to his home in the suburbs, where, between sips of the strong local coffee, we were treated to little tastes of diminutive coconut crepes topped with palm sugar and coconut cream, prepared by his wife.

FROM SOUP TO COCONUTS

The Guihs were a perfect Nonya and Baba couple. Their speech was slow, stately, and soft, their manners elegant and refined. Mr. Guih's composure became a kind of decorous enthusiasm when he began to describe a classic Nonya birthday celebration from the old days. As the guests arrived, bringing traditional presents of red candles, dozens of hen's eggs, dried rice vermicelli, and legs of pork, they were greeted with *ayer mata kuching*, an aromatic drink made from the pulp of the longan fruit. After a brief card game, the guests were seated at long dinner tables in rows of ten. The slurped down whole, and not bitten or chewed, since the strands represented longevity; a delicate dish of scrambled eggs and the valued shark's fin; and the obligatory rich coconut chicken curry borrowed

Dishes come with a selection of tongue-teasing sambals, hot and tangy condiments, or lime-scented, shredded salads. . .

dishes were subdivided in various categories beginning with the soupy dishes: dried fish maw soup, crab and pork ball broth with bamboo shoots, the mandatory delicacy bird's nest soup, and *buah keluak*, the curry made with Indonesian black nuts, vegetables, and chicken.

The second category consisted of *laok pingan panggang*, "food on large plates." These offerings included succulent Hainanese roast pork; rice noodles that had to be

from the Malays. Finally came the "food on medium plates," such as various bitingly hot-and-sour *acars*—succulent prawns stir-fried in a fiery Malay chile sauce, spicy barbecued pork strips, chicken in tart tamarind gravy, and pickled pineapple.

This was followed by a trip to the dessert table,

the pride of any Nonya household worth its chopsticks. The sweets were referred to as *kue chuchi mulot*, literally "cakes to wash the mouth with." The most symbolic birthday offering was the bright red *kueh koo*, a glutinous rice-flour cake with green-pea paste. Surrounding it would be coconut rolls, sweet-potato cake, *kueh lapis* (a European-style layer cake), sticky rice with egg custard, and carrot cake.

Led by three extraordinary guides from the hearts of the oldest and most revered Baba-Nonya communities in Melaka, Penang, and Singapore, we felt that we had been treated to a pure slice of living culinary history. Together, our guides—the passionate and eccentric Auntie Belle, the sophisticated habitués of the Dragon King on Penang Island, and the Guihs, who are an encyclopedia of Peranakan refinement in their own right—have given us an education in one of the greatest and most original fusion cuisines on earth.

Seared Steak with
Black Bean and Sherry Sauce

....

Steak with Chinese
Mustard and Honey Sauce

....

Tataki of Beef with
Artichoke and Olive Paste

....

Zarina's Mama Beefsteak

....

Vietnamese-Style London Broil

....

Grilled Herbed Skirt Steak

....

Red-Braised Beef with
Shiitake Mushrooms

....

Pot Roast with Asian Flavors

....

Beef Semur

....

Beef Rendang

....

Brochettes of Beef in Grape Leaves

....

Osso Buco of the Orient

....

Tandoori Veal Chops with Minted
Yogurt Sauce and Sautéed Apples

....

Veal Chops with a
Macadamia Nut Crust

....

Veal Scaloppine in Sake-Ginger Sauce

The East-West experiment in Asia—the haute cuisine aspect of it, at least—pretty much began with a steak. As Dietmar Sawyere, one of the chefs who pioneered fusion cuisine in the Pacific, told me, in the Asia of the early 1980s the worlds of Western-style fine dining and local cuisine were poles apart. Every posh hotel restaurant menu featured this or that from the tired mélange of international classics, with a selection of top-quality grilled steaks to please both Japanese and local businessmen. But when clients ordered their New York sirloin, they missed at least a suggestion of the familiar Asian tastes. So chefs began to marinate the steak in soy sauce or garnish it with a dab of chile or black bean sauce. The trend took off, and in just a decade or so developed into the wonderfully imaginative and sophisticated blending of Oriental and Occidental flavors.

Although beef is not as favored in Asia as pork or poultry, it marries extraordinarily well with a whole range of Eastern seasonings. My favorite way to serve good beef is to have it rare and succulent, either grilled over charcoal or quickly seared in a cast-iron pan or wok. The arsenal of Asian flavorings and marinades adds plenty of excitement to these simple preparations: the lively Thai mixture of cilantro, lime juice, and cracked white peppercorns; aromatic and piquant Chinese black bean sauce, with its suggestion of ginger; the slightly sweet, burnished Vietnamese glaze of brown sugar and fish sauce; or the simple, homey sauce of soy, tomato, and spices. Those who like their beef cooked slowly will be pleased with the red-braised beef, redolent of tangerine peel and star anise, and the deep, dusky flavor of shiitakes; or Asian pot roast, mellow with sweet spices and coconut milk.

As for veal, while almost unheard of in Asia, its delicate, white meat nevertheless lends itself beautifully to the gentler end of the Oriental seasoning spectrum: thin veal slices are finished in a delicate mirin sauce; classic Italian *osso buco* is enlivened with citrus, cilantro, and aromatics; and a juicy veal chop is marinated and baked tandoori-style and served with a tangy herbed yogurt sauce.

SEARED STEAK

with Black Bean and Sherry Sauce

The inspiration for this dish comes from the pungent and aromatic "black bean" stir-fries of Asia, only here the ginger-laced Chinese sauce is doused on a succulent sliced rare steak, and the rice wine is replaced with sherry. This is actually a typical ploy used in Asia's fancy international restaurants to maintain a local clientele—serve them something upscale and European in form (for example, steak or salmon), but dress it up with local flavors.

After you have tasted this versatile sauce with red meat, try it also with chicken or grilled firm fish steaks. With a good black bean sauce, it's hard to go wrong.

2 tablespoons olive oil

1 teaspoon minced garlic

1 tablespoon minced fresh ginger

1 large green bell pepper, stemmed,
    seeded, and diced

1 large red bell pepper, stemmed, seeded,
    and diced

1 small fresh hot chile, green or red stemmed,
    seeded, and chopped

2 tablespoons fermented black beans,
    rinsed

1 tablespoon dry sherry

1 tablespoon oyster sauce

⅔ cup Chicken Stock (page 384) or
    canned broth

½ teaspoon sugar, or more to taste

1½ teaspoons cornstarch, mixed with
    2 teaspoons cold water

1 sirloin steak (about 2 pounds),
    1½ inches thick

Salt, to taste

Sliced scallion greens, for garnish

1. Heat 1½ tablespoons of the oil in a wok, over medium-high heat until almost smoking. Add the garlic, ginger, bell peppers, and chile and stir-fry until softened, about 3 minutes. Add the black beans and cook for 1 minute longer. Add the sherry and cook until it almost evaporates. Stir in the oyster sauce, stock, and sugar and bring to a boil. Add the cornstarch mixture and cook until slightly thickened, about 2 minutes. Remove from the heat and keep warm.

2. Heat the remaining oil in a heavy skillet, over medium-high heat. Add the steak and cook until rare, about 7 minutes per side. Remove from the heat, cover with aluminum foil, and let stand for 5 minutes.

3. Spoon some sauce onto 4 plates. Cut the steak into ½-inch-thick slices and fan them out over the sauce, dividing evenly. Garnish with scallions.

SERVES 4

STEAK

with Chinese Mustard and Honey Sauce

The combination of Chinese mustard, honey, rice wine, and an accent of sesame oil provides a deliciously sweet and spicy foil for rare steak. Sautéed shiitake mushrooms would complete the picture nicely for a quick, but special, dinner for two. Brands of Chinese mustards vary in heat, so you might want to start out with 2 teaspoons and add more to taste, if you wish.

1 tablespoon vegetable oil

1 porterhouse steak (about 1¼ pounds)

3 tablespoons chopped shallots

1½ tablespoons Chinese rice wine or dry
    sherry

2 teaspoons Chinese mustard, or more
    to taste

⅓ cup Beef Stock, Chicken Stock (both
    page 384), or canned broth

2½ teaspoons soy sauce

¾ teaspoon honey

½ teaspoon cornstarch, mixed with
    1 teaspoon cold water

½ teaspoon Oriental sesame oil

2 teaspoons snipped fresh chives or
    chopped scallion greens

1. Heat the vegetable oil in a large heavy skillet over medium-high heat. Sauté the steak until medium-rare, about 5 minutes per side. Remove from the skillet, cover with aluminum foil, and let stand for 10 minutes.

2. Meanwhile, drain all but 2 teaspoons of fat from the skillet. Add the shallots and cook until softened, about 3 minutes. Add the rice wine and reduce for 1 minute. Stir in the mustard and stock and cook for 3 minutes. Add the soy sauce and honey and cook for 1 more minute. Stir in the cornstarch mixture and cook until the sauce thickens, about 1 minute longer. Stir in the sesame oil and chives.

3. Slice the steak and spoon the sauce over it to serve.

SERVES 2

TATAKI OF BEEF

with Artichoke and Olive Paste

In the high art of making East meet West, Sydney's Japanese-born chef, Tetsuya Wakuda, is a recognized master. Ever since his little restaurant in a fashionable suburb of Sydney has won the Remy Martin Australian Best Restaurant Award in 1994, a dinner there is the hottest meal ticket in town. Simple, clean, and fresh is how he describes his favorite food, and his own cooking is a delicate juggling of Mediterranean and Asian ingredients.

In this dish, seared rare slices of beef fillet are served accompanied by artichoke and olive paste and topped with a soy, rice wine, and ginger sauce. It makes an elegant cold entrée for 2 or a substantial appetizer for 4.

1 teaspoon olive oil
2 filet mignon steaks (about 8 ounces each),
    2 inches thick
3 tablespoons water
2 tablespoons mirin or medium-dry sherry
2 tablespoons soy sauce
1 teaspoon grated fresh ginger
2 cloves garlic, crushed through a press
½ cup chopped best-quality bottled marinated
    artichoke hearts
10 niçoise olives, pitted
Salt and freshly ground black pepper, to taste
Endive spears, for garnish
Frisée or chicory, for garnish
Julienned Japanese pink
    pickled ginger,
    for garnish

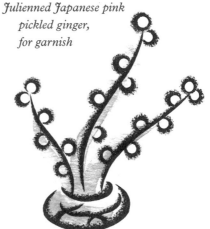

1. Heat the oil in a heavy skillet over medium-high heat. Add the beef and sear for 3 to 4 minutes on each side. Remove from the heat and cool to room temperature.

2. Combine the water, mirin, soy sauce, ginger, and half of the garlic in a small nonreactive saucepan and bring to a boil. Remove from the heat and cool to room temperature.

3. Process the artichoke hearts and olives to a paste in a food processor, scraping down the mixture from the sides of the bowl and processing again. Process in the remaining garlic and season with salt and pepper to taste.

4. Slice the beef into thin slices across the grain and fan them out on each of 2 plates. Arrange the endive, frisée, pickled ginger, and some artichoke paste next to the meat. Season the meat with salt and pepper and drizzle the meat and the greens with the mirin and soy mixture.

SERVES 2

ZARINA'S MAMA BEEFSTEAK

Sometimes you hunt down recipes for weeks and months, test them forever in the kitchen, and are lucky if you reach perfection in your own lifetime. Sometimes it's another story. I adapted the recipe for this delicious colonial dish of beef, potatoes, and peas, smothered in spicy tomato, soy, and Worcestershire sauce, from one I found in a marvelous cookbook I bought while waiting for a delayed flight at the Kuala Lumpur airport. It sounded so good and the directions were so precise I wanted to prepare it on the plane.

The book is *Zarina's Home Cooking.* It was written by Zarina Ibrahim, the Fanny Farmer of Southeast Asia, and it's chock-full of the great Indonesian, Indian, Malay, Chinese, and colonial recipes that make up the culinary landscape of the Malay Peninsula. As Zarina explains, "mama" is not actually her mother, but rather a nickname given to Indian Muslims by the Chinese and Malay populations of Singapore.

MARINADE

4 cloves garlic, crushed through a press

1 tablespoon grated fresh ginger

1½ teaspoons coarsely ground black pepper

1½ teaspoons ground coriander

1 teaspoon paprika

½ teaspoon ground cayenne pepper

¾ teaspoon five-spice powder

1½ tablespoons soy sauce

1 tablespoon Worcestershire sauce

1 teaspoon (packed) light brown sugar

1 sirloin (1¼ pounds), at least 1 inch thick, cut into thin slices against the grain

2½ tablespoons vegetable oil

2 cups thinly sliced onions

2 tablespoons Chinese rice wine or dry sherry

1 cup Beef Stock (page 384) or canned broth

1½ tablespoons tomato paste

1 tablespoon soy sauce

1½ teaspoons Worcestershire sauce

2 teaspoons rice vinegar

¾ teaspoon granulated sugar, or more to taste

3 medium firm, ripe tomatoes, peeled and quartered

4 peeled, cooked potatoes, quartered

1 cup fresh or frozen green peas, thawed if frozen

Salt, to taste

Chopped fresh parsley leaves, for garnish

1. In a large bowl, combine all the marinade ingredients. Add the beef and toss to coat with the marinade. Cover with plastic wrap and marinate in the refrigerator for 2 hours.

2. Heat the oil in a large heavy skillet over medium heat. Add the onions and cook, stirring occasionally, until soft and golden, about 10 minutes. Remove with a slotted spoon and set aside.

3. Reheat the skillet over high heat. Working in batches, sear the beef on all sides until brown on the outside and pink inside, about 2 minutes. Remove from the skillet.

4. Add the rice wine and deglaze the pan over high heat for 1 minute. Stir in the stock and tomato paste and cook until thickened a little, about 5 minutes. Add the soy sauce, Worcestershire sauce, rice vinegar, and granulated sugar and cook, stirring, for 1 more minute. Add the tomatoes and cook for 5 more minutes.

5. Return the onions and beef to the skillet and add the potatoes and peas. Toss carefully but thoroughly to combine all the ingredients, then cook until the potatoes are heated through and the peas are cooked, about 5 minutes. Season with salt to taste.

6. Transfer to a heated serving platter, garnish with parsley, and serve.

SERVES 4

VIETNAMESE-STYLE LONDON BROIL

Some days it's hard to get it all together. I remember one evening in particular in Australia. I had spent half the day preparing platters of elaborate finger foods and a complex soup, when I suddenly found myself in a conundrum. Eight guests were arriving shortly, and I hadn't even thought about, let alone purchased or prepared, my main course. I took a deep breath, sat down, and thought quickly. I knew it had to be something with a strong Asian theme, and it had to be beef. I rummaged around in my mental recipe index for something very simple and very quick, perhaps something my guests could watch

me put together. Then I saw it like a cartoon bubble hovering above the stove—enticing, light, and delicious Vietnamese grilled meats, with a sweet, slightly burnished glaze, served atop a bowl of light, chewy rice noodles and accompanied by an array of lively garnishes. It was a perfect solution, a "put-it-together-yourself" entrée that is also a great introduction to the light, fragrant flavors of Vietnam.

Serve the sliced meat on a bed of noodles. And set the table with bottles and jars of fish, chile, and hoisin sauces, sliced hot chiles, fresh herbs, lime wedges, and roasted peanuts for your guests to toss with the noodles and to use as condiments with the steak.

3 tablespoons Ketjap Manis (page 388) or sweet soy sauce
2 tablespoons Asian fish sauce, such as nam pla
2 teaspoons crushed garlic
1½ tablespoons (packed) light brown sugar
3 scallions, smashed
1 teaspoon freshly ground black pepper
2 London broil steaks (top sirloin; 2½ to 3 pounds each)
1 pound rice vermicelli
⅔ cup hot Chicken Stock (page 384), canned broth, or water

GARNISHES & ACCOMPANIMENTS
Thinly sliced fresh hot chiles, green or red
Red onions, quartered and thinly sliced
Chopped roasted peanuts
Fresh mint leaves
Fresh basil leaves, preferably Asian or purple
Fresh cilantro leaves
Lime wedges
Hoisin sauce
Sambal oelek (page 388) or Chinese chile paste with garlic
Asian fish sauce, such as nam pla

1. In a small bowl, combine the ketjap manis, fish sauce, garlic, sugar, scallions, and pepper and stir until the sugar is dissolved. Arrange the steaks in one or two shallow dishes. Brush the meat all over with the soy sauce mixture and refrigerate, covered, for 2 to 12 hours.

2. In a large bowl, soak the noodles in warm water to cover for 20 minutes. Drain thoroughly.

3. Preheat the broiler.

4. Broil the meat, 3 inches from the heat, until lightly charred on the outside and rare inside, 5 to 6 minutes per side. Remove from the broiler, cover loosely with aluminum foil, and let stand for 10 minutes.

5. Bring the stock to a boil in a large saucepan. Add the noodles and toss with the stock. Reduce the heat to low, cover, and cook until the liquid is absorbed, about 2 minutes. Transfer to a large serving platter and let cool slightly.

6. Cut the beef across the grain into thin slices and arrange over the noodles on the serving platter. Serve the garnishes in separate bowls and encourage your guests to add a little of each garnish and sauce to the noodles and the beef.

SERVES 8 TO 10

GRILLED HERBED SKIRT STEAK

The skirt steak is marinated in a heady mixture of cilantro, garlic, and white pepper that is typically Thai. Try to get fresh cilantro with the roots still on: its wonderfully earthy flavor is an essential taste of Thailand. If you can't find the roots, use the lower portion of the stem.

This meat also tastes great cold. Cut it into thin slices and serve with sliced colorful vegetables and a simple dressing for a light luncheon salad. The marinade works equally well with chicken breasts, swordfish, or tuna.

1 cup chopped fresh cilantro leaves, stems, and some roots
2 cloves garlic, chopped
1 tablespoon chopped fresh ginger
2 serrano chiles, stemmed, seeded, and chopped
2 teaspoons freshly ground white pepper
1 tablespoon distilled white vinegar
1½ tablespoons (packed) light brown sugar
¼ cup olive oil
4 pieces (about 6 ounces each) skirt steak
Salt, to taste

1. Combine the cilantro, garlic, ginger, chiles, pepper, vinegar, sugar and oil in a food processor and process to a paste.

2. Arrange the steaks in a large shallow dish and spread on all sides with the cilantro mixture. Cover and refrigerate at least 6 hours and up to 12. Bring to room temperature before grilling.

3. Prepare coals for grilling or preheat the broiler.

4. Arrange the steaks on the grill or on the rack in a broiler pan and grill or broil until lightly charred and cooked medium-rare, about 4 minutes per side. Let stand, covered with aluminum foil, for 5 minutes. Then season with salt and serve.

SERVES 4

RED-BRAISED BEEF

with Shiitake Mushrooms

Now, this is pot roast! It comes from Philip Searle, one of Sydney's most gifted and eccentric chefs (see box, facing page).

For best results, make the roast a day ahead to allow the flavors to mellow. Slice the meat while it is cold and heat it slowly in the sauce. I like to serve it with Lemony Mashed Turnips with Ginger and Chives (see Index) and a green vegetable.

1 tablespoon tamarind pulp, preferably from Thailand
⅓ cup boiling water
¼ cup peanut oil
1 tablespoon Oriental sesame oil
3½ pounds beef bottom round or chuck, in one piece, tied with kitchen string
6 ounces fresh shiitake mushroom caps, sliced
⅔ cup Chinese rice wine or dry sherry
7 tablespoons dark soy sauce
2½ tablespoons palm sugar or (packed) light brown sugar
3 slices (1 inch each) fresh ginger, smashed
10 dried shiitake mushrooms, well rinsed
1 star anise, broken into points; 20 lightly crushed black peppercorns; 20 lightly crushed coriander seeds; and 3 pieces dried tangerine peel tied in cheesecloth
4½ cups Beef Stock (page 384) or canned broth
2 teaspoons cornstarch, mixed with 1 tablespoon cold water
Julienned fresh ginger, for garnish
Julienned red bell pepper, for garnish
Fresh cilantro leaves, for garnish

CASUAL HEARTY CHINESE SUPPER

....

SPICE-CRUSTED CHICKEN LIVER NIBBLES

RED-BRAISED BEEF
with Shiitake Mushrooms

LEMONY MASHED TURNIPS
with Ginger and Chives

CHINESE GREENS WITH OYSTER SAUCE

ANDY WAI'S WATERMELON AND TAPIOCA SOUP

1. Soak the tamarind pulp in the boiling water off the heat for 15 minutes. Stir and mash the pulp with a fork to help it dissolve. Strain through a fine strainer into a bowl, pressing on the solids with the back of a wooden spoon to extract all the liquid. Set aside.

2. Preheat the oven to 325°F.

3. Heat the peanut and sesame oils in a large flameproof casserole or Dutch oven over medium-high heat. Brown the beef on all sides, about 10 minutes. Remove the beef from the casserole.

4. Add the fresh shiitakes to the casserole and stir-fry over high heat until tender, 3 to 5 minutes. Remove with a slotted spoon to a bowl and reserve.

5. Pour off the excess fat from the casserole. Pour the rice wine into the casserole and scrape up the browned pieces on the bottom with a wooden spoon. Cook over medium-high heat until reduced by half, about 7 minutes. Add the soy sauce, reserved tamarind liquid, sugar, ginger, dried shiitakes, cheesecloth bag, and stock and bring to a boil. Re-

We met Philip Searle one fall at his restaurant, Oasis Serros, located in an elegant old mansion on bustling, fashionable Oxford Street. Philip is a culinary fanatic, an intellectual, and an artist. There are plenty of good cooks who are none of these things, and very few who are all of them. But Philip is, and it was apparent in every gesture and comment he made. It's fair to say that Philip pioneered East-West cuisine Down Under almost a decade before it was on the drawing board in California. He thinks, feels, and cherishes food all at once, and the result is brazen experiment, lavish attention to detail, and some of the most exquisite successes of the Australian table.

Many of Philip's dishes are extravagant, complex, and demanding. His Red-Braised Beef (facing page) is a wonderful exception. Taking off from a classic Chinese dish, the meat is simmered in a flavorful liquid of stock, soy sauce, and rice wine, perfumed with mandarin orange peel, smashed ginger, and star anise. Philip adds fresh and dried shiitake mushrooms to deepen the flavor and texture, along with such typically Southeast Asian ingredients as tamarind and palm sugar. Come to think of it, this is a case of East meets East.

turn the beef to the casserole and bring the stock again to a boil.

6. Transfer the casserole to the oven and bake, covered, for 2 hours, turning the beef several times during the cooking. Uncover and cook until the beef is very tender and the liquid is thickened and reduced, about 30 minutes.

7. Remove the beef from the casserole to a cutting board and keep warm, covered with aluminum foil. Remove and discard the cheesecloth bag. With a slotted spoon, remove the dried mushrooms, and set aside until cool enough to handle. Cut off and discard the stems and slice the caps.

8. Over medium-high heat, bring the braising liquid to a boil. Add the cornstarch mixture and stir until thickened, about 1 minute. Stir in the reserved fresh and dried shiitake mushrooms and heat through for 1 minute more.

9. With a large sharp knife carefully slice the beef against the grain into thick slices, arrange on a serving platter, and pour the sauce over the slices. Sprinkle with the julienned ginger, bell pepper, and cilantro and serve at once.

SERVES 4 TO 6

POT ROAST
with Asian Flavors

Braised meats take especially well to a combination of sweet and pungent spices of the East since the long cooking time allows the flavors to mellow and really penetrate the texture of the meat. To my mind, pot roast can be a relatively boring proposition, but here the spices and coconut add both subtlety and excitement to the gravy, making this a perfect cold-weather meal.

Serve this roast with rice or another grain to sop up the juices, and Asparagus and Snow Peas with Mirin Sauce (see Index) for a splash of freshness and color.

2 tablespoons unsalted butter
3 tablespoons vegetable oil
2 cups chopped onion
2 carrots, peeled and chopped
1 small turnip, peeled and diced
2 teaspoons freshly ground black pepper
3 tablespoons all-purpose flour
3½ pounds boneless beef rump, trimmed
   of excess fat, tied with kitchen string
½ teaspoon ground turmeric
2 teaspoons ground coriander
½ teaspoon dried red pepper flakes
⅓ cup dry sherry
1 tablespoon rice vinegar
¾ cup canned unsweetened coconut milk,
   well stirred
1¾ cups Beef Stock (page 384) or canned
   broth
1 cinnamon stick; (3 inches) 2 cardamom
   pods, bruised; 1 star anise; and 2 bay
   leaves, tied in cheesecloth
Salt, to taste
Fresh parsley sprigs, for garnish

1. Preheat the oven to 325°F.

2. Melt the butter in 1 tablespoon of the oil in a large flameproof casserole or Dutch oven over medium heat. Add the onion, carrots, and turnip. Cook, stirring, until the vegetables soften, about 10 minutes. With a slotted spoon, remove the vegetables to a bowl and keep warm.

3. Spread the black pepper and flour on separate plates. Roll the meat first in the pepper, then dredge in the flour, shaking off the excess.

4. Add the remaining oil to the casserole.

Brown the meat well on all sides over medium-high heat, 7 to 8 minutes. Remove from the casserole. Add the turmeric, coriander, and pepper flakes and stir for 30 seconds. Stir in the sherry and vinegar and reduce by half, scraping the bottom of the casserole with a wooden spoon to deglaze.

5. Stir in the coconut milk and stock and bring to a boil over medium heat. Return the meat and vegetables to the casserole and add the cheesecloth bag. As soon as the liquid boils, transfer the casserole to the oven and bake, covered, until the meat is tender, about 2¼ hours, turning the meat occasionally.

6. Remove the meat from the cooking liquid, transfer to a cutting board and cover with aluminum foil to keep warm. On top of the stove, reduce the gravy slightly over medium-high heat, about 5 minutes. Remove the cheesecloth bag.

7. With a large sharp knife carefully cut the meat into thick slices across the grain and arrange on a serving platter. Ladle the gravy and vegetables over the meat, and garnish with parsley to serve.

SERVES 6

BEEF SEMUR

There's a marvelous bonus to hotel dining in Singapore that you do not often find in the West. Alongside the elegant five-star restaurants, which serve some of the most sophisticated and imaginative East-West cuisine in Asia, the lower-priced "coffee shop" menus sometimes offer some of the very best blends of Malay, Indian, and Chinese cuisines—the troika of tastes that make up Singapore's complex culinary mosaic. The hotels are fiercely competitive with each other, seeking out the most famous local chefs and home cooks to lure the discriminating local clientele with their authentic home-style dishes.

The Tradewinds Restaurant in the Singapore Hilton, overseen by a Muslim chef, is one of the best and most popular with the local Malays, who come in throngs, especially during the Muslim festivities of Hari Raya. It was there that I tasted this warming, long-cooked Malay stew, redolent of soy and sweet spices. Serve it with rice, egg noodles, or mashed potatoes.

3½ tablespoons peanut or vegetable oil
1 large onion, sliced
3 cloves garlic, crushed through a press
1½ teaspoons minced fresh ginger
1½ pounds boneless beef rump steak,
    cut into 1½-inch cubes
1 teaspoon freshly ground black pepper
1 teaspoon paprika
¼ to ½ teaspoon ground cayenne pepper
¼ teaspoon ground cinnamon
¼ teaspoon freshly grated nutmeg
1½ tablespoons Ketjap Manis (page 388)
    or sweet soy sauce
3½ tablespoons soy sauce
1½ teaspoons (packed) light brown
    sugar, or more to taste
1¾ cups Beef Stock (page 384) or
    canned broth
2 cups pearl onions, blanched and peeled

1. Heat the oil in a heavy flameproof casserole over medium heat. Add the onion and cook until translucent, about 5 minutes. Add the garlic and ginger and cook for 1 minute longer. Raise the heat to medium-high, add the meat, preferably in batches, and cook, stirring, until lightly browned, about 7 minutes. Return the meat to the casserole.

2. Stir the black pepper, paprika, cayenne, cinnamon, nutmeg, soy sauces, and sugar into the meat and cook, stirring, for 5 minutes. Pour in the stock and bring to a boil. Reduce the heat to low, cover, and simmer for 45 minutes.

3. Stir in the pearl onions and simmer, covered, until the meat is very tender, about 45 minutes more, stirring from time to time.

SERVES 4

BEEF RENDANG

A classic in Malaysia and Indonesia, *rendang* is a wondrous, dark, aromatic "dry curry" (meaning that the sauce is reduced from long, slow cooking), enhanced by a subtle blend of spices and toasted grated coconut. The best *rendang* I have tasted was made by the celebrity Malay chef Hassan Kassim, who runs the Terrace Restaurant at the luxurious Regent Hotel in Kuala Lumpur. On weekend afternoons Hassan prepares a magnificent high tea that features curries, noodles, and Indian breads, along with dainty European-style cakes. In colonial-minded Kuala Lumpur high society, this is *the* place to see and be seen on Sunday afternoons. Serve this *rendang* with rice or noodles.

1 small red bell pepper, stemmed, seeded, and
   chopped
4 dried red chiles (4 to 5 inches long),
   preferably Asian, seeded, soaked in warm
   water for 10 minutes, and chopped
5 cloves garlic, chopped
1/3 cup chopped red onion
2 tablespoons chopped fresh ginger
4 tablespoons peanut oil
1 cup fresh or dessicated (dried) coconut
3 1/2 pounds boneless beef chuck, cut into
   1-inch cubes
1 tablespoon ground cumin
1 tablespoon ground coriander
1 teaspoon freshly ground black pepper
1 1/2 tablespoons best-quality curry powder,
   preferably homemade (390)
1 1/2 cups unsweetened canned coconut milk,
   well stirred
1 1/2 cups Chicken Stock (page 384) or
   canned broth
2 1/2 teaspoons (packed) light brown sugar
2 stalks fresh lemongrass (3 inches of the
   lower stalk, tough outer leaves discarded),
   smashed
3 kaffir lime leaves, if available, bruised
1 piece (1 1/2 inches) cinnamon stick
Salt, to taste
Julienned red bell pepper, for garnish

1. Combine the bell pepper, chiles, garlic, onion, and ginger in a food processor and process into a fine paste, adding a little oil to assist blending if necessary. Scrape into a bowl and set aside. Clean the processor bowl.

2. Heat a wok or a heavy skillet over medium heat. Add the coconut and stir until deep golden, 2 to 3 minutes. Do not let it burn. Transfer to the processor and process until finely minced. Set aside.

3. Heat 3 tablespoons of the oil in heavy skillet over medium-high heat. Cook the meat, in batches, until browned on all sides, about 7 minutes.

4. Heat the remaining oil in a large flame-proof casserole or Dutch oven over low heat. Add the bell pepper paste, cumin, coriander, pepper, and curry powder. Cook over low heat, stirring, until the mixture no longer tastes raw, 5 to 7 minutes. Add the coconut milk, 1 teaspoon at a time, if the mixture begins to stick to the bottom.

5. Stir in half of the coconut milk, then turn the heat up to medium and cook until reduced a little, 5 minutes. Add the rest of the coconut milk and the stock and cook for 5 minutes. Stir in the sugar, beef, processed coconut, lemongrass, kaffir lime leaves, and cinnamon stick, and season with salt. Simmer, covered, over low heat for 1 hour.

6. Uncover and continue to simmer until the meat is very tender and the gravy reduced, another 30 to 40 minutes. Taste and correct the seasoning. Garnish with julienned red bell pepper. (In Southeast Asia, whole spices and aromatics are not usually removed before serving, but you can remove the lemongrass and cinnamon stick, if you wish.)

SERVES 6 TO 8

BROCHETTES OF BEEF
in Grape Leaves

Here is one of the most delectable Vietnamese dishes I know: sweet and spicy beef, wrapped in flavorful leaves and grilled. In Vietnam the beef is wrapped in a large round leaf called *la lot*. I first tasted this dish at a Vietnamese restaurant in Bangkok, where the English menu referred to *la lot* as "Good King Henry Leaf." In any event, this mysterious green is hard to come by in this country, so in Vietnamese restaurants and homes it is usually replaced by shiso or grape leaves.

These brochettes can be served as either a light main course or an appetizer. Serve them with Vietnamese Tangy Lime Dipping Sauce and/or Tamarind Dip (see Index).

3 shallots, chopped
1 tablespoon chopped fresh lemongrass
    (3 inches of the lower stalk, tough
    outer leaves discarded)
2 tablespoons chopped scallions
2 teaspoons sesame seeds
2 teaspoons chopped garlic
4 tablespoons Asian fish
    sauce, such as nam pla
3 tablespoons (packed) light
    brown sugar
1 pound ground beef
1 jar (16 ounces) grape leaves in brine

1. Soak 8 bamboo skewers in water for 30 minutes. Prepare coals for grilling or preheat the broiler.

2. Combine the shallots, lemongrass, scallions, sesame seeds, garlic, 2 tablespoons of the fish sauce, and 1 tablespoon of the sugar in a food processor and process until minced. Place the beef in a bowl and stir in the shallot mixture to mix well.

3. Select about 24 smaller grape leaves. Rinse well and scald in boiling water. Rinse in cold water and pat thoroughly dry.

4. Spread several leaves out on your work surface. Place some filling on each leave, closer to the stem, fold in the sides and roll up eggroll fashion. The rolls should be about 2¼ inches long. Repeat with the rest of the filling and leaves. Thread three rolls, lengthwise, on each skewer.

5. In a small bowl whisk together the re-maining fish sauce and sugar. Brush the rolls with the glaze, then grill or broil the rolls, 4 inches from the heat, until lightly charred and cooked through inside, about 5 minutes on each side. Serve with one of the sauces suggested in the headnote.

SERVES 8 AS AN APPETIZER, 4 AS A MAIN COURSE

OSSO BUCO OF THE ORIENT

This "Aussie buco" is the creation of Melbourne food writer Jeff Slattery. The preparation starts out straightforward, even "classic," but being a true Aussie—which means having a deft hand with Asian seasoning—Jeff couldn't resist adding a touch of lemongrass, galangal, and citrus zest and a splash of color from the red peppers. My own touch is a takeoff on the traditional Italian *gremolata* (minced parsley and lemon zest) that I prepare with cilantro, garlic, and orange zest and stir in at the end to add an accent of freshness to the dense, rich texture of the shanks. For best results, plan to make the shanks a day ahead, and serve over fresh fettuccine or rice.

Try a Marquès de Murrieta white Rioja with this dish. It's the last of the truly great Riojas, with an unctuous texture and a tropical fruit aftertaste that will go wonderfully with the refreshing suggestions of the Orient in the sauce. It is also a great value for the money.

BUSH TUCKER: THE OLDEST FOOD ON EARTH

With one of the oldest continuous cultures on earth, you'd expect the Aborigines of Australia to know a thing or two about food. Well, so they do. The quiet richness of their cuisine is intimately linked to the subtle blessings of the land, a fact that was entirely misunderstood by the first colonialists. One historian put it this way: "They [the first European arrivals] often concluded that the land was mean and hungry, not realizing that some regions provided a wider variety of foodstuffs than a gourmet in Paris would eat in an extravagant year."

Today we can only imagine this abundance. But twenty thousand years ago the earliest inhabitants of Australia made omelets with the blue-green eggs of the giant emu and winter casseroles with a hare-size marsupial called a battong. They feasted on freshwater shellfish, and roasted thirty-pound golden perch in hot ashes on the shores of Lake Mungo. Special nuts and the root-like stem of the lotus lily were their delicacies. Some of the preparations were quite elaborate. Ancient stone pounders and grinders have been found, which were presumably used for pulverizing seeds and other plant foods.

The Aborigines knew the coastal forests and the outback deserts by heart. Everything they ate was either gathered, fished, or hunted. It is not surprising that every stalk and twig and fruit that grows had a use—either ritualistic, medicinal, or for food. Some of the vast know-how and food experience of the Aboriginal people continues to this day and is being increasingly appreciated by the non-indigenous population.

WONGIS, OORAYS, AND LILLYPILLIES

The range of wild foods in Australia is remarkable. A rundown of just some of the fruits alone, which were given colorful names by the first settlers, reads like a hymn to the pickings of another planet: little gooseberry, corduroy tamarind, prickly and native currants, coffee berry, ooray (also known as Davidson's plum), the fruit of the persimmon-like sea ebony, the blue quandong, ruby saltbush, native kumquat or desert lemon (made by one traveler "into a dish very like gooseberry-fool"), the cherry-like fruit of the lillypilly, native guava, Moreton Bay and cluster figs, the fruit of the bread tree of the Lynd (the same traveler wrote that "when ripe it was slightly pulpy and acidulous, and reminded me of the taste of coarse German rye bread), muntries (native apples), emu berries, purple peas, the coastal wongi, finger-lime, native raspberries, yellow elderberries, native melons, grapes, and passion fruit.

The mecca of "bush tucker," as it is (quaintly) known in Australia, is in the vast, sparsely populated Northern Territory, where the restaurants of two hotels in the Red Centre, the Sheraton Alice Springs and the Four Seasons Resort, Ayers Rock, are pioneers. In the spectacular setting of the central Australian desert, and in the shadow of the great, glowing mountain the locals call Uluru, they have innovatively combined the most interesting tastes and textures from the bush with classical, nouvelle, and Australian preparations. Imagine a coulis flavored with wild rosella or quandong, lemon myrtle seasoning your vegetables, and a beurre blanc served on a warrigal leaf. You might be offered kangaroo consommé or camel carpaccio, crocodile steaks or roasted magpie goose.

These days a new boutique industry has sprung up around "bush tucker." Wattle-seed cakes, tiny jars of exotic fruit preserves and chutneys, luscious baby bush tomatoes, and wild bush lime crepes are all passed over the counters of specialty food shops in Melbourne and Sydney. The menu of a tasting we attended in Melbourne included emu egg meringues, barramundi (a wonderful tropical fish) stuffed with warrigal greens, damper bread (pan-baked unleavened bread) with a bush ragout of crocodile or water buffalo, banksia-smoked lamb with Illawara plum chutney, and carpaccio of emu with quandong chutney. Sometimes the hapless eater is made even more dizzy between the little known products of outback Australia and the over-familiar style of "nouvelle cuisine." We saw another menu with such offerings as crocodile and emu boudin with truffles served on a wild honey glaze. Eating native is suddenly the chic thing to do.

2 tablespoons unsalted butter
3 tablespoons light olive oil (do not use virgin or extra-virgin)
4 large, meaty 2-inch-thick veal shanks (10 to 12 ounces each), rinsed and patted dry
2 medium onions, coarsely chopped
1 cup chopped carrots
1 cup chopped parsnips
2 large cloves garlic, chopped
2 cups dry white wine
½ ham hock, rind removed and sawed in half (ask your butcher to do this for you)
2 fresh medium-hot red chiles, such as Fresno, stemmed, seeded, and chopped
2 cups Chicken Stock (page 384), or canned broth, or more as needed
Salt and freshly ground black pepper, to taste
2 stalks fresh lemongrass (3 inches of the lower stalk, tough outer leaves discarded), chopped
4 slices (1½ inches each) fresh ginger, crushed
½ cup fresh orange juice
2 roasted red bell peppers, cut into strips

GREMOLATA
2 teaspoons finely grated orange zest
3 tablespoons finely minced fresh cilantro leaves
2 teaspoons finely minced garlic

1. Make the veal shanks a day before you plan to serve them. Preheat the oven to 450°F.

2. Melt the butter in the oil in a large flameproof casserole or Dutch oven over medium-high heat. Brown the veal shanks well on all sides, about 7 minutes. Transfer the

casserole to the oven and roast the shanks for 20 minutes. Reduce the oven temperature to 350°F.

3. With a slotted spoon, remove the shanks from the casserole and pour off all but 3 tablespoons of the fat. Return the casserole to the stove, add the onions, carrots, parsnips, and garlic, and brown over medium heat. Add the wine to the casserole and increase the heat to high. Cook, scraping the bottom of the casserole with a wooden spoon, for about 5 minutes. Return the veal shanks to the casserole and add the ham hock and chiles. Add enough stock to barely cover the shanks and bring to a boil over high heat. Season to taste with salt and pepper.

4. Transfer the casserole to the oven and braise, covered, for 1¾ hours. Add the lemongrass, ginger, and orange juice, then return to the oven and braise, uncovered, for 1 hour longer.

5. Remove from the oven and let cool. Cover and refrigerate for several hours or overnight.

6. Skim off all the hardened fat and reheat the dish slowly. Right before serving, stir in the roasted peppers and *gremolata*.

SERVES 4

TANDOORI VEAL CHOPS

with Minted Yogurt Sauce and Sautéed Apples

The recipe for these moist, succulent veal chops, marinated and baked tandoori

style and served with minted yogurt sauce comes from Nutmegs, in Singapore's Hyatt Hotel, a restaurant known for its innovative cross-cultural cuisine, one that draws on Singapore's richly diverse ethnic heritage. Serve these chops on a bed of Spiced Red Lentils (see Index), if you wish, and/or with Buttered Basmati rice.

> 1½ cups low-fat plain yogurt
> 1 tablespoon grated onion
> 2 teaspoons grated fresh ginger
> 2 cloves garlic, crushed through a press
> ½ teaspoon pure chile powder
> 1 tablespoon ketchup
> 2 teaspoons best-quality curry powder
> 4½ tablespoons fresh lemon juice
> 6 veal chops (about 8 ounces each),
>   ¾ inch thick
> 3 tablespoons unsalted butter
> 2 large tart apples, such as Granny Smith,
>   peeled, cored, and cut into medium-thick
>   slices
> 1 tablespoon (packed) light brown sugar
> Minted Yogurt Sauce (recipe follows)

1. In a bowl, stir together the yogurt, grated onion, ginger, garlic, chile powder, ketchup, curry powder, and 3 tablespoons of the lemon juice. Arrange the veal chops in a shallow dish and coat on both sides with the yogurt mixture. Cover and refrigerate for 6 hours, turning once or twice. Bring to room temperature before roasting.

2. Preheat the oven to 450°F.

3. Brush off the excess marinade from the veal chops. Arrange the chops in one layer in a shallow roasting pan and bake until golden on the outside and just pink inside, 8 to 10 minutes per side.

4. While the veal chops are cooking, melt the butter in a large nonstick skillet over medium heat. Add the apples and cook, stirring gently with a wooden spoon, until softened, about 10 minutes. Sprinkle in the sugar and remaining lemon juice and swirl the pan until the apples are caramelized, 1 to 2 minutes.

5. Serve the veal chops as suggested in the headnote, accompanied by the apples and the Minted Yogurt Sauce.

SERVES 6

Minted Yogurt Sauce

2 cups low-fat plain yogurt
¾ cup shredded fresh mint leaves
5 tablespoons chopped fresh cilantro leaves
1 small serrano chile, stemmed, seeded, and finely chopped
1½ teaspoons finely chopped garlic
1½ teaspoons grated fresh ginger
2 tablespoons finely chopped red onion
Pinch of sugar, or more to taste
2 teaspoons fresh lemon juice, or more to taste
Salt and freshly ground black pepper, to taste

In a bowl, combine all the ingredients and stir well. Let stand at room temperature for 30 minutes for the flavors to develop.

MAKES ABOUT 2½ CUPS

VEAL CHOPS
with a Macadamia Nut Crust

For a dramatic tropical twist to the tired breaded veal chop, try this version with a crunchy crust of herbed macadamia nuts. It's very simple and very tasty when served with Carol Selvarajah's Vegetable Salad with Kiwi and Pickled Ginger (see Index), and washed down with a luscious, fruity German Riesling.

4 veal chops (about 8 ounces each), ¾ inch thick
Salt, to taste
2 tablespoons fresh lemon juice
1 large egg
½ cup fine dry bread crumbs
⅔ cup coarsely ground roasted macadamia nuts
¾ teaspoon crushed white peppercorns
¼ cup finely chopped fresh mint leaves
4½ tablespoons olive oil

1. Pound the veal chops between two sheets of waxed paper with a cleaver. Rub with salt, sprinkle with lemon juice, and let stand, at room temperature for 15 minutes.

2. In a shallow bowl, beat the egg lightly. On a large plate, mix the bread crumbs, macadamia nuts, peppercorns, and mint.

3. Dip the veal chops into the beaten egg and then coat them with the macadamia mixture.

4. Heat the oil in a skillet over medium heat and cook the veal chops until crispy, golden, and cooked through, 5 to 6 minutes per side. Quickly drain on paper towels and serve at once.

SERVES 4

VEAL SCALOPPINE

in Sake-Ginger Sauce

A quick and elegant veal dish with a sauce that will make your mouth tingle pleasurably with the perky flavors of ginger, citrus zests, and fresh green peppercorns. Try this idea with chicken breast fillets, too.

All-purpose flour, for dusting the scaloppine

1 pound veal scaloppine, pounded thin

2 tablespoons unsalted butter

1½ tablespoons peanut or canola oil

⅓ cup sake

9 tablespoons Chicken Stock (page 384) or canned broth

3 tablespoons heavy (or whipping) cream

½ teaspoon grated lime zest

1 teaspoon grated orange zest

2 teaspoons Ginger Juice (page 390)

1 teaspoon fresh lemon juice

Salt, to taste

Pinch of sugar, or to taste

1½ teaspoons whole green peppercorns in brine, drained and lightly crushed with the back of a spoon

1 tablespoon finely diced red bell pepper

2 teaspoons minced fresh parsley leaves, for garnish

1. Spread the flour on a large plate and dust the scaloppine lightly on both sides.

2. Melt the butter in the oil in a large skillet over medium-high heat. Add the scaloppine and cook until light golden, 1 to 1½ minutes per side. Remove from the skillet and keep warm.

3. Pour off the fat from the skillet and raise the heat to medium-high. Add the sake and reduce by half, 3 minutes. Add the stock and cream and reduce until the sauce is the consistency of heavy cream, 5 to 7 minutes. Stir in the zests, ginger juice, and lemon juice and cook for another 2 minutes. Add salt and sugar to taste, the peppercorns, and diced bell pepper and heat for 1 minute.

4. Divide the scaloppine among 4 plates and spoon the sauce around them. Garnish with parsley and serve at once.

SERVES 4

THE MAGIC OF MELAKA

From the city of Malacca ships sail also to the Isles of Maluco to take in cargoes of cloves. These ships sail also from Malacca to the islands which they call Bandan to get cargoes of nutmeg and mace, taking thither for sale Cambaya goods. They also sail to the Islands of Camatra, whence they bring pepper, silk, benzoin and gold. . . . This city of Malacca is the richest seaport with the greatest number of wholesale merchants and abundance of shipping and trade that can be found in the whole world.

—COLONIAL PORTUGUESE SAILOR

Anya and I drove from Kuala Lumpur to Melaka in Malaysia on a fresh, tangy day. While passing through a suburban jungle of five-story apartment buildings, our driver, Stephen, told us that the cooler ground-floor units commanded Western penthouse prices, while the top-floor apartments went for a song.

Just out of the city limits we motored through the Sungei Pesi, a lakeland reclamation area fashioned from inundated tin mines. Sungei Pesi boasted one of the largest open-cast mines in the world. It was a direct descendant of the Malaysian tin rush at the end of the last century that netted fabulous profits for the entrepreneurial few and launched the region's long march to industrial power.

On the right, a lush oil palm plantation cultivated by the Agricultural University of Malaysia rose out of a sandy earth that was the color of blood oranges. The palms fluttered in the light breeze like a conference of green emus. We passed by the Arab-Malaysian Industrial Park, the Nilai Memorial to the Prime Ministers of Malaysia, and a service station in Negri Province (home to many Sumatrans from across the Straits of Melaka), whose roof was pitched into two sharp points in imitation of buffalo horns.

Leaving the main highway at Alor Grajah, once the regional junction for elephant-transported cargo, we drove through the glittering ranks of stilted houses that make up the Melaka *kampangs* (villages). Each house is approached by a flight of colorfully tiled steps, and set off by a flowerpot garden lined up under the main window. We stopped at a tiny general store that doubled as a latex depot for the local rubber plantation, and wandered over to a nearby *lemang* stall for rice-in-bamboo, which we accompanied by a portion of delicious *chinchalok*—small preserved shrimps with raw onions and chiles. All the nearby mosques had three tiers, a style that was apparently favored by the Hindu prince from Sumatra who converted the area.

Rested and refreshed, we approached Melaka itself across a belt of flat land that used to serve as the town paddy fields. Nowadays the old-timers who own the land are selling it off to developers in blocks big enough for ten small houses, one of which is given to the former landlords as compensation. Stephen became quietly indignant at the suburbanization of the *kampangs* and the forced early retirement of the water buffalos.

The best entry into Melaka is along the coast road, which we joined a few miles north of the city. Stretching out to the right are the steamy Melaka Straits. Every now and then cracks in the haze would reveal a supertanker or a Chinese fishing junk sitting on the glassy surface. The road ran past a series of merchant mansions fronted by decorative gates and stone pillars. Most of these were in a state of elegiac disrepair. Those

"this place is the market of all India, of China, of the Moluccas, and of other islands round about…"

that weren't had been turned over to Japanese car dealerships.

IN COLONIAL HANDS

Melaka has many faces and many histories. Its fortunes have waxed and waned in time with the uncertain rhythms of colonial trade. At the height of its power in the first years of the sixteenth century, the Sultanate of Melaka earned so much that it attracted traders from all over Southeast Asia. But then the whole pattern of world trade was altered forever. Portuguese naval technology and centuries of maritime skill brought ships from the Iberian peninsula halfway around the world to the Straits of Melaka and soon transformed the tropical city into the center of the world's spice trade.

In the last year of the sixteenth century, an old traveler named Linschott wrote of Portuguese Melaka that "this place is the market of all India, of China, of the Moluccas, and of other islands round about from all which places, as well as from Banda, Java, Sumatra, Siam [Thailand], Pegu, Bengal, Coromandel, and India, arrive ships which come and go incessantly, charged with an infinity of merchandises." By now Melaka was also a sophisticated emporium. Linschott praised the

language of the Malays as "the most refined, exact and celebrated of all the East." And he thought that "the natives, both men and women, are very courteous, and are reckoned the most skillful in the world in compliments, and study much to compose and repeat verses and love-songs."

This was Melaka in its first colonial heyday—prosperous, refined, cosmopolitan. These conditions were repeated in their turn by the succeeding colonial powers, the Dutch who took over in 1641, and then the British to whom the port was ceded in exchange for Bencoolen in Sumatra just over a century and a half later. The Dutch constructed some wonderful public buildings, of which the most outstanding are the salmon-pink Stadthuys (meaning "town hall"), probably the oldest Dutch building in the East, and the graciously proportioned

Christ Church that stands at the other end of the main square dressed in a shock of red laterite. Yet by the summer of 1854, when the great naturalist and

adventurer Alfred Wallace traveled up from Singapore, Melaka had already reverted to the "picturesque town . . . crowded along the banks of the small river [and consisting of narrow streets of shops and dwelling houses, occupied by the descendants of the Portuguese and by Chinamen" that one can recognize today. Wallace found that "a vessel over a hundred tons hardly ever enters its port, and the trade is entirely confined to a few petty products of the forests."

MELAKA TODAY

Melaka has been something of a "sleepy hollow" (as the Malays still call it) for the last 150 years. Yet this lazy, languid atmosphere, the exquisite rows of shop houses on Jalan Tun Tan Cheng Lok (nicknamed Millionaires' Row), the dusty antique shops that line Jalan Hang Jebat (still known by its Dutch-era name of Jonkers Street), and the ruins of the three great civilizations, make the town one of the charmed spots of Southeast Asia.

We sat on the top of St. Paul's Hill (Bukit St. Paul) in a cloudy, purple light that was laced with busy flies. The ruined church behind us was originally a Portuguese-Catholic foundation. The famous missionary St. Francis Xavier stayed here. He was even buried here for the best part of a year, before his body was laid to rest in a grander grave. We browsed among the other tombstones, reading snatches of Dutch, Latin, Portu-guese, and English. Our favorite had no writing, just a serene bas-relief sailing sloop standing in a square, grainy slab.

There's no better way to watch the sun go down over Melaka than from Bukit China (China Hill), which rises behind the San Kong Temple.

You reach the summit of the hill by a stairway cut into the grassy slopes above the Porta de Santi-ago—the only surviving fragment of the Portuguese fort of A Famosa. The hill has the best view in Melaka. You can take in the city, its history, the Straits, the ships, and Sumatra with one turn of your head.

Looking south from St. Paul's, we peered down onto the late colo-nial Dunlop House, the local seat of the British rubber empire. Tucked into the inland side of the hill is a modern replica of the old sultan's palace, whose details and designs were painstakingly deduced from old European sketches and drawings. Between this and the Dunlop House, two foot-ball fields unfold on the foreshore flats. They are interrupted by a pristine model Malay house, a grandstand skewed at an odd angle away from the sea, and most curious of all, a giant, gaudily painted replica of a bullock cart, pulled by two bullocks and driven by an outsize woman. Crowning all this is a grand, double onion-domed colonial house, gaily painted in cream, blues, and sandy red, with a Franco-Malay garden laid out behind it and a 1957 Chevrolet convertible in front. This is post-colonial Malaysia.

AT DAY'S END

In addition to the super-tankers and the junks, we could also make

out the snail-paced Indonesian longboats that crisscross the Straits with mangrove logs for the Malaysian construction industry. At the end of the day, we met some of the boat boys squatting on their cargo at the mouth of the muddy Melaka River. They cooked up a watery-look-ing soup with vegetables they had brought with them from home. Seeing it was bubbling hot and emboldened by the gentleness of the after-noon, Anya had a quick sip. She said it was nutty and delicious. We tried to get a recipe translated from Indonesian to Malay to English, but gave up at the third impossibly obscure Sumatran vegetable.

In the late afternoon we wandered around old Melaka, past the Cheng Hoon Teng Temple (Tem-ple of the Evergreen Clouds), the oldest such Chinese foundation in Malaysia, and the Sumatran-in-fluenced Kam-pung Kling Mosque. The houses and shopfronts in the vicinity of the old square have been spruced up with coats of clay-red paint, similar in hue to the bright tan of the Dutch church. The authorities have even planted a model-village windmill on the traffic is-land.

There's no better way to watch the sun go down over Melaka than from Bukit China (China Hill), which rises behind the Sam Po Kong Temple. The temple is dedicated to the admiral-ambassador Cheng Ho, who arrived in Melaka in 1405 bearing promises of protection from the Chi-nese emperor that helped to secure the mercantile success of the port for the next 350 years. We strolled among the color-ful, flower-strewn circu-lar graves of the Chinese cemetery on the hill. With more than twelve thousand tombs scat-tered over the hill and reedy dale for some twenty-five hectares, (about 62 acres), this is supposedly the largest Chinese graveyard out-side China. The Chinese prefer hillside cemeteries because the ancestor spirits can command a good view of the goings-on of their earthly relatives, and evil winds can be fended off by the lay of the land. Then the sun set, lighting up the gorgeous little pocket of history that is Melaka, seeming to preserve it forever in crimson and gold.

Braised Lamb Shanks with Roasted
Baby Beets and Braised Mushrooms

Red-Braised Lamb Shanks

New Zealand Roast Lamb with
Emerald Sauce

Raffles Sunday Roast

Down-Under Roast Lamb Dinner

Chu-Chee Roast Lamb

Lamb Chops with
Fig and Tamarind Chutney

Lamb Chops with
Miso-Braised Eggplant

Roast Pork with
Gingered Sour Cherry Sauce

Pepper-Crusted Pork Tenderloin with
Pineapple Raisin Chutney

Lanna Thai Pork Stew

Chinese-Style Barbecued Pork

Stir-Fried Pork Ribbons with String
Beans and Basil-Chile-Garlic Sauce

Pork Chops with a
Mushroom Sauté and Arugula Pesto

Okra-Stuffed Pork Rolls with
Peanut Sauce

Spareribs with Mango Barbecue Sauce

Lion's Head

Lettuce Parcels with
Caramelized Grilled Pork Balls,
Herbs, and Pineapple

Minced Pork Curry

LAMB AND PORK

I will never forget my first spring in Melbourne. It was the beginning of September (remember the seasons are reversed Down Under), the bush was in bloom with banksia and wild rosellas, the sky was a crisp blue, and best of all, the markets were teeming with tender baby vegetables and the sweetest, whitest, most succulent lamb imaginable. I have traveled through the Mediterranean, Central Asia, and the Middle East and enjoyed some truly wonderful lamb, but I never knew it could taste this good. John and I had dinners with our friends Julie and Philip in their house by the sea. The air was still chilly and we enjoyed the lamb roasted with herbs from their garden, and accompanied by a luscious Shiraz, finishing the meal with a passion fruit pudding.

Lamb is the national meat Down Under, and needless to say, Australian and New Zealand chefs and home cooks prepare it with special flair, combining diverse influences and styles with skill and imagination. A grilled lamb chop might come with a lush accent of fig and tamarind chutney, or on a bed of miso-flavored eggplant stew. A moist, long-braised shank will be accompanied by roasted baby beets, in a sort of nouvelle English style, while for the traditional Sunday roast lamb, emerald kiwi purée might replace the traditional mint sauce.

When it comes to pork, I like to use prime cuts, such as loin or tenderloin, and brighten the lean white meat with a sweet and sour, aromatic chutney. Those who love barbecued ribs will enjoy the tangy, gingery Pacific barbecue sauce, while for a quick but intricate stir-fry, I have one of my favorite offerings from Thailand, delicate pork ribbons and string beans with a spirited sauce of lemongrass and chiles.

BRAISED LAMB
SHANKS

with
Roasted Baby Beets and
Braised Mushrooms

Lamb is the soul food of Australia, and like any culinary emblem, it arouses love and passion like nothing else. Australian lamb is tops in quality and low in price. And this has an effect at table. In the buoyant Australian food markets, a whole premium rack of loin lamb chops can be had for a song, so the humble shank, which often sells for as little as two for a dollar, has long been considered a cut far too poor for a good restaurant kitchen.

Thankfully all this has now changed. It was the "back to homey food" trend that helped resurrect the shank on Australian restaurant menus. What follows is both typical and marvelous—an Australian lamb shank dish from Taylor Square, one of the most fashionable of the Sydney bistros. Start the dish the day before so you can skim off any accumulated fat.

6 meaty lamb shanks (12 ounces each)

4 tablespoons olive oil

2 tablespoons unsalted butter

3 cups chopped onion

5 small carrots, peeled and chopped

8 cloves garlic, chopped

6 firm, ripe tomatoes, quartered

3 sprigs fresh rosemary, chopped, or 2
    teaspoons dried

5 cups Beef Stock (page 384) or canned
    broth

Salt and freshly ground black pepper,
    to taste

12 baby beets, trimmed but skins left on

18 large fresh white mushrooms, wiped with
    a damp cloth

4 tablespoons (½ stick) unsalted butter,
    melted

2 teaspoons minced garlic

1. Braise the shanks a day before you plan to serve them. Preheat the oven to 375°F.

2. Heat 3 tablespoons of the oil with the butter in a flameproof casserole or Dutch oven over medium-high heat. Brown the lamb shanks all over, about 10 minutes. With a slotted spoon, transfer them to a plate. Add the onion, carrots, garlic, and tomatoes to the casserole and cook, stirring, until the onions are soft, about 10 minutes. Stir in the rosemary.

3. Return the lamb shanks to the casserole. Add the stock and bring to a boil. Season to taste with salt and pepper. Transfer to the oven and braise, covered, until the meat is falling off the bones, 2 to 2½ hours.

4. Cool and refrigerate for at least 4 hours or overnight. Skim off the fat.

5. Preheat the oven to 350°F.

6. Toss the beets with the remaining olive oil. Place in a roasting pan and roast until the beets are tender, about 25 minutes. Remove from the oven, place in a plastic bag and close with a twist tie. Wrap well with a kitchen towel, and let sit for 20 minutes. Place

the beets in a colander and slip off the skins under cold running water.

7. You can cook the mushrooms at the same time as the beets. Toss the mushrooms with the melted butter, minced garlic, and salt and pepper. Place in a small roasting pan, stems facing up, and roast until golden and tender, about 30 minutes.

8. Return the casserole with the lamb shanks to medium heat and heat through. Remove the shanks and keep them warm. Over high heat, reduce the braising liquid to about 1½ cups, about 15 minutes. Strain through a fine strainer, pressing hard on the solids to extract all the liquid.

9. To serve, place a lamb shank on each plate. Arrange some beets and mushrooms around each and spoon some of the sauce over all.

SERVES 6

RED-BRAISED LAMB SHANKS

Chinese red braising (slow-simmering in liquid flavored with soy, sugar, rice wine, star anise, dried tangerine peel, and other aromatics) is ideal for rich gelatinous cuts of meat, such as pork hocks or lamb shanks. With lamb shanks so in vogue these days, this recipe won't fail to impress. These are best served with a dish of fried noodles and a vinaigrette-dressed salad.

4 meaty lamb shanks (about 1 pound each)

Large pinch of five-spice powder

2 teaspoons freshly ground black pepper

2 large cloves garlic, crushed through a press

2 tablespoons peanut or canola oil

2 medium carrots, peeled and cut into
*   1½-inch pieces*

12 ounces turnips or daikon radish, peeled
*   and cut into 1½-inch pieces*

½ cup Chinese rice wine or dry sherry

1 tablespoon rice vinegar

4½ cups Chicken Stock (page 384) or
*   canned broth*

2 cups soy sauce

3½ tablespoons sugar

Aromatics: 3 thick slices fresh ginger,
*   smashed; 4 pieces scallion (white part*
*   only), smashed; 1 star anise, broken into*
*   points; 2 teaspoons fennel seeds; 2*
*   teaspoons lightly crushed coriander seeds,*
*   2 pieces dried tangerine peel, tied in*
*   cheesecloth*

1 tablespoon cornstarch, mixed with
*   1½ tablespoons cold water*

Julienned fresh ginger, for garnish

Julienned red bell pepper, for garnish

Sliced scallions, for garnish

1. Rub the lamb shanks with five-spice powder, pepper, and garlic. Heat the oil in a large flameproof casserole or Dutch oven over medium-high heat. Brown the lamb shanks on all sides, about 5 minutes. Remove with a slotted spoon. Add the carrots and turnips to the drippings and brown for 3 minutes. Add the rice wine and vinegar and reduce over high heat for 2 minutes.

2. Return the lamb shanks to the casserole and add the stock, soy sauce, sugar, and the cheesecloth bag of aromatics. Bring to a boil. Reduce the heat to low, cover, and simmer until the meat is almost falling off the bones, about 3 hours.

3. With a large slotted spoon, remove the meat and vegetables to a serving platter and keep warm. Discard the aromatics.

4. Skim off the fat in the casserole and ladle about 2 cups of the braising liquid into a clean pot. Bring to a simmer. Slowly whisk in the cornstarch mixture and heat until it thickens, about 1 minute.

5. Pour the sauce over the lamb shanks. Serve garnished with julienned ginger and bell pepper and sliced scallions.

SERVES 4

NEW ZEALAND ROAST LAMB
with Emerald Sauce

This easy, quick recipe combining two of New Zealand's best-known exports, lamb and kiwi, is a creation of Jan Bilton, the recipe developer for the New Zealand Kiwi Fruit Board. Says Jan, the emerald-colored kiwi sauce gives an innovative twist to the vinegar-based mint sauce that is traditionally served with lamb.

¼ cup red currant jelly

1 leg of lamb (about 5½ pounds), trimmed
*   of excess fat*

Salt and freshly ground pepper, to taste

EMERALD SAUCE

8 firm, ripe kiwi

1 tablespoon sugar

1 tablespoon lemon juice

2 tablespoons rice vinegar

½ cup finely chopped fresh mint leaves

Salt, to taste

THE TRADITIONAL ROAST, SINGAPORE-STYLE

The Sunday roast has been a yeoman tradition in England since time immemorial. When the British went to Singapore, they were determined to bring it with them, and like so many other legacies from the colonial era, the tradition there became more British than in Britain. Little by little the tradition was augmented by local flavors, but through it all the roast has remained as quintessentially British as the Tower of London.

In the earliest colonial days, the Sunday roast caught on with the wealthier Indian population, for whom it was the perfect symbol of the Occidental luxury to which they aspired. On weekends and holidays, British clubs and colonial hotels served ever more elaborate buffet-style "tiffin" lunches, the lavish spread centering on a Western-style roast. As time went on, the magic wand of Southeast Asian cuisine was tipped on this little bit of England. The dish was pepped up with local spices, complemented by an array of traditional North Indian curries, and accompanied by innovative chutneys. Malay and Indonesian specialties began to appear alongside the Anglo-Indian centerpieces—intricately perfumed rich coconut curries, an impressive array of sambals (condiments), and dainty Straits Chinese cakes. For more on tiffin lunches, see page 283.

1. Preheat the oven to 350°F.

2. Melt the red currant jelly in a small nonreactive saucepan over low heat.

3. Rub the lamb with salt and pepper, place in a roasting pan, and brush with some of the melted jelly. Roast for 1½ hours for medium, brushing occasionally with the remaining melted jelly. Remove the lamb from the oven and let stand for 10 minutes, covered with aluminum foil, before carving.

4. Make the sauce: Combine the kiwi, sugar, lemon juice, and vinegar in a food processor and process, in pulses, until you get a coarse purée. Take care not to overprocess or the kiwi seeds will be crushed. Stir in the mint.

5. Serve the sauce in a sauceboat with the meat.

SERVES 6 TO 8

RAFFLES SUNDAY ROAST

The recipe for this marvelous roast comes from the Raffles Hotel, a legendary institution synonymous with colonial Singapore. The butterflied leg of lamb is marinated in a mixture of Indian spices and stuffed with a seductive blend of raisins, almonds, and candied citrus peel.

2 large cloves garlic, crushed through
  a press
1 tablespoon grated fresh ginger
1½ teaspoons ground turmeric
1 teaspoons pure chile powder
1½ teaspoons salt
1 tablespoon ground coriander
1½ teaspoons ground cumin
2½ tablespoons paprika
2 tablespoons olive oil, or more as
  needed
1 leg of lamb (6½ to 7 pounds), trimmed,
  boned, and butterflied (about 5 pounds
  boned weight)
¾ cup golden raisins
½ cup coarsely ground or slivered toasted
  almonds
⅓ cup mixed candied citrus peel
¼ cup slivered fresh mint leaves
1 large egg white, lightly beaten
1½ tablespoons fresh lemon juice

1. In a small bowl, combine the garlic, ginger, turmeric, ½ teaspoon chile powder, the salt, coriander, cumin, and 2 tablespoons paprika. Add enough olive oil to form a paste. Rub the lamb all over with this paste, cover with aluminum foil, and refrigerate for at least 2 hours or overnight. Bring to room temperature before roasting.

2. Preheat the oven to 400°F.

3. In a medium-size bowl, mix together the raisins, almonds, citrus peel, remaining chile powder, remaining paprika, mint, egg white, and lemon juice. Spread the stuffing over the inside of the lamb. Roll up carefully and tie with kitchen string. Place the lamb in a baking dish or roasting pan and roast for 20 minutes.

4. Reduce the oven temperature to 350°F and continue roasting the lamb for 1 hour and 10 minutes for medium doneness. Do not overcook. Brush with some olive oil if the lamb looks dry.

5. Remove from the oven, cover with aluminum foil, and let rest for 15 minutes before slicing. Discard the kitchen string and slice carefully, so that each serving includes some stuffing.

SERVES 6 TO 8

DOWN-UNDER ROAST LAMB DINNER

This is Julie Meyer's (see box, facing page) indisputably top-notch roast lamb. It is roasted with a whole host of root vegetables, so be sure to choose a large enough roasting pan.

1 leg of lamb (5 pounds), preferably spring
  lamb
1 large clove garlic, slivered
1 teaspoon chopped fresh rosemary leaves or
  1½ teaspoons dried
1 tablespoon olive oil
1 cup dry vermouth
½ cup plus 1 tablespoon all-purpose flour
1 teaspoon paprika
1 teaspoon freshly ground black pepper
Salt, to taste
6 to 8 small white onions (not pearl onions),
  peeled
6 to 8 medium Idaho potatoes, peeled and
  quartered
2 to 3 cups peeled, seeded, and cubed
  pumpkin or butternut squash
6 to 8 parsnips, peeled
1½ cups hot Chicken or Beef Stock (both
  page 384) or canned broth

PASSING THE CROWN

England and Australia have been energetically competitive since the earliest colonial days, the keenest issues in this endless rivalry being the mysterious game of cricket and the Sunday roast. After two years Down Under, John was finally forced to agree that Australia came out on top on both counts. Australian superiority in cricket was a matter of fact, but the question of the roast produced fierce debate and passionate partisanship. John was finally convinced at dinner with our friends Julie and Philip Meyer.

They live in the Melbourne seaside suburb of St. Kilda at the quiet end of Acland Street, one of the most cosmopolitan main streets in Australia. Julie and Philip Meyer are as Australian as eucalyptus. Julie is an artist and Philip a designer. They spend every minute of free time they can touring and hiking in the great Australian outback. Their wonderful home is crammed with Aboriginal objects, obscure rocks, smooth multicolored stones, and other trophies of their journeys and sojourns. The walls are hung with Julie's paintings of the Dry Lands and plastered with panoramic assemblages of color photos of the unearthly Australian landscape.

Needless to say, they cook and lay the table like the artist and designer they are.

They produce little vases with flowers from the garden or make rosettes from dry desert leaves. Julie might plait some delicate, patterned twigs she found in a dry riverbed into a delightful once-only napkin holder. Their table is always full of these lovely little gestures. Offstage, the kitchen is stacked to the ceiling with jars of pickles, jams, and preserves. There doesn't seem to be a single thing that grows in Australia that they can't eat or otherwise take delight in.

At the heart of our dinner with Julie and Philip was a dish that epitomizes early springtime in Australia, when the tenderest, sweetest lamb has just arrived in Melbourne's Victoria Market. The usual accompaniments at Acland Street are a dish of stuffed tomatoes and fresh peas laced with mint sauce. But Julie refuses to be precise about the vegetables. She cooks and shops just like she roams in the Australian wild, ad hoc and improvising on the run. But we know she always turns up the best seasonal root vegetables on her weekly rounds.

The recipe for the Down Under Roast Lamb Dinner is from Julie's mother. When you prepare it, you will know in an instant why John wasn't just convinced in the ancient dispute over cricket and the roast—he was bowled over.

1. Preheat the oven to 425°F.

2. With a sharp knife, make slits ¾ inch deep all over the lamb and insert a garlic sliver and some of the rosemary in each. Rub the lamb with olive oil and place in a large roasting pan.

3. Roast the lamb for 30 minutes. Reduce the oven temperature to 350°F and pour the vermouth over the lamb. Roast the lamb for another 30 minutes, basting every 10 to 15 minutes with the pan juices.

4. Spread ½ cup of the flour on a large

plate and mix with the paprika, the pepper, and salt to taste. Dredge the vegetables lightly with the flour and shake off the excess. After the lamb has roasted for 1 hour, add the vegetables to the roasting pan with the lamb. Spread them around the meat, stirring to coat them with the pan juices. Continue roasting the lamb and the vegetables until the vegetables are tender and the meat is cooked to medium, about 50 minutes (for well done lamb, roast an additional 10 to 15 minutes).

5. Remove the lamb from the roasting pan, cover with aluminum foil, and let stand for 15 minutes before carving. Remove the vegetables to a serving bowl and keep warm.

6. Sprinkle the pan with the remaining 1 tablespoon flour and stir over low heat. Slowly stir in the hot stock and bring to a boil, stirring until the gravy thickens.

7. Carve the lamb and serve with the vegetables. Pass the gravy separately in a sauceboat.

SERVES 6

C H U - C H E E
R O A S T   L A M B

The remarkable aromatic sauce served with this roast lamb provides a perfect foil for sliced roast leg of lamb. You can serve the Thai *chu-chee* sauce—thick red curry sauce, drizzled with coconut cream and accented with the fragrant kaffir lime— with almost any meat; next time try it with purchased Chinese roast duck. This dish was inspired by Prameran Krongkaew, the best Thai cook in New York City.

2 tablespoons vegetable oil
2 tablespoons soy sauce
1 tablespoon honey
1 small leg of lamb (4½ to 5 pounds), or
shank portion of a leg of lamb
1 teaspoon garlic powder
Salt and freshly ground black pepper,
to taste
Chu-Chee Sauce (recipe follows)
2 kaffir lime leaves, finely
shredded
Julienned red bell pepper, for garnish

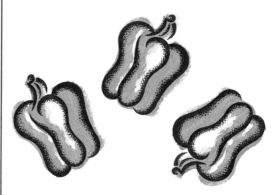

1. Preheat the oven to 450°F.

2. In a small bowl, whisk together the oil, soy sauce, and honey. Rub the lamb with garlic powder, salt and pepper and brush with the soy mixture. Place the lamb in a roasting pan and roast for 15 minutes. Reduce the oven temperature to 325°F and continue roasting the lamb for 1 hour longer for medium doneness.

3. Remove the lamb from the oven and let stand, covered with aluminum foil, for 10 minutes before carving.

4. To serve, carve the lamb into slices. Spoon the sauce onto a serving platter or individual plates and arrange the lamb slices on the sauce. Drizzle the reserved coconut cream mixture from the sauce recipe over the meat and sprinkle with kaffir lime and the julienned bell pepper.

SERVES 4 TO 6

Chu-Chee Sauce

2 tablespoons long-grain rice
1 can (13½ ounces) unsweetened coconut
   milk, refrigerated upright
½ cup water
½ teaspoon cornstarch, mixed with
   2 teaspoons water
1 tablespoon vegetable oil
1½ tablespoons Thai red curry paste, preferably homemade (268)
2 tablespoons Asian fish sauce, such as
   nam pla
2 tablespoons (packed) light brown sugar, or
   more to taste

1. Stir the rice in a small skillet over medium-low heat until golden brown. Let cool and grind in a coffee or spice grinder. You need 2½ teaspoons of the ground rice.

2. Open the can of coconut milk and remove to a small saucepan ½ cup of the thickened cream that has risen to the top. Stir the rest of the milk to blend it, then remove 1 cup of it to a bowl and mix with the water. Set aside. Heat the thickened cream, stir in the cornstarch mixture, and cook until thickened, about 2 minutes. (Cover the pan with a splatter screen if the milk splatters.) Reserve.

3. Heat the oil in a small heavy saucepan over medium-high heat. Add the curry paste and stir for 1 minute, breaking it up with a fork. Add the coconut milk mixture and cook for 5 minutes. Stir in the fish sauce, sugar, and ground rice and cook until thickened, about 3 minutes. Keep the sauce warm until ready to serve.

MAKES ABOUT 2 CUPS

LAMB CHOPS

with
Fig and Tamarind
Chutney

I am addicted to the intriguing tart and sweet flavor of tamarind and I use it generously in marinades, sauces, stews, curries, chutneys, and glazes. In this recipe—a take-off on the Indian chutney often served with tandoori dishes—the acidity of tamarind marries beautifully with the lush sweetness of the dried figs, providing just the right accompaniment for the grilled rare lamb. This versatile chutney goes well with just about any grilled or roasted meat or poultry. Make jars of it for the holiday season to intrigue your friends with a taste of the East.

8 rib lamb chops, cut ¾ inch thick (about
   2 pounds total)
3 cloves garlic, crushed through a press
1½ teaspoons freshly ground black
   pepper
Salt, to taste
Fig and Tamarind Chutney (recipe
   follows)

1. Prepare coals for grilling or preheat the broiler.

2. Rub the lamb chops with garlic, pepper, and salt. Grill or broil the chops, about 5 minutes on the first side and 4 minutes on the other side for medium doneness. Let stand, covered with aluminum foil, for 5 minutes.

3. Divide the lamb chops among 4 plates and spoon the chutney next to the lamb, or pass separately in a sauceboat.

SERVES 4

Fig and Tamarind Chutney

2½ tablespoons tamarind pulp, preferably
    from Thailand
1½ cups boiling Chicken Stock (page 384)
    or canned broth
1 tablespoon unsalted butter
½ cup chopped onion
5 dried figs, chopped medium fine
½ cup water
¼ teaspoon pure chile powder
¼ teaspoon ground ginger
½ teaspoon ground cumin
Salt, to taste
Pinch of sugar, or to taste (optional)
2½ tablespoons chopped fresh mint leaves

1. Soak the tamarind pulp in the boiling stock off the heat for 15 minutes. Stir and mash it with a fork to help it dissolve. Strain through a fine strainer into a bowl, pressing on the solids with the back of a wooden spoon to extract all the liquid.

2. Melt the butter in a heavy nonreactive saucepan over medium-low heat. Cook the onion until translucent, about 5 minutes. Add the figs, water, and the tamarind liquid and bring to a boil. Stir in the chile powder, ginger, and cumin, then cover and simmer over low heat, stirring occasionally, until the figs are soft, about 15 minutes. Uncover and simmer until the chutney thickens, about 5 minutes. Season with salt to taste and add a little sugar, if a sweeter chutney is desired. Stir in the mint right before serving. Serve warm.

MAKES ABOUT 1½ CUPS

LAMB CHOPS
with Miso-Braised Eggplant

The combination of lamb and eggplant is perfect for India or the Middle East, but it would raise a few eyebrows in Japan. Yet this didn't stop Sydney chef Tetsuya Wakuda from experimenting with exciting Japanese flavors to accompany the lamb of his adopted country. In this dish, juicy pan-fried lamb chops sit atop an Oriental goulash of eggplant cooked with two kinds of miso (red and white), Japanese rice wine, and a dash of soy sauce.

1½ pounds thin Chinese or Japanese
    eggplants, peeled, seeded if necessary, and
    cut into large 3- x ½-inch sticks
Salt, to taste
2 tablespoons lemon juice
1 tablespoon chopped shallots
2 cloves garlic, chopped
2 teaspoons grated fresh ginger
½ tablespoon dark miso (hatcho miso or
    aka miso)
1 tablespoon white miso (shiro miso)
⅓ cup Chicken Stock (page 384) or canned
    broth
3 tablespoons mirin or medium-dry sherry
1 teaspoon soy sauce
½ teaspoon sugar
¼ teaspoon ground sansho pepper
2 tablespoons olive oil
8 rib lamb chops, cut ¾ inch thick (about
    2 pounds total)

1. Bring a pot of salted water to a boil. Add the eggplant and lemon juice and cook, partially covered, until the eggplant is just tender, 8 to 10 minutes. Drain well.

2. In a bowl, combine the shallots, garlic, ginger, the two misos, stock, mirin, soy sauce, and sugar, and mix well with a wire whisk. Combine the miso mixture with the eggplant in a medium-size flameproof casserole and simmer over low heat about 10 minutes, stirring often with a wooden spoon. Season with *sansho* pepper and salt, if necessary. Set aside and keep warm.

3. Using two skillets or working in batches, heat the oil over medium-high heat. Sauté the lamb chops for about 5 minutes on each side for medium rare.

4. Divide the eggplant mixture among 4 plates and top each portion with 2 chops. Serve at once.

SERVES 4

ROAST PORK

with Gingered Sour Cherry Sauce

The beauty of this dish is its versatility. On a cold winter evening, it is a soul-warming roast dinner. On a hot summer afternoon, the pork, thinly sliced and served cold, makes a perfect outdoor treat for a lunch party or a picnic.

1 boneless pork loin (about 3½ pounds)
Salt and freshly ground black pepper,
    to taste
1 teaspoon minced garlic
1 tablespoon minced fresh ginger
2 tablespoons hoisin sauce
¾ cup Chicken Stock (page 384) or
    canned broth
Gingered Sour Cherry Sauce
    (recipe follows)

1. Preheat the oven to 350°F.

2. Rub the pork with salt and pepper. Combine the garlic, ginger, and hoisin and brush on the pork. Place the pork in a shallow roasting pan and pour in the stock. Cook, basting occasionally, until the juices run clear when you prick it with a tip of a knife, about 1 hour and 45 minutes.

3. Remove the pork from the oven, cover with aluminum foil, and let rest for 15 minutes before slicing. Pass the sauce separately in a sauceboat.

SERVES 6

Gingered Sour Cherry Sauce

The sour cherry sauce suffused with the flavors of garlic and aromatic herbs is best prepared a day ahead for all the flavors to ripen. I often serve it with roast turkey or with grilled chicken instead of roast pork.

Bottled sour cherries are available at specialty grocery shops and some supermarkets. I especially recommend the Adriatic brand.

3 cups pitted bottled sour cherries, juice reserved
1 dried hot red chile (1 inch), seeded and finely crumbled
1 tablespoon grated fresh ginger
2 large cloves garlic, crushed through a press
1 teaspoon mild paprika
1 teaspoon ground coriander
¼ teaspoon ground fenugreek
2 tablespoons fresh lime juice
2 teaspoons rice vinegar
Sugar, to taste
½ cup chopped fresh cilantro leaves
3 tablespoons chopped fresh mint leaves
Salt and freshly ground black pepper, to taste

1. Combine the cherries and ½ cup of the reserved juice in a food processor and process until puréed.

2. Transfer the puréed mixture to a nonreactive saucepan and cook over medium heat, skimming off the froth, until thickened and reduced, about 10 minutes.

3. Add the rest of the ingredients and mix well. Allow at least 2 hours for the flavors to blend. Serve cold or warm.

MAKES ABOUT 2 CUPS

PEPPER-CRUSTED PORK TENDERLOIN
with Pineapple Raisin Chutney

The chutney in this recipe—which takes its inspiration from the Indian migrant cuisine of Singapore—can also be served with sautéed pork chops, roast pork shoulder, turkey, or ham. Make it well ahead of time to have at hand for an improvised exotic island dinner.

1½ tablespoons black peppercorns, cracked
1½ tablespoons green peppercorns, cracked
1½ tablespoons pink peppercorns, cracked
4 pork tenderloins (6 ounces each)
2½ tablespoons olive oil
Salt, to taste
Pineapple Raisin Chutney (recipe follows)

1. Preheat the oven to 375°F.

2. Spread the cracked peppercorns on a board and press the pork tenderloins firmly into the peppercorns until they adhere on all sides.

3. Heat the oil in a large ovenproof skillet over medium-high heat. Add the pork and brown for 2 to 3 minutes per side. Transfer the skillet to the oven and bake for about 8 minutes for medium and 12 minutes for well done.

4. Season the pork with salt, cut into 1½-inch thick slices, and serve with the chutney.

SERVES 4

WALKING IN SINGAPORE WITH GERALDENE LOWE-ISMAIL

No one knows old Singapore better than Geraldene Lowe-Ismail. She has spent most of her life in the city and has an unquenchable passion for the history and the life of its streets. Geraldene has perfected the art of the informed wander. Whatever your interest—antiques, old buildings, Chinese temples, street foods, fine dining, masks and puppets, jewelry, literally anything—Geraldene will know how to find it. And what's more, she will find it five times over and make sure you have tea at a beautiful tearoom somewhere on the way.

If you can't find Geraldene herself (ask at the local tourist office) for a personalized tour, then look for her useful pamphlet "Six Walks at the Doorway to Chinatown," which she prepared for guests of the Hotel Furawa. Each walk begins and ends at the hotel. On the "blue" route you stroll along Club Street, which is lined with trade clubs (like guilds). Geraldene lists the well-known institutions used by gold- and silversmiths and restaurateurs. But she also lets you know the whereabouts of a club dedicated to "old amahs"—literally "old housemaids." Then she takes you along Gemill Lane, where several families still carve traditional Chinese deities out of sandalwood, and on to the late-afternoon "Thieves Market," brimming with bric-a-brac and curios.

On other walks you will meet a street scribe, still commissioned by the older inhabitants of Chinatown to read and write their correspondence; or visit the Padang with its quaint Singapore Cricket Club, founded in 1852; or you will find the best spot for gazing up at the OCBC Building—the tallest building outside the United States at the time of its completion—designed by Chinese-American I. M. Pei. En route you might take in a rarefied teahouse, a steamboat restaurant (serving a kind of Chinese fondue), a popiah pancake house, a bakery making festival cakes, or one of the few remaining authentic Chinese wine bars This is travel and food in an exquisite two-step—the way it should be.

Pineapple Raisin Chutney

2 tablespoons peanut oil

½ cup diced red onion

3 tablespoons chopped fresh ginger

1 clove garlic, minced

1 fresh mild green chile, such as Anaheim, stemmed, seeded, and diced

1 small red bell pepper, stemmed, seeded, and diced

¼ to ½ teaspoon pure chile powder

½ teaspoon ground turmeric

4 tablespoons sugar

5 tablespoons distilled white vinegar

¼ cup unsweetened pineapple juice

2 tablespoon fresh lime juice, or to taste

2 cups diced fresh pineapple

¼ cup golden raisins

2 tablespoons Chinese plum sauce (optional)

¼ cup chopped fresh cilantro leaves

Salt, to taste

1. Heat the oil in a medium-size nonreactive saucepan over medium heat. Add the onion and cook, stirring, for 3 minutes. Add the ginger, garlic, chile, bell pepper, chile powder, and turmeric and cook, stirring, for 2 minutes.

2. Add the sugar, vinegar, pineapple juice, lime juice, pineapple, raisins, and plum sauce. Bring to a simmer over low heat and cook, stirring, until the chutney has thickened and all the ingredients are soft, about 12 minutes. Add the salt.

3. Cool and let stand for at least 4 hours before using. Serve cold or warm. Stir in the cilantro just before serving. The chutney will keep up to 2 weeks, covered and refrigerated.

MAKES ABOUT 2¹/₂ CUPS

L A N N A   T H A I
P O R K   S T E W

The legendary Lanna kingdom of northern Thailand produced a cuisine that is much more earthy and austere than the zippy, extravagant cooking of the central plains of the south. Here the strongest influences come from neighboring Burma. The flavors of the curries are gentler and more blended, coconut milk is used less often, and mild and sweet spices have a more visible presence.

This tomato-based curry, enriched with sweet potatoes, is a lovely example of northern Thai cuisine. Traditionally it is eaten with sticky rice. If tamarind is unavailable, substitute with 1½ tablespoons fresh lemon or lime juice.

5 dried hot red chiles (2 to 3 inches), preferably Asian

4 stalks fresh lemongrass (3 inches of the lower stalk, tough outer leaves discarded), chopped

2 teaspoons anchovy paste

1½ tablespoons chopped fresh ginger

2 tablespoons chopped garlic

4 tablespoons vegetable oil, or more as needed

1½ tablespoons tamarind pulp, preferably from Thailand

½ cup boiling water

2 pounds pork loin or shoulder butt, cut into 1½-inch chunks

1½ cups chopped onion

1 tablespoon paprika

1½ teaspoons ground turmeric

2 tablespoons tomato paste

1 tablespoon (packed) dark brown sugar, or more to taste

3 cups water

Aromatics: 1 piece cinnamon stick (2 inches), 4 cloves, 2 bay leaves, and 2 cardamom pods, preferably unbleached (green), tied in cheesecloth

Salt, to taste

1 large sweet potato, peeled and cut into 1¼-inch cubes

1 tablespoon soy sauce

1. Stem the chiles and shake out the seeds. Using scissors, cut the chiles into pieces. Soak in warm water to cover for 10 minutes. Drain well.

2. Using a mortar and pestle or a small food processor, grind or process the lemongrass, anchovy paste, ginger, garlic, and chiles to a paste, adding a little vegetable oil if necessary to assist the blending. Set aside.

3. Soak the tamarind pulp in the ½ cup boiling water off the heat for 15 minutes. Stir and mash it with a fork to help it dissolve. Strain through a fine strainer into a bowl, pressing on the solids and with the back of a wooden spoon to extract all the liquid.

4. Heat 3 tablespoons of oil in a large heavy saucepan over medium heat. Add the pork in batches and cook until lightly browned on all sides, 5 to 7 minutes per batch. Drain the pork on paper towels.

5. In the same saucepan, heat the remaining oil over low heat. Add the onion and cook until translucent, about 5 minutes. Add the paprika, turmeric, and the spice paste and cook, stirring, until the mixture is fragrant and no longer tastes raw, about 5 minutes.

6. Stir in the tamarind liquid, tomato paste, sugar, and the 3 cups of water and bring to a simmer. Return the pork to the casserole and add the aromatics in the cheesecloth bag. Season with salt. Simmer, partially covered, for 1 hour.

7. Add the sweet potato and continue cooking, uncovered, over medium heat until the sweet potato is cooked and the pork is very tender, about 15 minutes. Stir in the soy sauce, more sugar if desired, and salt to taste.

8. Remove the cheesecloth bag and serve.

SERVES 6

CHINESE-STYLE BARBECUED PORK

This is an excellent home-style barbecue pork recipe, adapted and simplified from a recipe by the Chinese barbecue master, Chef Yee, of Harbor Village restau-

rant in San Francisco. Chef Yee marinates his pork in a far more complex sauce, consisting of very aromatic "rose dew" rice wine (*mui gwe lo*), hoisin, sesame paste, red bean curd, and bean paste. Then he roasts it, hung up in a traditional cylindrical oven, brushes it with a sweet maltose mixture, and hangs it up to dry. The following recipe produces very authentic-tasting results without the complicated ingredients and involved procedure.

The pork makes a great party platter, while the leftovers can be used for soups, salads, stir-fried noodles, vegetables, or rice. Any unused pork can be frozen, and the marinade will work equally well with spareribs.

1 boneless Boston pork butt or loin
    (2½ to 3 pounds)
Large pinch five-spice powder
½ cup hoisin sauce
⅓ cup sugar
3 tablespoons light soy sauce
2 tablespoons Chinese rice wine or dry sherry
1½ tablespoons hot bean paste (if available)
2 large cloves garlic, crushed through a press
2 to 3 drops red food coloring (optional)

1. Cut the pork with the grain into long slabs 1 inch thick and 2½-inches wide. Rub with five-spice powder.

2. In a bowl, mix all the remaining ingredients. Pour over the pork in a shallow dish and marinate for 1 hour, turning the pork pieces occasionally.

3. Preheat the oven to 500°F.

4. Place the pork on a rack in a roasting pan, reserving the marinade, and pour 1 cup of water into the pan. Roast the pork for 8 minutes. Turn the pork to the other side and roast for another 8 minutes. Reduce the oven temperature to 300°F and continue roasting the pork, turning halfway through the cooking time, and brushing with the marinade, until the juices run clear when you test it with a skewer, 40 to 45 minutes.

5. Let the pork cool slightly, then cut into thin slices and serve.

SERVES 8

STIR-FRIED PORK RIBBONS

with String Beans and Basil-Chile-Garlic Sauce

Here is a simple Thai stir-fry sparked with the radiant, eye-opening flavors of Thailand. I learned it at the cooking school at the Oriental Hotel in Bangkok. Try, if you can, to get sweet Thai basil for this dish. Chicken ribbons can be substituted for pork. Although fresh lemongrass and galangal are the core of a truly Thai taste, do not be put off from making this recipe if they are not easily found. In this case you can do without them and still come up with a tempting dish.

8 to 10 dried hot red chiles (2 to 3 inches), preferably Asian
6 large cloves garlic, chopped
¼ cup chopped shallots
2 teaspoons chopped fresh cilantro roots and/or stems
2 stalks fresh lemongrass (3 inches of the lower stalk, tough outer leaves discarded), chopped
2 teaspoons chopped fresh or frozen galangal (if unavailable, use fresh ginger)
1 teaspoon salt, plus more to taste
2 tablespoons peanut oil, or more as needed
1 pound string beans, trimmed
1½ pounds boneless pork loin chops, sliced lengthwise into ¼-inch-thick strips
2 tablespoons Asian fish sauce, such as nam pla, or more to taste
1½ teaspoons sugar
1 cup fresh basil leaves, preferably Thai or purple

1. Stem the chiles and shake out the seeds. Using scissors, cut the chiles into pieces. Soak in warm water to cover for 10 minutes. Drain well.

2. Combine the chiles, garlic, shallots, cilantro roots, lemongrass, galangal, and 1 teaspoon salt in a food processor and process to a paste, adding a little oil if necessary to assist the blending. Scrape into a bowl and set aside.

3. Blanch the beans in boiling salted water for 1 minute. Refresh under cold running water. Drain well and pat thoroughly dry with paper towels.

4. Brush a wok with a little oil and heat

over high heat. Working in small batches, sear the pork, stirring constantly, until just opaque, about 3 minutes per batch. Reheat the wok before each batch, pouring off any accumulated liquid. Remove the pork from the wok and set aside.

5. Add the beans to the wok and stir-fry for 5 minutes. Return the pork to the wok and stir to mix with the beans. Add the chile paste in batches, stirring each batch in thoroughly. Stir for 1 minute.

6. Stir in the fish sauce, sugar, basil, and salt to taste and cook for 2 minutes. Serve at once.

SERVES 4 TO 6

PORK CHOPS

with a Mushroom Sauté and Arugula Pesto

This is another dish from one of my favorite Sydney chefs, Tetsuya Wakuda. Japanese born and French trained, Tetsuya is the only chef I met in my long circuits around the Pacific who infallibly manages to pull off the most offbeat and unlikely Oriental-Mediterranean combinations.

Tetsuya prepares these chops with the wonderful Japanese *shimeji* mushrooms, which exude a delicate, musky flavor. They are not grown in Australia, so in his relentless pursuit of culinary perfection he persuaded a botany professor at the local university to grow them specially for his restaurant. If you can't find fresh *shimeji*, Tetsuya suggests substituting an equal quantity of button and shiitake mushrooms. Make the arugula pesto the day before you plan to serve the pork chops.

> 8 center-cut pork chops, ½ to ¾ inch
> thick (about 2½ pounds total),
> trimmed of most fat
> 1 tablespoon, plus 1 teaspoon virgin
> olive oil
> 7 ounces shimeji mushrooms, or substitute
> equal parts of button and shiitake
> mushrooms, sliced
> ¼ cup Chicken Stock (page 384) or
> canned broth
> 2 tablespoons Arugula Pesto
> (recipe follows)
> 1 teaspoon light soy sauce
> Salt and freshly ground black pepper,
> to taste

1. Preheat the grill or broiler.

2. Brush the pork chops with 1 teaspoon of the oil. Grill or broil for about 6 minutes on each side.

3. While the pork is cooking, prepare the mushrooms. Heat the remaining oil in a large nonstick skillet over medium heat. Add the mushrooms and sauté, stirring, for about 5 minutes. Add the stock, turn the heat up to high, and cook for 3 more minutes. Stir in 2 tablespoons of the arugula pesto and the soy sauce and cook to heat through, about 2 minutes. Season to taste with salt and pepper.

4. To serve, place 2 pork chops on each plate and top with the *shimeji* sauce.

SERVES 4

SOUTH AUSTRALIA: WINE AND WILDLIFE

No place explodes the myth that Australia is just a land of red desert, cuddly marsupials, canned beer, and meat pies better than South Australia, home to some of the most outstanding food and wine in the world. South Australia's Barossa Valley is an undulating, grape-growing plain whose culinary and viticultural offerings can match those of Burgundy, and which is within easy striking distance of the rugged outback of the Flinders Ranges and the unique wildlife of Kangaroo Island. This is one of our favorite regions in Australia. The state is the major wine-producing area in the country, and for several consecutive years, its best chefs and restaurants have taken top honors in the Australian food world.

A perfect week-long tour around South Australia should begin with a two-day sojourn in Adelaide, the state capital. Here you can explore the city's colonial architecture, take in the stunning collection of Aboriginal and Oceanic art, and gamble in the casino, located in a historic sandstone railway station. In the evenings you can meet with the locals in some of the finest historic pubs in Australia, then dine in one of those award-winning restaurants—perhaps the Pheasant Farm for outstanding local game, or Nediz-Tu for the best in East-meets-West.

Both Adelaide Hills and the Barossa valley are a short drive from Adelaide, and well worth a two- or three-day trip of bush-walking and winery tours, and high teas in the winsome villages founded by German settlers. The wineries range from huge international exporters to delightful, family-owned "boutique" concerns whose delicious wines can be tasted only in the valley. The larger-than-life personalities of the owners—chatty and eccentric Aussie farmers—make the tour vivid and eventful. They seem to have a special rapport with American visitors, who are often treated to a glass of "reserve" from the cellar. The winemakers are usually happy to show visitors around the wineries and will arrange international deliveries for those who want to take something home. The Barossa and the nearby Adelaide Hills offer a range of top-class inns and bed-and-breakfast places and exceptional country-style restaurants where food is lovingly matched with the local wines.

KANGAROO ISLAND

An absolute must to end any visit to South Australia is a day or two on Kangaroo Island, probably the best place in the country to see native animals in the wild. The sea lion beach, where you can wander among giant "king" lions and tiny white pups, and see pelicans and fairy penguins, is one of only two such places in the world. When Anya and I flew over to the island, we spent an hour or so on the beach, and then enjoyed a picnic in the bush, surrounded by emus, kangaroos, and wallabies. In the afternoon we took a glorious stroll through eucalyptus glades and flowery meadows, where we spotted koala bears, green-beaked Cape Barrant geese, a couple of utterly bizarre echidnas, and a rare black cockatoo.

Beyond the fringe of windblown dwarf forest that lines the rugged cliffs, the coastal scenery is both intimate and spectacular, with rolling, powder-white dunes, miles of pristine sandy beach, uncanny rock formations, caves, and gentle lagoons. If you stay, there are a couple of delightful family-run bed-and-breakfasts, with great views, delicious home-cooked meals, and personalized service.

MORE TEMPTING SIDE TRIPS

South Australia is just an hour away from Melbourne by air, and a visit there can easily be combined with one of the best sidetrips on the continent—the run up to Uluru (or Ayers Rock) and the Red Centre, which are linked to Adelaide by a restored nineteenth-century train route, still called the Ghan (after the Afghan camel-traders who once plied the central deserts).

Except for the wonderful Adelaide Arts Festival, when the place is thronging with international visitors and world-class cultural events, South Australia is seductively off the beaten track, even for Down Under. But you will find, year-round, that it serves up sophisticated food and wine, exotic fauna and infectious good humor in nicely equal measure.

Arugula Pesto

Use any leftover pesto served atop pasta or to flavor sauces.

1 small bunch arugula, washed, dried, trimmed, and chopped
¼ cup pine nuts
2 cloves garlic, chopped
1 tablespoon freshly grated Parmesan
3½ tablespoons extra-virgin olive oil
Salt and freshly ground white pepper, to taste

Combine the arugula, pine nuts, garlic, and Parmesan in a food processor and process to a paste. With the motor running, drizzle in the olive oil through the feed tube. Scrape the mixture into a bowl and season with salt and pepper. Cover with plastic wrap and refrigerate for at least 24 hours.

MAKES ABOUT ½ CUP

OKRA-STUFFED PORK ROLLS
with Peanut Sauce

Pork, peanuts, and okra are ingredients much loved in the American South. Here, soy sauce and coconut milk give the okra, pork, and sweet and spicy peanut sauce an unmistakable Southeast Asian inflection. So call this dish "South U.S.A. meets Southeast Asia" and enjoy it as much as we do.

Canola or peanut oil, for deep frying the
    okra, plus 2½ tablespoons
16 large okra pods, rinsed, patted dry, and
    trimmed
8 pork cutlets (about 1¼ pounds total),
    sliced thin
½ teaspoon ground cardamom
¾ teaspoon ground coriander
1 teaspoon freshly ground black pepper
¼ teaspoon ground cayenne pepper
Salt, to taste
1 large egg, lightly beaten
3 tablespoons rice wine or dry sherry
3 large plum tomatoes, chopped
Peanut Sauce (recipe follows)
Snipped fresh chives, for garnish

1. Pour oil to a depth of ½ inch into a medium-size skillet and fry the okra in batches over medium-high heat until golden, about 2 minutes. Drain on paper towels.

2. Lay each pork cutlet between 2 pieces of waxed paper and pound with the flat end of a meat pounder until thin.

3. In a small bowl, combine the cardamom, coriander, pepper, cayenne, and salt. Rub the pork with the mixture, then lay each cutlet flat on your work surface. Brush the entire surface of each with the beaten egg. Place two okra pods at one short end of each cutlet, roll up, and secure each roll with a toothpick.

4. Preheat the oven to 350°F.

5. In a large ovenproof skillet, heat the 2½ tablespoons oil over medium-high heat. Brown the rolls in batches on all sides, about 5 minutes, then remove from the skillet. Add the rice wine to the skillet and reduce by half, 30 seconds. Stir in the tomatoes and cook for 3 minutes. Replace the rolls in the skillet.

6. Bake the rolls, uncovered, for 10 minutes. Pour the peanut sauce over the rolls and bake, uncovered, for another 8 to 10 minutes.

7. To serve, arrange the rolls on a serving platter, discard the toothpicks, and sprinkle with the chives.

*SERVES 4
GENEROUSLY*

Peanut Sauce for Pork Rolls

1½ tablespoons peanut oil
½ cup chopped onion
1 teaspoon minced garlic
¼ teaspoon ground cayenne pepper, or more
    to taste
½ teaspoon paprika
⅛ teaspoon five-star powder
¼ cup crunchy unsalted, unsweetened peanut
    butter
½ cup canned unsweetened coconut milk, well
    stirred
½ cup Chicken Stock (page 384) or canned
    broth
2 teaspoons soy sauce, preferably tamari
1 tablespoon fresh lime juice, or more to taste
Salt, to taste (optional)

Heat the oil in a heavy medium-size saucepan over medium heat. Add the onion and sauté until limp, about 5 minutes. Stir in the garlic, cayenne, paprika, and five-spice powder and cook for another minute, stirring. Add the peanut butter, coconut milk, and stock. Stir well to blend and simmer, uncovered, until the sauce thickens and reduces a little, about 5 minutes. Stir in the soy sauce, lime juice, and salt to taste, if needed, and simmer for 1 more minute.

MAKES ABOUT 1¼ CUPS

VIETNAM AT YOUR TABLE

*T*hroughout years of upheaval and colonization, Vietnamese culture and cuisine have managed to retain their own unique expression and flavor. Vietnam may have only recently reopened as a travel destination, but a wave of immigration has brought Vietnamese expatriates to the United States. Many are now opening restaurants, giving Americans an excellent introduction to their extraordinary cuisine.

Vietnamese food is sophisticated, delicate, and subtle, characterized by clarity and a balance of flavors. The predominant tart, sweet, and salty tastes are always harmoniously orchestrated and cleverly set off against one another. These qualities, plus a cosmopolitan inflection gained from years of colonial French rule, make Vietnamese food especially attractive to Western diners and very accessible to a home cook.

The amber-colored salty fish sauce, nuoc mam, is a key to Vietnamese flavors. Both a condiment and a flavor base for many dishes, its sharp and slightly fishy character is skillfully balanced with other ingredients to produce a light, distinctive taste. When blended with lime juice, vinegar, sugar, chiles, garlic, and water, it becomes nuoc cham, a dynamic table sauce used to dress a variety of foods.

Rice paper (banh trang), a purely Vietnamese contribution to the culinary world, is another important ingredient. To prepare this edible wrapper, cooked rice is made into a dough, rolled paper-thin by machine, cut into rounds, placed on bamboo mats and left to dry in the sun. It is reconstituted with a little water, and used as a parchment-like wrapper for a variety of cold and hot foods. Rice-paper-wrapped fried and fresh filled rolls are some of the better-known offerings of the Vietnamese kitchen.

One of the world's great street foods is a Hanoi soup called pho bac. It is a wondrous long-simmered broth—slightly sweet from the hint of ginger and star anise—which is poured over thin slices of beef and homey broad rice noodles. The soup really comes to life when dressed with a whole range of palate teasers, including bean sprouts, scallions, mint and cilantro, lime wedges, a splash of fish sauce, and a hot chile sauce. In Vietnam it's the nourishing snack of choice and is sold by street vendors or at special pho shops, some of which boast pho prepared with up to a dozen cuts of meat, poultry, or offal.

The simplest way to serve a Vietnamese meal is South Vietnamese-style. Set the table with plates containing moistened rounds of rice paper, lettuce leaves, cubes of pineapple and cucumber, shredded carrots, bowls of nuoc cham, and bunches of herbs such as cilantro, mint, and Thai basil. Then present slices of grilled meat, chicken, or meatballs. Show your guests how to wrap the meats, vegetables, and herbs in lettuce leaves, and then in rice paper, before dipping them in the nuoc cham sauce. Also serve steamed rice or cooked rice vermicelli.

SPARERIBS

with Mango Barbecue Sauce

David Turner, a Chicago-born chef, came up with the recipe for the mango barbecue sauce. After stints in San Francisco and Hawaii, David is now in charge of the kitchen at one of the top hotel restaurants in Melbourne. The great barbecue traditions of Australia and the American heartland meet over a mango. What's more, it works like a dream.

The tangy mango sauce also works wonders with chicken or large shrimp.

MANGO BARBECUE SAUCE
1 tablespoon peanut oil
1½ tablespoons minced garlic
1½ teaspoons minced fresh ginger
¼ cup mirin or medium-dry sherry
1¼ cups puréed mango pulp (1 to 2 mangos)
2 tablespoons tomato paste
1 teaspoon (packed) light brown sugar, or
   more to taste
1½ tablespoons fresh lime juice
2 teaspoons red wine vinegar
1½ tablespoons Worcestershire sauce
2 teaspoons Dijon mustard
1 teaspoon Sambal Oelek (page 388) or
   Chinese chile paste with garlic
Salt and freshly ground black pepper, to taste

5 to 6 pounds meaty pork spareribs, cut into
   individual ribs

1. Make the barbecue sauce: Heat the oil in a saucepan over low heat. Add the garlic and ginger and stir until aromatic, about 30 seconds. Add the mirin and reduce over high heat for about 2 minutes.

2. Add the remaining sauce ingredients and simmer for about 10 minutes, stirring.

3. Arrange the spareribs in a large dish. Brush with generous amounts of the sauce and refrigerate for 12 hours or overnight.

4. Preheat the oven to 400°F.

5. Arrange the spareribs in a shallow baking pan and bake, brushing frequently with the remaining sauce, until the ribs are well browned, crisp, and cooked through, about 1¼ hours. Serve at once.

SERVES 4 TO 5

LION'S HEAD

Lions's Head, a dish of large pork meatballs cooked in a clay pot with napa cabbage is a glorious creation of the Shanghai kitchen. In its classic version, the pork is painstakingly chopped with fat and bacon rind, by hand, to produce unbelievably tender, fluffy balls that melt in your mouth but don't fall apart when cooked. This updated version (using tofu instead of the fat!) comes from San Francisco's China Bistro. The restaurant belongs to Joseph and Cecilia Chung (I have yet to encounter a more exotic and entertaining couple), and the Shanghai chef Leo serves up food that can be characterized as old-Shanghai-meets-nouvelle-California.

I have never had the privilege of tasting the original Lion's Head, but this version produces a strikingly light, delicate texture, making it the most outstanding meatball dish I've tasted so far.

To achieve good results, don't overstir

or press the meat. When adding tofu and other ingredients, gently massage them into the meat with your fingers, and then shape into balls between cupped hands. Strictly speaking, Lion's Head has to be cooked in a Chinese clay pot, but if you don't own one, use a heavy, even-cooking casserole instead.

MEATBALLS

1 pound lean pork, cut into cubes
1¼ cakes soft tofu, finely crumbled
1½ tablespoons Chinese rice wine or dry sherry
2½ tablespoons soy sauce
4 teaspoons sugar
1 tablespoon oyster sauce
1 teaspoon freshly ground white pepper
1 teaspoon salt
1½ tablespoons cornstarch, mixed with 2 tablespoons water

Peanut oil, for frying the meatballs
1 small head napa cabbage
1½ cups Chicken Stock (page 384) or canned broth
2 tablespoons soy sauce
1¾ teaspoons sugar
1½ teaspoons cornstarch, mixed with 2 teaspoons cold water
Salt, to taste

1. Working in batches, grind the pork in a food processor, until finely ground, but not made into a paste. Scrape into a large bowl.

2. With your fingers, gently massage the tofu into the pork, in upward motions, until well combined. Do not stir. Add the remaining meatball ingredients, one at a time, blending them in the same fashion until you have a fluffy, loose mixture.

3. Shape the mixture into 8 large meatballs by bouncing it gently between your cupped palms. (Your hands should not be far apart.)

4. Pour oil to a depth of 1 inch into a large wok and heat over medium heat. Add the meatballs in batches and brown on all sides, about 7 minutes per batch. Transfer the meatballs to paper towels to drain.

5. Trim off the upper third from the cabbage. Cut enough of the remaining cabbage into 2½-inch pieces to measure about 6 cups. Blanch the cabbage in boiling water for 30 seconds. Refresh under cold running water.

6. Bring the stock, soy sauce, and sugar in a small saucepan to a simmer over medium-low heat.

7. Arrange the cabbage on the bottom of a 2-quart Chinese clay pot or a heavy medium-size flameproof casserole. Place the meatballs on top and pour the stock mixture over. Bring to a simmer and drizzle in the cornstarch mixture. Stir gently, cover, and simmer for about 10 minutes, until the meatballs are cooked through.

8. Serve the dish from the clay pot or transfer to a serving dish. Serve at once.

SERVES 4 AS A MAIN COURSE, 8 WITH OTHER DISHES

LETTUCE PARCELS

with Caramelized Grilled Pork Balls, Herbs, and Pineapple

One of the extraordinary features of Vietnamese cuisine are the "caramelized" dishes, coated in a rich syrupy mixture of slightly burnt sugar mixed with water or fish sauce. Unconventionally, I use the caramel mixture inside the meatballs and as a glaze.

These pork balls, with their burnished sweet, salty glaze are at their best when served in typically Vietnamese fashion—rolled up in a crisp, cool lettuce leaf together with diced cucumbers and herb sprigs, and dipped in tangy sauce. Another traditional way of serving the pork balls is for lunch on a bed of warm rice vermicelli, with the sauce on the side.

¼ cup sugar

3 tablespoons Asian fish sauce, such as nam pla

1 pound ground pork

¼ cup finely minced shallots

3 cloves garlic, minced

1 tablespoon minced fresh lemongrass (3 inches of the lower stalk, tough outer leaves discarded)

1½ teaspoons cornstarch

1 tablespoon finely chopped fresh mint leaves

1½ tablespoons finely chopped fresh cilantro leaves

½ teaspoon salt

½ teaspoon freshly ground black pepper

FOR SERVING

Boston lettuce leaves, washed and dried, halved if large

½ cup peeled, finely diced firm cucumber

½ cup finely diced firm, ripe pineapple

Fresh mint sprigs

Fresh cilantro sprigs

Vietnamese Tangy Lime Dipping Sauce (page 15)

1. Heat the sugar in a small heavy saucepan over medium-low heat, stirring until it is melted and an amber colored caramel, 3 to 4 minutes. Stir in the fish sauce,

standing back as the mixture will splatter and smoke. Stir until all the lumps are dissolved. Remove from the heat and cool a little.

2. In a large bowl, stir together the pork, half of the caramel mixture, the shallots, garlic, lemongrass, cornstarch, mint, cilantro, salt, and pepper. Chill for 1 hour and bring to room temperature before grilling.

3. Prepare coals for grilling or preheat the broiler.

4. With oiled hands, shape the pork mixture into 1½-inch meatballs.

5. Place the meatballs on an oiled rack or in a broiler pan and brush with the remaining caramel mixture. Grill or broil, turning once and brushing the other side with the caramel mixture, for about 4 minutes on each side.

6. To eat, place a meatball on a lettuce leaf, add some cucumber and pineapple and a sprig each of mint and cilantro, and wrap into a parcel. Dip the parcel in the Tangy Lime Dipping Sauce and eat.

SERVES 6

MINCED PORK CURRY

A mandatory standby at most eateries in the Thai city of Chiang Mai is this warm ground pork dip, served with an assortment of cooked or raw vegetables, pork

CHIANG MAI

To my mind, the northern Thai city of Chiang Mai, located near the Burmese and Laotian borders, is the country's most enchanting city. Like the culture of the old Lanna kingdom, the cuisine of the north has a place all its own—sturdy and straightforward, as befits the cooler hill climate. Although the temperature in the north is actually only ten or so degrees cooler than the steamy central and southern districts, every self-respecting Thai woman treats a visit to the north like a trip to Siberia. She makes a show of bringing along a hat and shawl, and on her return to the balmy suburbs of Bangkok, is sure to complain how she nearly froze on the "mountainous" hills of Chiang Mai.

rind (which you can pick up at Hispanic markets where it goes under the name of *chicharón*), or sticky rice, the traditional northern Thai staple. As this is not, strictly speaking, a Western-style dip, I like serving it as I would a curry or stew over sticky or long-grain rice or Oriental noodles.

5 dried hot red chiles (2 to 3 inches),
    preferably Asian
1½ tablespoons minced shallots
1 tablespoon chopped garlic
1 tablespoon grated fresh ginger
2 teaspoons minced lemon zest
1 tablespoon minced cilantro roots and/or
    stems
2 teaspoons anchovy paste
2 tablespoons peanut oil, or more as needed
12 ounces ground pork
1 tablespoon paprika
1 cup water
6 canned plum tomatoes, drained and
    chopped
2 teaspoons fresh lime juice
1 tablespoon Asian fish sauce, such as
    nam pla
2 teaspoons sugar
¼ cup chopped fresh cilantro leaves

1. Stem the chiles and shake out the seeds. Using scissors, cut the chiles into pieces. Soak in warm water to cover for 10 minutes. Drain well.

2. Using a mortar and pestle or a small food processor, grind or process the chiles, shallots, garlic, ginger, lemon zest, cilantro roots, and anchovy paste to a paste, adding a little oil if necessary to assist the blending.

3. Heat the oil in a large skillet over medium-high heat and cook the pork for 5 minutes, breaking it up with a fork. Pour off most of the fat from the pan. Add the chile paste and paprika, turn the heat down to medium, and cook, stirring, for about 5 minutes. Add the water and tomatoes and continue cooking until the liquid reduces a little, about 10 more minutes.

4. Stir in the lime juice, fish sauce, and sugar and cook for 1 more minute. Off the heat, stir in the cilantro leaves. Transfer to a bowl and serve warm.

SERVES 2 TO 3

A TOUCH OF KUCHING

Kuching has been the capital of the Malaysian state of Sarawak in Borneo since the British adventurer James Brooke — the first "white rajah"— established a remarkable, century-long family dynasty in the region in the mid-1800s.

It only got its name (which means "cat," probably in reference to the wild felines that roamed nearby) in 1872, from the second rajah, Charles Brooke (nephew of James), who was also responsible for building the white, shingle-roofed Astana Palace and a local fort (called Margherita after his wife) to guard against the incursions of the fearsome Borneo pirates.

The early history of the kingdom was woven from the improbable threads of eccentric, if enlightened, despotism and vivid utopian dreams of colonial wealth and power.

It took a long time, but Sarawak's mineral and timber industries have indeed made the city boom. Modern Kuching is seductively laced with hibiscus, the national flower of Malaysia, and Cana lilies, which are the special flowers of the Sarawak capital. The main artery is the Sarawak River, which bounds the town to the north. A few bright, pastel-colored *tambangs*, the gondolas of Sarawak, still glide from bank to bank.

Twenty years ago there were three hundred of these river taxis, mostly worked by inland farmers between produce runs. Anyone in Kuching will tell you that they have cost a fixed "10 cents" for more than a generation, that you hardly ever see them anymore, and that when you do, you'll find that the tariff has been raised (again)—a clear sign of the end of the world.

SIGHTSEEING ON FOOT

One of the best ways to see Kuching is to make a tour of its outstanding nineteenth- and early-twentieth-century buildings. The local tourist office has a helpful pamphlet showing where they are and describing their main features. Anya and I started with the oldest structure in town, the pseudo-Tudor Bishop's House built around 1849. From here we wandered down to Jalan Carpenter (Carpenter Street), then headed for a couple of blocks over to Jalan Tun Haji Openg. This street is home to several of Kuching's architectural curios, including the ostentatious post office, with its endless Corinthian portico, and the peculiarly fenestrated Pavilion building (1907), which, unusually, combines the architecture of the American South with hints of English Renaissance style. At the far end of the street, near the main bazaar, the profile of a perfect, white, crenellated tower is etched on the river bank. It used to serve as the local prison, and then as a fortress and a dance hall. These days the Square Tower, as the locals call it, looks like a leftover from a Disney film set.

The Tua Pek Kong ("Grand Uncle" Temple), dedicated to the Cantonese guardian deity Loh Hong Pek, is the oldest Chinese temple in Sarawak. It sits on a rise at the busy intersection of Padugan Road and Jalan Tunku Abdul Rahman, overlooking the river and facing the Matang Mountains, and has been gorgeously overrestored so that its pristine lintels and jambs look as if they were selected from the latest Lego catalog.

The best place for a quick lunch is the Permata Food Center in southern Kuching. Here are ranks of neat, clean numbered stalls, each surrounded by plastic-covered tables and chairs, selling a full range of the national and regional specialties. One booth offers the delicious local fiddle-head ferns *(paku),* which you can eat like sticks of green licorice. Another has them worked into an appetizing fresh salad or stir-fried with a little *sambal.*

Nearby you can find tapioca-leaf *(ubi)* dishes, delicious tuna curries, a wonderful salty dried fish called *goneng,* and young, sweet, and delicate coconut shoots with mild coconut curry. The tapioca leaves, which taste a bit like vine leaves, have to be boiled to remove any trace of bitterness and then mixed with coconut milk and a dash of tiny salty anchovies and chiles. When this is properly done they can rival the apples in anybody's paradise. We were in an adventurous mood, so we sat down and tried as many unfamiliar tastes as we could find.

Observing our good spirits and that we were enjoying the local food with such relish, the hospitable, garrulous owner of Warang Abshah (kiosk number 13) came over to our table, delivered an impromptu lecture on the variety of bananas in Kuching, and told us the "monkey story," an anecdote he evidently reserved—adding just the right touch of irony—especially for foreigners.

"You are just like a monkey eating *blachan,*" he announced in Malaysian, surveying our indiscriminate consumption with well-practiced culinary misgiving. Then he translated: "That means a person who doesn't know his own station in life." It was his way of telling us we were lost in a labyrinth of new flavors.

Chastened by such wisdom and deliriously full of a dozen unknown culinary sensations, we took an hour's rest before heading out for the Sarawak Museum. The museum is justly acclaimed as one of the great collections of Southeast Asia. Founded over a hundred years ago, the old wing, curiously designed in the style of a Normandy townhouse, opened its doors in 1891. The early collection was formed in consultation with some of the best minds of the day. In the 1850s, James Brooke invited Alfred Wallace, a contemporary of Darwin and author of *The Malay Archipelago,* to spend a couple of years in Sarawak, based in his fledgling capital.

The original building houses a fabulous collection of ritual and everyday objects made by the local peoples, dozens of compelling ethnographic photographs, and intriguing vitrines full of shells, local wildlife, Chinese ceramics, and head-hunting trophies. Connected by a pedestrian bridge that traverses the Jalan Tun Haji Openg, the modern new wing opened in 1983. Most of the ground floor is devoted to a standing exhibition on the anecdotal history of cats. As we had already discovered, the word *kuching* means "cat" in Malay, and no effort has been spared in this sprawling diorama of cat lore and legend to bring to life what is surely the best collection of feline ephemera in the world.

Alexandre Dumas's pet cat, who lived in a ménage à trois with the writer and his mother, would meet Dumas on the street corner every evening . . .

Did you know, for example, that Florence Nightingale had sixty cats at a time, and never in her later life traveled without one; that Isaac Newton may be considered the inventor of the catdoor; that Albert Schweitzer, the missionary, who was left-handed, often wrote prescriptions with his right hand so as not to disturb his cat Suzi, who was accustomed to sleeping on his better arm; that Victor Hugo fashioned an armchair in the shape of a throne for his favorite cat; that Mysouff I, Alexandre

Dumas's pet cat, who lived in a ménage à trois with the writer and his mother, would meet Dumas on the street corner every evening and walk home with him; that Samuel Johnson would personally fetch fresh oysters for the enjoyment of his cat, Hodge? You can learn all this, and very much more, roaming through the great Cat Show of Kuching.

BAKO NATIONAL PARK

On our third day in Kuching we took a day trip to the Bako National Park. Driving north out of the city for about twelve miles, we waited for a car ferry over the river, before going on to Bako village, a small fishing settlement whose river banks were festooned with shrimp nets and buzzing with small craft. The village was edged by untouched jungle, which curled around it on all sides like a slumbering python. From here we signed into the visitors' book for the park and took a motor launch to the mouth of the South China Sea.

The coastal scenery is spectacular. Fringes of the inland mountain tumble into the white-blue water.

There are solitary fishermen, more shrimp stations, and dramatic, tree-strewn cliffs. We entered the park through a channel lit up on either side by precious stands of mangrove swamp that jutted deliriously from what was now the sparkling brown water.

Bako National Park is perfect for a two-day trip with an overnight in one of the simple cabins located near the Visitor's Center. With just twenty miles of well-marked and vividly varied trails, a good hiker can take in most of the area in two energetic days. The coastal and sandstone plateau scenery is gorgeous, the beaches pristine and romantically isolated, and there is a good chance of seeing long-tailed macaques, monitor lizards, wild boars, and the proboscis monkeys native to Borneo. On the shoreline, you might find fluorescent-colored crabs, amphibious mud-skippers, and mangrove otters; and overhead a rare white-bellied sea eagle or a barbet in its coat of many colors.

Like everything you taste, see, and feel in Sarawak, the creatures that move through the land, sea, and sky are all seductively different. Sitting on the sand, watching the sun set over the South China Sea, we ended our journey somehow happy that Warang Abash at kiosk number 13 had compared our eating habits to those of the monkey. Perhaps it was really a compliment.

257

Straits Devil Curry

....

Grilled Chicken Curry with Yogurt

....

Chicken and Pineapple Curry

....

Roast Duck with Pineapple in Thai Red Curry Sauce

....

Pan-Fried Quail in a Rich Curry Sauce

....

Appam Rajastani Rabbit Curry

....

Fragrant Ceylonese Fish Curry

....

Black Pepper Bluefish Curry

....

Salmon in Thai Green Curry Sauce

....

Curried La-Las

....

Muslim-Style Thai Beef and Potato Curry

....

Lamb Korma

....

Tradewinds Lentil and Vegetable Curry

....

Eggplant and Raisin Tamarind Curry

CURRIES

If one goes by a simple dictionary definition, a curry is essentially a method of simmering meats or vegetables in a thick liquid based on a blend of spices and aromatics. But anyone who has set foot in an Indian or Southeast Asian kitchen knows that curry is at the core of a whole culinary philosophy, providing the flavor and structure for a world of cuisine. Most cooks who are at least superficially familiar with Asian food will tell you that a real curry has nothing to do with the commercial mixed powder one picks up from a supermarket shelf. A good curry always starts out with freshly ground spices and pounded aromatics, and there are as many curry spice blends as there are dishes and cooks.

Homemade curry blends are much more flavorful than commercial mixes and do not take a long time to prepare. (If using commercial curry powder, use the best available brand. The best powders are obtainable at Indian or Southeast Asian groceries. If a recipe calls for as much as 1 tablespoon of curry powder, without a doubt, you should make your own.

GETTING STARTED

Depending on the country and the specific dish, a curry blend might be "dry," containing just spices, such as turmeric, coriander, cumin, and chile, or "wet," comprised of such aromatics as onion, shallots, ginger, garlic, chiles, and herbs. Thai curry pastes are the most intricate, an unmistakable bouquet of cilantro roots, shallots, lemongrass, galangal, chiles, and shrimp paste—augmented by spices, which change from dish to dish.

The best and most authentic utensil for making wet curry blends is a large, granite mortar and pestle. It can not be stressed

enough how much the result differs from the machine processed pastes. Manual pounding of the aromatics opens their pores and releases their flavor, while at the same time retaining some texture. A food processor, on the other hand, tears and shreds the ingredients and also tends to liquefy them. Despite this, the food processor swept through Asian kitchens like an electric storm, so you will not be violating any codes of authenticity by reverting to it from time to time. Since some of the recipes in this chapter call for relatively large amounts of curry pastes, you'll also save yourself from exhaustion by using a processor. For smaller amounts of pastes, a mortar and pestle or a small processor is ideal. Shake it often as you process the paste and add a little water or oil, as needed—this will make the job easier. You can also use a blender, using the pulse button and scraping the ingredients often from the sides of the jar.

Every curry begins with the aromatics being slowly cooked in oil or clarified butter. First of all, slow cooking tempers the harsh, raw effects of onions, garlic, and certain spices, then it brings out their flavors to the full. When cooking a curry paste, let your nose be the judge. Many Asian cookbooks will simply instruct you to cook the curry paste until "fragrant." But only when your kitchen is completely filled with a fragrant aroma and the mixture loses its raw taste are you ready to add the other ingredients. The cooking should be done over low

261

FOR AN AUTHENTIC PRESENTATION

In Asia, leaving whole spices such as cinnamon sticks, star anise, cardamom pods, and bay leaves in a finished dish is a part of the presentation aesthetic. To me the presence of whole spices is both authentic and exotic, but if you don't feel like biting into a cardamom pod or a star anise, you can remove them before serving.

heat and will take anywhere from 5 to 10 minutes, depending on the composition and the amount of curry paste. Don't trust recipes that tell you to cook the paste for 1 or 2 minutes. Any Asian home cook will tell you that the longer they cook, the more flavorful they become. In fact a "raw"-tasting curry paste is considered downright embarrassing for the cook. The curry paste should be stirred often to prevent it from sticking to the pan, and a little oil should be added if it looks too dry.

Thai curry pastes are first simmered in a small amount of thick oily coconut milk. As Thai pastes are very pungent, again it is important to allow plenty of time for the flavors to mellow and develop. A Thai curry paste is ready to go when it becomes very aromatic and the coconut milk in which it cooks "cracks" as its oil begins to separate.

CURRY QUICKSTEPS

Once you have located a shop that carries Asian groceries and have stocked up on essential ingredients, making a curry paste or powder is not much more

involved than, say, making a pesto. With canned coconut milk in your cupboard and a curry paste in your refrigerator or freezer, whipping up a curry can be an almost "instant" meal. Once you have mastered a few basics, Southeast Asian flavors will open up a whole new way of looking at food.

Here are a few tips that will save you time and make your curries a success:

▲ Wet curry pastes will keep refrigerated in an airtight container for about 2 weeks and in a freezer for several months. Dry curry powders should also be stored in airtight containers in the refrigerator, where they will keep for about 1 month without losing the intensity of their flavor. So, it's unnecessary to prepare the curry paste or powder at the same time that you prepare the actual curry. When I set out to make a curry paste or powder, I always make several extra portions to refrigerate or freeze. Make sure you label your containers clearly and if you are freezing the pastes do so in the portions you are going to use for one meal. This will save you defrosting and refreezing the unused curries. Defrost the curry pastes in the refrigerator or at room temperature.

▲ It is customary in India and Southeast Asia to toast whole spices before they are ground to bring out extra flavor. Grinding your own spices is a great practice since, in general, whole spices usually keep longer, and grinding them yourself results in a much more intense flavor; you know you are really getting the most out of your spice. It is best to toast and grind each spice separately at your leisure and keep them in well-labeled containers. If you already have good-quality, freshly ground spices on hand, of course you do not have to grind them specially for a specific recipe.

▲ If you are serving a curry as part of a Southeast Asian meal, it is likely that you will be using ingredients such as chiles, garlic, ginger, and shallots in other dishes as well. Read all the recipes carefully ahead of time and see if they require similar ingredients, in which case, peel your garlic, chop your ginger, and seed your chiles all at once.

▲ Many home cooks and restaurant chefs in Southeast Asia and India keep their crucial ingredients separately, all pounded and ready to go. If you are an aficionado of Southeast Asian cookery, you can have the following ingredients on hand, each pounded to a paste and kept in a separate clean container with a tight-fitting lid: garlic, ginger, lemongrass, chiles. You will be surprised how easy life will be and how often you will be able to prepare your favorite dishes in no time at all. Pounded aromatics usually will keep in a refrigerator for up to 2 weeks, if you add a little oil.

▲ If you make your own coconut milk, it can be frozen. Just make sure you store thick and thin coconut milk (see page 386) in separate containers.

▲ If a finished curry requires a garnish or chopped ingredients to be added at the end, prepare them ahead of time and keep on hand.

STRAITS DEVIL CURRY

I first met the Malaysian chef Christobelle Savage when she was doing a Nonya food promotion as a guest chef at the Hyatt Hotel in Melbourne. "When you come to Malaysia," she promised, "call me straight from the airport and I will show you how to make *kari devil*," a signature dish of Melaka and a culinary relic from a century of Portuguese rule. The original dish, a sweet-and-sour tomato-based stew, was brought over by Portuguese sea captains and eventually augmented with a whole pantry of local spices and aromatics. Christobelle kept her promise. She presided like a sultan over a kitchen empire—replete with high-tech equipment and a veritable harem of kitchen help—at the Sri Melaka restaurant in the Hyatt International Resort just outside of Kuala Lumpur. It was there that she initiated me into the secrets of the Straits cuisine, before dispatching me to the Melakan Portuguese settlement to continue my education (see page 273).

CURRY PASTE

*7 fresh mild red chiles, such as fresno,
    stemmed, seeded, and chopped (if mild red
    chiles are not easily found, use a
    combination of 3 small hot red chiles,
    ¼ cup chopped red bell pepper, and 1
    tablespoon mild paprika)*
⅓ cup chopped shallots or red onion
1½ tablespoons chopped fresh ginger
6 cloves garlic, chopped
*3 stalks fresh lemongrass (3 inches of the
    lower stalk, tough outer leaves discarded),
    chopped*
*1 tablespoon chopped fresh or frozen galangal
    (optional)*
6 raw (if possible) macadamia nuts, ground

2½ pounds chicken pieces
6 tablespoons peanut oil, or more as needed
1 large onion, thinly sliced
2 teaspoons yellow mustard seeds
*About 3 cups Chicken Stock (page 384) or
    canned broth*
*3 medium boiling potatoes, peeled and
    quartered*
2½ tablespoons ketchup
2 tablespoons tomato paste
Salt, to taste
2 tablespoons distilled white vinegar
*2 teaspoons (packed) light brown sugar, or
    more to taste*
Fresh cilantro leaves, for garnish

1. Make the curry paste: Process all the ingredients to a paste in a food processor, adding a little water if necessary to assist the blending. Set aside.

2. Rinse the chicken pieces well and pat thoroughly dry with paper towels.

3. Heat 4 tablespoons of the oil in a large heavy skillet over medium heat. Brown the chicken pieces on all sides, about 7 minutes. Remove the chicken from the skillet to paper towels to drain.

4. Heat the remaining oil in a flameproof casserole or Dutch oven. Add the onion and cook, stirring, for 5 minutes. Add the curry paste and mustard seeds and cook over low heat, stirring, until it no longer tastes raw, 8 to 10 minutes. Add a little oil if the mixture begins to stick to the bottom of the casserole.

5. Transfer the chicken to the casserole and add enough stock to barely cover. Add the potatoes, ketchup, tomato paste, and salt. Simmer, partially covered, until the chicken and potatoes are tender, 35 to 40 minutes.

6. Stir in the vinegar and sugar to taste and simmer for another 10 minutes. Transfer to a serving platter and garnish with cilantro.

SERVES 4

TRULY THAI

If you are making Thai curries for the first time, I can promise you will want to make them again and again. So prepare a double batch of red, green, or Muslim curry paste to keep in your freezer and stock canned coconut milk in your cupboard. You'll find that any of the curries (and most other Thai dishes) in this book will taste infinitely better than most of what you will eat at your local Thai restaurant. This is often true even of the restaurants in Bangkok.

The reason is that 99 percent of Thai restaurants in the United States (and in Thailand), use ready-made purchased curry pastes, frozen poultry and meat, canned coconut milk, and instant sauces. The fact that it still tastes wonderful is a true testimony to the greatness of Thai cuisine. But once you begin cooking the Thai recipes in this book, chances are you might never want to go back to the restaurant.

C A S U A L   C U R R Y   S U P P E R

· · · · · · · · · · · · · ·

SALMON AND SPINACH PAKORAS

GRILLED CHICKEN CURRY
with Yogurt

SPICED RED LENTILS

CAROL SELVARAJAH'S VEGETABLE SALAD
with Kiwi and Pickled Ginger

BUTTERED BASMATI RICE

CARDAMOM-COFFEE MOUSSE

G R I L L E D
C H I C K E N   C U R R Y
W I T H   Y O G U R T

Inspired by the Indian tandoori favorite, chicken tikka, this is a delicious, light summertime curry of grilled chicken breast and roasted bell peppers, in a tangy yogurt sauce. It's also delicious made with grilled lamb or jumbo shrimp. Serve with Zucchini and Red Pepper Pilaf and Chickpea, Tomato, and Cilantro Salad with Toasted Cumin Vinaigrette (see Index).

CHICKEN

2 pounds plump skinless, boneless chicken breasts
3 large cloves garlic, crushed through a press
1 teaspoon ground turmeric
1 teaspoon ground cayenne pepper
1 teaspoon paprika
1½ tablespoons light olive oil (do not use virgin or extra-virgin)
Salt, to taste

2 red bell peppers, stemmed, seeded, and halved
2 green bell peppers, stemmed, seeded, and halved
1 small red onion, cut into thick slices
1 tablespoon light olive oil (do not use virgin or extra-virgin)
3 tablespoons ghee or vegetable oil, or more as needed
3 cups thinly sliced yellow onion
3 cloves garlic, crushed through a press
1½ tablespoons grated fresh ginger
1 teaspoon best-quality curry powder
½ teaspoon ground cayenne pepper
¾ teaspoon ground cumin
1 teaspoon ground coriander
1 teaspoon Garam Masala (page 390)
¾ teaspoon ground fennel seeds
¾ teaspoon ground turmeric
1¼ cups Chicken Stock (page 384), canned broth, or water
⅓ cup heavy (or whipping) cream
Salt, to taste
1 cup low-fat plain yogurt
¼ teaspoon sugar, or more to taste

1. Make the chicken: Rinse the breasts well and pat dry with paper towels. Place in a shallow dish.

2. In a small bowl, combine the garlic, turmeric, cayenne, paprika, oil, and salt. Pour over the chicken breasts and toss to coat.

Cover with plastic wrap and marinate in the refrigerator for 2 hours.

3. Prepare coals for grilling or preheat the broiler.

4. Grill or broil the chicken until charred on the outside and juicy inside, about 5 minutes per side. Remove from the grill and keep the grill or broiler hot. When cool enough to handle, cut the chicken into bite-size strips.

5. Brush the peppers and red onion slices with olive oil. Grill or broil the peppers until charred and soft, about 10 minutes, and the onion until slightly charred, about 7 to 10 minutes. Cut the onion slices in half and separate into half rings. Place the peppers in a plastic bag, wrap in a towel, and let stand for 10 minutes. Peel and cut into strips.

6. Heat the *ghee* or vegetable oil in a heavy flameproof casserole or Dutch oven over medium-low heat. Add the yellow onion and cook, stirring, until softened, about 8 minutes. Add the garlic, ginger, curry powder, cayenne, cumin, coriander, garam masala, fennel seeds, and turmeric and stir 2 minutes more, adding a bit more oil if the mixture sticks. Stir in the stock and cream, bring to a simmer, and cook, uncovered, for 10 minutes. Season with salt to taste.

7. Stir in the yogurt and simmer until heated through over low heat, without allowing it to boil. Stir in the grilled chicken, red onion and peppers and simmer for 5 minutes. Add sugar and additional salt, if needed.

SERVES 6

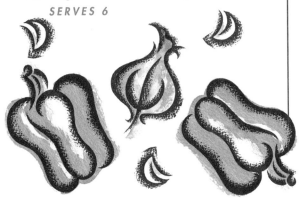

CHICKEN AND PINEAPPLE CURRY

This curry is inspired by a dish I tasted at Akkash, a tiny Fijian-Indian restaurant in an ethnic suburb of Sydney. John and I were dispatched there one Saturday evening by two of Sydney's most celebrated restaurateurs. Both chefs talked as vividly about Akkash as they did about their own menus. What's more, they took their own staffs there when they weren't working.

The place was painted in electric blue, and the owner's husband, a famous exiled musician, was pounding a tropical beat on a set of Fijian drums. The food was prepared by the owner and her mother in a tiny kitchen without even so much as a dishwasher. When I went in the back, the mother was stirring a curry in a black cauldron that looked like it belonged in another century. Her face had the studied concentration of an alchemist. "The secret of a good curry, luv," she said, "is to grind all the spices right before you add 'em to the dish." And so she did, using a grinding block and something resembling a rolling pin that looked as if it weighed a hundred pounds. She was preparing a Kashmiri chicken curry that she served to us with coconut rice.

Fiji has a large Indian population, and the food there is a blend of Indian spices and local tropical produce, such as this curry, which contains fresh pineapple and its juice and is sparked up with fresh cilantro. It's delicious over Coconut Rice (see Index).

CURRY BLEND

1 teaspoon cumin seeds

2 teaspoons coriander seeds

3 cardamom pods, preferably unbleached
   (green)

6 whole cloves

1 piece (1 inch) cinnamon stick

8 black peppercorns

½ teaspoon ground turmeric

½ cup chopped fresh cilantro leaves

½ onion, chopped

5 cloves garlic, chopped

1 tablespoon chopped fresh ginger

1 small fresh hot chile, green or red, with
   seeds, stemmed and chopped

Vegetable oil (optional)

5 tablespoons vegetable oil, or more as
   needed

1 chicken (2½ pounds), cut into serving
   pieces

2 large onions, thinly sliced

3 large cloves garlic, sliced

1½ tablespoons grated fresh ginger

1½ cups Chicken Stock (page 384) or
   canned broth

2 large firm, ripe tomatoes, peeled and
   seeded

½ cup unsweetened pineapple juice

Salt, to taste

1 cup diced fresh pineapple

2 teaspoons fresh lemon juice, or more
   to taste

¼ cup chopped fresh cilantro leaves

1. Make the curry blend: Heat a small skillet over medium heat. Add the cumin seeds, coriander seeds, cardamom pods, cloves, cinnamon stick, and peppercorns and toast, stirring occasionally, until fragrant, about 2 minutes. Cool the spices, then grind in a spice grinder with the turmeric until fine. Set aside.

2. Combine the cilantro, onion, garlic,

ginger, and chile in a food processor, and process to a paste, adding a little oil if necessary to assist the blending.

3. Rinse the chicken pieces well and pat thoroughly dry with paper towels.

4. Heat 3 tablespoons of the oil in a large heavy skillet over medium heat. Brown the chicken, in batches, for about 7 minutes and remove from the skillet with a slotted spoon. Drain on paper towels.

5. Heat the remaining oil in a large heavy flameproof casserole or Dutch oven over medium heat. Add the onion, garlic, and ginger and cook until the onion is translucent, about 7 minutes. Add the curry blend and stir for 1 minute. Add the cilantro paste and cook over very low heat, stirring, until it no longer tastes raw, about 7 minutes. Add oil, a little at a time, if the mixture begins to stick to the bottom of the casserole.

6. Add the stock, tomatoes, and pineapple juice, then season with salt and bring to a simmer over medium heat. Add the chicken, reduce the heat to low, and cook, covered, until the chicken is cooked through, about 35 minutes.

7. Remove the chicken from the casserole and keep warm. Reduce the cooking juices over high heat for 5 minutes. Stir in the pineapple, lower the heat to medium, and cook for another 5 minutes. Stir in the lemon juice and cilantro, then adjust the seasoning and return the chicken to the casserole, stirring to coat with the juices.

SERVES 4

KITCHEN AEROBICS

I got my red curry demonstration in the kitchens of the exquisite Benjarong restaurant, located in Bangkok's renowned Dusit Thani Hotel. It all seemed very simple: throw a few ingredients together into a heavy stone mortar and pound them into a paste. The pounding seemed especially easy when performed by the tiny lady sous chef. But when I gave it a go, the smiles on the faces of the kitchen staff turned into uncontrollable giggles as I struggled to lift the enormous heavy mortar, splattering bits of chile and garlic all over the kitchen. The polite head chef kindly suggested that the food processor, although far inferior to the traditional utensil, would make a perfectly acceptable substitute, unless I was particularly interested in developing the necessary arm muscles.

ROAST DUCK WITH PINEAPPLE

in Thai Red Curry Sauce

In Thailand, duck is prepared with great gusto in salads, soups, and curries. This curry crowns the repertoire of Thai curries, and is best prepared with purchased hacked Chinese roast duck, the most au-

thentic, simple, and delicious way to make this dish. However, for those who don't have a Chinese barbecue shop nearby, I include instructions for roasting the duck. It is a party dish par excellence and I love the leftover gravy spooned over carved roast turkey or roast pork loin. Serve the duck with Steamed Jasmine Rice (see Index).

½ large Chinese barbecue duck (about 3 pounds), hacked by the butcher into dainty serving pieces, or 1 uncooked duckling

3 cans (13½ ounces each) coconut milk, chilled upright

9 tablespoons Red Curry Paste (recipe follows), or 6 tablespoons purchased Thai red curry paste

4 tablespoons Asian fish sauce, such as nam pla

1½ tablespoons palm sugar or (packed) light brown sugar

1½ teaspoons fresh lime juice

10 cherry tomatoes, halved

10 Thai pea eggplants, or ½ cup fresh or frozen green peas, thawed if frozen

1 red bell pepper, stemmed, seeded, and julienned

1¼ cups ripe but firm pineapple wedges

1 cup torn fresh basil leaves, preferably Thai

6 kaffir lime leaves, cut into very fine shreds (if available)

Salt, to taste

2 tablespoons chopped fresh cilantro leaves, for garnish

1. If using purchased duck, omit this and step 2. For uncooked duck, preheat the oven to 400°F. Remove the excess fat from the duck's cavities, then rinse the duck well, and pat thoroughly dry with paper towels. Rub the duck, inside and out, with salt and pepper. Prick the skin all over with the tines of a fork. Place the duck on a rack in a roasting pan, breast side up, and roast for 20 minutes.

2. Reduce the oven temperature to 350°F. Pour off the accumulated fat and continue roasting until the duck is cooked through, 1¼ hours. (To test for doneness, prick the skin of the duck with a fork; the juices should run clear. And, the leg should twist easily in its socket.) Remove the duck from the oven, cover loosely with aluminum foil, and let rest for 10 minutes. Gently pat the duck with paper towels to remove excess fat. With a sharp large knife or a Chinese cleaver, cut the duck into bite-size pieces. Set aside.

3. Open the cans of chilled coconut milk. Carefully spoon out a total of 2 cups of the thick cream that has risen to the top, and place it in a large, heavy saucepan or wok. In a bowl, stir all the remaining coconut milk together, then measure out and reserve 2¾ cups, saving the rest for another use. Add 1 cup of water to the reserved coconut milk to make thin coconut milk.

4. Boil the thick coconut cream over medium-high heat until thickened and the oil begins to separate from the white solids, about 8 minutes. (Use a splatter screen if the cream splatters.) Stir in the curry paste and cook until the mixture looks cracked and no longer tastes raw, 7 to 8 minutes. Add the thin coconut milk, 1 tablespoon at a time, if the paste begins to stick.

5. Add the remaining thin coconut milk and bring to a simmer over medium heat. Add the duck and cook until heated through. Add the fish sauce, sugar, lime juice, tomatoes, eggplants or peas, bell pepper, and pineapple, and cook for 4 to 5 minutes. Stir in the basil, kaffir lime leaves, and salt, and cook for 1 minute more.

6. Garnish with cilantro leaves and serve the curry over rice.

SERVES 6 OR 8 WITH OTHER DISHES

Red Curry Paste

Red curry paste, made from dried red chilies and other Thai essentials, is a staple ingredient in the Thai kitchen. It's used not only as a base for red coconut curries, but in a whole range of classic dishes. You can use it as a flavor base for sauces, stir-fries, and marinades, add it to fish cake or meatball mixtures, or stir it into soups and stews to heighten the flavor.

If you like your food really hot, seed only half of the chiles. This recipe makes a rather large amount of the paste, which freezes well and is great to have on hand, so don't let the large amount of chiles alarm you. In any event, once the dried chiles are seeded and soaked, much of the heat will be gone.

1½ teaspoons Thai shrimp paste or
*   1 tablespoon anchovy paste*
24 to 26 dried hot red chiles (2 inches long),
*   preferably Asian*
½ cup chopped shallots or red onion
½ cup chopped garlic
¼ cup thinly sliced fresh lemongrass (3 inches
*   of the lower stalk, tough outer leaves*
*   discarded)*
1 tablespoon chopped peeled fresh or frozen
*   galangal, or fresh ginger*
3 tablespoons chopped cilantro roots and/or
*   stems*
2 teaspoons finely grated kaffir lime zest or
*   regular lime zest*
2 teaspoons white peppercorns, toasted and
*   ground*
1 teaspoon cumin seeds, toasted and ground
2 teaspoons coriander seeds, toasted and
*   ground*
1½ teaspoons paprika
1 teaspoon freshly grated nutmeg
1½ tablespoons peanut oil

1. If using shrimp paste, wrap it in a double layer of aluminum foil and dry-roast it in a heavy skillet over medium-high heat for 2 minutes on each side.

2. Cut the stems off the chiles and shake out the seeds. Using scissors, cut the chiles into 1½-inch lengths. Place in a bowl, cover with warm water, and soak for 20 minutes. Drain well, reserving 1 tablespoon of the soaking liquid.

3. In a food processor, in batches if necessary, purée the chiles with the reserved soaking liquid, the shrimp or anchovy paste, and all the remaining ingredients to a very fine paste. Scrape into a container with a tight-fitting lid. The paste will keep in the refrigerator for up to 2 weeks and in a freezer for up to 2 months.

MAKES ABOUT 1 CUP

PAN-FRIED QUAIL
in a Rich Curry Sauce

This preparation was inspired by a quail curry I saw demonstrated at the Thai Cooking School at the Oriental Hotel in Bangkok. Although I thought the aromatic sauce went very well with quail, since it is not a bird we eat often, it seemed a bit of a pity to drown its flavor completely in the sauce. I prefer to pan-fry the quail separately and serve it in a pool of the pink,

richly scented curry sauce. Ask your butcher to partially bone the quail for you, keeping the legs intact. And there is no reason why you shouldn't use the sauce with roast chicken, sautéed lamb or pork chops, or even fish. A good curry is democratic with respect to the meat used.

5 dried hot red chiles (2 inches long), preferably Asian
½ red bell pepper, stemmed, seeded, and chopped
6 cloves garlic, chopped
¼ cup chopped shallots
1 tablespoon chopped cilantro roots and/or stems
2 tablespoons chopped fresh ginger
1 tablespoon chopped fresh lemongrass (3 inches of the lower stalk, tough outer leaves discarded)
2 teaspoons grated lime zest
2 teaspoons grated lemon zest
1 teaspoon anchovy paste or mashed anchovies
4 tablespoons light olive oil (do not use virgin or extra-virgin), or more as needed
2 cups canned unsweetened coconut milk, well stirred
½ cup heavy (or whipping) cream
1 cup Chicken Stock (page 384) or canned broth
2 tablespoons Asian fish sauce, such as nam pla
1 teaspoon sugar, or more to taste
1 cup fresh basil leaves, preferably Thai
8 partially boned quail (6 to 8 ounces each, before boning)
⅓ cup all-purpose flour
½ teaspoon salt
Large pinch of cayenne

1. Make the sauce: Stem the chiles and shake out the seeds. Using scissors, cut the

chiles into pieces. Soak in warm water to cover for 10 minutes. Drain well.

2. Combine the chiles, bell pepper, garlic, shallots, cilantro, ginger, lime and lemon zests, and anchovy paste in a food processor, and process to a paste, adding a little of the olive oil if necessary to assist the blending. Set aside.

3. Cook 1 cup of the coconut milk in a large, heavy saucepan over medium-high heat until it thickens and the oil begins to separate, 8 to 10 minutes. (Use a splatter screen if the cream splatters.)

4. Add the chile paste to the coconut milk and cook over low heat, stirring, until the color deepens and the oil again begins to separate, about 7 minutes. Add a tablespoon of the remaining coconut milk if the mixture begins to look dry.

5. Stir in the remaining coconut milk, the cream, and stock and cook, uncovered, over medium heat for 10 minutes. Stir in the fish sauce, sugar, and half of the basil and remove from the heat. Keep warm while preparing the quail.

6. Rinse the quail well and pat thoroughly dry with paper towels.

7. Divide the 4 tablespoons olive oil between 2 large skillets and heat well over medium heat. On a large plate, mix the flour, salt, and cayenne. Roll the quail in the mixture and shake off the excess. Cook the quail, breast side first, until golden and cooked through, about 5 minutes on each side.

8. Place 2 quail on each serving plate. Stir the remaining ½ cup basil into the sauce and pour the sauce around the quail.

SERVES 4

APPAM RAJASTANI RABBIT CURRY

At Appam, an Indian restaurant in San Francisco, this curry, perfumed with sweet spices, is cooked in the ancient *Dumpokt* method—steamed in clay pots under a lid of dough. Here is a home-style version—less dramatic, but supremely flavorful. Serve with Buttered Basmati Rice or Tomato-Flavored Basmati Rice with Sweet Spices (see Index).

1 rabbit (about 2½ pounds), cut into
    smallish serving-size pieces
Salt, to taste
6 tablespoons canola oil
1½ cups thinly sliced onion
6 cardamom pods, preferably unbleached
    (green), crushed
2 bay leaves
1 cinnamon stick (3 inches)
1 tablespoon grated fresh ginger
1 tablespoon crushed garlic
1 teaspoon ground turmeric
    1½ teaspoons paprika
    ½ teaspoon freshly grated nutmeg, plus
        more for garnish
    ¾ teaspoon ground cumin
    1 cup finely chopped peeled fresh
        tomatoes
    ½ cup water
    ½ cup low-fat plain yogurt
    Pinch of sugar, or to taste
    Fresh cilantro leaves, for garnish

1. Rinse the rabbit pieces and pat thoroughly dry with paper towels. Rub the rabbit all over with salt.

2. Heat 2 tablespoons of the oil in a large heavy skillet over medium-high heat. Brown the rabbit pieces, in batches, until golden, 3 to 4 minutes on each side. Remove to paper towels to drain.

3. Wipe out the skillet and heat the remaining oil over medium-low heat. Add the onion and cook until softened, about 5 minutes. Add the cardamom, bay leaves, cinnamon stick, ginger, and garlic and cook for another 5 minutes. Add the turmeric, paprika, nutmeg, and cumin and stir until fragrant, about 1 minute.

4. Stir in the tomatoes and water and cook, stirring, until the tomatoes throw off their juice, about 7 minutes. Gently fold in the yogurt and sugar and stir to combine. Return the rabbit pieces to the skillet. Cover and cook, stirring occasionally, until the rabbit is tender, about 20 minutes.

5. Remove from the heat and let the curry rest for 1 to 2 hours. Reheat slowly and serve, garnished with cilantro leaves and a sprinkling of freshly grated nutmeg.

SERVES 4

FRAGRANT CEYLONESE FISH CURRY

The intriguing cuisine of Ceylon (Sri Lanka) is not exactly a Pacific one, but one that is a crucial bridge between Indian and Southeast Asian culinary traditions. This delicate fish curry, perfumed with lemongrass, is a typical Ceylonese blend of Indian and Asian influences. As the taste is mild and the preparation quite simple, this is a good dish for curry beginners, and a fine introduction to the joys of curry making in general. If you are near an Indian shop, it is worth inquiring whether they carry Ceylonese curry powder. It is similar to Indian, but includes certain Ceylonese spices, such as dried pandanus leaf, that make this dish even more heavenly.

For best results, make the curry a few hours before you are going to serve it. This allows the fish to soak up the delicious juices. Reheat slowly before serving time. A simple, colorful pilaf, such as Zucchini and Red Pepper Pilaf (see Index) is just the right match for this special dish.

4 firm, white fish steaks, such as snapper or halibut (about 6 ounces each), ¾ inch thick

1½ teaspoons ground turmeric

1 teaspoon salt, plus additional to taste

1 large onion, coarsely chopped

3 cloves garlic, chopped

2 teaspoons chopped fresh ginger

2 stalks fresh lemongrass (3 inches of the lower stalk, tough outer leaves discarded), chopped

2 medium firm, ripe tomatoes, chopped

1 small fresh hot chile, green or red, stemmed, seeded, and chopped

2½ tablespoons peanut oil, or more as needed

2 teaspoons ground coriander

1½ teaspoons ground cumin

2 teaspoons best-quality curry powder

1 cup canned unsweetened coconut milk, well stirred

1 cup Fish Stock (page 385)

1 tablespoon fresh lemon juice

1. Rinse the fish well and pat thoroughly dry with paper towels.

2. In a small bowl, combine the turmeric and salt. Rub the fish with the mixture and let stand for 10 minutes.

3. Combine the onion, garlic, ginger, lemongrass, tomato, and chile in a food processor, and process to a paste, adding a little oil if necessary to assist the blending.

4. In a heavy flameproof casserole or Dutch oven large enough to accommodate all the fish in one layer, heat 2 tablespoons of the oil over medium-high heat. Add the fish and cook for about 1 minute per side. Remove from the casserole to paper towels to drain.

5. Add the remaining oil to the saucepan and heat over medium-low heat for one minute. Add the coriander, cumin, and curry powder and stir for 1 minute until fragrant. Add the onion paste and cook, stirring, until it no longer tastes raw, about 7 minutes. Stir in the coconut milk and stock and bring the mixture to a simmer, stirring. Cook until the mixture thickens a little, about 7 minutes, and add the lemon juice.

6. Add the fish and gently stir it in so that it is submerged in the liquid. Cover and simmer over low heat until the fish is cooked through and flakes when tested with a fork, about 6 minutes. Do not overcook. With a metal spatula carefully transfer the fish to a deep serving dish and spoon the sauce over it.

SERVES 4

BLACK PEPPER BLUEFISH CURRY

For Auntie Belle's (see box, facing page) fish curry recipe, I like to use bluefish, whose taste has a hint of the slightly oily *ikan tengiri,* or Spanish mackerel, used in the region. The tart tamarind sauce will cut nicely across its rich texture. Serve over rice.

2 pounds thick skinless bluefish fillets, cut
    into 2½-inch pieces
1½ teaspoons ground turmeric
Salt, to taste
2½ cups Fish Stock (page 385) or bottled
    clam juice
1½ tablespoons tamarind pulp, preferably
    from Thailand
6 dried red chiles (2 inches), preferably Asian
¼ cup chopped shallots or red onion
5 large cloves garlic, chopped
3 tablespoons chopped red bell pepper
1 tablespoon chopped fresh ginger
1½ teaspoons anchovy paste or mashed
    anchovies
¼ cup ground raw (if possible) macadamia
    nuts
3½ tablespoons peanut oil, plus more for
    deep frying the okra
1 tablespoon cracked or coarsely ground
    black pepper
¾ cup canned unsweetened coconut milk,
    well stirred
1½ cups fresh okra, trimmed
3 firm, ripe plum tomatoes, peeled and
    quartered
1½ teaspoons sugar, or more to taste
Fresh cilantro or mint leaves, for garnish

AUNTIE BELLE

Before Christobelle Savage (otherwise known as Auntie Belle) became a celebrity chef and went to cook for golfers and rajas at the posh Sri Melaka restaurant in the Hyatt International resort near Kuala Lumpur, she lived with her large family in the Portuguese settlement of Melaka. When I came for a cooking demonstration at her kitchens at the Hyatt, she made plans to continue my culinary apprenticeship at her house in Melaka, where she went once a week to visit her husband and children. The house didn't have a phone, but she instructed John and me to appear on the main square of the Portuguese settlement and ask for Auntie Belle. "An' you better sleep at my house," she said emphatically. "You didn't come all the way to Malaysia to be stuck in a hotel, like a couple of pigeons in a cage."

We did exactly as she suggested. When we appeared on the square, we were greeted by a group of young men, stretched out on the shady pavement, playing dominoes. All of them turned out to be related in one way or another to Auntie Belle. Yes, they were expecting us, a couple from Australia in search of the best "devil curry."

"Auntie Belle did not come after all," they apologized. "She had to cook a function for a top, top VIP, we think a sultan." They lowered their voices. "But the whole family is waiting, and her daughter Elizabeth will show you the special black pepper curry, which she makes as well as Auntie Belle herself."

Elizabeth insisted that the delicious tart fish curry with okra and tomatoes that she was preparing for us that afternoon was typically Portuguese-Malay, but the minute I spotted the okra and tamarind I recognized that it also had southern Indian influences, typical in this land of culinary exchange and appropriation. The dish, which combined three food cultures, was an extraordinary introduction to Malaysia's multiethnic cuisine.

1. Rinse the fish pieces well and pat thoroughly dry with paper towels. Rub the pieces with 1 teaspoon of the turmeric and sprinkle with salt. Let stand for 15 minutes.

2. Heat 1 cup of the stock; pour over the tamarind pulp in a bowl. Soak for 15 minutes. Stir and mash the pulp with a fork to help it dissolve. Strain through a fine strainer into a bowl, pressing on the solids with the back of a wooden spoon to extract all the liquid.

3. Stem the chiles and shake out the seeds. Using scissors, cut the chiles into pieces. Soak in warm water to cover for 10 minutes. Drain well.

4. Combine the chiles, shallots, garlic, bell pepper, ginger, anchovy paste, and macadamia nuts in a food processor and process to a paste, adding a little water if necessary to assist the blending.

5. Heat 2 tablespoons of the oil in a large skillet over medium heat and brown the fish on both sides for about 3 minutes. Drain on paper towels and set aside.

6. Heat the remaining oil in a heavy flameproof casserole or Dutch oven over low heat. Add the chile paste and black pepper and cook until the mixture no longer tastes raw, about 7 minutes. Add a little oil if the mixture begins to stick to the bottom of the casserole.

7. Add the tamarind liquid, the remaining fish stock, and the coconut milk and bring to a simmer over low heat. Cook, uncovered, for 10 minutes.

8. Pour oil to a depth of 1 inch in a heavy, medium-size skillet and heat over medium-high heat to 360°F. Deep-fry the okra, in batches, until light golden. Transfer with a slotted spoon to paper towels to drain.

9. Return the fish to the casserole along with the okra, tomatoes, and sugar. Cook for 5 minutes longer. Garnish with cilantro or mint and serve.

SERVES 4 TO 6

SALMON IN THAI GREEN CURRY SAUCE

If you make the green curry paste yourself and follow the recipe carefully, you will end up with a curry that is infinitely superior to anything you might have encountered under this rubric, even in the best Thai restaurants, both here and in Thailand.

Green curry sauce is also excellent with chicken or seafood. To make it with chicken, substitute 1½ pounds boneless chicken breasts, cut into bite-size strips, for the salmon. The chicken will take about 8 to 10 minutes to cook. To make it with seafood, use 1½ pounds of shrimp or scallops, or a combination, and cook for about 4 to 5 minutes in total. This recipe can eas-

ily be doubled for a large crowd. Serve any green curry with Steamed Jasmine Rice. (see Index).

> 2 cans (13½ ounces each) unsweetened coconut milk, one of the cans refrigerated upright (the other can remain in the cupboard)
> ½ cup water
> 7 tablespoons Green Curry Paste (recipe follows)
> 1½ pounds boneless skinless salmon fillets, cut into 2-inch chunks
> 2 teaspoons palm or (packed) light brown sugar, or more to taste
> 3 tablespoons Asian fish sauce, such as nam pla
> 1 tablespoon fresh lime juice
> Salt, to taste
> 1 red bell pepper, stemmed, seeded, and julienned
> ¾ cup drained canned straw mushrooms, or ½ cup sliced white mushrooms
> 8 to 10 Thai pea eggplants, or 5 white Thai eggplants, quartered (optional)
> ½ cup torn basil leaves, preferably Thai
> 3 kaffir lime leaves, finely shredded

1. Open the refrigerated can of coconut milk and spoon off ¾ to 1 cup of the cream that has risen to the top. Place it in a large, heavy saucepan or wok. Before opening the can from the cupboard, shake it well. In a bowl, combine the rest of the milk in the refrigerated can with ½ cup of the milk from the cupboard can, then stir in the water.

2. Boil the thick coconut cream over medium-high heat until it thickens and the oil begins to separate from the white solids, about 8 minutes. (Use a splatter screen if it splatters.) Stir in the curry paste and cook, stirring, until the curry looks cracked and no longer tastes raw, 7 to 8 minutes. Add the thin coconut milk, 1 tablespoon at a time, if the paste begins to stick.

3. Add the salmon and stir for 2 minutes. Stir in the remaining thin coconut milk and cook, uncovered, until the salmon is cooked through, about 5 minutes. Stir in the sugar, fish sauce, lime juice, and salt and cook for 2 minutes. Add the bell pepper, mushrooms, eggplants, and basil and lime leaves and cook for 2 minutes more.

S E R V E S   6

Note: The beauty of Thai green curry is the intense herby freshness of the paste, which is all but lost by using commercial paste. If you want to use purchased curry paste for this recipe, use only about 4 tablespoons (as it tends to be very pungent) and freshen it up with 2 tablespoons of pounded fresh cilantro roots and/or stems.

THAI CURRIES

Thai curries are made with thick and thin coconut milk, the oily thick milk being used as a medium in which to cook the curry paste until it loses its harsh "raw" taste. A proper thick coconut milk is difficult to reproduce at home, but the thick cream that rises to the surface of canned coconut milk is quite suitable. Therefore I prefer to make Thai curries with canned milk.

Green
Curry Paste

The intensely flavored aromatic green curry paste, *nam prig gaeng khiew warn*, is the flavor base for Thai green curry

dishes, which are superb when made with seafood, or chicken—although the Thais also prepare it with beef or duck.

1 teaspoon Thai shrimp paste, or 2 teaspoons anchovy paste
3 tablespoons chopped, seeded, small hot green chiles
4 large fresh mild green chiles, such as Anaheim, seeded and chopped
½ cup chopped red onion
6 large cloves garlic, chopped
3 large stalks fresh lemongrass (3 inches of the lower stalk, tough outer leaves discarded), chopped
1 tablespoon frozen or fresh chopped galangal, or fresh ginger
2 tablespoons chopped cilantro stems and/or roots
2 teaspoons freshly ground white peppercorns
1½ teaspoons ground coriander
½ teaspoon ground cloves
Grated zest of 1 lime, preferably kaffir
1 tablespoon peanut oil, or more if needed

1. If using shrimp paste, wrap it in a double layer of aluminum foil and dry-roast it in a heavy skillet over medium-high heat for 2 minutes on each side.

2. In a food processor, in batches if necessary, purée the shrimp or anchovy paste with all the remaining ingredients to a very fine paste. If necessary, add a little more oil to assist the blending. Scrape into a container with a tight-fitting lid. The paste will keep in the refrigerator for up to 2 weeks and in a freezer for up to 2 months.

MAKES ABOUT 1 CUP

CURRIED LA-LAS

The waters of Southeast Asia abound in all kinds of clams, from the tiny periwinkles, so wonderful when bathed in black bean sauce, to the oblong *la-las* (razor clams), which are often cooked in one or another type of curry. The best *la-la* curry I tasted was at a street stall in Kuching, the capital of the jungle state of Sarawak, in Malaysian Borneo. To accompany the curry we had young, delicate coconut shoots, cooked in turmeric-hued coconut sauce, and *paku*, a buttery textured indigenous jungle fern, stir-fried with a blistering sauce of dried chiles and salty shrimp paste.

I recommend razor clams for this dish, but it will also work with Manila clams or littlenecks. For a Western touch, I like to add a little white wine and cream to the aromatic curry mixture. Serve these in deep bowls for an appetizer or light main course, with crusty bread to sop up the juices or over pasta, Chinese noodles, or steamed rice.

1 tablespoon unsalted butter
1 tablespoon canola or peanut oil
¼ cup chopped shallots
3 cloves garlic, minced
2 fresh hot chiles, green or red, stemmed, seeded, and minced
1½ teaspoons best-quality curry powder
⅓ cup dry white wine
½ cup heavy (or whipping) cream
1 cup Fish Stock, Light and Aromatic Shrimp Stock (both page 385), or bottled clam juice
Salt, to taste
1½ teaspoons fresh lemon juice, or to taste
1½ pounds razor clams, cleaned, shelled, and halved crosswise, or 2 pounds Manila or littleneck clams, shells well scrubbed under cold running water
1 large red bell pepper, cut into strips
1 fresh mild green chile, such as Anaheim, stemmed, seeded, and cut into strips
1 cup fresh baby corn or sliced canned bamboo shoots
¾ cup fresh or frozen green peas, thawed if frozen
2 tablespoons fresh cilantro leaves, for garnish

1. Melt the butter in the oil in a deep, heavy skillet over medium-low heat. Add the shallots, garlic, and chiles and cook over low heat until the shallots are translucent, about 3 minutes. Add the curry powder and cook, stirring, for 1 minute.

2. Raise the heat to high, add the wine, and reduce for 3 minutes. Stir in the cream and fish stock and cook over medium heat until slightly thickened and reduced, 5 to 7 minutes. Season with salt and add lemon juice to taste.

3. Stir in the clams, bell pepper, mild chile, corn, and peas and cook until the razor clams, if using, are tender, 3 to 4 minutes. (If using Manilas or littlenecks, cook, covered, shaking the skillet, until the clams open, about 5 minutes. Discard any that do not open.)

4. Divide the clams among 4 bowls and spoon the liquid and vegetables on top. Garnish with cilantro leaves.

SERVES 4

MUSLIM-STYLE THAI BEEF
and Potato Curry

Mussaman, the name of this southern Thai curry paste, translates as "Muslim." The sweet spices in the paste—mace, cardamom, and cloves—reveal the Indian influences that spread into Thailand from Muslim Malaysia via the Isthmus of Kra—a narrow strip of land that connects the country to the Malay Peninsula.

THE OLD-FASHIONED WAY

David Thompson, a chef I met in Sydney, Australia, lived in Thailand, learned the language and has dedicated his life to recreating true Royal Thai cuisine which, with the introduction of pre-prepared curry mixes and canned coconut milk, is all but extinct. His bold, vibrant flavors come from years of research and the lengthy and painstaking preparation on which the cuisine relies.

When he gave me the recipe for Muslim-Style Thai Beef and Potato Curry, David emphatically insisted that the onions and potatoes should be deep fried before they are added to the curry, so that their texture is maintained. When I went to buy the ingredients in my neighborhood Thai grocery in New York, the owner, in her usual fashion, inquired what I was cooking. "Gaeng mussaman," I told her cheerfully. She twisted her face in an expression of polite compassion. As I fended off her offers of canned coconut milk and instant mussaman paste, she asked me, as she often does, how exactly I was going to execute the recipe. I began reciting David's recipe for her, and when I got to the part about deep-frying all the ingredients first, the polite look on her face turned to true horror. In Thailand cooking carries little prestige, and it was obviously inconceivable to her that a relatively young woman, who didn't seem to be at the very bottom of the social ladder, was prepared to spend this amount of time in the kitchen, instead of pursuing more noble endeavors, such as rearing children or opening a small business. "Fry too much, just boil, okay," she pronounced decisively. I thought long and hard about this and decided that roasting the onions and potatoes would be an acceptable compromise. Try this delicious curry (see above)—and I think you'll agree.

The recipe for this historic dish comes from Sydney chef David Thompson. For best results, prepare the curry a day ahead. If you do it this way, the peanuts and pineapple should be added after you have reheated the dish. The curry paste can be made way ahead of time and refrigerated or frozen. Serve the curry over Steamed Jasmine Rice (see Index).

3 cans (13½ ounces each) coconut milk, chilled upright

5 tablespoons peanut oil

4 pounds beef round, cut into 1½-inch chunks

1 cinnamon stick (3 inches)

Salt, to taste

8 medium potatoes, peeled and quartered

1½ pounds pearl onions, blanched and peeled

3 tablespoons tamarind pulp, preferably from Thailand

½ cup boiling water

¾ cup Mussaman Curry Paste (recipe follows)

⅓ cup Asian fish sauce, such as nam pla

2½ tablespoons palm sugar or (packed) light brown sugar

5 bay leaves

½ cup whole roasted peanuts

¾ cup diced fresh pineapple, puréed in a food processor

1. Open the cans of coconut milk and spoon off 1¾ cups of the thick cream that has risen to the top. Place in a bowl, cover, and refrigerate until ready to use. Measure the rest of the canned milk, and place it in another bowl with enough water to make 6 cups. Set aside.

2. Heat 3½ tablespoons of the oil in a large, heavy flameproof casserole or Dutch oven over medium-high heat. Brown the beef, in batches, until well browned on all sides,

about 10 minutes. Remove to paper towels to drain and wipe out the casserole.

3. Return the beef to the casserole and add the thin coconut milk and cinnamon stick and bring to a boil over medium heat. Reduce the heat to low, season with salt, and simmer, covered, until the beef is tender, about 1½ hours. While the beef is simmering, prepare the next steps.

4. Preheat the oven to 350°F.

5. Place the potatoes and onions on a large baking sheet, brush with the remaining oil, and bake until the onions are browned, about 25 minutes. Remove the onions from the baking sheet and continue to roast the potatoes until tender, another 10 minutes.

6. While the vegetables are cooking, soak the tamarind pulp in the boiling water off the heat for 15 minutes. Stir and mash it with a fork to help it dissolve. Strain through a fine strainer into a bowl, pressing on the solids with the back of a wooden spoon to extract all the liquid. Set aside.

7. When the beef is almost cooked, cook the thick coconut cream in a large, heavy saucepan over medium-high heat until it thickens and the oil begins to separate, 8 to 10 minutes. (Use a splatter screen if the cream splatters.)

8. Stir the curry paste into the coconut cream and cook over medium heat, stirring often, until the mixture is very fragrant and the color deepens, about 10 minutes. Add some of the cooking liquid from the beef if the mixture looks dry. Stir in the tamarind liquid, fish sauce, and sugar and cook, stirring constantly, for 5 more minutes.

9. Add the curry-coconut mixture to the beef and stir to combine. Add the potatoes, onions, and bay leaves and simmer for 5 to 7 minutes for the flavors to blend. Stir in the peanuts and pineapple purée and simmer for 2 minutes to heat through before serving.

SERVES 8 TO 10

Mussaman Curry Paste

This fragrant paste, made from dry-roasted aromatics, is also delicious stirred into stews or sauces to heighten the flavor. This paste will keep, tightly covered and refrigerated, for up to 2 weeks, or it can be frozen for up to 2 months.

2 teaspoons Thai shrimp paste, or 4 teaspoons
   anchovy paste
15 dried red chiles (2 inches long), preferably
   Asian
1½ cups sliced red onion
1 cup sliced garlic (about 2 small heads)
1 tablespoon white peppercorns
2 tablespoons coriander seeds
Seeds from 7 cardamom pods
1 tablespoon cumin seeds
1½ teaspoons ground mace
½ cup sliced fresh lemongrass (3 inches
   of the lower stalk, tough outer leaves
   discarded)
½ cup chopped cilantro roots and/or stems
¼ cup chopped fresh or frozen galangal
   (optional)
1 piece (3 inches) fresh ginger, chopped
2 teaspoons salt
Peanut oil (optional)

1. If using shrimp paste, wrap it in a double layer of aluminum foil and dry-roast it in a heavy skillet over medium-high heat for 2 minutes on each side.

2. Stem the chiles and shake out the seeds. Using scissors, cut the chiles into pieces. Soak in warm water to cover for 10 minutes. Drain well.

3. Heat a wok or heavy skillet over medium heat. Add the onion, garlic, and chiles and stir until just softened and slightly charred, about 6 minutes. You might have to do this in batches.

4. Toast the peppercorns, coriander seeds, cardamom seeds, and cumin seeds in a small skillet over low heat, stirring until browned and fragrant, about 3 minutes. Grind in a spice grinder until fine.

5. In a medium-size bowl, combine the onion mixture, toasted spices, the mace, lemongrass, cilantro, galangal, ginger, and salt. Working in batches, process the mixture to a fine paste in a food processor. Use small amounts of oil if necessary to assist the blending.

**MAKES ABOUT
1½ CUPS**

LAMB KORMA

This mild Indian *korma* curry, rich with sweet spices and coconut milk, is a classic in Malaysia, where it is often served not with rice, which I suggest here, but with a delicious layered fried bread, called *roti chanai*. Don't be put off by the long list of ingredients; most of them are easily obtainable spices and aromatics. You can make the spice paste up to several days ahead of time. Keep it covered in the refrigerator.

SPICE PASTE

6 shallots, chopped

7 large cloves garlic, chopped

1 piece (2 inches) fresh ginger, chopped

1½ teaspoons freshly ground white pepper

1 tablespoon fennel seeds, ground (preferably freshly ground)

1½ teaspoons ground cumin seeds

1½ teaspoons ground coriander seeds, preferably freshly ground

1 teaspoon paprika

½ teaspoon ground cayenne pepper

5½ tablespoons peanut oil, or more as needed

1½ cups sliced onion

2 cloves garlic, sliced

2 teaspoons grated fresh ginger

1½ tablespoons homemade (page 390) or best-quality curry powder

1½ cups canned unsweetened coconut milk, well stirred

1 cup water

2½ pounds boneless lamb shoulder, cut into 1½-inch chunks

1 star anise, broken into points

6 cardamom pods, preferably unbleached (green), lightly crushed

1 cinnamon stick (3 inches)

½ teaspoon freshly grated nutmeg

Salt, to taste

¼ cup low-fat plain yogurt

Fried Shallots (page 389), for garnish, optional

Julienned red bell pepper, for garnish

Scallion flowers, for garnish (see Note, page 135)

1. Make the spice paste: Combine the shallots, garlic, ginger, white pepper, fennel, cumin, coriander, paprika and cayenne in a food processor and process to a paste, adding a little water to assist blending. Set aside.

2. Heat 3 tablespoons of the oil in a large, heavy flameproof casserole, Dutch oven, or heavy skillet over low heat. Add the onion, garlic, and ginger and cook, stirring, for 5 minutes. Add the curry powder and stir for 1 minute. Add the spice paste and cook over very low heat, stirring, until the mixture no longer tastes raw, about 7 minutes. Add a little oil if the mixture begins to stick to the bottom of the casserole.

3. Stir in the coconut milk and cook over medium heat, stirring, for 5 minutes. Stir in the water and cook for another 5 minutes.

4. While the sauce is cooking, heat the remaining oil in a large skillet and brown the lamb lightly in batches. Remove to paper towels to drain well.

5. Add the lamb to the sauce along with the star anise, cardamom, cinnamon stick, and nutmeg. Season with salt. Reduce the heat to low, cover, and simmer for 1 hour. Uncover and continue cooking, stirring, until the lamb is very tender, about 30 minutes more. Stir in the yogurt and simmer for 5 minutes more.

6. Serve the curry garnished with fried shallots, julienned bell pepper, and scallion flowers.

SERVES 6

TRADEWINDS LENTIL AND VEGETABLE CURRY

When I tasted this tart soupy North-ern Indian curry at Tradewinds restaurant in Singapore, I knew this was a dish I wanted to cook often, just for myself and close friends for a cozy, unpretentious Sunday dinner. Some versions of this dish use small amounts of lamb or chicken to enhance and deepen the flavor. Red lentils can be used instead of brown. Serve with Buttered Basmati Rice and a cooling Raita (see Index).

½ cup brown or red lentils

2 tablespoons tamarind pulp, preferably from Thailand

2½ cups boiling water

Vegetable oil, for frying

1 pound slender Chinese or Japanese eggplants, halved lengthwise and cut into 1½ inch pieces

2 medium onions, thinly sliced

1 tablespoon grated fresh ginger

1 tablespoon minced garlic

1½ tablespoons homemade (page 390) or best-quality curry powder

½ to 1 teaspoon pure chile powder, to taste

4 fresh or dried curry leaves (optional)

2 fresh hot red chiles, stemmed, seeded, and halved

3 fresh mild green chiles, such as Anaheim, stemmed, seeded, and cut into chunks

2 slender carrots, peeled and cut into 3-inch lengths

2 medium potatoes, peeled and cut into large dice

1¼ cups canned unsweetened coconut milk, well stirred

4 medium firm, ripe tomatoes, peeled and cut into large chunks

2 teaspoons sugar, or more to taste

Salt, to taste

¼ cup chopped fresh cilantro leaves, for garnish

1. Place the lentils in a strainer and rinse under cold running water. Place in a bowl and soak in warm water to cover for 2 hours. Drain well and set aside. If using red lentils, pick over carefully and soak for only 30 minutes.

2. Soak the tamarind pulp in the boiling water off the heat for 15 minutes. Stir and mash it with a fork to help it dissolve. Strain through a fine strainer into a bowl, pressing on the solids with the back of a wooden spoon to extract all the liquid.

3. Pour oil to a depth of 1½ inches into a large, heavy flameproof casserole or Dutch oven and heat over medium-high heat to 360°F. Add the eggplant, in batches, and cook until softened, about 7 minutes. Remove with a slotted spoon and drain on paper towels.

4. Pour off all but 3 tablespoons of oil from the casserole, and reduce the heat to low. Add the onions, ginger, and garlic and cook, stirring, until the onions are softened, about 7 minutes. Add a little more oil if the mixture sticks to the bottom.

5. Add the curry and chile powders, curry leaves, if using, and red and green chiles and stir for 2 minutes. Add the carrots and potatoes and stir for about 5 minutes. Add the lentils and eggplants, then stir in the coconut milk, tamarind liquid, and tomatoes. Bring to a simmer, cover, and cook until the potatoes and lentils are tender, about 20 minutes. Add the sugar and correct the seasoning.

6. Serve hot or warm, garnished with the cilantro.

SERVES 4 TO 6

EGGPLANT AND RAISIN TAMARIND CURRY

This curry with its winning combination of sweet, sour, and spicy flavors is one of my absolutely favorite ways to prepare eggplant. Serve it as a part of a curry meal, or as an accompaniment to grilled poultry or meat. It is also excellent at room temperature. When cooking the eggplant, make sure you drain it thoroughly of all excess oil. If you like, you can grill the eggplant slices instead of frying them.

2 eggplants (about 1½ pounds total), sliced medium thick

1½ tablespoons tamarind pulp, preferably from Thailand

Coarse (kosher) salt

⅔ cup water

¼ cup plus 3 tablespoons peanut oil

2 cups thinly sliced onion

3 cloves garlic, crushed through a press

1 tablespoon grated fresh ginger

1 teaspoon ground coriander

½ teaspoon best-quality curry powder

¼ teaspoon ground cayenne pepper, or more to taste

½ teaspoon freshly ground black pepper

Pinch of ground cinnamon

½ cup golden raisins

1½ teaspoons (packed) light brown sugar, or more to taste

Salt, to taste

½ teaspoon Garam Masala (page 390)

Fresh cilantro leaves, for garnish

1. Place the eggplant in a colander, sprinkle with the coarse salt and leave for 30 minutes. Rinse thoroughly and dry well with paper towels.

2. Soak the tamarind pulp in ⅓ cup boiling water, off the heat, for 15 minutes. Stir and mash it with a fork to help it dissolve. Strain through a fine strainer into a bowl, pressing on the solids with the back of a wooden spoon to extract all the liquid.

3. Heat ¼ cup of the oil in a large, deep skillet over medium heat. In batches, cook the eggplant until golden on both sides, about 7 minutes per batch, transferring the cooked eggplant to paper towels to drain. Drain thoroughly, changing the paper towels with each batch.

4. Heat the remaining oil in a large, heavy flameproof casserole or Dutch oven, over medium heat. Add the onion and cook, stirring, until golden, about 10 minutes. Reduce the heat to low. Add the garlic, ginger, coriander, curry powder, cayenne, black pepper, and cinnamon and stir for 1 minute.

5. Add the remaining water, tamarind liquid, raisins, and sugar and salt to taste and simmer over low heat until the mixture reduces and thickens, 5 to 7 minutes. Add the eggplant slices, tossing them gently in the sauce, and simmer for another 5 minutes. Add the garam masala and cook for another minute. Serve garnished with cilantro leaves.

SERVES 4 TO 6

A TIFFIN AT RAFFLES

If we had to name the most classic, enduring, and beloved colonial institution in Singapore, it would certainly be the Sunday tiffin curry lunch at Raffles Hotel. This is as true in the 1990s as it was a century ago. The great storyteller Rudyard Kipling didn't mince words after visiting the hotel's restaurant: "Feed at Raffles when visiting Singapore," he said. That was all, and that was enough.

The origin of the tiffin lunch lies in the first days of colonialism. The word "tiffin" refers to a stacked series of containers used to carry and deliver hot lunches. The tradition began in India and caught on like wildfire throughout the British colonies, eventually becoming synonymous with lunch itself. The male Europeans working in Singapore for one of the many colonial companies or burgeoning government institutions, usually came out on three- or four-year contracts. They were typically forbidden to get married until two contracts had elapsed, sometimes as long as eight years. Until then they were condemned to live in "messes," shabby shared bachelor flats that provided them only half-board. The wealthier workers could afford an *amah* (housekeeper), who would stuff tiffin carriers with curries and delicacies. The rest had to eat their tiffin out, and Raffles served the tiffin of choice.

THE GOOD LIFE

Before World War I, colonial clerks and businessmen in Singapore arrived at their offices at or before six in the morning, and would typically leave at around one in the afternoon. The hours from two to four were jealously reserved for the tiffin. During tiffin time, no one could be contacted or called, and no business whatsoever conducted. After lunch the happy workers would take a nap stretched out on planter chairs provided by Raffles Hotel. By late afternoon, when the heat subsided, they would go to the *padang* (square), the social center of old Singapore. Here they would swap gossip and play croquet until high tea, at six o'clock.

east monsoon to blow them back.

As the tradition developed, British clubs and colonial hotels served table d'hôte buffet tiffin lunches on weekends, too. As one crusty old account put it, these were meant to "expurgate the body of the previous night's debauched intake of

sambals (condiments); and dainty Straits Chinese cakes.

LONG LIVE THIS QUEEN

> *Dishes are laid out on silver platters and trays in one of the most splendid colonial dining rooms under the sun.*

In those days 8:00 P.M. was curfew, and most members of colonial society were safely tucked in bed soon afterward. It was considered uncouth—and unsafe—to rub shoulders with the sailors and "riff-raff" who arrived from Britain with the monsoons, often waiting for months for an

'rubbish.' " Upscale tiffin spreads often included a Western-style roast pepped up with local spices; an array of traditional North Indian curries, mildly seasoned to suit the Occidental palate; chutneys; such Malay and Indonesian specialties as intricately perfumed rich coconut curries; an impressive array of

With the reopening of the legendary Raffles Hotel in 1991, the tiffin room has been restored to its nostalgic colonial splendor. It is run by the venerable Baliram Sangkaran, who in his search for classic tastes, might pass six versions of mulligatawny soup through his staff a day, and overseen by the seventy-five-year-old Mr. Goh, who worked his way up from the British army canteen to the Raffles tiffin room half a century ago and still remembers the luncheon preferences of Charlie Chaplin and the young Elizabeth Taylor.

Raffles is the crown jewel of colonial hotels. With its ceiling fans, wicker chairs, balconies, impeccable service, famous cocktails (like the Singapore Sling) in its famous long bar, there is a sense of time standing still, and great novels being penned in the corner. All that we associate with the grand hospitality of the Empire has come home to roost in the newly refurbished queen of them all.

The tiffin restaurant is a miracle conjured from the best of Indian, Chinese, Malay, and British culinary traditions. Dishes are laid out on silver platters and trays in one of the most splendid colonial dining rooms under the sun. This is Singapore dining at its very best.

Depending on the chef's whim, the soup of the day might be a rich, curried mulligatawny, a homey cream of chicken with a faint accent of Eastern seasoning, or a refreshing Thai hot and sour soup. On weekends, the centerpiece of the buffet is usually a roast, either a succulent leg of lamb coated in Indian spices and stuffed with almonds and raisins or, on a more British note, a juicy rare roast beef. Around it congregate small bowls of chutneys, pickles, and *sambals* of all colors and provenances. There are tender pickled green gingers spiked with chiles; Malay *acar kunung*, a mixed pickle laced with dozens of spices; sweet, sour, and plump mango and pineapple chutneys; bright-green mint chutney; amber-colored tamarind; the fiery Malay *sambal* of pure pounded chiles; and the incredibly tart but pleasing local lime pickle.

Lifting the lids on the curries is like releasing a genie from its bottle. As soon as the steam dances out, you are momentarily lost in the heady aromas of the East. It might be a pineapple and prawn curry, thick with coconut milk, aromatics, and pounded nuts; a richly spiced creamy spinach curry; or the more traditional Indian and Malay offerings, like lamb korma or chicken Masala. To accompany the curries, you might opt for a classic Malay coconut rice; an impeccably steamed buttered basmati; or a variety of *biriyanis,* rice dishes studded with morsels of curried meats, vegetables, raisins, and nuts. And as if this were not enough, there are always platters of Chinese delicacies like tender stuffed bean curd in spicy pork sauce.

The dessert selection alone could make up several high teas and still leave room for more. Best of all are the Nonya (the Straits Chinese of Singapore) dishes. Well known for their dainty cakes and pastries, called *kueh,* often made with rice flour, palm sugar, and coconut milk, these heavenly offerings are displayed in all their glory, standing on a little dais next to rice and sago puddings, cream puffs, and Western cakes—all lovingly enhanced with tropical flavors.

285

Asparagus and Snow Peas with Mirin Dressing

Steamed Broccoli with Miso Sauce

Broccoli and Cauliflower with Lemon Sauce

String Beans and Carrots with Shredded Coconut

Carrots Braised with Ginger and Pineapple

Eggplant in Cilantro Sauce

**Roasted Eggplant Stuffed with
Ground Chicken and Miso**

Orangey Fennel and Red Pepper Stir-Fry

Grilled Leeks Glazed with Soy and Orange

Spiced Red Lentils

Oriental Mushroom Fricassee with Pine Nuts

Indian Okra Sauté

Potatoes Stuffed with Keema

Crispy Curried Roast Potatoes

Borneo Pumpkin Stew

Stir-Fried Spinach in a Pungent Sauce

Chinese Greens with Oyster Sauce

**Stir-Fried Spinach with
Pork Cracklings and Crispy Garlic**

Spicy Tomato Chutney

Lemony Mashed Turnips with Ginger and Chives

Vegetable Mélange with Coconut Milk and Basil

Stir-Fried Mixed Vegetables with Shredded Pork

Vegetable Medley with Indonesian Peanut Dip

VEGE- TABLES

There are few culinary experiences that gratify the senses more than a stroll through an Asian market, be it in India, Thailand, Hong Kong, or a Chinatown in the United States. And in any good market, pride of place is allotted to a colorful lineup of vegetable stalls. What a pleasure it is to stroll amid rows of radiant Chinese greens, adorable fresh baby corn, tender asparagus stalks, long beans, bright red peppers, delicate crunchy snow peas, fuzzy okra, many varieties of eggplant, and funny-looking bitter melons—all just begging to jump into a wok, steamer, or deep fryer.

In this chapter I take my inspiration from two great Asian culinary traditions, both of which excel in preparing fresh vegetables. My first approach is based on the Chinese method of quickly stir frying garden-fresh vegetables over intense heat, and enhancing them with a quick boost of flavor from garlic, chiles, and soy or oyster sauce. Precision and simplicity are the key here.

When I am looking for a more complex preparation, I turn to an Indian tradition, a long and distinguished one, stemming from the richness and diversity of the southern Indian vegetarian cuisines. Here vegetables are coupled with rich spices and made into patties and fritters, stuffed into breads or lentil pancakes, and slow-cooked in warming curries. This is great for sturdy winter vegetables and legumes. Thai vegetable curries, although distinctive in taste, are essentially variations on the same theme.

To bring it all together, I've adopted the Californian penchant for beautifully and colorfully presented fresh vegetables designed to add a splash of color excitement to main courses.

ASPARAGUS AND SNOW PEAS
with Mirin Dressing

These slightly crispy, delicately sauced vegetables will add a tasty splash of jade to any main course. Mirin is a sweet Japanese rice wine, great for enhancing sauces. If you can't find it, substitute sake or medium-dry sherry.

1 tablespoon peanut oil

1½ teaspoons Oriental sesame oil

1¼ pounds slender asparagus, trimmed and cut diagonally into 2-inch lengths

2 cups snow peas, trimmed

1½ tablespoons sesame seeds

3 tablespoons mirin

1½ tablespoons fresh lemon juice

1 tablespoon soy sauce

3 tablespoons Chicken Stock (page 384), canned broth, or water

½ teaspoon sugar

Salt, to taste

1. Heat the peanut and sesame oils in a wok over medium-high heat. Swirl the wok to coat with the oil. Add the asparagus and cook, stirring until the stalks turn bright green, about 2 minutes. Add the snow peas and sesame seeds and stir until the vegetables are bright green and crisp-tender, 2 to 3 minutes. With a slotted spoon, remove the vegetables to a bowl and keep warm.

2. Add the mirin to the skillet and reduce by half over high heat, about 1 minute. Stir in the lemon juice, soy sauce, stock, and sugar and cook until the sauce is slightly thickened and reduced, about 5 minutes. Return the vegetables to the skillet and toss to coat with the sauce. Season to taste with salt and serve at once.

SERVES 4

STEAMED BROCCOLI
with Miso Sauce

The first time I made this broccoli it didn't make it to the dinner table, having been devoured en route by my friend's teenage children. Despite my annoyance at being left without a vegetable course, I was pleasantly surprised to see teenagers gulp down broccoli in a strange sauce with such vigor. I've made this dish often since, and have had almost equal success with the over-sixteens—at least they wait for it to arrive at the table.

If you are looking for a healthy, flavorful way to thicken sauces and vinaigrettes, you should definitely give miso a try. This sauce can dress a range of steamed or boiled vegetables. Try it with cauliflower, Brussels sprouts, asparagus, or green beans, or a warm salad of mixed winter greens.

The broccoli can be served either cold or warm.

MISO SAUCE
2 tablespoons white miso (shiro miso)
1 tablespoon tamari soy sauce
1 tablespoon cider vinegar
1 clove garlic, crushed through a press
1½ teaspoons Dijon mustard
¾ teaspoon sugar, or more to taste
⅔ cup Chicken stock (page 384) or
    canned broth
2 teaspoons Oriental sesame oil
Salt and freshly ground black pepper, to taste

1 bunch broccoli (about 2½ pounds), woody
    stems trimmed and discarded, cut into
    serving pieces

1. Make the sauce: In a bowl, combine the miso, soy sauce, vinegar, garlic, mustard, and sugar and whisk until the miso is no longer lumpy. Slowly drizzle in the stock, whisking until the dressing is creamy. Whisk in the sesame oil and season to taste with salt and pepper.

2. Steam the broccoli, covered, on a steaming rack set over simmering water, until bright green and fork-tender, about 8 minutes.

3. Transfer the broccoli to a serving bowl and let cool a little. Toss or drizzle with the sauce. Serve warm or cold.

SERVES 4 TO 6

BROCCOLI AND CAULIFLOWER

with Lemon Sauce

Nourishing broccoli and cauliflower, dressed up in a tart yet sweet sherried lemon sauce, is a lovely fall dish that goes well with the Thanksgiving turkey.

1 bunch broccoli (about 1½ pounds)
1 head cauliflower (about 1½ pounds)
1 tablespoon unsalted butter
1 tablespoon minced fresh ginger
3 tablespoons dry sherry
⅓ cup Chicken Stock (page 384) or canned broth
3 tablespoons fresh lemon juice
1¼ teaspoons sugar
1 teaspoon grated lemon zest
1 teaspoon soy sauce
Salt, to taste (optional)
1½ teaspoons cornstarch, mixed with 2 teaspoons cold water
¼ teaspoon lemon extract (optional)

1. Trim the stems off the broccoli and cauliflower and reserve for another use. Cut the broccoli and cauliflower into medium-size flowerets.

2. Bring a large pot of salted water to a boil. Cook the cauliflower for 2 minutes. Add the broccoli and cook until both are just tender, 2 to 3 minutes. Drain and keep warm while making the sauce.

3. Melt the butter in a medium-size nonreactive saucepan over medium-low heat. Add the ginger and stir for 30 seconds. Add the sherry and cook over high heat until reduced by half, about 1 minute. Add the stock, lemon juice, sugar, and lemon zest and cook for 3 minutes. Stir in the soy sauce and salt, if needed. Drizzle in the cornstarch mixture and cook, stirring, until the mixture thickens, about 1 minute. Stir in the extract, if using.

4. Place the broccoli and cauliflower in a serving bowl and toss with the sauce. Serve at once.

SERVES 6

BROCCOLI AND JADE

Almost everything in the natural world is a symbol for the Chinese, and they will eat anything so long as they believe it brings good fortune or good health. Green vegetables, such as peas or broccoli, recall the color of jade and are associated with youth and healthfulness. Red things are full of good fortune. Gold, the color of money and the sun, is prized above all, so golden-fried foods, oranges, kumquats, and tangerines are revered. The round, yellow pomelo and the grapefruit are thought to resemble the full moon, and thus bring (still more) good fortune.

STRING BEANS AND CARROTS

with Shredded Coconut

Ginger, garlic, rich Indian spices, and shredded coconut are a perky and innovative way to dress up this green and orange vegetable combo. If you prefer, you can substitute julienned red bell peppers for the carrot.

¾ pound green beans, trimmed

3 tablespoons peanut oil

1 teaspoon yellow mustard seeds

1 medium onion, thinly sliced

1 teaspoon minced garlic

1 teaspoon minced fresh ginger

1 teaspoon ground turmeric

¼ to ½ teaspoon pure chile powder

3 carrots, cut into 1½ x ¼-inch sticks

½ cup Chicken Stock (page 384) or water

Salt, to taste

⅓ cup dessicated (dried) coconut

1. Bring a pot of salted water to a boil and blanch the green beans for 1½ minutes. Refresh under cold running water. Drain and pat dry.

2. Heat the oil in a large skillet over medium heat. Add the mustard seeds and cook, covered, until they pop, about 1½ minutes. Add the onion, garlic, ginger, turmeric, and chile powder and cook, stirring, until the onion is translucent, about 5 minutes.

3. Add the beans and carrots and cook, stirring, until the beans are bright green and a little crunchy, 7 minutes. Add the stock and salt to taste, then cover, and continue to cook until the vegetables are tender, about 5 minutes more. Stir in the coconut and cook for another 2 minutes before serving.

SERVES 4

CARROTS BRAISED

with Ginger and Pineapple

Braising brings out the natural sweetness of the carrots, accented here with fresh ginger, and the acidity of pineapple. I like to add herbs as well, but the choice depends on the mood of the entrée and how "aromatic" you want this side dish to be. Mint or basil will make it very perfumey, which is good for a simple main course; cilantro will add a bit of character; and parsley will keep it more or less neutral.

3 tablespoons unsalted butter

1 small onion, chopped

1 pound young, slender carrots, peeled and cut on the diagonal into ¾-inch-thick slices

2 cloves garlic, minced

1½ teaspoons grated fresh ginger

3 tablespoons water, or more as needed

¼ cup unsweetened pineapple juice

1 teaspoon soy sauce

½ teaspoon rice vinegar

Salt and freshly ground black pepper, to taste

3 tablespoons chopped fresh mint, basil, cilantro, or parsley leaves

1. Melt the butter in a heavy skillet over medium heat. Add the onion and cook until translucent, about 5 minutes. Add the carrots and cook, stirring, for 5 minutes.

2. Add the garlic and ginger and stir for 1 minute. Add the water and pineapple juice and cook, covered, until the carrots are almost tender, about 15 minutes, shaking the skillet occasionally.

PENANG

*L*ying like a giant water lily just off the north-western coast of Malaysia, Penang is the enchanted isle of Southeast Asian colonialism. Deeply veined with migrations from near and far (Dutch, British, Chinese, Indian, Thai), its main city, Georgetown, is alive with the latter-day vitality of these peoples. Unlike the great cities of the region (Singapore, Kuala Lumpur, Jakarta), the communities, districts, architectures, and cuisines of Penang are still local and intimate.

Penang has a rich and varied history. The Chinese immigrants who flooded into the Malaysian Peninsula in the late nineteenth century soon organized themselves into special groups and name clans. Many of the clans preserved their own rituals, supported their solidarity, and showed off their wealth by building clan halls. Here members of the clan could come to worship, pay their respects to the clan notables from all over the world who had donated plaques and mementos, and indulge in annual feasts and celebrations. The clan house combined the functions of church, social club, and kitchen. The most magnificent of these is the fabulously overdecorated Khoo Clan House, whose entrance colonnade is adorned with snakes, fishes, and ecstatic figures riding boars and birds.

Penang also has a wonderful Little India. Anya and I wandered around the home-style Tamil restaurants on New Year's Street, arriving at four in the afternoon, just as the bread vendor was making his third round of the day and hawking Chinese buns from a bright blue tricycle. A southern Indian Muslim sauntered by. He was clutching an umbrella from Harrod's, the London department store, and sporting an old-style Islamic cap. At the intersection of Lebuh Queen and Pasar Street, the roti-chanai makers were frantically slapping and pulling their breads.

Farther up we passed the gaudy, elaborate pyramidal gopuram of the Sri Mariamman Temple, founded in 1833. The temple is the heartbeat of Penang's Indian community. Dedicated to "the mother of the universe" and centered on the idol of Muthu Mariamman, which was brought from a famous temple near Trichi in India, the temple took its present form only in 1933, a hundred years after its foundation. The gopuram tower over the main entrance is delightfully festooned with statues of gods, goddesses and swans.

While there have been Indians in Penang for many hundreds of years, there was a major influx of immigrants from the subcontinent after the establishment of Penang as a British trading post in 1786. The first wave were laborers brought over by the British East India Company, but they were soon joined by traders and shopkeepers. By 1835 the Chitis, as they are known in Malaysia, made up no less than a quarter of the population of Penang Island, with the Tamils, who were responsible for founding the temple, predominating.

Lording over the native Malays and immigrant Chinese and Tamils (for two centuries) were the British colonists, who, as ever, left be-

hind dozens of monuments to their trade, religion, and pleasure. Like Singapore and Rangoon (the capital of Burma), Penang is home to one of the great old colonial hotels of Southeast Asia, the ramshackle Eastern & Oriental. Billed in an advertisement from 1922, which still hangs near the entrance, as the "premier hotel east of Suez," the Eastern & Oriental is the most winsome and sentimental place in town. Seventy years ago, dinner and the cabaret cost a mere $3. If you were lucky, you could have watched members of the Diaghilev Ballet perform. These days the E & O (as it's known by everyone in town) is the venerable old dowager of the peninsula's hotels. Not much remains of the original structure of 1885, but some fittings, furniture, and lion-pawed metal bathtubs are preserved in the guest rooms. Best of all is the marvelous, outsize circular lobby, built in the 1920s. The rhythmic sweep of the white canopy overhead is dizzying and delightful. Sitting there, gathering enough energy to brave the humidity outside, as everyone seems to do, we felt as if we were pausing in an observation tank from another world.

3. Stir in the soy sauce and vinegar, season with salt and pepper, and continue cooking until the carrots are just tender. If the liquid reduces too much, add water a tablespoon at a time. Stir in the herbs and serve.

SERVES 4

EGGPLANT
in Cilantro Sauce

When I called Charmaine Solomon —a legend in food journalist circles, whose *Complete Asian Cookbook* has sold over a million copies worldwide—for an interview, she immediately invited me to lunch in her house in Sydney. "Don't expect anything much," she warned, "I will be just testing and photographing a few recipes for a magazine article." When I arrived, Charmaine, her husband, and her assistant were busy preparing this dish of fried tender Japanese eggplants, finished in a lovely Thai-inspired sauce of cilantro, spices, and coconut milk.

Charmaine was such a fascinating hostess—a Sri Lankan, born in Malaysia, married to a Burmese Jew, a culinary cult figure in Australia, and a walking encyclopedia of Asian cooking—that I quite forgot to ask for the eggplant recipe. I recreated it from memory and think it's a deliciously close approximation. The effect here is the contrasting textures of crispy deep-fried eggplant and the mellow velvety sauce. To achieve this, the eggplant should be added to the sauce right before it goes to the table.

¼ cup chopped onion

3 cloves garlic, chopped

1½ teaspoons chopped fresh ginger

1 teaspoon freshly ground white pepper

1 cup chopped fresh cilantro leaves

1½ tablespoons peanut or canola oil,
plus more for deep frying the
eggplant

½ cup canned unsweetened coconut
milk, well stirred

½ cup Chicken Stock (page 384), canned
broth, or water

1 tablespoon Asian fish sauce, such as
nam pla

1 teaspoon palm sugar or (packed) light
brown sugar

2 teaspoons fresh lemon juice

Salt, to taste

4 to 5 slender Chinese or Japanese eggplants
(about 1½ pounds total), trimmed, and
cut into ½-inch-thick slices

¼ cup cornstarch

Fresh cilantro leaves, for garnish

1. Using a mortar and pestle or a small food processor, grind or process the onion, garlic, ginger, white pepper, and cilantro to a paste, adding a little oil if necessary to assist the blending.

2. Heat 1½ tablespoons oil in a heavy medium-size pot over medium-low heat. Add the cilantro paste and cook, stirring, until it is fragrant and no longer tastes raw, about 5 minutes. Add the coconut milk and stock and simmer over low heat for 7 minutes. Stir in the fish sauce, sugar, and lemon juice and season to taste with salt.

3. Pour oil to a depth of 2 inches into a wok or a large skillet and heat over medium-high heat until hot but not smoking.

4. Place the eggplant in a paper bag and add the cornstarch. Shake the bag to dust the eggplant with the cornstarch. Working in batches, fry the eggplant until golden, about 7

minutes. With a slotted spoon, remove to paper towels to drain.

5. Reheat the sauce and pour into a large shallow serving dish. Add the eggplants and serve at once, garnished with cilantro.

SERVES 4 TO 6

ROASTED EGGPLANT

Stuffed with Ground Chicken and Miso

This is my rendition of a recipe for a delectable dish I tasted in the trendy Japengo restaurant, at the Hyatt Regency Hotel in San Diego. In my adaptation, roasted Chinese eggplants are stuffed with a flavorful mixture of ground chicken, miso, and sake. Present the dish on an attractive bed of greens, sprinkled with toasted pine nuts.

4 medium Chinese or Japanese eggplants
(about 4 ounces each), trimmed and
halved lengthwise

7 teaspoons light olive oil (do not use virgin
or extra-virgin)

Salt and freshly ground black pepper

8 ounces ground chicken

⅓ cup red miso (aka miso)

⅓ cup sake

2 teaspoons sugar

3 tablespoons pine nuts, for garnish

3 to 4 cups frisée leaves or other tender,
young greens

Snipped fresh chives, for garnish

1. Preheat the oven to 450° F.

2. Brush the cut side of each eggplant half with about ½ teaspoon of the oil and season with salt and pepper. Place on a baking sheet, cut side up, and roast until soft, about 20 minutes.

3. While the eggplants are roasting, prepare the chicken. Heat the remaining oil in a medium-size skillet over medium-high heat until almost smoking. Add the chicken and cook, breaking it up with a fork, until cooked through, about 5 minutes. With a slotted spoon transfer the chicken to a medium-size bowl.

4. In a small bowl, whisk together the miso, sake, and sugar until smooth. Stir three-fourths of the mixture into the chicken.

5. Remove the eggplant from the oven and top each half with some of the chicken mixture. Return to the oven and bake until the chicken is lightly browned, about 8 minutes, sprinkling once with the remaining miso mixture.

6. Dry-roast the pine nuts in a small skillet over medium heat, stirring, until deep golden, 3 to 4 minutes.

7. To serve, arrange the frisée on a serving platter, top with the eggplant halves, and sprinkle with pine nuts and chives.

SERVES 4 AS AN APPETIZER OR A LIGHT ENTREE

ORANGEY FENNEL AND RED PEPPER STIR-FRY

Colorful and sophisticated, this stir-fry is great served as a full side dish, a zesty relish, or as a bed for grilled or pan-fried chicken breasts or fish.

2 teaspoons minced orange zest
2 teaspoons soy sauce
3 tablespoons fresh orange juice
1½ teaspoons rice vinegar
1½ tablespoons water
1 teaspoon cornstarch, mixed with
    2 teaspoons cold water
1½ tablespoons olive oil
1 medium onion, halved and sliced thin
2 cloves garlic, minced
3 large red bell peppers, stemmed, seeded, and cut into julienne strips
1 fennel bulb, trimmed and cut into julienne strips
¼ cup sliced scallions
Pinch of sugar, or to taste
Salt and freshly ground black pepper, to taste

1. In a small bowl, combine the orange zest, soy sauce, orange juice, vinegar, water, and cornstarch mixture and whisk to combine.

2. Heat the oil in a wok over medium-high heat. Add the onion and stir-fry until translucent, about 3 minutes. Add the garlic, bell peppers, and fennel and stir-fry for 3 minutes. Add the orange mixture, turn the heat down to low, and cook until the vegeta-

bles are cooked through but still crisp and the sauce thickens, about 3 more minutes. Stir in the scallions and salt and pepper, and serve at once.

SERVES 4

GRILLED LEEKS
Glazed with Soy and Orange

Young slender leeks are lovely in just about any form, but especially when grilled with a tangy soy and orange glaze. Serve these with Veal Chops with a Macadamia-Nut Crust or Pan-Fried Salmon with Sesame Crust (see Index).

3 tablespoons soy sauce
2 tablespoons fresh orange juice
1½ teaspoons rice vinegar
1½ tablespoons honey
10 to 12 slender leeks, with ½-inch green
*   part on, thoroughly rinsed and dried*

1. Prepare coals for grilling or preheat the broiler.

2. Combine the soy sauce, orange juice, vinegar, and honey in a small nonreactive saucepan and stir over medium heat until the honey is dissolved and the glaze thickens, about 3 minutes.

3. Brush the leeks all over with this mixture and grill until tender and deep golden, about 12 minutes, turning the leeks halfway through the cooking time and brushing with the glaze. Serve at once.

SERVES 4 TO 6

SPICED RED LENTILS

Red lentils are tasty, nutritious, colorful, and easily cooked, and they blend beautifully with various spices. This dish is essentially a version of *dal*, the soupy Indian side dish of lentils, eaten with curry and rice. I have made it a thicker consistency so that it can be served as a side dish, without the rice. If you increase the amount of stock to about 6 cups, you can transform these lentils into a delicious spicy soup.

1 cup red lentils
4 tablespoons vegetable oil
½ cup finely chopped onion
2 teaspoons grated fresh ginger
2 cloves garlic, chopped
1 fresh serrano chile, stemmed, seeded, and
*   chopped*
2½ cups Chicken Stock (page 384), canned
*   broth, or water*
1½ tablespoons fresh lemon juice, or more to
*   taste*
Salt, to taste
½ teaspoon garam masala
½ teaspoon ground ginger
½ teaspoon ground cayenne pepper
½ teaspoon ground cumin
1 teaspoon yellow mustard seeds

1. Pick over the lentils. Place in a colander and rinse under cold running water. Place in a bowl, cover with cold water, and soak for 30 minutes. Drain.

2. Heat 2 tablespoons oil in a heavy saucepan over medium-low heat. Add the onion, ginger, garlic, and chile and cook until the onion is softened, about 8 minutes. Add the lentils and stock and bring to a boil. Skim, if necessary. Reduce the heat to low, add the lemon juice and salt, and simmer, partially covered, until the lentils are tender, 25 to 30 minutes.

3. Heat the remaining oil in a small skillet over low heat. Add the garam masala, ground ginger, cayenne, cumin, and mustard seeds and cover. Holding onto the lid, shake the pan for 1½ minutes, or until the mustard seeds pop. Swirl the spiced oil into the lentils. Adjust the amount of salt and lemon juice, if needed, and serve at once.

SERVES 4

O R I E N T A L
M U S H R O O M
F R I C A S S E E
with Pine Nuts

This fricassee is a luxurious medley of various Asian mushrooms—Chinese black mushrooms, shiitakes, oyster, and enoki—with a piquant, faintly sweet Asian sauce and a sprinkling of toasted pine nuts.

You can serve these mushrooms as a vegetable dish; as a light appetizer on a bed of wild greens; spooned atop grilled chicken or steak; or, on toast points or deep-fried wonton skins, as an elegant hors d'oeuvre.

8 Chinese dried black or shiitake mushrooms

3 tablespoons vegetable oil, or more as needed

6 shallots, chopped

2 teaspoons chopped garlic

¾ pound fresh shiitake mushrooms, stems discarded, caps sliced

6 ounces fresh oyster mushrooms, sliced in half lengthwise, if large

3 ounces fresh enoki mushrooms, trimmed

¼ teaspoon ground cayenne pepper

1 teaspoon paprika

¼ to ½ teaspoon five-spice powder

Salt, to taste

3 tablespoons dry sherry

1½ tablespoons soy sauce

1 tablespoon Ketjap Manis (page 388) or sweet soy sauce

1½ teaspoons oyster sauce

2 teaspoons fresh lemon juice

1 teaspoon rice vinegar

½ teaspoon sugar, or more to taste

⅓ cup toasted pine nuts (page 389)

4 teaspoons minced fresh parsley leaves

1. Soak the dried mushrooms in hot water to cover for 30 minutes. Remove and discard the stems and thinly slice the caps. Reserve ¼ cup of the soaking liquid.

2. Heat the oil in a large skillet over medium-high heat. Add the shallots, garlic, and dried mushrooms and sauté, stirring, for 3 minutes. Add the fresh shiitake mushrooms and sauté for another 3 minutes, adding more oil if necessary. Add the oyster and enoki mushrooms, cayenne, paprika, and five-spice powder and cook, stirring, until the mushrooms are tender, about 3 minutes. Season with salt. With a slotted spoon, remove the mushrooms and keep warm.

3. Add the sherry to the skillet and reduce to 1 tablespoon, about 1 minute. Add the reserved mushroom soaking liquid, soy sauces, oyster sauce, lemon juice, vinegar, and sugar and cook until the sauce is slightly reduced and thickened, 3 to 4 minutes.

4. Return the mushrooms to the skillet, add the pine nuts, and toss to heat through in the sauce. Sprinkle with parsley and serve at once.

SERVES 4 GENEROUSLY AS A FIRST COURSE

INDIAN OKRA SAUTE

In this tasty Indian recipe, which comes from Singapore's famous Raffles Hotel, the okra is first deep fried in hot oil, so that it retains its texture (an excellent tip to remember when cooking okra), and then finished in a flavorful sauce of onions, chiles, tomatoes, and spices. The best okra is often found at ethnic markets. Look for firm, bright green pods. If the okra looks limp and discolored, give it a miss altogether.

Vegetable oil for deep frying the okra, plus
   1 tablespoon
1 pound okra, trimmed, rinsed, and patted
   thoroughly dry
1 large onion, chopped
1 large fresh mild green chile, such as
   Anaheim, stemmed, seeded, and chopped
1 teaspoon grated fresh ginger
3 cloves garlic, minced
¼ to ½ teaspoon ground cumin
½ teaspoon ground turmeric
1 large ripe tomato, peeled, seeded, and
   chopped
4 teaspoons fresh lemon juice
Pinch of sugar
Salt and freshly ground black pepper, to taste
2 tablespoons chopped fresh parsley leaves

1. Pour oil to a depth of 1½ inches into a heavy saucepan and heat over medium-high heat until hot but not smoking. In batches, fry the okra until light golden, about 5 minutes. Remove with a slotted spoon to paper towels to drain.

2. Heat 1 tablespoon oil in a large skillet over medium-low heat. Sauté the onion, chile, ginger, and garlic until the onion is translucent, about 5 minutes.

3. Stir in the cumin and turmeric and stir for 1 minute. Add the tomato, lemon juice, and sugar and cook, stirring, until the tomato is softened, about 7 minutes. Add the okra, stir to coat with the sauce, and cook for another 3 to 4 minutes. Season to taste with salt and pepper and serve garnished with parsley.

SERVES 4 TO 6

POTATOES STUFFED WITH KEEMA

I am always impressed with the way Indians prepare potatoes, pairing them with other root vegetables in rich, warming curries, stuffing them into breads or *dosai*, the South Indian lentil-flour pancakes. This is my variation on an Indian theme—baked potatoes stuffed with a piquant mixture of lamb and vegetables. They make a great light entrée or party food.

4 large Idaho potatoes, scrubbed and patted
    dry
2 tablespoons light olive oil
    (do not use virgin or extra-virgin)
1 cup chopped onion
1 tablespoon minced garlic
1 tablespoon grated fresh ginger
8 ounces ground lamb
1 teaspoon best-quality curry powder
1 teaspoon ground coriander
1 teaspoon cumin seeds
¼ teaspoon ground allspice
¼ teaspoon dried red pepper flakes, or more
    to taste
1 large mild fresh green chile, such as
    Anaheim, stemmed, seeded, and diced
½ cup fresh or frozen green peas, thawed
    if frozen
5 firm, ripe plum tomatoes, seeded and
    chopped
⅔ cup Chicken Stock (page 384) or canned
    broth
Salt, to taste
3 tablespoons chopped fresh cilantro leaves
Raita (page 112) or plain yogurt, for
    serving

1. Preheat the oven to 375° F.

2. Prick the potatoes all over with the tines of a fork and place them on a baking sheet. Bake until soft, about 1¼ hours. Remove the potatoes but leave the oven on.

3. When the potatoes are cool enough to handle, halve them lengthwise and remove the pulp, being careful not to mash it up too much. Dice enough potato pulp to measure 1 cup and reserve the rest for another use. Reserve the shells.

4. Heat the oil in a large skillet over medium heat. Add the onion and cook until softened, about 5 minutes. Add the garlic and ginger and cook for 1 minute more.

5. Turn the heat up to medium-high, add the lamb, and cook, breaking it up with a fork, until it is no longer pink. Stir in the curry powder, coriander, cumin seeds, allspice, and pepper flakes and cook for 2 minutes. Stir in the chiles, peas, tomatoes, reserved potato pulp, and stock. Stir well and cook for 5 minutes. Season with salt to taste and stir in the cilantro.

6. Place the potato shells on a baking sheet and divide the meat mixture among them. Bake until the tops are lightly browned, 10 to 15 minutes. Serve accompanied by Raita or yogurt.

SERVES 4 AS A MAIN COURSE OR 8 WITH OTHER DISHES

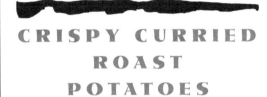

CRISPY CURRIED ROAST POTATOES

Potatoes are to a cook what a blank canvas is to a painter (as Brillat-Savarin once said about chicken)—raw material for inspiration. These are flavored with a palette of Indian spices and passed under a broiler before serving, for extra crunch.

¼ cup vegetable oil
1 teaspoon ground cumin
½ teaspoon pure chile powder
1 teaspoon best-quality curry powder
1 tablespoon paprika
½ teaspoon ground cayenne pepper
1 teaspoon ground ginger
1 tablespoon minced garlic
Salt, to taste
5 Idaho potatoes, peeled and cut
    lengthwise into wedges

1. Preheat the oven to 400° F.

2. Heat the oil in a large skillet over medium heat. Add the spices and garlic and stir for 1 minute. Add the potatoes and toss to coat with the oil. Season with salt.

3. Arrange the potatoes on a baking sheet and bake until tender, about 35 minutes, tossing them several times.

4. Preheat the broiler.

5. Place the baking sheet under the broiler and broil until the potatoes are crisp, 3 to 5 minutes. Serve at once.

SERVES 4 TO 5

BORNEO PUMPKIN STEW

Pumpkins, squash, and sweet potatoes abound in Southeast Asia and are prepared with flair in soups, curries, and desserts. I first tasted *pengat*, a stew sweet from the flavors of pumpkin, coconut, and cardamom and spicy from the blending of chiles, garlic, and coriander, at a roadside stall on the exotic island of Borneo. I now make it as often as possible during pumpkin season. Serve the stew with plain rice, Basmati Rice Pilaf with Sweet Spices, or Zucchini and Red Pepper Pilaf (see Index).

4 dried hot red chiles (2 to 3 inches),
  preferably Asian
¼ cup chopped shallots
2 teaspoons chopped garlic
2 stalks fresh lemongrass (3 inches of the
  lower stalk, tough outer leaves discarded),
  chopped
1½ tablespoons peanut oil, or more as needed
2 teaspoons ground coriander
½ teaspoon ground turmeric
1 teaspoon paprika
¾ cup canned unsweetened coconut milk, well
  stirred
¾ cup Chicken Stock (page 384), canned
  broth, or water
1½ pounds pumpkin or butternut squash,
  peeled, seeded, and cut into 2-inch chunks
2 cardamom pods, preferably unbleached
  (green), crushed
1 piece (1 inch) cinnamon stick
Salt, to taste
1 small red bell pepper, stemmed, seeded, and
  julienned
1½ tablespoons soy sauce
1½ teaspoons (packed) light brown sugar
1½ teaspoons lemon juice, or more to taste
2 tablespoons fresh cilantro leaves,
  for garnish

1. Stem the chiles and shake out the seeds. Using scissors, cut the chiles into pieces. Soak in warm water to cover for 10 minutes. Drain well.

2. Using a mortar and pestle or a small food processor, grind or process the chiles, shallots, garlic, and lemongrass to a paste; add a little oil if necessary to assist blending.

3. Heat 1½ tablespoons oil in a heavy medium-size saucepan over medium-low heat. Add the chile paste and cook, stirring, until it is fragrant and no longer tastes raw, about 5 minutes. Add the coriander, turmeric, and paprika and stir for 1 minute. Add the coconut milk and simmer, stirring, for 5 minutes.

4. Stir in the stock and bring to a simmer. Reduce the heat to low, add the pumpkin, cardamom, cinnamon stick, and salt to taste and simmer, partially covered, until the pumpkin is tender and the sauce is reduced, 20 to 25 minutes.

5. Add the bell pepper and cook for 3 minutes longer. Stir in the soy sauce, sugar, and lemon juice and simmer for another 2 minutes. Serve garnished with cilantro leaves.

SERVES 4 TO 6

STIR-FRIED SPINACH

in a Pungent Sauce

The pungent Malaysian paste, *sambal blacan*, made with shrimp paste, chiles, and garlic, provides a perfect foil for countless vegetables. This is one of my all-time favorite vegetable preparations, and besides spinach the sauce will go with any stir-fried vegetables, from asparagus to zucchini. I suggest substituting anchovy paste for the infamous *blacan*. It's actually quite wonderful when roasted and blended with other ingredients, but, alas, many Westerners—including expatriate chefs who have spent decades in Southeast Asia—find its smell just too overwhelming. Anyway, those who look for authentic tastes and have a well-ventilated kitchen can find the shrimp paste under either the name of *blacan* or *kapi*, its milder Thai equivalent. If you are going to substitute anchovy paste for the dried shrimp paste, omit step 2.

Steps 1 to 3 can be prepared up to two days in advance. Keep the mixture tightly covered, in the refrigerator.

*4 dried hot red chiles (2 to 3 inches),
    preferably Asian*
*½ teaspoon dried shrimp paste or
    1½ teaspoons anchovy paste*
*1 tablespoon chopped fresh lemongrass
    (3 inches of the lower stalk, tough outer
    leaves discarded)*
3 tablespoons chopped red onion
*½ medium red bell pepper, stemmed, seeded,
    and chopped*
3 large cloves garlic, chopped
5 teaspoons peanut oil, or more as needed
*2 bunches fresh spinach (2 pounds total),
    tough stems removed, leaves well rinsed,
    and patted thoroughly dry*

1. Stem the chiles and shake out the seeds. Using scissors, cut the chiles into pieces. Soak in warm water to cover for 10 minutes. Drain well.

2. Wrap the shrimp paste in a double layer of aluminum foil and dry-roast in a skillet over medium-high heat for about 2 minutes on each side.

3. Combine the chiles, shrimp paste, lemongrass, onion, bell pepper, and garlic in a food processor and process to a paste, adding a little oil if necessary to assist blending.

4. Heat 3 teaspoons of the oil in a medium-size skillet over low heat. Add the chile paste and cook, stirring, until it is fragrant and no longer tastes raw, 5 to 7 minutes. Add oil, a little at a time, if the mixture begins to stick to the bottom of the skillet. Set aside.

5. Heat the remaining oil in a wok or skillet over high heat. Add the spinach and cook, stirring, until wilted, about 3 minutes. Stir in the chile paste and toss for 1 minute. Serve at once.

SERVES 4

CHINESE GREENS
with Oyster Sauce

One of the most common Chinese vegetable preparations, this is a great way to prepare greens. Use any green Chinese vegetable—bok choy, *choy sum, kai lan,* or snake beans—you can find fresh at the market. If you don't have an Asian vegetable market close by, choose any easy-to-stir-fry green such as spinach, chard, mustard greens, or broccoli rabe. If using greens with meaty but edible stems, such as bok choy, cook the stems first for a couple of minutes and add the leaves later. Don't forget to wash, drain, and dry your greens beforehand so that they are completely dry before they go into the wok.

4½ teaspoons soy sauce
2½ teaspoons oyster sauce
½ teaspoon Chinese rice wine or
   dry sherry
½ cup Chicken Stock (page 384),
   canned broth, or water
1½ teaspoons cornstarch, mixed with
   1 tablespoon cold water
1 tablespoon peanut oil
1½ teaspoons minced garlic
2 shallots, chopped
1 teaspoon grated fresh ginger
2 pounds Chinese or other greens,
   trimmed, rinsed, and patted
   thoroughly dry

1. In a small bowl, stir together the soy sauce, oyster sauce, rice wine, stock, and cornstarch mixture. Set aside.

2. Heat the oil in a wok until almost smoking. Swirl the wok to coat with the oil. Add the garlic, shallots, and ginger and stir for 30 seconds. Add the greens and stir-fry until the greens are wilted. (The time will depend on the type of greens used). Slowly drizzle in the soy sauce mixture and toss with the greens until slightly thickened, about 1 minute. Serve at once.

SERVES 4

STIR-FRIED SPINACH
with Pork Cracklings and Crispy Garlic

There is nothing better that good Chinese stir-fried vegetables, and the mere thought of these wok-fried greens with crispy garlic and savory cracklings makes my mouth water. This is one of my all-time favorites! If you are near an Asian market, use Chinese greens. Otherwise the preparation will still be wonderful with spinach or another Western green.

4 ounces pork fatback, chopped
1½ tablespoons peanut or canola oil
4 large garlic cloves, smashed
2 teaspoons minced garlic
½ teaspoon Chinese chile paste with
   garlic
2 bunches fresh spinach (about 2 pounds
   total), tough stems removed,
   leaves well rinsed and patted
   thoroughly dry
1½ tablespoons soy sauce
Salt, to taste

1. Cook the chopped fatback in a medium-size skillet over medium-high heat until it has rendered all its fat and the cracklings are crisp, about 5 minutes. With a slotted spoon, remove the cracklings to drain on paper towels and discard the fat.

2. Heat the oil in a wok over high heat. Add the smashed garlic and cook for 30 seconds. Add the minced garlic and chile paste and stir for 10 seconds. Add the spinach and stir-fry until tender and bright green, about 2 minutes. Drizzle in the soy sauce and stir for another minute. Stir in the reserved cracklings. Season with salt and serve at once.

SERVES 4

SPICY TOMATO CHUTNEY

This beautifully spiced Indian chutney, devised by the San Francisco restaurateur Irene Trias, can be put to many uses in the kitchen. Warm, it is a lively side dish with rice and meat. Cold, it can be served as a party dip with finger food; a condiment with grilled fish, chicken, or meat; or spread on sandwiches. And finally, mixed with some water or stock, it becomes a flavorful poaching liquid for fish.

> 2 tablespoons peanut or canola oil
> ¼ teaspoon black onion seeds or
>   black mustard seeds
> Pinch of asafetida (hing; optional)
> 1 medium onion, chopped
> 1½ tablespoons grated fresh ginger
> 2½ teaspoons paprika
> 1 teaspoon ground turmeric
> 2 teaspoons sugar, or more to taste
> 2 large fresh mild green chiles, such as
>   Anaheim, stemmed, seeded, and diced
> 4 large firm, ripe tomatoes (about 2
>   pounds), peeled and chopped
> 3 tablespoons fresh lemon juice
> Salt, to taste

1. Heat the oil in a medium-size heavy saucepan over medium heat until it shimmers. Add the onion or mustard seeds and stir for about 1 minute. When the seeds begin to pop, remove the saucepan from the heat. Cover and let stand, until the seeds stop popping.

2. Return the saucepan to heat and stir in the asafetida, if using. Add the chopped onion and ginger and cook, stirring, until the onion is softened, about 5 minutes. Stir in the paprika, turmeric, and sugar and stir for 30 seconds.

3. Add the chiles, tomatoes, and lemon juice. Cover and simmer, stirring occasionally, until the tomatoes are thoroughly softened and the liquid is reduced, 15 to 20 minutes. Season with salt to taste and add more sugar, if desired.

4. Serve warm or cold. The chutney will keep in an airtight container, refrigerated, for up to a week.

MAKES ABOUT 3 CUPS

*L*ike the coconut trees of the Pacific islands, bamboo is one of those extraordinary natural products whose usefulness has no end. All over Southeast Asia, wherever it grows, the local people put it to work a hundred times a day. Arriving on the island of Borneo, naturalist Alfred Russell Wallace was immediately struck by the versatility of the bamboo trunks he saw all around him. His account in The Malay Archipelago, is like a poem to the magic wands of bamboo.

Their strength, lightness, smoothness, straightness, roundness, and hollowness, the facility and regularity with which they can be split, their many different sizes, the varying lengths of their joints, the ease with which they can be cut and with which holes can be made through them, their hardness outside, their freedom from any pronounced taste or smell, their great abundance, and the rapidity of their growth and increase, are all qualities which render them useful for a hundred different purposes. . . . The bamboo is one of the most wonderful and beautiful productions of the tropics, and one of nature's most valuable gifts. . .

The natives of Borneo lived in bamboo huts with bamboo roofs, they built bridges with it, they slept on bamboo mats. They even used it to make pegs for climbing trees. Its domestic uses were no less varied. Wallace was eagle-eyed here, as well.

The outer rind of the bamboo, split and shaved thin, is the strongest material for baskets; hen-coops, bird-cages and conical fish traps are very quickly made from a single joint by splitting off the skin in narrow strips left attached to one end, while rings of the same material or rattan are twisted in at regular distances. Water is brought to the houses by little aqueducts formed of large bamboo split in half and supported on crossed sticks of various heights so as to give it a regular fall. Thin long-jointed bamboos form the Dyak's [Dayak's; the general name for the natives of Borneo] only water-vessels and a dozen of them stand in the corner of every house. They are clean, light and easily carried, and are in many ways superior to earthen vessels for the same purpose. They also make excellent cooking utensils; vegetables and rice can be boiled in them to perfection, and they are often used when travelling. Salted fruit or fish, sugar, vinegar and honey are preserved in them instead of in jars or bottles. In a small bamboo case prettily carved and ornamented, the Dyak carries his sirah and lime for betel-chewing, and his little long-bladed knife has a bamboo sheath.

Even when they took time off, the men of Borneo still looked to bamboo. Their favorite pipe was a "hubble-bubble," improvised in a few minutes by inserting a small piece of bamboo for a hole obliquely into a large cylinder about six inches from the bottom containing water, through which the smoke passes to a long slender bamboo tube.

LEMONY MASHED TURNIPS

with Ginger and Chives

This sophisticated East-West purée should be presented as an exciting alternative to mashed potatoes. And if you don't want to give up the spuds, you can use them instead of the turnips. Just increase the amount of butter until you get the consistency you like, and mash them by hand. These are great with Pot Roast with Asian Flavors or Yin and Yang Chicken Stew (see Index).

4 medium turnips, peeled and cut
    into large chunks
2 medium Idaho potatoes, peeled
    and cut into large chunks
Salt
3½ tablespoons unsalted butter
6 to 7 shallots, sliced
1½ tablespoons grated fresh
    ginger
1 teaspoon grated lemon zest
2 tablespoons fresh lemon juice
Pinch of sugar, or to taste
¼ cup finely snipped fresh chives
Freshly ground white pepper,
    to taste

1. Cook the turnips and potatoes together in boiling salted water to cover until tender, 20 to 25 minutes. Drain.

2. Melt the butter in a small skillet over medium-low heat. Add the shallots and ginger and cook, stirring, until translucent, about 5 minutes.

3. Combine the turnips, potatoes, and shallot mixture with the butter in a food processor. Process, using on and off pulses, until the mixture is just puréed. You will probably have to do it in two batches.

4. Transfer the mixture to a saucepan, stir in the lemon zest and juice, sugar, and chives and cook until warmed through, 3 minutes. Season with salt and pepper to taste.

SERVES 4

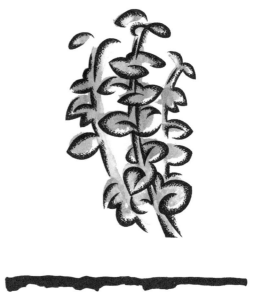

VEGETABLE MELANGE

with Coconut Milk and Basil

You can throw just about any colorful, market-fresh vegetables into this mouth-watering Southeast Asian curry. Make sure to add them to the sauce separately, depending on individual cooking time. This dish is a vegetarian's dream, especially when "beefed up" with some tofu. Serve it over rice, pasta, or Asian noodles.

¼ cup chopped shallots

1 tablespoon chopped garlic

2 teaspoons chopped fresh ginger

2½ tablespoons vegetable oil

1½ teaspoons ground turmeric

½ teaspoon cayenne pepper

½ teaspoon ground cumin

1 teaspoon ground coriander

1 teaspoon ground fennel

1½ cups canned unsweetened coconut milk,
    well stirred

1½ cups Chicken Stock (page 384),
    canned broth, or water

Salt, to taste

1½ cups cauliflower flowerets

2 slender carrots, peeled and sliced diagonally
    into ¾-inch thick slices

1½ cups broccoli flowerets

1½ cups green beans, trimmed and
    halved crosswise

1 cup quartered mushroom caps

1 large red bell pepper, stemmed, seeded, and
    cut into strips

1 tablespoon Asian fish sauce, such as
    nam pla

1½ teaspoons sugar

½ cup fresh basil leaves, preferably Thai,
    small ones left whole, large ones torn

1. Using a mortar and pestle or a small food processor, grind or process the shallots, garlic, and ginger to a paste, adding a little water if necessary to assist blending.

2. Heat the oil in a large heavy saucepan over medium-low heat. Add the shallot paste and cook, stirring often, until it is fragrant and no longer tastes raw, about 5 minutes. Stir in the turmeric, cayenne, cumin, coriander, and fennel and stir for 1 minute.

3. Stir in the coconut milk and stock and bring to a simmer over medium heat. Season with salt and simmer for 10 minutes. Add the cauliflower and carrots and cook for 3 minutes. Add the broccoli and beans and cook for

another 3 minutes. Add the mushrooms and bell pepper and cook for another 3 minutes. Stir in the fish sauce, sugar, and basil leaves and cook for 1 minute. Serve hot.

SERVES 4 TO 6

STIR-FRIED MIXED VEGETABLES
with Shredded Pork

This comforting dish of vegetables, pork ribbons, and rice vermicelli is tasty, healthy, nourishing, and authentically home-style Chinese. With some steamed rice, it makes a great light lunch, or you can offer it as a part of a multicourse Chinese dinner.

SAUCE

2 teaspoons light soy sauce

1 tablespoon dark soy sauce

1½ teaspoons oyster sauce

1 teaspoon sugar

1½ teaspoons
    cornstarch, mixed
    with 1 tablespoon
    cold water

½ cup Chicken Stock
    (page 384)

PORK AND VEGETABLES

1 tablespoon Chinese rice wine or
*   dry sherry*
1½ teaspoons cornstarch
3 tablespoons plus 1 teaspoon peanut oil
1½ teaspoons light soy sauce
2 boneless loin pork chops (about
*   7 ounces total), cut into*
*   ribbons*
6 dried Chinese black mushrooms or
*   shiitake mushrooms*
About 2 ounces rice vermicelli
1½ cups broccoli flowerets
2 teaspoons minced fresh ginger
1 teaspoon minced garlic
1 tablespoon finely sliced scallion
1 cup carrots, cut into matchsticks
2 cups shredded napa cabbage
1 cup mung bean sprouts, rinsed and
*   patted dry*
Salt, to taste (optional)

1. Whisk together all the sauce ingredients in a small bowl, set aside.

2. In a medium-size bowl, whisk together the rice wine, cornstarch, the 1 teaspoon oil, and the soy sauce. Add the pork, toss, and let marinate while you prepare the mushrooms and vermicelli.

3. Soak the dried mushrooms in hot water to cover for 30 minutes. In a separate bowl, soak the vermicelli in hot water to cover for 20 minutes.

4. Drain the mushrooms and pat dry with paper towels. Remove and discard the stems. Cut the caps into thin slices and reserve.

5. Drain the vermicelli, cut it into 2 inch lengths, and reserve.

6. Blanch the broccoli in boiling water for 30 seconds. Refresh under cold running water. Then drain and pat dry with paper towels.

7. Heat 1 tablespoon of the oil in a wok until almost smoking. Swirl the wok to coat with the oil. Add the pork in batches and stir until it is no longer pink, about 2 minutes. Remove from the wok and keep warm.

8. Add the remaining 2 tablespoons oil and heat until almost smoking. Swirl the wok to coat with the oil. Add the ginger, garlic, and scallion and stir for 30 seconds. Add the broccoli, carrots, and reserved mushrooms and stir-fry for 3 minutes. Add the cabbage and bean sprouts and stir-fry for 2 minutes. Return the pork to the wok.

9. Add the vermicelli and sauce and bring to a boil. Reduce the heat to low and simmer for 3 minutes. Season with salt, if necessary, and serve at once.

SERVES 4 AS A MAIN COURSE OR 6 AS PART OF A BUFFET

VEGETABLE MEDLEY

with Indonesian Peanut Dip

One of the Indonesian classics, *gado-gado* is a vibrant salad that combines raw and cooked vegetables, hard-cooked eggs, and tofu, dressed in a piquant, creamy peanut-coconut sauce. It is a wonderful dish to serve as a party platter with the dip in the middle, surrounded by colorful rows of vegetables. For an authentic presentation, place some vegetables and eggs on each plate and drizzle with the dressing. Deep-fried tofu is also part of the original recipe.

PEANUT DIP

4 large cloves garlic, minced

1 tablespoon grated fresh ginger

¾ teaspoon salt

2 teaspoons paprika

¼ teaspoon ground cayenne pepper, or more to taste

½ teaspoon ground turmeric

1 tablespoon plus 1 teaspoon peanut or canola oil

1½ cups canned unsweetened coconut milk, well stirred

1⅔ cups water

1¼ cups smooth unsalted, unsweetened peanut butter

1½ tablespoons dark soy sauce

1 tablespoon (packed) light brown sugar or more, to taste

2½ tablespoons fresh lime juice, or more to taste

Salt, to taste (optional)

VEGETABLES

4 medium red potatoes, scrubbed

1 pound green beans or wax beans, (or a combination), trimmed

2 large carrots, peeled and cut into 2 x ¼-inch pieces

1 small head cauliflower, separated into flowerets

1 small bunch asparagus, trimmed

3 small cucumbers, peeled, quartered lengthwise, and seeded

4 hard-cooked eggs, quartered

Red kale or lettuce leaves, for garnish

1. Make the dip: Using a mortar and pestle or a small food processor, grind or process the garlic, ginger, salt, paprika, cayenne, and turmeric to a paste with 1 teaspoon of the oil. Set aside.

2. Heat the remaining oil in a saucepan over medium-low heat. Add the garlic paste and stir for 1 minute. Stir in the coconut milk and water and bring to a boil. Simmer until the mixture thickens slightly, about 5 minutes. Place the peanut butter in a bowl and whisk in about 1½ cups of the hot liquid. Stir well and whisk the mixture back into the saucepan. Cook for 5 minutes. Remove from the heat and stir in the soy sauce, sugar, lime juice, and salt, if needed. Let stand to cool and for the flavors to develop, 30 minutes.

3. Cook the potatoes in salted water until tender, then drain them. When cool enough to handle, drain and cut the potatoes into quarters. Cook the beans in boiling salted water until crisp-tender, 4 to 5 minutes. Remove with a slotted spoon and rinse under cold running water. Bring the water back to a boil and blanch the carrot sticks for 1 minute. Remove the sticks with the slotted spoon and rinse under cold running water. In the same water, cook the cauliflower until almost tender, but still slightly crisp to the bite, 3 to 4 minutes. Drain and rinse under cold running water.

4. To serve, line a decorative serving platter with red kale or lettuce leaves. Transfer the peanut dip to a bowl and place in the middle of the platter. Arrange the vegetables and the eggs, each in a neat separate row, around the dip.

SERVES 8 TO 10 AS A PART OF A BUFFET

BORNEO FARE

In Borneo many people still eat by the law of the jungle, and almost anything goes. In the state of Sarawak, for example, you can feast on the traditional delicacies of the Dayaks, the largest indigenous group. These delicacies include jungle ferns, sago worms, snake head, porcupine, flying fox, monitor lizard, mouse deer, and giant local snails.

When consumed in the jungle, food is placed in large bamboo tubes lined with banana leaves, which impart a green sappy flavor, and steamed over indirect heat. The drink of choice is tuak, the Dayak rice wine, prepared from glutinous rice that is fermented with palm sugar and a type of homemade yeast for at least fifteen days.

These days the give-and-take that character-izes food cultures all over Southeast Asia is actively encouraged by the Sarawak government. The local department of agriculture sends envoys to remote longhouses to teach the locals to cook their jungle produce using traditional Chinese, Indian, and Malay prepa-rations. In turn it pro-motes the highly nutri-tious jungle products among the Chinese, Indian, and Malay popu-lations of the cities of Malaysian Borneo.

Some of my favorites from the jungle menu include paku, a delicate buttery fern that is the local green of choice. It is prepared in a variety of guises but is probably best stir-fried and tossed with *sambal blachan*, a paste made with red chiles and pungent, salty shrimp paste. When John and I visited the Bako National Park, near Kuching, the capital of Sarawak, we passed through fishing villages devoted to the produc-tion of this paste, whose aroma filled the seaside air for miles in every direction.

In tribal villages we enjoyed *urum*, deep-fried cakes made from tapioca and sugar prepared by the Iban, and cakes of sago mixed with eggs, coconut, and sugar wrapped in banana leaf and baked in a clay oven by the Melanau, a tribe that subsists mostly on sago.

A MECCA OF TASTES

The great covered market in Kuching, the capital of Sarawak, is the mecca for all the local tastes. There are booths groaning with fresh jungle vegetables: Dayak eggplant, which looks like a persimmon, and grows on trees like a fruit, and

that teams up perfectly with sour *asam* (tamarind) fish curry because it absorbs the flavors so well. There are Dayak

But most seductive of all were the condiment stalls diplaying multicolored wares...

lychees, which are flower shaped, sweet and sour, and great to munch on raw, dipped in a little *blachan* or preserved in sugar syrup. We snacked on *tapai*, palm leaf triangles enclosing packets of sweet fermented rice that reminded us of tuak. We found dried sago balls, which can be snacked on like nuts, and palm leaves used as cigarette wrappers. But most seductive of all were the condiment stalls displaying multicolored wares neatly hung up in small plastic bags: the black dried skins of an unidentifiable fruit, which supposedly cures dandruff; pink *cincalo*, pungent preserved tiny shrimp from Melaka; brown preserved tama-

rind, which should be cooked in water and used to massage the stomach in case of an ache; betel nut leaves and bags of

moistened white limestone to be mixed with the nuts and chewed; bark to cure sprained ankles; palm salt; and dozens of shapes and substances we could only guess at.

No less intriguing were the Tamil vendors, who sold a variety of wet curry pastes, spooning off the requested amount into banana-leaf wrappers: The white paste was ground candlenut; brick-colored was made from hot chiles; orange was turmeric, used for fish curries; and the chocolate-hued paste was of roasted, pounded coconut, used to thicken traditional Malay curries. Nearby were hot food stalls serving *bak kut teh* soup, a pork version of bouillabaisse, and *kacang ma,* chicken simmered with rice wine and a variety of local herbs—including the special one that gives the dish its name and is reserved for women in confinement.

The Chinese food in Kuching includes the staple Malaysian Cantonese, Hokkien, and Hainanese

fare, with its infinite varieties of noodle dishes, as well as the hearty peasant cuisine of Hakka and Foochow migrants who make up a substantial proportion of Sarawak's Chinese population.

A CHINESE FEAST AT THE PERMATA

We had been told that in the evening the Permata Food Center dresses up for dinner, transforming itself into a seafood paradise. So, on our last night we ate at Ah Seng, stall number 28, reputed to be one of Sarawak's best seafood joints. The fare here was laid out like a "salad bar" assortment. Spectacular shellfish were encased in ice, and all the components for traditional Chinese hotpots lay beside them, with pairs of tongs for piling one's choices high onto a plastic plate. One can choose from half a dozen varieties of prawns; long, slender, tubular bamboo snails; sweet, succulent yabbies (lobster-like crustaceans); the freshest imaginable crayfish; and mud crab, turtles, sea cucumber, mussels, and clams. There

is a real salad bar, too, offering all the hotpot essentials: crunchy elephant's ear mushrooms, fresh and dried shiitakes, large and meaty oyster mushrooms, spotty quail's eggs, pieces of chicken breast, springy

delicate fish balls, an assortment of tofu, and a cornucopia of green vegetables.

The food is weighed and priced, then cooked according to the customer's preference. It can be boiled in a delicate fish broth, stir-fried with garlic, chile, oyster sauce, or *sambal blachan,* or wrapped in a leaf and steamed. Once the food is cooking, you take a seat, order a beer or young coconut juice served in the shell or one of many freshly squeezed exotic fruit juices, and wait for your incredible feast to arrive.

Zucchini and Red Pepper Pilaf

....

Indonesian Fried Rice

....

Malaysian Chicken Biriyani

....

Salmon Biriyani from San Francisco

....

Shrimp Risotto with Snow Peas,
Shiitake Mushrooms, and Crispy Ginger

....

Pineapple Fried Rice

....

Steamed Coconut Rice with Cashews

....

Steamed Sticky Rice with Swordfish and Shiitakes

....

Grilled Sticky Rice Cakes with
Black Sesame Seeds

....

Tomato-Flavored Basmatic Rice with Sweet Spices

....

Noodles, Chicken, and Clams in
Spiced Coconut Broth

....

Ma Po Tofu Noodles

....

Linguine with Grilled Chile Chicken and Spinach

....

Oritalia Gnocchi

....

Seafood Tagliatelle with Coconut-Saffron Sauce

....

Cold Noodles with Asian Pesto

....

Singapore Noodles

....

Mee Krob

....

Indian-Style Noodles with Lamb and Peanuts

....

Nori Saffron Pasta

....

Staff Dinner Rice Vermicelli with
Minced Pork and Mustard Greens

....

Curried Glass Noodle and Seafood Hotpot

....

Broad Rice Noodles
with Chinese Sausage and Shrimp

RICE
AND
NOODLES

To Asians, food *is* rice. A common greeting in Southeast Asia translates as "Have you eaten?" which means, literally, "Have you eaten rice?" the word for food being synonymous with the word for rice. A cookbook I brought back from Bangkok sums up not just the Thai attitude toward rice but the feelings of an entire continent: "Although Thailand contains many jewels, no gem can rival the pearly white rice which is produced in abundance and which has staved off famine throughout Thai history."

Rice rules everywhere and at all times of the day. A bowl of *congee* (rice porridge) starts the morning for the Chinese. The Malays like their breakfast rice cooked in rich coconut milk, while the Thais prefer to begin the day with a bowl of comforting rice soup called *khao tom*. An afternoon snack might be a plate of stir-fried leftover rice studded with vegetables and meats or a bowl of chicken rice, a mound of the grain accompanied by succulent "white-cooked" chicken and condiments. And for the evening meal, no matter what other dishes might be served, perfectly steamed rice is the nucleus around which other dishes grow and multiply according to the occasion. As expected, rice is treated with great reverence and respect. Throwing it out is strictly taboo in most Asian cultures, and no guest would ever take more rice than he or she would actually eat.

While in most Asian countries today, noodles hold second place in popularity to rice, to the Chinese they are the very stuff of life. A special dish of yellow egg noodles is served for birthdays and other family occasions, and the etiquette is to slurp the noodles loudly rather than bite them. Breaking the noodles is a potential break in a long lifeline.

Frequent trips to Asia have left me addicted to noodles of all kinds. When pangs of hunger strike, I reach in my cupboard, stocked with different varieties of noodles, and combine them effortlessly with whatever else I might find in the fridge for a quick soup, salad, or stir-fry. I soak some rice vermicelli and mix it with chicken stock and garnishes for a delicious quick soup. Or I toss some leftover lamb and peppery mustard greens with egg noodles and a flavorful sauce for a satisfying one-dish meal. To sound a more elaborate note, or for a festive but casual buffet, I prepare a *laksa*—scented coconut broth containing two varieties of noodles, chicken, and clams.

When Western pasta is the order of the day, I still like to keep to an Asian theme. For that special occasion, tender tagliatelle is served with a beguiling sauce of saffron-scented coconut milk and an assortment of seafood, linguine is tossed with roasted chiles and ginger-flavored chicken, while chilled pasta gets dressed up with an Oriental pesto.

Rice, noodles, or pasta—the recipes that follow will make these pantry favorites dance.

ZUCCHINI AND RED PEPPER PILAF

A simple and colorful pilaf, this is great to serve either with a rich, coconut-based curry or alongside a succulent roast. For best results use good-quality basmati rice found at Indian groceries and some specialty stores.

1½ cups basmati rice, preferably Pari or
  Elephant brand
3 tablespoons unsalted butter
1 medium onion, chopped
2 small zucchini (about 5 ounces total),
  cut into medium dice
1 small red bell pepper, stemmed, seeded,
  and diced
2 teaspoons best-quality curry
  powder
½ teaspoon ground turmeric
¼ teaspoon ground cayenne
  pepper
2¾ cups hot Chicken Stock (page 384) or
  canned broth
Salt, to taste

1. Place the rice in a strainer and rinse under lukewarm running water until the water runs clear. Drain the rice, place in a bowl, and soak in cold water to cover for 30 minutes. Drain and rinse well, then drain again.

2. Melt the butter in a medium-size heavy pot over medium heat. Add the onion and cook, stirring, until translucent, about 5 minutes. Add the zucchini and bell pepper and cook for another 5 minutes. Stir in the curry powder, turmeric, and cayenne and stir until the mixture is fragrant, 1 minute.

3. Add the rice and toss gently until the grains are coated with oil. Add the hot stock and bring to a boil. Add salt, then reduce the heat to low, cover, and cook until the rice is tender and the liquid is absorbed, about 17 minutes. Remove from the heat and let stand, covered, without disturbing for 15 minutes. Fluff with a fork, transfer to a serving bowl and serve at once.

SERVES 4 TO 6

INDONESIAN FRIED RICE

There are an unbelievable 13,000 islands that make up the Indonesian archipelago, and there are almost as many cooking styles and varieties. From Java and Sumatra in the west, to Bali in the south, from the Spice Islands in the Banda and Molucca seas, to Irian Jaya (in New Guinea), 2,000 miles to the east of the capital, Jakarta, the diversity of Indonesian cultures and cuisines is staggering.

But if there's an Indonesian "national dish" that is at home almost anywhere in this fragmented country, it would have to be *nasi goreng*, elaborately garnished fried rice studded with vegetables, chicken, and shrimp and dressed with flavorful, sweet Indonesian soy sauce.

If you want to make a quick family-style meal, you can forgo the garnishes of egg strips and fried shallots.

2 small fresh hot chiles, green or red, stemmed, seeded, and finely chopped

1½ teaspoons minced garlic

1 tablespoon minced fresh ginger

5 shallots, minced

3 tablespoons peanut oil, or more as needed

1 onion, halved and sliced

1 large red bell pepper, stemmed, seeded, and diced

1 small green bell pepper, stemmed, seeded, and diced

2½ cups diced cooked chicken, pork, or cooked small shrimp, or a combination

⅔ cup chopped scallions

1¼ cups bean sprouts

1½ tablespoons Ketjap Manis (page 388) or sweet soy sauce

1½ tablespoons soy sauce

2 tablespoons Chicken Stock (page 384), canned broth, or water

5 cups cooked long-grain rice

Salt, to taste

2 large firm, ripe tomatoes, cut into wedges

Fried Shallots (page 389)

Omelet Strips (page 106)

1. Using a mortar and pestle or small food processor, grind or process the chiles, garlic, ginger, and shallots to a paste, adding a little oil if necessary to assist the blending. Set aside.

2. Heat 2 tablespoons of the oil in a wok over medium-high heat until almost smoking. Swirl the wok to coat with the oil. Add the onion and cook for 2 minutes, stirring. Add the red and green peppers and cook for 2 minutes more, stirring. Add the chicken, scallions, and bean sprouts and stir for 1 minute more. With a slotted spoon, remove all the ingredients from the wok and keep warm.

3. Heat the remaining oil in the wok over medium-low heat. Add the chile paste and cook, stirring until fragrant, about 2 minutes. Add the soy sauces and stock and cook for 1

minute. Stir in the rice, then turn the heat up to high and toss until heated through and coated with the sauce. Season with salt. Stir in the chicken and vegetable mixture and toss until well distributed.

4. To serve, mound the rice on a serving platter and garnish with tomatoes, Fried Shallots, and Omelet Strips.

SERVES 6

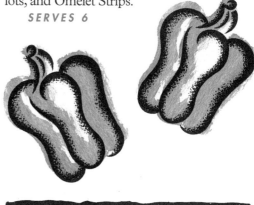

MALAYSIAN CHICKEN BIRIYANI

Indian dishes are an integral part of Malaysian cuisine, prepared with gusto not only by the Hindu population but also by Chinese and Malay cooks. *Biriyani* is an intricate dish of rice, simmered with rich spices and meats, which Malaysian cooks prepare with coconut milk, giving it the characteristic flavor of a Southeast Asian curry. I offer a lighter, simpler version, using just a touch of coconut milk or chicken stock, and neat bite-size chunks of juicy chicken breasts.

I like to serve this *biriyani* with one or more curries or as part of an elaborate buffet. But it would also do well as a basic one-dish meal, and you can certainly increase the amount of chicken.

1½ cups basmati rice, preferably Pari or
    Elephant brand

5 shallots, chopped

1½ tablespoons grated fresh ginger

3 cloves garlic, chopped

Vegetable oil (optional)

1 tablespoon chopped fresh lemongrass
    (3 inches of the lower stalk, tough outer
    leaves discarded)

1¼ pounds skinless, boneless chicken breasts

3 tablespoons ghee or clarified butter

1¼ cups chopped onion

1 cinnamon stick (3 inches)

1 whole star anise

4 cardamom pods, preferably unbleached
    (green), crushed

5 to 6 dried curry leaves (optional)

2 teaspoons ground turmeric

1 teaspoon paprika

¼ teaspoon ground cayenne pepper

¼ cup low-fat plain yogurt

⅓ cup canned unsweetened coconut milk,
    well stirred, or Chicken Stock (page 384)
    or canned broth

1 large fresh mild green chile, such as
    Anaheim, seeded and diced

3 small firm, ripe tomatoes, quartered

1½ tablespoons slivered almonds, toasted
    (page 389) for garnish

2 tablespoons cashew nuts, toasted
    (page 389) for garnish

1. Place the rice in a strainer and rinse under lukewarm running water until the water runs clear. Drain the rice, place in a bowl, and soak in cold water to cover for 30 minutes. Drain and rinse well, then drain again.

2. Using a mortar and pestle or small food processor, grind or process the shallots, ginger, garlic, and lemongrass to a paste, adding a little oil if necessary to assist the blending. Set aside.

3. Rinse the chicken breasts well and pat

thoroughly dry with paper towels. Cut into 1-inch chunks and set aside.

4. Heat the ghee in a large heavy casserole over medium-low heat. Add the onion and sauté until translucent, about 5 minutes. Stir in the shallot paste and cook, stirring, for 5 minutes. Stir in the cinnamon stick, star anise, cardamom, curry leaves, turmeric, paprika, and cayenne and stir for 1 minute. Stir in the yogurt, coconut milk, chile, and tomatoes. Add the chicken, bring to a simmer, and cook until the chicken is just tender, about 5 minutes. Remove from the heat.

5. Preheat the oven to 325° F.

6. Bring a large saucepan of salted water to a boil over medium-high heat. Add the rice in a slow steady stream. Cook, uncovered, at a rolling boil, stirring once, until the rice is tender but still slightly al dente, 7 to 8 minutes. Drain well.

7. Add the rice to the chicken mixture in the casserole, tossing with two forks and taking care not to damage the grains. Cover tightly and place in the oven until the rice is fully cooked, about 15 minutes.

8. Transfer to a serving platter, garnish with almonds and cashews, and serve.

SERVES 6 AS A SIDE DISH

SALMON
BIRIYANI
from San Francisco

Irene Trias, who runs two Indian restaurants in San Francisco, is a truly Californian chef. While remaining faithful to the origins of her cuisine, she lightens it and sparks it up with untraditional ingredients. For instance, her delicate version of the famous Indian rice dish uses salmon. It can be served as a light main course, or presented with a curry or other meat dish.

RICE

1½ cups basmati rice, preferably Pari or
    Elephant brand
2½ cups water
2 tablespoons peanut or canola oil
5 cardamom pods, preferably unbleached
    (green), crushed
2 bay leaves
4 whole cloves
1 cinnamon stick
    (3 inches)
Pinch of
    pulverized
    saffron
    threads

SALMON

3 tablespoons peanut or canola oil
Pinch of black onion seeds or cumin
    seeds
Pinch of asafetida (hing; optional)
¾ cup diced onion
2 large fresh mild green chiles, such
    as Anaheim, stemmed, seeded,
    and diced
1 tablespoon garlic, crushed through
    a press
1 tablespoon grated fresh ginger
1 pound skinless salmon fillets, cut
    crosswise into 1½-inch pieces
½ cup Chicken Stock (page 384) or
    canned broth
Salt, to taste
Pinch of freshly grated nutmeg
2 tablespoons torn fresh cilantro leaves,
    for garnish

1. Place the rice in a strainer and rinse under lukewarm running water until the water runs clear. Drain the rice, place in a bowl, and soak in cold water to cover for 30 minutes. Drain and rinse well, then drain again.

2. Combine the water, oil, cardamom, bay leaves, cloves, cinnamon stick, and saffron in a large pot with a tight-fitting lid. Bring to a rolling boil, then pour in the rice in a slow steady stream. Return the water to a boil, reduce the heat to medium, and cook, stirring only once, until the water is almost absorbed and bubbles appear on the surface of the rice. Reduce the heat to very low, cover tightly, and steam until the rice is tender, about 15 minutes. Remove from the heat and let stand, covered, while preparing the salmon.

3. In a saucepan large enough to accommodate the rice later, heat the oil over medium-high heat until it shimmers. Add the onion seeds and stir for 30 seconds. Reduce the heat to low and add the asafetida if using. Add the onion and cook, stirring, until softened, about 5 minutes. Add the garlic and ginger and stir for 1 minute more.

4. Add the salmon and stir gently for 1 minute. Add the stock, cover, and cook until the salmon is cooked through, 3 to 4 minutes. With a slotted spoon, remove the salmon pieces from the saucepan to drain on paper towels.

5. Fluff the rice gently with a fork and carefully stir into the spice mixture left from cooking the fish. Using two forks, gently but thoroughly toss the rice with the contents of the saucepan.

6. To serve, arrange the rice on a serving platter or on individual plates. Top the rice with several salmon pieces, sprinkle with some freshly grated nutmeg, and garnish with cilantro.

SERVES 4

SHRIMP RISOTTO

with Snow Peas, Shiitake Mushrooms, and Crispy Ginger

While I am wholeheartedly behind the concept of cross-cultural cuisine, I am not an advocate of randomly mixing alien flavors into established ethnic classics. However, when it comes to rice and pasta dishes, the affinity with Asia is so undeniable that it's hard to resist tampering just a little. This dish is a case in point. In it, a touch of curry and ginger and the lively crunch of snow peas and crisp ginger garnish happily disrupt the homogenous creaminess of the Italian classic. The result is a delicious, innovative risotto.

7 dried shiitake mushrooms

½ cup cold sake

¼ cup light olive oil (do not use virgin or extra-virgin

1 cup chopped onions

¼ cup chopped shallots

2 teaspoons minced fresh ginger

2 teaspoons best-quality curry powder

1½ cups Arborio rice

6 cups Chicken Stock (page 384) or canned broth, kept at a simmer

Peanut oil, for deep frying the ginger

2 heaping tablespoons julienned fresh ginger

10 ounces medium shrimp, peeled and deveined

4 ounces snow peas, trimmed

Salt, to taste

1. Soak the dried shiitakes in the cold sake for 1 hour. Drain, reserving the soaking liquid. Remove and discard the stems and cut the caps into thin slices.

2. Heat the olive oil in a large heavy pot over medium heat. Add the onions, shiitakes, shallots, and minced ginger and cook, stirring, for 5 minutes. Add the curry powder and stir for 1 minute. Add the rice and cook, stirring, for another 3 minutes. Add the reserved mushroom-soaking liquid, then raise the heat to medium-high and cook, stirring continuously, until the liquid evaporates, about 4 minutes.

3. Slowly stir ½ cup of the simmering stock into the rice. Reduce the heat to low and keep at a simmer. Cook the rice, stirring frequently to keep it from sticking to the pan, until the stock is absorbed. Continue adding more stock, ½ cup at a time and stirring frequently until it is absorbed and there is 1 cup of stock remaining, 15 to 20 minutes.

4. While the risotto is cooking, prepare the fried ginger. Pour peanut oil to a depth of 1 inch into a small skillet and heat to 375° F. Add the ginger and cook until crisp, about 2 minutes. With a slotted spoon, remove to paper towels to drain.

5. Stir the shrimp into the risotto, and continue adding the remaining 1 cup stock, ¼ cup at a time, for 10 minutes. Stir in the snow peas and salt to taste. Cook until the shrimp is cooked through and the rice is creamy, but still slightly al dente, about 5 minutes more. Divide among 6 serving bowls and garnish with the fried ginger.

SERVES 6

BASMATI RICE

*F*ew dishes can taste more delicious than a plate of perfectly cooked buttered basmati rice, the very long-grained, exquisitely perfumed variety used in Indian and Persian cooking. Basmati rice is widely available in health food stores, specialty food stores, and some supermarkets, but grades vary quite considerably in quality. As with olive oil, it is truly worthwhile to seek out the best there is. Indian and Middle Eastern groceries usually carry a good selection, and the best kind comes in sealed 5- or 11-pound coarse linen bags. My favorite brands are Pari, Elephant, or Super Sadhu, all from India. Basmati rice should be rinsed thoroughly in several changes of water and soaked for 30 minutes before cooking to get rid of the excess starch, which makes the rice mushy when cooked. I like to intensify its natural fragrance by adding a few sweet spices, such as cinnamon, cardamom, and star anise to the cooking liquid.

STICKY RICE

*S*ticky rice, also called glutinous or sweet rice, is Asia's comfort food. It is popular throughout Asia, and is often steamed with various other ingredients, shaped into cakes, used for sweets, or ground into a sticky dough. It should be soaked for at least 8 hours before cooking; the best way to cook it is to steam it in a bamboo steamer lined with cheesecloth. Replenish the water in the steamer and moisten the rice with additional water as it steams. (I like cooking sticky rice briefly—1 cup of water to 1 cup soaked rice—to plump it up before steaming. I find this unconventional method makes for a moister rice.) Sticky rice is available in large bags at most Asian markets.

BLACK RICE

*B*lack rice is a member of the glutinous rice family. It grows predominantly in Southeast Asia, where it is mainly used in dessert dishes. Black rice has a somewhat nutty taste and long dark-brown grains that become ink-purple when the rice is cooked, making it a dramatic side dish. As with white sticky rice, it has to be soaked for at least 8 hours before cooking, and then cooked until tender in about 1⅔ cups liquid to 1 cup rice. Black rice is quite flavorless on its own, so it's a good idea to cook it in some kind of tasty liquid spiked with various aromatics. Black rice can be found at good Southeast Asian groceries and is sold in bulk.

PINEAPPLE FRIED RICE

Chinese in origin, this rice, served in pineapple shells, has became a classic Thai restaurant dish. It is as decorative as it is delicious and I often serve it as a centerpiece for an Oriental buffet.

1 pineapple (about 4 pounds), leaves
    attached
2½ tablespoons peanut or vegetable oil
4 to 5 ounces small shrimp, peeled and
    deveined
1½ cups diced leftover roast pork
    or ham
1½ teaspoons minced garlic
1 small onion, diced
½ teaspoon ground turmeric
5 cups cooked long-grain rice
1 tablespoon dark soy sauce
1½ teaspoons Asian fish sauce, such as
    nam pla, or more to taste
3 tablespoons thinly sliced scallions
Salt, to taste (optional)
¼ cup chopped roasted peanuts,
    for garnish
Julienned red bell pepper, for garnish

1. Preheat the oven to 425° F.

2. Halve the pineapple lengthwise and cut out the flesh, leaving about ½ inch of pulp in the shell. Trim away the core, then cut enough pineapple into ½-inch dice to measure ¾ cup and reserve the rest for another use.

3. Place the pineapple shells on a baking sheet and bake while preparing the next 2 steps, 7 to 10 minutes. (This will seal the juices and prevent them from leaking into the rice when it is placed in the shells.)

4. Heat 1 tablespoon of the oil in a wok over medium-high heat until almost smoking. Swirl the wok to coat with the oil. Add the shrimp and pork and stir-fry until the shrimp just turn pink, about 2 minutes. With a slotted spoon, remove the shrimp and pork from the wok and keep warm.

5. Add the remaining oil to the wok and heat over medium-high heat until almost smoking. Swirl the wok to coat with the oil. Add the garlic and onion and stir for 2 minutes. Add the ¾ cup pineapple and turmeric and stir for 1 minute. Add the rice and stir for about 2 more minutes. Add the soy and fish sauces and scallions and stir in the reserved pork and shrimp. Cook for 1 to 2 minutes more, tossing and stirring to make sure all the ingredients are evenly distributed. Taste and correct the seasoning for salt, if necessary.

6. Remove the pineapple shells from the oven and arrange on a platter. Scoop as much of the rice mixture as will fit into the shells and arrange the rest around them. Garnish with peanuts and julienned red pepper and serve at once.

SERVES 4 TO 6

STEAMED COCONUT RICE
with Cashews

In Malaysia, *nasi lemak* (coconut rice), a traditional dish of rice, perfumed with aromatics and steamed in coconut milk, is much more than just a side dish. In the morning it is the nucleus of a wonderful local breakfast, the rice being served with a whole array of savory dishes—dark brown, aromatic beef stew, chicken curry, grilled fish, crisp fried anchovies, quartered hard-cooked eggs, and a palette of spicy condiments called *sambals*. The quick way to consume *nasi lemak* is to buy it before going to work from a street vendor, who sells it neatly packaged in a banana leaf together with chile sauce, sliced egg, fried dried anchovies, lime wedges, and cucumber slices. In Kuala Lumpur, the street food capital of the world, if you see a huge line at rush hour, you can bet your last coconut it's for *nasi lemak*.

Strictly speaking, the rice should be steamed with plain thin coconut milk, but I like to add some of the shredded dried coconut to the rice and then garnish the finished product with cashews. By the way, do not attempt to make coconut rice with thick canned coconut milk, as this is one liquid the rice will not absorb properly.

1 cup desiccated (dried) coconut
3 cups boiling water
1 piece (1 inch) cinnamon stick
Salt, to taste
1½ cups jasmine or long-grain rice, well rinsed and drained
¼ cup roasted cashews, for garnish

1. In a heatproof bowl, soak the coconut in the boiling water for 20 minutes. Strain through a fine strainer into another bowl, squeezing to extract as much liquid as possible. Discard two-thirds of the coconut and add the rest to the liquid.

2. Combine the coconut liquid with the reserved coconut and cinnamon stick in a heavy medium-size pot and bring to a boil. Season with salt. Add the rice in a slow, steady stream and cook, uncovered, over medium heat, stirring once, until the water is almost

absorbed and bubbles appear on the surface. Reduce the heat to very low, then cover tightly and steam until the rice is tender, about 10 minutes. Remove from the heat and let stand, covered, without disturbing, for 15 minutes.

3. Fluff the rice with a fork, transfer to a serving platter, and serve garnished with cashews.

SERVE 4 TO 6

STEAMED STICKY RICE
with Swordfish and Shiitakes

Anyone who tastes sticky rice instantly recognizes it as comfort food *par excellence*. Those already addicted to its soothing taste will applaud this dish of soy- and shiitake-flavored rice enhanced with neat cubes of swordfish and quail eggs. For a novice, it will be a great introduction to the pleasures of sticky rice. This recipe was inspired by Nekko Edamoto, a food writer from Tokyo. The rice can be served as a light meal, or with other dishes. Note that the sticky rice needs at least 8 hours to soak, so start ahead.

1½ cups sweet (glutinous) rice

8 medium dried shiitake mushrooms

1½ tablespoons peanut oil

2 tablespoons Oriental sesame oil

2 teaspoons grated fresh ginger

1 tablespoon chopped scallions, plus more
    for garnish

2 tablespoons Chinese rice wine or sake

2½ tablespoon tamari soy sauce

1¼ cups Chicken Stock (page 384),
    canned broth, or water

8 ounces swordfish steak, cut into
    1-inch cubes

6 to 8 hard-cooked quail eggs (optional)

1. Place the sticky rice in a strainer and rinse under cold running water until the water runs clear. Place in a bowl, add water to cover, and soak for 8 hours or overnight. Rinse and drain the rice before using.

2. Soak the mushrooms in cold water for 1 hour. Remove and discard the stems and chop the caps coarsely.

3. Heat the peanut oil and 1 tablespoon of the sesame oil in a heavy saucepan over medium heat. Add the ginger and scallions and cook for 1 minute. Add the shiitakes and cook, stirring, for 3 minutes. Add the rice and stir until the grains are translucent. Add the rice wine, soy sauce, and half of the stock. Cook over high heat, stirring gently, until the liquid is absorbed, 3 to 5 minutes. Add the remaining stock, then turn the heat down to medium and cook until the liquid is absorbed, about 5 minutes more.

4. While the rice is cooking, heat the remaining sesame oil in a heavy skillet over medium-high heat and quickly sear the swordfish on both sides, about 1 minute.

5. Gently stir the swordfish and quail eggs into the rice. Transfer the rice mixture to a plate in a bamboo or other steamer, set over simmering water. Cover and steam until the rice is tender, about 10 minutes.

6. Transfer the rice to a serving platter and garnish with scallions.

SERVES 4

GRILLED STICKY RICE CAKES
with Black Sesame Seeds

It seems that the wind of gastronomic fashion have blown sticky rice cakes (along with *katsu*, *gobo* root, and seared ahi) into the kitchen of every East/West restaurant on the west coast of the United States. These cakes dotted with black sesame seeds and scallions are crispy on the outside and soft within, and they make a wonderful accompaniment to a saucy stir-fry or light stew. If black sesame seeds are not readily found, substitute toasted white sesame seeds.

1½ cups sweet (glutinous) rice

Salt, to taste

1½ tablespoons black sesame seeds

2 tablespoons Chicken Stock (page 384),
    canned broth, or water

1 tablespoon rice vinegar

1¼ teaspoons sugar

3 tablespoons thinly sliced scallions

1 tablespoon Oriental sesame oil

1½ teaspoons peanut oil

1. Place the sticky rice in a strainer and rinse under cold running water until the water runs clear. Place in a bowl, add water to cover, and soak for 8 hours or overnight. Rinse and drain the rice before using.

2. Line a bamboo or other steamer with cheesecloth and set over simmering water. Spread the rice in the steamer. Cover with cheesecloth or a kitchen towel and steam until the rice is tender, about 40 minutes. Check and replenish the water every 10 minutes or so. Transfer the rice to a bowl, season with salt, and cool until easy to handle.

3. Prepare coals for grilling or preheat the broiler.

4. Toast the sesame seeds in a small skillet over medium heat until fragrant, 1 minute.

5. Stir the stock, vinegar, and sugar in a small nonreactive saucepan over medium heat until the sugar is dissolved.

6. Add the scallions, sesame seeds, sesame oil, and vinegar mixture to the rice, using your hands to stir the ingredients in. Shape the rice into 6 cakes, each about 3 inches in diameter. Brush lightly with peanut oil and grill until the cakes are crispy and lightly browned, 2 to 3 minutes on each side.

SERVES 6

TOMATO-
FLAVORED
BASMATI RICE
with Sweet Spices

This intensely aromatic, rose-hued rice dish will make a soul-satisfying companion to a wintry stew, roast, or curry. I love the sweet, heady fragrance that star anise imparts to food, but for some it's an acquired taste. If you don't like star anise, or just aren't sure, you might want to reduce the amount given in the recipe.

1½ cups basmati rice, preferably Pari or
*   Elephant brand*
1½ tablespoons tomato paste
2½ cups Chicken Stock (page 384), canned
*   broth, or water*
3 tablespoons peanut oil
2 bay leaves
1 whole cinnamon stick (3 inches)
1 whole star anise (or to taste),
*   broken into points*
4 cardamom pods, preferably unbleached
*   (green), crushed*
4 whole cloves
Salt, to taste
3 tablespoons evaporated milk
Freshly grated nutmeg, for garnish

1. Place the rice in a strainer and rinse under lukewarm running water until the water runs clear. Drain the rice, place in a bowl, and soak in cold water to cover for 30 minutes. Drain and rinse well, then drain again.

2. Dilute the tomato paste in 2 tablespoons of the stock. In a large pot with a tight-fitting lid combine the remaining stock, tomato paste, oil, bay leaves, cinnamon stick, star anise, cardamom, cloves, and salt. Bring to a rolling boil and pour in the rice in a slow, steady stream. Return to a boil, then reduce the heat to medium and cook uncovered, stirring only once, until the water is almost absorbed and bubbles appear on the surface of the rice.

3. Add the evaporated milk. Reduce the heat to very low, cover tightly, and steam until the rice is tender, about 15 minutes. Remove from the heat and let stand, covered, without disturbing, for 15 minutes.

4. To serve, fluff the rice with a fork and transfer to a serving bowl. Sprinkle with freshly grated nutmeg.

SERVES 4 TO 6

N O O D L E S , C H I C K E N , A N D C L A M S

in Spiced Coconut Broth

This dish, called *kari laksa,* is a wondrous Malaysian concoction of infused coconut broth, two kinds of noodles, morsels of chicken, fresh clams, crisp green vegetables, and elaborate garnishes. It is one of the world's great one-dish meals and certainly deserves the same recognition in culinary circles as bouillabaisse or paella.

Kari laksa is an ideal all-in-one meal to serve at a buffet dinner party, but it can also double as a soup or entrée. Although it involves many ingredients and steps, the steps are easy and the ingredients—except for a couple—are readily available.

In Malaysia, the preparation of *laksa* varies from state to state and from cook to cook. Once you have tried the original version, experiment with various kinds of seafood and garnishes. You can also substitute spaghetti for the rice noodles as is done in some parts of Malaysia.

2 pounds Manila or littleneck clams
1½ pounds skinless, boneless chicken breasts
2½ tablespoons peanut oil, or more if needed
1 recipe Laksa Paste (recipe follows)
2 teaspoons best-quality curry powder
½ teaspoon freshly ground white pepper
3 cups Chicken Stock (page 384), canned broth, or water
3 cups canned unsweetened coconut milk, well stirred
6 ounces rice vermicelli
¾ pound fresh flat Chinese egg noodles or dried fettuccine
2 cups green beans, trimmed and cut into 1½-inch lengths
2 cups bean sprouts
Salt, to taste
Large pinch of sugar, or more to taste

GARNISHES
3 tablespoons sliced scallion greens
3 to 4 tablespoons fresh cilantro leaves
1 lime, cut into thin wedges
3 fresh hot red chiles, stemmed, seeded, and thinly sliced
1 medium cucumber, diced
Sambal oelek (page 388) or Chinese chile paste with garlic

1. Scrub the clams well under cold running water. Drain and set aside.

2. Rinse the chicken breasts well and pat thoroughly dry with paper towels. Set aside in the refrigerator.

3. Heat the oil in a large heavy pot over medium-low heat. Add the Laksa Paste, curry powder, and white pepper and cook, stirring often, until the mixture no longer tastes raw, about 7 minutes. Add more oil, a little at a time, if the mixture begins to stick. Add the stock and coconut milk, bring to a boil, and simmer for 15 minutes. Strain through a fine strainer, into another large heavy saucepan, pressing on the solids to extract all the liquid. Set aside.

4. Soak the rice vermicelli in warm water to cover for 20 minutes. Bring a pot of salted water to a boil. Drain the vermicelli, add it to the boiling water, and cook until tender about 30 seconds. Remove the vermicelli with a wire mesh skimmer, rinse under cold running water, and drain again. Set aside. Add the egg noodles to the boiling water and cook until just tender, about 1½ minutes for fresh, 6 to 8 minutes for dried. Remove the noodles with a slotted spoon. Rinse under cold running water, and drain. Set aside.

5. Blanch the green beans in the boiling water for 1 minute. Remove with a slotted spoon, rinse under cold running water, and drain. Set aside. Blanch the bean sprouts in the boiling water for 15 seconds. Drain, rinse under cold running water, and drain again.

6. Season the reserved coconut liquid with salt and sugar. Add the clams and cook, covered, over medium heat until they open, about 8 minutes. With a slotted spoon, remove the clams from the liquid and reserve, covered with plastic wrap, so they don't dry out. Discard any clams that haven't opened.

7. To the coconut liquid add the chicken breasts and cook over medium-low heat until cooked through, 10 to 15 minutes. Remove from the liquid and cut into bite-size pieces.

8. To the coconut liquid, add the clams, chicken, green beans, and bean sprouts, and cook until heated through, about 1 minute.

9. To serve, divide the rice vermicelli and egg noodles among 6 to 8 large soup bowls. Ladle some of the liquid over the noodles and add chicken, clams, green beans, and bean sprouts. Garnish individual portions with scallions, cilantro, lime wedges, fresh chiles, cucumber, and *sambal oelek* or pass small bowls of the garnishes at the table.

SERVES 6 TO 8

Laksa Paste

5 dried red chiles (2 to 3 inches), preferably Asian
¾ teaspoon Thai shrimp paste or 1½ teaspoons anchovy paste
8 cloves garlic, chopped
1 piece (2 inches) fresh ginger, chopped
2 tablespoons minced fresh lemongrass (3 inches of the lower stalk, tough outer leaves discarded)
½ cup chopped onion
1½ teaspoons paprika
Peanut oil, if needed

1. Stem the chiles and shake out the seeds. Using scissors, cut the chiles into pieces. Soak in warm water to cover for 10 minutes. Drain well.

2. Wrap the shrimp paste in a double layer of aluminum foil. Roast in a small skillet over high heat for 2 minutes on each side. (Omit this step if using anchovy paste.)

3. Combine the chiles, shrimp paste, garlic, ginger, lemongrass, onion, and paprika in a food processor and process to a smooth paste, adding a little oil to assist blending. Set aside until ready to use.

MAKES ABOUT ⅓ CUP

MA PO TOFU NOODLES

Here's a delightfully spicy tofu dish given to me by my favorite Chinese chef, Andy Wai, who cooks at the Harbor Village restaurant in San Francisco. This is what Andy says about his noodles: "My recipe is an updated version of a popular northern Chinese dish, *ma po tofu,* that I loved as a child growing up in Hong Kong. The recipe uses very little meat, but is a flavorful, aromatic dish, making it especially good on a chilly evening. Best of all, it is quick and easy to prepare." I can add that the tofu sauce is equally good over linguine, broad Chinese noodles, or rice.

MARINADE

1⅓ cups Chicken Stock (page 384), canned broth, or water
1 tablespoon hot bean paste (chile bean paste)
2½ tablespoons tomato paste
1 teaspoon Oriental sesame oil
2 teaspoons sugar
2 teaspoons rice vinegar
½ teaspoon salt
1 tablespoon cornstarch, diluted in 1½ tablespoons cold water
¼ cup sliced scallions
½ teaspoon crushed Szechuan peppercorns

2 cakes soft tofu (8 ounces each), cut into ¼-inch dice
1 tablespoon peanut oil
2 large cloves garlic, finely minced
8 ounces lean ground pork or beef
Salt, to taste
8 ounces linguine
1 tablespoon oyster sauce
1 teaspoon Oriental sesame oil
Sliced scallions, for garnish

1. In a large bowl combine all the marinade ingredients and stir to mix. Add the tofu and let stand for 30 minutes.

2. Bring a large pot of salted water to a boil.

3. Meanwhile, heat the oil in a large heavy skillet over medium-high heat. Add the garlic and sauté, stirring, for 30 seconds. Add the pork and cook, breaking it up with a fork, until opaque, about 2 minutes. Add the tofu and the marinade and bring to a simmer. Reduce the heat to low, cover, and simmer the sauce for 15 minutes, stirring occasionally.

4. Cook the linguine at a rolling boil in the salted water until al dente. Drain and rinse under warm running water. Drain again. In a large bowl, toss the linguine with the oyster sauce and sesame oil. Arrange the linguine on a large serving platter and pour the sauce over it. Garnish with scallions and serve at once.

SERVES 4

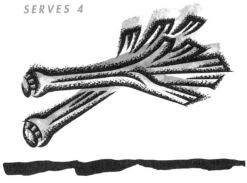

LINGUINE

with Grilled Chile Chicken and Spinach

This colorful pasta dish is a cross between Asian fried noodle dishes and the fashionable pasta salads we enjoy so much in the summer. One of its attractions is versatility: It can be served hot, warm, or cold, as a first course, main course, or a simple luncheon salad. And if you like, you can use thin Chinese noodles in place of linguine.

The pasta is tossed with olive oil, which is flavored with dried chiles, garlic, and ginger. This works well if you use a mild olive oil. Don't use virgin or extra-virgin oil, as this will result in an ethnic clash.

CHICKEN AND MARINADE

4 skinless, boneless chicken breast halves
    (about 1½ pounds total)
1½ tablespoons grated fresh ginger
¼ cup chopped onion
2 dried red chiles (2 to 3 inches), preferably
    Asian, seeded and crumbled
3 cloves garlic, chopped
¼ cup chopped fresh cilantro leaves
¼ cup soy sauce
2 tablespoons light olive oil (do not use virgin
    or extra-virgin)
1½ teaspoons (packed) light brown sugar

3 dried red chiles (2 to 3 inches), preferably
    Asian
2 tablespoons chopped sun-dried tomatoes
1½ teaspoons chopped fresh ginger
2½ teaspoons chopped garlic
½ cup light olive oil (do not use virgin or
    extra-virgin), or more as needed
1 onion, finely chopped
1 small red bell pepper, stemmed, seeded, and
    cut into strips
3 cups (tightly packed) coarsely chopped
    spinach leaves, rinsed well and patted dry
Salt, to taste
8 ounces linguine
1 tablespoon soy sauce
2 teaspoons Oriental sesame oil

1. Rinse the chicken breasts well and pat dry with paper towels. Set aside.

2. Process all the marinade ingredients in a food processor. Transfer to a large bowl, add the chicken, toss to coat and marinate, covered, in the refrigerator for 2 to 6 hours, turning occasionally.

3. Prepare coals for grilling or preheat the broiler.

4. Drain the chicken, and grill or broil, basting with the marinade, until cooked through but still moist, about 4 minutes per side. When slightly cooled, cut the chicken into ½-inch slices. Set aside, covered loosely with aluminum foil to keep warm.

5. Stem the chiles and shake out the seeds. Using scissors, cut the chiles into pieces. Soak, together with the sun-dried tomatoes, in warm water to cover for 10 minutes. Drain well.

6. Using a mortar and pestle or small food processor, grind or process the chiles, sun-dried tomatoes, ginger, and garlic to a paste, adding a little oil if necessary to assist the blending. Set aside.

7. Bring a large pot of salted water to a boil.

8. Meanwhile, heat the oil in a wok or large skillet over medium heat. Add the onion and sauté until translucent, about 5 minutes. Add the chile paste and cook for 5 minutes, stirring, without letting it brown. Add the bell pepper and cook, stirring, for another 2 minutes. Stir in the spinach and cook until just wilted. Stir in the chicken slices.

9. Cook the linguine at a rolling boil in the salted water until al dente. Drain. Transfer to a serving bowl and toss with the soy sauce and sesame oil, and then with the chicken-spinach mixture. Serve hot, warm, or cold.

SERVES 4

ORITALIA
GNOCCHI

When mixing Asian and European flavors, flights of fancy should be combined with prudence and restraint. The food of chef Bruce Hill of Oritalia restaurant in San Francisco displays these virtues in abundance. He stays within the classical European idiom, using Asian tastes as an extra dimension of flavor. His diminutive gnocchi with ginger cream, garnished with shrimp and Japanese Tobiko caviar, are a perfect case in point—an Italian would applaud.

GNOCCHI

1 cup cooked, cubed potatoes

¼ cup plus 1 tablespoon all-purpose flour

1 large egg yolk

2 tablespoons freshly grated Parmesan cheese

1 teaspoon salt

1 teaspoon freshly ground black pepper,
*   or to taste*

GINGER CREAM SAUCE

2 teaspoons peanut oil

12 large shrimp (preferably rock shrimp),
*   peeled and deveined*

1 tablespoon minced fresh ginger

1 clove garlic, minced

⅓ cup dry white wine

1 teaspoon tomato paste

⅔ cup heavy (or whipping) cream

⅓ cup crème fraîche

2 tablespoons chopped fresh cilantro leaves,
*   for garnish*

2 tablespoons snipped fresh chives, for garnish

1 tablespoon Tobiko caviar (small red
*   lumpfish caviar), for garnish*

1. Make the gnocchi: Rice the potatoes through a ricer into a bowl. Add the flour, egg yolk, Parmesan, and salt and pepper. Mix gently but thoroughly with your hands. Turn onto a floured surface and knead gently. Roll the dough into 4 long ropes about ½ inch thick, then cut the ropes into 1-inch-long pieces. Place the gnocchi on a floured baking sheet, sprinkle lightly with flour, cover with plastic wrap, and and set aside until ready to cook.

2. Bring a large pot of salted water to a boil.

3. Meanwhile, make the ginger cream: Heat the oil in a large skillet over high heat. Add the shrimp and sear on both sides until they just turn pink but are not yet fully cooked, about 1 minute. Remove the shrimp from the skillet and set aside. To the skillet add the ginger and garlic and stir for 15 seconds. Add the wine and reduce by half over high heat, about 3 minutes. Add the tomato paste, stirring until dissolved. Reduce the heat to medium and stir in the cream and crème fraîche, cooking until slightly thickened and reduced, about 5 minutes. Return the shrimp to the skillet and cook for 1 minute more.

4. Drop the gnocchi in the boiling water and cook until they float to the surface, about 1½ minutes. Drain.

5. Divide the gnocchi between 2 individual serving bowls and toss with the sauce and shrimp. Garnish with chives, cilantro, and Tobiko caviar and serve at once.

SERVES 2

SEAFOOD TAGLIATELLE
with Coconut-Saffron Sauce

Pasta with seafood is one of those elegant dishes that spell out "special occasion." But even natural elegance can be improved. When the sauce is subtly enhanced by the hovering taste of coconut milk and a hint of Asian seasonings, it becomes truly luxurious.

Serve the pasta in large, deep bowls with crusty bread to sop up the fabulous sauce.

2 tablespoons vegetable oil, or more if needed

1 tablespoon unsalted butter, or more if needed

12 medium shrimp, peeled and deveined

8 sea scallops, halved crosswise, if large

8 ounces skinless salmon fillet, cut into 1-inch cubes

12 mussels, scrubbed and debearded (see Note)

⅓ cup finely chopped shallots

2 teaspoons minced garlic

1 small fresh hot chile, green or red, seeded and chopped

⅓ cup dry white wine

⅔ cup Fish Stock (page 385) or bottled clam juice

1⅓ cups canned unsweetened coconut milk, well stirred

8 to 10 saffron threads, soaked in 1 teaspoon warm water

3 medium firm, ripe plum tomatoes, peeled, seeded, and diced

¼ teaspoon ground cayenne pepper

Salt and freshly ground black pepper, to taste

2 tablespoons chopped fresh cilantro leaves, plus additional for garnish

12 ounces cooked fresh tagliatelle

Julienned red bell pepper, for garnish

1. Heat 1 tablespoon of the oil with the butter in a large heavy nonstick skillet over medium heat. Add the shrimp and cook on both sides until they just turn pink, about 3 minutes. Using a slotted spoon, remove the shrimp from the skillet to a large bowl. Add the scallops to the skillet and cook on both sides until just opaque, about 2 minutes. Remove to the same bowl. Add a little more oil and butter, if needed, and cook the salmon on both sides until opaque, about 3 minutes. Transfer to the bowl.

2. In a steamer set over boiling water, steam the mussels until they open, 3 to 5 minutes. Discard any that don't open. Add the mussels to the rest of the seafood in the bowl.

3. To the skillet in which you cooked the seafood, add the remaining 1 tablespoon oil and sauté the shallots, garlic, and chile over medium-low heat until the shallots are translucent. Raise the heat to medium-high and add the wine. Cook until reduced by half, about 3 minutes. Add the fish stock and 1 cup of the coconut milk and reduce by half, about 7 minutes. Add the saffron, tomatoes, and cayenne and cook for another 5 minutes. Season to taste with salt and pepper.

4. Stir in the remaining coconut milk and the seafood with the accumulated juices. Cook over low heat until heated through. Stir in the cilantro.

5. Divide the pasta among 4 warmed bowls, and spoon equal portions of seafood and sauce on top. Garnish each portion with julienned pepper and cilantro.

SERVES 4

Note: Debeard mussels right before cooking to prevent spoilage.

COLD NOODLES

with Asian Pesto

Try these next time you are looking for a great cold pasta dish to replace the tired sesame noodles standby. For a more substantial summertime entrée, "fill up" the pasta with cold poached seafood, diced cooked chicken breast, or colorful raw or blanched vegetables such as red bell peppers, zucchini, pattypan squash, asparagus, or cherry tomatoes.

Salt, to taste
1 pound fresh thin Chinese egg noodles or
*   capellini*
2½ teaspoons Oriental sesame oil
1½ cups Asian Pesto (recipe follows)
Red and yellow cherry tomatoes, halved, for
*   garnish*
Chopped roasted peanuts, for garnish

1. Bring 3 quarts of salted water to a rolling boil.

2. Fluff the noodles with a fork to untangle, add to the boiling water, and cook until just slightly al dente, 2 to 3 minutes, separating the noodle strands that are stuck together.

3. Drain and rinse the noodles in cold water. Place in a large bowl and toss with the sesame oil. Cool to room temperature.

4. Place the noodles in a large serving bowl and toss in the pesto, a little at a time. Serve garnished with cherry tomatoes and peanuts.

SERVES 6

Asian Pesto

This pesto is great to toss into noodles, pasta or rice, add to salad dressings, rub on food for the grill or heighten the flavor of soups or coconut-based curries. Experiment with various ingredients. Try cashews, peanuts, shredded coconut, Asian basil or mint, or flavored oils. Seed the chiles or not, depending on the degree of heat desired. It's hard to go wrong.

The pesto will keep in the refrigerator for up to 2 weeks or in the freezer for several months.

1¼ cups roasted peanuts (or a combination
*   of peanuts, cashews, and macadamia*
*   nuts)*
¼ cup chopped garlic
3 tablespoons chopped fresh ginger
5 serrano chiles, stemmed, seeded (if desired),
*   and chopped*
2 cups fresh mint leaves
2 cups fresh cilantro leaves
2 cups fresh basil leaves, preferably Thai
1½ cups peanut or canola oil
2 tablespoons grated orange zest
1 tablespoon grated lime zest
2 teaspoons Oriental sesame oil, or more to
*   taste*
Salt, to taste

1. Make the pesto in two batches. Place half of the nuts, garlic, ginger, and chiles in a food processor and process to a paste.

2. Add half of the mint, cilantro, and basil and process until minced. Add half of the peanut oil or canola oil in a thin steady stream. Scrape into a bowl.

3. Repeat the procedure with the remaining peanuts, garlic, ginger, chiles, herbs, and oil. Combine with the first batch.

4. Add the orange and lime zests, sesame oil, and salt to taste. Scrape into a jar and store in the refrigerator.

MAKES ABOUT 3 CUPS

NOODLES, UNTANGLED

RICE NOODLES

Delicately flavored, alabaster-colored rice noodles are made from rice flour and water, and come in a variety of sizes and shapes. The most common are the thin rice vermicelli, also referred to as rice sticks. These are sold dried, in 1-pound plastic-wrapped packages; they are divided into 3 or 4 skeins, each weighing 4 to 6 ounces. The wider dried rice noodles favored in Thai and Vietnamese cuisine are the size of fettuccine and come in large 1-pound plastic bags. Dried rice noodles should be soaked in cold or warm water to soften before cooking them very briefly in a wok or boiling water. Both are favorites for stir-frying and soups. The thin rice vermicelli can also be deep-fried in hot oil until puffed and crispy and used as a garnish, a bed for stir-fried dishes, or a base for mee krob. Cold thin rice vermicelli is wonderful for summer salads, with vegetables, and meats and a dressing of fish sauce, lime juice, and sugar.

One of Southeast Asia's all-time road-stall favorites is qwai tew, fat (about 2 inches wide), pillowy fresh rice noodles, available in smallish plastic packages at good Thai, Vietnamese, and sometimes Chinese groceries. These are glorious when stir-fried with seafood, tofu, egg, and a soy-based sauce.

BEAN THREAD NOODLES

Also known as cellophane noodles and glass noodles, bean thread noodles are made from mung bean flour and water. They are clear and hard and come in packets of small bundles. When cooked, they become pleasingly slippery. As bean thread noodles have little flavor of their own and readily absorb others, they are best simmered with other ingredients in a well-seasoned liquid. I like them best in soups, curries, and vegetable stir-fries. Bean threads should be soaked in warm or hot water until pliable, cut into manageable lengths, and then slowly simmered in the desired liquid until soft. Note that these noodles will absorb quite a lot of liquid as they cook.

WHEAT NOODLES

Chinese wheat noodles are made from wheat flour, water, and often eggs. The best wheat noodles are fresh. As they freeze quite well, I usually stock up on a month's supply when shopping at Chinese grocery stores, where they are available fresh and frozen. Both thin and thicker (fettuccine-size) fresh noodles should be untangled with a fork and cooked in a large pot of boiling water for 2 to 4 minutes, depending on the desired degree of doneness. Do not leave them unattended and keep tasting a strand or two, as you would pasta. Dried capellini is a good substitute for thin Chinese noodles, while fresh fettuccine makes an acceptable standby for the wider noodles. Fresh Chinese noodles will keep in the refrigerator for several days; if frozen they should be thawed before cooking.

SINGAPORE NOODLES

Known as Singapore noodles every where except Singapore, these delicate, lightly curried rice noodles dotted with seafood, chicken, and colorful vegetables nevertheless capture the spirit of this exotic island. With a big green salad they make a wonderful lunchtime meal.

8 ounces rice vermicelli

8 ounces skinless, boneless chicken
*   breasts*

1½ cups broccoli flowerets

3 tablespoons peanut oil

5 ounces small shrimp, peeled and
*   deveined*

2 small fresh hot chiles, green or red,
*   stemmed, seeded, and minced*

1 teaspoon minced garlic

1½ teaspoons minced fresh ginger

1 medium onion, quartered and sliced

1 slender small carrot, peeled, and sliced
*   crosswise on the diagonal*

½ cup julienned red bell pepper

½ cup julienned green bell pepper

2 tablespoons sliced scallions

2 teaspoons best-quality curry powder

½ teaspoon ground turmeric

½ teaspoon ground cayenne pepper

2½ tablespoons soy sauce

6 tablespoons Chicken Stock (page 384)
*   or canned broth*

Salt, to taste (optional)

Chopped roasted peanuts, for garnish

Lime wedges, for garnish

1. Soak the rice vermicelli in warm water to cover for 20 minutes. Drain well.

2. Meanwhile, rinse the chicken breasts well and pat thoroughly dry with paper towels. Cut into dice and set aside.

3. Blanch the broccoli in boiling water for 45 seconds. Drain, refresh under cold running water, and pat gently dry with paper towels.

4. Heat 2 tablespoons of the oil in a wok over high heat until almost smoking. Swirl the wok to coat with the oil. Add the chicken pieces and stir until they just turn opaque, about 2 minutes. Add the shrimp and stir until they turn pink, about 2 minutes. Remove the chicken and shrimp from the wok with a slotted spoon and keep warm.

5. Add the remaining oil to the wok and heat until almost smoking. Add the chiles, garlic, and ginger and stir for 30 seconds. Add the onion and toss for 1 minute. Add the carrot and toss for another minute. Add the broccoli, peppers, and scallions and stir for 2 more minutes.

6. Stir in the curry powder, turmeric, and cayenne and stir for 15 seconds. Return the reserved chicken and shrimp to the wok along with the noodles and toss and stir until combined with the other ingredients. Add the soy sauce, stock, and salt to taste, if needed. Reduce the heat to low and cook until the liquid is absorbed, 2 to 3 minutes. Serve at once, garnished with peanuts and lime wedges.

SERVES 6

MEE KROB

Crispy Rice Noodles with Pork, Chicken, and Shrimp

The authentic *mee krob*, which is nowadays hard to come by even in Thailand, is a far cry from the gooey sweet concoction—sort of a Thai equivalent of Chinese sweet-and-sour pork—one encounters in restaurants. It is thus a bit ironic that one of the most sophisticated and elaborate dishes of the Royal Thai table has become almost a fast-food cliché.

A true *mee krob* is made from cooked rice noodles that are scrupulously dried and fried to a crisp. Then the noodles are quickly tossed with fried tofu strips, crispy garlic and shallots, shrimp, chicken, and minced pork (the last three are actually optional), a caramelized sauce, and crushed preserved soy beans. The resulting dish is mounded on a plate and garnished with an elaborate fried egg net, sweet pickled garlic, chile and scallion flowers, and citrus zest. The dish is not as much a meal as an edible centerpiece at important banquets, celebrations, and Buddhist gatherings.

To create a true *mee krob* requires an incredible amount of time and effort, but the simplified version I present here is a very tasty alternative. It retains the integrity of flavor, while forgoing the time-consuming garnishes and complex techniques. As *mee krob* is supposed to be served at room temperature, you can prepare it ahead of time, but toss the noodles with the remaining ingredients literally moments before serving. If making the sauce ahead of time, reheat gently before tossing into the noodles.

8 ounces rice vermicelli

Peanut oil for deep frying the vermicelli plus ¼ cup

¼ cup thinly sliced garlic

¼ cup thinly sliced shallots

1 cup diced firm tofu

6 ounces small shrimp, peeled and deveined

4 ounces boneless chicken breast, diced

4 ounces lean ground pork

¼ cup Asian fish sauce, such as nam pla

2 tablespoons Thai yellow bean sauce (tao jiaw; optional)

2½ tablespoons rice vinegar

3 tablespoons fresh lime juice

1 teaspoon ketchup

1½ teaspoons soy sauce

2 tablespoons water

5 tablespoons granulated sugar

1½ tablespoons (packed) light brown sugar

1 dried red chile (1 inch), finely crumbled

Salt, to taste

GARNISHES

Fresh cilantro leaves

Lime wedges

Julienned red bell pepper or mild red chile

Scallion flowers (optional; see Note, page 135)

Sliced sweet Thai pickled garlic (optional)

1. Break the rice vermicelli into 3-inch lengths and separate into small handfuls. Line 2 large baking sheets with a double layer of paper towels.

2. Pour oil to a depth of 3 inches into a large wok or deep fryer and heat over medium-high heat to 375°F. The oil is ready when a few noodles dropped in puff immediately to 2 to 3 times their original size. Fry the noodles, small handfuls at a time, until puffed and light golden, about 5 seconds per batch. The noodles will form into a cake. Quickly turn each cake with a large slotted spoon or a wire mesh spoon and fry for several seconds on the other side. Using the slotted spoon, transfer the cooked batches to the prepared baking sheets to drain. (You can make these noodles up to a day in advance. Store in an airtight container and keep in a dry place.)

3. Discard the oil and wipe the wok clean. Carefully heat the ¼ cup oil over high heat until almost smoking. Set out several more layers of paper towels. Add the garlic and shallots to the oil (do this carefully, too; the oil may splatter) and cook until golden and slightly crispy 1 to 2 minutes. Remove with a slotted spoon to drain on paper towels. Add the tofu and fry on all sides until golden, about 3 minutes. Remove to drain on paper towels.

4. Drain all but about 1½ tablespoons of the oil from the wok. Reheat the oil in the wok until hot but not smoking. Add the shrimp, chicken, and pork, and stir-fry over high heat until the shrimp and chicken are opaque and the pork is lightly browned, 2 to 3 minutes. Using a slotted spoon, transfer the contents of the wok to a large bowl.

5. To the wok add the fish sauce, bean sauce, vinegar, lime juice, ketchup, soy sauce, water, both sugars, and chile. Cook over medium heat, stirring, until the mixture becomes syrupy, 4 to 5 minutes. Stir in the reserved garlic and shallots, tofu, shrimp, chicken, and pork. Season with salt, to taste.

6. Working in a very large bowl or two large bowls, toss the noodles, about one quarter at a time with portions of the sauce mixture, tossing it carefully but thoroughly with two forks. When all the noodles and sauce have been combined, quickly transfer them to a large serving platter, mounding them into a cone shape. Garnish with the cilantro leaves, limes wedges, bell pepper, scallion flowers, and pickled garlic. Serve at once.

SERVES 8 AS AN APPETIZER OR PART OF A BUFFET

INDIAN-STYLE NOODLES
with Lamb and Peanuts

The best noodle dishes in Southeast Asia are to be found at the colorful hawkers' stalls that line the streets of every town and village. "Indian *mee goreng*"—fried noodles with lamb, vegetables and potatoes, bound with eggs, flavored with spicy tomato sauce, and garnished with peanuts—is beloved in Singapore and Malaysia, but unheard of in India. It's not hard to find the reason why. *Mee goreng* (fried noodles) is clearly a Chinese-originated dish that has been adopted by the local Indian population to suit its own palate, and then, in one of those marvelous culinary give-and-takes, is embraced again by the local Chinese. Throughout the Malay peninsula one finds elderly barefoot, Tamil vendors wearing white tunics and high turbans, piling delicious mounds of these homey fried noodles onto take-out plastic plates.

I always make this dish the day after serving roast leg of lamb, but almost any cut of cooked lamb will do as nicely.

Salt, to taste

1 pound fresh or ¾ pound dried wide
     Chinese egg noodles or fettuccine

1 teaspoon plus 3 tablespoons peanut oil

2 cups diced or sliced cooked lamb

2 tablespoons plus 2 teaspoons
     soy sauce

1 large egg, beaten

1 teaspoon Oriental sesame oil

1 medium onion, sliced

1½ teaspoons best-quality curry powder

¾ to 1 teaspoon pure chile powder

1 fresh large mild green chile, such as
     Anaheim, stemmed, seeded, and sliced

2 firm, ripe tomatoes, cut into thin wedges

¾ cup diced cooked potatoes

1½ cups bean sprouts

2 cups mustard greens, bok choy, or Swiss
     chard cut into 1-inch lengths

¼ cup Chicken Stock (page 384) or
     canned broth

2 tablespoons ketchup

¼ cup chopped roasted peanuts

3 tablespoons chopped fresh cilantro leaves

1. Bring a pot of salted water to a boil.

2. If using fresh noodles, separate with a fork to untangle. Add the noodles to the boiling water and cook until just slightly al dente, about 1½ minutes. (If using dried noodles, cook for 6 to 8 minutes.) Drain, rinse under cold running water, and toss with the 1 teaspoon oil. Set aside.

3. Toss the lamb with the 2 teaspoons soy sauce. Set aside.

4. In a bowl, beat the egg with the sesame oil and set aside.

5. Heat the remaining oil in a wok over high heat until almost smoking. Swirl the wok to coat with the oil. Add the onion and stir-fry for 3 minutes. Stir in the curry and chile powders. Stir in the lamb, chile, tomatoes, potatoes, bean sprouts, and mustard greens and stir for 2 minutes.

6. Add the noodles and cook, stirring and tossing, until they are heated through.

7. Push the noodles to the side of the wok and drizzle in the egg mixture. Cook, stirring, until the egg begins to set and then toss with the noodles.

8. Turn the heat down to medium and add the stock, ketchup, and the remaining soy sauce. Cook, tossing and stirring, until the noodles are dry, abut 3 minutes more. Transfer the noodles to a large serving platter and sprinkle with peanuts and cilantro.

SERVES 4 TO 6

NORI SAFFRON PASTA

Here is an intriguingly flavored fresh fettuccine to expand your repertoire of homemade pastas. The recipe uses nori, the toasted Japanese seaweed used for sushi. It is readily available in health food stores and quality grocery stores.

This pasta will go nicely with a very simple sauce that doesn't overpower its delicate taste. Try melted butter with a touch of lemon juice, parsley, and toasted pine nuts. You can also serve it just with butter, as an accompaniment to grilled poultry or fish.

3 large eggs

½ teaspoon saffron threads, crumbled

2¼ cups unbleached all-purpose
     flour

½ cup finely chopped, unsoaked dried
     toasted nori

4 tablespoons (½ stick) unsalted butter, cut
     into small pieces

1. Place the eggs in a bowl and beat in the saffron.

2. Place the flour in the food processor. With the motor running, slowly add the egg mixture. Process for another 10 seconds.

3. Turn the dough out onto a lightly floured surface. Sprinkle the nori over the dough and knead to incorporate. Continue kneading until the dough has formed a smooth ball, about 5 minutes.

4. Cover with a kitchen towel and let rest for 30 minutes.

5. Divide the dough into 6 parts. Take one piece of dough and keep the rest covered. Flatten the piece lightly with a rolling pin. Flour the dough lightly on both sides.

6. Set a pasta machine to the widest opening. Roll the dough through the machine. Fold it in thirds and run through the machine again. Repeat another 3 times, folding the dough in thirds each time.

7. Continue rolling the pasta through the machine, gradually making the opening smaller each time, until you arrive at the third thinnest setting. Run the pasta through the machine one more time. Set aside on a clean kitchen towel. Repeat with the remaining pieces of dough.

8. Allow the flattened pasta sheets to dry on the clean kitchen towels for 10 minutes, turning the sheets over from time to time.

9. To cut the pasta, use the broad cutters on the machine to make fettuccine.

10. Bring a large pot of salted water to a boil.

11. Add the fettucine to the salted water and cook at a rolling boil until al dente, 1½ to 2 minutes. Drain and toss with the butter. Serve at once.

SERVES 6

STAFF DINNER RICE VERMICELLI

with Minced Pork and Mustard Greens

While searching for recipes in Bangkok I observed many great chefs in action and sampled hundreds of exquisite and painstakingly prepared delicacies in the city's top restaurants. Thai food, however, is not all royal. It has another side that is quick, simple, unpretentious, and utterly delicious. These delicate, yet filling, noodles are inspired by the many staff meals I was fortunate enough to share with cooks backstage in their hotel and restaurant kitchens.

8 ounces rice vermicelli
1½ tablespoons peanut oil
6 ounces small shrimp, peeled and
   deveined
½ teaspoon minced fresh hot green or
   red chile
2 teaspoons crushed garlic
6 ounces lean ground pork
1 bunch mustard greens, trimmed and
   coarsely chopped (3 cups)
⅓ cup Chicken Stock (page 384), canned
   broth, or water
2½ tablespoons Asian fish sauce, such as
   nam pla
1 tablespoon dark soy sauce
1 tablespoon fresh lime juice
¾ teaspoon sugar, or more to taste
3 tablespoons chopped roasted peanuts,
   for garnish
Fresh cilantro leaves, for garnish

1. In a large bowl, soak the rice vermicelli, in warm water to cover for 20 minutes. Drain thoroughly.

2. Heat the oil in a wok over high heat until almost smoking. Swirl the wok to coat with the oil. Add the shrimp and cook until they turn pink, about 2 minutes. Remove with a slotted spoon and set aside.

3. Add the chile and garlic and stir for 30 seconds. Add the pork and cook, breaking it up with a fork, until opaque, about 2 minutes. Add the mustard greens and stir for 2 more minutes.

4. Stir in the noodles and shrimp and toss and stir until well combined, about 1 minute. Reduce the heat to medium-low and stir in the stock, fish sauce, soy sauce, lime juice, and sugar. Cook, stirring and tossing, until the noodles are dry, about 3 minutes. Serve at once, garnished with peanuts and cilantro.

SERVES 4 TO 6

CURRIED GLASS NOODLE AND SEAFOOD HOTPOT

Glass noodles, also known as mung bean threads or cellophane noodles, are the thin transparent noodles, made from mung bean flour, that are packaged in small bundles. Don't confuse them with rice vermicelli! As glass noodles readily absorb other flavors, they are especially delicious in a dish such as this—where they are simmered in a mild, flavorful Thai coconut curry, with various seafood and vegetables.

If you have a Chinese sand pot or clay pot, it will add to the presentation. Otherwise use a casserole and carefully transfer the dish to a deep, decorative bowl.

2 skeins (bundles) glass noodles (mung bean threads; about 3½ to 4 ounces total)
1½ cups canned unsweetened coconut milk, well stirred
2 tablespoons Thai red curry paste, preferably homemade (page 268)
2 teaspoons ground turmeric
1½ cups Chicken Stock (page 384) Fish Stock (page 385), or canned broth
2 tablespoons Asian fish sauce, such as nam pla
¾ teaspoon sugar
1 pound mixed seafood, such as peeled, deveined shrimp, scallops, chunks of fish, mussels, or clams (see Note)
1 red bell pepper, stemmed, seeded, and diced
¾ cup snow peas, trimmed
6 to 8 ounces fresh spinach, rinsed well and patted dry, tough stems discarded
8 to 10 canned straw mushrooms, drained
⅓ cup (tightly packed) fresh basil leaves, preferably Thai
Fresh cilantro leaves, for garnish

1. Soak the noodles in warm water to cover for 30 minutes. Drain and cut into 4-inch lengths. Set aside.

2. In a heavy flameproof casserole or Dutch oven, heat ¼ cup of the coconut milk over high heat. Add the curry paste and turmeric and cook, breaking the curry paste up with a fork, for 5 minutes. Add the rest of the coconut milk and the stock and bring to a simmer. Add the fish sauce and sugar.

3. Stir in the noodles and simmer over low heat for 3 minutes. About two thirds of the liquid should be absorbed. Add the seafood (except the shellfish, if using) and bell pepper, stirring them gently into the noodles.

Cover and simmer for 3 minutes. Add the snow peas, spinach, and mushrooms, stirring them in gently. Cover and cook for another 3 minutes, shaking the casserole gently. Stir in the shellfish, if using, and the basil.

4. If using a sand pot, bring it straight to the table. Otherwise, carefully transfer the dish to a serving bowl and serve, garnished with cilantro.

SERVES 4

Note: If using mussels and/or clams, scrub them well, debearding the mussels right before cooking. Steam them open in a large covered pot, filled to a depth of 1 inch with boiling water. Add them to the dish where noted in step 3.

BROAD RICE NOODLES

with Chinese Sausage and Shrimp

Of all the noodles dishes of Southeast Asia, nothing makes me more nostalgic for the roadside stalls of Malaysia and Singapore than *chow kway teo,* flat, pillowy rice noodles, slightly charred from the wok and tossed with sausage, shrimp, fish cakes, eggs, and a dark, sweet and spicy sauce.

This dish was made for me by the Nonya chef Jenny Fong, from San Francisco's Straits Café, as we stood in her kitchen reminiscing about the gastronomic delights of her native Penang.

1½ tablespoons Ketjap Manis (page 388) or sweet soy sauce
2 to 3 teaspoons Sriracha chile sauce or Chinese chile paste with garlic
1 tablespoon soy sauce
1½ tablespoons water
2 tablespoons peanut oil
1 large clove garlic, crushed through a press
4 ounces large shrimp, peeled, deveined, and cut in half lengthwise
2 Chinese sausage links, sliced diagonally
½ cake firm tofu, cut into 1-inch dice
¾ pound flat broad noodles (kway teo), available fresh from Asian markets, or dried flat rice noodles, soaked in water to cover for 20 minutes and drained
1 large egg, lightly beaten
½ cup bean sprouts
2 scallions, trimmed and cut into 2-inch lengths
2 tablespoons chopped roasted peanuts, for garnish
Lime wedges, for garnish

1. In a small bowl, mix the ketjap manis, chile sauce, soy sauce, and water. Set aside.

2. Heat the oil in a wok over high heat until almost smoking. Swirl the wok to coat with the oil. Add the garlic and stir for 30 seconds. Add the shrimp, sausages, and tofu and stir over high heat until the shrimp are pink, about 2 minutes.

3. Add the noodles and toss and stir for 1 minute. Add the soy mixture and toss thoroughly. Push the noodles to the side of the wok and add the beaten egg. Cook until the egg begins to set, about 25 seconds, and stir in the bean sprouts and scallions. Toss the egg into the noodles.

4. Transfer to a serving platter and garnish with peanuts and lime wedges.

SERVES 4

BREAKFAST IN SINGAPORE'S CHINATOWN

Anya and I had heard that Chinatown is the place for breakfast in Singapore. So we headed out early one morning on a quest through the ornate streets, past dragon-topped temples and rows of exquisitely decorated shop houses. We took with us a hot tip on the best places in town from one of our friends. She had recommended two eateries on Mosque Street, but had put an asterisk by the second.

As it turned out we walked by the unstarred restaurant first, and though we had resolved to try her preferred choice, we couldn't resist peeking in. It was famous in Singapore for traditional, hearty, peasant fare from Teochew, a region in Southeast China.

The place was filled with the sweet, gingery odor of red-braising, the trademark of Teochew cuisine. It was a braiser's paradise. At the counter we saw whole braised geese laid out next to huge slabs of bacon and a pig's head. These were offered with bean curd and braised peanuts and the favorite side dish of cabbage braised with pork crackling and lily flower. We joked that if we were in Paris this joint would surely be called a "brasserie!" There were also deep-fried prawn rolls and the ubiquitous *congee,* rice porridge, served plain or with deep-fried salted eggs. Many patrons were breakfasting on the Taiwanese version of *congee,* with chunks of sweet potatoes mixed in, accompanied by different kinds of omelets. It was wonderful and overwhelming—and, all in all, a bit too much for breakfast.

ANOTHER DISTRACTION

So we hurried off down the street to choice number one. But such are the seductions of Chinatown that we couldn't refrain from one more stop—at an ancient medicinal shop packed with antique jars full of an incredible selection of herbs, roots, flowers, twigs, and sundry dried creatures that the health-obsessed Chinese treat as restoratives and tonics to build themselves up in every possible way. Every time we stared at a particular jar brimming with unlikely powdered parts of an obscure animal, our curiosity was rewarded with advice from the owner as he launched unstoppably into a long explanation.

"Ah, yes, the dried crocodile meat is mixed into soups to cure asthma . . . and the sea horse is best boiled with ginger, in which case it acts like an antibiotic for people plagued by wounds and

scars . . . and this dried snake should be soaked in rice wine and taken for muscular aches and pains. . . ."

341

> *". . .the dried crocodile meat is mixed into soups to cure asthma . . . and the sea horse is best boiled with ginger. . ."*

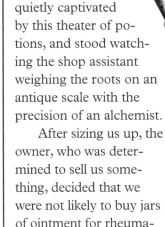

We were quietly captivated by this theater of potions, and stood watching the shop assistant weighing the roots on an antique scale with the precision of an alchemist.

After sizing us up, the owner, who was determined to sell us something, decided that we were not likely to buy jars of ointment for rheuma-

tism, nor were we about to spend our money on one of the bundles of holy pig's nipple flowers strewn on the counter. So instead

he pushed forward twenty different kinds of aphrodisiac. While he was reaching for the last of these, we thanked him politely and made a dash for the door. Our recommended destination was very close by, and this place was not a good one for a pre-breakfast appetizer.

A STEP BACK IN TIME

The Tai Tong Hoikee Coffee Shop was everything we had

dreamed of—a little moon cake and *dim sum* heaven. One of the few old eateries that still looks much as it did in the 1920s, it was packed with old-timers exchanging the week's gossip across marble-topped round tables with cast-iron legs.

dim sum circuses with their cartloads of food, huge groups of diners, screaming children, and general commotion. It was the Chinatown equivalent of a working-class Parisian café.

We sat down at the only table with space,

men was tucking into egg custard and chicken's feet. His friend worked in a coffee shop on the other side of town. The third was in his late eighties and had worked for most of the century as an ice-cream hawker one block away. He described his favorite flavors—coconut and red bean—in poetic Cantonese that we could neither fully understand nor properly translate. He told us they had been congregating there for breakfast for forty years.

Our new companions consumed vast amounts of extra-strong tea and happily reminisced about Singapore's Chinatown in its heyday sixty years ago. The new high rises and the rent hikes that went with them were beyond their comprehension. All the while, the powerful fans hanging from the high corrugated-zinc ceiling failed to ruffle a single receding strand of their thoroughly brilliantined hair.

Tai Tong Hoikee was the kind of place where the first bowl of tea is put in front of you before your rear end hits the seat.

The menu was laid out along a green- and white-tiled wall in red and yellow banner headlines. Here and there were old fans, piles of wooden crates, and utensils that ignored the electronic age. The air was thick with orders and opinions. Tai Tong Hoikee was the antithesis of huge, Cantonese-style family

next to three old men wearing wrinkled faces and white T-shirts. They seemed delighted to talk to us and quite happy not to—whatever our preference—in that unnerving Chinese way. One of the

Tai Tong Hoikee was the kind of place where the first bowl of tea is put in front of you before your rear end hits the seat. And one of the ubiquitous logo-bearing, plastic-wrapped wet towels follows suit before you can possibly take a sip. Customers select their chopsticks from a white and blue ceramic vase on the table, measuring the lengths without looking, to find a proper pair.

PERFECTING AN EATING TECHNIQUE

Actual eating, of course, was a whole ritual in itself. The ice-cream vendor had the most captivating technique. Using his fingers, he flattened the rice in his bowl and then mixed it vigorously with his spoon. Then he poured tea from the pot into his cup, exchanged a few lines of conversation to the right or the left, repoured the tea back into the pot; and repeated the decanting cycle once again. Next he sorted carefully but quickly through his portion of braised pork, poured some sauce onto his rice, and started to eat and drink in rhythmic alternation between his rice, pork, and tea cup.

The *dim sum* was steamed in enormous bamboo steamers, and rather than the cart coming to you, you had to go over to a counter and

pick it up yourself—which just added to the fun and the exchange. We opted for the plump and succulent pork *shiew mai*, chewy and gelatinous pork ribs braised in ginger and garlic-laced brown sauce, and the *chee chong fun*, a rice-flour crepe filled with generous portions of spiced pork. The chicken (and what good chicken it was, straight from the nearby market) came in two guises, velveted and steamed, and roasted with a pronounced flavor of soy. The chicken and pork were accompanied by *no mai fun*, steamed glutinous rice, faintly sweet, sticky, and comforting.

We sat and chatted with the old men, who kept pouring just a little bit of tea (as the tea drinking etiquette requires) into our cups, lamenting further about the changes in the Chinatown.

Sitting in on this perfectly choreographed meal made us ever more eager to know just what the wiry old man really thought of red bean ice cream.

Passion Fruit Ginger Cheesecake

Orange Cake with Passion Fruit Icing

Mango Mousse Cake

Spice Route Coconut Cake

Quince Galette

Seduction Pineapple Upside-Down Cake

Banana Fudge Cake (!!!)

Elizabeth Pederson's Pavlova

Thai-Inspired Pumpkin Tart

Tropical Trifle

Banana and Kiwi Spring Rolls

Tropical Fruit in Scented Coconut Milk

Cresside Colette's Coconut and Palm Sugar Custard

Licorice Cream with Passion Fruit and Meringue

Ginger Crème Brûlée

Mango Gratin with Champagne Sabayon

Cardamom-Coffee Mousse

Piña Colada Parfaits

Banana and Lime Soufflés

Peaches in Pink Ginger Syrup

Steamed Kumquat Puddings with
Orange Custard Cream

Andy Wai's Watermelon and Tapioca Soup

Javanese Black Rice Pudding

Fragrant Fruit Compote

Kiwi Tiramisù

Jasmine Jazz Tiramisù

Frozen Pineapple Soufflés

Papaya-Lime-Coconut Sorbet

Kiwi and Gewürztraminer Sorbet

Passion Fruit and Gin Granita

Frozen Toasted Coconut and
Mango Terrine with Coconut Wafers

In this age of great desserts, it is difficult to startle and surprise. But a new taste—intensely perfumed tropical fruit or an unexpected sweet spice that hovers gently in the back of the palate—can make even a simple dessert into a dramatic showcase. And with no effort at all! My strategy for desserts is straightforward: Keep the preparation as simple as possible and use enticing, exotic flavors that leave guests delighted and slightly bemused but not oversaturated. The desserts in this chapter are light, tart, and almost never rich—seduction minus the sin.

A passion fruit icing transforms an ordinary orange cake into something special; ripe peaches float in a refreshing ginger-infused syrup; a simple custard surprises with its blend of palm sugar and coconut milk; and trifle comes alive with the radiant flavors of tropical fruit and citrusy *crème anglaise*. And for the dog days of summer, there are beguiling iced combinations: papaya, lime, and coconut; passion fruit and gin; kiwi and Gewürztraminer.

Almost every chapter in this book took its inspiration from a rainbow of different cultures and culinary traditions—there are salads from Thailand, curries from Malaysia, noodles from China, vegetables from India. The desserts here are a tribute to the ingenuity of chefs and home cooks from Australia and New Zealand. Southeast Asia does not have a dessert tradition to speak of. France and Britain do, but they lack the cornucopia of exotic tastes that bless the tropical climates. The antipodeans, on the other hand, have the best of both worlds. They treasure their trifles, puddings, pastries, mousses, and *gelati* and they enjoy an astonishing selection of tropical flavors. It is in the delicious wizardry of dessert making that these sweet-tooth magicians really put their natural bounty to use. I am forever indebted to my friends and colleagues Down Under for making this chapter sparkle.

PASSION FRUIT GINGER CHEESECAKE

Light, fresh, and exotic, this cheesecake is seduction in its purest form. Passion fruit has exactly the right fragrance and acidity to enliven and cut through the lush creamy texture of the ricotta and cream cheese filling. I have also added yogurt for extra tang. For decoration you can pipe some whipped cream around the edges of the cake and drizzle with fresh passion fruit pulp.

CRUST
1½ cups ground gingersnaps or other plain ginger cookies
¼ cup sugar
5 tablespoons unsalted butter, melted

FILLING

12 ounces cream cheese, at room temperature,
    cut into pieces

¾ cup ricotta cheese

½ cup low-fat plain yogurt

⅔ cup sugar, or more to taste

2 teaspoons fresh lemon juice

Pulp from 5 fresh passion fruit, or ⅓ cup
    thawed frozen passion fruit pulp

1½ tablespoons syrup from minced ginger
    packed in syrup

3 large eggs

2½ tablespoons minced ginger in syrup
    (syrup drained)

1. Prepare the crust: Combine the ground gingersnaps and sugar in a large bowl and mix well. Pour in the butter and mix in thoroughly with a fork.

2. Press the mixture evenly over the bottom of an 8½-inch springform pan, covering it completely. Chill for 15 minutes.

3. Preheat the oven to 375°F.

4. Prepare the filling: Combine the cheeses, yogurt, sugar, lemon juice, passion fruit pulp, and ginger syrup in a food processor and process thoroughly. Taste and add more sugar if needed. Add the eggs, one at a time, processing until well blended after each addition. Transfer the mixture to a large bowl, scraping off the sides of the processor with a spatula, and stir in the minced ginger.

5. Pour the mixture into the prepared pan and bake until the cheesecake is set, about 50 minutes. To test for doneness, insert a toothpick in the center of the cake. It should come out fairly clean, although the filling will jiggle a little. Open the oven door and cool the cheesecake in the oven for 1 hour. Refrigerate at least 6 hours before serving. Remove the sides of the springform pan at serving time.

SERVES 6 TO 8

ORANGE CAKE
with Passion Fruit Icing

The intense, mysterious taste of passion fruit transforms a delicious but unassuming Australian buttercake into a memorable treat. The cake is lovely with juicy diced oranges alongside. I like to keep some of the passion fruit seeds in the icing; it gives the cake an unusual hedgehog appearance and a bit of crunch. If you can't find fresh passion fruit, use frozen pulp, available from Hispanic grocery stores.

The cake tastes best when made a day ahead to let the flavors ripen.

1⅔ cups all-purpose flour

2 teaspoons baking powder

Pinch of salt

¾ cup granulated sugar

¼ cup fresh orange juice

3 large eggs, separated

2 tablespoons milk

Grated zest from 1 orange

10 tablespoons (1¼ sticks) unsalted butter,
    melted and cooled

PASSION FRUIT ICING

4 fresh passion fruit (if unavailable, use
    4 tablespoons thawed frozen passion
    fruit pulp)

1½ cups confectioners' sugar

1 tablespoon unsalted butter, at room
    temperature

1. Preheat the oven to 350°F and lightly grease an 8-inch square baking pan.

2. Sift together the flour, baking powder, salt, and sugar into a large bowl.

3. In another bowl, whisk the orange

juice with the egg yolks. In a third bowl, whisk the milk with the egg whites. Make a well in the dry ingredients and stir in the yolk mixture. With an electric mixer, beat at low speed until combined. Add the melted butter and beat at high speed until fluffy. Add the egg white mixture and beat for 5 minutes, until the mixture is light and fluffy.

4. Pour the batter into the prepared pan and bake in the middle of the oven until the top is golden and a cake tester comes out clean, 40 to 45 minutes. Cool on a rack, then remove it from the pan.

5. Make the icing: If using fresh passion fruit, halve them and scoop out the pulp into a bowl. Strain through a fine strainer into a 2-cup glass measure, pressing thoroughly on the solids to extract all the liquid. Stir half of the strained seeds back into the liquid. Pour the liquid into the sugar in a bowl, stirring well. Stir in the melted butter.

6. With a rubber spatula, spread the icing over the top and sides of the cooled cake. When the icing is set and cooled, carefully insert toothpicks in the top of the cake, then cover it loosely with plastic wrap, and let stand for several hours or overnight. Remove the plastic wrap and toothpicks before serving.

SERVES 8

MANGO MOUSSE CAKE

I don't believe in serving rich cakes after a filling meal, opting instead for light, acidic, palate-refreshing conclusions. This cake, however, offers a perfect compromise. It combines all the grandness we rightly expect from a cake with the refreshing lightness of a sorbet or mousse. And if you are not in the mood for making the génoise base, the mango mousse is delicious on its own, especially when topped with fresh raspberry or blackberry sauce.

For the glaze I use Goya brand mango jelly which can be found at many supermarkets and Hispanic grocery stores. Make sure you use ripe, intensely flavored mangoes for the mousse, otherwise the taste will be watery and thin. Plan to make the cake a day ahead.

CAKE
4 large eggs
⅔ cup sugar
1 teaspoon vanilla extract
¼ cup clarified butter (page 390)
⅔ cup all-purpose flour
Pinch of salt

SYRUP
½ cup fresh orange juice
3 tablespoons sugar
2 tablespoons Grand Marnier
    (orange liqueur)

Mango Mousse (recipe follows)

GLAZE
3 tablespoons water
1 teaspoon unflavored gelatin
⅔ cup mango jelly
3 tablespoons fresh orange juice
1 tablespoon fresh lemon juice

6 thin mango slices, for garnish

1. Preheat the oven to 350°F. Line the bottom of a 9-inch springform pan with waxed paper. Grease the waxed paper and dust lightly with flour, shaking off the excess.

2. Make the cake: In the top of a double boiler set over simmering water, whisk the eggs and sugar until the mixture is warm and the sugar is dissolved. Scrape into a large bowl and beat with an electric mixer at medium speed until tripled in volume, about 7 minutes. Beat in the vanilla and clarified butter.

3. Sift together the flour and salt into a small bowl. Fold gently into the egg mixture until just combined.

4. Pour the batter into the prepared pan and smooth the top with a spatula. Bake in the middle of the oven until the top is golden and a cake tester comes out clean. Remove from the oven and let stand for 5 minutes. Carefully remove the sides of the pan, invert the cake onto a cake rack, and remove the bottom of the pan. Carefully peel off the waxed paper. Reinvert the cake onto another rack and cool.

5. Make the syrup: Combine the syrup ingredients in a small nonreactive saucepan and bring to a simmer over medium heat, stirring to dissolve the sugar. Remove from the heat and let cool to room temperature.

6. With a large serrated knife, cut a thin layer off the top of the cake. Nibble on it as you finish preparing the recipe.

7. Put the remaining cake layer back into the springform pan, cut side up, and brush with the syrup. Pour all the Mango Mousse on the cake and smooth the top with a spatula. Refrigerate until set, about 4 hours.

8. Make the glaze: In a small bowl, sprinkle the water over the gelatin and let soften for 3 minutes. Combine the mango jelly with the orange and lemon juices in a small saucepan, and bring to a boil over medium heat, stirring. Cook for 1 minute. Remove from the heat, add the gelatin mixture, and stir until dissolved. Cool slightly.

9. Arrange the mango slices in a fan in the middle of the cake. Pour the glaze evenly all over the top of the cake. Carefully insert toothpicks in the top of the cake, then cover it with plastic wrap (the toothpicks should prevent the wrap from touching the top of the cake). Refrigerate the cake until the glaze is set, about 1 hour. Remove the plastic wrap and the toothpicks. Carefully remove the sides of the springform and place the cake, still on the pan bottom, on a cake platter.

SERVES 8

Mango Mousse

2 tablespoons Grand Marnier
  (orange liqueur)
1½ tablespoons unflavored gelatin
2 teaspoons grated orange zest
¾ cup fresh orange juice
1½ tablespoons fresh lemon juice
Flesh from 3 medium ripe mangoes,
  coarsely chopped
½ cup milk
¼ cup sugar
¾ cup heavy (or whipping) cream,
  chilled

1. Pour the Grand Marnier over the gelatin in a nonreactive saucepan and let soften for 2 minutes. Stir in the orange zest and orange juice.

2. Combine the mango flesh and milk in a food processor and process until smooth. Strain through a fine strainer into the gelatin mixture. Add the sugar, stir well, and bring just to a boil over medium heat, stirring constantly. Remove from the heat and cool to room temperature.

3. In a small bowl, beat the cream with an electric mixer at medium speed until soft

THE WELL-ROUNDED COCONUT

*T*he coconut palm, with its characteristic cluster of nuts, is an unfussy species that grows all around the equator, lapping up plenty of sun and quite content with occasional rain. The large brownish-green coconuts from which one sips at a tropical beach are the unripe nuts, still in their husk. They have a delicious jelly-like pulp, which solidifies as the coconut matures to form the firm, juicy, white flesh of a mature hairy brown coconut. When the grated flesh is squeezed, with or without water, it produces what's known as coconut milk—not to be confused with the clear liquid inside the young coconut. Some gourmet markets now sell coquitos, marble-size, shelled baby coconuts, imported from Chile. These should be treated as regular nuts—eaten straight out of the package or grated and sprinkled on desserts.

Fresh coconuts are sensitive to heat and spoil easily, so when choosing one, follow these guidelines. Look for a medium-size nut which feels heavy for its size: This means that there is plenty of liquid inside. Make sure there are no cracks, and then carefully examine the "eyes," the three dots around the top. They should be completely dry without any sign of mold. The brown hairs should look healthy and shiny. Once you've cracked the nut, taste the liquid inside. If the taste is off, discard the nut and start again. As coconuts are inexpensive, you would do well to buy an extra one just in case. Once you bring the coconuts home, store them in a cool, dry place.

GETTING TO THE MEAT

Coconuts are rather like my Russian babushka, richly benevolent on the inside, but tough as nails on the surface. And so, just as it was for me in Moscow when I wanted some extra rubles for candy, when it comes to cracking one open and extracting the milk, there is simply no easy solution. But while the milk is most flavorful when extracted from a freshly opened coconut, the trouble of prying the meat out of the shell, peeling off the brown skin, and grating it is hardly worth the effort. Baking the coconut in the oven first, helps the skin separate from the shell. But for those with access to ethnic grocery stores, the best bet for making milk is the grated fresh coconut, sold packaged and frozen at many Southeast Asian and Hispanic markets. Let it defrost, purée in a blender for a minute or so, with 1 cup boiling water to 1 cup grated coconut, let stand for 5 minutes and strain through a sieve, pressing hard on the solids. If desiccated (dried) coconut is your only option, pour 1½ cups boiling water for each cup of coconut, let stand for 15 minutes, blend, and strain. Coconut milk should refrigerated and used within two days. Like stock, it will keep in a freezer indefinitely.

As homemade coconut milk will always taste somewhat thin, a canned substitute is often best. (Some purists argue that the difference between the two is like the one between canned and freshly made stock. My answer:

Just imagine if you had to pluck the chicken to make the stock!) Canned coconut milk is denser and richer than homemade and, in most cases, needs to be thinned out with water or broth. Use ¾ to 1 cup water for every 14-ounce can of coconut milk.

The difference in quality between brands is quite considerable. Of the types that are most commonly available, Chaokoh from Thailand is the most reliable. Goya—which can now be found at many supermarkets in areas with large Latin populations—is fine too, as is the Goya frozen shredded coconut, which can be spotted in the freezer section. If you refrigerate a can of coconut milk upright, you will find that the thick cream will rise to the surface. For Thai recipes that call for thick and thin milk, skim off the desired amount of the thick cream and dilute the rest with water. Many Southeast Asian grocery stores also carry frozen fresh coconut milk. Thick and flavorful, it really is the best solution to the riddle of coconut milk. Again, thin it out with water to the consistency of heavy cream.

Mild, soothing, with an irresistibly exotic suggestion, coconut milk invites culinary drama and is best when coupled with pungent seasoning and fragrant aromatics. Coconut milk isn't low in fat and I like to use it sparingly, just as I would cream. If you add it to puréed soups or pasta sauce, along with a handful of spices, ordinary dishes will glow with exotica—like a piece of drab linen transformed into a shimmering Thai silk.

peaks form. Fold gently into the cooled mango mixture.

4. If using the mousse for the cake, follow the instructions in step 7 of the cake recipe (page 349). Otherwise, pour into serving glasses and chill until set, about 4 hours.

SERVES 6 ON ITS OWN

SPICE ROUTE COCONUT CAKE

While busy buying, planting, and exporting the exotic spices of Malaysia, Indonesia, and Singapore, the Dutch, Portuguese and British colonists introduced European cooking to the lush tropical lands. In so doing they contributed further twists and turns to the fascinating kaleidoscope of culinary traditions and styles that light up Southeast Asia. The British brought Sunday roast and Worcestershire sauce; the Portuguese contributed chiles, pineapples, and tomato-based stews, and the Dutch spread the tradition of European holiday baking. Here, then, is a typical tropical colonial cake, rich with the indigenous flavors of coconut, sweet spices, and nuts (by now, all staples in our postcolonial kitchens). Rose water adds an exotic touch.

This cake is best served slightly warm, with a dollop of cream and a tropical fruit sorbet. Using freshly ground spices will make the taste more vivid and refined at the same time.

1²⁄₃ cups all-purpose flour

1 teaspoon freshly ground cardamom

1¹⁄₂ teaspoons freshly ground cinnamon

¹⁄₂ teaspoon freshly ground cloves

¹⁄₂ teaspoon freshly grated nutmeg

1¹⁄₂ teaspoons baking powder

¹⁄₂ teaspoon baking soda

11 tablespoons unsalted butter, at room temperature

³⁄₄ cup granulated sugar

2 large eggs

²⁄₃ cup canned unsweetened coconut milk, well stirred

2 teaspoons rose water

³⁄₄ cup grated fresh or dessicated (dried) coconut

²⁄₃ cup chopped toasted (page 389) macadamia or cashew nuts

Confectioners' sugar for dusting the cake

1. Preheat the oven to 350°F and grease a 9-inch square baking pan.

2. Sift together the flour, cardamom, cinnamon, cloves, nutmeg, baking powder, and baking soda into a medium-size bowl.

3. In a large bowl, beat the butter with the sugar using an electric mixer until fluffy. Beat in the eggs, one at a time, then beat in the coconut milk and rose water.

4. Beat in the dry ingredients just until blended. Stir in the coconut and macadamias. Pour the batter into the prepared pan and bake in the middle of the oven until the top is golden and a cake tester comes out clean, about 45 minutes.

5. Cool the cake on a wire rack, then remove it from the pan. Dust with confectioners' sugar and serve slightly warm.

SERVES 8

QUINCE GALETTE

This dessert takes its inspiration from the Middle East, but goes particularly well after an Asian meal. It's a cinch to prepare—it's just sliced quinces layered over a sheet of purchased puff pastry. What makes it special is the striking caramelized mixture of palm sugar, cinnamon, and rose water, sprinkled over the quinces. Serve it warm with whipped cream or ice cream.

3 large quinces, scrubbed lightly, washed, cut in half lengthwise, and cored

1 cup water

¹⁄₂ cup granulated sugar

6 tablespoons (³⁄₄ stick) unsalted butter

¹⁄₄ cup palm sugar or (packed) light brown sugar

1¹⁄₂ teaspoons ground cinnamon

1 teaspoon rose water

1 sheet frozen puff pastry, thawed

1. Preheat the oven to 400°F.

2. Arrange the quinces in a baking dish, cut sides down. Mix the water with the granulated sugar and pour into the baking dish. Bake until the quinces are almost tender, about 30 minutes, turning once. Remove from the liquid, reserving the liquid, then, when cool enough to handle, cut the quinces into ¼-inch-thick slices. Set aside to cool completely. (This can be done a day ahead. Cover with plastic wrap and refrigerate. Bring to room temperature before proceeding.)

3. Reduce the oven temperature to 350°F. Lightly grease a baking sheet.

4. Melt the butter in a small saucepan over medium heat. Stir in the palm sugar, cinnamon, and rose water and cook, stirring, until the sugar is dissolved.

5. Roll the puff pastry into a rectangle about 12 x 9 inches. Hang the pastry over a rolling pin and transfer to the prepared baking sheet. Arrange the quince slices on the pastry, leaving a 1½-inch border. Fold in the edges and crimp decoratively. Brush the quinces with the butter mixture, reserving about 1 tablespoon of it, then bake until the quinces are soft and golden, about 35 minutes. About halfway through the baking, sprinkle about 2 tablespoons of the reserved quince baking liquid all over the galette.

6. Preheat the broiler.

7. Reheat the reserved butter mixture. Brush the quinces with it and pass under the broiler to caramelize, 30 seconds to 1 minute. (Watch closely or the galette will burn.) Serve warm.

SERVES 8

SEDUCTION PINEAPPLE UPSIDE-DOWN CAKE

The story of this cake is one of seduction. Literally. When chef Bruce Hill first met his fiancée at his San Francisco restaurant, Oritalia, he knew she was the woman of his dreams. She, however, was not so sure. He kept asking her out, but she refused—that is, until she tasted his pineapple cake. Her heart was his.

The batter for the cake is quite unconventional, and when you make it, you will

be convinced there is a mistake, since before the egg whites are added it will be more like a pastry dough than a batter. Keep at it—it works!

8 tablespoons (1 stick) unsalted butter, at
*   room temperature*
5 tablespoons (packed) light brown sugar
4 to 6 fresh pineapple rings
2 cups all-purpose flour
1¾ teaspoons baking powder
1½ cups plus 2 tablespoons granulated sugar
5 large eggs, separated
2 teaspoons vanilla extract
Coconut-Rum Whipped Cream
*   (recipe follows)*

1. Preheat the oven to 325°F.

2. Melt 6 tablespoons of the butter in a 10-inch cast-iron or other ovenproof skillet over medium heat. Add the brown sugar and stir until it dissolves. Off the heat, place a whole pineapple ring in the middle of the skillet. Cut the other rings in half and place them decoratively around the whole ring. Set the skillet aside.

3. Sift together the flour and baking powder into a medium-size bowl. Set the bowl aside.

4. In a large bowl, beat the 1½ cups granulated sugar with the remaining butter, then add the egg yolks and beat until pale yellow and fluffy. Beat in the vanilla extract, then gradually beat in the flour mixture. You will have something that resembles more a pastry dough than a batter.

5. In another large bowl using clean, dry beaters, beat the egg whites with the remaining sugar until stiff peaks form. Little by little, fold the whites into the stiff batter, stirring gently but thoroughly with a wooden spoon until the mixture is smooth and lighter but still thick.

6. Pour the batter over the pineapple,

using a spatula to help spread it evenly. Bake until the cake is golden and a tester comes out clean, about 55 minutes. Cover loosely with aluminum foil if it begins to brown too quickly.

7. Run a knife around the edges of the skillet and invert the cake onto a cake platter. Serve slightly warm with the Coconut-Rum Whipped Cream.

SERVES 8 TO 10

Coconut-Rum Whipped Cream

1½ cups heavy (or whipping) cream, chilled
1 tablespoon sugar
1½ tablespoons dark rum
¼ cup sweetened flaked coconut

In a large bowl, beat the cream and sugar with an electric mixer at medium speed until soft peaks form. Gently fold in the rum and the coconut.

MAKES ABOUT 2 CUPS

BANANA FUDGE CAKE (!!!)

When I interviewed Elizabeth Pederson, one of New Zealand's top food writers, she praised her country's meats and seafood, she had exciting things to say about its young chefs, but she just couldn't stop raving about the old-fash-ioned country baked goods, produced by the wives of farmers and sheep shearers. She gave me the recipe for this cake and marked it with three exclamation points. My adaptation retains the luscious quality of the chocolate-banana filling while assuring a moist, delicious cake that needs no icing.

FILLING
2 tablespoons unsweetened cocoa
   powder
¼ cup (packed) light brown sugar
¼ cup granulated sugar
½ cup sweetened flaked coconut
3 medium firm, ripe bananas

CAKE
10 tablespoons (1¼ sticks) unsalted
   butter, at room temperature
1 cup granulated sugar
½ teaspoon vanilla extract
3 large eggs
2¼ cups all-purpose flour
2 teaspoons baking powder
Pinch of salt
1 cup milk
3 tablespoons unsalted butter, melted
Confectioners' sugar

1. Preheat the oven to 350°F. Grease and lightly flour a 10-inch springform pan and line the bottom with greased parchment paper.

2. Make the filling: In a large bowl, sift together the cocoa, brown and granulated sugars, and stir in the coconut. Set aside. Thinly slice the bananas. Set aside.

3. Make the cake: In a large bowl, beat

the butter and sugar with an electric mixer at medium speed until fluffy. Beat in the vanilla, then the eggs, one at a time, beating well after each addition.

4. Sift together the flour, baking powder, and salt into a medium-size bowl. Beat the dry ingredients into the butter mixture, alternating with the milk.

5. With a wet spatula, spread a third of the batter in the prepared pan. Sprinkle half of the cocoa mixture over the batter and arrange half of the bananas over it. Drizzle with half the melted butter. Carefully spread on another third of the batter and repeat the layers of filling, banana, and butter. Evenly spread the remaining batter on top.

6. Bake the cake in the middle of the oven until a tester comes out clean and the top is golden, 55 to 60 minutes. Remove the sides of the pan and invert the cake onto a wire rack. Remove the pan bottom and peel

off the parchment. Reinvert the cake onto another rack and cool for 20 minutes.

7. Dust the cake with confectioners' sugar and serve slightly warm.

SERVES 8 TO 10

ELIZABETH PEDERSON'S PAVLOVA

Pavlova, the meringue dessert named after the legendary Russian ballerina, is to Australia and New Zealand what apple pie is to America or Sunday roast is to

BANANA BELIEFS

The familiar and beloved banana is cultivated in many tropical countries, but is actually native to Southeast Asia. The sun-colored, horn-shaped fruit made its way over to Africa about 1,500 years ago, and from there migrated to Arabia. It was idolized everywhere it went.

From great religions of the world, the banana received glowing reports. The plant is referred to in the Koran as the Tree of Paradise, while in early Christian mythology it was known as the tree of knowledge. In Southeast Asia the banana is even more revered; in fact, it's almost a cult. To Thais the tall banana plant is the guardian of good fortune, and banana trees are planted on temple

grounds. Thais believe that if you pray by a banana tree during a full moon, you will be rewarded with the vision of a long-haired beauty with a flower above her ear.

Filipinos, who prefer their banana trees short, believe that you shouldn't look up while planting a banana tree. What's more, to ensure thin peel it should only be planted by a bare-chested man, and it should also be planted at low tide, when there are many stones on the shore, to ensure that the harvest is as abundant as the stones. In Bali the banana is a symbol of fertility: A gift of twin bananas will bring a pregnant woman twins. And for single souls, it can also be used as a charm to win someone's affection.

Great Britain—a national classic. Invite an antipodean to a party and you will be sure to hear "I'll bring the pav, luv."

The idea for this recipe comes from Elizabeth Pederson, a food writer for the *New Zealand Herald*, the country's main newspaper, and actually originated with her mother, Cathy.

Elizabeth, raised on a farm in New Zealand's South Island, told me that the eggs used for a good pav should be no more and no less than 3 to 4 days old. Another luxury available to antipodeans is fresh passion fruit, whose pulp, along with kiwi and strawberries, forms the classic decoration for the pavlova. If you can't find it fresh, try looking for frozen passion fruit pulp at a Hispanic grocery store.

4 large egg whites, at room temperature
Pinch of salt
1 1/3 cups superfine sugar
2 1/2 teaspoons cornstarch
1 teaspoon distilled white vinegar
1 teaspoon vanilla extract
2 cups heavy (or whipping) cream
Sliced kiwi, for garnish
Fresh or thawed frozen passion fruit pulp,
*   for garnish*
Sliced fresh strawberries, for garnish

1. Preheat the oven to 250°F. Lightly grease and flour a large nonstick baking sheet.

2. Beat the egg whites and salt with an electric mixer at medium speed until soft peaks form. Increase the speed to high, and while beating, gradually add the sugar. Beat until stiff and glossy, about 8 minutes. Beat in the cornstarch, vinegar, and vanilla.

3. Spoon the mixture into a pastry bag fitted with a 3/4-inch round tip, and pipe it onto the sheet, forming a 10-inch circle about 1 inch thick. Place in the oven and bake for 1 1/2 hours. Turn off the oven and leave the pavlova

in the oven for 1 hour with the door slightly ajar. Using two large metal spatulas, carefully transfer the pavlova to a serving platter.

4. Whip the cream until soft peaks form. Spoon the whipped cream into a clean pastry bag fitted with a decorative tip. Pipe the cream over the top of the pavlova. Decorate with fruit.

SERVES 8

THAI-INSPIRED PUMPKIN TART

This tart is inspired by the flavors of *sangkhyaa fak thong*, a classic Thai dessert of a soothing, rich coconut custard baked inside a small pumpkin. I enlivened the mellow flavors of coconut and pumpkin with sweet spices and bake the custard in a buttery pastry shell. Serving it for Thanksgiving will add allure to your holiday table.

2 large eggs
3 large egg yolks
2/3 cup palm sugar or (packed) light brown
*   sugar*
1 3/4 cups puréed cooked fresh or canned
*   pumpkin*
2/3 cup canned unsweetened coconut milk,
*   well stirred*
1/2 teaspoon ground cardamom
1/2 teaspoon freshly grated nutmeg
1/2 teaspoon ground ginger
Pinch of freshly ground white pepper
2 tablespoons dark rum
Prebaked Tart Shell (recipe follows)

1. Preheat the oven to 325°F.

2. In a large bowl, whisk the eggs, egg yolks, and sugar until foamy. Add the pumpkin, coconut milk, cardamom, nutmeg, ginger, pepper, and rum and stir well.

3. Pour the mixture into the tart shell. Bake in the lower third of the oven until the filling is set, about 50 minutes. Serve the tart warm or at room temperature.

SERVES 8

Prebaked Tart Shell

1⅓ cups all-purpose flour
3 tablespoons confectioners' sugar
8 tablespoons (1 stick) unsalted butter,
*   chilled and cut into pieces*
1 large egg yolk, beaten with 1½ tablespoons
*   heavy (or whipping) cream, chilled*
Ice water (optional)

1. Sift together the flour and confectioners' sugar into a large bowl. Add the butter, and using a pastry blender, two knives, or your fingertips, cut it into the flour until the mixture resembles coarse crumbs.

2. Add the egg yolk-cream mixture and quickly blend into the pastry, using your fingertips. If the pastry doesn't quite hold together, add a few drops of ice water. Shape the pastry into a ball and press into a thick disk. Wrap in plastic wrap and refrigerate for 2 hours.

3. Preheat the oven to 400°F.

4. On a well-floured surface with a floured rolling pin, roll out the disk to an 11-inch circle, about ⅛-inch thick. Drape over a rolling pin and fit into a 9-inch tart pan with a removable bottom, pressing the pastry gently into the corners and against the sides of the pan. Roll the rolling pin over the top of the pan to trim off the crust.

5. Prick the bottom of the pastry with a fork, line with aluminum foil, and fill with pie weights, dried beans, or rice. Bake the crust until light golden, about 20 minutes.

6. Remove from the oven and remove the foil and the weights. Cool before filling.

MAKES ONE 9-INCH TART SHELL

TROPICAL TRIFLE

Despite the name, which conjures up azure skies, palm trees, and continuous sunshine, this dessert was inspired by a Melbourne winter—which is, in a way, very Brrr . . . itish, with badly heated Victorian houses and weeks of relentless drizzle. (Yes, of course it has its bright side, with warming fires and dainty glasses of sherry.) Anyway, on one of these days I sat home, writing, and dreamed of Singapore. My only consolation was the thought of weekend trips to the market where, even in winter, one can find a cornucopia of exotic fruit, flown in from the tropical North.

Between the winter, the writing, and my

daydreams, I came up with this typical Melbourne dessert. It's English to the core, but with that welcome suggestion of the tropics.

Using a homemade sponge cake is, of course, preferable, and you can do so if you wish. I, however, don't believe dessert should become a daunting undertaking. By the time the cake is soaked through with rum and fruit juices, frankly it's hard to tell the difference anyway. If passion fruit is available, do add some.

1 sponge cake (about 16 ounces), preferably homemade
½ cup dark rum
1½ cups puréed mango flesh
3 kiwi, peeled and diced, plus slices for decorating
2½ cups diced ripe fresh pineapple, plus more for decorating
1¼ cups fresh raspberries, plus more for decorating
Citrus Custard Cream (recipe follows)
1½ cups heavy (or whipping) cream, chilled
1 tablespoon confectioners' sugar

1. Cut the sponge cake into ½-inch-thick slices. Line the bottom of a large glass serving bowl with them, trimming the slices to fit the bowl. Drizzle the rum over the cake and let stand for 15 minutes.

2. Spread the mango purée over the cake. Scatter on a layer of kiwi, then pineapple, and then top with raspberries.

3. Pour the Citrus Custard Cream over the fruit. Cover the trifle with plastic wrap and chill for at least 4 hours or overnight.

4. In a chilled bowl, whip the cream with the confectioners' sugar until soft peaks form. Transfer the whipped cream to a pastry bag and pipe in swirls over the trifle. Decorate with the remaining kiwi, pineapple, and raspberries.

SERVES 6 TO 8

FORTUNATE FRUIT

The Chinese believe that planting citrus trees in their gardens will bring prosperity and matrimonial harmony. Mandarins signify gold and great wealth, and tangerine and orange plants are given as New Year presents, for luck. Pineapples are also signs of prosperity, while bananas bring luck first thing in the morning.

Fruits with a lot of seeds, such as melons or pomegranates, betoken fertility.

Citrus Custard Cream

This is a versatile, fresh-tasting custard cream that can be served with a range of desserts: chocolate cakes, fruit tarts, and scrumptious winter puddings.

6 large egg yolks
½ cup sugar
1½ cups milk
½ cup heavy (or whipping) cream
Grated zest of 1 orange
Grated zest of 1 lemon
¼ cup fresh orange juice

1. Whisk the egg yolks and sugar in a medium-size bowl until the mixture is light and thick, about 2 minutes.

2. Combine the milk and cream in a medium-size heavy saucepan and heat until small bubbles form around the edge of the pan. Remove from the heat and gradually add to the egg yolk mixture, whisking constantly.

3. Pour the mixture back into the

saucepan. Cook over low heat, stirring constantly with a wooden spoon, until the custard is thick enough to coat the back of the spoon. Do not allow it to boil.

4. Strain the custard through a fine strainer into a bowl. Stir in the citrus zests and orange juice. Cover the surface directly with plastic wrap to prevent a skin from forming and allow to cool to room temperature.

MAKES ABOUT 2 CUPS

BANANA AND KIWI SPRING ROLLS

If you see a throng of Southeast Asian children lining up by a street stall after school, you can bet it's for their favorite snack of deep-fried bananas. This is my own more formal variation on the theme: a whole banana wrapped in a spring roll wrapper, with a kiwi tucked inside it for a splash of acidity and color. Present these rolls on dark plates, dusted with confectioners' sugar, with Coconut-Rum Whipped Cream (see Index), or in a pool of cool mango or raspberry sauce.

3 large firm, ripe bananas
3 to 4 medium firm, ripe kiwi, peeled and
   sliced
6 spring roll wrappers (6½ inches each),
   thawed if frozen
3 tablespoons (packed) light brown sugar
1 large egg white, lightly beaten
Peanut oil, for deep frying
Confectioners' sugar, for dusting the rolls

1. Cut a banana in half lengthwise. Place one banana half, cut side up, on your work surface, and on it position 3 to 5 of the kiwi slices, or as many as will fit without overlapping the slices. Top with the other banana half. Holding the banana firmly, cut it in half crosswise. Repeat with the remaining bananas and kiwi.

2. Place a spring roll wrapper on the work surface with a corner facing you. Place a stuffed banana half horizontally across the middle of the wrapper. Sprinkle the banana with 1½ teaspoons of the brown sugar. Fold the bottom corner of the wrapper over the banana and tuck it under. Fold in the sides and roll the banana almost up to the end. Brush the top corner with a little egg white, roll up, and press firmly to seal. Prepare the rest of the rolls in the same fashion.

3. Pour oil to a depth of 2 inches into a wok or deep skillet and heat over medium-high heat to 375°F. Fry the rolls, 3 at a time, until deep golden, about 4 minutes. Turn several times during the frying process. Using tongs or a slotted spoon, transfer to a double layer of paper towels to drain. Repeat with the rest of the rolls.

4. Place the rolls on individual plates, sprinkle with confectioners' sugar, and serve at once.

SERVES 6

TROPICAL FRUIT

in Scented Coconut Milk

This falls somewhere between a soup and a fruit salad, and it makes a wonderful dessert. I also love the scented coconut milk with morning granola and bananas. The flavor of the coconut milk, infused with aromatics, is very delicate, so I wouldn't use assertively acidic fruit here. You can use either a combination of fruits or a single flavor, such as ripe mango or papaya, brightened with raspberries. Skinned ripe peach halves work very nicely, too. I would try to use fresh coconut milk here, but if you have to use canned, dilute a 13½-ounce can with ⅔ cup water.

3 cups fresh coconut milk (page 386)
3 tablespoons sugar
1½ teaspoons cream of coconut,
*   such as Coco Lopez, well stirred*
6 cardamon pods, preferably unbleached
*   (green), lightly crushed*
2 stalks fresh lemongrass, chopped (3 inches
*   of the lower stalk, tough outer leaves*
*   discarded; if unavailable, use dried*
*   lemongrass)*
2 slices (1 inch) fresh ginger, smashed
1 vanilla bean, split lengthwise
3 cups sliced or diced fresh fruit (such
*   as mango, papaya, cantaloupe,*
*   bananas, watermelon, lychees, or star*
*   fruits)*
½ cup fresh raspberries
Fresh mint leaves, for garnish

1. Combine the coconut milk, sugar, cream of coconut, cardamom, lemongrass, ginger and the vanilla bean in a medium-size saucepan and bring to a simmer. Remove from the heat, cool, and chill for at least 6 hours or overnight.

2. Strain and discard the solids, then stir the coconut liquid well. Divide the fruit among serving bowls (glass bowls are nice) and pour some coconut liquid over them. Garnish with mint sprigs.

SERVES 3 TO 4

CRESSIDE COLETTE'S COCONUT AND PALM SUGAR CUSTARD

During my stay in Melbourne I became friendly with a group of Sri Lankan women, all of them extraordinary cooks. Their repertoire of intricate, richly spiced dishes seemed never-ending, but this remarkable dessert always completed the meal. It's a pudding that proves why pudding is a pure comfort food. The deep, coffeelike taste produced by palm sugar is wonderfully enhanced by the rousing scent of cardamom and rose water. The recipe was given to me by Cresside Colette, to whom I am grateful for a perfect and generous first introduction to Ceylonese food.

You will find palm sugar at most Asian, Indian, or Latin grocery stores. If you have a choice, use the soft, deep amber kind, available at Indian grocery stores.

¾ cup palm sugar, preferably dark, or
(packed) dark brown sugar
⅓ cup water
5 large eggs
2 large egg yolks
2 cups canned unsweetened coconut
milk, well stirred
⅔ cup canned evaporated milk
¼ cup strongly brewed coffee
¼ teaspoon ground cloves
½ teaspoon ground cardamom,
preferably freshly ground
2 teaspoons rose water
Whipped cream, for serving, if desired

1. Combine the palm sugar and water in a small saucepan and heat, stirring, until the sugar is completely dissolved. Remove from the heat and let cool. Strain through a fine strainer if it seems a little lumpy.

2. Preheat the oven to 325°F.

3. In a large bowl, whisk the whole eggs with the egg yolks until foamy. Add the palm sugar mixture and the coconut milk. Whisk in the evaporated milk, coffee, cloves, cardamom, and rose water. Transfer the mixture to a medium-size soufflé dish or other round ovenproof dish.

4. Set the soufflé dish in a larger pan and add enough boiling water to reach three-fourths of the way up the sides of the soufflé dish. Place in the oven and bake until the custard is set, about 50 minutes.

5. Remove from the oven and let cool to warm. Serve with whipped cream, if desired.

SERVES 6 TO 8

LICORICE CREAM
with Passion Fruit and Meringue

This dessert is stunning—velvety, light licorice-infused custard, drizzled with tart passion fruit pulp, topped with a fluffy meringue, and passed under a broiler. It sounds quite unusual, but when you try it you'll see that it is sheer perfection. This masterpiece is the brainchild of Girard Madani, a French chef I met in Sydney.

Try to use the real licorice root, which is available at Chinese markets, herbal shops, and good spice shops. If you can't find it, black-licorice stick candy will also work, but you will have to reduce the amount of sugar by about 1 tablespoon and infuse the milk for only 5 to 6 minutes.

2 cups milk
2 tablespoons finely chopped licorice
root, soaked in warm water to cover
for 30 minutes, or black-licorice stick
candy
5 large egg yolks
⅓ cup (packed) light brown sugar
1 tablespoon cornstarch
7 tablespoons heavy (or whipping) cream
2 large egg whites
½ cup superfine sugar
Pulp from 4 passion fruit (about ¼ cup), or
¼ cup thawed frozen passion fruit pulp
Granulated sugar, for sprinkling

1. Bring the milk and licorice to a boil in a medium-size saucepan over medium-high

heat. Remove from the heat and let stand for 10 minutes to infuse. Strain, discarding the licorice root.

2. Whisk the egg yolks, brown sugar, and cornstarch in a medium-size saucepan until blended. Whisking constantly, stir in the infused milk. Set the mixture over low heat and heat, stirring constantly with a wooden spoon, until the mixture thickens, about 5 minutes. Remove the pan from the heat and stir in the cream, then strain the mixture into eight ⅔-cup ramekins or soufflé molds. Each should be three quarters full. Cool and refrigerate until completely chilled and set.

3. In a large bowl, beat the egg whites with an electric mixer at medium speed until soft peaks form. Stir in the superfine sugar and beat until the mixture is stiff and glossy. Gently fold half of the passion fruit pulp into the meringue.

4. Preheat the broiler.

5. Divide the remaining passion fruit pulp among the ramekins. Top with the meringue mixture, smoothing the tops with the back of a spoon, and sprinkle with granulated sugar. Place under the broiler and broil just long enough to brown the surface, about 30 seconds to 1 minute. Cool to room temperature and refrigerate until chilled.

SERVES 8

GINGER CREME BRULEE

This smooth, velvety crème brûlée has a lingering suggestion of ginger and lime. For crème brûlée to be a success, the brown sugar topping needs to caramelize very quickly under a broiler. You must use shallow individual ramekins (scallop-edged porcelain dishes are perfect), make sure the custards are completely chilled, and take care that your brown sugar is dry and not lumpy. In addition, the custards have to broil as close to the source of heat as possible. To achieve the last goal, you might want to place an inverted shallow baking sheet on your broiler rack to elevate it closer to the flame. Place the ramekins on it. If you don't manage to place the crème brûlées very close to the heat, place the ramekins in a baking pan half-filled with cold water and ice cubes. This will prevent the custard from curdling slightly.

> 6 large egg yolks
> ⅓ cup sugar
> 1 cup half-and-half
> 1⅔ cups heavy (or whipping) cream
> 1 vanilla bean, split lengthwise
> ¼ cup grated fresh ginger
> 1 tablespoon grated lime zest
> 2 tablespoons fresh lime juice
> 3 tablespoons (packed) dark brown sugar, air- or oven-dried, then well sifted

1. In a large bowl, whisk the egg yolks with the sugar and half-and-half until frothy.

2. Heat the cream with the vanilla bean, ginger, and lime zest in a medium-size saucepan over low heat for 5 minutes. Do not let the mixture boil. Slowly and carefully, whisk the cream into the egg yolk mixture. Cover with plastic wrap and let stand for 20 minutes.

3. Preheat the oven to 325°F.

4. Strain the cream mixture into a bowl and stir in the lime juice. Ladle the mixture into six ½-cup ramekins or soufflé molds. Place the ramekins in a baking pan and pour in enough boiling water to reach halfway up the sides of the ramekins. Bake until the custards are just set, 45 to 50 minutes. Do not overcook.

5. Cool the custards a little, cover each with plastic wrap, and refrigerate until the custards are completely chilled, 4 hours or overnight.

6. Preheat the broiler.

7. Sprinkle the top of each custard evenly with 1½ teaspoons brown sugar. Broil, as close to the heat as possible, until the sugar melts and bubbles. This could take anywhere from 45 seconds to 1½ minutes, depending how close to the heat the crème brûlées are. Remove from the broiler, cool until the topping hardens, and serve.

SERVES 6

MANGO GRATIN
with Champagne Sabayon

This very simple and lovely *à la minute* dessert of ethereal sabayon layered over juicy mangoes was created by Girard Madani, a dashing young French chef I met in Sydney. The dessert is gratinéed in individual ovenproof plates. If you are not sure whether your plates can be passed under a broiler, use a large gratin dish and apportion the dessert after it comes out of the broiler.

Good-quality Champagne will make a difference. All you need is ⅔ cup—use it as an excuse to sip the rest.

4 large egg yolks
5 tablespoons granulated sugar
⅔ cup good-quality Champagne
6 medium ripe mangoes, sliced
3 tablespoons sliced almonds
Confectioners' sugar, for dusting the gratins

1. Preheat the broiler.

2. In a medium-size bowl combine the egg yolks and sugar and whisk until thick and pale, about 2 to 3 minutes.

3. Add the Champagne, whisking constantly. Transfer the sabayon mixture to the top of a double boiler set over simmering water and carefully beat with a hand mixer at high speed until the mixture is frothy and has doubled in volume, about 5 minutes.

4. Arrange the mango slices in a fan on each of 6 ovenproof plates. Pour equal amounts of the sabayon on top and sprinkle with the almonds. Working with 2 plates at a time, pass under a broiler, about 2 inches away from the heat, until the topping is golden brown, about 1 minute.

5. Remove from the broiler and let cool a little. Serve sprinkled with confectioners' sugar.

SERVES 6

CARDAMOM-COFFEE MOUSSE

Cardamom, one of the favorite Asian spices, can perfume a dish like nothing else. To me, this simple mousse has a romantic suggestion of India and Java, of spice routes and pirates. Although I think the glowing scent of cardamom needs little else, if you are a chocolate addict, you can chill the mousses in molds, unmold onto a dessert plate, and serve in a pool of your favorite chocolate sauce.

> 4 cardamom pods, preferably unbleached
>   (green)
> 2 cups evaporated milk
> ⅔ cup strongly brewed coffee
> ⅔ cup (packed) light brown sugar
> 3 large egg yolks
> 1 envelope unflavored gelatin
> 3 tablespoons cold water
> 1½ cup heavy (or whipping) cream,
>   chilled
> 6 to 8 unsalted roasted cashews, for
>   garnish

1. Open the cardamom pods and extract the seeds. Crush the seeds with a mortar and pestle or the flat side of a knife and reserve.

2. Combine the evaporated milk, coffee, sugar, and cardamom in a small saucepan, and heat until small bubbles form around the edges of the pan, stirring with a wooden spoon to dissolve the sugar.

3. In a large bowl, whisk the egg yolks until pale yellow. Slowly whisk in the hot milk mixture. Transfer the mixture to the top of a double boiler set over simmering water and cook, stirring constantly, until thick enough to coat the back of the spoon, about 7 minutes. Do not allow to boil. Transfer to a bowl.

4. In a small bowl, sprinkle the gelatin over the cold water and soften for 5 minutes.

5. Stir the softened gelatin thoroughly into the custard. Refrigerate the mixture until it begins to set, about 1 hour.

6. Whip the cream until soft peaks form. Gently fold the cream into the chilled mousse mixture. Divide among 6 to 8 dessert glasses and chill for at least 4 hours. Garnish each portion with a cashew before serving.

SERVES 6 TO 8

PINA COLADA PARFAITS

I have combined the flavors of a favorite tropical drink—rum, coconut, and fresh pineapple—in a winning dessert. Serve it in tall parfait glasses after a light outdoor luncheon.

> 1 envelope unflavored
>   gelatin
> 4 tablespoons light rum
> 3 large egg yolks
> 5 tablespoons plus 1
>   teaspoon sugar
> ⅓ cup cream of coconut,
>   such as Coco Lopez, well
>   stirred
> ⅓ cup thawed frozen pineapple
>   juice concentrate
> 3 tablespoons plus 2 teaspoons
>   fresh lime juice
> 2 large egg whites (see Note)
> 1 cup heavy (or whipping)
>   cream
> 1¾ cups diced ripe fresh
>   pineapple
> Whipped cream, for garnish
> 2 tablespoons toasted sweetened
>   flaked coconut, for garnish

1. In a small bowl, sprinkle the gelatin over 3 tablespoons of the rum and let stand for 5 minutes.

2. In the top of double boiler set over simmering water, beat the egg yolks with 3 tablespoons of the sugar until thick and pale, about 5 minutes. Scrape into a large bowl. Add the gelatin to the egg yolk mixture while it is still warm and stir until completely dissolved. Cool the mixture.

3. Blend the cream of coconut, pineapple juice concentrate, and 3 tablespoons lime juice in a blender. Whisk the mixture into the egg yolks.

4. In a medium-size bowl, beat the egg whites with an electric mixer at medium speed until soft peaks form. Sprinkle 2 tablespoons of the sugar into the whites and continue beating until stiff.

5. In another bowl, beat the cream until soft peaks form, then, using a rubber spatula, fold gently into the yolk mixture. Fold in the egg whites.

6. Toss the pineapple with the remaining sugar, rum, and lime juice. Divide the pineapple among 6 tall parfait glasses. Top with the mousse and refrigerate until set.

7. Serve garnished with dollops of whipped cream and a sprinkling of toasted coconut.

SERVES 6

Note: The egg whites in this parfait remain uncooked. Raw eggs have been known to be a source of a serious salmonella infection. If you are unsure of the quality of the eggs you buy, avoid recipes that use them raw.

BANANA AND LIME SOUFFLES

Bananas and limes are a happy tropical match, the sweetness of one balancing the acidity of the other. These soufflés are light yet nourishing, and they make an uplifting conclusion for either a rich or a light meal.

2 tablespoons granulated sugar
2 large egg yolks
2 teaspoons all-purpose flour
1 cup milk
1 heaping teaspoon grated lime zest
3½ tablespoons fresh lime juice
3½ tablespoons superfine sugar, plus more for coating the soufflé molds
6 large egg whites, at room temperature
1 large firm, ripe banana, thinly sliced
Confectioners' sugar, for dusting the soufflés

1. In a medium-size bowl, whisk the granulated sugar with the egg yolks until thick and pale, about 2 minutes. Whisk in the flour until blended.

2. Bring the milk to a boil in a small saucepan over medium-high heat. Remove from the heat and whisk slowly into the egg mixture. Transfer the mixture to the top of a double boiler and cook over simmering water until thickened, about 5 minutes, whisking constantly. Stir in the lime zest and juice and let cool to room temperature.

3. Preheat the oven to 400°F. Grease eight ½-cup soufflé molds and dust evenly with superfine sugar.

4. In a medium-size bowl, beat the egg whites with an electric mixer at medium speed until soft peaks form. Beat in 3½ tablespoons superfine sugar until the whites are stiff but not dry. Using a wooden spoon, fold one third of the whites gently into the yolk mixture. Fold in the rest.

5. Pour half of the mixture into the prepared molds. Arrange a layer of banana slices on the mixture and top with the remaining souffle mixture. Run your little finger around the edge of each soufflé to score.

6. Bake until puffed and pale brown, 10 to 12 minutes. Dust with confectioners' sugar, cool slightly, and serve.

SERVES 8

PEACHES
in Pink Ginger Syrup

Luscious ripe peaches—especially white ones—are delicious served in this mouth-tingling spiced ginger syrup with a touch of Cointreau. Another great way to serve peaches is to brush them lightly with a brown sugar and butter mixture, pass under a broiler, and serve in a pool of Scented Coconut Milk (page 360).

1 cup sugar
3 cups water
Grated zest from 1 lemon
5 cardamom pods, preferably unbleached
*   (green), lightly crushed*
4 slices (each 1 inch thick) fresh ginger,
*   smashed*
¼ cup fresh lemon juice
⅓ cup Cointreau (orange liqueur)
3 tablespoons finely julienned Japanese pink
*   pickled ginger*
6 firm, ripe peaches
Whipped cream, for serving

1. Combine the sugar, water, lemon zest, cardamom pods, fresh ginger, lemon juice, Cointreau, and pickled ginger in a medium-size nonreactive saucepan and bring to a simmer over medium-low heat, stirring until the sugar is dissolved. Simmer for 5 minutes. Remove from the heat and let stand for 2 hours.

2. Cut the peaches in half and carefully remove the pits. Blanch the peaches in boiling water for 30 seconds, then plunge into cold water. Remove and discard the skins.

3. Strain the syrup and pour over the peaches in a bowl. Toss gently to coat and re-frigerate for 2 hours, tossing occasionally. Serve in glass bowls, with whipped cream.

SERVES 6

STEAMED KUMQUAT PUDDINGS
with Orange Custard Cream

I love the way Australian chefs layer and juxtapose flavors to add fresh, innovative accents to traditional classics. This dessert is a quintessential comfort food, but instead of being predictable it virtually explodes at you with bright, unusual flavors. It is a creation of the extraordinarily talented Chris Manfield—a virtuoso when it comes to blending diverse culinary cultures into a brilliant and original style. The Chinese white rice wine used for the kumquats is available at most liquor stores; do not substitute *shao xing*, the yellow rice wine.

You will have some candied kumquats left over. They are delicious spooned over ice cream or on slices of sponge cake.

KUMQUATS
1 vanilla bean, split lengthwise
1 cup Cognac
1 cup Chinese white rice wine or sake
3 cups water
2 cups granulated
*   sugar*
2 pounds unpeeled
*   kumquats, scrubbed*

PUDDING

Confectioners' sugar, for dusting the ramekins

2 large eggs, separated

½ cup granulated sugar

1 teaspoon vanilla extract

1 cup milk

1¾ cups all-purpose flour

1½ teaspoons baking powder

1 tablespoon unsalted butter, melted

Orange Custard Cream (recipe follows)

1. Prepare the kumquats: In a large, heavy nonreactive saucepan, combine the vanilla bean, Cognac, rice wine, water, and sugar and bring to a boil over medium-high heat. Add the kumquats, reduce the heat to medium-low, and cook, partially covered, until the fruit is tender and the skins are translucent, 25 to 30 minutes.

2. With a slotted spoon, remove the kumquats from the syrup, leaving the syrup in the pan. When cool enough to handle, cut in half crosswise and scoop out the seeds. Return the kumquats to the syrup and continue to cook over medium-low heat until the liquid turns into a thick syrup and the fruit is candied, about 45 minutes. Remove from the heat and allow to cool in the syrup. Remove the vanilla bean. (This step can be prepared a day ahead).

3. Make the pudding: Preheat the oven to 375°F. Grease eight ¾-cup ramekins or soufflé molds and dust with confectioners' sugar.

4. In a large bowl, beat the egg yolks and sugar with an electric mixer at medium speed until the mixture is light and thick, about 3 minutes. Stir in the vanilla, milk, flour, baking powder, and butter. In a separate bowl with clean, dry beaters, beat the egg whites until stiff and fold into the batter with a wooden spoon.

5. Place 2 tablespoons of the kumquats and 1½ tablespoons of the syrup on the bottom of each ramekin. Pour the pudding mixture over the kumquats. Set the ramekins in a baking dish and pour in enough boiling water to reach two thirds of the way up the sides of the ramekins. Cover the ramekins with aluminum foil, place the baking dish in the oven, and bake until a skewer inserted in the center of a pudding comes out clean, 30 to 35 minutes.

6. To serve, run a knife around the edges of the ramekins. Turn the puddings out onto 8 warmed plates and pour the Orange Custard Cream around them.

SERVES 8

Orange Custard Cream

1 cup heavy (or whipping) cream

5 tablespoons strained fresh orange juice

2 tablespoons milk

1 tablespoon Cognac

4 large egg yolks

⅓ cup sugar

1. In the top of a double boiler over simmering water, heat the cream, orange juice, milk, and Cognac together until just warm, about 100°F.

2. In a bowl, whisk together the egg yolks and the sugar until thick and pale, about 2 minutes. Pour the cream mixture into the eggs, whisking constantly. Return the mixture to the double boiler and continue to whisk over simmering water until the mixture reaches custard consistency (thick enough to coat the back of a spoon), 5 to 7 minutes.

MAKES ABOUT 1½ CUPS

DURIAN

What smells like hell and tastes like heaven?
— *popular Asian riddle*

In Southeast Asia, the durian, a spiky creature with a white custard-like flesh, is the "king of fruits," and there is a whole culture, almost a religion, devoted to growing, gathering, tasting, and preparing it. There are many different kinds and sizes of durians, but by and large durian connoisseurs will confirm what has long been known on the street—the worse the smell, the better the taste. So powerful is the smell that durians are officially prohibited from elevators, hotel lobbies, airports, and other public places, usually signaled by a "No Durian Allowed" sign. Yet despite the smell, families begin to save up long before the durian season, as one top-quality fruit will fetch a small fortune at Southeast Asian markets. It is difficult to describe the taste, but it could be compared to an ambrosial custard, with the faint perfume of a smelly French cheese.

The durian season is from August to September. Unlike most other fruits, durians are not picked but allowed to fall off a tree. Such are the weight and the proportions of the fruit, however, that mature trees have to be carefully supported by ropes and struts, and multicolored netting is arranged underneath their falling arc. The gatherers start out at dawn and customarily wear a helmet (usually the one that goes with their motorbike) for protection.

The famous naturalist and explorer, Alfred Wallace got hooked on durians during a visit to Sarawak in the mid-1850s. He left a wonderful record of the fruit in his book The Malay Archipelago *(1869):*

Doctor Paludanus [writes]: "This fruit is of a hot and humid nature. To those not used to it, it seems at first to smell like rotten onions, but immediately they taste it they prefer it to all other food. The natives give it honourable titles, exalt it, and make verses on it." When brought into a house the smell is often so offensive that some persons can never bear to taste it. This was my own case when I first tried it in Malacca, but in Borneo I found a ripe fruit on the ground, and, eating it out-of-doors, I at once became a confirmed durion eater. A rich, butter-like custard, highly flavored with almonds gives the best general idea of it, but intermingled with it come wafts of flavor that call to mind cream-cheese, onion-sauce, brown-sherry, and other incongruities. Then there is a rich glutinous smoothness in the pulp which nothing else possesses, but which adds to its delicacy. It is neither acid, nor sweet, nor juicy, yet one feels the want of none of these qualities, for it is perfect as it is. It produces no nausea or other bad effect, and the more you eat of it the less you feel inclined to stop. In fact, to eat durions, is a new sensation worth a voyage to the East to experience.

Terrific Pacific Desserts

ANDY WAI'S WATERMELON AND TAPIOCA SOUP

Most Chinese desserts are an acquired taste, but this soup—watermelon blended with ice and thickened with pearl tapioca—immediately appeals. It's lovely and refreshing, with a touch of mystique, and is excellent served at the end of an al fresco luncheon or as a finale to a complex meal. You can also use other ripe fruit in season, such as strawberries, mango, honeydew melon, or peaches. If using other fruit, adjust the amounts of sugar syrup and tapioca, depending on the sweetness and thickness of the fruit purée. Small pearl tapioca is available at Asian grocery stores, but you can use quick-cooking tapioca.

1¼ cups small pearl tapioca or quick-cooking
tapioca
¼ cup sugar
3 tablespoons water
5 cups diced firm, ripe watermelon, seeded
1 cup crushed ice
Fresh mint leaves, for garnish

1. Bring a large pot of water to a boil over medium-high heat. Add the tapioca in a slow, steady stream and stir to prevent it from sticking to the bottom of the pot. Cook until the tapioca is translucent, 12 to 15 minutes. Drain in a strainer and rinse thoroughly under cold running water. Shake the strainer well to drain out all the water, then set the tapioca aside.

2. Heat the sugar and water in a small saucepan over medium heat, stirring until the sugar dissolves. Cool.

3. In a blender, blend the watermelon with the ice. Transfer to a large serving bowl and stir in the sugar syrup, 1 tablespoon at a time. The amount depends on your taste and the sweetness of the watermelon. Stir in the reserved tapioca. Serve garnished with mint leaves.

SERVES 6

JAVANESE BLACK RICE PUDDING

The Southeast Asian dessert repertoire is fairly small, usually limited to various coconut custards, fried bananas, and sweet sticky rice dishes. Of the latter, the extraordinary Indonesian black rice pudding certainly gets my vote. Black rice, which grows predominantly in Indonesia and the Philippines, belongs to the "glutinous rice" variety, with long, dark brown grains that turn a dramatic inky purple when cooked. It is very inexpensive and can be obtained easily from most Southeast Asian grocery stores.

The traditional dessert consists of sweet, simply cooked black rice, topped with a touch of very lightly salted coconut

milk. (The salt is actually used to stabilize the coconut milk and protect it from curdling, but it has been worked into the flavor of the dish.) I have elaborated on this theme by infusing unsalted coconut milk with aromatics and spiking the rice with Cointreau. Serve the pudding in light-colored bowls to offset its intriguing color, and keep your guests guessing as to what it is.

1¼ cups canned unsweetened coconut milk,
    well stirred
2 tablespoons grated lemon zest
2 tablespoons grated lime zest
4 cardamom pods, preferably unbleached
    (green), lightly crushed
1 stalk fresh lemongrass (3 inches of the
    lower stalk, tough outer leaves discarded;
    optional), smashed
2 kaffir lime leaves (optional), lightly
    crushed
⅔ cup plus 2 tablespoons sugar
1 cup black rice
3 cups water, or more as needed
2 tablespoons Cointreau (orange liqueur)
Whipped cream, for garnish
Toasted Coconut (page 389), for garnish

1. Combine the coconut milk, lemon and lime zests, cardamom pods, lemongrass, kaffir lime leaves, and the 2 tablespoons sugar in a small saucepan and bring to a boil over medium-high heat. Remove from the heat and let stand for 1 hour, then refrigerate for at least 3 and up to 24 hours. Strain.

2. Place the rice in a strainer and rinse in several changes of water. Soak in tepid water to cover 8 to 12 hours or overnight. Drain and rinse well, then rinse again.

3. In a large saucepan with a tight-fitting lid, combine the rice, water, and remaining sugar and bring to a boil over high heat. Reduce the heat to low, cover, and simmer until the rice is tender, 35 to 45 minutes. Add up to

¼ cup more water if the pudding is too thick. Stir in the Cointreau and simmer for another 10 minutes. Let the rice cool to warm.

4. Spoon into dessert bowls, cover with several tablespoons of the coconut cream mixture, top with whipped cream, and sprinkle with toasted coconut.

SERVES 6

FRAGRANT
FRUIT COMPOTE

Add or substitute whatever tropical fruit you like—guava, passion fruit, star fruit, and cactus pear are all welcome in this compote. Serve the compote with a dollop of crème fraîche or with a tart sorbet.

SYRUP
1 lime
1 lemon
1⅔ cups sugar
3 cups water
3 slices fresh ginger (each ½ inch thick),
    smashed
3 stalks fresh lemongrass (3 inches of the
    lower stalk, tough outer leaves discarded;
    optional), smashed

1 nashi (Asian) pear, peeled, cored, and
    diced
1 cup diced fresh pineapple
3 kiwis, peeled and diced
1 small papaya, peeled, seeded, and sliced
1 cup fresh raspberries
2 firm, ripe bananas, diced
2 small mangos, diced
Fresh basil or mint leaves, for garnish

1. Make the syrup: With a vegetable peeler, remove the zest from the lime and lemon, taking care not to include the bitter white pith. Save the lemon for another use and squeeze and reserve the juice from the lime.

2. Combine the sugar, water, lime and lemon zest, ginger, and lemongrass in a small nonreactive saucepan and heat over low heat until the sugar is dissolved. Simmer for 5 minutes. Stir in 1 tablespoon of the reserved lime juice. Remove from the heat and let stand for 1 hour to infuse the syrup with ginger and citrus flavors. Strain.

3. Arrange the fruit in a glass bowl. Pour the syrup over the fruit and refrigerate for 1 to 4 hours.

4. Serve in glass bowls, garnished with basil leaves.

SERVES 4 TO 6

K I W I
T I R A M I S U

The first person who greeted me in New Zealand, as I arrived on my recipe collection odyssey, was Jan Bilton, a well-known food writer and a recipe developer for the New Zealand Kiwifruit Board. Jan looked after me for the duration of my visit and entrusted me with an enormous heap of fabulous kiwi recipes, including this one, for a New Zealand tiramisù.

The kiwi look startling in a glass bowl and add much needed freshness and astringency to the scrumptuously rich Italian classic. Because mascarpone is not always readily available in Auckland, Jan uses light cream cheese, which makes the dessert lighter and tarter than the original Italian version.

3 egg large yolks
½ cup confectioners' sugar
⅓ cup Tia Maria (coffee liqueur)
12 ounces light cream cheese, at room temperature
1½ cups heavy (or whipping) cream, chilled
3 tablespoons granulated sugar
¼ teaspoon vanilla extract
4 to 6 kiwi, peeled and sliced
1 package (7 ounces) ladyfingers
1¼ cups espresso or other strong brewed coffee, sweetened to taste
1 tablespoon unsweetened cocoa powder

1. In the top of a double boiler, whisk the egg yolks with the confectioners' sugar until thick and pale, about 2 minutes. Set over simmering water, stir in the Tia Maria, and simmer over low heat, whisking constantly, until the mixture is thick enough to coat the back of a spoon, about 4 minutes. Cool.

2. In a large bowl, beat the cream cheese with an electric mixer on low speed. Beat in the yolk mixture.

3. In another bowl, beat the cream, with the sugar and vanilla, until soft peaks form. Fold into the cream cheese mixture.

4. Decoratively line the bottom and sides of an 8-inch glass bowl with the kiwi. Dip the ladyfingers in the coffee just to moisten. Using one third of the ladyfingers, line the bottom of the bowl. Spread one third of the cream cheese mixture on top, taking care not to disturb the kiwi. Top with another layer of ladyfingers, then a layer of cream cheese mixture, then ladyfingers, and top with a final layer of cream cheese mixture.

5. Refrigerate for at least 2 hours or overnight. Sprinkle the top with cocoa powder before serving.

SERVES 8

JASMINE JAZZ TIRAMISU

Another innovative tiramisù with a Pacific Rim inflection, this one from Oritalia, a restaurant in San Francisco.

LADYFINGER CAKE
4 large eggs, 3 of them separated
½ cup plus 2 tablespoons sugar
1 teaspoon vanilla extract
⅔ cup cake flour

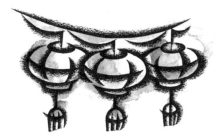

FILLING
⅓ cup jasmine tea leaves, preferably Republic of Tea "Jasmine Jazz" tea
1 cup heavy (or whipping) cream
10 ounces mascarpone cheese
⅓ cup sugar
⅓ cup dark rum
Custard Cream (recipe follows)
Sweetened cocoa powder
Fresh mint leaves, for garnish

1. Preheat the oven to 350°F. Line a 18 x 12-inch baking sheet with well-greased parchment.

2. Make the cake: In a large bowl, beat the whole egg, egg yolks, and the ½ cup sugar with an electric mixer at medium speed until thick and pale, about 2 minutes. Beat in the vanilla and flour until blended.

3. With clean, dry beaters, beat the egg whites with the remaining 2 tablespoons sugar until stiff peaks form. Fold one third of the whites into the egg yolk mixture and then gently fold in the rest. Spread the batter evenly on the prepared parchment. Bake in the middle of the oven until golden and springy to the touch, about 15 minutes. When cool enough to handle, invert the cake onto a rack and gently peel off the parchment. Cut the cake into three equal-size rectangles, trim the edges, and set aside.

4. Make the filling: Combine the tea with the cream in a small saucepan and heat over medium heat to 180°F for 2 to 3 minutes. Strain the cream into a clean bowl, discarding the tea leaves. Refrigerate until cold, about 2 hours.

5. In a large bowl, gently whisk the mascarpone with the cold flavored cream and sugar until fluffy. Refrigerate until cold, about 2 hours.

6. To assemble the tiramisù, brush the first cake layer with half of the rum and ⅓ cup of the Custard Cream. Spread with half of the filling mixture. Place another cake layer on top and repeat with the rum, custard, and filling. Top with the remaining cake layer.

7. Cover the dessert with plastic wrap and refrigerate for 2 hours. Refrigerate the remaining Custard Cream.

8. To serve, dust the top of the cake generously with cocoa. Cut into squares. Place a piece of tiramisù on a plate, drizzle some of the remaining Custard Cream around it and garnish with a mint leaf.

SERVES 6

Custard Cream

5 large egg yolks
⅓ cup sugar
2 cups milk
½ vanilla bean, split lengthwise

1. In a bowl, whisk the egg yolks and sugar until the mixture is thick and pale, about 2 minutes.

2. Heat the milk and vanilla bean in a heavy medium-size saucepan over medium heat until small bubbles form around the edges of the pan. Off the heat, gradually add one third of the hot milk to the egg yolk mixture, whisking constantly. Whisk in the remaining milk.

3. Return the mixture to the saucepan. Cook over low heat, stirring constantly with a wooden spoon, until the custard is thick enough to coat the back of the spoon. Do not allow the mixture to boil.

4. Strain the custard through a fine strainer into a bowl, discarding the vanilla bean. Cover the surface directly with plastic wrap to prevent a skin from forming and refrigerate at least 2 hours.

MAKES ABOUT 2 CUPS

FROZEN PINEAPPLE SOUFFLES

The Asians rightly believe that a ripe pineapple is a perfect way to cleanse the palate and aid digestion. After a rich meal, I can't think of anything better than these refreshing soufflés, bright with the taste of fresh pineapple. Chose ripe, fragrant fruit, and if you taste the soufflé mixture and discover that the flavor is still thin, add an extra tablespoon or so of the frozen pineapple juice concentrate. (See the Note at the end of this recipe.)

2 large egg yolks
¼ cup plus 2 tablespoons sugar, plus more for sprinkling the soufflé molds
1¾ cups chopped fresh ripe pineapple
⅓ cup frozen pineapple juice concentrate
2¼ cups heavy (or whipping) cream, chilled
½ teaspoon vanilla extract
3 large egg whites, at room temperature
Pinch of cream of tartar
6 tablespoons finely diced fresh pineapple

1. In the top of a double boiler set over simmering water, whisk the egg yolks with ¼ cup sugar until the mixture is thick and pale, about 3 minutes. Scrape into a large bowl and let cool.

2. Purée the chopped pineapple with the frozen concentrate in a food processor.

3. Lightly butter six ½-cup soufflé molds and sprinkle them with sugar. Tear off strips of waxed paper long enough to wrap around the dishes and fold them in half lengthwise. Using rubber bands or Scotch tape, secure the strips around the dishes so they form a collar extending 2 inches above the rim.

4. In a large bowl, beat the cream and vanilla extract with an electric mixer at medium speed until soft peaks form.

5. With clean, dry beaters, beat the egg whites with the cream of tartar until soft peaks form. While beating, sprinkle in the remaining 2 tablespoons sugar and beat until glossy, 30 seconds more.

6. Gently but thoroughly fold the egg white mixture into the yolk mixture. Gently but thoroughly fold in all but ½ cup of the whipped cream, then the puréed and diced pineapple. Reserve the extra whipped cream in the refrigerator.

7. Divide the mixture among the prepared soufflé molds and place in the freezer until completely frozen, about 4 hours.

8. To serve, remove the waxed paper strips from the frozen soufflés, and top each with a dollop of reserved whipped cream.

MAKES 6 SOUFFLES

Note: These soufflés are made with raw eggs, which have been known to cause a serious salmonella infection. If you are unsure of the quality of the eggs you buy, it's best to avoid recipes that use them raw.

PAPAYA-LIME-COCONUT SORBET

This tasty sorbet juggles all the favorite flavors of the tropics, the heady sweetness of papaya, the tang of lime, and the richness of coconut.

½ cup water
½ cup plus 1 tablespoon sugar
2 tablespoons Cointreau (orange liqueur)
1½ tablespoons grated lime zest
3½ tablespoons fresh lime juice
3½ cups diced papayas
3 tablespoons cream of coconut, such
*   as Coco Lopez, well stirred*

1. Combine the water, sugar, Cointreau, and lime zest in a small nonreactive saucepan

and simmer over low heat, stirring, until the sugar is dissolved, 5 minutes. Stir in the lime juice and let the mixture cool completely.

2. Purée the papaya with the cream of coconut in a food processor until smooth. Transfer to a large bowl, scraping the sides with a rubber spatula, and add the syrup. Stir well. Cover and refrigerate the mixture until cold, about 2 hours.

3. Freeze the mixture in an ice-cream maker according to manufacturer's instructions.

MAKES ABOUT 4 CUPS

KIWI AND GERWURZTRAMINER SORBET

This is another New Zealand creation from Auckland food writer Jan Bilton. I was lucky to have Jan as my guide to the Auckland food scene, and on my very first evening she invited me to a New Zealand Gerwürztraminer tasting and dinner. To me the evening was a great introduction to the country's culinary bounty: We sipped the fruity, cool-climate Gerwürz and feasted on pristine local salmon and venison, and for dessert we enjoyed this sophisticated, jade-colored sorbet that Jan devised especially for the occasion.

Freshly squeezed juice of 2 lemons
⅔ cup sugar
10 large kiwi, peeled and coarsely chopped
1½ cups good-quality Gerwürztraminer
*   wine*

1. Combine the lemon juice and sugar in a small nonreactive saucepan and simmer over low heat, stirring, until the sugar is dissolved, 5 minutes. Cool completely.

2. Working in batches if necessary, purée the kiwi with the syrup in a food processor. Do not overprocess or the seeds will be crushed.

3. Strain into a bowl through a fine strainer to remove the seeds. Add the wine and stir well to combine. Cover and refrigerate the mixture until cold, about 2 hours.

4. Transfer the mixture to an ice-cream maker and freeze according to manufacturer's instructions.

MAKES ABOUT 4 CUPS

PASSION FRUIT AND GIN GRANITA

Offer this elegant and unusual granita in martini glasses either as a mid-meal palate refresher or as a light dessert.

You can make it with frozen South American passion fruit pulp, but in this case you might want to adjust the amount of sugar, as the pulp tends to be very tart. Keep tasting until you get it right.

2 cups water
½ cup superfine sugar, or more to taste
¾ cup fresh or thawed frozen passion fruit
*   pulp (about 10 passion fruit)*
½ cup plus 2 tablespoons good-quality gin

1. Bring the water and sugar to a boil in a medium-size nonreactive saucepan over medium heat, stirring to dissolve the sugar. Remove from the heat, stir in the passion fruit pulp and gin, and cool.

2. Transfer the cooled mixture to a shallow dish, cover, and freeze for 1½ hours. Stir the granita to break it up, then return it to the freezer for another hour. Stir it again, return it to the freezer, then stir it a final time after another hour. Allow it to freeze until completely firm, at least 2 hours more or overnight.

3. Using a large, sturdy metal spoon, scrape the granita into chilled glasses and serve at once.

SERVE 6

FROZEN TOASTED COCONUT AND MANGO TERRINE
with Coconut Wafers

A stunning summertime dessert of tart mango sorbet nestled between two layers of luscious toasted coconut ice cream, this is a creation of Sydney chef Chris Manfield that has been featured on the cover of Australian *Vogue Entertaining*. When making her famous ice creams Chris likes to use liquid glucose, instead of the sugar syrup, to give the ice cream a perfectly smooth, blended consistency. It is available in most drug stores and is very inexpensive. I use light corn syrup instead.

You can make the ice cream and the mango sorbet up to several days ahead—they will have to be done in turns, unless you have two ice-cream makers—and assemble the terrine several hours before serving. This is three recipes in one, and the sorbet, ice cream, and coconut wafers can each be served on their own.

MANGO SORBET

½ cup water
⅓ cup granulated sugar
¼ cup light corn syrup
2½ tablespoons lime juice
2 cups puréed ripe mango

TOASTED COCONUT ICE CREAM

1½ cups heavy (or whipping)
*   cream*
1½ cups milk
⅓ cup Toasted Coconut (page 389)
⅔ cup coconut sugar, palm sugar, or
*   (packed) light brown sugar*
5 large egg yolks

Coconut Wafers (recipe follows)

1. Make the sorbet: Combine the water, sugar, and corn syrup in a small nonreactive saucepan and simmer over low heat for 5 minutes. Cool completely.

2. Transfer the cooled syrup to a large bowl and stir in the lime juice and mango. Cover and refrigerate until cold, about 2 hours. Transfer to an ice-cream maker and freeze according to manufacturer's instructions. When ready, transfer to another container and return to the freezer.

3. Make the ice cream: Combine the cream, milk, coconut, and sugar in a medium-size saucepan. Bring to a simmer over medium heat, stirring to dissolve the sugar. Remove from the heat and allow to stand in a warm place for at least 2 hours to allow the flavors to develop. Strain through a fine strainer into the top of a double boiler, discarding the coconut.

4. In a medium-size bowl, whisk the egg yolks until pale yellow and frothy and pour into the cream mixture. Set the pan over simmering water and cook, stirring with a wooden spoon, until the mixture thickens enough to coat the back of the spoon. Allow the mixture to cool thoroughly, then transfer to the ice-cream maker and freeze according to manufacturer's instructions.

5. To assemble the terrine, line an 8½ x 4½ x 2½-inch loaf pan with plastic wrap, leaving a 2-inch overhang. Spoon half of the coconut ice cream into the pan and smooth with a spatula. Place all of the mango sorbet on top and smooth the top. Top with a layer of the remaining coconut ice cream and smooth the top. Cover with plastic wrap and freeze for 4 hours.

6. Unmold the terrine by running a knife around the edges and pulling gently on the plastic. Invert onto a large serving platter. To serve, dip a large knife into hot water and cut into 1½-inch-thick slices. Serve with Coconut Wafers.

SERVES 8 TO 10

Coconut Wafers

7 tablespoons unsalted butter
3 tablespoons light corn syrup
½ cup sugar
⅔ cup all-purpose flour
3 tablespoons Toasted Coconut (page 389)

1. In the top of a double boiler set over simmering water, melt the butter in the corn syrup, stirring. Transfer to a bowl and add the sugar, flour, and coconut and stir well to combine. Cover and refrigerate until cold, about 2 hours.

2. Preheat the oven to 350°F and grease 2 baking sheets.

3. Form the wafer mixture into 8 balls. Flatten the balls with the palm of your hand and place 4 of them on one of the baking sheets, spacing them about 3 inches apart. Cover with a sheet of baking parchment, and using a rolling pin, roll the wafers into 4-inch circles. Remove the parchment. Repeat with the remaining balls on the second baking sheet.

4. Bake the wafers until golden, about 15 minutes. Remove the baking sheets from the oven and let stand until the wafers cool slightly, about 4 minutes. Do not allow them to harden. Use a spatula to transfer the wafers to a wire rack to cool completely.

MAKES 8 WAFERS

THE TEA CHAPTER IN SINGAPORE

Prolonged taking of bitter tea can tranquillize the heart and invigorate the qi (vital energy) . . . cleanse the body and hold back ageing.

—SHEN NONG,
CANON OF MATERIA MEDICA

Unlike its more famous Japanese counterpart, the Chinese tea ceremony is relatively unknown in this country—even though it was the Chinese who first introduced tea drinking to the world. While strolling through the impeccably restored Tanjong Pagar conservation area in Singapore, a district lit up with the gorgeous pastel colors of its traditional, turn-of-the-century shop houses, John and I stumbled across a beautifully refurbished storefront with an intriguing sign outside. It was called The Tea Chapter. There was no hint from the street of what was going on inside, so we cautiously peeked in, and in five minutes had gone through the looking glass into another world.

The Tea Chapter epitomizes the stylish combination of old and new that characterizes today's Singapore. Its three intimate floors were devoted to serving an ancient Chinese tea ceremony that was as authentic as they come. The place was packed with Singapore's trendy teens, squatting at low tables equipped with all the necessary tea paraphernalia and munching on "tea eggs"—eggs boiled with soy sauce, five-spice powder, cinnamon, and tea leaves. This was obviously them in place to be. All around us the walls were plastered with rave reviews from the Singapore press and photographs of Queen Elizabeth's 1989 visit to the teahouse. Having taken all this in, we climbed up to the top floor of the establishment, fashioned after a teahouse of the Tang dynasty.

The ancient Chinese emperor Shen Nong, the father of agriculture and the patron saint of herbal medicine, is credited by the Chinese as the discoverer of tea. Known as the Divine Healer, Shen Nong also revealed the medicinal properties of many herbs. The legend goes that one evening in 2737 B.C. Shen Nong was sitting in contemplation before a fire made up of the leaves and branches of a camellia-like tree. All of a sudden, the fire cracked and the scorched leaves swirled up into the air. Some of these fell into a flask of water boiling on the fire, and as a beautiful aroma rose up, he tasted the infusion and was overwhelmed by the clear, astringent, and refreshing taste. Shen Nong went on to experiment with similar types of leaves, which we know today as tea.

The Chinese tea ceremony can be traced back to Lu Yu, a Chinese scholar who, in the eighth century, wrote the imposing ten-part, three-volume *Ch'a Ching Tea Classics.* The attitude toward tea drinking he encouraged was "to esteem nature, to advocate the delightful serenity of seclusion, to cultivate the virtue of patience, regardless of its form and etiquette."

When we reached the top floor, we sat down with Mr. Ho,

the soft-spoken young computer specialist who was co-owner, along with eighteen partners, of The Tea Chapter. All were dedicated to reviving the ancient Chinese traditions of Singapore. He explained that the Chinese tea ceremony is not just about the taste but is equally concerned with the "self-restraint of physical action" involved in the whole tea-making process—from selecting pots, purchasing the tea, boiling the water,

Mr. Ho presented us with the menu. It listed thirty-one kinds of tea, of which there are six main types: white, green, flower, fermented, semifermented, and heavily fermented. Most were imported from China, and the varieties were but a small sampling of what was available there. He went through each kind, adding comments and opinions like a connoisseur of art. The jasmine and other flower tea options he quickly

The ancient Chinese emperor Shen Nong, the patron saint of herbal medicine, is credited by the Chinese as the discoverer of tea.

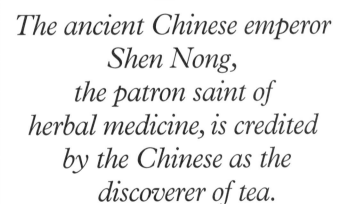

to brewing, sampling, and discussing the tea. In China, he said, the activity of tea drinking has long been associated with learning and culture.

dismissed as an amateur's choice, as they tended to be too "flowery" and overpowering. So was the green tea, high in vitamin C but favored mostly, he noted quite severely, by young girls who value it for what it does for their complexions. He advised us to try the Golden Cassia—a tea that was presented to Queen Elizabeth during her visit—so we did. Then we chose *tienguanyin,* which

and the other, which was smaller and differently shaped, simply for sniffing. (Enjoying tea by its smell is crucial to the experience, and in this regard good tea is treated with the same kind of respect that Europeans lav-

water between each round of tea tasting. It was set with a long wooden spoon for measuring the leaves; a spatula to get them out of the container; and wooden tongs to hold the cup once it has been scalded. The clay used for the service is very special, and one must never wash the tea set with soap or detergent for fear that it will absorb the scent of the cleansers.

John and I sat as reverentially as if we were in the reserve cellar at Château Margaux, staring and sniffing away at our tea cups, contemplating the flavors, after each round of different teas.

The ceremony begins with perfectly dry tea leaves. The quantity depends on the type of tea, but one third pot of leaves to two thirds pot of water is about right. It is important not to let the water boil for too long, and the ideal temperature is 158° F. If it's higher, the leaves will spoil; if lower, they will not infuse properly. The first round of tea is poured into the "sniffer" cup, for a preliminary sample. As the tea con-

translates as "The Goddess of Mercy" and which we picked for its name (though we gave our host no hint of our "amateur" motives).

A few moments later an elaborate tea set was laid out in front of us. It consisted of two tea pots, one for water and another for brewing, and two sets of cups, one for drinking

ish on fine wine). Nearby was a tray perforated with holes, and mounted on a drainage stand, which was used to rinse the cups and kettle with hot

tinues to brew, and your palate becomes acquainted with the taste, every round of the same tea develops a different fragrance. John and I sat as reverentially as if we were in the reserve cellar at Château Margaux, staring and sniffing away at our tea cups, contemplating the flavors, and slowly discussing the tastes and aftertastes of each round of different teas. After a prolonged and passionate discussion (the kind of passion, it must be said, that comes from leisurely politeness and mild stimulation) we finally managed to come to the consensus that the aftertaste of our Golden Cassia had veered from "creamy" to "peachy." Mr. Ho was visibly delighted with our progress, pronounced us converts to the ritual, and laid elaborate plans for our continuing tea education.

Connoisseurs seldom take more than three rounds of the same tea, since it dulls the palate. They usually observe a strict progression from bitter and more assertive to sweeter, more fragrant teas. The very last round of tea should bring a sweet lingering aftertaste and make one salivate. Drinking too much tea is considered impolite, and the phrase "tea drunk" is applied to offenders.

The tiny tasting cup has to be finished in three sips—and, not surprising in a culture where words and images flow together much more easily

than they do in the West, the Chinese character for "sip" is three dots. The etiquette and finesse are almost endless. Mr. Ho was still instructing us on little details two hours into our "let's-peek-inside" visit. Your four fingers, he said, have to be on the cup while you taste. This is so no one sees

your mouth as you are drinking. In the old days, a young woman would be expected to mask her mouth with the sleeve of her gown to achieve the same effect of modesty and decorum. Above all, drink lightly and slowly and indulge in graceful, learned conversation about the tea.

This we did. And it was wonderfully peaceful and refreshing. As we walked down the stairs, John remarked that it would be difficult ever to have a cup of tea "English-style" again.

Chicken Stock

....

Beef Stock

....

Light and Aromatic Shrimp Stock

....

Fish Stock

....

Fresh Coconut Milk

....

Buttered Basmati Rice

....

Steamed Jasmine Rice

....

Sambal Oelek

....

Ketjap Manis

....

Fried Shallots

....

Toasted Coconut

....

Toasted Nuts

....

Clarified Butter

....

Ginger Juice

....

Garam Masala

....

Curry Powder

CHICKEN STOCK

You will find that Pacific recipes require stocks that are lighter and less concentrated than their European counterparts. There is no roasting of bones, no long simmering, no strong-tasting ingredients, no reducing. In a pinch, you can substitute a good-quality canned low-sodium broth for homemade stock.

If you plan to make this stock primarily for Asian and East-West recipes, add a tablespoon of soy sauce at the end.

2½ to 3 pounds chicken backs, necks, and wings, well rinsed
3 quarts water
Salt, to taste
1 carrot, peeled and halved
2 medium onions, sliced
1 turnip, peeled and quartered
1 bunch fresh flat-leaf parsley, tied with kitchen string
5 unpeeled cloves garlic, smashed
2 slices (each ½-inch thick) ginger, smashed
3 scallions, smashed
3 whole stalks fresh lemongrass (optional), smashed
15 black peppercorns

1. Place the chicken pieces and water in a large heavy pot and bring to a boil over high heat. Skim off the foam as it rises to the surface.

2. Add the remaining ingredients, then reduce the heat to low, cover, and simmer, skimming occasionally, for 2 hours.

3. Strain the stock. Cool and refrigerate up to 3 days, degreasing the stock before using. Freeze for longer storage.

MAKES ABOUT 2 QUARTS

BEEF STOCK

4 pounds beef stewing bones with marrow
3 quarts water
2 leeks, well rinsed and halved lengthwise
2 ribs celery with leaves, halved
2 parsnips, peeled and halved
6 unpeeled cloves garlic, smashed
2 scallions, smashed
1 small bunch fresh flat-leaf parsley, tied with kitchen string
4 whole cloves
3 points star anise (optional)
1 tablespoon black peppercorns

1. Place the bones and water in a large heavy pot and bring to a boil over high heat. Skim off the foam as it rises to the surface.

2. Add the remaining ingredients, then reduce the heat to low, cover, and simmer, skimming occasionally, for 3 hours.

3. Strain the stock. Cool and refrigerate, up to 3 days, degreasing the stock before using. Freeze for longer storage.

MAKES ABOUT 2 QUARTS

LIGHT AND AROMATIC SHRIMP STOCK

For many Asian soups and curries, a Western-style fish stock would be a bit too heavy. Whenever you peel shrimp, save the heads (if still attached) and shells and make this quick stock. It will keep indefinitely in a freezer.

Shells and heads from 2 pounds large
    or medium shrimp
3/4 cup sliced shallots
1 lemon, halved
2 teaspoons white peppercorns, lightly
    crushed
5 whole stalks fresh lemongrass,
    smashed
5 slices (1/2 inch each) fresh ginger,
    smashed
5 scallions, smashed
1 teaspoon grated lemon zest
1 teaspoon grated lime zest
10 cups water
1 1/4 teaspoons salt, or more to taste

1. Rinse the shrimp shells under cold running water. Combine the shrimp shells with all the remaining ingredients in a large heavy pot. Bring to a boil over high heat. Skim off the foam as it rises to the top.

2. Reduce the heat to low and simmer for 15 minutes. Turn the heat up to medium and simmer, uncovered, for another 20 minutes. Strain. Cool and refrigerate the stock until ready to use. Freeze for longer storage.

MAKES 10 CUPS

FISH STOCK

2 1/2 tablespoons unsalted butter
1 cup chopped onion
5 cloves garlic, sliced
2 carrots, peeled and diced
2 pounds fish trimmings, such as heads, tails
    and frames, well rinsed
8 cups water
1/2 cup dry white wine
2 tablespoons fresh lemon juice
1 bunch fresh flat-leaf parsley
1 teaspoon black peppercorns
Salt, to taste

1. Melt the butter in a large heavy soup pot over medium heat. Add the onion, garlic, carrots, and fish trimmings. Stir, then cover and steam for 5 minutes.

2. Add the remaining ingredients and bring to a boil. Skim off the foam as it rises to the top. Reduce the heat to low, cover, and simmer for 20 minutes.

3. Strain through a fine strainer, pressing on the solids with the back of a spoon to extract as much liquid as possible. Cool and refrigerate the stock until ready to use. Freeze for longer storage.

MAKES 2 QUARTS

FRESH COCONUT MILK

While any Southeast Asian cook can expertly cleave a fresh coconut, extract and grate the flesh, and squeeze out the milk in a matter of minutes, most prefer to buy fresh coconut milk at the market, where the job is done by powerful machines. I find the procedure of making fresh coconut milk rather laborious and the resulting milk quite thin. So, in most cases, I opt for a good brand of canned or frozen milk instead. However if you'd like to give it a try, here is the procedure. Coconuts spoil easily, and as they are inexpensive, it is a good idea to buy an extra one just in case.

1 large mature coconut, without any cracks
Boiling water

1. Preheat the oven to 425°F.

2. Using an ice pick or a sturdy skewer, pierce 2 of the 3 "eyes" of the coconut. Drain off the liquid and save for another use. Place the coconut on a baking sheet and bake for about 12 minutes. Then, remove it from the oven.

3. When cool enough to handle, break the coconut with a hammer into several pieces. With a sharp, small knife remove the flesh from the coconut, prying it away from the shell. Peel off the brown skin with a vegetable peeler. Cut into small pieces. Process the flesh in a food processor until finely minced. You should have 2½ to 3 cups grated coconut.

4. In a blender, blend equal amounts of coconut and boiling water for 1 minute. Transfer the mixture to a bowl. Let the mix-

ture cool to lukewarm. Working in small batches squeeze out as much liquid as you can through a fine sieve set over a clean bowl. Fresh coconut milk will keep in a refrigerator for about 2 days, and indefinitely in the freezer.

MAKES 2½ TO 3 CUPS COCONUT MILK

Thick Coconut Milk

Some Thai recipes call for thick and/or thin coconut milk. The thick milk is used as oil to fry curry pastes; the thin milk used as a cooking liquid.

To make thick coconut milk, follow the procedure above, using ½ cup boiling water per 1 cup freshly grated coconut. One coconut will yield 1¼ to 1½ cups thick coconut milk.

Thin Coconut Milk

Thin coconut milk is made by reusing the grated coconut left after making either regular or thick coconut milk. In a blender, blend the grated coconut with an equal amount of boiling water for 1 minute. Squeeze out the milk as directed in the Fresh Coconut Milk recipe. One coconut will yield 2½ to 3 cups thin coconut milk.

BUTTERED BASMATI RICE

Rice is the centerpiece of a Pacific meal. The exact ratio of rice to water might differ slightly depending on the brand of rice you use, the type of pot you cook it in, and even the water in which it is cooked. Consistency is your key to making moist, fluffy rice. Choose a good brand and a capacious heavy-bottomed saucepan, and stay with them. After a few tries, you'll get it just right.

If you get good-quality basmati rice and take the time to rinse and soak it carefully, you will end up with a dish that you simply can't stop eating. I recommend Pari or Elephant brand, or any brand (imported from India, not Pakistan) that comes in a sealed linen or burlap bag.

2 cups basmati rice, (preferably Pari or
*   Elephant brand)*
3¹/₂ cups Chicken Stock (page 384),
*   canned broth, or water*
1¹/₂ tablespoons vegetable oil
2 bay leaves
1 whole cinnamon stick
1 whole star anise, broken into points, or to
*   taste*
4 cardamom pods, preferably unbleached
*   (green), lightly crushed*
4 whole cloves
Salt, to taste
2¹/₂ tablespoons unsalted butter, cut into
*   small pieces*

1. Place the rice in a sieve and rinse thoroughly in several changes of cold water, scooping and sifting the rice through your fingers. Drain the rice, place in a bowl and soak in cold water to cover for 30 minutes. Drain and rinse well.

2. Combine the stock, oil, bay leaves, star anise, cardamom, cloves, and salt in a large pot with a tight-fitting lid. Bring to a rolling boil and pour in the rice in a slow steady stream. Return the water to a boil, reduce the heat to medium-low and cook, uncovered, stirring only once, until the water is almost absorbed and air bubbles appear on the surface of the rice, about 7 minutes.

3. Reduce the heat to as low as possible, cover tightly, and let the rice steam for 15 minutes. Remove from the heat and let stand, undisturbed, for 15 to 20 minutes.

4. Fluff the rice with a fork and transfer to a serving bowl. Gently stir in the butter using 2 forks.

SERVES 6

STEAMED JASMINE RICE

Each Asian cook has a slightly different method of cooking jasmine rice (usually with rice and water measurements expressed in terms of "knuckles" or "fingers"), but I find the following one tasty and reliable. Nothing, however, guarantees a better result than an electric rice cooker. It is convenient and relatively inexpensive, and if you eat rice often, it's an absolute must for your kitchen. Note that if you increase the amount of rice, the amount of water does not always double. For larger amounts of rice, make sure the water covers it by 1 inch, about 1 knuckle.

> 2 cups jasmine rice
> 3¼ cups water
> Salt, to taste

1. Place the rice in a strainer and rinse thoroughly in several changes of cold water, scooping and sifting the rice through your fingers.

2. Bring the rice with the water to a boil in a heavy saucepan over medium heat. Allow to boil until small air bubbles form on the surface. Add salt, then reduce the heat to very low, cover, and cook the rice until it is tender and all the liquid has been absorbed, about 15 minutes. Remove from the heat and let stand, covered, for 15 minutes.

SERVES 6

Terrific Pacific Basics

SAMBAL OELEK

(Indonesian Hot Chile Sauce)

If you can find them, meaty, red (ripe) jalapeños are the best to use for this fiery Indonesian condiment. If you can't, use red bird's eye or cayenne chiles, or fresnos (for a milder taste), or a combination. If you can't find any red chiles at all, use serranos, though you won't get the color or the slight suggestion of sweetness that the red chiles produce. Note that homemade *sambal oelek* is hotter than the store-bought version (es-

pecially if you use green chiles), so if you make your own, do not use the full amount called for in the recipes. Add it to taste. The chiles should be seeded to taste as well.

> 1 cup finely chopped fresh hot chiles, preferably ripe jalapeños, fresnos or bird's eye, seeded to taste
> 6 cloves garlic, chopped
> 1 teaspoon salt
> Scant 1 teaspoon sugar
> 1½ teaspoons distilled white vinegar
> 1½ teaspoons fresh lime juice

Using a mortar and pestle or small food processor, grind or process the chiles, garlic, and salt to a coarse paste. Scrape into a bowl. Stir in the sugar, vinegar, and lime juice then transfer to a jar with a tight-fitting lid. The sauce will keep in the refrigerator for up to 2 weeks.

MAKES ABOUT ¾ CUP

KETJAP MANIS

(Thick and sweet Indonesian soy sauce)

Dark, and syrupy, with a characteristic sweet-salty taste, *ketjap manis* is a wonderful ingredient to add to marinades, sauces, and stir-fries. If you can't find it or Chinese sweet soy sauce in Asian grocery stores, prepare the simple version below. It's not as thick and rich as the original, but is very tasty, and makes a more than adequate substitute. I especially like the version below as a glaze for grilled meats and poultry.

⅔ cup (packed) dark brown sugar
¼ cup water
¾ cup unsulfured molasses
1 cup dark soy sauce
½ teaspoon ground coriander
¼ teaspoon five-spice powder

1. Combine the sugar and water in a heavy saucepan and bring to a boil over medium heat. Cook, stirring, until the sugar is dissolved.

2. Stir in the molasses, soy sauce, coriander, and five-spice powder and simmer for 5 minutes. Strain through a fine strainer into a jar with a tight-fitting lid. It will keep for several months in the refrigerator.

MAKES ABOUT 2 CUPS

FRIED SHALLOTS

Peanut oil, for deep frying
1 cup very thinly sliced shallots

Pour oil to a depth of 1½ inches into a medium skillet or deep fryer and heat over medium-high heat to 375°F. Add the shallots in batches, and fry, stirring gently, until the shallots are golden and crisp, about 1½ to 2 minutes. With a slotted spoon, transfer to paper towels to drain. Store in an airtight container. They will keep for up to 1 week.

MAKES ABOUT ⅔ CUP

TOASTED COCONUT

Dessicated (dried) coconut or sweetened or unsweetened flaked coconut

Heat a wok or a heavy skillet over medium-low heat. Add the coconut and stir with a wooden spoon until deep golden, 2 to 3 minutes for dried coconut, slightly longer for fresh. Cool and store in an airtight container in a cool, dry place.

TOASTED NUTS

Toasted nuts are used frequently, so toast them ahead of time and at your leisure. Store the toasted nuts in an airtight container.

At least ½ cup shelled whole nuts or nuts in large pieces

1. Preheat the oven to 350°F.

2. Spread the nuts in one layer in a shallow baking pan like a jelly-roll pan. Toast in the oven until they are golden, shaking the pan once or twice. This should take up to 5 to 7 minutes. Do not leave the nuts unattended—once they begin to deepen in color, they will toast very quickly. Remove the nuts from the oven and let cool in the pan. Store the toasted nuts in an airtight container in a cool, dry place.

CLARIFIED BUTTER

2 sticks (½ pound) unsalted butter

1. Melt the butter in a medium-size saucepan over low heat. When the butter forms a white foam on the surface, remove the pan from the heat and let stand until the milk solids settle on the bottom, 3 to 5 minutes.

2. Carefully pour off the clear butter, leaving the solids in the saucepan. Strain the solids through several layers of cheesecloth to remove as much clarified butter as possible. The butter will keep in the refrigerator for up to 3 weeks.

MAKES ABOUT ¾ CUP

GINGER JUICE

½ cup finely grated fresh ginger

Working in batches, squeeze the ginger through a very clean garlic press into a small bowl.

MAKES ABOUT 2 TABLESPOONS

GARAM MASALA

2 tablespoons coriander seeds
2 tablespoons regular cumin seeds
½ teaspoon black cumin seeds (if available)
1½ tablespoons black peppercorns
1 tablespoon whole cloves
1½ tablespoons cardamom seeds, preferably from unbleached (green) pods
1 piece (2 inches) cinnamon stick, crushed into pieces with a mortar and pestle
¼ teaspoon freshly grated nutmeg

1. Heat a small skillet over medium-low heat. Add all the spices except the nutmeg and dry-roast, stirring, until fragrant and several shades darker, about 2 minutes. Add the nutmeg and remove from the heat. Let the spices cool to room temperature.

2. Grind the spices in a spice grinder until fine, about 1 minute. Store in a tightly covered jar in a cool, dry place. The mixture will keep for 1 month without losing its fragrance.

MAKES ABOUT ¼ CUP

CURRY POWDER

This is a very nice, quite mild, all-purpose curry powder, and much better than anything you can buy in a store. I highly recommend making your own, especially since it doesn't take any longer than shopping for the best available brand. You should certainly use the homemade version for any recipe that calls for more than 1 tablespoon of curry powder.

If you want to make the powder hotter, increase the amount of dried chiles to 4 or 5. For a sweeter accent (good for many Malaysian or Singaporian curried dishes), add a teaspoon of cardamom seeds, several whole cloves, and a grating of fresh nutmeg. Ground spices begin to lose their pungency and aroma after about 1 month, and I usually make a new batch every 3 weeks or so.

¼ cup coriander seeds

2 tablespoons cumin seeds

2 teaspoons fennel seeds

1½ tablespoons yellow mustard seeds

1 teaspoon fenugreek seeds

1 piece (2 inches) cinnamon, crushed into
   pieces with a mortar and pestle

2 to 3 dried chiles (2 to 3 inches), seeds
   shaken out, broken into pieces

1 teaspoon black peppercorns

2½ tablespoons ground turmeric

1 teaspoon ground ginger

Pinch of asafetida (hing)

1. Heat a small skillet over medium-low heat. Add all the ingredients except the turmeric, ginger, and asafetida and dry-roast, stirring, until fragrant and several shades darker, about 3 minutes. Add the turmeric, ginger, and asafetida and remove from the heat. Let the mixture cool to room temperature.

2. Working in batches, grind the mixture in a spice grinder until fine, about 1 minute. Store in a tightly covered jar in a cool, dry place. It will keep for 1 month without losing its fragrance.

MAKES ABOUT 1 CUP

CHILES

The fire of Pacific cuisines, chiles are landing in the American markets in seemingly infinite varieties. So much so, that specifying a particular type is often more confusing than it is helpful. Generally, when small fresh hot chiles are required, I use the hot and fragrant ½-inch bird's eye (or Thai) chiles. The slightly milder green serranos are also a good option. For less fiery, sweeter and meatier chiles, which are still hot, I prefer fresnos. They are wonderful in aromatic pastes, and sliced thin, as a garnish. Where a recipe calls for large green chiles, use the 5- to 6-inch Anaheims. Jalapeños don't really add a Pacific flavor, but they would work fine in some recipes, if you can't find other hot chiles. Use half a small jalapeño for each small hot chile called for in the recipe.

For dried chiles, I like the Thai *phrik kii noo*, which are small and very hot, or the milder 2-inch *phrik chiifaa*. These are available at Asian grocery stores. Mexican arbol or japones chiles (which are sold in small plastic bags in gourmet food stores and sometimes in supermarkets) make a fine substitute for the latter. With Mexican chiles, it's a good idea to toast them in a dry skillet until they turn several shades darker. Dried chile flakes can substitute for small hot dried chiles, which are crumbled into sauces and salad dressings. The larger dried chiles are often used as a base for curry and other aromatic pastes, and should be soaked in water before using. Fresh or dried chiles should be seeded according to the desired degree of heat (the more seeds, the

hotter your dish will be). Wear rubber gloves when seeding chiles and avoid contact with your eyes.

COCONUT

The flavor of coconut is central to Pacific cooking. Its liquid is sipped as a refreshing beverage, the milk used in curries and desserts, and the flesh added to a variety of sweet and savory dishes. For use in cakes and other sweets, nothing beats the juicy flesh of freshly grated coconut, but you can substitute grated frozen coconut, available from Goya. For coating deep-fried foods, and for sprinkling on as a garnish, I usually use shredded, unsweetened, dessicated (dried) coconut, available in health food stores. I almost never use the sweetened dried coconut often used in baking in the United States.

COCONUT MILK

Ideally, coconut milk should be made at home by soaking the grated flesh of the coconut in boiling water and squeezing out the liquid. However, it is a rather arduous task, and I find the resulting milk not as thick and creamy as a good brand of canned coconut milk. If you want to make fresh coconut milk but would rather save yourself the trouble of cracking and grating a fresh coconut, look for Goya's brand of frozen grated coconut in Latin grocery stores or frozen food sections of some supermarkets. (Because of contamination warnings, I do not recommend using brands of grated coconut or fresh-frozen coconut milk from Southeast Asia.)

Most of the time, a good brand of canned unsweetened coconut milk is a fine substitute for fresh. It can be found at Asian and specialty markets, and many supermarkets throughout the United States. Brands of coconut milk vary quite considerably in quality. I find Chaokoh the most reliable of the more widely available ones. Goya, found in the Hispanic section of many supermarkets, is also fine. Canned coconut milk should be stirred well before using. Once opened, canned coconut milk will keep in the refrigerator 2 to 3 days, and in the freezer indefinitely.

CURRY POWDERS AND PASTES

As I explain in the Curries chapter of this book, curry is really a method rather than a packet of spices. For the most part, commercially available curry powder tends to be of inferior quality, so I always make my own (see page 390) and urge you to do the same. If you use a commercial curry powder, try to buy it at an Indian market or a gourmet grocery. If shopping at an Indian market, also look for jarred Madras-style curry paste, which has a more vivid taste than the powdered variety.

As with powders, I prefer homemade curry pastes. If using commercial Indian or Thai curry pastes, you should "freshen" them up with an extra dose of pounded garlic, chiles, and ginger. If buying "red," "green," or "mussaman" Thai curry pastes, look for ones in small cans. They are fresher tasting than ones packaged in plastic jars.

FERMENTED BLACK BEANS

The salted Chinese black beans, which are usually cooked with garlic, ginger, sugar, and rice wine, add a lively pungent note to stir-fries and sauces. Good Chinese chefs recommend using them sparingly, so as not to overpower the taste of other ingredients. Try to find fermented black beans that come in yellow cardboard containers, as they are of much higher quality than those that come in a plastic bag. If you cannot find fermented black beans, use jarred black bean sauce, which has the aromatics already mixed in. Once opened, black beans should be stored in an airtight container on the lowest shelf of a refrigerator or in a dark, cool place. They will keep indefinitely.

FISH SAUCE

Fish sauce (*nam pla* in Thai, *nuoc mam* in Vietnamese) is the salt of Southeast Asia. It is made by fermenting layers of anchovies in salt in large stone or wooden barrels and draining off the thin pungent liquid. Fish sauce has a characteristic piquant fishy smell, which disappears when the sauce is blended with other ingredients, such as lime juice and sugar. This is one of the most essential ingredients in Southeast Asian cooking, used in salad dressings, curries, stir fries, sauces, and dips. It is sold very cheaply at any Asian grocery store, and with the increasing popularity of Thai cuisine, is now sold at gourmet stores and many supermarkets. If you don't make frequent trips to Asian markets, stock up on several bottles, as you will be using it often. Look for fish sauce imported from Vietnam or Thailand, which is light amber in color. I like Squid or Tiparos brand. There is no real substitute for fish sauce, but if a recipe calls for a small quantity, and push comes to shove, you can use light soy sauce.

HERBS

Fresh aromatic herbs are the very heart of Pacific cooking and are used with flair and imagination. The herbs I use most frequently are cilantro, Italian basil, mint, chives, and Asian basil. When fresh herbs are called for in the recipe, do not substitute dried—they may work in some European dishes, but they are out of the question in Asian cuisine, where herbs are valued for their accent of bright, crisp freshness as much as for their aroma. If the fresh herb required in a recipe is not available, substitute another one. There is usually enough flexibility in the recipes to allow for this. If herbs are scarce and you have to freeze yours, wash, dry, and keep whole sprigs in the freezer. While not great for salads or garnishes, frozen herbs can be used to flavor soups, stews, and curries.

GALANGAL

Galangal (*kha* in Thai) is a rhizome of the ginger family with a tingling aftertaste of bubblegum. It is an essential ingredient in the Thai kitchen, where it is used to flavor curries and soups. It is quite difficult to find fresh galangal even at Thai markets, where it is usually available frozen. If using frozen galangal, you don't need to defrost it. Just slice it with a large sharp knife, or pound with other aromatics. Dried galangal is much less flavorful than fresh but can be used as a last resort. Sometimes galangal comes powdered, in which form it is known as "laos." Laos powder to fresh galangal is what ground ginger is to fresh ginger, another taste altogether. While not really suitable to use in authentic Thai dishes, it can be used to add zest to certain dishes. Fresh ginger is not really a suitable substitute for galangal, but it can be used as an additional aromatic in recipes that call for a small amount of galangal.

GINGER

Ginger has become so popular in the United States in recent years that it hardly needs an introduction. Often mistakenly called a root, ginger is a rhizome, a tuber with roots of its own. Most of the fresh ginger on the American market comes from Hawaii. When buying fresh ginger, look for very firm tubers with slightly shiny, smooth skin. When you cut off a piece of ginger, the cut end of the ginger is likely to dry out. Trim it off before re-using the ginger. I prefer to purchase a small amount and not keep it for too long. Store fresh ginger in the refrigerator or in a cool, dark place. To extract ginger juice, see page 390.

KAFFIR LIME

Kaffir lime (*makrut* in Thai) is a light green, knobby, bumpy citrus fruit whose zest and, especially, leaves give a unique flavor and fragrance to Thai food. The grated zest is used as one of the ingredients in Thai curry pastes, and the bright green leaves are finely shredded and added to dishes at the last minute to impart an exquisite scent.

Both kaffir lime and its leaves freeze well and are usually available frozen at Thai grocery stores. Common lime can be substituted for the zest and juice of the kaffir, but the fragrance of kaffir leaves is pretty unique, and there is no real substitute.

KETJAP MANIS

Ketjap manis is a sweet, thick, malty Indonesian soy sauce, great to use in a sauce for fried rice, stir-fried noodles, or marinades. It can be found in some Asian grocery stores, but if it is not available, substitute Chinese sweet soy sauce or make it yourself, following the instructions on page 388.

LEMONGRASS

Lemongrass, which looks like a pale-green, hard scallion, has the unmistakable sweet yet zesty perfume of citrus, essential to many Southeast Asian and Pacific Rim dishes. Thinly sliced or minced, it can be used in salads; bruised whole stalks can infuse liquids; when pounded, it flavors curries and marinades. I love infusing dishes with its citrusy fragrance, so I often boil sliced fresh lemongrass with water, (about 1 cup sliced lemongrass for 1½ cups water), cook to reduce by half, let steep for 1 hour, then strain. You can add this aromatic liquid to anything from sauces to vinaigrettes to ice creams and other desserts.

Choose firm stalks that do not appear withered or wilted. Discard the tough outer leaves and use only the juicy 3 to 4 inches of the inner core. If you like, you can save and dry the tops to use to brew delicious lemongrass tea (see Index). Lemongrass is very fibrous, so the stalks need to be thinly sliced, finely chopped, or pounded in a mortar.

Lemongrass can be found at most Asian markets, and with its growing popularity, is becoming available at gourmet groceries and specialty markets in large cities. Lemongrass freezes well, so when you see it, buy a large quantity and freeze. I use dried lemongrass stalks only if a recipe calls for whole stalks to infuse soups or stews. Chopped or pounded lemongrass may be substituted with grated lemon zest although the fragrance will be lost. Use 1 teaspoon lemon zest for 1 stalk fresh lemongrass.

MIRIN

Mirin is the delicate sweet Japanese rice wine, great to use for sauces and salad dressings. If not available, substitute medium-dry sherry.

MISO

Long associated with good health and nutrition, miso—the protein-laden Japanese fermented soybean paste—is wonderful in soups, salad dressings, marinades, and poaching liquids. Miso comes in various colors and can be found at Japanese and Korean markets and some better health food stores. For the recipes in this book, I use the rust-colored salty red miso (called *aka miso*) and the yellowish, more delicate white miso *(shiro miso)*. Miso is best mixed with the sweet Japanese wine mirin or sugar, to balance its saltiness, and a touch of soy to give it depth.

PALM SUGAR

Palm sugar is a rich-tasting, brown-colored sugar, obtained from the sap of the palmyra or sugar palm tree. This is the sugar traditionally used in most Southeast Asian dishes and you will love its deep, comforting taste. It can be obtained from a number of sources; it is even available in a line of Thai products currently on the shelves of some supermarkets. At Thai groceries it is often sold in glass jars or plastic containers. Thai palm sugar is light in color, looking somewhat like solidified honey. At Indian markets (where it is sometimes referred to as jaggery), it is sold in solid cakes and is dark amber in color. You can also find palm sugar in Hispanic and Jamaican markets.

Like dried out brown sugar, palm sugar is hard and lumpy. For easy use I like to break it up with a hammer or a handle of a large knife and process in a food processor.

If palm sugar is unavailable, substitute light brown sugar, although the taste will not be the same. For Southeast Asian salad dressings—usually a combination of lime juice, fish sauce, and palm sugar—I often use a good maple syrup instead.

RICE WINE

Chinese rice wine, called *shao-hsing*, is widely used for marinades, sauces, and braising liquids. As with any cooking wine, do not use anything you would not drink. And certainly stay away from the *"shao-hsing* cooking wine," sold at some Chinese grocery stores. *Shao-hsing* should be purchased from liquor stores. If it is unavailable, substitute with dry sherry, dry vermouth, or Scotch.

SAMBAL OELEK

Sambal oelek (also spelled *ulek* or *olek*) is a blistering Indonesian sauce of crushed red chiles preserved with a little vinegar and salt. In Asia it is placed on the table as a condiment, or added to marinades, stir-fries, and stews. If not available, you can make it yourself (see page 388) or substitute with Chinese chile paste, or chile paste with garlic.

SHRIMP PASTE

Kapi in Thai, *terasi* in Vietnamese or *blachan* in Malay, shrimp paste is used in many Southeast Asian dishes to add pungency and bite. Its smell is as notorious as that of durian (a fruit), but it does provide an essential "kick" to curries and sauces. I like to use the Thai variety, which comes in small tin jars with a plastic lid. Once opened

(and if using it for the first time, you will inevitably stand back), it should be tightly closed and kept in a cool, dark place, wrapped in several plastic bags, or placed in another container. Before cooking, it should be wrapped in 2 layers of foil and dry roasted for several minutes. Any true aficionado of Thai cuisine will swear by it, and I urge you to try it. But if after your first experiment you find the smell too offensive, substitute anchovy paste.

SPICES

Spices are the true essence of Pacific cuisine. Once a precious and luxurious commodity, most spices are now readily available almost anywhere in the United States. Nevertheless, good spices should be treated with the reverence and respect they deserve. In Asia, despite the fact that spices are used in great profusion, no self-respecting cook would ever resort to commercial ground varieties. They are always ground at home (except for the occasion when enormous amounts are required, in which case they are sent off to a spice mill) and I urge you to do the same. Those of us who use a pepper mill will never go back to commercial ground pepper. It's the same with spices.

Begin with buying whole spices at a good spice shop. To grind them you will need a spice grinder or a small coffee grinder used only for grinding spices. It isn't a good idea to grind spices in the machine you are using for coffee (unless you want an aftertaste of chile in your morning cup). Coffee or spice grinders are inexpensive and are a must for every kitchen. Separately grind a relatively small amount of the spices you use most often and keep them in sealed, labeled spice jars. I usually grind about a week's supply.

Indian and many Southeast Asian cooks toast spices before grinding. To do so, heat a small skillet over medium heat. Add the spices and stir until they are fragrant and turn several shades darker. Toasting spices really heightens their flavor.

Store whole spices in airtight containers. Good Asian cooks often keep their ground spices in the refrigerator. It is not always convenient, but it keeps them tasting fresher.

SOY SAUCE

Soy sauce is made from a mixture of fermented soybeans and a roasted grain such as wheat or barley, which is injected with yeast, then salted and left to marinate in vats.

There are light and dark varieties of soy sauce. Light soy sauce is lighter, thinner, and more pungent. The dark variety, which is deeper in color, more robust, but less salty in flavor, is light soy sauce with the addition of caramel or molasses. When a recipe calls for soy sauce, use the dark variety, unless otherwise specified. For sauces and condiments I like the sweeter, more refined taste of a Japanese variety of soy sauce often referred to in this country as tamari. If shopping for soy sauce at an Asian grocery store, look for better-quality, more expensive brands.

Sweet soy sauce is another thing altogether. It is essentially a syruplike molasses. I use it to flavor marinades and Southeast Asian stir-fries, when *ketjap manis,* sweet Indonesian soy sauce, is not available.

TAMARIND

Tamarind is my favorite tropical ingredient. Its pulp comes from the pods of the tamarind tree and has a sticky texture and a wonderfully deep, rich, sour taste with a faint suggestion of sweetness. I use it prodigiously for sauces, glazes, chutneys, curries, and marinades, and I especially like to combine it with the rich sweetness of palm sugar or honey.

The best tamarind pulp comes from Thailand. It is quite soft and comes packaged in rectangular blocks, wrapped in plastic. Once opened, keep the tamarind pulp in small zip-lock bags, or wrap tightly in plastic wrap. It will keep almost indefinitely. To use, soak the pulp in boiling water off the heat for 30 minutes to soften. Pass the resulting thick liquid through a fine sieve to get rid of the fibers and seeds. I like the Indian tamarind concentrate much less; its color is darker and the flavor is almost aggressively sour. As it still has to be soaked to soften, it isn't really much of a time saver. Many Hispanic grocery stores actually carry fresh tamarind pods—just ask for *tamarindo.* Fresh pods should be cracked open, the flesh and the seeds scooped into a bowl, then strained through a fine sieve. Fresh lime or lemon juice can substitute for a small amount of tamarind.

WASABI

Often called Japanese horseradish, it is the hot and pungent root of the wasabi plant. It is best known when mixed with soy sauce and used as a dipping sauce for sushi and sashimi. But it can be put to use in many imaginative ways—as a flavoring for mayonnaise, as a rub for meats, and as an addition to salad dressings. It is very hot, so use it sparingly.

Wasabi can be bought in powdered form and mixed with water (which is preferable) or as a paste, packaged in a tube.

INDEX

Terrific Pacific Index

Terrific Pacific Index

Terrific Pacific Index

Terrific Pacific Index

Terrific Pacific Index

419

Terrific Pacific Index